THE MORALITY OF WAR

CLASSICAL AND CONTEMPORARY READINGS

Larry May, Eric Rovie, and Steve Viner
Washington University in St. Louis

PEARSON
Prentice
Hall

UPPER SADDLE RIVER, NEW JERSEY 07458

Library of Congress Cataloging-in-Publication Data

May, Larry.
  The morality of war : classical and contemporary readings / Larry May, Eric Rovie,
and Steve Viner.-- 1st ed.
    p. cm.
  ISBN 0-13-148770-1
  1. War--Moral and ethical aspects.   2. Just war doctrine.   I. Rovie, Eric.
II. Viner, Steve. III. Title.

  U22.M39 2005
  172'.42--dc22

                                                                      2004023983

Editorial Director: Charlyce Jones-Owen
Senior Acquisitions Editor: Ross Miller
Assistant Editor: Wendy B. Yurash
Editorial Assistant: Carla Worner
Marketing Manager: Kara Kindstrom
Production Liaison: Joanne Hakim
Manufacturing Buyer: Christina Helder
Cover Art Director and Cover Design: Jayne Conte
Manager, Cover Visual Research & Permissions: Karen Sanatar
Cover Photo: Getty Images
Composition/Full-Service Project Management: Linda Duarte/Pine Tree Composition, Inc.
Printer/Binder: The Courier Companies

Credits and acknowledgments borrowed from other sources and reproduced, with permission, in
this textbook appear on pages 461–463.

Pearson Prentice Hall™ is a trademark of Pearson Education, Inc.
Pearson® is a registered trademark of Pearson plc
Prentice Hall® is a registered trademark of Pearson Education, Inc.

Pearson Education LTD., London
Pearson Education Singapore, Pte. Ltd
Pearson Education, Canada, Ltd
Pearson Education–Japan
Pearson Education Australia PTY, Limited

Pearson Education North Asia Ltd
Pearson Educación de Mexico, S.A. de C.V.
Pearson Education Malaysia, Pte. Ltd
Pearson Education, Upper Saddle River, New Jersey

PEARSON
Prentice
Hall

10 9 8 7 6 5 4 3 2 1
ISBN 0-13-148770-1

Contents

PREFACE vii

GENERAL INTRODUCTION ix

Part I Historical Origins 1

    A. The Just War Theory 1

        Cicero,
            On Duties 5

        Seneca,
            On Mercy 8

        Tertullian,
            "The Soldier's Chaplet" 12

        Augustine,
            The City of God 15

        Averroes (Ibn Rushd),
            "Jihad" 21

        Thomas Aquinas,
            Summa Theologica 26

    B. The Natural Law of Nations 34

        Francisco de Vitoria,
            On the Law of War 38

Alberico Gentili,
The Law of War   49

Francisco Suarez,
"On War"   58

Hugo Grotius,
The Law of War and Peace   66

Thomas Hobbes,
Leviathan   80

Samuel Pufendorf,
On The Law of Nature and Nations   89

C. The Moralists vs. The Realists   96

Emer de Vattel,
The Law of Nations or the Principles of Natural Law   99

Immanuel Kant,
"Perpetual Peace"   110

Carl von Clausewitz,
On the Art of War   115

Henry David Thoreau,
"On the Duty of Civil Disobedience"   122

Part II Contemporary Moral Foundations   131

A. Pacifism and the Credibility of the Just War Tradition   131

William James,
"The Moral Equivalent of War"   134

Jan Narveson,
"Pacifism: A Philosophical Analysis"   141

Stanley Hauerwas,
"Pacifism: Some Philosophical Considerations"   148

John Howard Yoder,
When War Is Unjust: Being Honest in Just-War Thinking   153

B. The Doctrine of Double Effect   160

Joseph M. Boyle, Jr.,
"Toward Understanding the Principle of Double Effect"   164

Warren S. Quinn,
    "Actions, Intentions, and Consequences: The Doctrine of Double Effect" 174

Jonathan Bennett,
    "Morality and Consequences" 187

Michael Walzer,
    "Double Effect and Double Intentions" 193

C. Absolutists and Consequentialists   200

G. E. M. Anscombe,
    "War and Murder" 203

George I. Mavrodes,
    "Conventions and the Morality of War" 212

Thomas Nagel,
    "War and Massacre" 222

Richard B. Brandt,
    "Utilitarianism and the Rules of War" 234

D. Self-Defense   246

Michael Walzer,
    Just and Unjust Wars 250

David Rodin,
    War and Self-Defense. 261

David Luban,
    "Just War and Human Rights" 272

Paul Woodruff,
    "Justification or Excuse: Saving Soldiers at the Expense of Civilians" 281

Part III Recent Applications 293

A. Terrorism   293

Michael Walzer,
    "Terrorism: A Critique of Excuses" 296

Robert Fullinwider,
    "Understanding Terrorism" 305

Andrew Valls,
    "Can Terrorism be Justified?" 315

Joseph Boyle,
"Just War Doctrine and the Military Response to Terrorism" 326

B. Humanitarian Intervention and the Just War   339

David Luban,
"The Romance of the Nation-State" 343

Fernando Teson,
"The Liberal Case for Humanitarian Intervention" 347

Burleigh Wilkins,
"Humanitarian Interventions: Some Doubts" 360

George R. Lucas, Jr.,
"From Jus ad Bellum *to* Jus ad Pacem*: Rethinking Just-War Criteria for the Use of Military Force for Humanitarian Ends"* 368

C. Recent Armed Conflicts   380

Georg Meggle,
"Is this War [in Kosovo] Good? An Ethical Commentary" 384

Miriam Sapiro,
"Iraq: The Shifting Sands of Preemptive Self-Defense" 395

William Galston,
"The Perils of Preemptive War" 406

David Luban,
"The War on Terrorism and the End of Human Rights" 412

D. After War   421

R. M. Hare,
"Can I Be Blamed for Obeying Orders?" 424

Larry May,
"Superior Orders, Duress, and Moral Perception" 429

David Cooper,
"Collective Responsibility, 'Moral Luck,' and Reconciliation" 438

Elizabeth Kiss,
"Moral Ambition Within and Beyond Political Constraints: Reflections on Restorative Justice" 447

Credits   461

Preface

War is always with us, and as Cicero observed over two thousand years ago, this is why we need "humane laws" that restrict war. The morality of war is a subject traceable at least to the time of Cicero, and encompasses both what counts as a legitimate basis for going to war in the first place, and what counts as legitimate tactics to employ once war has begun. For almost every thinker who has written about morality and politics, from as far back as recorded history, war has been a central topic of concern. This is because war is seen as necessary, at least when a State is being invaded, but also highly suspect, because it always involves the intentional killing of others, normally thought to be one of the most seriously immoral of acts. Justifying war is both a puzzle and commonplace.

This book arose as the result of two causes. The first is the state of the world, in which war is once again seen as an instrument of foreign policy, and in which there is even more of a need to discuss humane laws of war. The second is student demand; courses are oversubscribed when they merely mention the word war in the title, whereas just a few years ago such courses were consigned to mere "historical" interest. Here in St. Louis, squarely in the middle (geographically and politically) of the United States, our students are consumed with war, and most importantly with questions of what makes wars morally acceptable or unacceptable. This book was inspired by our inability to find a good book of readings that challenged students and gave them a sense of the historical and theoretical debates about whether and when war is justified.

The first part of the book, which could stand on its own as the basis of a course, deals with the historical debates about so-called Just Wars. Here we see very early debates between church fathers who were pacifists and those, like Augustine, who argued that some defensive wars must be justifiable. We see the medieval theorists develop the idea of Jihad, holy war, and also the first attempt to formulate distinct moral rules for war, culminating in Aquinas's doctrine. We also see debates between the first international lawyers, Gentili and Grotius, about what a secular Just War would be based on. In the second part of the book, we see recent theoretical debates about pacifism and realism as well as positions in between, where the doctrines of self-defense and double effect are rigorously challenged. And in the third part of the book, we see how these theoretical positions play themselves out in recent controversies about terrorism and humanitarian intervention in such places as Iraq and Kosovo. And we end with questions about what it is moral to do in the aftermath of war.

We are very grateful to Ross Miller from Prentice-Hall who showed such strong interest in this project at its inception. Ross's own expertise in this area has been of enormous help to us. We also wish to thank Jeff McMahan, Andrew Rehfeld, and Andrew Valls who gave us good suggestions about what to include and what to exclude in this reader. Likewise we are grateful to the reviewers for Prentice-Hall who also gave us support and suggestions at a crucial stage in the process: Fariborz L. Mokhtari, National Defense University, Kenneth T. Osborne, Roger Williams University, and Bradley C. S. Watson, Saint Vincent College. Marilyn Friedman, Emily Crookston, Jeff Brown, Emily Austin, Justin Cox, and Marisa Mizus also were helpful to us in conceptualizing this anthology. The book can be used in either an undergraduate or graduate class in such fields as philosophy, religious studies, political science, peace studies, and elsewhere.

Larry May
Eric Rovie
Steve Viner

General Introduction

In the recent debates about whether the United States should have waged war against Iraq, the Just War tradition was explicitly or implicitly consulted as a kind of moral compass. The philosopher, Matthias Lutz-Bachmann tells the story of being called by the German chancellor to advise him about Just War Theory just before he met with President Bush. Bush never called any American philosophers before he met with the German chancellor, although many people in the United States spoke of the Iraq war in Just War terms. There are two reasons why many people appeal to this tradition. First, this tradition extends back in time, at least to the writings of Augustine who confronted the pacifism of the early Church Fathers. Of course, that a doctrine is of ancient origins does not make it right, but that it has stood the "test of time" is a strong indicator that it is not a bad starting point. Second, and perhaps more persuasive is the idea that the Just War tradition seems to capture deep-seated intuitions, held by many people in diverse cultures. Again, that a doctrine is cross-culturally acceptable also does not make it right. But it is often hard to figure out where to start a moral inquiry, and most of us choose as a starting point positions that seem, from an intuitive standpoint, relatively uncontroversial. In the shifting sands of moral foundations, positions that are highly intuitive seem at least to be pretty good starting points, even if not themselves rock solid.

From across the political spectrum, politicians today appeal to the Just War tradition. The libertarian presidential candidate, Pat Buchanan, used the terms of this tradition when he argued for a more isolationist U.S. foreign policy; and the liberal, former President Jimmy Carter, also invoked the Just War tradition when he recently condemned President Bush's attack on Iraq. We also regard the Just War tradition as a good starting-point. To answer the question of whether one state might be justifiable to go to war against another state, a question that initially seems daunting, we ask about what we would consider justifiable if we, as individuals, were interacting with a stranger who had threatened us.

We will first consider briefly two important controversies within this tradition to give a flavor of the richness of the Just War tradition and its continuing appeal today, as well as its potentially problematic aspects when we are regarding that tradition not just as a starting point, but also as an end point of our deliberations. We will discuss the debates about the justifiability of preventive or preemptive war. Here we can learn a lot that is useful for such controversies as that concerning Iraq. Then we will discuss the debates about whether the parties to a war could both act justly in waging war. Here we might wish to try to move beyond the Just War tradition, but not as far away from that tradition as some might have supposed.

The Just War tradition seeks a moral consensus concerning the justifiable grounds for waging war. Moral justification of war is necessary since war involves the intentional taking of human life, an act that is universally considered prima facie unjustifiable. This is why pacifists have argued that war is never justified. The Just War tradition, both in philosophy and law, extends back at least to the time of Rome. An analogy was developed between what was justifiable for states and what would be justifiable for individuals to do to one another. In the case of individual persons, it seemed obvious that pacifism was not morally required, for if one is attacked and can only save one's life by fighting back, surely this is justifiable. While it might be virtuous to turn the other cheek in such cases, few have argued over the ages that a person is morally required to do so. But beyond this point of near consensus, namely, that everyone has the right to strike back against another when necessary for self-defense, things get murky quickly.

Hugo Grotius, arguably the founder of modern international law, reminds us that there have been many reasons given for going to war, but only some of them are justifiable. Grotius warns against going to war on unjustified pretexts, that is, going to war "through what is expedient" rather than "what is right."[1] Among the unjustified pretexts for war was "the unjust cause of fear of something uncertain."[2] Preventive war is no more justified than is the killing of an individual who we merely fear may attack us. In this respect, Grotius was opposed by Alberico Gentili, the other leading international legal theorist of Grotius's time. Gentili argued that it is unreasonable to expect someone to wait to be attacked, or to be on the verge of attack, before it is justifiable to launch a preemptive attack of one's own. The debate between Gentili and Grotius closely mirrors the debate in the United States about the invasion of Iraq in 2003.

The main difficulty is to discern whether the adversary is merely meditating on doing evil or whether the adversary really is making serious preparatory attempts to attack. For, as Grotius pointed out, "those who accept fear of any sort as justifying anticipatory slaying are themselves greatly deceived."[3] Violence among persons, and war among states, is simply too important a matter to be allowable when mere fear exists, since "complete security is never guaranteed to us."[4] The better rule is not to attack "if the danger can in any other way be avoided."[5] This led Grotius to propose what is still accepted in international law today, namely, that the danger must be "immediate and imminent in point of time."[6] To establish this condition, evidence of planning that is virtually completed needs to be shown.

This brings us to the current intense dispute about whether President George W. Bush had sufficient grounds for going to war against Iraq. He claimed that he was justified so as to prevent (really to preempt) Iraq from attacking the United States. But such talk of prevention is imprecise, for it may refer either to a necessary preemption of an impending attack or merely to an unjustified fear as a pretext for war based on other motivations. In his 2003 State of the Union speech, Bush said that "The British government has learned that Saddam Hussein recently sought significant quantities of uranium from Africa." Such a claim was meant to show that Iraq posed an imminent, not merely a speculative threat to the United States. In addition, Bush said that he was not required to wait for the United States to be attacked, or even to wait for all of the evidence needed to show that Iraq might attack. But, in Grotius's view, Bush was not justified in going to war against Iraq on this basis. Rather, what was needed was something like what British Prime Minister Tony Blair said he had evidence for, namely, that Iraq could launch a nuclear attack on Britain in forty-five minutes, and that Saddam was planning to do so.

So, we can see the importance of the issue of whether Iraq had weapons of mass destruction, especially nuclear weapons that it was nearly ready to launch against Britain or the United States. Anticipatory or preemptive strikes against Iraq could have been justified if it could be shown that Iraq did indeed pose such an "immediate and imminent" danger. It was not sufficient merely to show that Iraq needed to be prevented from eventually posing such a threat, for then war would be waged on the basis of an unjustified fear and probably waged for a pretext. The United Nations was set up to deal with adjudicating disputes between states so as to prevent the escalation to war and in this respect the United Nations is founded in the legacy of both Gentili and Grotius. The basis of international law, the so-called laws of humanity, require that wars only be conducted to fend off attack or in the face of imminent threat of attack, not for mere prevention of what is feared, especially if this is pretext for other actual causes of war, such as oil.

Now let us turn to the second issue. One of the central ideas behind the Just War tradition is that there must be a just cause for war to be justifiable. The Jesuit schoolman, Francisco Suarez, went so far as to say that it was patently absurd that both sides could fight with just cause. If it turned out that two parties to a war could both be fighting for a just cause, then it would be impossible to determine which side was in the right and which side was in the wrong. The reason why this issue so vexed the adherents of the Just War tradition was that that tradition presumed that just cause was the key to determining if war was being waged justly. If this could not be determined, then the proposition expressed so well by Aquinas and reiterated by Francisco de Vitoria, namely, that "There is a single and only just cause for commencing a war, namely a wrong received" also could not be determined, and some wars would seemingly be neither just nor unjust. This issue is of pressing concern in today's pluralistic society where there is such a wide array of views about morality.

Vitoria, writing at the beginning of the sixteenth century, addressed this issue forthrightly, if not completely satisfactorily. Vitoria asked whether "a war can be just on both sides" and answered: "Apart from ignorance the case clearly cannot occur, for if the right and justice of each side be certain, it is unlawful to fight against it, either in offense or defense."[7] He says that what appears to be a just cause on both sides turns out to be at most a true just cause on one side and, because of ignorance, "the war is excused from sin by reason of good faith, because invincible ignorance is a complete excuse."[8] Vitoria seemingly did not see this as especially problematical.

Gentili, writing at the end of the sixteenth century seems to follow Vitoria, but ultimately both identifies the problem and seemingly gives it its due. He argues that there are several significant ways that it can be true that both sides in a war fight with just cause. Nonetheless, Gentili argues that only one side can properly have a just cause; the other side may, through "justifiable ignorance," believe that it also fights for a just cause, and hence "there may be reasonable doubt as to the justice of the cause."[9] If one side fights justly, and the other side believes that it has been unjustly attacked, then it may be that, in a sense, both sides fight with just cause. Here is one of his examples: "Thus led by the voice of God, the Jews justly made war against the Canaanites, and the Canaanites also justly resisted the Jews through ignorance of the divine utterance, acting in self-defense."[10] But if this argument is accepted, there are serious consequences for the very idea of distinguishing between just and unjust wars. For, as Gentili says, "it is the nature of wars for both sides to maintain that they are supporting a just cause." And Gentili forthrightly admits that "In general it may be true that neither of the two disputants is unjust."[11] Gentili seems to admit what Vitoria could not see, namely, the strong possibility in many cases that war could be waged where neither side is truly unjust. This admission, I will argue, should give us pause in accepting Just War theory as more than just a starting point to our reflections on war.

If Gentili is right, and his view seems quite plausible indeed, that both sides to a war often claim to both be in the right, where one side attacks for what it believes is a just cause and the other side defends on what it believes are good grounds namely, self-defense, then Just War theory needs to be very clear on what does and does not count as justifiable beliefs of rightness (or just cause). Think of the Iraq war. Even if it could be argued that the United States waged a Just War against Iraq, the preceding discussion illustrates that this does not mean that Iraq would therefore act unjustly in fighting back. Indeed, the whole attempt to portray Iraqi resistance to the United States–led invasion of Iraq as unjustified, perhaps even as acts of terrorists, is undermined by the strong possibility that the Iraqis believed that they were justified in acting in self-defense to counter the aggressive acts of the United States, and that this belief was not culpable. If Genitili is right, then the main issue will not be whether there is just cause on the side of one party rather than another, but whether one side's beliefs of just cause are culpably or non-culpably ignorant.

After Aquinas, the Just War tradition took a decidedly secular turn. Most especially, even clerical schoolmen like Vitoria argued that "Difference of religion is not a cause of just war."[12] But in Vitoria's day, as well as in our own, religion can promote beliefs that could, non-culpably, make one prone to war. The Islamic idea of a "Holy War" is probably not all that distant from the idea of a "Just War" coming out of the Christian tradition.[13] But if the religious belief that one has a right to resist infidels is a non-culpable belief, then difference of religion may unfortunately still give rise to just causes, at least non-culpable ignorance about just causes. In this way, the Just War tradition may not stand as a bulwark against religious zealotry, thereby undermining the most intuitively appealing aspect of Just War theory, namely the use of reason rather than emotion in determinations of whether it is justified to go to war.

How might non-culpable ignorance be reigned in? Let us just say that the Just War tradition does have some preliminary answers. Suarez argues that one should apply something like the same standard as that used to determine primary intent in doctrine of double effect cases. We should ask whether the resort to war was truly a last resort. Couldn't heretics and infidels be countered in many other ways than by waging wars? If so, then religious beliefs may be mere pretexts for waging war unjustifiably. But this probably won't help in the Iraq case, since the only way to stop the putative U.S. aggression was by waging war, first in normal battlefields and then in the streets. Hence, Just War theory seems to provide, once again, a good beginning to our deliberations. As we try to sort out truly non-culpable ignorance from culpable pretext, we won't have to go far from Suarez's interpretation of the Just War tradition. But obviously, this will not take us quite far enough either. This illustrates why in rethinking the Just War tradition we have come to realize that it is still a serviceable place to start to think about the moral justifiability of war, but it is rarely the place to end such reflections.

In the remainder of this introduction, we will briefly discuss what our book hopes to accomplish. As one can see from the Table of Contents, the first large part of the anthology is devoted to historical origins, with essays from Roman times until the middle of the nineteenth century. We begin with Cicero and end with Henry David Thoreau. The remaining parts of the book are devoted to the debates in the twentieth and early twenty-first centuries. We begin with William James and end with recent essays on Kosovo and Iraq. The various essays discuss many issues, including: why self-defense matters for the justification of wars and whether it is the only legitimate justificatory basis for war; and why poisonings but not bombing have been outlawed for a thousand years or more. There are many such puzzles and debates found in our book—arguably the most comprehensive treatment of the subject.

These essays create a multiparty dialogue on the subject of what counts as a Just War and how such a war should be conducted. Kant proposes that we think of the possibility of perpetual peace, but Clausewitz says that wars will always be with us. At very least, war will continue to plague us over the course of our natural lives. The anthology we have constructed aims to help people come to terms with war from the perspective of morality so that perhaps it will make more sense, or at very least, we will see what needs to be done to our world to make living there, even with our plague of wars, more endurable and humane.

Notes

1. Hugo Grotius, *De Jure Belli ac Pacis,* [1625] translated by Francis W. Kelsey, Oxford: Clarendon Press, 1925. Pretexts, for Grotius, are publicly declared reasons.
2. Ibid., p. 549.
3. Grotius, De Jure Belli ac Pacis, p. 173.
4. Ibid., p. 184.
5. Ibid., p. 175.
6. Ibid., p. 173.
7. Francisco de Vitoria, *De Indis et de De Ivre Belli Relectiones* [1557], translated by John Pawley Bate, edited by Ernest Nys, Washington: Carnegie Institution of Washington, 1917, p. 177.
8. Ibid.
9. Alberico Gentili, *De Jure Belli* [1598], trans. by John C. Rolfe, Oxford: Oxford U. P. 1933, p. 31.
10. Ibid.
11. Ibid.
12. Vitoria, *De Indus et de Ivre Belli Relectiones,* p. 170.
13. See for instance the striking parallels between Averroes's ideas about Jihad and Aquinas's views about Just War.

PART I

HISTORICAL ORIGINS

A. The Just War Theory

Discussion of war goes back at least to the time when discussion itself first began. The dilemma is that war seems to be justified, even necessary, especially in self-defense, but that war necessarily involves killing or risking death, which itself seems to be unjustified. Roman writers were clearly bothered by the demands of justice and mercy that both seemed to make it difficult, although not impossible, to justify war. Cicero concerns himself with justice and puts limits on how war can be justified, while Seneca, concerning himself more with mercy than justice, comes close to pacifism when he contemplates a world state in which sparing life is the greatest virtue. Early Christian writers sought to resolve the dilemma by forbidding war altogether, even in self-defense, as the epitome of Jesus's injunction to "Turn the other cheek." Tertullian embodies this tradition. And Augustine is the first major Christian theorist to confront the early Christian pacifists by arguing that some wars can be justifiably waged if there is a "just cause." In the late Middle Ages, Averroes and Aquinas refined what came to be called the "Just War Theory" in very different ways, at least in part because of the different experiences they drew upon.

There are two large categories of issues in what has come to be called The Just War Theory:

Jus ad bellum—under what conditions can war be justifiably initiated?
Jus in bello—what tactics may be justifiably employed in war?

Cicero, the most famous Roman philosopher and statesman, provides a brief and very early discussion of each of these categories. He contends that the "rights of war must be strictly observed" since humans have moral duties "even to those who have wronged us." War can only justifiably be fought when

1

"discussion" has failed or is not possible. And the "only excuse, therefore, for going to war is that we may live in peace unharmed." Concerning tactics, Cicero maintains that there is "a limit to retribution" and that "we should spare those who are not bloodthirsty and barbarous in their warfare." According to Cicero, justice demands that "humane laws" be adhered to even in war. Such restraint should be shown, again, even when we are dealing with our enemies. Cicero talks of the importance of fighting a "just war" and hence sets the stage for the more formal treatment of Just War Theory in later centuries.

Seneca, a Roman poet and orator, perhaps the greatest of the Stoic philosophers, writes of mercy as the most humane of virtues. The use of strength to cause harm is "pernicious." Humans by nature seek peace, but they do so under a common head. They seek to preserve themselves by combining together. But even, and especially, rulers must show mercy since the commonwealths over which they rule are merely the bodies of which the rulers are the minds. And no one is so foolish as to act harshly instead of mercifully to one's own body. Hence, the great minds must rise above petty feelings and display the greatest of the virtues. Taking life is the easy path; but sparing life when one can easily take it is the path of virtue. And given that there are not only individual states, but also a world state, mercy must be shown to all people, not merely to one's fellow nationals. Seneca thus comes to a position close to pacifism when he argues that sparing life is the greatest of virtues. But Seneca worries about what true pacifism will do to the Roman empire, just as he worries what will become of that empire if it does not show mercy.

Tertullian, one of the most uncompromising pacifists of the early Church fathers, makes his case for pacifism on the basis of Jesus's injunctions to turn away from the Old Testament vengeance standard—an eye for an eye. He likens military service to desertion from God's camp, the camp of Light, and the turn into the camp of Darkness. Tertullian's extremism can be seen when he admits that Christians should be ready to be martyrs rather than ever to take up arms. Even torture and punishment must be forborne out of respect for what Tertullian calls "the law of Christianity." In the final page of this brief excerpt, Tertullian suggests other bases for Christian pacifism: tombs, corpses, and the tears of wives and mothers are all that clearly follows from war; one cannot serve two masters, both God and Caesar. Tertullian also argues that any public service is problematic on similar grounds to service in war, since in both cases a person suffers from dirty hands.

According to Augustine, Bishop of Hippo in the fourth century, war can be justified if it is made by authority of God: either ordered by God directly, or prescribed by God's law, that is "by a just law." In such circumstances, a warrior is then the instrument of God, and "does not himself kill." This is an interesting way to get out of the predicament that Tertullian described. Notice, though, that without this proviso, acts of war are indeed instances of killing and perhaps even murder. In Book 19 of *The City of God*, Augustine speaks of "the necessity of waging just wars." This is the origin of the idea of Just War Theory that continues to our present day to be the most important theoretical position on the morality of war. Even though war involves "slaughter of human beings, [with] all the blood that is shed," if there is sufficient "evil" or "injustice" to be combated, then God's law compels war. The chief desire (and what Aquinas calls the primary intention) must be to maintain peace. So, initially, war is justified to sustain that peace, that is, to stymy an aggressor. This is later called "defensive" wars and is the easiest to justify, namely as a form of self-defense. Augustine derides the peace of the unjust, as "not being worth the name peace."

What is curious is that Augustine also goes on to defend "offensive" wars. Two principles are articulated: do no harm, and help everyone wherever possible. So, if one person sins by wronging another person, war may be justified to punish or gain recompense for the victim. Augustine seems to support the disturbing view that war can be rightly waged to replace one form of peace with another that merely "suits the wishes" of a given state. Such war is justified according to the laws of war as Augustine understands them. These laws are pretty clearly moral in two senses: as conventionally or customarily understood, and as justified by reference to God's higher law.

Both Augustine and Aquinas see war as justified if it is waged to convert infidels, since the infidels harm self and others. This is also the view of the famous Medieval Islamic philosopher, Averroes. Averroes uses the term Jihad, or holy war, to refer to war that is justified on religious grounds as saving infidels from false or ruinous theological beliefs. For Averroes, waging holy war is a collective rather than a personal obligation. Jihad can be seen as defensive, defending the faith, or offensive, since it is not really aimed at defending lives under physical attack. The main focus of Jihad are those who are polytheists, although some monotheists, such as Christians, are also mentioned as people who might be justifiably attacked so they can be converted to the true religion. Either the unbelievers must convert, or they must pay a tax to show homage to the true religion and so as to spare themselves from being justifiably killed.

Averroes asks about tactics as well as about waging war, and he takes a surprising position concerning who can justifiably be killed in wars: "Muslims agree that in times of war, all adult, able-bodied, unbelieving males may be slain." The idea seems to be that it is not only justifiable to kill members of army units, but also those who might be replacements in those armies. Contemporary Just War theorists confront this view by making a significant distinction between combatants and civilians.

Aquinas, the greatest theologian of the late Middle Ages, codifies the religiously oriented Just War tradition's consensus in remarkably clear terms and also anticipates much of the later debates. In our short selection from his massive *Summa Theologica*, we learn that for war to be just three things are necessary:

(a) War must be waged by a sovereign [now called a "competent authority"];
(b) War must be waged for a just cause;
(c) War must be waged with rightful intention.

Other elements will be added by subsequent theorists, but this formulation has served as the rudimentary model of the Just War Theory for almost a millennium.

Aquinas also has a very clear discussion of whether ambushes and other tactics are justified, discussing such issues in terms of the rights of war, even the rights of one's enemies. This idea, that in war all parties have certain rights that should not be violated, is the cornerstone of the *jus ad bello* prong of the Just War Theory. Aquinas is also the first to discuss an enormously influential doctrine, the doctrine of double effect. Tactics may be justified even if they lead to the intentional killing of a person, as long as the primary intention of those tactics is to further a just cause. If one's intention is to save one's life, not to slay the other, such slaying can be justified because the killing of the other is not directly intended. Finally, Aquinas also briefly mentions another important principle, proportionality, namely, that a person cannot be justified in using more than necessary violence even in wartime.

The Just War tradition was launched in these Roman and Medieval texts. Significant refinements were made in the sixteenth and seventeenth centuries, most especially in providing a secular basis for what had been a purely religious doctrine in the Middle Ages. But the elements, especially those identified by Aquinas, remained pretty much intact, although debates broke out regularly about how to understand both the justification for going to war, as well as the justification for the use of various tactics, as we will see in the next section of readings.

On Duties

(C. 45 B.C.)

Cicero

Marcus Tullius Cicero (106–43 B.C.) was one of the most famous Roman orators and statesmen who also wrote significant works in philosophy, law, and politics. Among his most influential works are De Re Publica *and* De Officiis *(On Duties).*

BOOK I. X.–XIV.

XI. Again, there are certain duties that we owe even to those who have wronged us. For there is a limit to retribution and to punishment; or rather, I am inclined to think, it is sufficient that the aggressor should be brought to repent of his wrongdoing, in order that he may not repeat the offence and that others may be deterred from doing wrong.

Then, too, in the case of a state in its external relations, the rights of war must be strictly observed. For since there are two ways of settling a dispute: first, by discussion; second, by physical force; and since the former is characteristic of man, the latter of the brute, we must resort to force only in case we may not avail ourselves of discussion. The only excuse, therefore, for going to war is that we may live in peace unharmed; and when the victory is won, we should spare those who have not been blood-thirsty and barbarous in their warfare. For instance, our forefathers actually admitted to full rights of citizenship the Tusculans, Aequians, Volscians, Sabines, and Hernicians, but they razed Carthage and Numantia to the ground. I wish they had not destroyed Corinth; but I believe they had some special reason for what they did—its convenient situation, probably—and feared that its very location might some day furnish a temptation to renew the war. In my opinion, at least, we should always strive to secure a peace that shall not admit of guile. And if my advice had been heeded on this point, we should still have at least some sort of constitutional government, if not the best in the world, whereas, as it is, we have none at all.

Not only must we show consideration for those whom we have conquered by force of arms but we must also ensure protection to those who lay down their arms and throw themselves upon the mercy of our generals, even though the battering-ram has hammered at their walls. And among our countrymen justice has been observed so conscientiously in this direction, that those who have given promise of protection to states or nations subdued in war become, after the custom of our forefathers, the patrons of those states.

As for war, humane laws touching it are drawn up in the fetial code of the Roman People under all the guarantees of

5

religion; and from this it may be gathered that no war is just, unless it is entered upon after an official demand for satisfaction has been submitted or warning has been given and a formal declaration made. Popilius was general in command of a province. In his army Cato's son was serving on his first campaign. When Popilius decided to disband one of his legions, he discharged also young Cato, who was serving in that same legion. But when the young man out of love for the service stayed on in the field, his father wrote to Popilius to say that if he let him stay in the army, he should swear him into service with a new oath of allegiance, for in view of the voidance of his former oath he could not legally fight the foe. So extremely scrupulous was the observance of the laws in regard to the conduct of war. There is extant, too, a letter of the elder Marcus Cato to his son Marcus, in which he writes that he has heard that the youth has been discharged by the consul,[a] when he was serving in Macedonia in the war with Perseus. He warns him, therefore, to be careful not to go into battle; for, he says, the man who is not legally a soldier has no right to be fighting the foe.

XII. This also I observe—that he who would properly have been called "a fighting enemy" (*perduellis*) was called "a guest" (*hostis*), thus relieving the ugliness of the fact by a softened expression; for "enemy" (*hostis*) meant to our ancestors what we now call "stranger" (*peregrinus*). This is proved by the usage in the Twelve Tables: "Or a day fixed for trial with a stranger" (*hostis*). And again: "Right of ownership is inalienable for ever in dealings with a stranger" (*hostis*). What can exceed such charity, when he with whom one is at war is called by so gentle a name?

And yet long lapse of time has given that word a harsher meaning: for it has lost its signification of "stranger" and has taken on the technical connotation of "an enemy under arms."

But when a war is fought out for supremacy and when glory is the object of war, it must still not fail to start from the same motives which I said a moment ago were the only righteous grounds for going to war. But those wars which have glory for their end must be carried on with less bitterness. For we contend, for example, with a fellow-citizen in one way, if he is a personal enemy, in another, if he is a rival: with the rival it is a struggle for office and position, with the enemy for life and honour. So with the Celtiberians and the Cimbrians we fought as with deadly enemies, not to determine which should be supreme, but which should survive; but with the Latins, Sabines, Samnites, Carthaginians, and Pyrrhus we fought for supremacy. The Carthaginians violated treaties; Hannibal was cruel; the others were more merciful. From Pyrrhus we have this famous speech on the exchange of prisoners:

> "Gold will I none, nor price shall ye give; for I ask none;
> Come, let us not be chaff'rers of war, but warriors embattled.
> Nay; let us venture our lives, and the sword, not gold, weigh the outcome.
> Make we the trial by valour in arms and see if Dame Fortune
> Wills it that ye shall prevail or I, or what be her judgment.
> Hear thou, too, this word, good Fabricius: whose valour soever
> Spared hath been by the fortune of war— their freedom I grant them.
> Such my resolve. I give and present them to you, my brave Romans;
> Take them back to their homes; the great gods' blessings attend you."

A right kingly sentiment this and worthy a scion of the Aeacidae.

XIII. Again, if under stress of circumstances individuals have made any promise to the enemy, they are bound to keep their word even then. For instance, in the First Punic War, when Regulus was taken prisoner by the Carthaginians, he was sent to Rome on parole to negotiate an exchange of prisoners; he came and, in the first place, it was he that made the motion in the Senate that the prisoners should not be restored; and in the second place, when his relatives and friends would have kept him back, he chose to return to a death by torture rather than prove false to his promise, though given to an enemy.

And again in the Second Punic War, after the Battle of Cannae, Hannibal sent to Rome ten Roman captives bound by an oath to return to him, if they did not succeed in ransoming his prisoners; and as long as any one of them lived, the censors kept them all degraded and disfranchised, because they were guilty of perjury in not returning. And they punished in like manner the one who had incurred guilt by an evasion of his oath: with Hannibal's permission this man left the camp and returned a little later on the pretext that he had forgotten something or other; and then, when he left the camp the second time, he claimed that he was released from the obligation of his oath; and so he was, according to the letter of it, but not according to the spirit. In the matter of a promise one must always consider the meaning and not the mere words.

Our forefathers have given us another striking example of justice toward an enemy: when a deserter from Pyrrhus promised the Senate to administer poison to the king and thus work his death, the Senate and Gaius Fabricius delivered the deserter up to Pyrrhus. Thus they stamped with their disapproval the treacherous murder even of an enemy who was at once powerful, unprovoked, aggressive, and successful.

With this I will close my discussion of the duties connected with war.

But let us remember that we must have regard for justice even towards the humblest. Now the humblest station and the poorest fortune are those of slaves; and they give us no bad rule who bid us treat our slaves as we should our employees: they must be required to work; they must be given their dues.

While wrong may be done, then, in either of two ways, that is, by force or by fraud, both are bestial: fraud seems to belong to the cunning fox, force to the lion; both are wholly unworthy of man, but fraud is the more contemptible. But of all forms of injustice, none is more flagrant than that of the hypocrite who, at the very moment when he is most false, makes it his business to appear virtuous.

This must conclude our discussion of justice.

On Mercy

(c. 56)

Seneca

Lucius Annaeus Seneca (c. 4 B.C.–65 A.D.) was tutor and political advisor to the young emperor Nero. He is also one of the best known Stoic philosophers. His works include his Letters *and* De Clementia *(On Mercy), which is dedicated to Nero.*

THE EXCELLENCE OF MERCY

Mercy the Royal Virtue

(2) Of all the virtues, in truth, none befits a human being more, since none is more humane. That is a necessary point of agreement not only among ourselves with our view that man should be seen as a social animal born for the common good, but also among those who give man over to pleasure and whose every word and action looks to their own advantage. For if a man seeks calm and leisure, he acquires here a virtue which, with its love of peace and restraint on action, suits his nature. (3) Of all men, however, mercy becomes no one more than a king or a prince. What gives great might its grace and glory is its power for good; strength to harm is simply pernicious force. He alone has a firm, well-founded greatness whom all know to be not only above them but also for them, whose vigilant care for the safety of each and every one they experience every day, whose approach is not like the leap of an evil, dangerous beast from its lair, before which they scatter in flight, but rather that of a bright and kindly star. Racing each other they fly towards him, in total readiness to throw themselves on to the blades of those who lie in wait for him, to cast their own bodies to the ground if human slaughter is needed to provide the foundation of his road to safety. They watch over his sleep at night. They protect his person, making themselves a barrier to encircle it. As danger approaches, they interpose. (4) There is reason behind this unanimity of peoples and cities in their protection and love of kings, in their sacrifice of themselves and their own, whenever the safety of their commander requires it. It is not through lack of self-esteem or of sanity that thousands face the sword for one person and rescue, by a multitude of deaths, one life—sometimes that of a feeble old man. (5) Compare the way in which the body is entirely at the service of the mind. It may be ever so much larger and more impressive. The mind may remain hidden and tiny, its very location uncertain. Yet hands, feet and eyes do its business. The skin that we see protects it. At its command, we lie still. Or else we run restlessly about, when it has given the order. If its avarice masters us, we scan the sea for material gain. Its lust for glory has long since led us to thrust our right hand into the flame or plunge of our own free will into the earth. In the same way, this

vast multitude of men surrounds one man as though he were its mind, ruled by his spirit, guided by his reason; it would crush and shatter itself by its own strength, without the support of his discernment.

4 (I) Their own safety is thus what men have at heart when for one man they lead ten legions into battle, rushing at the front line and baring their breasts to the wounds, lest their emperor's standards be overthrown. For he is the bond which holds the commonwealth together; he is the breath of life drawn by these several thousands. They themselves would be nothing but a burden, a prey, were that mind of the empire to be withdrawn.

> While he survives, in concord and content
> The commons live, by no divisions rent,
> But the great monarch's death dissolves
> 　the government.

(2) Such a disaster would be the end of the Roman peace, driving the fortunes of our great people to ruin. That people will only escape the danger for so long as it can endure the reins. Should it break them, should it find them shaken off and not allow them to be put on again, the unified structure of this far-flung empire will shatter into a multitude of parts, and this city's dominance will have ended with its willingness to obey. (3) No wonder, then, that princes and kings and whatever other title there may be for guardians of public order, should meet with a love surpassing even the bonds of private affinity. For if men of sense put public interests before private, it follows that their affection will also be greater for one on whom the whole commonwealth turns. Long ago, in fact, Caesar so worked himself into the commonwealth, that neither could be separated without the ruin of the other. He needs the strength, and the commonwealth needs a head.

5 (I) My discourse may seem to have digressed some way from its subject. In truth, it bears closely on the real question. For if, as has just been shown, your commonwealth is your body and you are its mind, you can see, I think, how necessary mercy is. You are sparing yourself, when you appear to spare another. So even culpable citizens should be spared in the same way as unsound limbs. If ever there is need for blood to be let, you should stay the knife, lest it cut beyond what is needed. (2) Mercy, as I said, is natural to all human beings. Yet it most becomes emperors, finding when among them more to save and greater scope for revealing itself. How tiny is the harm done by the cruelty of private individuals! But the raging of princes means war. (3) There is, to be sure, a concord among the virtues. Each of them is as good and honourable as the other. Yet one may be more suitable to some people. Greatness of mind befits any mortal, even the poorest—is anything greater or braver than to beat back the force of ill fortune? But this greatness of mind has freer scope in good fortune, and is shown to better effect up on the magistrate's bench than down on the floor. (4) Mercy, whatever house it enters, will make it happy and calm. In a palace, its rarity renders it the more amazing. For what is more remarkable than that one whose anger has nothing to resist it, whose severest sentence commands the assent of the very people who perish by it, whom no one is going to sue or even entreat, if he has been too fiercely incensed—that this very man should take hold of himself, putting his power to better, more peaceful use with this very thought: 'Anyone can break the law in order to take a life. No one except for me can do so to save a life!'? (5) A great mind is an adornment to great fortune, but

it must rise to it and stand above it—or else bring down fortune, too, to the ground. Now the characteristic of a great mind is to be peaceful and calm, looking down from above at injuries and affronts. It is for women to rave in anger, for wild beasts—and not even the noble ones at that—to bite and worry the fallen. Elephants and lions walk past what they have struck down; relentlessness is the mark of an ignoble animal. (6) Savage, inexorable anger is not becoming to a king. He cannot tower much above any person on whose level he has placed himself by growing angry. But if he grants life and dignity to men who have risked and deserve to lose them, he does what none save a man of power can do. One can take the life of even a superior; one cannot grant it to anyone except an inferior. (7) To save life is the prerogative of high good fortune, never more admirable than when it attains the same power as the gods, by whose favour we are brought into the light of day, good men and bad alike. So a prince should adopt as his own the attitude of the gods. Some citizens, because they are useful and good, he should look upon with pleasure, others he should leave to make up the number, rejoicing in the existence of some, enduring that of the others.

6 (I) Consider this city where the crowd flows without pause through its broadest streets, crushed if anything stands in the way to hold back the swift current of its movement, where the capacities of three whole theatres are required at one and the same time, where produce grown all over the world is consumed—think what an empty waste there would be if nothing were left of it save those whom a stern judge would acquit! (2) How few investigators there are who would not be found guilty under the very law by which they make their investigation! How few ac-

cusers are blameless! Is anyone more reluctant, I wonder, to grant pardon than he who has all too often had reason to seek it? (3) We have all done wrong, some seriously, some more trivially, some on purpose, some perhaps under impulse or led astray by the wickedness of others. Some of us were not firm enough in our good intentions, losing our innocence unwillingly, clutching at it as we lost it. Nor have we merely transgressed—to the end of our lives we shall continue to transgress. (4) Suppose, indeed, that someone has so purged his mind as to be beyond further reach of confusion or deception. His innocence has been reached, none the less, through doing wrong.

7 (I) Having mentioned the gods, I can do no better than to make them a model for the prince: he should wish to be to the citizens as he would wish the gods to be to him. Can it be good that the powers of heaven should be inexorably set against sin and error, hostile to the very point of our final destruction? Could any king in that case be safely assured that his limbs would not have to be gathered together by the sooth-sayers? (2) But if the gods, neither implacable nor unreasonable, are not given to pursuing the crimes of potentates immediately with their thunderbolts, how much more reasonable is it for a man set in authority over men to exercise his command in a gentle spirit and to reflect: When is the world's state more pleasing to the eye and lovelier? On a day serene and bright? Or when all is shaken by frequent thunderbolts and the lightning flashes hither and thither? And yet the look of a calm, well-ordered empire is like that of the sky serene and shining. (3) A reign that is cruel is troubled and overcast. All there tremble and start up at any sudden noise. Nor is the cause of the universal disturbance himself unshaken.

Private individuals are more easily pardoned if they avenge themselves relentlessly. They can be hurt; they are open to pain from wrongs done to them. Besides, they are afraid of contempt, and not to pay back in kind those who harm them looks like weakness, not mercy. But those to whom vengeance is easy can do without it and gain sure praise for their gentleness. (4) Men of humble position are free to use violence, go to law, rush into brawls and indulge their anger—blows between equals are slight. For a king, it hardly accords with his majesty so much as to raise his voice or use intemperate language.

8 (I) You may think it hard that kings should be deprived of that freedom in speaking which even the humblest enjoy. 'This is *slavery*,' you may say, 'not supreme command.' What! Are you not aware that this supreme command means *noble* slavery for you? The situation is different for those who lurk in the crowd without leaving it, whose virtues have to fight long to come into the open and whose vices have the cover of darkness. But what you say and do is seized on by rumour; and that is why none should care more about their reputation than those whose reputation, whatever their deserts may be, is going to be great. (2) How much there is that you are forbidden but we, thanks to you, are allowed! I can walk without fear wherever I will in the city, with no escort to follow me, with no sword either at home or at my side. You, in the peace that you guarantee, must live under arms. You cannot escape your lot. It besets you; wherever you descend, it follows you with its mass of trappings. (3) The slavery of being supremely great lies in the impossibility of ever becoming anything less. But this constraint is one which you share with the gods. They too are held bound to the heavens. No more is it granted to them than it would be safe for you to come down. You are fixed to your pinnacle. (4) When we move, few notice. We can go, come back, change costume unnoticed by the public. You have no more chance than the sun of not being seen. A flood of light meets you face to face, and the eyes of all are turned towards it. You think you are setting out—in fact, you are rising. (5) You cannot speak without your voice being heard by the nations everywhere; you cannot show anger without everything trembling at it, since you cannot strike anyone without throwing whatever is around him into turmoil. When thunderbolts fall, few are endangered, but all are terrified. In the same way, punishments by mighty potentates cause more terror than harm—and not without reason: it is not what he has done, but what he may do, that people consider in the case of one who can do anything.

(6) Consider this, too. Private individuals are likelier to have wrongs done to them by putting up with wrongs which already have been done. For kings, however, the surer way to security is through gentleness, since frequent punishment, while it crushes hatred in a few, arouses it in everyone. (7) The wish to rage should cease, sooner than the occasion. Otherwise, in the same way that trees which have been chopped down sprout again with a multitude of branches and many plants are pruned to make them grow thicker, the cruelty of a king increases the number of his enemies by removing them. Parents and children of those slain, kinsmen and friends, take the place of each single victim.

The Soldier's Chaplet

(c. 210)

Tertullian

Quintus Septimus Florens Tertullian (c. 160–220) was an African Church father. Born in Carthage and trained in Roman law, he converted to Christianity, only to break with other Church fathers toward the end of his life, when The Soldier's Chaplet *was written.*

CHAPTER 11

(1) Now, to come down to the very heart of this question about the soldier's crown, should we not really first examine the right of a Christian to be in the military service at all? In other words, why discuss the merely accidental detail, when the foundation on which it rests is deserving of censure? Are we to believe it lawful to take an oath of allegiance to a mere human being over and above the oath of fidelity to God? Can we obey another master, having chosen Christ? Can we forsake father, mother, and all our relatives? By divine law we must honor them and our love for them is second only to that which we have toward God. The Gospel also bids us honor our parents, placing none but Christ Himself above them. (2) Is it likely we are permitted to carry a sword when our Lord said that he who takes the sword will perish by the sword? Will the son of peace who is forbidden to engage in a lawsuit espouse the deeds of war? Will a Christian, taught to turn the other cheek when struck unjustly, guard prisoners in chains, and administer torture and capital punishment? (3) Will he rather mount guard for others than for Christ on station days? And what about the Lord's Day? Will he not even then do it for Christ? Will he stand guard before temples, that he has renounced? Will he eat at pagan banquets, which the Apostle forbids? Will he protect by night those very demons whom in the daytime he has put to flight by his exorcisms, leaning on a lance such as pierced the side of Christ [on the cross]? Will he bear, too, a standard that is hostile to Christ, and will he ask the watch-word from his commander-in-chief—he who has already received one from God? Moreover, after death, will he be disturbed by the horn of the trumpeter—he who expects to be aroused by the trumpet of the angel? Will his corpse be cremated according to military custom—when he, a Christian, was not permitted to burn incense in sacrifice, when to him Christ remitted the eternal punishment by fire he had deserved?

(4) Yes, these and many other offenses can be observed in the discharge of military duties—offenses that must be interpreted as acts of desertion. To leave the camp of Light and enlist in the camp of Darkness means going over to the enemy.

To be sure, the case is different for those who are converted after they have been bound to military service. St. John admitted soldiers to baptism; then there were the two most faithful centurions: the one whom Christ praised, and the other whom Peter instructed. But, once we have embraced the faith and have been baptized, we either must immediately leave military service (as many have done); or we must resort to all kinds of excuses in order to avoid any action which is also forbidden in civilian life, lest we offend God; or, last of all, for the sake of God we must suffer the fate which a mere citizen-faith was no less ready to accept.

(5) For, military service offers neither exemption from punishment of sins nor relief from martyrdom. The Gospel is one and the same for the Christian at all times whatever his occupation in life. Jesus will deny those who deny Him and confess those who confess Him; He will save the life that has been lost for His Name's sake, but He will destroy the one that has been gained against His Name. With Him the faithful citizen is a soldier, just as the faithful soldier is a citizen. (6) The state of faith admits no plea of compulsion. Those are under no compulsion to sin whose sole obligation is not to sin. A Christian may be pressed to the offering of sacrifice and to the straight denial of Christ under threat of torture and punishment. Yet, the law of Christianity does not excuse even that compulsion, since there is a stronger obligation to dread the denial of the faith and to undergo martyrdom than to escape suffering and to perform the sacrificial rite required. (7) Moreover, that kind of argument destroys the very essence of our sacramental oath, since it would loosen the fetters for voluntary sins. For, it will be possible to maintain that inclination is a compulsion, too, since there is, indeed, some sort of compelling force in it. The foregoing principles I wish to have also applied to the other occasions for wearing crowns in some official capacity (it is with reference to such occasions especially that people are wont to plead compulsion), since for this very reason we must either refuse public offices lest we fall into sin, or we must endure martyrdom in order to sever our connection with them.

CHAPTER 12

(1) I will not waste any more words over the essential point of the question, namely, the unlawfulness of military life itself, but return to the secondary point of the matter. Indeed, if, employing all my efforts, I do away with military service altogether, there will be little point in issuing a challenge on the military crown. Let us assume, then, that military service is permitted up to the point of wearing a crown. Let me say, first, a word about the crown itself. We know from Claudius that the laurel crown (such as the one in question) is sacred to Apollo as the god of archery and to Bacchus as the god of triumphs. (2) He also tells us that soldiers were often garlanded with myrtle. 'For the myrtle,' he writes, 'belongs to Venus, the mother of the descendants of Aeneas, the mistress also of Mars, who through Ilia and her twins is Roman herself.' But I myself do not believe that Venus shares in this respect the friendly feelings of Mars for Rome, in view of the god's dealing with a concubine. Moreover, when a soldier is crowned with an olive wreath, he commits idolatry to Minerva, who is also a goddess of arms,

even though she crowned her head with an olive branch to celebrate her peace with Neptune. In all these relations we see the defiled and all-defiling superstitious character of the military crown. In fact, I think that the very motives for wearing it causes its defilement.

(3) Take the annual public pronouncement of vows. What do you think of it? The first takes place in the general's quarters; the second, in heathen temples. In addition to the places, note the words, also; 'We promise to give to you, then, O Jupiter, an ox with golden horns.' What is the real sense of that pronouncement? Is it not a denial of the faith? Even though the Christian says nothing on that occãsion with his mouth, he makes his response by having the crown on his head. The wearing of the laurel crown is likewise enjoined at the distribution of a largess, though, plainly, you do not attend this ceremony without making a profit.

(4) Idolater! Do you not see that you are selling Christ for a few pieces of gold, just as Judas sold him for silver? It is written: 'You cannot serve God and mammon.' Does this perhaps mean that you can do both things: reach out your hand to mammon and stand on the side of God? And what about 'Render to Caesar the things that are Caesar's and to God the things that are God's? Does this perhaps mean that you can withhold the man from God and take the denarius from Caesar? Is the laurel of triumph made of leaves, or of corpses? Is it adorned with ribbons, or with tombs? Is it anointed with perfumes, or with the tears of wives and mothers, some of them, perhaps, Christian women, for we know that Christianity has also spread among the barbarians. (5) Has the man who wears a crown as a symbol of glory not actually fought in battle? There is yet another kind of military service—that of the bodyguard in the imperial household. For these men, too, are called 'soldiers of the camp,' and they perform services in connection with the ceremonial observed in the imperial court. But, even then you are still the soldier and servant of another, and if of two masters—God and Caesar—then, certainly, not of Caesar, when you owe yourself to God, who, I am inclined to believe, has a higher claim even in matters in which both have an interest.

The City of God

(c. 420)

Augustine

Augustine (354–430) was born in North Africa and trained in Roman rhetoric and Neo-platonism. In 386, he converted to Christianity, becoming a priest and then Bishop of Hippo. He wrote The City of God, *as well* The Confessions.

Book I, Chapter 22

21. All homicide is not murder

There are however certain exceptions to the law against killing, made by the authority of God himself. There are some whose killing God orders, either by a law, or by an express command to a particular person at a particular time. In fact one who owes a duty of obedience to the giver of the command does not himself 'kill'—he is an instrument, a sword in its user's hand. For this reason the commandment forbidding killing was not broken by those who have waged wars on the authority of God, or those who have imposed the death-penalty on criminals when representing the authority of the State in accordance with the laws of the State, the justest and most reasonable source of power. When Abraham was ready to kill his son, so far from being blamed for cruelty he was praised for his devotion; it was not an act of crime, but of obedience. One is justified in asking whether Jephtha is to be regarded as obeying a command of God in killing his daughter, when he had vowed to sacrifice to God the first thing he met when returning victorious from battle. And when Samson destroyed himself, with his enemies, by the demolition of the building, this can only be excused on the ground that the Spirit, which performed miracles through him, secretly ordered him to do so. With the exception of these killings prescribed generally by a just law, or specially commanded by God himself—the source of justice—anyone who kills a human being, whether himself or anyone else, is involved in a charge of murder. . . .

BOOK XIX

1. The philosophic debate on the Supreme Good and Evil

It is clear to me that my next task is to discuss the appointed ends of these two cities, the earthly and the heavenly. Hence I must first explain, as far as is allowed by the limits I have designed for this work, the arguments advanced by mortal men in their endeavour to create happiness for themselves amidst the unhappiness of this life.

•••

7. Human society divided by differences of language. The misery of war, even when just

After the city or town comes the world, which the philosophers reckon as the third level of human society. They begin with the household, proceed to the city, and then arrive at the world. Now the world, being like a confluence of waters, is obviously more full of danger than the other communities by reason of its greater size. To begin with, on this level the diversity of languages separates man from man. For if two men meet, and are forced by some compelling reason not to pass on but to stay in company, then if neither knows the other's language, it is easier for dumb animals, even of different kinds, to associate together than these men, although both are human beings. For when men cannot communicate their thoughts to each other, simply because of difference of language, all the similarity of their common human nature is of no avail to unite them in fellowship. So true is this that a man would be more cheerful with his dog for company than with a foreigner. I shall be told that the Imperial City has been at pains to impose on conquered peoples not only her yoke but her language also, as a bond of peace and fellowship, so that there should be no lack of interpreters but even a profusion of them. True; but think of the cost of this achievement! Consider the scale of those wars, with all that slaughter of human beings, all the human blood that was shed!

Those wars are now past history; and yet the misery of these evils is not yet ended. For although there has been, and still is, no lack of enemies among foreign nations, against whom wars have always been waged, and are still being waged, yet the very extent of the Empire has given rise to wars of a worse kind, namely, social and civil wars, by which mankind is more lamentably disquieted either when fighting is going on in the hope of bringing hostilities eventually to a peaceful end, or when there are fears that hostilities will break out again. If I were to try to describe, with an eloquence worthy of the subject, the many and multifarious disasters, the dour and dire necessities, I could not possibly be adequate to the theme, and there would be no end to this protracted discussion. But the wise man, they say, will wage just wars. Surely, if he remembers that he is a human being, he will rather lament the fact that he is faced with the necessity of waging just wars; for if they were not just, he would not have to engage in them, and consequently there would be no wars for a wise man. For it is the injustice of the opposing side that lays on the wise man the duty of waging wars; and this injustice is assuredly to be deplored by a human being, since it is the injustice of human beings, even though no necessity for war should arise from it. And so everyone who reflects with sorrow on such grievous evils, in all their horror and cruelty, must acknowledge the misery of them. And yet a man who experiences such evils, or even thinks about them, without heartfelt grief, is assuredly in a far more pitiable condition, if he thinks himself happy simply because he has lost all human feeling.

• • •

12. Peace is the instinctive aim of all creatures, and is even the ultimate purpose of war

Anyone who joins me in an examination, however slight, of human affairs, and the human nature we all share, recognizes that just as there is no man who does not wish for joy, so there is no man who does not wish for peace. Indeed, even when men choose war, their only wish is for victory; which shows that their desire in fighting is for peace with glory. For what is victory but the conquest of the opposing side? And when this is achieved, there will be peace. Even wars, then, are waged with peace as their object, even when they are waged by those who are concerned to exercise their warlike prowess, either in command or in the actual fighting. Hence it is an established fact that peace is the desired end of war. For every man is in quest of peace, even in waging war, whereas no one is in quest of war when making peace. In fact, even when men wish a present state of peace to be disturbed they do so not because they hate peace, but because they desire the present peace to be exchanged for one that suits their wishes. Thus their desire is not that there should not be peace but that it should be the kind of peace they wish for. Even in the extreme case when they have separated themselves from others by sedition, they cannot achieve their aim unless they maintain some sort of semblance of peace with their confederates in conspiracy. Moreover, even robbers, to ensure greater efficiency and security in their assaults on the peace of the rest of mankind, desire to preserve peace with their associates.

Indeed, one robber may be so unequalled in strength and so wary of having anyone to share his plans that he does not trust any associate, but plots his crimes and achieves his successes by himself, carrying off his booty after overcoming and dispatching such as he can; yet even so he maintains some kind of shadow of peace, at least with those whom he cannot kill, and from whom he wishes to conceal his activities. At the same time, he is anxious, of course, to be at peace in his own home, with his wife and children and any other members of his household; without doubt he is delighted to have them obedient to his beck and call. For if this does not happen, he is indignant; he scolds and punishes; and, if need be, he employs savage measures to impose on his household a peace which, he feels, cannot exist unless all the other elements in the same domestic society are subject to one head; and this head, in his own home, is himself. Thus, if he were offered the servitude of a larger number, of a city, maybe, or a whole nation, on the condition that they should all show the same subservience he had demanded from his household, then he would no longer lurk like a brigand in his hide-out; he would raise himself on high as a king for all to see—although the same greed and malignity would persist in him.

We see, then, that all men desire to be at peace with their own people, while wishing to impose their will upon those people's lives. For even when they wage war on others, their wish is to make those opponents their own people, if they can— to subject them, and to impose on them their own conditions of peace.

Let us, however, suppose such a man as is described in the verse or epic legends, a creature so unsociable and savage that they perhaps preferred to call him a semi-human rather than a human being. Now although his kingdom was the solitude of a dreadful cavern, and although he was so unequalled in wickedness that a name was found for him derived from that quality (he was called Cacus, and *kakos* is the Greek word for 'wicked'); although he had no wife with whom to exchange endearments, no children to play with when little or to give orders to when they were a little bigger, no friends with whom to enjoy a chat, not even his father, Vulcan (he was happier than his father only in this important respect—that he did not beget another such monster as himself); although he never gave anything to anyone, but took what he wanted from anyone he could and removed, when he could, anyone he wished to remove; despite all this, in the very solitude of his cave, the floor of which, in the poet's description

> reeked ever with the blood of recent
> slaughter

his only desire was for a peace in which no one should disturb him, and no man's violence, or the dread of it, should trouble his repose.

• • •

It comes to this, then; a man who has learnt to prefer right to wrong and the rightly ordered to the perverted, sees that the peace of the unjust, compared with the peace of the just, is not worthy even of the name of peace. Yet even what is perverted must of necessity be in, or derived from, or associated with—that is, in a sense, at peace with—some part of the order of things among which it has its being or of which it consists. Otherwise it would not exist at all. For instance if anyone were to hang upside-down, this position of the body and arrangement of the limbs is undoubtedly perverted, because what should be on top, according to the dictates of nature, is underneath, and what nature intends to be underneath is on top. This perverted attitude disturbs the peace of the flesh, and causes distress for that reason. For all that, the breath is at peace with its body and is busily engaged for its preservation; that is why there is something to endure the pain. And even if the breath is finally driven from the body by its distresses, still, as long as the framework of the limbs holds together, what remains retains a kind of peace among the bodily parts; hence there is still something to hang there. And in that the earthly body pulls towards the earth, and pulls against the binding rope that holds it suspended, it tends towards the position of its own peace, and by what might be called the appeal of its weight, it demands a place where it may rest. And so even when it is by now lifeless and devoid of all sensation it does not depart from the peace of its natural position, either while possessed of it or while tending towards it. Again, if treatment with embalming fluids is applied to prevent the dissolution and disintegration of the corpse in its present shape, a kind of peace still connects the parts with one another and keeps the whole mass fixed in its earthly condition, an appropriate, and therefore a peaceable state.

• • •

14. The order and law, earthly or heavenly, by which government serves the interests of human society

Now God, our master, teaches two chief precepts, love of God and love of neighbour; and in them man finds three objects for his love: God, himself, and his neighbour; and a man who loves God is not wrong in loving himself. It follows, therefore, that he will be concerned also that his neighbour should love God, since he is told to love his neighbour as himself; and the same is true of his concern for his wife, his children, for the members of his household, and for all other men, so far as is possible. And, for the same end, he will wish his neighbour to be concerned for him, if he happens to need that concern. For this reason he will be at peace, as far as lies in him, with all men, in that peace among men, that ordered harmony; and the basis of this order is the observance of two rules: first, to do no harm to anyone, and, secondly, to help everyone whenever possible. To begin with, therefore, a man has a responsibility for his own household—obviously, both in the order of nature and in the framework of human society, he has easier and more immediate contact with them; he can exercise his concern for them. That is why the Apostle says, 'Anyone who does not take care of his own people, especially those in his own household, is worse than an unbeliever—he is a renegade.' This is where domestic peace starts, the ordered harmony about giving and obeying orders among those who live in the same house. For the orders are given by those who are concerned for the interests of others; thus the husband gives orders to the wife, parents to children, masters to servants. While those who are the objects of this concern obey orders; for example, wives obey husbands, the children obey their parents, the servants their masters. But in the household of the just man who 'lives on the basis of faith' and who is still on pilgrimage, far from that Heavenly City, even those who give orders are the servants of those whom they appear to command. For they do not give orders because of a lust for domination but from a dutiful concern for the interests of others, not with pride in taking precedence over others, but with compassion in taking care of others.

15. Man's natural freedom; and the slavery caused by sin

This relationship is prescribed by the order of nature, and it is in this situation that God created man. For he says, 'Let him have lordship over the fish of the sea, the birds of the sky . . . and all the reptiles that crawl on the earth.' He did not wish the rational being, made in his own image, to have dominion over any but irrational creatures, not man over man, but man over the beasts. Hence the first just men were set up as shepherds of flocks, rather than as kings of men, so that in this way also God might convey the message of

what was required by the order of nature, and what was demanded by the deserts of sinners—for it is understood, of course, that the condition of slavery is justly imposed on the sinner. That is why we do not hear of a slave anywhere in the Scriptures until Noah, the just man, punished his son's sin with this word; and so that son deserved this name because of his misdeed, not because of his nature. The origin of the Latin word for slave, *servus,* is believed to be derived from the fact that those who by the laws of war could rightly be put to death by the conquerors, became *servi,* slaves, when they were preserved, receiving this name from their preservation. But even this enslavement could not have happened, if it were not for the deserts of sin. For even when a just war is fought it is in defence of his sin that the other side is contending; and victory, even when the victory falls to the wicked, is a humiliation visited on the conquered by divine judgement, either to correct or to punish their sins. We have a witness to this in Daniel, a man of God, who in captivity confesses to God his own sins and the sins of his people, and in devout grief testifies that they are the cause of that captivity. The first cause of slavery, then, is sin, whereby man was subjected to man in the condition of bondage; and this can only happen by the judgement of God, with whom there is no injustice, and who knows how to allot different punishments according to the deserts of the offenders.

16. Equity in the relation of master and slave

However, if anyone in the household is, through his disobedience, an enemy to the domestic peace, he is reproved by a word, or by a blow, or any other kind of punishment that is just and legitimate, to the extent allowed by human society; but this is for the benefit of the offender, intended to readjust him to the domestic peace from which he had broken away. For just as it is not an act of kindness to help a man, when the effect of the help is to make him lose a greater good, so it is not a blameless act to spare a man, when by so doing you let him fall into a greater sin. Hence the duty of anyone who would be blameless includes not only doing no harm to anyone but also restraining a man from sin or punishing his sin, so that either the man who is chastised may be corrected by his experience, or others may be deterred by his example. Now a man's house ought to be the beginning, or rather a small component part of the city, and every beginning is directed to some end of its own kind, and every component part contributes to the completeness of the whole of which it forms a part. The implication is quite apparent, that domestic peace contributes to the peace of the city—that is, the ordered harmony of those who live together in a house in the matter of giving and obeying orders, contributes to the ordered harmony concerning authority and obedience obtaining among the citizens. Consequently it is fitting that the father of a household should take his rules from the law of the city, and govern his household in such a way that it fits in with the peace of the city.

• • •

28. The end of the wicked

In contrast with this, however, the wretchedness of those who do not belong to this City of God will be everlasting. This is called also 'the second death', because the soul cannot be said to be alive in that state, when it is separated from the life of God, nor can the body, when it is subjected to eternal torments. And this is precisely the reason why this 'second death' will be harder to bear, because it cannot come to an end in death. But here a question arises; for just as wretchedness is the opposite of blessedness, and death of life, so war is evidently the opposite of peace. And the question is rightly asked: What war, or what kind of war, can be understood to exist in the final state of the wicked, corresponding, by way of contrast, to that peace which is proclaimed with joyful praises in the final state of the good? Now anyone who puts this question should observe what it is that is harmful and destructive in war; and he will see that it is precisely the mutual opposition and conflict of the forces engaged. What war, then, can be imagined more serious and more bitter than a struggle in which the will is so at odds with the feelings and the feelings with the will, that their hostility cannot be ended by the victory of either—a struggle in which the violence of pain is in such conflict with the nature of the body that neither can yield to the other? For in this life, when such a conflict occurs, either pain wins, and death takes away feeling, or nature conquers, and health removes the pain. But in that other life, pain continues to torment, while nature lasts to feel the pain. Neither ceases to exist, lest the punishment also should cease.

These, then, are the final states of good and evil. The first we should seek to attain, the latter we should strive to escape. And since it is through a judgement that the good will pass to the one, and the evil to the other, it is of this judgement that I shall deal, as far as God grants, in the book which follows.

Jihad

(c. 1167)

Averroes

Averroes, Ibn-Rushd (c. 1126–1198) was born in the Arabic town of Cordoba. He was trained in Islamic theology and law. He held positions as judge, court physician, and philosopher. He wrote the legal handbook Al-Bidaya, *in which the essay on Jihad is contained.*

PAR. 1. THE LEGAL QUALIFICATION (*HUKM*) OF THIS ACTIVITY AND THE PERSONS OBLIGED TO TAKE PART IN IT

Scholars agree that the jihad is a collective not a personal obligation. Only ʿAbd Allāh Ibn al-Ḥasan professed it to be a recommendable act. According to the majority of scholars, the compulsory nature of the jihad is founded on [2:216]: *"Prescribed for you is fighting, though it be hateful to you."* That this obligation is a collective and not a personal one, i.e. that the obligation, when it can be properly carried out by a limited number of individuals, is cancelled for the remaining Muslims, is founded on [9:122]: *"It is not for the believers to go forth totally"* on [4:95]: *"Yet to each God has promised the reward most fair"* and, lastly, on the fact that the Prophet never went to battle without leaving some people behind. All this together implies that this activity is a collective obligation. The obligation to participate in the jihad applies to adult free men who have the means at their disposal to go to war and who are healthy, that is, not ill or suffering from chronic dis-

eases. There is absolutely no controversy about the latter restriction because of [48:17]: *"There is no fault in the blind, and there is no fault in the lame, and there is no fault in the sick"* and because of [9:91]: *"There is no fault in the weak and the sick and those who find nothing to expend."* Nor do I know of any dissentient views as regards the rule that this obligation applies only to free men. Nearly all scholars agree that this obligation is conditional on permission granted by the parents. Only in the case that the obligation has become a personal one, for instance because there is nobody else to carry it out, can this permission be dispensed with. This prerequisite of permission is based on the following authentic Tradition: *"Once a man said to the Messenger of God: 'I wish to take part in the jihad.' The Messenger said to him: 'Are both your parents still alive?' When he answered in the affirmative, the Messenger said: 'Then perform the jihad for their sake.'"* Scholars are not agreed whether this permission is also required of parents who are polytheists. There is controversy, too, about the question whether the creditor's permission has to be asked when a person has run into debt. An argument in favour of this can be found in the following Tradition: *"A man said to the Prophet: 'Will God forgive me my sins if I shall sacrifice myself patiently and shall be killed in the way of God (i.e. by taking part in the jihad)?' The Prophet said: 'Yes, with the exception of your debts. This Jibrīl has told me before.'"* The majority of scholars do not consider it obligatory, especially not when the debtor leaves enough behind to serve as payment for his debts.

PAR. 2. THE ENEMY

Scholars agree that all polytheists should be fought. This is founded on [8:39]: *"Fight them until there is no persecution and the religion is God's entirely."* However, it has been related by Mālik that it would not be allowed to attack the Ethiopians and the Turks on the strength of the Tradition of the Prophet: *"Leave the Ethiopians in peace as long as they leave you in peace."* Questioned as to the authenticity of this Tradition, Mālik did not acknowledge it, but said: "People still avoid attacking them."

PAR. 3. THE DAMAGE ALLOWED TO BE INFLICTED UPON THE DIFFERENT CATEGORIES OF ENEMIES

Damage inflicted upon the enemy may consist in damage to his property, injury to his person or violation of his personal liberty, i.e. that he is made a slave and is appropriated. This may be done, according to the *Consensus (ijmāʿ)* to all polytheists: men, women, young and old, important and unimportant. Only with regard to monks do opinions vary; for some take it that they must be left in peace and that

they must not be captured, but allowed to go unscathed and that they may not be enslaved. In support of their opinion they bring forward the words of the Prophet: *"Leave them in peace and also that to which they have dedicated themselves,"* as well as the practice of Abū Bakr.

Most scholars are agreed that, in his dealings with captives, various policies are open to the Imam [head of the Islamic state, caliph]. He may pardon them, enslave them, kill them, or release them either on ransom or as *dhimmī* [non-Moslem subject of the Islamic state], in which latter case the released captive is obliged to pay poll-tax (*jizya*). Some scholars, however, have taught that captives may never be slain. According to al-Ḥasan Ibn Muhammad al-Tamīmī, this was even the *Consensus (ijmāʿ)* of the Ṣaḥāba [contemporaries of Mohammed that have known him]. This controversy has arisen because, firstly, the Koran-verses contradict each other in this respect; secondly, practice [of the Prophet and the first caliphs] was inconsistent; and lastly, the obvious interpretation of the Koran is at variance with the Prophet's deeds. The obvious interpretation of [47:4]: *"When you meet the unbelievers, smite their necks, then, when you have made wide slaughter among them, tie fast the bonds"* is that the Imam is only entitled to pardon captives or to release them on ransom. On the other hand, [8:67]: *"It is not for any Prophet to have prisoners until he make wide slaughter in the land,"* as well as the occasion when this verse was revealed [viz. the captives of Badr] would go to prove that it is better to slay captives than to enslave them. The Prophet himself would in some cases slay captives outside the field of battle, while he would pardon them in others. Women he used to enslave. Abū Ubayd has related that the Prophet never enslaved male Arabs. After him, the Ṣaḥāba reached unanimity about the rule that the People of the Book *(ahl al-kitāb),* both male and female, might be enslaved. Those who are of the opinion that the verse which prohibits slaying [K 47:4] abrogates the Prophet's example, maintain that captives may not be slain. Others profess, however, that this verse does not concern itself with the slaughter of captives and that it was by no means intended to restrict the number of policies possible with regard to captives. On the contrary, they say, the fact that the Prophet used to slay captives adds a supplementing rule to the verse in question [K 47:4] and thus removes the occasion for the complaint that he omitted to kill the captives of Badr. These, now, do profess that the killing of captives is allowed.

It is only allowed to slay the enemy on the condition that *amān* [safe-conduct] has not been granted. There is no dissension about this among the Muslims. There is controversy, however, concerning the question who is entitled to grant *amān.* Everyone is agreed that the Imam is entitled to this. The majority of scholars are of the opinion that free Muslim males are also entitled to grant it, but Ibn Mājishūn maintains that in this case, it is subject to authorization by the Imam. Similarly, there is controversy concerning the *amān* granted by women and slaves. Ibn Mājishūn and Saḥnūn hold that *amān* granted by a woman is also subject to authorization by the Imam. Abū Ḥanīfa has taught that the *amān* granted by a slave is only valid when the slave is allowed to join in the fighting. The source of the controversy is that a general rule is in conflict with the analogous interpretation of another rule. The general rule is founded on the words of the Prophet: *"The blood(money) of all Muslims is equal. Even the humblest strives for their protection. Together, they make up a unity against the others."* These words, in their universality, imply that *amān* granted by a slave is valid. The conflicting analogy is that in order to be able to grant *amān* full legal capacity is required. Now, a slave has only partial legal capacity by the very fact of his being a slave. By analogy, the fact that he is a slave should counteract the validity of his *amān,* as it does with regard to numerous other legal acts. The general rule, then, should be restricted by analogy.

The controversy about the validity of *amān* granted by a woman owes its origin to two different readings of the words of the Prophet: *"We grant protection to those to whom you have granted protection, Umm Hāni'"* as well as to the question whether women are to be put on a par with men by analogy. Some read in the words of the Prophet an authorization of the *amān* granted by Umm Hāni', not a confirmation of its validity, and they infer that her *amān* would have had no legal effects had the Prophet not authorized it. Consequently, they maintain that *amān* granted by a woman is only valid when the Imam has authorized it. Others hold that the Prophet confirmed the *amān* granted by Umm Hāni' in the sense that he approved something which already existed and had legal effects, not in the sense that the act was only validated by his authorization. Thus, the latter group maintains that a woman is entitled to grant valid *amān.* This view finds also favour with those who, in this respect, put women on a par with men and feel that there is no difference between them here. Others, who are of the opinion that a woman is inferior to a man, consider an *amān* granted by her invalid. Anyhow, *amān* does not afford protection against enslavement but only against death. The controversy [about the validity of *amān* granted by women] might also be explained by the divergent opinions about the use of the male plural: does this include women or not? All this, of course, according to legal usage.

As regards injury to the person, that is, the slaying of the enemy, the Muslims agree that in times of war, all adult, able-bodied, unbelieving males may be slain. As to the question whether the enemy may also be slain after he has been captured, there is the above-mentioned controversy. There is no disagreement about the rule that it is forbidden to slay women and children, provided that they are not fighting, for then women, in any case, may be slain. This rule is founded on the fact that, according to authoritative Traditions, the Prophet prohibited the slaughter of women and children and once said about a woman who had been slain: "*She was not one who would have fought.*"

• • •

PAR. 5. THE MAXIMUM NUMBER OF ENEMIES AGAINST WHICH ONE IS OBLIGED TO STAND ONE'S GROUND

The maximum number of enemies against which one is obliged to stand one's ground is twice the number [of one's own troops]. About this, everybody agrees on account of [8:66]: "*Now God has lightened it for you, knowing that there is weakness in you.*" Ibn Mājishūn maintains, on the authority of Mālik, that the actual force, rather than the number, is to be considered and that it might be allowed for a single man to flee before another if the latter should possess a superior horse, superior weapons and superior physical strength.

PAR. 6. TRUCE

The conclusion of truce is considered by some to be permitted from the very outset and without an immediate occasion, provided that the Imam deems it in the interest of the Muslims. Others maintain that it is only allowed when the Muslims are pressed by sheer necessity, such as a civil war and the like. As a condition for truce, it may be stipulated that the enemy pay a certain amount of money to the Muslims. This is not poll-tax (*jizya*), because for that it would be required that they come under Islamic rule [which is not the case here]. Such a stipulation [the payment of a tribute], however, is not obligatory. Awzāʿī even considered it admissible that the Imam should conclude a truce with the stipulation that the Muslims pay a certain amount to the enemy, should this be forced upon them by emergency, such as a civil war and the like. Shāfiʿī's opinion is that the Muslims may never give anything to the unbelievers, unless they are in mortal fear of being extinguished, on account of the enemy's superiority or because they are being harrassed by disasters. Among those who profess that the Imam is entitled to conclude a truce when he considers it in the interest [of the Muslims] are Mālik, Shāfiʿī and Abū Ḥanīfa. Shāfiʿī maintains that a truce may not be concluded for a period longer than that of the truce which the Prophet concluded with the unbelievers in the year of Ḥudaybiyya. The controversy about the question whether the conclusion of truce is also allowed without a compulsive reason, is rooted in the fact that the obvious interpretation of [9:5]: "*Slay the idolaters wherever you find them,*" and that of [9:29]: "*Fight those who believe not in God and the Last Day,*" contradict that of [8:61]: "*And if they incline to peace, do thou incline to it."* Some hold that the verse which commands the Muslims to fight the polytheists until they have been converted or until they pay poll-tax (*jizya*) [K 9:29] abrogates the Peace-verse [K 8:61]. Consequently, they maintain that truce is only admissible in cases of necessity. Others are of the opinion that the Peace-verse [K 8:61] supplements the other two verses and they consider the concluding of truce allowed if the Imam deems it right. They also argue, in support of their view, that the Prophet acted accordingly, as the truce of Ḥudaybiyya had not been concluded from necessity. According to Shāfiʿī, the principle is that polytheists must be fought until they have been converted or until they are willing to pay poll-tax (*jizya*). The acts of the Prophet in the year of Ḥudaybiyya are an exception to this [principle]. Therefore, says Shāfiʿī, a truce may never exceed the period for which the Prophet concluded truce in the case of Ḥudaybiyya. Still, there is controversy about the duration of this period. According to some it amounts to four years, but according to others three or ten years. Shāfiʿī opts for the latter. As to the view of some, that in cases of emergency such as civil war and the like, the Muslims may conclude a truce on the stipulation that they pay the enemy a certain amount of money, this is based on the Prophet's example, for it has been related that he was seriously contemplating to bestow a third of the date-harvest of Medina upon a group of polytheists belonging to the Confederates with a view to induce them to move off. However, before he had had time to reach an agreement on the basis of the quantity of dates he had been allowed [by the people of Medina] to give away, God granted him the victory. The opinion of those who profess that a truce may only be

concluded when the Muslims are in mortal fear of extinction, is founded on analogous application of the rule that Muslim captives may be ransomed; for when Muslims have been reduced to such a state they are in the position of captives.

PAR. 7. THE AIMS OF WARFARE

The Muslims are agreed that the aim of warfare against the People of the Book, with the exception of those belonging to the Quraysh-tribe and Arab Christians, is twofold: either conversion to Islam, or payment of poll-tax (*jizya*). This is based on [9:29]: *"Fight those who believe not in God and the Last Day and do not forbid what God and His Messenger have forbidden— such men as practise not the religion of truth, being of those who have been given the Book—until they pay the tribute out of hand and have been humbled."* Most lawyers likewise agree that poll-tax (*jizya*) may also be collected from Zoroastrians (*madjūs*) on the strength of the words of the Prophet: *"Treat them like the People of the Book."* There is, however, controversy with regard to polytheists who are not People of the Book: is it allowed to accept poll-tax (*jizya*) from them or not? Some, like Mālik, have taught that it may be collected from any polytheist. Others make an exception for the polytheist Arabs. Shāfiʿī, Abū Thawr and a few others maintain that poll-tax (*jizya*) may only be accepted from People of the Book and Zoroastrians. The controversy is again brought about by the fact that a general rule conflicts with a particular one. The general rule is derived from [2:193 and 8:39]: *"Fight them until there is no persecution and the religion is God's (entirely),"* and from the Tradition: *"I have been commanded to fight the people until they say: 'There is no god but God.' When they say that, then their lives and property are inviolable to me, except [in the case when] the [law of] Islam allows it [to take them]. They will be answerable to God.*" The particular rule is founded on the Tradition mentioned earlier, viz. that Mohammed used to say to the leaders of troops which he sent out to the polytheist Arabs: "*When ye will encounter your polytheist foes, then summon them to three things,*" etc. In this Tradition, poll-tax (*jizya*) is also mentioned. Now, some scholars hold that a general rule cancels a particular one if the general rule was revealed at a later date. These do not accept poll-tax (*jizya*) from others than People of the Book, since the verses prescribing, in general terms, to fight them are of a more recent date than the Tradition mentioned; for the general command to fight the polytheists is to be found in the *Sūrat Barā'a* which was revealed in the year of the conquest of Mecca. The Tradition in question, on the other hand, dates back from before the conquest of Mecca, in view of the fact that it contains a summons to emigration.

Others, however, maintain that general rules should always be interpreted in association with the particular rules, no matter whether the one is more recent than the other or whether this is unknown. The latter group, accordingly, accepts poll-tax (*jizya*) from any polytheist. The People of the Book are in an exceptional position with respect to the other polytheists because they have been excluded from the general rule just mentioned, on the strength of the particular rule given in [9:29]: "*. . . being of those who have been given the Book—until they pay the tribute out of hand and have been humbled.*" The poll-tax (*jizya*) itself and the rules related to it will be dealt with in the next chapter. So much for the principles of warfare. One famous question remains to be touched upon in this connection: that whether it is prohibited to march into hostile territory carrying a copy of the Koran. Most scholars do not consider it allowed because an authoritative rule to this effect has been handed down from the Prophet in an authentic Tradition.

Summa Theologica

(c. 1265)

Thomas Aquinas

Thomas Aquinas (c. 1224–1274) was born in Italy and became a Benedictine monk. He was professor of theology in Paris and Rome. He wrote his great treatise on philosophy and theology, Summa Theologica, *over a several-year period around 1265.*

QUESTION XL. OF WAR. (IN FOUR ARTICLES.)

WE must now consider war, under which head there are four points of inquiry: (1) Whether some kind of war is lawful? (2) Whether it is lawful for clerics to fight? (3) Whether it is lawful for belligerents to lay ambushes? (4) Whether it is lawful to fight on holy days?

First Article. Whether it is Always Sinful to Wage War?

We proceed thus to the First Article:—

Objection 1. It would seem that it is always sinful to wage war. Because punishment is not inflicted except for sin. Now those who wage war are threatened by Our Lord with punishment, according to Matth. xxvi. 52: *All that take the sword shall perish with the sword.* Therefore all wars are unlawful.

Obj. 2. Further, Whatever is contrary to a Divine precept is a sin. But war is contrary to a Divine precept, for is written (Matth. v. 39): *But I say to you not to resist evil;* and (Rom. xii. 19): *Not revenging yourselves, my dearly beloved, but give place unto wrath.* Therefore war is always sinful.

Obj. 3. Further, Nothing, except sin, is contrary to an act of virtue. But war is contrary to peace. Therefore war is always a sin.

Obj. 4. Further, The exercise of a lawful thing is itself lawful, as is evident in scientific exercises. But warlike exercises which take place in tournaments are forbidden by the Church, since those who are slain in these trials are deprived of ecclesiastical burial. Therefore it seems that war is a sin in itself.

On the contrary, Augustine says in a sermon on the son of the centurion: *If the Christian Religion forbade war altogether,* those who sought salutary advice in the Gospel would rather have been counselled to cast aside their arms, and to give up soldiering altogether. On the contrary, they were told: 'Do violence to no man; . . . and be content with your pay.' If he commanded them to be content with their pay, he did not forbid soldiering.

I answer that, In order for a war to be just, three things are necessary. First, the authority of the sovereign by whose command the war is to be waged. For it is not the business of a private individual to declare war, because he can seek for redress of his rights from the tribunal of his superior. Moreover it is not the business of a private individual to summon together the people, which has to be done in wartime. And as the care of the common weal is committed to those who are in authority, it is their business to watch over the common weal of the city, kingdom or province subject to them. And just as it is lawful for them to have recourse to the sword in defending that common weal against internal disturbances, when they punish evil-doers, according to the words of the Apostle (Rom. xiii. 4): *He beareth not the sword in vain: for he is God's minister, an avenger to execute wrath upon him that doth evil;* so too, it is their business to have recourse to the sword of war in defending the common weal against external enemies. Hence it is said to those who are in authority (Ps. lxxxi. 4): *Rescue the poor: and deliver the needy out of the hand of the sinner;* and for this reason Augustine says (*Contra Faust.* xxii. 75): *The natural order conducive to peace among mortals demands that the power to declare and counsel war should be in the hands of those who hold the supreme authority.*

Secondly, a just cause is required, namely that those who are attacked, should be attacked because they deserve it on account of some fault. Wherefore Augustine says (*QQ. in Hept.*, qu. x., *super Jos.*): *A just war is wont to be described as one that avenges wrongs, when a nation or state has to be punished, for refusing to make amends for the wrongs inflicted by its subjects, or to restore what it has seized unjustly.*

Thirdly, it is necessary that the belligerents should have a rightful intention, so that they intend the advancement of good, or the avoidance of evil. Hence Augustine says (*De Verb. Dom.*): *True religion looks upon as peaceful those wars that are waged not for motives of aggrandisement, or cruelty, but with the object of securing peace, of punishing evil-doers, and of uplifting the good.* For it may happen that the war is declared by the legitimate authority, and for a just cause, and yet be rendered unlawful through a wicked intention. Hence Augustine says (*Contra Faust.* xxii. 74): *The passion for inflicting harm, the cruel thirst for vengeance, an unpacific and relentless spirit, the fever of revolt, the lust of power, and suchlike things, all these are rightly condemned in war.*

Reply Obj. 1. As Augustine says (*Contra Faust.* xxii. 70): *To take the sword is to arm oneself in order to take the life of anyone, without the command or permission of superior or lawful authority.* On the other hand, to have recourse to the sword (as a private person) by the authority of the sovereign or judge, or (as a public person) through zeal for justice, and by the authority, so to speak, of God, is not to *take the sword,* but to use it as commissioned by another, wherefore it does not deserve punishment. And yet even those who make sinful use of the sword are not always slain with the sword, yet they always perish with their own sword, because, unless they repent, they are punished eternally for their sinful use of the sword.

Reply Obj. 2. Suchlike precepts, as Augustine observes (*De Serm. Dom. in Monte*

i. 19), should always be borne in readiness of mind, so that we be ready to obey them, and, if necessary, to refrain from resistance or self-defence. Nevertheless it is necessary sometimes for a man to act otherwise for the common good, or for the good of those with whom he is fighting. Hence Augustine says (*Ep. ad Marcellin.* cxxxviii.): *Those whom we have to punish with a kindly severity, it is necessary to handle in many ways against their will. For when we are stripping a man of the lawlessness of sin, it is good for him to be vanquished, since nothing is more hopeless than the happiness of sinners, whence arises a guilty impunity; and an evil will, like an internal enemy.*

Reply Obj. 3. Those who wage war justly aim at peace, and so they are not opposed to peace, except to the evil peace, which Our Lord *came not to send upon earth* (Matth. x. 34). Hence Augustine says (*Ep. ad Bonif.* clxxxix.): *We do not seek peace in order to be at war, but we go to war that we may have peace. Be peaceful, therefore, in warring, so that you may vanquish those whom you war against, and bring them to the prosperity of peace.*

Reply Obj. 4. Manly exercises in warlike feats of arms are not all forbidden, but those which are inordinate and perilous, and end in slaying or plundering. In olden times warlike exercises presented no such danger, and hence they were called *exercises of arms* or *bloodless wars,* as Jerome states in an epistle.

• • •

Third Article. Whether it is Lawful to Lay Ambushes in War?

We proceed thus to the Third Article:—

Objection 1. It would seem that it is unlawful to lay ambushes in war. For it is written (Deut. xvi. 20): *Thou shalt follow justly after that which is just.* But ambushes, since they are a kind of deception, seem to pertain to injustice. Therefore it is unlawful to lay ambushes even in a just war.

Obj. 2. Further, Ambushes and deception seem to be opposed to faithfulness even as lies are. But since we are bound to keep faith with all men, it is wrong to lie to anyone, as Augustine states (*Contra Mend.* xv.). Therefore, as one is bound to keep faith with one's enemy, as Augustine states (*Ep. ad Bonifac.* clxxxix.), it seems that it is unlawful to lay ambushes for one's enemies.

Obj. 3. Further, It is written (Matth. vii. 12): *Whatsoever you would that men should do to you, do you also to them:* and we ought to observe this in all our dealings with our neighbour. Now our enemy is our neighbour. Therefore, since no man wishes ambushes or deceptions to be prepared for himself, it seems that no one ought to carry on war by laying ambushes.

On the contrary, Augustine says (*QQ. in Heptateuch.,* qu. x., *super Jos.*): *Provided the war be just, it is no concern of justice whether it be carried on openly or by ambushes:* and he proves this by the authority of the Lord, Who commanded Joshua to lay ambushes for the city of Hai (Jos. viii. 2).

I answer that, The object of laying ambushes is in order to deceive the enemy. Now a man may be deceived by another's word or deed in two ways. First, through being told something false, or through the breaking of a promise, and this is always unlawful. No one ought to deceive the enemy in this way, for there are certain *rights of war and covenants, which ought to be observed even among enemies,* as Ambrose states (*De Offic.* i.).

Secondly, a man may be deceived by what we say or do, because we do not declare our purpose or meaning to him. Now we are not always bound to do this, since

even in the Sacred Doctrine many things have to be concealed, especially from unbelievers, lest they deride it, according to Matth. vii. 6: *Give not that which is holy, to dogs.* Wherefore much more ought the plan of campaign to be hidden from the enemy. For this reason among other things that a soldier has to learn is the art of concealing his purpose lest it come to the enemy's knowledge, as stated in the Book on *Strategy* by Frontinus. Suchlike concealment is what is meant by an ambush which may be lawfully employed in a just war.

Nor can these ambushes be properly called deceptions, nor are they contrary to justice or to a well-ordered will. For a man would have an inordinate will if he were unwilling that others should hide anything from him.

This suffices for the *Replies* to the *Objections.*

• • •

QUESTION LXIV.

Third Article. Whether it is Lawful for a Private Individual to Kill a Man who has Sinned?

We proceed thus to the Third Article:—

Objection 1. It would seem lawful for a private individual to kill a man who has sinned. For nothing unlawful is commanded in the Divine law. Yet, on account of the sin of the molten calf, Moses commanded (Exod. xxxii. 27): *Let every man kill his brother, and friend, and neighbour.* Therefore it is lawful for private individuals to kill a sinner.

Obj. 2. Further, As stated above (A. 2, *ad* 3), man, on account of sin, is compared to the beasts. Now it is lawful for any private individual to kill a wild beast, especially if it be harmful. Therefore for the same reason, it is lawful for any private individual to kill a man who has sinned.

Obj. 3. Further, A man, though a private individual, deserves praise for doing what is useful for the common good. Now the slaying of evildoers is useful for the common good, as stated above (A. 2). Therefore it is deserving of praise if even private individuals kill evildoers.

On the contrary, Augustine says (*De Civ. Dei* i.): *A man who, without exercising public authority, kills an evildoer, shall be judged guilty of murder, and all the more, since he has dared to usurp a power which God has not given him.*

I answer that, As stated above (A. 2), it is lawful to kill an evildoer in so far as it is directed to the welfare of the whole community, so that it belongs to him alone who has charge of the community's welfare. Thus it belongs to a physician to cut off a decayed limb, when he has been entrusted with the care of the health of the whole body. Now the care of the common good is entrusted to persons of rank having public authority: wherefore they alone, and not private individuals, can lawfully put evildoers to death.

Reply Obj. 1. The person by whose authority a thing is done really does the thing, as Dionysius declares (*Coel. Hier.* iii.). Hence according to Augustine (*De Civ. Dei* i. 21), *He slays not who owes his service to one who commands him, even as a sword is merely the instrument to him that wields it.* Wherefore those who, at the Lord's command, slew their neighbours and friends, would seem not to have done this themselves, but rather He by whose authority they acted thus: just as a soldier slays the foe by the authority of his sovereign, and the executioner slays the robber by the authority of the judge.

Reply Obj. 2. A beast is by nature distinct from man, wherefore in the case of a wild beast, there is no need for an author-ity to kill it; whereas, in the case of domestic animals, such authority is required, not for their sake, but on account of the owner's loss. On the other hand a man who has sinned is not by nature distinct from good men; hence a public authority is requisite in order to condemn him to death for the common good.

Reply Obj. 3. It is lawful for any private individual to do anything for the common good, provided it harm nobody: but if it be harmful to some other, it cannot be done, except by virtue of the judgment of the person to whom it pertains to decide what is to be taken from the parts for the welfare of the whole.

• • •

Sixth Article. Whether it is ever Lawful to Kill the Innocent?

We proceed thus to the Sixth Article:—

Objection 1. It would seem that in some cases it is lawful to kill the innocent. The fear of God is never manifested by sin, since on the contrary *the fear of the Lord driveth out sin* (Ecclus. i. 27). Now Abraham was commended in that he feared the Lord, since he was willing to slay his innocent son. Therefore one may, without sin, kill an innocent person.

Obj. 2. Further, Among those sins that are committed against one's neighbour, the more grievous seem to be those whereby a more grievous injury is inflicted on the person sinned against. Now to be killed is a greater injury to a sinful than to an innocent person, because the latter, by death, passes forthwith from the unhappiness of this life to the glory of heaven. Since then it is lawful in certain cases to kill a sinful man, much more is it lawful to slay an innocent or a righteous person.

Obj. 3. Further, What is done in keeping with the order of justice is not a sin.

But sometimes a man is forced, according to the order of justice, to slay an innocent person: for instance, when a judge, who is bound to judge according to the evidence, condemns to death a man whom he knows to be innocent, but who is convicted by false witnesses; and again the executioner, who in obedience to the judge puts to death the man who has been unjustly sentenced.

On the contrary, It is written (Exod. xxiii. 7): *The innocent and just person thou shalt not put to death.*

I answer that, An individual man may be considered in two ways: first, in himself; secondly, in relation to something else. If we consider a man in himself, it is unlawful to kill any man, since in every man though he be sinful, we ought to love the nature which God has made, and which is destroyed by slaying him. Nevertheless, as stated above (A. 2) the slaying of a sinner becomes lawful in relation to the common good, which is corrupted by sin. On the other hand the life of righteous men preserves and forwards the common good, since they are the chief part of the community. Therefore it is in no way lawful to slay the innocent.

Reply Obj. 1. God is Lord of death and life, for by His decree both the sinful and the righteous die. Hence he who at God's command kills an innocent man does not sin, as neither does God Whose behest he executes: indeed his obedience to God's commands is a proof that he fears Him.

Reply Obj. 2. In weighing the gravity of a sin we must consider the essential rather than the accidental. Wherefore he who kills a just man, sins more grievously than he who slays a sinful man: first, because he injures one whom he should love more, and so acts more in opposition to charity: secondly, because he inflicts an injury on a man who is less deserving of one, and so acts more in opposition to justice:

thirdly, because he deprives the community of a greater good: fourthly, because he despises God more, according to Luke x. 16, *He that despiseth you despiseth Me.* On the other hand it is accidental to the slaying that the just man whose life is taken be received by God into glory.

Reply Obj. 3. If the judge knows that a man who has been convicted by false witnesses, is innocent he must, like Daniel, examine the witnesses with great care, so as to find a motive for acquitting the innocent: but if he cannot do this he should remit him for judgment by a higher tribunal. If even this is impossible, he does not sin if he pronounce sentence in accordance with the evidence, for it is not he that puts the innocent man to death, but they who stated him to be guilty. He that carries out the sentence of the judge who has condemned an innocent man, if the sentence contains an inexcusable error, he should not obey, else there would be an excuse for the executions of the martyrs: if however it contain no manifest injustice, he does not sin by carrying out the sentence, because he has no right to discuss the judgment of his superior; nor is it he who slays the innocent man, but the judge whose minister he is.

Seventh Article. Whether it is Lawful to Kill a Man in Self-defence?

We proceed thus to the Seventh Article:—

Objection 1. It would seem that nobody may lawfully kill a man in self-defence. For Augustine says to Publicola (*Ep.* xlvii.): *I do not agree with the opinion that one may kill a man lest one be killed by him; unless one be a soldier, or exercise a public office, so that one does it not for oneself but for others, having the power to do so, provided it be in keeping with one's person.* Now he who kills a man in self-defence, kills him lest he be killed by him. Therefore this would seem to be unlawful.

Obj. 2. Further, He says (*De Lib. Arb.* i. 5): *How are they free from sin in sight of Divine providence, who are guilty of taking a man's life for the sake of these contemptible things?* Now among contemptible things he reckons *those which men may forfeit unwillingly,* as appears from the context (*ibid.*): and the chief of these is the life of the body. Therefore it is unlawful for any man to take another's life for the sake of the life of his own body.

Obj. 3. Further, Pope Nicolas says in the Decretals: *Concerning the clerics about whom you have consulted Us, those, namely, who have killed a pagan in self-defence, as to whether, after making amends by repenting, they may return to their former state, or rise to a higher degree; know that in no case is it lawful for them to kill any man under any circumstances whatever.* Now clerics and laymen are alike bound to observe the moral precepts. Therefore neither is it lawful for laymen to kill anyone in self-defence.

Obj. 4. Further, Murder is a more grievous sin than fornication or adultery. Now nobody may lawfully commit simple fornication or adultery or any other mortal sin in order to save his own life; since the spiritual life is to be preferred to the life of the body. Therefore no man may lawfully take another's life in self-defence in order to save his own life.

Obj. 5. Further, If the tree be evil, so is the fruit, according to Matth. vii. 17. Now self-defence itself seems to be unlawful, according to Rom. xii. 19: *Not defending* (Douay,—*revenging*) *yourselves, my dearly beloved.* Therefore its result, which is the slaying of a man, is also unlawful.

On the contrary, It is written (Exod. xxii. 2): *If a thief be found breaking into a house or undermining it, and be wounded so as to die; he that slew him shall not be guilty of blood.* Now it is much more lawful to defend one's life than one's house. Therefore neither is a man guilty of murder if he kill another in defence of his own life.

I answer that, Nothing hinders one act from having two effects, only one of which is intended, while the other is beside the intention. Now moral acts take their species according to what is intended, and not according to what is beside the intention, since this is accidental as explained above (Q. XLIII., A. 3: I.-II., Q. LXXII., A. 1). Accordingly the act of self-defence may have two effects, one is the saving of one's life, the other is the slaying of the aggressor. Therefore this act, since one's intention is to save one's own life, is not unlawful, seeing that it is natural to everything to keep itself in *being,* as far as possible. And yet, though proceeding from a good intention, an act may be rendered unlawful, if it be out of proportion to the end. Wherefore if a man, in self-defence, uses more than necessary violence, it will be unlawful: whereas if he repel force with moderation his defence will be lawful, because according to the jurists, *it is lawful to repel force by force, provided one does not exceed the limits of a blameless defence.* Nor is it necessary for salvation that a man omit the act of moderate self-defence in order to avoid killing the other man, since one is bound to take more care of one's own life than of another's. But as it is unlawful to take a man's life, except for the public authority acting for the common good, as stated above (A. 3), it is not lawful for a man to intend killing a man in self-defence, except for such as have public authority, who while intending to kill a man in self-defence, refer this to the public good, as in the case of a soldier fighting against the foe, and in the minister of the judge struggling with robbers, although even these sin if they be moved by private animosity.

Reply Obj. 1. The words quoted from Augustine refer to the case when one man intends to kill another to save himself from death. The passage quoted in the *Second Objection* is to be understood in the same sense. Hence he says pointedly, *for the sake of these things,* whereby he indicates the intention. This suffices for the *Reply* to the *Second Objection.*

Reply Obj. 3. Irregularity results from the act though sinless of taking a man's life, as appears in the case of a judge who justly condemns a man to death. For this reason a cleric, though he kill a man in self-defence, is irregular, albeit he intends not to kill him, but to defend himself.

Reply Obj. 4. The act of fornication or adultery is not necessarily directed to the preservation of one's own life, as is the act whence sometimes results the taking of a man's life.

Reply Obj. 5. The defence forbidden in this passage is that which comes from revengeful spite. Hence a gloss says: *Not defending yourselves,—that is, not striking your enemy back.*

• • •

QUESTION LXIX

Fourth Article. Whether a Man who is Condemned to Death may Lawfully Defend Himself if he can?

We proceed thus to the Fourth Article:—

Objection 1. It would seem that a man who is condemned to death may lawfully defend himself if he can. For it is always lawful to do that to which nature inclines us, as being of natural right, so to speak. Now, to resist corruption is an inclination of nature not only in men and animals but also in things devoid of sense. Therefore if

he can do so, the accused, after condemnation, may lawfully resist being put to death.

Obj. 2. Further, Just as a man, by resistance, escapes the death to which he has been condemned, so does he by flight. Now it is lawful seemingly to escape death by flight, according to Ecclus. ix. 18, *Keep thee far from the man that hath power to kill [and not to quicken].* Therefore it is also lawful for the accused to resist.

Obj. 3. Further, It is written (Prov. xxiv. II): *Deliver them that are led to death: and those that are drawn to death forbear not to deliver.* Now a man is under greater obligation to himself than to another. Therefore it is lawful for a condemned man to defend himself from being put to death.

On the contrary, The Apostle says (Rom. xiii. 2): *He that resisteth the power, resisteth the ordinance of God: and they that resist, purchase to themselves damnation.* Now a condemned man, by defending himself, resists the power in the point of its being ordained by God *for the punishment of evil-doers, and for the praise of the good.* Therefore he sins in defending himself.

I answer that, A man may be condemned to death in two ways. First justly, and then it is not lawful for the condemned to defend himself, because it is lawful for the judge to combat his resistance by force, so that on his part the fight is unjust, and consequently without any doubt he sins.

Secondly a man is condemned unjustly: and such a sentence is like the violence of robbers, according to Ezech. xxii. 27, *Her princes in the midst of her are like wolves ravening the prey to shed blood.* Wherefore even as it is lawful to resist robbers, so is it lawful, in a like case, to resist wicked princes; except perhaps in order to avoid scandal, whence some grave disturbance might be feared to arise.

B. The Natural Law of Nations

In the sixteenth and seventeenth centuries, lawyers, theologians, and philosophers followed Aquinas in search of a basis of a "just cause" for war. All of the theorists in this section, even the theologians, are trying to address the idea of a just war in a secular way, although still connected to the basis of the earlier religious conceptions by reference to the idea of a natural law. For Aquinas, the natural law was simply God's eternal law as applied to the creatures of nature, especially humans who choose how they should live their lives. On the secular construal, natural law is the voice of conscience that appeals to our inbred sense of justice. Vitoria and Suarez, as Catholic clerics, follow Aquinas most closely, but even the Protestant lawyers, Gentili and Grotius, as well as the philosophers Hobbes and Pufendorf, are inspired by the idea of natural law, especially by the idea that there can be a natural law for nations that will govern conduct in war.

Francisco Vitoria is the first modern theorist to address the idea of just wars. He begins by worrying about the conquest of the Native Americans by his fellow Spaniards. Vitoria is clear in arguing that "difference of religion" cannot justify fighting a war, nor can "extension of empire," nor "the personal glory of the prince," all reasons given to justify the Conquistadors. Instead, Vitoria argues that the "only just cause for commencing a war" is "a wrong done." With this as background, Vitoria provides the first sustained attempt to provide arguments for specific limitations on the tactics of war. He argues that the "deliberate slaughter of the innocent is never lawful" and generally that such killing can only be justified as "collateral circumstances." This harkens back to Aquinas' doctrine of double effect, although giving it much more substance. Concerning claims like Averroes' about the justified killing of all adult males, Vitoria worries that this is to hold someone guilty for "their future conduct." Vitoria also argues that enslaving or confining of hostages must only occur according to "the necessity of war." In general, Vitoria enunciates the modern humanitarian principle that war must not be waged to ruin people, but must only be waged to protect rights, and always conducted with moderation.

Gentili, a famous international lawyer who often defended Spanish conquest, is in many ways the closest to contemporary politicians in America who defend many wars, even preemptive attacks, but he argues that there are still moral limitations on war nonetheless. Gentili says that if a magistrate has been given a sword to protect his citizens from harm at home, why not allow the magistrate to ward off harm that comes from outside as well. Gentili criticizes Tertullian for looking only at the horror of the tactics of war and not at the legitimate aims of war, which can be good independent of the destruction that war causes. To justify his claim, Gentitli uses an analogy to the two-person case. He starts by claiming that there is a natural right to defend oneself. It is just to kill in self-defense even though one may flee one's attacker "without danger." The reason here is that it would be disgraceful to flee or retreat.

Curiously, even if we have provoked the war, as long as the war is necessary for self-defense, it is justified. But what does "necessary" mean here? Gentili says he means an extreme situation, based on whatever causes, in which one needs to defend oneself from attack in a way that does not lose one's honor. Gentili then argues that it would be foolish to expect people to wait to be struck before they strike at a likely assailant. Gentili says that suspicion is not enough, but real fear is required. Yet fear is enough "even though there is no great and clear cause of fear, and even if there is no real danger, but only a legitimate cause of fear." The startling image is this: "we kill a snake as soon as we see one, even though it has not injured us and perhaps will not harm us." George W. Bush could have uttered these words four hundred years after Gentili, although not with such engaging argumentation. And Gentili also argues that war can be justified if one is nonculpably ignorant that justice is not on your side. This is similar to the issue of fear: As long as one is sincere in one's beliefs, and the beliefs have some basis, this is enough for justification of going to war.

Francisco Suarez, a Jesuit theologian and last of the great Scholastic philosophers, is more cautious here than Gentili. Honor requires that we hate not individuals but their actions. Indeed, honor requires that we forgive our enemies, and give them the benefit of the doubt. Aggressive war cannot be justified on the basis of fear, but may be justified nonetheless in terms of defense of possessions if not defense of lives. Indeed, Suarez contends that "if the cause in question should cease to exist, the justice of war would also cease to exist."

Protecting the innocent is one of the hallmarks of the *jus in bello* prong of the Just War Theory. And Suarez makes some important contributions to this doctrine. He says that "the method of its conduct must be proper; and due proportion must be observed." Proportionality has been one of the most important principles of the *jus in bello* doctrine. Armed force should not be used in greater strength and lethalness than what is in keeping with the aim of a just war. And Suarez also spends much time arguing that innocent persons must not be slain, and including in the innocent those "who are able to bear arms but who do not share in the crime nor in the unjust war." This raises questions about the justifiability of killing enemy soldiers who have been conscripted and who are not currently aiming their guns at us.

Hugo Grotius, the greatest of the seventeenth century international lawyers and theorists, goes farther than Suarez in this respect, arguing that no one can be justifiably killed if the danger can in any way be avoided, or if the person is not guilty. Grotius gives a very long list of those who should not be killed due to their innocence, including large numbers of soldiers who are compelled to serve, or who end up as soldiers due to their ill-fortune, or those who do not know what they are fighting for. Thus, Grotius seemingly rules out the killing of most soldiers. He does so from the standpoint of mercy rather than justice, to harken back to the contrast between the essays by Cicero and Seneca. Indeed, it seems to us that like Seneca, Grotius comes close to pacifism and sets the stage for the contemporary international doctrine that has outlawed most wars.

Grotius is also concerned about justice, especially concerning the decision to initiate war. Here Grotius agrees with Suarez that war is permitted in a strictly legal way even in defense of one's possessions, but then Grotius addresses Gentili directly. He tries to defend the view that anticipatory war is only justified when "the danger, again, must be immediate and imminent in point of time." This is the view still held in international law today. Grotius disputes those views, like that of Gentili, that allow fear to be enough to justify war. In part, this is because Grotius thinks that "consideration for others [is] on a level with consideration for ourselves," and this view "does not permit the injuring of the innocent even" for protection of one's life. Grotius argues that "the person who is attacked ought to prefer to do anything possible to frighten away or weaken the assailant, rather than cause his death." The main justification of this view is that Grotius has a very different view of honor than does Gentili. Honor involves doing more than what is narrowly permitted; rather it involves doing what is just in a larger frame, the frame of one's conscience. This means avoiding what is shameful as well as what is strictly wrong, "for that which is more just and better."

The philosopher Thomas Hobbes provides a somewhat contrasting view of natural law and the role of conscience to that of Grotius. Hobbes depicts the state of nature, over which the laws of nature hold sway, as "solitary, poor, nasty, brutish, and short." Justice means only giving to each what is due, and in the state of nature nothing is due since property requires consent. The laws of nature are indeed the dictates of conscience, but they bind only in our hearts, and not as proper laws. And the interactions of nations are thus governed by nonbinding prudential exhortations. In this domain, nations are seemingly not bound by justice, and may rightly do to each other as they see fit. There are no rights here, since to have rights there must be law and to have law there must be a sovereign. Contrary to Seneca, Hobbes denies that there is anything like a world state to enforce the natural law and to make sure that nations follow principles of natural justice.

But Hobbes somewhat modifies this view because he perceives that each person, and each nation, has a strong need for peace and self-preservation, and the only way that such peace can be secured is by voluntarily restraining oneself. Principles of equity and mercy enter into the equation, urging that we restrain our war-like tendencies so as to live peaceably together. On this construal, the laws of nature are mere theorems concerning what conduces to the best life for us all. And those laws, while not properly binding, are nonetheless to be abandoned at our peril, for there would only follow the war of all against all. To achieve security, if not because of a concern for justice proper, people should restrain themselves and not go to war for frivolous reasons, or take advantage of one another when they can seemingly get away with it. This gives a different although compatible basis for the rules of war to those provided by Grotius and other more traditional natural law theorists.

Samuel Pufendorf draws on both Grotius and Hobbes to form a highly plausible basis for the natural law of nations. Pufendorf agrees with Hobbes that peace is the state that all humans most prefer but differs from Hobbes in thinking that peace is the natural state of humans. For Pufendorf, war is permitted by natural law "on the condition that he who wages it shall have as his end the establishment of peace." Our natural instincts move us both toward defending ourselves by force but also toward restraining ourselves from doing harm to others. But peace is always the legitimate goal. Like Grotius, Pufendorf argues that "fear alone does not suffice as a just cause for war, unless it is established with moral and evident certitude that there is an intent to injure us." Both prudence and natural virtue should combine to restrain the use of violence by one state against another, in most situations.

This plausible picture is partially stained by Pufendorf's attempt to prove that nearly any tactic can be justified as long as defensive, or even offensive, wars can be justified by reference to natural law. Indeed, Pufendorf claims, echoing many earlier Just War theorists, that to secure what is rightfully mine, "it is permissible to use whatever means I think will best prevail against such a person" who has tried to deprive me of it. Indeed, Pufendorf suggests that a person can literally never be said to do no injury to someone who has already inflicted an injury on him. And while it is true that Pufendorf then returns to the higher sounding "law of humanity" he does not seem to realize that he has portrayed war as the most dire of Hobbesian states of nature, in which it seems that all is permissible.

Natural Law Theory provides the crucial moral foundation for Just War Theory. But as we have seen, there is a significant debate in the late sixteenth and seventeenth centuries about what natural law requires of humans. At least in part, this mirrors the Roman disputes about whether it is justice or mercy that is the greatest virtue. In Natural Law Theory, this debate is only partially reformulated to be a question of which is more natural: the desire for self-defense or the desire for peace. And while it is possible to combine these together, á la Hobbes or Pufendorf, there are still multiple answers possible to the question of which wars are justified and which tactics can legitimately be used.

On the Law of War

(c. 1532)

Francisco de Vitoria

Francisco de Vitoria (c. 1480–1546), a Spanish Dominican, priest and philosopher, was justly famous for condemning the Conquistadors who waged war against the Indians in South America. His major work was published posthumously.

7. Now, the whole difficulty is in the questions: What is a State, and who can properly be called a sovereign prince? I will briefly reply to them by saying that a State is properly called a perfect community. But the essence of the difficulty is in saying what a perfect community is. By way of solution be it noted that a thing is called perfect when it is a completed whole, for that is imperfect in which there is something wanting, and, on the other hand, that is perfect from which nothing is wanting. A perfect State or community, therefore, is one which is complete in itself, that is, which is not a part of another community, but has its own laws and its own council and its own magistrates, such as is the Kingdom of Castile and Aragon and the Republic of Venice and other the like. For there is no obstacle to many principalities and perfect States being under one prince. Such a State, then, or the prince thereof, has authority to declare war, and no one else.

8. Here, however, a doubt may well arise whether, when a number of States of this kind or a number of princes have one common lord or prince, they can make war of themselves and without the authorization of their superior lord. My answer is that they can do so undoubtedly, just as the kings who are subordinate to the Emperor can make war on one another without waiting for the Emperor's authorization, for (as has been said) a State ought to be self-sufficient, and this it would not be, if it had not the faculty in question.

9. Hence it follows and is plain that other petty rulers and princes, who are not at the head of a perfect State, but are parts of another State, can not begin to carry on a war. Such is the Duke of Alva or the Count of Benevento, for they are parts of the Kingdom of Castile and consequently have not perfect States. As, however, these matters are for a great part governed by the law of nations or by human law, Custom can give power and authority to make war. And so if any State or prince has obtained by ancient custom the right to make war of itself or himself, this authority can not be gain-said, even if in other respects the State be not a perfect one. So, also, necessity can confer this license and authority. For if within one and the same realm one city should take up arms against another, or one of the dukes against another duke, and the king should

neglect or should lack courage to exact redress for the wrongs that have been done, the aggrieved city or duke may not only resort to self-defense, but may also commence war and take measures against the enemy and even kill the wrongdoers, there being no other adequate means of self-defense. For the enemy would not cease from outrage, if the victims thereof were content merely with self-defense. On this principle a private person also may begin an attack on his foe, if there is no other way of safeguarding himself from wrong. This is enough on the present question.

10. Third question: What may be a reason and cause of just war? It is particularly necessary to ask this in connection with the case of the Indian aborigines, which is now before us. Here my first proposition is: Difference of religion is not a cause of just war. This was shown at length in the preceding Relectio, when we demolished the fourth alleged title for taking possession of the Indians, namely, their refusal to accept Christianity. And it is the opinion of St. Thomas (*Secunda Secundae,* qu. 66, art. 8), and the common opinion of the doctors—indeed, I know of no one of the opposite way of thinking.

11. Second proposition: Extension of empire is not a just cause of war. This is too well known to need proof, for otherwise each of the two belligerents might have an equally just cause and so both would be innocent. This in its turn would involve the consequence that it would not be lawful to kill them and so imply a contradiction, because it would be a just war.

12. Third proposition: Neither the personal glory of the prince nor any other advantage to him is a just cause of war. This, too, is notorious. For a prince ought to subordinate both peace and war to the common weal of his State and not spend public revenues in quest of his own glory or gain, much less expose his subjects to danger on that account. Herein, indeed, is the difference between a lawful king and a tyrant, that the latter directs his government towards his individual profit and advantage, but a king to the public welfare, as Aristotle says (*Politics,* bk. 4, ch. 10). Also, the prince derives his authority from the State. Therefore he ought to use it for the good of the State. Also, laws ought "not to be enacted for the private good of any individual, but in the common interest of all the citizens," as is ruled in can. 2, Dist. 4, a citation from Isadore. Therefore the rules relating to war ought to be for the common good of all and not for the private good of the prince. Again, this is the difference between freemen and slaves, as Aristotle says (*Politics,* bk. I, ch. 3 and 4) that masters exploit slaves for their own good and not for the good of the slaves, while freemen do not exist in the interest of others, but in their own interest. And so, were a prince to misuse his subjects by compelling them to go soldiering and to contribute money for his campaigns, not for the public good, but for his own private gain, this would be to make slaves of them.

13. Fourth proposition: There is a single and only just cause for commencing a war, namely, a wrong received. The proof of this rests in the first place on the authority of St. Augustine (*Liber 83 Quaestionum,* "Those wars are described as just wars," etc., as above), and it is the conclusion arrived at by St. Thomas (*Secunda Secundae,* qu. 40, art. I) and the opinion of all the doctors. Also, an offensive war is for the purpose of avenging a wrong and of taking measures against an enemy, as said above. But there can be no vengeance where there is no preceding fault and wrong. Therefore. Also, a prince has no

greater authority over foreigners than over his own subjects. But he may not draw his sword against his own subjects, unless they have done some wrong. Therefore not against foreigners either. This is confirmed by the text already cited from St. Paul (*Romans,* ch. 13) about a prince: "He beareth not the sword in vain: for he is the minister of God, a revenger to execute wrath upon him that doeth evil." Hence it is clear that we may not turn our sword against those who do us no harm, the killing of the innocent being forbidden by natural law. I omit here any injunctions inconsistent herewith which God has given in special cases, for He is the Lord of life and death and it is within His competence to vary His dispositions.

14. Fifth proposition: Not every kind and degree of wrong can suffice for commencing a war. The proof of this is that not even upon one's own fellow-countrymen is it lawful for every offense to exact atrocious punishments, such as death or banishment or confiscation of property. As, then, the evils inflicted in war are all of a severe and atrocious character, such as slaughter and fire and devastation, it is not lawful for slight wrongs to pursue the authors of the wrongs with war, seeing that the degree of the punishment ought to correspond to the measure of the offence (*Deuteronomy,* ch. 25).

15. The fourth question is about the law of war, namely, what kind and degree of stress is lawful in a just war. Here let my first proposition be: In war everything is lawful which the defense of the common weal requires. This is notorious, for the end and aim of war is the defense and preservation of the State. Also, a private person may do this in self-defense, as has been proved. Therefore much more may a State and a prince.

16. Second proposition: It is permissible to recapt everything that has been lost and any part of the same. This is too notorious to need proof. For war is begun or undertaken with this object.

17. Third proposition: It is lawful to make good out of enemy property the expenses of the war and all damages wrongfully caused by the enemy. This is clear, for the enemy who has done the wrong is bound to give all this redress. Therefore the prince can claim it all and exact it all by war. Also, as before, there is the argument that, when no other way lies open, a private creditor can seize the amount of his debt from the debtor. Also, if there were any competent judge over the two belligerents, he would have to condemn the unjust aggressors and authors of wrong, not only to make restitution of what they have carried off, but also to make good the expenses of the war to the other side, and also all damages. But a prince who is carrying on a just war is as it were his own judge in matters touching the war, as we shall forthwith show. Therefore he can enforce all these claims upon his enemy. . . .

34. With regard to another question, namely, what degree of stress is lawful in a just war, there are also many doubts. The first is: Whether it is lawful in war to kill the innocent. It seems that it is; because, in the first place, the Sons of Israel slew children at Jericho, as appears from *Joshua,* ch. 6, and afterwards Saul slew children in Amalek (I *Samuel,* ch. 15), and in both these cases it was by the authority and at the bidding of God. "Now, whatever is written is written for our instruction," as appears from *Romans,* ch. 15. Therefore, if a war of the present day be just, it will be lawful to kill the innocent.

35. With regard to this doubt, let my first proposition be: The deliberate slaugh-

ter of the innocent is never lawful in itself. This is proved, firstly, by *Exodus,* ch. 23: "The innocent and righteous slay thou not." Secondly, the basis of a just war is a wrong done, as has been shown above. But wrong is not done by an innocent person. Therefore war may not be employed against him. Thirdly, it is not lawful within a State to punish the innocent for the wrongdoing of the guilty. Therefore this is not lawful among enemies. Fourthly, were this not so, a war would be just on both sides, although there was no ignorance, a thing which, as has been shown, is impossible. And the consequence is manifest, because it is certain that innocent folk may defend themselves against any who try to kill them. And all this is confirmed by *Deuteronomy,* ch. 20, where the Sons of Israel were ordered to take a certain city by force and to slay every one except women and little ones.

36. Hence it follows that even in war with the Turks it is not allowable to kill children. This is clear, because they are innocent. Aye, and the same holds with regard to the women of unbelievers. This is clear, because so far as the war is concerned, they are presumed innocent; but it does not hold in the case of any individual woman who is certainly guilty. Aye, and this same pronouncement must be made among Christians with regard to harmless agricultural folk, and also with regard to the rest of the peaceable civilian population, for all these are presumed innocent until the contrary is shown. On this principle it follows that it is not lawful to slay either foreigners or guests who are sojourning among the enemy, for they are presumed innocent, and in truth they are not enemies. The same principle applies to clerics and members of a religious order, for they in war are presumed innocent unless the contrary be shown, as when they engage in actual fighting.

37. Second proposition: Sometimes it is right, in virtue of collateral circumstances, to slay the innocent even knowingly, as when a fortress or city is stormed in a just war, although it is known that there are a number of innocent people in it and although cannon and other engines of war can not be discharged or fire applied to buildings without destroying innocent together with guilty. The proof is that war could not otherwise be waged against even the guilty and the justice of belligerents would be balked. In the same way, conversely, if a town be wrongfully besieged and rightfully defended, it is lawful to fire cannon-shot and other missiles on the besiegers and into the hostile camp, even though we assume that there are some children and innocent people there.

Great attention, however, must be paid to the point already taken, namely, the obligation to see that greater evils do not arise out of the war than the war would avert. For if little effect upon the ultimate issue of the war is to be expected from the storming of a fortress or fortified town wherein are many innocent folk, it would not be right, for the purpose of assailing a few guilty, to slay the many innocent by use of fire or engines of war or other means likely to overwhelm indifferently both innocent and guilty. In sum, it is never right to slay the guiltless, even as an indirect and unintended result, except when there is no other means of carrying on the operations of a just war, according to the passage (*St. Matthew,* ch. 13) "Let the tares grow, lest while ye gather up the tares ye root up also the wheat with them."

38. Here a doubt may arise whether the killing of guiltless persons is lawful when they may be expected to cause danger in

the future; thus, for example, the children of Saracens are guiltless, but there is good reason to fear that when grown up they will fight against Christians and bring on them all the hazards of war. Moreover, although the adult male civilians of the enemy who are not soldiers are presumed to be innocent, yet they will hereafter carry a soldier's arms and cause the hazard named. Now, is it lawful to slay these youths? It seems so, on the same principle which justifies the incidental killing of other guiltless persons. Also (*Deuteronomy*, ch. 20) the Sons of Israel were ordered when assaulting any city to slay "every adult male." Now, it can not be presumed that all of these would be guilty.

My answer is that although this killing may possibly be defended, yet I believe that it is in no wise right, seeing that evil is not to be done even in order to avoid greater evil still, and it is intolerable that any one should be killed for a future fault. There are, moreover, other available measures of precaution against their future conduct, namely, captivity, exile, etc., as we shall forthwith show. Hence it follows that, whether victory has already been won or the war is still in progress, if the innocence of any soldier is evident and the soldiers can let him go free, they are bound to do so.

To the argument on the opposite side my rejoinder is that the slaughter in the instances named was at the special command of God, who was wroth against the people in question and wished to destroy them utterly, just as he sent fire on Sodom and Gomorrah which devoured both guiltless and guilty together. He, however, is Lord of all and has not given this license as a common law. And the same answer might be made to that passage in *Deuteronomy,* ch. 20. But, inasmuch as what is there enjoined is in the form of a common law of war for all future time, it would

rather seem that the Lord enjoined it because all adult males in an enemy State are deemed guilty, and guiltless can not be distinguished from guilty. Therefore all may be killed.

39. The second doubtful point is whether in a just war it is lawful to despoil innocent enemy-subjects. Let my first proposition be: It is certainly lawful to despoil the innocent of goods and things which the enemy would use against us, such as arms, ships, and engines of war. This is clear, because otherwise we could not gain the victory, which is the aim of war. Nay, it is also lawful to take the money of the innocent and to burn and destroy their grain and kill their horses, if this is requisite in order to sap the enemy's strength. Hence follows the corollary that if the war goes on for an indefinitely long time it is lawful utterly to despoil all enemy-subjects, guilty and guiltless alike, for it is from their resources that the enemy is feeding an unjust war, and, on the other hand, his strength is sapped by this spoliation of his citizens.

40. Second proposition: If a war can be carried on effectively enough without the spoliation of the agricultural population and other innocent folk, they ought not to be despoiled. Sylvester maintains this (under the word *bellum,* I, § 10) on the ground that war is founded on a wrong done, and therefore the rights of war may not be enforced against the innocent if the wrong can be redressed in another quarter. Aye, and Sylvester adds that, even if there were good reason to despoil the innocent, yet when the war is over the victor is bound to restore to them whatever is left. This, however, I do not think necessary, because, as said above, whatever is done in right of war receives the construction most favorable to the claims of those engaged in a just war. Hence, whatever has been law-

fully seized is not in my opinion subject to restitution. All the same, Sylvester's remark is a pious one and not indefensible. But the spoliation of foreigners and travelers on enemy soil, unless they are obviously at fault, is in no wise lawful, they not being enemies.

41. Third proposition: If the enemy refuse to restore things wrongfully seized by them and the injured party can not otherwise properly recoup himself, he may do so wherever satisfaction is obtainable, whether from guilty or from innocent. For instance, if French brigands made a raid into Spanish territory and the French King would not, though able, compel them to restore their booty, the Spanish might, on the authorization of their sovereign, despoil French merchants or farmers, however innocent these might be. This is because, although the French State or Sovereign might initially be blameless, yet it is a breach of duty, as St. Augustine says, for them to neglect to vindicate the right against the wrongdoing of their subjects, and the injured sovereign can take satisfaction from every member and portion of their State. There is, accordingly, no inherent injustice in the letters of marque and reprisals which princes often issue in such cases, because it is on account of the neglect and breach of duty of the other prince that the prince of the injured party grants him this right to recoup himself even from innocent folk. These letters are, however, hazardous and open the way to plunder.

42. The third doubtful point is: Assuming the unlawfulness of the slaughter of children and other innocent parties, is it permissible, at any rate, to carry them off into capitivity and slavery? This can be cleared up in a single proposition, namely: It is in precisely the same way permissible to carry the innocent off into captivity as to despoil them, liberty and slavery being included among the good things of Fortune. And so when a war is at that pass that the indiscriminate spoliation of all enemy-subjects alike and the seizure of all their goods are justifiable, then it is also justifiable to carry all enemy-subjects off into captivity, whether they be guilty or guiltless. And inasmuch as war with pagans is of this type, seeing that it is perpetual and that they can never make amends for the wrongs and damages they have wrought, it is indubitably lawful to carry off both the children and the women of the Saracens into captivity and slavery. But inasmuch as, by the law of nations, it is a received rule of Christendom that Christians do not become slaves in right of war, this enslaving is not lawful in a war between Christians; but if it is necessary having regard to the end and aim of war, it would be lawful to carry away even innocent captives, such as children and women, not indeed into slavery, but so that we may receive a money-ransom for them. This, however, must not be pushed beyond what the necessity of the war may demand and what the custom of lawful belligerents has allowed.

43. The fourth doubtful point is: Whether it is lawful at any rate to kill hostages who have been taken from the enemy, either in time of truce or on the conclusion of a war, if the enemy break faith and do not abide by their undertakings. My answer is in a single proposition: If the hostages are in other respects among the guilty, as, for instance, because they have borne arms, they may rightfully be killed in that case; if, however, they are innocent, as, for instance, if they be children or women or other innocent folk, it is obvious from what has been said above that they can not be killed.

44. The fifth doubt is: Whether in a just war it is lawful to kill, at any rate, all

the guilty. Prefatory to an answer be it noted that, as is shown by what has been said above, war is waged: Firstly, in defense of ourselves and what belongs to us; secondly, to recover things taken from us; thirdly, to avenge a wrong suffered by us; fourthly, to secure peace and security.

45. This premised, let my first proposition be: In the actual heat of battle, either in the storming or in the defense of a city, all who resist may be killed indiscriminately; and, briefly, this is so as long as affairs are in peril. This is manifest, because combatants could not properly effect their purpose save by removing all who hinder and resist them. All the doubt and difficulty, however, is to know whether, when we have won our victory and the enemy is no longer any danger to us, we may kill all who have borne arms against us. Manifestly, yes. For, as shown above, one of the military precepts given by the Lord (*Deuteronomy,* ch. 20) was that when a city of the enemy had been taken all dwellers in it were to be killed. The words of the passage are: "When thou comest nigh unto a place to fight against it, then proclaim peace unto it. And it shall be if it make thee answer of peace, and open unto thee, that all the people that is found therein shall be saved and shall be tributaries unto thee and shall serve thee. But if it will make no peace with thee, but will make war against thee, then thou shalt besiege it. And when the Lord thy God hath delivered it into thine hands, thou shalt smite every male thereof with the edge of the sword, but not the women and the little ones."

46. Second proposition: Even when victory has been won and no danger remains, it is lawful to kill the guilty. The proof is that, as said above, war is ordained not only for the recovery of property, but also for the avenging of wrongs. Therefore the

authors of a past wrong may be killed therefor. Again, this is permissible against our own wrongdoing citizens. Therefore also against foreigners; for, as said above, a prince when at war has by right of war the same authority over the enemy as if he were their lawful judge and prince. And a further reason is that, although there be no present danger from the enemy, yet security for the future can not be had, unless the enemy be restrained by the fear of punishment.

47. Third proposition: Merely by way of avenging a wrong it is not always lawful to kill all the guilty. The proof is that even among citizens it would not be lawful, not even where the wrong was done by the whole city or district, to kill all the delinquents; nor in a common rebellion would it be permissible to slay and destroy the whole population. Accordingly, for such a deed, St. Ambrose interdicted Theodosius from the church. For such conduct would not be for the public good, which is nevertheless the end and aim of both war and peace. Therefore, it is not right to kill all the guilty among the enemy. We ought, then, to take into account the nature of the wrong done by the enemy and of the damage they have caused and of their other offenses, and from that standpoint to move to our revenge and punishment, without any cruelty and inhumanity. In this connection Cicero says (*Offices,* bk. 2) that the punishment which we inflict on the guilty must be such as equity and humanity allow. And Sallust says: "Our ancestors, the most religious of men, took naught from those they conquered save what was authorized by the nature of their offenses."

48. Fourth proposition: Sometimes it is lawful and expedient to kill all the guilty. The proof is that war is waged in order to get peace and security. But there are times when security can not be got save by de-

stroying all one's enemies: and this is especially the case against unbelievers, from whom it is useless ever to hope for a just peace on any terms. And as the only remedy is to destroy all of them who can bear arms against us, provided they have already been in fault. That is how the injunction in *Deuteronomy*, ch. 20, is to be interpreted. Otherwise, however, in a war with Christians, where I do not think this would be allowable. For, as it needs must be that scandals come (*St. Matthew*, ch. 18) and also wars between princes, it would involve the ruin of mankind and of Christianity if the victor always slew all his enemies, and the world would soon be reduced to solitude, and wars would not be waged for the public good, but to the utter ruin of the public. The measure of the punishment, then, must be proportionate to the offense, and vengeance ought to go no further, and herein account must be taken of the consideration that, as said above, subjects are not bound, and ought not, to scrutinize the causes of a war, but can follow their prince to it in reliance on his authority and on public counsels. Hence in the majority of cases, although the war be unjust on the other side, yet the troops engaged in it and who defend or attack cities are innocent on both sides. And therefore after their defeat, when no further danger is present, I think that they may not be killed, not only not all of them, but not even one of them, if the presumption is that they entered on the strife in good faith.

49. Sixth doubt: Whether it is lawful to slay those who have surrendered or been captured, supposing them also to have been guilty. My answer is that, speaking absolutely, there is nothing to prevent the killing of those who have surrendered or been captured in a just war so long as abstract equity is observed. Many of the rules of war have, however, been fashioned by the law of nations, and it seems to be received in the use and custom of war that captives, after victory has been won (unless perchance they have been routed) and all danger is over, are not to be killed, and the law of nations must be respected, as is the wont among good people. But I do not read or hear of any such custom with regard to those who have surrendered; nay, on the capitulation of a fortress or city it is usual for those who surrender to try and provide for themselves in the conditions of the capitulation, as that their heads shall be safe and that they shall be let go in safety; that is, they fear that an unconditional surrender would mean their deaths. We read of this being several times done. Accordingly, it does not seem unjust that, if a city capitulates without taking any such precautions, the more notorious offenders should be put to death on the order of the prince or a judge.

50. Seventh doubt: Whether everything that is captured in a just war becomes the property of the captor and seizor. My first proposition hereon is: There is no doubt that everything captured in a just war vests in the seizor up to the amount which provides satisfaction for the things that have been wrongfully seized and which covers expenses also. This needs no proof, for that is the end and aim of war. But, apart from all consideration both of restitution and satisfaction, and looking at the matter from the standpoint of the law of war, we must distinguish according as the things captured in war are movables (like money, garments, silver, and gold), or are immovables (like lands, cities, and fortresses).

51. This being assumed, let my second proposition be: All movables vest in the seizor by the law of nations, even if in amount they exceed what will compensate for damages sustained. This is clear from

Dig., 49, 15, 28 and 24, and from can. 9, Dist. 1, and it is more expressly laid down in *Inst.,* 2, 1, 17, where it is said that "by the law of nations whatever is taken from the enemy immediately becomes ours, even so far as that free persons may be made our slaves." And St. Ambrose says (*Liber de Patriarchis*) that when Abraham slew the four kings their spoil belonged to him as the conqueror, although he refused to take it (*Genesis,* ch. 14, and can. 25, C. 23, qu. 5). And this is confirmed by the authority of the Lord (*Deuteronomy,* ch. 20), where He says concerning the storming of a town: "All the spoil thereof thou shalt divide with the army and thou shalt eat of the spoil of thine enemies." Adrian holds this opinion in his *quaestio* on restitution, in the special *quaestio* on war. So, also, Sylvester, under the word *bellum,* § 1 and § 9, where he says that he who fights a just cause is not bound to give back his booty (can. 2, C. 23, qu. 7). "Hence it follows that what is taken in war is not used as a set-off against the principal debt, as the Archdeacon also holds (can. 2, C. 23, qu. 2)." And Bartolus is of the same opinion, in his comment on *Dig.,* 49, 15, 28. And this is understood to be so even if the enemy be ready to make amends in other ways for the damages and wrongs suffered. Sylvester, however, limits this, and rightly, allowing it only until a satisfaction sufficient in equity has been taken for the damages and wrongs suffered. For it is not to be imagined that, if the French have ravaged some one district or insignificant town in Spain, the Spanish might also, if they could, ravage the whole of France; they can only retort in a manner proportionate in kind and degree to the wrong done, according to the estimate of a good man.

52. But on this conclusion a doubt arises, namely, whether it is right to give a city up to the soldiery to sack. My answer is, and let this be my third proposition: This is not unlawful in itself, if necessary for the conduct of the war or as a deterrent to the enemy or as a spur to the courage of the troops. So Sylvester, under the word *bellum,* § 10. It is on the same principle as that which justifies the burning of a city for reasonable cause. Nevertheless, inasmuch as such authorization to sack results in many horrors and cruelties, enacted beyond all humane limits by a barbarous soldiery, such as slaughter and torture of the innocent, rape of virgins, dishonor of matrons, and looting of temples, it is undoubtedly unjust in the extreme to deliver up a city, especially a Christian city, to be sacked, without the greatest necessity and weightiest reason. If, however, the necessities of war require it, it is not unlawful, even if it be likely that the troops will perpetrate foul misdeeds of this kind, which their generals are none the less bound to forbid and, as far as they can, to prevent.

53. Fourth proposition: Despite all this, soldiers may not, without the authority of their prince or general, go looting or burning, because they are themselves not judges, but executive officers; and those who do otherwise are bound to make restitution.

54. Now, with regard to immovable property and things, the difficulty is greater, and let my fifth proposition be: There is no doubt about the lawfulness of seizing and holding the land and for-tresses and towns of the enemy, so far as is necessary to obtain compensation for the damages he has caused. For instance, if the enemy has destroyed a fortress of ours, or has burnt a city or vineyards or olive gardens, we may in turn seize his land or fortress or city and hold it. For if it is lawful to exact compensation from the enemy for the things of ours which he has taken, it is cer-

tain that by the divine law and natural law it is not more lawful to take recompense therefore in movables than in immovables.

55. Sixth proposition: In order to obtain security and avoid danger from our enemy it is also lawful to seize and hold a fortress or city belonging to him which is necessary for our defense or for taking away from him an opportunity of hurting us.

56. Seventh proposition: It is also lawful, in return for a wrong received and by way of punishment, that is, in revenge, to mulct the enemy of a part of his territory in proportion to the character of the wrong, or even on this ground to seize a fortress or town. This, however, must be done within due limits, as already said, and not as utterly far as our strength and armed force enable us to go in seizing and storming. And if necessity and the principle of war require the seizure of the larger part of the enemy's land, and the capture of numerous cities, they ought to be restored when the strife is adjusted and the war is over, only so much being retained as is just, in way of compensation for damages caused and expenses incurred and of vengeance for wrongs done, and with due regard for equity and humanity, seeing that punishment ought to be proportionate to the fault. Thus it would be intolerable that, if the French raided the flocks of the Spanish or burnt a single district, the latter should be allowed to seize the whole Kingdom of France. Now, the lawfulness of seizing on this score either a part of enemy territory or an enemy city appears from *Deuteronomy,* ch. 20, where permission is granted in war to seize a city that has refused to accept terms of peace. Again, internal wrongdoers may be punished in this way, that is, they may be deprived of house or land or a fortress, in proportion to the

character of the circumstances. Therefore foreigner wrongdoers also. Again, a superior judge has competence to mulct the author of a wrong by taking away from him a city (for instance) or a fortress. Therefore a prince who has suffered wrong can do this too, because by the law of war he is put in the position of a judge. Again, it was in this way and by this title that the Roman Empire grew and developed, that is, by occupation, in right of war, of cities and provinces belonging to enemies who had injured them, and yet the Roman Empire is defended as just and lawful by St. Augustine, St. Jerome, St. Ambrose, St. Thomas, and other reverend doctors. Nay, it might be held approved by God in the passage, "Render unto Caesar the things that are Caesar's," and by St. Paul, who appealed unto Caesar and who in *Romans,* ch. 13, gave an admonition to be subject to the higher powers and to princes and to pay tribute to those who at that time, all of them, derived their authority from the Roman Empire.

57. Eighth doubt: Whether it is lawful to impose a tribute on conquered enemies. My answer is that it is undoubtedly lawful, not only in order to recoup damages, but also as a punishment and by way of revenge. This is clear enough from what has been said above and from the passage in *Deuteronomy,* ch. 20, which says that when the Jews have approached a city with good cause in order to attack it, if the city receives them and opens its gates, all the people therin shall be saved and shall serve the Jews with payment of tribute. And this law and usage of war has prevailed.

58. Ninth doubt: Whether it is lawful to depose the princes of the enemy and appoint new ones or keep the princedom for oneself. First proposition: This is not unqualifiedly permissible, nor for any and

every cause of just war, as appears from what has been said. For punishment should not exceed the degree and nature of the offense. Nay, punishments should be awarded restrictively, and rewards extensively. This is not a rule of human law only, but also of natural and divine law. Therefore, even assuming that the enemy's offense is a sufficient cause of war, it will not always suffice to justify the overthrow of the enemy's sovereignty and the deposition of lawful and natural princes; for these would be utterly savage and inhumane measures.

59. Second proposition: It is undeniable that there may sometimes arise sufficient and lawful causes for effecting a change of princes or for seizing a sovereignty; and this may be either because of the number and aggravated quality of the damages and wrongs which have been wrought or, especially, when security and peace can not otherwise be had of the enemy and grave danger from them would threaten the State if this were not done. This is obvious, for if the seizure of a city is lawful for good cause, as has been said, it follows that the removal of its prince is also lawful. And the same holds good of a province and the prince of a province, if proportionately graver cause arise.

Note, however, with regard to Doubts VI to IX, that sometimes, nay, frequently, not only subjects, but princes, too, who in reality have no just cause of war, may nevertheless be waging war in good faith, with such good faith, I say, as to free them from fault; as, for instance, if the war is made after a careful examination and in accordance with the opinion of learned and upright men. And since no one who has not committed a fault should be punished, in that case, although the victor may recoup himself for things that have been taken

from him and for any expenses of the war, yet, just as it is unlawful to go on killing after victory in the war has been won, so the victor ought not to make seizures or exactions in temporal matters beyond the limits of just satisfaction, seeing that anything beyond these limits could only be justified as a punishment, such as could not be visited on the innocent.

60. All this can be summarized in a few canons or rules of warfare. First canon: Assuming that a prince has authority to make war, he should first of all not go seeking occasions and causes of war, but should, if possible, live in peace with all men, as St. Paul enjoins on us (*Romans,* ch. 12). Moreover, he should reflect that others are his neighbors, whom we are bound to love as ourselves, and that we all have one common Lord, before whose tribunal we shall have to render our account. For it is the extreme of savagery to seek for and rejoice in grounds for killing and destroying men whom God has created and for whom Christ died. But only under compulsion and reluctantly should he come to the necessity of war.

Second canon: When war for a just cause has broken out, it must not be waged so as to ruin the people against whom it is directed, but only so as to obtain one's rights and the defense of one's country and in order that from that war peace and security may in time result.

Third canon: When victory has been won and the war is over; the victory should be utilized with moderation and Christian humility, and the victor ought to deem that he is sitting as judge between two States, the one which has been wronged and the one which has done the wrong, so that it will be as judge and not as accuser that he will deliver the judgment whereby the injured state can obtain satisfaction, and this, so far as possible should involve the offending state in the least degree of calamity and misfortune, the offending individuals being chastised within lawful limits; and an especial reason for this is that in general among Christians all the fault is to be laid at the door of their princes, for subjects when fighting for their princes act in good faith and it is thoroughly unjust, in the words of the poet, that—

> Quidquid delirant reges, plectantur Achivi.
> (For every folly their Kings commit the punishment should fall upon the Greeks.)

The Law of War

(1598)

Alberico Gentili

Alberico Genitli (1552–1608) was born in Italy. He was trained as a lawyer, specializing in international law. He was a judge in Italy and a professor at Heidelberg and Oxford. Gentili defended the Spanish ambassador, convincing the English government to send him back to Spain rather that to execute him for treason.

CHAPTER V IT IS JUST TO WAGE WAR

Now let us first inquire as to the justice of war, whether it is lawful to wage it. For if war, as Cicero says, is characteristic of beasts, and hence has its name from the beasts (*belluis*), it may well appear that war does not become mankind.

Hear the words of Seneca: 'We repress homicide and the murder of individuals. What of wars and the glorious crime of destroying nations? Avarice and cruelty know no bounds. By decree of the Senate and by vote of the people savagery is practised and officially ordered, although it is prohibited to individuals. Crimes punishable with death are praised because they are committed in a general's uniform.

Mankind, though a kindly race, is not ashamed to revel in the blood of its fellows, to wage wars and transmit them to its children to carry on, although even the dumb and savage beasts keep peace among themselves.'

This is a strong argument; for if dumb beasts, which cannot make speeches and argue about the reasons for their anger, and which because of their innate ferocity are averse to peace and inclined to battle, yet live in peace; how much the more ought human beings to do this, unless they wish to seem more bestial than the very beasts.

Cyprian too expresses himself in language like that of Seneca: 'When individuals commit homicide, it is a crime. It is called valour, when war is waged by the state, and impunity is granted to crimes, not out of regard for their blamelessness, but for the greatness of their cruelty.' And on another point, which, however, bears upon our present topic, he says: 'The laws have formed a conspiracy with crime, and what is public is beginning to be regarded as lawful.' Seneca says in another place: 'Slight acts of sacrilege are punished, great ones are honoured with triumphs.' Tertullian too said that injustice was a characteristic of wars, and forbade the Christians to take up military service. Lactantius asserted that the just man might not serve as a soldier; moreover, that whatever is argued about the duties relating to military life cannot be reconciled with justice nor with true virtue, but pertains to this life and to civil usage. And other utterances of the kind are numerous.

The canon of the great Basil is also cited, by which those who had slain an enemy in battle were excommunicated for three years. In Gregory's *Decree* we read these words: 'Were it not that those carnal wars bore a likeness to the spiritual conflicts, never in my opinion would those books of Jewish history have been handed down by the Apostles, to be read in the churches by the disciples of Christ, who came into the world to teach peace.' And what shall I say of Erasmus, who in a long digression in his *Proverbs* assails the injustice of war?

Others perhaps would not condemn every war, but only one which is undertaken for another motive than honour or defence. So Cicero, who says that no war is undertaken by a well-ordered state except to defend its honour or for self-protection. They also condemn a war undertaken without provocation. Thus, for example, Ambrose records that David never made war unprovoked. And our friend Baldus

writes that war is contrary to nature's laws, unless the necessity for defence arises. 'Warfare is bestial, when you make war; when you defend your country, it is human,' says Scaliger. And other statements of the kind might be added.

But this view is rejected by all the theologians after Augustine. Opposed to it too are all our jurists and all the philosophers of every time. And rightly; for if a sword has been given to a magistrate to protect his citizens against harm, why should he not ward off injury which comes from without, as well as that which exists within? Is a war of defence, which is prompted by nature, also unlawful? But there is an abundance of arguments in its favour from those who have undertaken its advocacy, and they will appear in the course of our discussion.

We will now make reply to our opponents. And first we shall say to Seneca and to Pauli-Festus that their etymology of *bellum* is not the correct one, any more than that other derivation of the grammarians by contraries from the adjective *bellus,* 'pretty', as if war were 'the ugly thing' (*minime bellum*). And even though their etymology were correct, it would prove nothing as to the injustice of the thing itself except in so far as the Latins are concerned, for among the Greeks πόλεμος, 'war', derives its name from πολύς, 'the multitude', and in other languages from other concepts.

To Cicero, who maintains that war is opposed to some law of humanity, by which we were born for union and not for discord, we may reply that war is not contrary to all human law; for example, that which provides that those who revolt from society and do not keep men's laws should be punished and forced to conform to those laws, statutes, and customs. This fact too has a bearing upon our investigation, that wars are just even though so many things which come from them are evil, because their final aim is good, after the rebels have been forced to submit to reason. And since its aim is good, war itself is also good and just. And because all things have their own bounds, etc., all of which is from Aristotle.

Moreover, the purpose of war is peace, to which end and to justice (such is said to be the decree of nature) one cannot attain except through bloodshed and those evils arising from strife. In the same way, too, slavery is contrary to nature, and yet at the same time in accord with nature, because those who act contrary to nature have no right to enjoy her blessing of liberty. This subject I shall discuss more fully in my Third Book.

Cicero himself will be found to agree with this view, nor does Seneca hold a different opinion. They are both referring to unjust wars; for Seneca commends the wars of Hercules, which he believes to be just. Tertullian too, in saying that injustice was characteristic of war, had in mind the things which are too often wont to happen in war and which are unjust. But we are inquiring what ought to be done in war, and also what can be done, has been done, and is regularly done by good men. Furthermore, Tertullian's condemnation of military service is particularly directed against the idolatry which at that time was connected with the oath of allegiance and with the veneration of the images of the emperors, as is clearly seen in his works.

I shall now make reply in the same manner to Lactantius, Cyprian, Gregory, and even to Erasmus himself. For he tells us in his commentary on Cyprian how that holy man assailed wars on the ground that they were nearly all unjust; nay, were absolutely all unjust as they were usually

carried on at that time. Starting with that preconception, Erasmus himself forms his opinions and declaims them in such wise that Bellarmino may well term his manner of argument childish. In fact, some cite Erasmus in our favour, others on the opposite side. Perhaps a third view will be nearer the truth, that the flighty dilettante did not know what he thought.

It seems to me also that the other Church Fathers have not always been consistent on this point. We have heard what Gregory says; yet there is to be found in his *Decree* even more that is favourable to war. Theophylactus says that it is less of an evil for soldiers to make war than to busy themselves with worse things. Tertullian expresses the view that one ought not to enter upon military service after being baptized, and other writers express various opinions of that kind, which unequivocally condemn war; and they have not always been satisfactorily answered by later writers.

What are we to say to Basil? Are we to assail the canons of such a man? Or are we to see in them something of a sacerdotal nature, since the Churchman ever spitefully assails the pagan and the enemy? Or has he followed Phocylides when he sang: 'Even if it is an enemy whom you slay, you defile your hand.' They shrink from what is lawful because of the proximity of what is unlawful (in this case because such a connexion is usual) just as they shrink from an oath and other lawful acts.

Be it therefore established as a fact, that even a war of vengeance and an offensive war may be waged justly. For I shall show that in the case of these also there is always a defensive aspect, if they are just. As Marcus Tullius says: 'Certain it is that those wrongs which are inflicted intentionally, with the design of doing harm, often proceed from fear, since one who plans to injure another fears that, if he does not do so, he will himself suffer some damage.' In this way we must understand Baldus, that he may not be assumed wrongly to disapprove of every war except one of defence. So with Scaliger, who believes that the attempts of Aeneas were lawful, although he was trying to get possession of what belonged to another, since he was trying to bring his gods into Latium.

CHAPTER VI THAT WAR MAY BE WAGED JUSTLY BY BOTH SIDES

But may a war be waged with justice on both sides? The learned Piccolomini raises this question somewhere, but does not answer it. Among our jurists Fulgosius maintained the affirmative against the opinion of the others. Alciati has followed Fulgosius in more than one place. I too follow him, but with the proviso that there may be reasonable doubt as to the justice of the cause. This same point has been made by our other jurists and by our theologians, who declare that there is justice on one side in reality, but on the other and on both through justifiable ignorance. Thus, led by the voice of God, the Jews justly made war upon the Canaanites, and the Canaanites also justly resisted the Jews through ignorance of the divine utterance, acting in self-defence. And so Pius the Second wisely replied to the Hungarian envoys, who spoke against the emperor, that he thought that the King of Hungary was not departing from what was honourable; while he also knew that the emperor was a lover of justice, however much the two might differ as to the sovereignty. For neither of them thought that he had an unjust cause.

It is the nature of wars for both sides to maintain that they are supporting a just cause. In general, it may be true in nearly every kind of dispute, that neither of the two disputants is unjust. Aristotle makes an exception only when the inquiry is 'whether the act took place'. And indeed in the case of one's own act our jurists are not in the habit of admitting ignorance as a defence. But they do admit it in the case of another's act, because that happens under different conditions. We are driven to this distinction by the weakness of our human nature, because of which we see everything dimly, and are not cognizant of that purest and truest form of justice, which cannot conceive of both parties to a dispute being in the right. For why, says Maximus of Tyre in this connexion, should those whose purposes are just engage in strife with one another? And in fact it is either the unjust who fight with one another or the unjust with the just.

But we for the most part are unacquainted with that truth. Therefore we aim at justice as it appears from man's standpoint. In this way we avoid the objection of Baldus, that when war arises among contending parties, it is absolutely inevitable that one side or the other is in the wrong. Accordingly we say that if it is evident that one party is contending without any adequate reason, that party is surely practising brigandage and not waging war. All agree on this point, and rightly. And it is quite true that the cause of the party which is in the right receives additional justification from that fact. 'The injustice of an adversary makes wars just', writes Augustine, and referring to the Romans he says: 'The injustice of others furnished them with adversaries with whom they could wage just wars.'

But if it is doubtful on which side justice is, and if each side aims at justice, neither can be called unjust. Thus Baldus himself maintains that war between kings is just, whenever the aim on both sides is to retain majesty and justice. Those who contend in the litigation of the Forum justly, that is to say, on a plausible ground, either as defendants or plaintiffs, and lose their case and the verdict, are not judged guilty of injustice. And yet the oath regarding false accusation is taken by both parties. Why should the decision be different in this kind of dispute and in a contest of arms?

In particular Bartolus, Baldus, and some others apply arguments derived from those bloodless contests of the Forum to the strife of arms and the duel. For example, some point is obscure and it is not clear whether a thing belongs to Titius or Sempronius; and since each lays claim to it, each tries to take it from the other. Will you find one of them guilty of injustice?

Baldus says, and it is perfectly evident, that no one ought to surrender his rights without a struggle, but that every possible effort should be made to maintain them. Cicero appropriately says of the two factions of Julius Caesar and of Pompey: 'There was an element of uncertainty and a contest between leaders of distinction. Many were in doubt as to what was best, many wondered what would be to their advantage, many what was proper, some even what was lawful.' And when the struggle is between expediency and honour, there is no slight degree of uncertainty as to which we ought to follow. We may add to the above the words of Severus to Albinus: 'When we fought against Niger, we did not have such specious reasons for our hostilities; for the empire was the prize of victory, and each of us with equal eagerness strove to win it, even while its lawful possession was still a matter of dispute.'

I add here the cases in which one renders aid to allies, friends, kindred, neighbours and others whom one is under obligations to assist, and yet in so doing justly rouses against himself the arms of the adversary whom he is attacking. Thus Livy relates of the people of Caere that they espoused the cause of the men of Tarquinii against the Romans through compassion for their kinsfolk, and as the historian makes their own envoys say, not through design, but through the compulsion of necessity.

This will, moreover, give rise to a third variety of the question, when the war is just on one side, but on the other is still more just. Such a case is of course possible, inasmuch as one man does not cease to be in the right because his opponent has a juster cause. The virtues admit of greater or less degrees, and the middle ground of a virtue has length and breadth and is not limited to a point.

I shall add other instances and other causes for war from time to time and take note of them. Of all our laws, however, that one seems to me the clearest which grants the rights of war to both contestants, makes what is taken on each side the property of the captors, and regards the prisoners of both parties as slaves. While others are endeavouring to evade this law, in opposition to Fulgosius, they are unquestionably indulging in a pleasurable madness; as was demonstrated by Alciati, who also insists on that equality among enemies of which we made note before.

But although it may sometimes happen (it will not occur very often, as you will learn forthwith) that injustice is clearly evident on one of the two sides, nevertheless this ought not to affect the general principle, and prevent the laws of war from applying to both parties. For laws are not based upon rare instances and adapted to them; that is to say, on events which are rare in their own class, and which take place only occasionally, contrary to the general nature of the case. This is the doctrine of many of our learned men, and they maintain that the general rule (as I say) is not affected. 'No law is altogether adapted to every one', said Marcus Cato. Therefore no change must be made in this law of the enemy and of war; for it is impartial to both sides, just as in the contests of the Forum the law is impartial towards each of the litigants, until sentence has been pronounced in favour of one or the other of them. And then the defeated party, who contended unjustly, will suffer severe punishment at the hands of the victor because of his injustice.

But if the unjust man gain the victory, neither in a contention in arms nor in the strife carried on in the garb of peace is there any help for it. Yet it is not the law which is at fault, but the execution of the law. As Paulus says: 'The law is not to blame, but its application.'

Perhaps you may console yourself by saying with the theologians and the philosophers that there is no sin without retribution, since every wicked deed is its own punishment. As Seneca puts it, 'the first and greatest penalty for sinners is to have sinned'. Fear too is a chastisement, as the same philosopher points out, when he says: 'Fortune exempts many from punishment, but none from fear.' Besides, there is ill repute in the eyes of others and remorse in one's own heart, as the philosophers have made clear. There is also Hell, of which the philosophers have told us by induction, and the theologians from knowledge.

• • •

CHAPTER XIII OF NECESSARY DEFENCE

Now although I maintain that no natural cause for war exists, yet there are reasons because of which we undertake wars under Nature's guidance. For example, for defence and when we make war because something is refused us which Nature herself has bestowed upon mankind; and therefore war is resorted to, because a law of nature is violated. We call defence, now necessary, now expedient, now honourable; yet in every case we should regard it as necessary. 'He who defends himself is said to act through compulsion.' So says Baldus, who refuses to distinguish whether one is defending oneself, one's possessions, or one's subjects; or whether what is defended is near or at a distance. Thus one who is attacked by an armed enemy makes a necessary defence, and his action is that of necessary defence; and so also does one against whom an enemy has been making preparations. And that such a one ought to be helped by his allies is rightly maintained by the aforementioned Baldus, while others hold the same opinion.

It was for this reason, we may say, that war was made on Mithridates in days gone by, and in response to his formidable preparations for war. For it was not right for prudent men to wait until he had declared himself their enemy; but to consider his deeds rather than his words. Thus in speaking of necessity we are not speaking with absolute accuracy, but we mean that which is not uncommon in human relations, and which is ordinarily called necessity; it may, however, not be true and absolute necessity. For instance, when the Romans made a hostile invasion of their territories, the people of Tusculum acted in a peaceful and conciliatory manner, opening their gates and showing themselves friendly in every way; and they declared that they preferred anything whatever rather than war. And by this submission they gained peace at the time, and shortly afterwards citizenship.

Amalassuntha, queen of the Goths, tried the same tactics, replying to the envoys of Justinian, when they threatened war, that she had no desire to contend with arms and that he who began a contest with one who made no resistance gained a victory without honour. In fact, it is a most unfair struggle, when one party attacks and the other merely suffers. The same statement was made by the envoys of the Gepidi, namely, that those could not justly be assailed who were willing to accept another's terms.

But these things have nothing to do with justice. For to kill in self-defence is just, even though the one who kills may flee without danger and so save himself; and regardless of the question whether the one who slays in self-defence is of such condition that it would be disgraceful for him to flee, or not disgraceful. These views have been admitted in the case of private individuals, and I consider them still more valid with regard to states. Even the brutes are given the right of defence by nature, and we are persuaded and convinced of this right not by argument, but by some innate power. And it is a necessary right; for what can be done against violence, says Cicero, without resort to violence? This is the most generally accepted of all rights. All laws and all codes allow the repelling of force by force. There is one rule which endures for ever, to maintain one's safety by any and every means. 'Every method of securing safety is honourable. This has been taught to philosophers by reason, to barbarians by necessity, to the nations by custom, to wild animals by Nature herself. This law is not written, but inborn.' And there are other statements of the same kind.

But I am not speaking at present of the manner and method of defence, a subject which belongs to my following Books. To defend our own property is a necessary defence, as I have said. And even though we have provoked the war which is made upon us, this is a just cause, both in the view of other men and also in that of Paul de Castro. I myself subscribe to this opinion, adding the thought that the right of war, or the violence of war, is not ended by the recovery of what was previously demanded, but goes on at the will of the victor. 'Who, pray, is satisfied with a punishment commensurate with the wrong which he has suffered?' says Augustine, and all admit that he speaks truly. But escape from this conclusion may be made rightly by all who are not subjects, and can therefore defend themselves against it by arms. Hostile witnesses and jurors are rejected, even though those against whom they are summoned have given cause for hostility. The fact of having himself given cause for the hostility is not to the disadvantage of one who asks that he be protected against being wronged. 'He who refuses what is just to one who is armed gives up everything,' said Caesar.

And here it is not a question of that justifiable control where there is no superior. These theories are therefore evaded. Accordingly, in my opinion the cause of Romulus will rightly be called just, when he defended himself with arms against the invasion of the Sabines, although he had himself given cause for anger and war by carrying off the Sabine women contrary to all precedent. This matter I discuss at length in the Second Book of my treatise *On the Wars of the Romans.* 'Under the pressure of arms the power of necessity is so great, that even what is unjust appears wholly just', as Bodin well puts it. 'War is just for those for whom it is necessary, and arms are righteous for those who have no hope left except in arms.'

In fact, extreme necessity forms an exception to every law. Yet I do not restrict our present principle to that extreme necessity; or at least I understand (as I have said) 'extreme' from the standpoint of human conditions. For granting that what can be avoided is not a necessity, and that Romulus might have avoided war by giving up the stolen women; yet he also had the right to defend himself against enemies who were presently going to attack him. I do not greatly concern myself about that principle. For it is a question of civil law whether a bandit, who may be attacked with impunity, may nevertheless defend himself.

CHAPTER XIV OF DEFENCE ON GROUNDS OF EXPEDIENCY

I CALL it a defence dictated by expediency, when we make war through fear that we may ourselves be attacked. No one is more quickly laid low than one who has no fear, and a sense of security is the most common cause of disaster. This to begin with. Then, we ought not to wait for violence to be offered us, if it is safer to meet it halfway. 'The man who attacks has greater hope and greater courage than one who defends himself', says Livy, and again: 'He who causes danger has more courage than he who wards it off.' So also Vegetius says: 'If the enemy has once anticipated us, general confusion results from fear.' Therefore (according to Nicephorus, a historian of no

mean authority) those who desire to live without danger ought to meet impending evils and anticipate them.

One ought not to delay, or wait to avenge at one's peril an injury which one has received, if one may at once strike at the root of the growing plant and check the attempts of an adversary who is meditating evil. Suidas, or rather Demosthenes, says that we ought not to delay but ought to press hostilities, for fear that we may be compelled to defend ourselves against violence after having first suffered wrongs. As Cicero, the Latin Demosthenes, says, it is also a disgrace to prefer to find a remedy for present ills, when one might have anticipated them before they happened. So, too, that inexperienced youth in Terence says (so true is it that Nature herself suggests that law): 'I prefer that we should be on our guard, rather than that I should punish him after we have suffered wrong.' That is an excellent saying of Philo's, that we kill a snake as soon as we see one, even though it has not injured us and will perhaps not harm us. For thus we protect ourselves before it attacks us.

Am I tiresome to you in naming those authorities, who are not of our own country? Yet the agreement of many different authorities is a strong argument. We always consider every argument in connexion with the authority for it, and the authorities who have been cited are thoroughly pertinent to our subject, since they are well acquainted with the matters of which we are treating. Cicero indeed was a distinguished jurist, as Baldus says, and he cites him as such. Cicero was not only the greatest of orators, but also of jurists, as Duaren declares.

But is there any one who does not know this thing? I have much more reason to fear that I may be trying to make clear what is already clear, and thus waste my time in the effort to prove what no one doubts. Yet I shall not omit some things which have almost become proverbial and so indicate a great deal by a mere hint, such as 'Meet a disease half-way', 'Check it at the start, otherwise remedies are prepared too late.' 'Neglected fires always spread.' There are others that come from legal authorities: 'It is better to keep the laws intact than to look for a cure when it is too late. It is better to provide in time than to take vengeance after the event.' It is lawful to anticipate a wrong. It is lawful for me to attack a man who is making ready to attack me. And there are other rules of the same kind, which are said to have been laid down for the benefit of humanity and confirmed in the courts.

No one ought to expose himself to danger. No one ought to wait to be struck, unless he is a fool. One ought to provide not only against an offence which is being committed, but also against one which may possibly be committed. Force must be repelled and kept aloof by force. Therefore one should not wait for it to come; for in this waiting there are the undoubted disadvantages which have been enumerated above and also the considerations which are mentioned in the suits of private individuals: that we may not fall by submitting to the first blow, and that we may not give ground in flight, and be overwhelmed when prostrate. But to flee is not to defend oneself. This may be understood from the testimony of learned men and also from the facts themselves; and this our jurists also tell us. These things are clear and well established and thoroughly adapted to a treatise on war.

What follows is more doubtful, namely, the question when a matter may be said to have reached the point where it is necessary to resort to that expedient defence. A just cause for fear is demanded; suspicion is not enough. Now a just fear is defined as the fear of a greater evil, a fear which might properly be felt even by a man of great courage. Yet in the case of great empires I cannot readily accept that definition, which applies to private affairs. For if a private citizen commit some offence against a fellow citizen, reparation may be secured through the authority of a magistrate. But what a sovereign has done to a sovereign, no one will make good.

But in this argument based upon fear we must not depart from those definitions of fear, which are not designed to show what we ought to do through fear of a coming evil in order to avert the evil (which is the object of our present study), but rather, if we have been subjected to fear and have therefore done anything to our disadvantage, what legal remedy we have for our act and for the fear which was inspired in us. Here we should take our definitions rather from another chapter of the civil law, which stipulates that damage shall not be inflicted and which stipulates in such a way as to see that precaution is taken even when it may happen that no damage is done; even though there is no great and clear cause for fear, and even if there really is no danger, but only a legitimate cause for fear.

This does not apply, however (as Euripides says), to cases when one fears without reason. For who is there who can prevent a man from being afraid of his own shadow? I read in Cicero: 'I do not inquire whether anything ought to be feared. I think every man ought to have the privilege of fearing what he chooses.' Similar are the well-known words of Matius to Cicero, that even slaves had always been at liberty to fear at their own discretion, rather than according to the mandate of another. You may also apply here the saying of the law: one must not dictate to any one what he is to fear. Cicero says: 'If I were to inquire into all the particulars of these great dangers, I should hear many; I should not believe in them all, but I should guard against all of them.' So, too, Seneca says: 'When you shudder at great dangers which you think cannot exist, you fear them none the less.'

In fact this principle must be admitted at this point touching the greater evil, about which I shall speak later. But with regard to anticipating danger these words of Gellius are noteworthy: 'In all cases where caution is necessary the reason is not the same, nor are the affairs, the actions, and the duties of human life the same whether they oblige us to anticipate or defer or take vengeance or be on our guard. The gladiator who is ready for battle is confronted with the alternative of killing, if he is quick, or of being killed, if he is too slow. But the life of men is not circumscribed by such unjust and inevitable necessities that you must be the first to in-

flict injury, in order to avoid suffering injury in case you do not inflict it.' And Cicero says: 'Who ever made such a law as this, or to whom could this be conceded without the greatest danger to all men, that it should be right for a man to kill one at whose hand he said that he himself feared death at a later time?'

Yet the reply of the people of Mytilene to the Athenians was reasonable: 'If we seem to any one unjust, because we revolted first, without waiting until we knew clearly whether they would do us any harm, such a man does not consider well; for if we had been equally strong, so that we could have plotted against them in turn and could have delayed with safety, then his words would be just. But since they always have the opportunity of doing harm, we ought to have the privilege of anticipating our defence.' What then are we to ask of men like Bartolus and Baldus; or on whose bare names are we to rely? Are we not to value more highly the defence of a most famous state, nay, the opinion of Thucydides, an eminent and wise man; an opinion confirmed also by reason?

On War

(c. 1610)

Francisco Suarez

Francisco Suarez (1548–1617), a Spanish Jesuit priest and philosopher, taught in Rome and Salamanca. It is said that he once defended the infamous Spanish Inquisition. His work on war was published as part of a larger work on Charity.

DISPUTATION XIII ON WAR

An external contest at arms which is incompatible with external peace is properly called war, when carried on between two sovereign princes or between two states. When, however, it is a contest between a prince and his own state, or between citizens and their state, it is termed sedition. When it is between private individuals it is called a quarrel or a duel. The difference between these various kinds of contest appears to be material rather than formal, and we shall discuss them all, as did St. Thomas (II.-II, qq. 40, 41, 42) and others who will be mentioned below.

Section I Is War Intrinsically Evil?

1. The first heresy [in connexion with this subject] consists in the assertion that it is intrinsically evil and contrary to charity to wage war. Such is the heretical belief attributed by Augustine to the Manichaeans (*Against Faustus*, Bk. XXII, chap. lxxiv), whom Wycliffe followed, according to the testimony of Waldensis (*De Sacramentalibus* [which is Vol. III of *Doctrinale Antiquitatum Fidei*] last title, next to last chapter). The second error is the assertion that war is specifically forbidden to Christians, and especially, war against Christians. So Eck maintains (*Enchiridion Locorum Communium*, Chap. xxii); and other persons of our own time, who are heretics, advance the same contention. They distinguish, however, two kinds of war, the defensive and the aggressive, which we shall discuss in Sub-section 6 of this Section. The conclusions that follow will elucidate the matter.

2. Our first conclusion is that war, absolutely speaking, is not intrinsically evil, nor is it forbidden to Christians. This conclusion is a matter of faith and is laid down in the Scriptures, for in the Old Testament, wars waged by most holy men are praised (*Genesis*, Chap. xiv [, vv. 19–20]): 'Blessed be Abram [. . . .] And blessed be God by whose protection the enemies are in thy hands.' We find similar passages concerning Moses, Josue, Samson, Gedeon, David, the Machabees, and others, whom God often ordered to wage war upon the enemies of the Hebrews. Moreover, the apostle Paul (*Hebrews*, Chap. xi[, v. 33]) said that by faith the saints conquered kingdoms. The same principle is confirmed by further testimony, that of the Fathers quoted by Gratian (*Decretum*, Pt. II, causa XXIII, qq. 1 and 2), and also that of Ambrose (*On Duties*, various chapters).

However, one may object, in the first place, that the Lord said to David [*I Paralipomenon*, Chap. xxviii, v. 3]: 'Thou shalt not build my temple because thou art a man who has shed blood.

Secondly, it will be objected that Christ said to Peter (*John*, Chap. xviii [, v. 11]): 'Put up thy sword into the scabbard,' &c.; and that Isaias also said (*Isaias*, Chap. ii [, v. 4]): 'They shall turn their swords into ploughshares [. . .] neither shall they be exercised any more to war'; and, in another Chapter (Chap. xi [, v. 9]): 'They shall not hurt nor shall they kill in all [my] holy mountain.' The Prophet is speaking, indeed, of the time of the coming of the Messiah, at which time, especially, it will be made clear, what is permissible and what is not permissible.

Thirdly, at the Council of Nicaea (Chap. xi [, can. xii]), a penalty was imposed upon Christians who, after having received the faith, enrolled themselves for military service. Furthermore, Pope Leo (*Letters*, xcii [Letter clxvii, inquis. xii.]) wrote that war was forbidden to Christians, after a solemn penance.

Fourthly, war morally brings with it innumerable sins; and a given course of action is considered in itself evil and forbidden, if it is practically always accompanied by unseemly circumstances and harm to one's neighbours. [Furthermore,] one may add that war is opposed to peace, to the love of one's enemies, and to the forgiveness of injuries.

3. We reply to the first objection that [the Scriptural passage in question] is based upon the unjust slaying of Uriah; and, also, upon the particularly great reverence owed to the Temple.

[As for the second objection, we may answer, first, that] Christ our Lord is speaking of one who on his own initiative wishes to use the sword, and in particular, of one who so desires, against the will of his prince. Moreover, the words of Isaias, especially in Chap. xi, are usually understood as referring to the state of glory. Secondly, it is said that future peace was symbolized in the coming of the Messiah, as is explained by Jerome on this point [on *Isaias,* Chap. xi], Eusebius (*Demonstrations,* Bk. I, chap. i), and other Fathers [of the Church]; or, at least, that Isaias is referring to the spiritual warfare of the Apostles and of the preachers of the Gospel, who have conquered the world not by a material but by a spiritual sword. This is the interpretation found in Justin Martyr, in his *Second Apology* for the Christians, and in other writers.

The Council of Nicaea, indeed, dealt especially with those Christians who, for a second time, were assuming the uniform of pagan soldiers which they had once cast off. And Pope Leo, as the Gloss (on *Decretum,* Pt. II, causa XXXIII, qu. iii (*De Paenitentia*), dist. v, cans. iv and iii) explains, was speaking of those Christians who, after a public penance had been imposed upon them, were returning to war, before the penance had been completed. Furthermore, it may have been expedient for the early Church to forbid those who had recently been converted to the faith, to engage in military service immediately, in company with unbelievers, and under pagan officers.

To the argument drawn from reason, Augustine replies (*On the City of God,* Bk. XIX, last chapter [Chap. vii]) that he deems it advisable to avoid war in so far as is possible, and to undertake it only in cases of extreme necessity, when no alternative remains; but he also holds that war is not entirely evil, since the fact that evils follow upon war is incidental, and since greater evils would result if war were never allowed.

Wherefore, in reply to the confirmation of the argument in question one may deny that war is opposed to an honourable peace; rather, it is opposed to an unjust peace, for it is more truly a means of attaining peace that is real and secure. Similarly, war is not opposed to the love of one's enemies; for whoever wages war honourably hates, not individuals, but the actions which he justly punishes. And the same reasoning is true of the forgiveness of injuries, especially since this forgiveness is not enjoined under every circumstance, for punishment may sometimes be exacted, by legitimate means, without injustice.

4. Secondly, I hold that defensive war not only is permitted, but sometimes is even commanded. The first part of this proposition follows from the first conclusion, which even the Doctors cited above accept; and it holds true not only for public officials, but also for private individuals, since all laws allow the repelling of force with force (*Decretals,* Bk. V, tit. XXXIX, chap. iii). The reason supporting it is that the

right of self-defence is natural and necessary. Whence the second part of our second proposition is easily proved. For self-defence may sometimes be prescribed, at least in accordance with the order of charity; a fact which I have elsewhere pointed out, in Disputation IX [: *De Ordine circa Personas Servando in Praecepto Charitatis,* &c., Chaps. xxv, xl, § 3]. The same is true of the defence of the state, especially if such defence is an official duty. See the statement of Ambrose (*On Duties,* Bk. I, chap. vii). If any one objects that in the *Epistle to the Romans* (Chap. xii [, v. 19]) these words are found: 'Revenge not yourselves, my dearly beloved', and that this saying is in harmony with the passage (*Matthew,* Chap. v [, v. 39]): 'If one strike thee on the right cheek, turn to him also the other', we shall reply with respect to the first passage, that the reference is to vengeance, so that another version reads [*Romans,* Chap. xii, v. 19]: 'Not avenging yourselves', and that the Greek word, ἐκδικοῦντες, has both significations; but the meaning is clear from what follows: 'For it is written: Revenge is mine', &c. The meaning of the second passage cited is the same, if it is interpreted as a precept; although it may also be understood, in accordance with Augustine's explanation (Vol. IV in the book *On Lying,* Chap. xv and elsewhere), as referring to the preparation of the soul, at least when such a process is necessary; for otherwise [the passage in question is] merely a counsel [of perfection, and not a commandment].

5. My third conclusion is, that even when war is aggressive, it is not an evil in itself, but may be right and necessary. This is clear from the passages of Scripture cited above, which make no distinction [between aggressive and defensive wars]. The same fact is evidenced by the custom of the Church, one that has quite frequently been approved by the Fathers and the Popes, according to an extensive collection of all such instances, made by Roffensis (*Contra Lutherum* [*Assertionis Lutheranae Confutationem,*] Art. 4 [Art. 34]). In this connexion, we may refer also to Torquemada (on *Decretum,* Pt. II, causa XXIII, qu. i, nos. 1 and 2), as well as to many other passages, in *Decretum, ibid.,* qu. viii, cans. vii *et seq.*

The reason supporting our third conclusion is that such a war is often necessary to a state, in order to ward off acts of injustice and to hold enemies in check. Nor would it be possible, without these wars, for states to be maintained in peace. Hence, this kind of warfare is allowed by natural law; and even by the law of the Gospel, which derogates in no way from natural law, and contains no new divine commands save those regarding faith and the Sacraments. The statement of Luther that it is not lawful to resist the punishment of God is indeed ridiculous; for God does not will the evils [against which war is waged,] but merely permits them; and therefore He does not forbid that they should be justly repelled.

6. It remains for us to explain what constitutes an aggressive war, and what, on the other hand, constitutes a defensive war; for sometimes that which is merely an act of defence may present the appearance of an aggressive act. Thus, for example, if enemies seize the houses or the property of others, but have themselves suffered invasion from the latter, that is no aggression but defence. To this extent, civil laws (*Code,* VIII. iv. 1 and *Digest,* XLIII. xvi. 1 and 3) are justified in conscience also, when they provide that if any one tries to dispossess me of my property, it is lawful for me to repel force with force. For such an act is not aggression, but defence,

and may be lawfully undertaken even on one's own authority. The laws in question are extended to apply to him who, while absent, has been ejected from a tenure which they call a natural one, and who, upon his return, is prevented from recovering that tenure. For [the same laws decree] that any one who has been despoiled may, even on his own authority, have recourse to arms, because such an act is not really aggression, but a defence of one's legal possession. This rule is laid down in *Decretals,* Bk. II, tit. XIII, chap. xii.

Consequently, we have to consider whether the injustice is, practically speaking, simply about to take place; or whether it has already done so, and redress is sought through war. In this second case, the war is aggressive. In the former case, war has the character of self-defence, provided that it is waged with a moderation of defence which is blameless. Now the injury is considered as beginning, when the unjust act itself, even physically regarded, is beginning; as when a man has not been entirely deprived of his rightful possession; or even when he has been so deprived, but immediately—that is, without noteworthy delay—attempts to defend himself and to reinstate himself in possession. The reason for this is as follows: When any one is, to all intents and purposes, in the very act of resisting, and attempts—in so far as is possible—to protect his right, he is not considered as having, in an absolute sense, suffered wrong, nor as having been deprived of his possession. This is the common opinion of the Doctors as stated by Sylvester (word *bellum,* Pt. II), and also by Bartolus and the jurists on the aforesaid *Digest,* XLIII. xvi. 3, § 9 [§ § 1 *et seq.*].

7. Our fourth proposition is this: in order that a war may be justly waged, a number of conditions must be observed, which may be grouped under three heads.

First, the war must be waged by a legitimate power; secondly, the cause itself and the reason must be just; thirdly, the method of its conduct must be proper, and due proportion must be observed at its beginning, during its prosecution and after victory. All of this will be made clear in the following sections. The underlying principle of this general conclusion, indeed, is that, while a war is not in itself evil, nevertheless, on account of the many misfortunes which it brings in its train, it is one of those undertakings that are often carried on in evil fashion; and that therefore, it requires many [justifying] circumstances to make it righteous.

SECTION II WHO HAS THE LEGITIMATE POWER OF DECLARING WAR?

1. Our question relates to aggressive war; for the power of defending oneself against an unjust aggressor is conceded to all.

I hold first: that a sovereign prince who has no superior in temporal affairs, or a state which has retained for itself a like jurisdiction, has by natural law legitimate power to declare war. This is the opinion held by St. Thomas (II.-II, qu. 40, art. 1); and he is supported by all. Reference may be made to Covarruvias (on *Sext,* rule *peccatum,* Pt. 11, § 9), who cites many laws, as well as certain theological divines.

A reason in support of this conclusion is, first, that this sort of war is at times permitted by the natural law, as we have demonstrated; hence, the power of declaring such a war must rest with some one; and therefore it must rest, most of all, with the possessor of sovereign power, for it is particularly his function to protect the state, and to command the inferior princes [within the realm].

A second reason is that the power of declaring war is (so to speak) a power of jurisdiction, the exercise of which pertains to punitive justice, which is especially necessary to a state for the purpose of constraining wrongdoers; wherefore, just as the sovereign prince may punish his own subjects when they offend others, so may he avenge himself on another prince or state which by reason of some offence becomes subject to him; and this vengeance cannot be sought at the hands of another judge, because the prince of whom we are speaking has no superior in temporal affairs; therefore, if that offender is not prepared to give satisfaction, he may be compelled by war to do so.

In this first conclusion, I used the words, 'or a state', in order that I might include every kind of polity; for the same reasoning holds true of all polities. Only it must be noted of a monarchical régime that, after a state has transferred its power to some one person, it cannot declare war without that person's consent, because it is no longer supreme; unless the prince should chance to be so negligent in avenging or defending the state as to cause public and very grave harm to that state, for, in such a case, the commonwealth as a whole could take vengeance and deprive the sovereign of the authority in question. For the state is always regarded as retaining this power within itself, if the prince fails in his duty.

2. I hold, secondly, that an inferior prince, or an imperfect state, or whosoever in temporal affairs is under a superior, cannot justly declare war without the authorization of that superior. A reason for the conclusion is, first, that a prince of this kind can claim his right from his superior, and therefore has not the right to declare war; since, in this respect, he has the character of a private person. For it is because of the reason stated that private persons cannot declare war. A second reason in support of this same conclusion is that such a declaration of war is opposed to the rights of the sovereign prince, to whom that power has been specially entrusted; for without such power he could not govern peacefully and suitably.

Victoria [*De Iure Belli,* no. 9], indeed, sets certain limitations to what has been here stated, and Cajetan and others seem to hold the same opinion.

• • •

SECTION IV WHAT IS A JUST CAUSE OF WAR, ON THE BASIS OF NATURAL REASON?

There was an old error current among the Gentiles, who thought that the rights of nations were based on military strength, and that it was permissible to make war solely to acquire prestige and wealth; a belief which, even from the standpoint of natural reason, is most absurd.

1. Therefore I hold, first: that there can be no just war without an underlying cause of a legitimate and necessary nature. The truth of this conclusion is indubitable and clearly evident. Now, that just and sufficient reason for war is the infliction of a grave injustice which cannot be avenged or repaired in any other way. This, the consensus of opinion of all the theologians, is also to be deduced from the *Decretum* (Pt. II, tit. XXIII, chap. ii) and from a mass of evidence collected by Covarruvias on the *Constitutions of Clement,* c. *si furiosus,* Pt. II, § 3, no. 2].

The first reason in support of such a conclusion is the fact that war is permissible [only] that a state may guard itself from molestation; for in other respects, war is opposed to the welfare of the human race on account of the slaughter, material losses, and other misfortunes which it involves; and therefore, if the cause in question should cease to exist, the justice of war would also cease to exist.

Secondly, in war, men are despoiled of their property, their liberty, and their lives; and to do such things without just cause is absolutely iniquitous, for if this were permissible, men could kill one another without cause.

Thirdly, the sort of war which we are chiefly discussing is aggressive war, and it is frequently waged against non-subjects. Consequently, it is necessary that the latter shall have committed some wrong on account of which they render themselves subjects. Otherwise, on what ground could they be deserving of punishment or subject to an alien jurisdiction?

Furthermore, if the grounds or purposes which the Gentiles had in view (for example, ambition, avarice, and even vainglory or a display of ferocity) were legitimate and sufficient, any state whatsoever could aspire to these ends; and hence, a war would be just on both sides, essentially and apart from any element of ignorance. This supposition is entirely absurd; for two mutually conflicting rights cannot both be just.

2. But in order that this matter may be explained more clearly, there are several points which should be noted.

First, it is not every cause that is sufficient to justify war, but only those causes which are serious and commensurate with the losses that the war would occasion. For it would be contrary to reason to inflict very grave harm because of a slight injustice. In like manner, a judge can punish, not all offences whatsoever, but only those which are opposed to the common peace and to the welfare of the realm. In this connexion, however, we must remember that not infrequently a wrong which appears to be slight is in fact serious, if all the circumstances are weighed, or if other and similar wrongs are permitted [as a consequence], since thereby great harm may gradually ensue. Thus, for example, to seize even the smallest town, or to make raids, &c., may sometimes constitute a grave injustice, especially when the prince who has done the wrong treats with scorn the protest that is made.

3. Secondly, it must be noted that there are various kinds of injuries which are causes of a just war. These may be grouped under three heads. One of the heads would be the seizure by a prince of another's property, and his refusal to restore it. Another head would be his denial, without reasonable cause, of the common rights of nations, such as the right of transit over highways, trading in common, &c. The third would be any grave injury to one's reputation or honour. It should be added that it is a sufficient cause for war if an injury of this kind be inflicted either upon a prince himself or upon his subjects; for the prince is guardian of his state and also of his subjects. Furthermore, the cause is sufficient if the wrong be inflicted upon any one who has placed himself under the protection of a prince, or even if it be inflicted upon allies or friends, as may be seen in the case of Abraham (*Genesis,* Chap. xiv), and in that of David (*1 Kings,* Chap. xxviii). 'For a friend is a second self', says Aristotle (*Nicomachean Ethics,* Bk. IX, chaps. iv and ix). But it must be understood that such a circumstance justifies war only on condition that the friend him-

self would be justified in waging the war, and consents thereto, either expressly or by implication. The reason for this limitation is that a wrong done to another does not give me the right to avenge him, unless he would be justified in avenging himself and actually proposes to do so. Assuming, however, that these conditions exist, my aid to him is an act of co-operation in a good and just deed; but if [the injured party] does not entertain such a wish, no one else may intervene, since he who committed the wrong has made himself subject not to every one indiscriminately, but only to the person who has been wronged. Wherefore, the assertion made by some writers, that sovereign kings have the power of avenging injuries done in any part of the world, is entirely false, and throws into confusion all the orderly distinctions of jurisdiction; for such power was not [expressly] granted by God and its existence is not to be inferred by any process of reasoning.

4. Thirdly, we must note that, in regard to an injury inflicted, two arguments may be alleged, [to justify a declaration of war]. The first is [that such a declaration is justifiable], in order that reparation for the losses suffered should be made to the injured party. For this cause, indeed, it is not to be questioned that war may legitimately be declared; for if this declaration is to be permitted because of an injury [already done], then it is in the highest degree permissible when the object is that each one may secure himself against loss. Many examples illustrating this point are to be found in the Scriptures (*Genesis,* Chap. xiv, and similar passages). The other argument is [that war should be declared]

in order that the offender may be duly punished; a contention which presents its own difficulty.

5. Secondly, then, I hold that a war may also be justified on the ground that he who has inflicted an injury should be justly punished, if he refuses to give just satisfaction for that injury, without resort to war. This conclusion is commonly accepted. In connexion with it, and with the preceding conclusion, we must assume that the opposing party is not ready to make restitution, or to give satisfaction; for if he were so disposed, the warlike aggression would become unjust, as we shall demonstrate in the following sections.

The conclusion is proved, first, by certain Scriptural passages (*Numbers,* Chap. xxv; *2 Kings,* Chaps. x and xi), according to which, unconditional punishment for offences was carried into execution, by the command of God.

The reason in support of this same conclusion is that, just as within a state some lawful power to punish crimes is necessary to the preservation of domestic peace; so in the world as a whole, there must exist, in order that the various states may dwell in concord, some power for the punishment of injuries inflicted by one state upon another; and this power is not to be found in any superior, for we assume that these states have no commonly acknowledged superior; therefore, the power in question must reside in the sovereign prince of the injured state, to whom, by reason of that injury, the opposing prince is made subject; and consequently, war of the kind in question has been instituted in place of a tribunal administering just punishment.

The Law of War and Peace

(1625)

Hugo Grotius

Hugo Grotius, Hugo de Groot (1583–1645), was born in Holland and trained as a lawyer, specializing in international law. Grotius famously defended Holland for keeping the booty seized from pirate ships.

CHAPTER II WHETHER IT IS EVER LAWFUL TO WAGE WAR

I.—That War is not in Conflict with the Law of Nature is Proved by Several Considerations

1. Having seen what the sources of law are, let us come to the first and most general question, which is this: whether any war is lawful, or whether it is ever permissible to war. This question, as also the others which will follow, must first be taken up from the point of view of the law of nature.

Marcus Tullius Cicero, both in the third book of his treatise *On Ends* and in other places, following Stoic writings learnedly argues that there are certain first principles of nature—'first according to nature', as the Greeks phrased it—and certain other principles which are later manifest but which are to have the preference over those first principles. He calls first principles of nature those in accordance with which every animal from the moment of its birth has regard for itself and is impelled to preserve itself, to have zealous considera-tion for its own condition and for those things which tend to preserve it, and also shrinks from destruction and things which appear likely to cause destruction. Hence also it happens, he says, that there is no one who, if the choice were presented to him, would not prefer to have all the parts of his body in proper order and whole rather than dwarfed or deformed; and that it is one's first duty to keep oneself in the condition which nature gave to him, then to hold to those things which are in confor-mity with nature and reject those things that are contrary thereto.

2. But after these things have received due consideration [Cicero continues], there follows a notion of the conformity of things with reason, which is superior to the body. Now this conformity, in which moral good-ness becomes the paramount object, ought to be accounted of higher import than the things to which alone instinct first di-rected itself, because the first principles of nature commend us to right reason, and right reason ought to be more dear to us than those things through whose instru-mentality we have been brought to it.

Since this is true and without other demonstration would easily receive the assent of all who are endowed with sound judgement, it follows that in investigating the law of nature it is necessary first to see what is consistent with those fundamental principles of nature, and then to come to that which, though of later origin, is nevertheless more worthy—that which ought not only to be grasped, if it appear, but to be sought out by every effort.

3. According to the diversity of the matter, that which we call moral goodness at times consists of a point, so to speak, so that if you depart from it even the least possible distance you turn aside in the direction of wrong-doing; at times it has a wider range, so that an act may be praiseworthy if performed, yet if it be omitted altogether or performed in some other way no blame would attach, the distinction being generally without an intermediate stage, like the transition from being to not-being. [16] Between things opposed in a different way, however, as white and black, a mean may be found either by effecting a combination of the two or by finding an intermediate between them.

It is with this latter class of actions that both divine and human laws are wont to concern themselves, in order that those acts which were in themselves merely praiseworthy might become also obligatory. But we said above, in discussing the law of nature, that the question is this, whether an act can be performed without injustice; and injustice is understood to be that which is utterly repugnant to a rational and social nature.

4. In the first principles of nature there is nothing which is opposed to war; rather, all points are in its favour. The end and aim of war being the preservation of life and limb, and the keeping or acquiring of things useful to life, war is in perfect accord with those first principles of nature. If in order to achieve these ends it is necessary to use force, no inconsistency with the first principles of nature is involved, since nature has given to each animal strength sufficient for self-defence and self-assistance. 'All kinds of animals', says Xenophon, 'understand some mode of fighting, and they have learned this from no other source than nature.' In the fragment of the *Piscation* we read:

> To all has it been given
> To recognize a foe, likewise to know
> Their safeguards each its own, and power
>   and use
> Each of its weapon.

Horace had said:

> With tooth the wolf, with horn the bull attacks;
> And why, unless by inner feeling guided?

Lucretius presents the thought more fully:

> Each creature feels the strength which it
>   can use.
> Felt by the calf his horns are, ere they stand
> Upon his forehead; and with them he butts
> Angrily, and, threatening, forward thrusts.

The same idea is thus expressed by Galen: 'We see that each animal uses for its protection that in which it is strongest. For the calf whose horns have not yet sprouted threatens with that part, and the colt kicks before its hoofs are hard, and the puppy tries to bite when its teeth are not yet strong.' Galen also remarks (*On the Use of Parts,* 1) that man is an animal born for peace and war. Weapons, to be sure, are not born with him, but he has hands suited for fashioning and handling weapons; and we see that babies of their own accord, and without being taught by any one, use their hands in place of weapons. So Aristotle, too

(*On the Parts of Animals*, IV. 10), says that in the case of man the hand has the place of spear, sword, and all other weapons, because he is able to take and hold everything with the hand.

5. Right reason, moreover, and the nature of society, which must be studied in the second place and are of even greater importance, do not prohibit all use of force, but only that use of force which is in conflict with society, that is which attempts to take away the rights of another. For society has in view this object, that through community of resource and effort each individual be safeguarded in the possession of what belongs to him.

It is easy to understand that this consideration would hold even if private ownership (as we now call it) had not been introduced; for life, limbs, and liberty would in that case be the possessions belonging to each, and no attack could be made upon these by another without injustice. Under such conditions the first one taking possession would have the right to use things not claimed and to consume them up to the limit of his needs, and any one depriving him of that right [17] would commit an unjust act. But now that private ownership has by law or usage assumed a definite form, the matter is much easier to understand. I shall express the thought in the words of Cicero:

> Just as, in case each member of the body should have a feeling of its own, so that it might think that it could gain in vigour by drawing to itself the vigour of the nearest member, the whole body would of necessity be weakened and utterly perish, so, if every one of us should seize upon the possessions of others for himself and carry off from each whatever he could, for his own gain, human society and the community of life would of necessity be absolutely destroyed. For, since nature does not oppose, it has been granted

that each prefer that whatever contributes to the advantage of life be acquired for himself rather than for another; but nature does not allow us to increase our means of subsistence, our resources, and our riches, from the spoil of others.

6. It is not, then, contrary to the nature of society to look out for oneself and advance one's own interests, provided the rights of others are not infringed; and consequently the use of force which does not violate the rights of others is not unjust. This thought also Cicero has presented: 'Since there are two ways of settling a difference, the one by argument, the other by force, and since the former is characteristic of man, the latter of brutes, we should have recourse to the second only when it is not permitted to use the first.' 'What can be done', says the same writer in another passage, 'against force without force?

In Ulpian we read: 'Cassius writes that it is permissible to repel force by force, and this right is bestowed by nature. From this moreover it appears, he says, that it is permissible to repel arms by means of arms.' Ovid had said:

> The laws permit arms 'gainst armed men
>   to bear.

II.–That War is not in Conflict with the Law of Nature is Proved from History

1. Our statement that not all war is in conflict with the law of nature is more fully proved from sacred history. For Abraham with his servants and allies had taken up arms and had won the victory over the four kings who had sacked Sodom; and God approved the deed through his priest Melchizedek. Thus in fact Melchizedek addressed him (*Genesis,* xiv. 20): 'Praise be to God Most High, who has delivered thine enemies into thine hand.' But Abraham had taken up arms, as is evident from the

narrative, without a special command of God; in accordance with the law of nature, therefore, did he act, a man not only most holy but also most wise—so recognized even by the testimony of foreigners, Berosus and Orpheus.

I shall not appeal to the history of the seven peoples whom God delivered to the Israelites to be destroyed; for in that case there was a special command to execute a judgement of God upon peoples guilty of the greatest crimes. These wars therefore in holy writ are properly called the wars of God, since they were undertaken by the command of God, not at the discretion of men. Having a more direct bearing on our subject is the war in which the Jews, under the leadership of Moses and Joshua, by arms repelled the Amalekites who were attacking them (*Exodus,* xvii). This act, which God had not commanded in advance, He approved afterward.

2. But further, God laid down for His own people general and perpetual laws in regard to the mode of carrying on war (*Deuteronomy,* xx. 10, 15), showing by this very act that a war can be just even without having been specifically commanded by Him. For in these passages He plainly distinguishes the case of the seven peoples from that of other peoples; and since in the same passages He presents no ordinance dealing with the just causes for undertaking war, by this very fact He shows that these are clearly enough known from nature. A just cause of war, for example, is the defence of territory, in the war of Jephthah against the Ammonites (*Judges,* xi); another is the maltreatment of envoys, in the war of David against the same people (*2 Samuel,* x).

In the same connexion we should note what the inspired writer to the Hebrews says, that Gideon, Barak, Samson, Jephthah, David, Samuel, and others 'through faith subdued kingdoms, waxed valiant in fight, turned to flight the armies of the aliens' (*Hebrews,* xi. 33, 34). In this passage, as the context makes plain, he includes in the term 'faith' the conviction that [18] what is done is pleasing to God. So also a wise woman says that David 'fights the battles of God' (*1 Samuel,* xxv. 28), that is, battles that are righteous and just.

• • •

CHAPTER I THE CAUSES OF WAR: FIRST, DEFENCE OF SELF AND PROPERTY

I.–What Causes of War may be called Justifiable

1. LET us proceed to the causes of war—I mean justifiable causes; for there are also other causes which influence men through regard for what is expedient and differ from those that influence men through regard for what is right.

The two kinds of causes Polybius accurately distinguishes from each other and from beginnings of war, such as the [wounding of the] stag was in the war between Aeneas and Turnus. Although the distinction between these matters is clear, nevertheless the words applied to them are often confused. For what we call justifiable causes Livy, in the speech of the Rhodians, called beginnings: 'You certainly are Romans who claim that your wars are so fortunate because they are just, and pride yourselves not so much on their outcome, in that you gain the victory, as upon their beginnings, because you do not undertake wars without cause.'

In the same sense also Aelian (in Book XII, chapter liii) speaks of the beginnings of wars, and Diodorus Siculus (Book XIV), giving an account of the war of the

Lacedaemonians against the Eleans, expresses the same idea by using the words 'pretexts' and 'beginnings'.

2. These justifiable causes are the special subject of our discussion. Pertinent thereto is the famous saying of Coriolanus quoted by Dionysius of Halicarnassus: 'This, I think, ought to be your first concern, that you have a cause for war which is free from reproach and just.' Similarly Demosthenes says: 'As the substructures of houses, the framework of ships, and similar things ought to be most firm, so, in the case of actions, the causes and fundamental reasons ought to be in accord with justice and truth.' Equally pertinent is the statement of Dio Cassius: [101] 'We must give the fullest consideration to justice. With justice on our side, military prowess warrants good hope; without it, we have nothing sure, even if the first successes equal our desires.' Cicero also says, 'Those wars are unjust which have been undertaken without cause'; and in another passage he criticizes Crassus because Crassus had determined to cross the Euphrates without any cause for war.

3. What has been said is no less true of public than of private wars. Hence the complaint of Seneca:

> We try to restrain murders and the killing of individuals. Why are wars and the crime of slaughtering nations full of glory? Avarice and cruelty know no bounds. In accordance with decrees of the Senate and orders of the people atrocities are committed, and actions forbidden to private citizens are commanded in the name of the state.

Wars that are undertaken by public authority have, it is true, in some respects a legal effect, as do judicial decisions, which we shall need to discuss later; but they are not on that account more free from wrong if they are undertaken without

cause. Thus Alexander, if he commenced war on the Persians and other peoples without cause, was deservedly called a brigand by the Scythians, according to Curtius, as also by Seneca; likewise by Lucan he was styled a robber, and by the sages of India 'a man given over to wickedness', while a pirate once put Alexander in the same class with himself. Similarly, Justin tells how two kings of Thrace were deprived of their royal power by Alexander's father, Philip, who exemplified the deceit and wickedness of a brigand. In this connexion belongs the saying of Augustine: 'If you take away justice, what are empires if not vast robberies?' In full accord with such expressions is the statement of Lactantius: 'Ensnared by the appearance of empty glory, men give to their crimes the name of virtue.'

4. No other just cause for undertaking war can there be excepting injury received. 'Unfairness of the opposing side occasions just wars,' said the same Augustine, using 'unfairness' when he meant 'injury', as if he had confused the Greek words for these two concepts. In the formula used by the Roman fetial are the words, 'I call you to witness that that people is unjust and does not do what is right in making restitution.'

II.–Justifiable Causes Include Defence, the Obtaining of that which Belongs to us or is our Due, and the Inflicting of Punishment

1. It is evident that the sources from which wars arise are as numerous as those from which lawsuits spring; for where judicial settlement fails, war begins. Actions, furthermore, lie either for wrongs not yet committed, or for wrongs already done.

An action lies for a wrong not yet committed in cases where a guarantee is sought against a threatened wrong, or security against an anticipated injury, or an interdict of a different sort against the use of violence. An action for a wrong committed lies where a reparation for injury, or the punishment of the wrong-doer, is sought.

These two sources of legal obligations were rightly distinguished by Plato, in the ninth book of the *Laws*. Reparation is concerned either with what is or has been ours, giving rise to actions involving property interests, and certain personal actions; or with what is owed to us by contract, or in consequence of a criminal act; or by operation of law, a category to which must be referred also cases arising from implied contracts and constructive crimes. Under these subdivisions the rest of the personal actions fall. An act deserving punishment opens the way to accusation and public trial.

2. Authorities generally assign to wars three justifiable causes, defence, recovery of property, and punishment. All three you may find in Camillus's declaration with reference to the Gauls: 'All things which it is right to defend, to recover, and to avenge.' In this enumeration the obtaining of what is owed to us was omitted, unless the word 'recover' is used rather freely. But this was not omitted by Plato when he said that wars are waged not only in case one is attacked, or despoiled of his possessions, but also if one has been deceived. In harmony with this is a sentence of Seneca: 'Perfectly fair, and in complete accord with the law of nations, is the maxim, "Pay what you owe."' The thought was expressed also in the formula of the fetial: 'Things which they have not given, nor paid, nor done, which things ought to have been given, to have been done, to have been paid'; in the words of Sallust, in his *Histories:* 'I demand restitution in accordance with the law of nations.'

When, however, Augustine said, 'Those wars are wont to be defined as just which avenge wrongs,' he used the word 'avenge' in a rather general way [102] to mean 'exact requital for'. This is shown by what follows, for therein we find not a logical subdivision but a citation of examples: 'War, then, ought to be undertaken against that people and state which has either neglected to exact punishment for wrongs done by its members, or to return what has been wrongfully taken away.'

3. It was in accordance with this natural principle that a king of India, according to Diodorus, brought against Semiramis the charge 'that she commenced war without having suffered any wrong'. So also the Romans demanded of the Senones that they should not attack a people at whose hands they had received no injury. Aristotle in his *Analytics,* Book II, chapter 11, says: 'It is customary to make war on those who were the first to inflict injury.' Of the Abians, who were Scythians, Curtius says: 'It was agreed that of barbarians they were the most just; they refrained from war unless attacked.'

The first cause of a justifiable war, then, is an injury not yet inflicted, which menaces either person or property.

III.—War for the Defence of Life is Permissible

We said above that if an attack by violence is made on one's person, endangering life, and no other way of escape is open, under such circumstances war is permissible, even though it involve the slaying of the assailant. As a consequence of the general acceptance of this principle we showed that in some cases a private war may be lawful.

This right of self-defence, it should be observed, has its origin directly, and chiefly, in the fact that nature commits to each his own protection, not in the injustice or crime of the aggressor. Wherefore, even if the assailant be blameless, as for instance a soldier acting in good faith, or one who mistakes me for some one else, or one who is rendered irresponsible by madness or by sleeplessness—this, we read, has actually happened to some—the right of self-defence is not thereby taken away; it is enough that I am not under obligation to suffer what such an assailant attempts, any more than I should be if attacked by an animal belonging to another.

IV.–War in Defence of Life is Permissible only Against an Actual Assailant

1. It is a disputed question whether innocent persons can be cut down or trampled upon when by getting in the way they hinder the defence or flight by which alone death can be averted. That this is permissible, is maintained even by some theologians. And certainly, if we look to nature alone, in nature there is much less regard for society than concern for the preservation of the individual. But the law of love, especially as set forth in the Gospel, which puts consideration for others on a level with consideration for ourselves, clearly does not permit the injuring of the innocent even under such conditions.

2. It has been well said by Thomas—if he is rightly understood—that if a man in true self-defence kills his assailant the slaying is not intentional. The reason is not that, if no other means of safety is at hand, it is not sometimes permissible to do with set purpose that which will cause the death of the assailant; it is, rather, that in such a case the inflicting of death is not the primary intent, as it is in the case of procedure by process of law, but the only

resource available at the time. Even under such circumstances the person who is attacked ought to prefer to do anything possible to frighten away or weaken the assailant, rather than cause his death.

V.–War in Defence of Life is Permissible only when the Danger is Immediate and Certain, not when it is Merely Assumed

1. The danger, again, must be immediate and imminent in point of time. I admit, to be sure, that if the assailant seizes weapons in such a way that his intent to kill is manifest the crime can be forestalled; for in morals as in material things a point is not to be found which does not have a certain breadth. But those who accept fear of any sort as justifying anticipatory slaying are themselves greatly deceived, and deceive others. Cicero said truly, in his first book *On Duties,* that most wrongs have their origin in fear, since he who plans to do wrong to another fears that, if he does not accomplish his purpose, he may himself suffer harm. In Xenophon, Clearchus says: [103] 'I have known men who, becoming afraid of one another, in consequence of calumny or suspicion, and purposing to inflict injury before receiving injury, have done the most dreadful wrongs to those who had had no such intention, and had not even thought of such a thing.' Cato, in his speech for the Rhodians, asks: 'Shall we be the first to do what we say they wished to do?' There is a notable expression of the thought in Gellius:

> When a gladiator is equipped for fighting, the alternatives offered by combat are these, either to kill, if he shall have made the first decisive stroke, or to fall, if he shall have failed. But the life of men generally is not hedged about by a necessity so unfair and so relentless that you are obliged to

strike the first blow, and may suffer if you shall have failed to be first to strike.

In another passage Cicero says, not less rightly: 'Who has ever established this principle, or to whom without the gravest danger to all men can it be granted, that he shall have the right to kill a man by whom he says he fears that he himself later may be killed?' In this connexion we may quote the well-known verses of Euripides:

If, as you say, your husband wished to take
Your life, wishing were then your part as
   well,
Until the time should come.

A parallel is found in Thucydides: 'The future is still uncertain, and no one, influenced by that thought, should arouse enmities which are not future but certain.' Thucydides, further, in the passage in which he sets forth the evils arising from the manifestations of party-spirit in the Greek states, reckons as a fault also this: 'The man was praised who had himself been first to commit the evil deed which another was going to commit.' 'In the effort to guard against fear,' says Livy, 'men cause themselves to be feared, and we inflict upon others the injury which has been warded off from ourselves, as if it were necessary either to do or to suffer wrong.' To such men the query of Vibius Crispus, which Quintilian praised, is applicable: 'Who has permitted you to harbour so great fear?' According to Dio, Livia said that they do not escape disgrace who are first to do the deed that they fear.

2. Further, if a man is not planning an immediate attack, but it has been ascertained that he has formed a plot, or is preparing an ambuscade, or that he is putting poison in our way, or that he is making ready a false accusation and false evidence, and is corrupting the judicial procedure, I maintain that he cannot lawfully be killed, either if the danger can in any other way be avoided, or if it is not altogether certain that the danger cannot be otherwise avoided. Generally, in fact, the delay that will intervene affords opportunity to apply many remedies, to take advantage of many accidental occurrences; as the proverb runs, 'There's many a slip 'twixt cup and lip.' There are, it is true, theologians and jurists who would extend their indulgence somewhat further; but the opinion stated, which is better and safer, does not lack the support of authorities.

VI.–Defence of Limb against Injury is also Justifiable

What shall we say about the danger of injury to a part of the body?

Truly the loss of a limb, especially if it is one of the principal limbs, is an extremely serious matter, and in a sense comparable to loss of life; further, we cannot be sure that injury to a part of the body will not bring danger of death. If, therefore, the injury cannot be avoided in any other way, I should think that he who is on the point of inflicting such injury can be rightly slain.

VII.–The Defence of Chastity is in the Highest Degree Justifiable

That the same right to kill should be conceded also in defence of chastity is hardly open to question; not only the general opinion of men, but also the divine law puts chastity on a plane with life. Thus Paul the jurist said that virtue could properly be defended by such an act.

We find an example in Cicero and Quintilian; the case was that of a tribune of Marius, who was killed by a soldier. In the histories there are also some examples

[104] of men who were slain by women. The killing of a man under such circumstances is called by Chariclea, in Heliodorus, 'a justifiable defence for warding off a violation of chastity.'

• • •

At this point we must add that war cannot permissibly be waged by him who knows that he has a just cause but has not adequate proofs to convince the possessor of the injustice of his possession; the reason is that he does not have the right to compel the other to surrender possession.

[398] XII.—When the Doubt on Either side is Equal, if Neither Party is in Possession the Thing Under Dispute should be Divided

In cases in which the right is in doubt, and neither party is in possession, or each holds possession in an equal measure, he is to be considered in the wrong who rejects a proposed division of the thing under dispute.

XIII.—The Question Whether a War may be Just from the View-Point of Both Parties is Discussed, with many Qualifications

1. From what we have said it is possible to reach a decision regarding the question, which has been discussed by many, whether, if we take into consideration the prime movers, a war may be considered just from the point of view of each of the opposing sides.

We must distinguish various interpretations of the word 'just'. Now a thing is called just either from its cause, or because of its effects; and again, if from its cause, either in the particular sense of justice, or in the general sense in which all right conduct comes under this name. Further, the particular sense may cover either that which concerns the deed, or that which concerns the doer; for sometimes the doer

himself is said to act justly so long as he does not act unjustly, even if that which he does is not just. This distinction between 'acting wrongly' ($\tau o\ \dot{\alpha}\delta\iota\kappa\epsilon\hat{\iota}\nu$) and 'doing that which is unjust' ($\tau o\ \dot{\alpha}\delta\iota\kappa o\nu\ \pi\rho\dot{\alpha}\tau\tau\epsilon\iota\nu$) is rightly made by Aristotle.

2. In the particular sense and with reference to the thing itself, a war cannot be just on both sides, just as a legal claim cannot; the reason is that by the very nature of the case a moral quality cannot be given to opposites as to doing and restraining. Yet it may actually happen that neither of the warring parties does wrong. No one acts unjustly without knowing that he is doing an unjust thing, but in this respect many are ignorant. Thus either party may justly, that is in good faith, plead his case. For both in law and in fact many things out of which a right arises ordinarily escape the notice of men.

3. In the general sense that is usually called just which is free from all blame on the part of the doer. However, many things are done without right and yet without guilt, because of unavoidable ignorance. An example of this is the case of those who fail to observe a law of which they are ignorant through no fault of their own, after the law itself has been promulgated and a sufficient time has elapsed for them to know of it. So it may happen in the case of legal claims also, that each party is guiltless, not only of injustice, but also of any other fault; this is especially true where each party, or even one of the two, pleads not in his own name but in the name of another, for example because of his duty as a guardian, which cannot abandon a right even if it is uncertain.

In this sense Aristotle declares that in suits concerning a disputed right neither party is dishonourable or, as he says, 'wicked'. In agreement therewith Quintilian says that it may happen that an orator, that is a good man, may speak on either side. Furthermore Aristotle also says that a judge is said to judge justly in a twofold sense, for this means that he judges either 'as he ought', without any ignorance, or 'in accordance with his own judgement'. And in another place he says: 'If a judge has rendered judgement through ignorance, he is not unjust.'

4. In the case of war, however, it is scarcely possible that rashness and lack of kindly feeling should not play some part, because of the seriousness of the business. The seriousness of war is in all respects such that, not satisfied with merely acceptable causes, it demands causes that are perfectly evident.

5. If we interpret the word 'just' in relation to certain legal effects, in this sense surely it may be admitted that a war may be just from the point of view of either side; this will appear from what we shall have to say later regarding a formal public war. So, in fact, a judgement not rendered according to law, and possession without right, have certain legal effects.

• • •

CHAPTER X CAUTIONS IN REGARD TO THINGS WHICH ARE DONE IN AN UNLAWFUL WAR

I.–With what Meaning a Sense of Honour may be said to Forbid what the Law Permits

1. I must retrace my steps, and must deprive those who wage war of nearly all the privileges which I seemed to grant, yet did not grant to them. For when I first set out to explain this part of the law of nations I bore witness that many things are said to be 'lawful' or 'permissible' for the reason that they are done with impunity, in part also because coactive tribunals lend to them their authority; things which, nevertheless, either deviate from the rule of right (whether this has its basis in law strictly so called, or in the admonitions of other virtues), or at any rate may be omitted on higher grounds and with greater praise among good men.

2. In the *Trojan Women* of Seneca, when Pyrrhus says:

> No law the captive spares, nor punishment restrains,

Agamemnon makes answer:

> What law permits, this sense of shame forbids to do.

In this passage the sense of shame signifies not so much a regard for men and reputation as a regard for what is just and good, or at any rate for that which is more just and better.

So in the *Institutes* of Justinian we read: 'Bequests in trust (*fideicommissa*) were so called, because they rested not upon a legal obligation, but only upon the sense of honour in those who were asked to take charge of them.' In Quintilian the Father, again: 'The creditor goes to the surety, without violating his sense of honour, only in case he is unable to recover from the debtor.' With this meaning you may often see justice associated with the sense of honour. [Thus Ovid]:

> Not yet had justice fled before men's guilt;
> Last of divinities she left the earth,
> And sense of honour in the place of fear
> Ruled o'er the people without force.

Hesiod sang:

> Nowhere a sense of honour, nowhere golden Justice;
> The base assail the better wantonly.

The sentence of Plato, in the twelfth book of his *Laws*, 'For Justice is called, and truly called, the virgin daughter of Honour' (παρθένος γὰρ αἰδοῦς Δίλη λέγεταί τε καὶ ὄντως εἴρηται), I would emend by πάρεδρος, so that the sense would be: 'Justice is called the councillor of honour, and this has been said with truth.' For in another place Plato also speaks thus: 'The deity, fearing for the human race, lest it should utterly perish, endowed men with a sense of honour and justice, in order that there might be adornments of cities and bonds of friendship.'

In like manner Plutarch calls 'justice' a 'house-companion of the sense of honour,' and elsewhere he connects 'sense of honour' and 'justice'. In Dionysius of Halicarnassus, 'sense of honour and justice' are mentioned together. Likewise Josephus also links 'sense of honour and equity'. Paul the jurist, too, associates the law of nature and the sense of honour. Moreover Cicero draws the boundary line between justice and a sense of reverence (*verecundia*) in this way, that it is the function of justice not to do violence to men, that of the sense of reverence not to offend them.

3. The verse which we quoted from Seneca is in complete agreement with a statement in his philosophical works: 'How limited the innocence to be innocent merely according to the letter of the law? How much more widely extend the rules of duty than the rules of law? How many things are demanded by devotion to gods, country and kin, by kindness, generosity, justice, and good faith? Yet all these requirements are outside the statutes of the law.' Here you see 'law' distinguished from 'justice', because he considers as law that which is in force in external judgements.

The same writer elsewhere well illustrates this by taking as an example the right of the master over slaves: 'In the case of a slave you must consider, not how much he may be made to suffer with impunity, but how far such treatment is permitted by the nature of justice and goodness, which bids us to spare even captives and those bought for a price.' Then: 'Although all things are permissible against a slave, yet there is something which the common law of living things forbids to be permissible against a human being.' In this passage we must again note the different interpretations of the term 'to be permissible', the one external, the other internal.

II.—The Principle Stated is Applied to the things which we said were Permitted by the Law of Nations

1. Of the same effect is the distinction which was drawn by Marcellus in the Roman Senate: 'What I have done does not enter into the discussion, for the law of war defends me in whatever I did to the enemy, but what they deserved to suffer'; that is, according to the standard of that which is just and good.

Aristotle approves the same distinction when he is discussing whether the slavery which originates in war ought to be called just: 'Certain people, regarding only a part of what is just (for a law is something just), declare that slavery arising through war is just. But they do not say absolutely just; for it may happen that the cause of war was not just.' Similar is the saying of Thucydides in the speech of the Thebans: 'We do not thus complain regarding those whom you slew in battle; for that fate befell them in accordance with a kind of law.'

2. Thus the Roman jurists themselves at times characterize as a wrong what they often define as the right of captivity; and they contrast it with natural right. Seneca, having in mind what often occurs,

says that the name of slave has sprung from a wrong. In Livy also the Italians, who retained the things which they had taken in war from the Syracusans, are called stubborn in retaining their wrongful gains. Dio of Prusa, having said that those captured in war recovered their liberty if they returned to their own people, [510] adds, 'just as those who were wrongfully in servitude'.

Lactantius, in speaking of philosophers, says: 'When they are discussing the duties that belong to the military life their whole argument is adapted not to justice, nor to true virtue, but to this life and to the practice of states.' Shortly after, he says that wrongs have been legally inflicted by the Romans.

III.—What is done by Reason of an Unjust War is Unjust from the Point of View of Moral Injustice

In the first place, then, we say that if the cause of a war should be unjust, even if the war should have been undertaken in a lawful way, all acts which arise therefrom are unjust from the point of view of moral injustice (*interna iniustitia*). In consequence the persons who knowingly perform such acts, or co-operate in them, are to be considered of the number of those who cannot reach the Kingdom of Heaven without repentance. True repentance, again, if time and means are adequate, absolutely requires that he who inflicted the wrong, whether by killing, by destroying property, or by taking booty, should make good the wrong done.

Thus God says He is not pleased with the fasting of those who held prisoners that had been wrongfully captured; and the king of Nineveh, in proclaiming a public mourning, ordered that men should cleanse their hands of plunder, being led

by nature to recognize the fact that, without such restitution, repentance would be false and in vain. We see that this is the opinion not merely of Jews and Christians, but also of Mohammedans.

IV.—Who are Bound to make Restitution, and to What Extent

Furthermore, according to the principles which in general terms we have elsewhere set forth, those persons are bound to make restitution who have brought about the war, either by the exercise of their power, or through their advice. Their accountability concerns all those things, of course, which ordinarily follow in the train of war; and even unusual things, if they have ordered or advised any such thing, or have failed to prevent it when they might have done so.

Thus also generals are responsible for the things which have been done while they were in command; and all the soldiers that have participated in some common act, as the burning of a city, are responsible for the total damage. In the case of separate acts each is responsible for the loss of which he was the sole cause, or at any rate was one of the causes.

CHAPTER XI MODERATION WITH RESPECT TO THE RIGHT OF KILLING IN A LAWFUL WAR

I.—In a Lawful War Certain Acts are Devoid of Moral Justice; a Condition which is Explained

1. Not even in a lawful war ought we to admit that which is said in the line,

> He, who refuses what is just, yields all.

Cicero's point of view is better: 'There are certain duties which must be performed even toward those from whom you have received an injury. There is in fact a limit to vengeance and to punishment.' The same writer praises the ancient days of Rome, when the issues of wars were either mild or in accordance with necessity.

Seneca calls those persons cruel who 'have a reason for punishing, but observe no limit'. Aristides, in his second speech *On Leuctra,* says: 'Men may, men may indeed be unjust in avenging themselves, if they carry vengeance beyond measure. He, who in punishing goes so far as to do what is unjust, becomes a second wrongdoer.' Thus, in the judgement of Ovid, a certain king,

> Avenging himself to excess,
> And slaughtering the guilty, guilty himself
>   became.

2. In a speech of Isocrates the Plataeans ask, 'Whether it is just to exact so severe and unjust penalties for so trivial wrongdoings?' The same Aristides, whom we have cited above, in his second oration *On Peace,* says: 'Do not merely consider the causes for which you are going to exact punishment, but also who they are from whom the punishment is to be exacted, [513] who we ourselves are, and what is the just limit of punishments.' Minos is praised in Propertius because,

> Although a victor, just to the foe he was;

and also by Ovid;

> Lawgiver most upright,
> He laws imposed upon his conquered foes.

II.—Who may be Killed in Accordance with Moral Justice

When it is just to kill—for this must be our starting point—in a lawful war in accordance with moral justice (*iustitia interna*) and when it is not just to do so, may

be understood from the explanations which were given by us in the first chapter of this book.

Now a person is killed either intentionally or unintentionally. No one can justly be killed intentionally, except as a just penalty or in case we are able in no other way to protect our life and property; although the killing of a man on account of transitory things, even if it is not at variance with justice in a strict sense, nevertheless is not in harmony with the law of love. However that punishment may be just, it is necessary that he who is killed shall himself have done wrong, and in a matter punishable with the penalty of death on the decision of a fair judge. But we shall here say less on this point, because we think that what needs to be known has been sufficiently set forth in the chapter on punishments.

III.—No one may Rightly be Killed Because of His Ill Fortune; for example, those who take sides Under Compulsion

1. Previously, in discussing suppliants—for there are suppliants in war as well as in peace—we distinguished 'ill-fortune' (ἀτύχημα) and 'wrong' (ἀδίκημα). Gylippus, in the passage of Diodorus Siculus which we then quoted in part, asks in which class the Athenians should be placed, in that of the unfortunate or that of the unjust. He declares that they cannot be regarded as victims of ill-fortune, seeing that, of their own accord, and unprovoked by any wrong, they had waged war upon the Syracusans. He concludes that, since of their own initiative they had undertaken the war, they must also in their own persons endure the evils of the war.

An example of the victims of ill-fortune are those who are in the ranks of the enemy without hostile intent, as the Athenians were in the time of Mithridates. Of these Velleius Paterculus speaks thus:

> If any one blames the Athenians for this period of rebellion, when Athens was stormed by Sulla, he is indeed ignorant both of the truth and of antiquity. So steadfast was the loyalty of the Athenians to the Romans, that at all times and in every matter the Romans declared that whatever was carried out in good faith was done with Attic loyalty. But at that time, oppressed by the forces of Mithridates, the men of Athens were in a most pitiable condition. While they were in the grasp of the enemy, they were besieged by their friends, and they had their hearts outside the walls while their bodies, by constraint of necessity, were within.

The end of the quotation may seem to have been adapted from Livy; in this author the Spaniard Indibil says that, although his body was with the Carthaginians, his heart was with the Romans.

2. 'Beyond doubt', as Cicero says, 'all men whose lives are placed in the power of another more often think what he, under whose authority and sway they are, is able to do, than what he ought to do.' The same author, in his speech *For Ligarius,* declares: 'There is a third time, when he remained in Africa after the arrival of Varus; but if that is criminal, it is a crime of necessity, not of will.' The principle was applied by Julian in the case of the Aquileians, as we learn from Ammianus. This author, after recounting the punishment of a few persons, adds: 'All the rest departed unharmed; necessity, not intention, had driven them into the madness of strife.'

On the passage of Thucydides regarding the Corcyraean prisoners who had been sold, an ancient commentator remarks: 'He reveals a clemency worthy of the Greek character; for it is cruel to kill prisoners after a battle, especially slaves, who do not wage war of their own will.' In the speech of Isocrates, already mentioned, the Plataeans assert: [514] 'We served them' (the Lacedaemonians) 'not willingly, but under compulsion.' The same writer says of others of the Greeks: 'These were compelled to follow their side' (that of the Lacedaemonians) 'in body, but in spirit they were with us.' Herodotus had previously said of the Phocians: 'They sided with the Medes, not willingly, but by force of necessity.'

As Arrian relates, Alexander spared the Zelites 'because they had been compelled to serve on the side of the barbarians'. In Diodorus, Nicolaus of Syracuse says in his speech on behalf of the prisoners: 'The allies are compelled to take the field by the power of those who have authority over them; therefore, as it is fair to punish those who do wrong with intention, so it is right to pardon those who do wrong against their will.' Similarly, in Livy the Syracusans, in clearing themselves before the Romans, say that they had broken the peace because they were confused by fear and treachery. For a like reason Antigonus declared that he had been at war with Cleomenes, not with the Spartans.

Leviathan

(1651)

Thomas Hobbes

Thomas Hobbes (1588–1679) was born in England and employed as a teacher and as a tutor to members of the royal family. When Charles I was beheaded, Hobbes fled to the continent where he met Descartes among others. Leviathan *was his most important work.*

CHAPTER XIII OF THE NATURAL CONDITION OF MANKIND, AS CONCERNING THEIR FELICITY, AND MISERY

[1] Nature hath made men so equal in the faculties of body and mind as that, though there be found one man sometimes manifestly stronger in body or of quicker mind than another, yet when all is reckoned together the difference between man and man is not so considerable as that one man can thereupon claim to himself any benefit to which another may not pretend as well as he. For as to the strength of body, the weakest has strength enough to kill the strongest, either by secret machination, or by confederacy with others that are in the same danger with himself.

[2] And as to the faculties of the mind—setting aside the arts grounded upon words, and especially that skill of proceeding upon general and infallible rules called science (which very few have, and but in few things), as being not a native faculty (born with us), nor attained (as prudence) while we look after somewhat else—I find yet a greater equality amongst men than that of strength. For prudence is but experience, which equal time equally bestows on all men in those things they equally apply themselves unto. That which may perhaps make such equality incredible is but a vain conceit of one's own wisdom, which almost all men think they have in a greater degree than the vulgar, that is, than all men but themselves and a few others whom, by fame or for concurring with themselves, they approve. For such is the nature of men that howsoever they may acknowledge many others to be more witty, or more eloquent, or more learned, yet they will hardly believe there be many so wise as themselves. For they see their own wit at hand, and other men's at a distance. But this proveth rather that men are in that point equal, than unequal. For there is not ordinarily a greater sign of the equal distribution of anything than that every man is contented with his share.

[3] From this equality of ability ariseth equality of hope in the attaining of our ends. And therefore, if any two men desire the same thing, which nevertheless they cannot both enjoy, they become enemies; and in the way to their end, which is principally their own conservation, and sometimes their delectation only, endeavour to destroy or subdue one another. And from

hence it comes to pass that, where an invader hath no more to fear than another man's single power, if one plant, sow, build, or possess a convenient seat, others may probably be expected to come prepared with forces united, to dispossess and deprive him, not only of the fruit of his labour, but also of his life or liberty. And the invader again is in the like danger of another.

[4] And from this diffidence of one another, there is no way for any man to secure himself so reasonable as anticipation, that is, by force or wiles to master the persons of all men he can, so long till he see no other power great enough to endanger him. And this is no more than his own conservation requireth, and is generally allowed. Also, because there be some that taking pleasure in contemplating their own power in the acts of conquest, which they pursue farther than their security requires, if others (that otherwise would be glad to be at ease within modest bounds) should not by invasion increase their power, they would not be able, long time, by standing only on their defence, to subsist. And by consequence, such augmentation of dominion over men being necessary to a man's conservation, it ought to be allowed him.

[5] Again, men have no pleasure, but on the contrary a great deal of grief, in keeping company where there is no power able to over-awe them all. For every man looketh that his companion should value him at the same rate he sets upon himself, and upon all signs of contempt, or undervaluing, naturally endeavours, as far as he dares (which amongst them that have no common power to keep them in quiet, is far enough to make them destroy each other), to extort a greater value from his contemners, by damage, and from others, by the example.

[6] So that in the nature of man we find three principal causes of quarrel: first, competition; secondly, diffidence; thirdly, glory.

[7] The first maketh men invade for gain; the second, for safety; and the third, for reputation. The first use violence to make themselves masters of other men's persons, wives, children, and cattle; the second, to defend them; the third, for trifles, as a word, a smile, a different opinion, and any other sign of undervalue, either direct in their persons, or by reflection in their kindred, their friends, their nation, their profession, or their name.

[8] Hereby it is manifest that during the time men live without a common power to keep them all in awe, they are in that condition which is called war, and such a war as is of every man against every man. For WAR consisteth not in battle only, or the act of fighting, but in a tract of time wherein the will to contend by battle is sufficiently known. And therefore, the notion of *time* is to be considered in the nature of war, as it is in the nature of weather. For as the nature of foul weather lieth not in a shower or two of rain, but in an inclination thereto of many days together, so the nature of war consisteth not in actual fighting, but in the known disposition thereto during all the time there is no assurance to the contrary. All other time is PEACE.

[9] Whatsoever therefore is consequent to a time of war, where every man is enemy to every man, the same is consequent to the time wherein men live without other security than what their own strength and their own invention shall furnish them withal. In such condition there is no place for industry, because the fruit thereof is uncertain, and consequently, no culture of the earth, no navigation, nor use

of the commodities that may be imported by sea, no commodious building, no instruments of moving and removing such things as require much force, no knowledge of the face of the earth, no account of time, no arts, no letters, no society, and which is worst of all, continual fear and danger of violent death, and the life of man, solitary, poor, nasty, brutish, and short.

[10] It may seem strange, to some man that has not well weighed these things, that nature should thus dissociate, and render men apt to invade and destroy one another. And he may, therefore, not trusting to this inference made from the passions, desire perhaps to have the same confirmed by experience. Let him therefore consider with himself—when taking a journey, he arms himself, and seeks to go well accompanied; when going to sleep, he locks his doors; when even in his house, he locks his chests; and this when he knows there be laws, and public officers, armed, to revenge all injuries shall be done him— what opinion he has of his fellow subjects, when he rides armed; of his fellow citizens, when he locks his doors; and of his children and servants, when he locks his chests. Does he not there as much accuse mankind by his actions, as I do by my words? But neither of us accuse man's nature in it. The desires and other passions of man are in themselves no sin. No more are the actions that proceed from those passions, till they know a law that forbids them—which till laws be made they cannot know. Nor can any law be made, till they have agreed upon the person that shall make it.

[11] It may peradventure be thought, there was never such a time nor condition of war as this; and I believe it was never generally so, over all the world. But there are many places where they live so now.

For the savage people in many places of *America* (except the government of small families, the concord whereof dependeth on natural lust) have no government at all, and live at this day in that brutish manner as I said before. Howsoever, it may be perceived what manner of life there would be where there were no common power to fear, by the manner of life which men that have formerly lived under a peaceful government use to degenerate into, in a civil war.

[12] But though there had never been any time wherein particular men were in a condition of war one against another, yet in all times kings and persons of sovereign authority, because of their independency, are in continual jealousies and in the state and posture of gladiators, having their weapons pointing and their eyes fixed on one another, that is, their forts, garrisons, and guns upon the frontiers of their kingdoms, and continual spies upon their neighbours, which is a posture of war. But because they uphold thereby the industry of their subjects, there does not follow from it that misery which accompanies the liberty of particular men.

[13] To this war of every man against every man, this also is consequent: that nothing can be unjust. The notions of right and wrong, justice and injustice, have there no place. Where there is no common power, there is no law; where no law, no injustice. Force and fraud are in war the two cardinal virtues. Justice and injustice are none of the faculties neither of the body, nor mind. If they were, they might be in a man that were alone in the world, as well as his senses and passions. They are qualities that relate to men in society, not in solitude. It is consequent also to the same condition that there be no propriety, no dominion, no *mine* and *thine* distinct, but

only that to be every man's that he can get, and for so long as he can keep it. And thus much for the ill condition which man by mere nature is actually placed in, though with a possibility to come out of it, consisting partly in the passions, partly in his reason.

[14] The passions that incline men to peace are fear of death, desire of such things as are necessary to commodious living, and a hope by their industry to obtain them. And reason suggesteth convenient articles of peace, upon which men may be drawn to agreement. These articles are they which otherwise are called the Laws of Nature, whereof I shall speak more particularly in the two following chapters.

CHAPTER XIV OF THE FIRST AND SECOND NATURAL LAWS AND OF CONTRACTS

[1] The RIGHT OF NATURE, which writers commonly call *jus naturale,* is the liberty each man hath to use his own power, as he will himself, for the preservation of his own nature, that is to say, of his own life, and consequently of doing anything which, in his own judgment and reason, he shall conceive to be the aptest means thereunto.

[2] By LIBERTY is understood, according to the proper signification of the word, the absence of external impediments, which impediments may oft take away part of a man's power to do what he would, but cannot hinder him from using the power left him, according as his judgment and reason shall dictate to him.

[3] A LAW OF NATURE (*lex naturalis*) is a precept or general rule, found out by reason, by which a man is forbidden to do that which is destructive of his life or taketh away the means of preserving the same,

and to omit that by which he thinketh it may be best preserved. For though they that speak of this subject use to confound *jus* and *lex* (*right* and *law*), yet they ought to be distinguished, because RIGHT consisteth in liberty to do or to forbear, whereas LAW determineth and bindeth to one of them; so that law and right differ as much as obligation and liberty, which in one and the same matter are inconsistent.

[4] And because the condition of man (as hath been declared in the precedent chapter) is a condition of war of everyone against everyone (in which case everyone is governed by his own reason and there is nothing he can make use of that may not be a help unto him in preserving his life against his enemies), it followeth that in such a condition every man has a right to everything, even to one another's body. And therefore, as long as this natural right of every man to everything endureth, there can be no security to any man (how strong or wise soever he be) of living out the time which nature ordinarily alloweth men to live. And consequently it is a precept, or general rule, of reason *that every man ought to endeavour peace, as far as he has hope of obtaining it, and when he cannot obtain it, that he may seek and use all helps and advantages of war.* The first branch of which rule containeth the first and fundamental law of nature, which is *to seek peace, and follow it.* The second, the sum of the right of nature, which is *by all means we can, to defend ourselves.*

[5] From this fundamental law of nature, by which men are commanded to endeavour peace, is derived this second law: *that a man be willing, when others are so too, as far-forth as for peace and defence of himself he shall think it necessary, to lay down this right to all things, and be contented with so much liberty against other*

men, as he would allow other men against himself. For as long as every man holdeth this right of doing anything he liketh, so long are all men in the condition of war. But if other men will not lay down their right as well as he, then there is no reason for anyone to divest himself of his; for that were to expose himself to prey (which no man is bound to), rather than to dispose himself to peace. This is that law of the Gospel: "whatsoever you require that others should do to you, that do ye to them." And that law of all men: *quod tibi fieri non vis, alteri ne feceris.*

[6] To *lay down* a man's *right* to anything is to *divest* himself of the *liberty* of hindering another of the benefit of his own right to the same. For he that renounceth or passeth away his right giveth not to any other man a right which he had not before (because there is nothing to which every man had not right by nature), but only standeth out of his way, that he may enjoy his own original right without hindrance from him, not without hindrance from another. So that the effect which redoundeth to one man by another man's defect of right is but so much diminution of impediments to the use of his own right original.

[7] Right is laid aside either by simply renouncing it or by transferring it to another. By *simply* RENOUNCING, when he cares not to whom the benefit thereof redoundeth. By TRANSFERRING, when he intendeth the benefit thereof to some certain person or persons. And when a man hath in either manner abandoned or granted away his right, then is he said to be OBLIGED or BOUND not to hinder those to whom such right is granted or abandoned from the benefit of it; and [it is said] that he *ought,* and it is his DUTY, not to make void that voluntary act of his own, and that such hindrance is INJUSTICE, and

INJURY, as being *sine jure* [without right], the right being before renounced or transferred. So that *injury* or *injustice,* in the controversies of the world, is somewhat like to that which in the disputations of scholars is called absurdity. For as it is there called an *absurdity* to contradict what one maintained in the beginning, so in the world it is called injustice and injury voluntarily to undo that which from the beginning he had voluntarily done.

The way by which a man either simply renounceth or transferreth his right is a declaration, or signification by some voluntary and sufficient sign or signs, that he doth so renounce or transfer, or hath so renounced or transferred the same, to him that accepteth it. And these signs are either words only, or actions only, or (as it happeneth most often) both words and actions. And the same are the BONDS by which men are bound and obliged, bonds that have their strength, not from their own nature (for nothing is more easily broken than a man's word) but from fear of some evil consequence upon the rupture.

[8] Whensoever a man transferreth his right or renounceth it, it is either in consideration of some right reciprocally transferred to himself or for some other good he hopeth for thereby. For it is a voluntary act, and of the voluntary acts of every man the object is some *good to himself.* And therefore there be some rights which no man can be understood by any words or other signs to have abandoned or transferred. As, first, a man cannot lay down the right of resisting them that assault him by force, to take away his life, because he cannot be understood to aim thereby at any good to himself. [Second], the same may be said of wounds, and chains, and imprisonment, both because there is no benefit consequent to such patience (as

there is to the patience of suffering another to be wounded or imprisoned), as
also because a man cannot tell, when he
seeth men proceed against him by violence, whether they intend his death or
not. [Third] and lastly, the motive and end
for which this renouncing and transferring
of right is introduced, is nothing else but
the security of a man's person, in his life
and in the means of so preserving life as
not to be weary of it. And therefore if a
man by words or other signs seem to despoil himself of the end for which those
signs were intended, he is not to be understood as if he meant it, or that it was his
will, but that he was ignorant of how such
words and actions were to be interpreted.

• • •

CHAPTER XV OF OTHER LAWS OF NATURE

[1] From that law of nature by which we
are obliged to transfer to another such
rights as, being retained, hinder the peace
of mankind, there followeth a third, which
is this *that men perform their convenants
made,* without which covenants are in
vain, and but empty words, and the right
of all men to all things remaining, we are
still in the condition of war.

[2] And in this law of nature consisteth
the fountain and original of JUSTICE. For
where no covenant hath preceded, there
hath no right been transferred, and every
man has right to everything; and consequently, no action can be unjust. But when
a covenant is made, then to break it is
unjust; and the definition of INJUSTICE is no
other than *the not performance of covenant.*
And whatsoever is not unjust, is *just.*

[3] But because covenants of mutual
trust where there is a fear of not performance on either part (as hath been said in

the former chapter [xiv, 18–20]) are invalid, though the original of justice be the
making of covenants, yet injustice actually
there can be none till the cause of such
fear be taken away, which, while men are
in the natural condition of war, cannot be
done. Therefore, before the names of just
and unjust can have place, there must be
some coercive power to compel men equally
to the performance of their covenants, by
the terror of some punishment greater
than the benefit they expect by the breach
of their covenant, and to make good that
propriety which by mutual contract men
acquire, in recompense of the universal
right they abandon; and such power there
is none before the erection of a commonwealth. And this is also to be gathered out
of the ordinary definition of justice in the
Schools; for they say that *justice is the constant will of giving to every man his own.*
And therefore where there is no *own,* that
is, no propriety, there is no injustice; and
where there is no coercive power erected,
that is, where there is no commonwealth,
there is no propriety, all men having right
to all things; therefore where there is no
commonwealth, there nothing is unjust. So
that the nature of justice consisteth in
keeping of valid covenants; but the validity
of covenants begins not but with the constitution of a civil power sufficient to compel men to keep them; and then it is also
that propriety begins.

[4] The fool hath said in his heart:
"there is no such thing as justice"; and
sometimes also with his tongue, seriously
alleging that: "every man's conservation
and contentment being committed to his
own care, there could be no reason why
every man might not do what he thought
conduced thereunto, and therefore also to
make or not make, keep or not keep,
covenants was not against reason, when it

conduced to one's benefit." He does not therein deny that there be covenants, and that they are sometimes broken, sometimes kept, and that such breach of them may be called injustice, and the observance of them justice; but he questioneth whether injustice, taking away the fear of God (for the same fool hath said in his heart there is no God), may not sometimes stand with that reason which dictateth to every man his own good; and particularly then, when it conduceth to such a benefit as shall put a man in a condition to neglect, not only the dispraise and revilings, but also the power of other men.

"The kingdom of God is gotten by violence; but what if it could be gotten by unjust violence? were it against [OL: right] reason so to get it, when it is impossible to receive hurt by it [OL: but only the supreme good]? and if it be not against reason, it is not against justice; or else justice is not to be approved for good."

From such reasoning as this, successful wickedness hath obtained the name of virtue, and some that in all other things have disallowed the violation of faith, yet have allowed it when it is for the getting of a kingdom. And the heathen that believed that *Saturn* was deposed by his son *Jupiter* believed nevertheless the same *Jupiter* to be the avenger of injustice, somewhat like to a piece of law in *Coke's* Commentaries on *Littleton,* where he says: if the right heir of the crown be attainted of treason, yet the crown shall descend to him, and *eo instante* [immediately] the attainder be void; from which instances a man will be very prone to infer that "when the heir apparent of a kingdom shall kill him that is in possession, though his father, you may call it injustice, or by what other name you will, yet it can never be against reason, seeing all the voluntary actions of men tend to the benefit of themselves, and those actions are most reasonable that conduce most to their ends." This specious reasoning is nevertheless false.

[5] For the question is not of promises mutual where there is no security of performance on either side (as when there is no civil power erected over the parties promising), for such promises are no covenants, but either where one of the parties has performed already, or where there is a power to make him perform, there is the question whether it be against reason, that is, against the benefit of the other to perform or not. And I say it is not against reason. For the manifestation whereof we are to consider: first, that when a man doth a thing which, notwithstanding anything can be foreseen and reckoned on, tendeth to his own destruction (howsoever some accident which he could not expect, arriving, may turn it to his benefit), yet such events do not make it reasonably or wisely done. Secondly, that in a condition of war wherein every man to every man (for want of a common power to keep them all in awe) is an enemy, there is no man can hope by his own strength or wit to defend himself from destruction without the help of confederates (where everyone expects the same defence by the confederation that anyone else does); and therefore, he which declares he thinks it reason to deceive those that help him can in reason expect no other means of safety than what can be had from his own single power. He, therefore, that breaketh his covenant, and consequently declareth that he thinks he may with reason do so, cannot be received into any society that unite themselves for peace and defence but by the error of them that receive him; nor when he is received, be retained in it without seeing the danger of their error; which errors a man cannot reasonably reckon upon as the means of his security; and therefore, if he be left or

cast out of society, he perisheth; and if he live in society, it is by the errors of other men, which he could not foresee nor reckon upon; and consequently [he has acted] against the reason of his preservation, and so as all men that contribute not to his destruction forbear him only out of ignorance of what is good for themselves.

[6] As for the instance of gaining the secure and perpetual felicity of heaven by any way, it is frivolous, there being but one way imaginable, and that is not breaking, but keeping of covenant.

[7] And for the other instance of attaining sovereignty by rebellion, it is manifest that, though the event follow, yet because it cannot reasonably be expected (but rather the contrary), and because (by gaining it so) others are taught to gain the same in like manner, the attempt thereof is against reason. Justice, therefore, that is to say, keeping of covenant, is a rule of reason by which we are forbidden to do anything destructive to our life, and consequently a law of nature.

• • •

[34] These are the laws of nature dictating peace for a means of the conservation of men in multitudes; and which only concern the doctrine of civil society. There be other things tending to the destruction of particular men (as drunkenness and all other parts of intemperance), which may therefore also be reckoned amongst those things which the law of nature hath forbidden; but are not necessary to be mentioned, nor are pertinent enough to this place.

[35] And though this may seem too subtle a deduction of the laws of nature to be taken notice of by all men (whereof the most part are too busy in getting food, and the rest too negligent, to understand), yet to leave all men inexcusable they have been contracted into one easy sum, intelligible even to the meanest capacity, and

that is *Do not that to another, which thou wouldst not have done to thyself;* which sheweth him that he has no more to do in learning the laws of nature but (when, weighing the actions of other men with his own, they seem too heavy) to put them into the other part of the balance, and his own into their place, that his own passions and self-love may add nothing to the weight; and then there is none of these laws of nature that will not appear unto him very reasonable.

[36] The laws of nature oblige *in foro interno,* that is to say, they bind to a desire they should take place; but *in foro externo,* that is, to the putting them in act, not always. For he that should be modest and tractable, and perform all he promises, in such time and place where no man else should do so, should but make himself a prey to others, and procure his own certain ruin, contrary to the ground of all laws of nature, which tend to nature's preservation. And again, he that having sufficient security that others shall observe the same laws towards him, observes them not himself, seeketh not peace, but war, and consequently the destruction of his nature by violence.

[37] And whatsoever laws bind *in foro interno* may be broken, not only by a fact contrary to the law, but also by a fact according to it, in case a man think it contrary. For though his action in this case be according to the law, yet his purpose was against the law, which, where the obligation is *in foro interno,* is a breach.

[38] The laws of nature are immutable and eternal; for injustice, ingratitude, arrogance, pride, iniquity, acception of persons, and the rest, can never be made lawful. For it can never be that war shall preserve life, and peace destroy it.

[39] The same laws, because they oblige only to a desire and endeavour (I mean an

unfeigned and constant endeavour) are easy to be observed. For in that they require nothing but endeavour, he that endeavoureth their performance fulfilleth them; and he that fulfilleth the law is just.

[40] And the science of them [the laws of nature] is the true and only moral philosophy. For moral philosophy is nothing else but the science of what is *good* and *evil* in the conversation and society of mankind. *Good* and *evil* are names that signify our appetites and aversions, which in different tempers, customs, and doctrines of men are different; and divers men differ not only in their judgment on the senses (of what is pleasant and unpleasant to the taste, smell, hearing, touch, and sight), but also of what is conformable or disagreeable to reason in the actions of common life. Nay, the same man in divers times differs from himself, and one time praiseth (that is, calleth good) what another time he dispraiseth (and calleth evil); from whence arise disputes, controversies, and at last war. And therefore so long a man is in the condition of mere nature (which is a condition of war) as private appetite is the measure of good and evil; and consequently, all men agree on this, that peace is good; and therefore also the way or means of peace (which, as I have shewed before, are *justice, gratitude, modesty, equity, mercy,* and the rest of the laws of nature) are good (that is to say, *moral virtues*), and their contrary vices, evil.

Now the science of virtue and vice is moral philosophy; and therefore the true doctrine of the laws of nature is the true moral philosophy. But the writers of moral philosophy, though they acknowledge the same virtues and vices, yet not seeing wherein consisted their goodness, nor that they come to be praised as the means of peaceable, sociable, and comfortable living, place them in a mediocrity of passions (as if not the cause, but the degree of daring, made fortitude; or not the cause, but the quantity of a gift, made liberality).

[41] These dictates of reason men use to call by the name of laws, but improperly; for they are but conclusions or theorems concerning what conduceth to the conservation and defence of themselves, whereas law, properly, is the word of him that by right hath command over others. But yet if we consider the same theorems, as delivered in the word of God, that by right commandeth all things; then are they properly called laws.

On the Law of Nature and Nations

(1672)

Samuel Pufendorf

Samuel Puffendorf (1632–1694) was a German philosopher and jurist. He taught at Heidelberg and Lund, Sweden, where he held the first chair in international law. He was also renowned as a historian and political scientist.

CHAPTER VI ON THE LAW OF WAR

SINCE individuals who live in natural liberty have no less power accorded them than states to defend themselves against an unjust threat of violence, and to have recourse to force in maintaining their rights, when they have been infringed upon or denied by others, I feel that it would be fitting to examine first, what the wars of individuals and states have in common, and secondly, what belongs in a special way to the latter by their nature, or by the customs of nations.

2. Now it is one of the first principles of natural law that no one unjustly do another hurt or damage, as well as that men should perform for each other the duties of humanity, and show especial zeal to fulfil the matters upon which they have entered into particular agreements. When men observe these duties in their relations one with another, it is called peace, which is a state most highly agreeable to human nature and fitted to preserve it, the creation and preservation of which constitutes one of the chief reasons for the law of nature being placed in the hearts of men. Add Polybius, Bk. XII, chap. xiv. Nay, peace is a state especially reserved to human nature as such, since it springs from a principle which belongs to man, as distinct from animals, while war arises from a principle common to them both. Of course, even animals depend upon a natural instinct to defend and preserve themselves by force, but man alone understands the genius of peace. For it is characteristic of him voluntarily to do something for another, and to refrain from injury, by reason of a certain obligation residing in one, and of a certain right residing in another person, all of which is unintelligible without the use of reason. Of course domestic animals perform services for their masters, but that is due to a fear of blows, or an expectation of food, and not to any obligation, which, indeed, is beyond their powers to comprehend. Animals also refrain from doing harm to men and to other animals, but that is due to weakness, or to the fact that they find in them nothing to whet their appetite. Finally, there are some that show affection for one another or render mutual assistance, but that does not mean that they understand that they are obligated to act in that way. This is illustrated by a passage in Quintilian, *Declamations,* ix [13]:

Nature first put a certain sociableness into our minds beyond other creatures, whereby we are taught to rejoice in one another's company, to gather a people, to build cities, and though she hath furnished our minds with several inclinations, yet she hath given us no affection better than kindness one to another. For what would be more happy than we men, if all of us were friends? For then wars, seditions, robberies, and other mischiefs that arise from ourselves, would not also come upon us on the score of fortune. But because God thinks it not fit to bestow so great a blessing on us, yet certainly at all times and amongst all nations, 'twas ever held one of the greatest and as it were most sacred offices, for men to agree together in honest principles, to observe truth and faithfulness, and return love for love. (W.*)

Despite all this war is lawful and sometimes even necessary for man, when another with evil intent threatens me with injury, or withholds what is my due. For under such circumstances my care for my own safety gives me the power to maintain and defend myself and mine by any means at my disposal, even to the injury of my assailant, or, as Ulysses says in Dictys Cretensis, Bk. II [xxi]: 'To extort by force a right which cannot be secured by friendly means.' Here belongs the statement of Maximus of Tyre, *Dissertations,* xiv [xxiv. II e]: 'Consequently to the just war appears a necessity, to the unjust a voluntary act.' Add Boecler on Grotius, Bk. I, chap. iii, § 1. A further consideration lies in the fact that nature has not only instilled in the minds of men a bitter sense of injuries, so that they avoid in every way being harassed by the injuries of others, but has also given his body for its protection such agility and strength of hands that he may not be forced to bear them in patience. And yet nature permits war, on the condition that he who wages it shall have as his end

the establishment of peace. Aristotle, *Nicomachean Ethics,* Bk. X, chap. vi [X. vii. 6]:

> [. . .] The object of war is the enjoyment of peace. [. . .] Nobody desires war, or prepares to go to war, for its own sake. A person would be regarded as absolutely bloodthirsty, if he were to make enemies of his friends for the mere sake of fighting and bloodshed. (W.)

Themistius, *Orations,* x [p. 131 A]: 'The prize of war is peace. Moreover, men fight because they have to, not in order that they may spend their days in fighting, but that they may rest in safety.' Tacitus, *Histories,* Bk. IV [lxxvi]: 'No man was so addicted to arms as not to prefer the same reward for repose to incurring danger for it.' (O.) Therefore, you would never approve the character of those described in the lines of Silius Italicus, Bk. III [330–1]: 'They cannot endure life without war; because the only purpose for living lay in arms, and a peaceful existence stands condemned in their eyes.' Furthermore, although he who has injured me gives me by that act the fullest power to find recourse against him in war, yet I should consider how much good or evil such a course will probably contain for me, or for others who have not injured me. For I need not fly to arms to avenge such injuries as do not mean my utter ruin, if that will mean greater disadvantages than advantages to me and mine, or if others with whom I am still at peace will by reason of my war suffer great losses, which I should, by the law of humanity, have warded off from them by allowing such an injury as was done me to go unpunished. Therefore, if a man feels that the avenging of an injury done him will mean more evil than good, he acts in a just and praiseworthy manner in refusing to punish it by recourse to war.

3. The causes of just wars may be reduced to the following heads: To preserve and protect ourselves and our possessions against others who attempt to injure us, or take from us or destroy what we have; to assert our claim to whatever others may owe us by a perfect right, when they refuse to perform it for us of their own accord; and, finally, to obtain reparation for losses which we have suffered by injuries, and to extort from him who did the injury guarantees that he will not so offend in the future. As a result of these causes we have the division of just wars into offensive and defensive, of which we consider the latter to be those in which we defend and strive to retain what is ours, the former those by which we extort debts which are denied us, or undertake to recover what has been unjustly taken from us, and to seek guarantees for the future. Although sometimes the credit for defence stands with him who is the first to take up arms against another, if, for instance, a man has been troubled time and again with sudden border raids, the enemy always retiring on his approach, or if by a swift movement he overcomes an enemy who is already bent upon attacking him, but is still engaged in his preparations. See Justin, II. iii. 12.

4. But in general the causes of wars, and of offensive wars in particular, should be clear and leave no chance for doubt. For time and again doubts arise on this point, either from ignorance of fact, when it is not clearly established whether a thing was done or not, or what was the purpose of the doing, or from an obscure comparison of strict right with the law of charity, or from an uncertain balancing of the advantages which are likely to follow upon the declaration or avoidance of war. Therefore, in the matter before us, neither should we rashly advance any vague claim,

nor, on the other hand, fly at once to arms; but we should by all means try one of three courses in order to prevent the affair from breaking out into open war, to wit, either a conference between the parties concerned or their representatives; or an appeal to arbitrators; or, finally, the use of the lot. Valerius Flaccus [*Argonautica*], Bk. V [563 ff.]: 'Should we never have given ear to prayers or sought treaties with the king, but turned our every effort to blind battle? That is the life of Thracians.' See Grotius, Bk. II, chap. xxiii, §§ 7, 11. [Especially should such amicable settlements be sought by him who is the plaintiff, since there is some reason for the favour which regularly attends possession.] But however clear be the cause of war, every wise man before rushing to arms should carefully weigh the observations of Grotius, Bk. II, chap. xxiv. No less should he bear in mind that it is great folly both in individuals and states to be unable to reach a settlement while their fortunes are still unscathed. 'But when they have used each other severely, they separate of their own accord without the need of any one's intervention.' (F.) Isocrates, *To Philip* [38].

5. The unjust causes for wars are reviewed by Grotius, Bk. II, chap. xxii, of which some have no grounds at all, while some have a slight foundation, though weak at the best. To the first belong avarice and the lust for superfluous possessions, ambition and a craving to lord it over others, and a burning desire to gather fame from the oppression of their fellows. Yet men usually go to much labour to conceal the first of these, because it betokens a sordid mind, although many a man puts forth the last as a proof of greatness, 'calling it praise fit for a king to battle for another's goods'. Yet all kings should take to

themselves the words of Philiscus to Alexander: 'Be mindful of glory; yet be not a pestilence, nor some great disorder, but a bringer of peace and health.' [Aelian, *Varia Historia*, XIV. xi.] For although God often uses war to drain away, as it were, the dregs of mankind, as we find in Euripides, *Helena* [39–40], Jupiter saying that he raised up the Greeks and Phrygians against each other:

> [. . .] To disburden so
> Earth-mother of her straitened throngs
> of men; (W.)

still it is unlawful for princes to rush into war for that reason, when no other cause can be found. And yet the Hebrews held that they were permitted, in order to increase the majesty of their nation, to attack other peoples and reduce them and their property to subjection for no other reason than that their Sanhedrin had seen fit to declare a war. Selden, *De Jure Naturali et Gentium*, Bk. VI, chaps. iii and xii.

To the second class belongs fear of the strength and power of a neighbour, and 'when men deem that will is equal to power'. Lucan, Bk. III [101]. Yet fear alone does not suffice as a just cause for war, unless it is established with moral and evident certitude that there is an intent to injure us. For an uncertain suspicion of peril can, of course, persuade you to surround yourself in advance with defences, but it cannot give you a right to be the first to force the other by violence to give a real guarantee, as it is called, not to offend. Gellius, Bk. VIII, chap. iii [VI. iii. 31–2]:

> For the fortune of gladiators prepared to engage, was of this kind, either to kill if they should conquer, or to die if they should yield. But the life of men is not circumscribed by such unjust or insuperable necessity, that you ought first to commit an injury, lest, by not doing so, you should endure it. (B.)

For so long as a man has not injured me, and is not caught in open preparation to do so (for sometimes an incompleted injury can be avenged by a war no less than a completed one), it should be presumed that he will perform his duty in the future, especially when he confirms it by protestations and his pledged word. But it would be unjust to extort a real guarantee from such a one through force, since by such a procedure his condition would be worse than ours, in that he is required to abide by our mere given word. But supposing there exists a just cause for war, in that case an unusual increase in a neighbour's power comes in for serious consideration in the debates upon war, since experience well shows that most men, as their strength increases, grow more eager to lord it over others. Add Cumberland, *De Legibus Naturae,* chap. ii, § 15, towards the end; Bacon, *Essays,* chap. xix. Seneca, *Oedipus* [542–3]:

> There stands a mighty tree
> And with its heavy shade it overwhelms
> The lesser trees. (M.*)

Procopius, *Gothic War,* Bk. IV [xx]:

> Men naturally are restive when there is any neighbouring power which has attained great size and is prepared to inflict injury. For the extremely powerful are never at a loss for excuses upon which to bring war against their neighbours, no matter how innocent these may be.

Herodes, *De Republica* [13]:

> Neighbouring nations are not displeased when peoples near them are torn with internal strife. Weaker ones see that thus they will not be subdued; those of equal strength think they will be the stronger; powerful ones hope that they will subdue them the more easily.

Polybius, Bk. I, chap. lxxxiii: 'It is never right [. . .] to help any one to build up so preponderating a power as to make resistance to it impossible, however just the cause.' (S.) Appian of Alexandria, *Bellum Lybicum* [lxi]: 'Although he be a friend, not even he should become so powerful.' Yet it would be impudent to allot *utility* the same right over the property of others as necessity, as Thucydides, Bk. I [lxxvi], represents the Athenians maintaining: 'No one ever put justice before force and refrained from taking advantage, when opportunity offered, of securing something by main strength' (S.); especially since mankind would surely fare ill for the future, if it was introduced as a right, that I could take by force from another, against his will, whatever I think will be of use to me. For others will surely employ the same licence against me that I use against them.

On the other pretexts adduced by Grotius in the passage cited above, we must reach the same conclusion. Thus we cannot agree with Bacon of Verulam, *The Advancement of Learning,* p. 348, when he holds that sufficient cause for waging war upon the Americans can be found in the fact that they can be held condemned by the very law of nature, because it is their custom to sacrifice men and eat human flesh. On this matter we should carefully consider whether a Christian prince can attack the Indians, as men condemned by nature, merely because they eat human flesh like any other food, or because they eat the flesh of men of their own religion, or because they eat that of strangers. And in connexion with their treatment of strangers we must again inquire, whether those foreigners come to their shores as enemies and robbers, or come as innocent guests, or driven by storms. For only in the last case does a right of war lie with those whose citizens are treated with such cruelty, not in the others.

6. There is also this one feature common to all wars, that, although their method and genius, as it were, is force and intimidation, one may still use craft or deceit against an enemy, provided that this does not entail perfidy and the violation of pacts and pledged faith. Agesilaus says in Plutarch, *Agesilaus* [*Laconian Apophthegms,* p. 209 B]: 'To break one's promise is indeed impious; but to outwit an enemy is not only just and glorious, but profitable and sweet.' (G.) And especially appropriate in this connexion is the saying of Cleandrides in Polyaenus, *Strategemata,* Bk. II, [x. 5]: 'When the lion's skin fails, one must put on also the fox's.' Silius Italicus, Bk. I [219]: 'He had no confidence in the sword alone without guile.' Add Xenophon, *Training of Cyrus,* Bk. I [vi. 19]; Livy, Bk. XLII, chap. xlvii; Grotius, Bk. III, chap. i, § 9; and above Bk. IV, chap. i, §§ 12 and 19.

7. But if we are correctly to understand how far we may proceed with violence against an enemy and his possessions, we should observe that the licence to be used against an enemy is one thing, as it arises from a simple state of hostility, and another, as the mercifulness of natural law orders control and temperance in its indulgence. That is, since according to the law of nature there should be a mutual performance of the duties of peace, whoever takes the first step in violating them against me, has, so far as he is able, freed me from my performance of the duties of peace, and therefore, in confessing that he is my enemy, he allows me a licence to use force against him to any degree, or so far as I may think desirable. This is especially true because the end of war, whether offensive or defensive, could not be gained without this licence, if it were necessary to hold the use of force against an enemy within a certain limit, and never to proceed to extremities. For this reason even open wars

partake somewhat of the nature of a contract like this: 'Try whatever you can, I will likewise use every means at my disposal.' And this holds good not merely if an enemy has undertaken to use every extremity against me, but also if he simply wishes to injure me within certain limits, for he has no greater right to do me a slight injury than a severe one. Therefore, not only may I use force against an enemy until I have warded off the peril with which he threatened me, or have received or extorted from him what he had unjustly robbed me of, or refused to furnish, but I can also proceed so far as to secure guarantees for the future. And if he allows that to be forced from him, he shows clearly enough that he still intends to injure me again in the future. Nor is it in fact always unjust to return a greater evil for a less, for the objection made by some that retribution should be rendered in proportion to the injury, is true only of civil tribunals, where punishments are meted out by superiors. But the evils inflicted by right of war have properly no relation to punishments, since they neither proceed from a superior as such, nor have as their direct object the reform of the guilty party or others, but the defence and assertion of my safety, my property, and my rights. To secure such ends it is permissible to use whatever means I think will best prevail against such a person, who, by the injury done me, has made it impossible for me to do him an injury, however I may treat him, until we have come to a new agreement to refrain from injuries for the future.

But now the law of humanity would not only have one consider how much an enemy can suffer without injury, but also what should be the deeds of a humane and, above all, a generous victor. Therefore, we should take care that, so far as it is possible, and as our defence and future security allow, we suit the evils inflicted upon an enemy to the process usually observed by a civil court in meting out justice in offences and other quarrels. This proportion and measure is treated in detail by Grotius, Bk. III, chaps. xi–xvi, just as the understanding of the licence of war is greatly aided by the three rules laid down by the same author in Bk. III, chap. i, §§ 2–4. It often happens, as well, that the uncertainty of the outcome of a war leads us to temper its licence, for fear the examples we have set may by the hand of fortune be turned against us. See Diodorus Siculus, Bk. XIV, chap. xlvii. Vergil, *Aeneid,* Bk. X [533]: 'By the death of Pallas, Turnus had first removed all friendly intercourse of war.' (B.) Here belongs an incident found in Anton. Gratianus, *De Bello Cyprio,* Bk. V, to the effect that when Colonna gave orders for the Turks captured in the battle of Lepanto to be accorded generous treatment in Rome, he turned to Mohammed and said, 'Learn humanity of us, you who are regularly so harsh and cruel to Christian captives'. To which the infidel replied, 'You should forgive us, for it has never yet been our fortune to be captured and fall into the hands of our enemies; in fact we Turks have only learned how to make captive, not how to be captives ourselves'.

What is permissible against such as only furnish an enemy with supplies is also to be seen in Grotius, Bk. III, chap. i, § 5, and chap. xvii.

8. Let us now consider the questions which concern in a peculiar way wars waged by states and their heads. Here we must observe, at the outset, that the right of war which accompanies a natural state is taken away from individuals in a commonwealth, and that therefore individuals can no longer revenge injuries done them

with the means at their own disposal and at their own discretion, or extort with violence of their own doing anything owed them when it is denied, but on such matters they must have recourse to a magistrate, whose function it is to secure to injured persons reparation for damage and guarantees for the future, as well as to make it possible for every man to enjoy his own right. On this point bear *Digest,* L. xvii. 176; IV. ii. 11 at end, 12, 13; XLIII. xxiv. 7, § 3; *Code,* I. ix. 14. And although individuals in a state are sometimes permitted to defend themselves by their own strength, that cannot properly be called a right to make war. For that right is summed up in this: That a man can commence a war at his own judgement, continue it so long as he pleases, and conclude pacts with the enemy. But citizens are allowed to use violence in their own defence only in case of an unavoidable peril, and then not after it has been warded off, just as there is no necessity for individuals drawing up pacts for peace, when that is already secured well enough by the authority of the supreme sovereignty. Nay, even though a quarrel may have been settled between private citizens, that does not prevent a magistrate from having a free hand in settling the injury which gave rise to the altercation between the citizens.

C. The Moralists vs. The Realists

In the eighteenth and nineteenth centuries, there were two different reactions to the Just War Theory and its grounding in Natural Law Theory. The first reaction was from a group that we will call "the moralists." These theorists wanted to go beyond the "minimal morality" of secular Natural Law theorists like Grotius and Hobbes, to a much more robust morality that would either lead to more severe restrictions on war, or to its complete elimination. In the former camp is the diplomat and minister, Emer de Vattel, and in the latter camp was the greatest of the modern philosophers, Immanuel Kant. The other reaction was to be highly skeptical of even a minimalist moral project, arguing that the reality of war is best seen in political rather than moral terms. In this camp, we find the soldier and military leader, Carl von Clausewitz. And then, disagreeing with both the moral idealists and the realists, we find the anarchist Henry David Thoreau, who argued for the right of individuals to resist war and all forms of state power, not on grounds of abstract right but individual, egoistic conscience. Because of his rejection of moral idealism, Thoreau's own moralism is quite different from Vattel and Kant and is best seen as closer to the realists as he urges that individuals approach war in their own terms rather than looking to higher ideals.

Vattel is quite explicit in providing an interpretation of the laws of nature that contains principles "very inconsistent with the policies of cabinet ministers." He begins with the principle that all humans have duties of mutual assistance toward each other. Such duties extend to a nation that "should give its aid to further the advancement of other Nations and save them from disaster and ruin, so far as it can do so without running too great a risk." Vattel anticipates contemporary debates about humanitarian wars when he says that nations should come to the aid of peoples who are suffering from famines or find themselves in other "dire straits." Vattel also argues though that states are not justified in interfering in the affairs of other states merely to punish, but only when the state's own rights or safety are jeopardized.

In general, Vattel urges that nations regard each other as "brothers" and greatly restrict the use of war. But this does not mean that states cannot act in self-defense and even engage in anticipatory attacks, "being careful, however, not to act upon vague and doubtful suspicions." The nations of the world should band together to aid in the prevention of hostile war making, because "a general contempt for justice is a wrong to all Nations." This final doctrine anticipates the contemporary doctrine of universal jurisdiction that will be discussed in later sections of this book.

Kant goes further than Vattel and argues that states should work toward a cosmopolitan order where war is virtually eliminated. Kant sets out six articles or principles that would lead to lasting peace. The second article prohibits the acquiring of one state by another, and the third calls for the gradual abolition of standing armies. This strong rejection of most war is based on a moral concern for the rights of individuals. On this view, "war is only a regrettable expedient for asserting one's rights" when no other avenues are open to a person. Kant does not, though, call for the elimination of all wars since there will still be situations where war must be relied on as a last resort. But this must remain an option that is indeed regrettable. For despite what the practical politician might say, morality dictates that peace must be pursued, and pursued in a way that makes it not merely temporary but lasting for the overall betterment of humanity.

Clausewitz responds to Kant and other idealistic theorists, arguing that political reality is such that war is inevitable, for "the tendency to destroy the adversary which lies at the bottom of the conception of War is in no way changed or modified through the progress of civilization." This does not mean that limits should not be placed on war, but only that we should not seek such limits in humanitarian sentiments, but rather in prudential political considerations. Prisoners are not put to death because of prudential calculations rather than a concern for humanity or other self-imposed moral restrictions. War should be understood as a duel writ large. "War therefore is an act of violence intended to compel our opponent to fulfill our will." While in the abstract there is reason to be optimistic, in reality there is no basis to think that war can be eliminated. War is most like a game, in which each side calculates the probabilities that it can gain an advantage over the other. In this respect, what is most important is to master the "art of war." And hence "courage and self-reliance," "boldness, even to rashness" should be seen as necessary and even the "noblest of military virtues." The reality that war is always with us makes theoretical speculations about ending war ring false.

Thoreau is at odds with both the extreme moralism of Kant and the extreme realism of Clausewitz. In their place, Thoreau advocates another form of extremism, extreme individualism. Thoreau begins his essay by linking the arguments against a standing army, as we saw manifested in Kant's essay, with his own arguments against a standing government. And contrary to Vattel and others, Thoreau says that the only rights one has are the right to do what one thinks to be right. Yet armies are often composed of men marching "over hill and dale to the wars, against their wills, aye, against their common sense and consciences" even though "they are all peaceably inclined." Thoreau entreats his fellow citizens to overthrow the yoke that government imposes, whether it be through slavery or war. Unlike Clausewitz, Thoreau argues that it is the duty of each person to reject what the government demands of us. Not only should soldiers refuse to serve in an unjust war, they should also "refuse to sustain the unjust government which makes the war." So, for Thoreau morality has its place; not the morality of all humanity, but the morality of the individual conscience that will not let the individual be forced into wars against the individual's own principles.

Clausewitz would say to the idealistic moralists, as well as to Thoreau, that their theoretical views were inapplicable to reality. Yet, in the case of Thoreau, it took only a little more than half a century for Mahatma Gandhi to follow Thoreau's model and construct a form of nonviolent resistance that was extremely effective politically. And some would say that in our contemporary times the ideas espoused by Vattel and Kant have had a profound impact on international legal institutions such as the International Criminal Court. The debate between moralists and realists continues in our own day as well. Realists continue to think that war is inevitable and that moral considerations do not function to limit war. But, as Clausewitz knew all too well, prudential considerations argue for limitations on both the decision to go to war and on how war will be conducted. At a certain point, self-interest shades into morality—and it is there that our consciences may indeed be our best guide.

The Law of Nations or the Principles of Natural Law

(1758)

Emer de Vattel

Emer de Vattel (1714–1767) was a Swiss jurist and philosopher. At one point, he was Privy Councilor to the King of Saxony. He supported himself with various ministerial positions.

CHAPTER I. COMMON DUTIES, OR OFFICES OF HUMANITY, BETWEEN NATIONS.

The principles we are about to lay down will seem very inconsistent with the policies of cabinet ministers, and, unhappily for the human race, many of those astute leaders of Nations will turn into ridicule the doctrines in this chapter. Nevertheless, let us boldly set forth the duties which the Law of Nature imposes upon Nations. Shall we fear ridicule when Cicero has spoken before us? That great man held the reins of the most powerful State that ever existed and he never showed his greatness more than when he spoke as a jurist. He considered that the safest policy for a State lay in an exact observance of the Law of Nature. I have already quoted in the preface this noble passage: *Nihil est quod de republica putem dictum, et quo possim longius progredi, nisi sit confirmatum, non modo falsum esse illud, sine injuria non posse, sed hoc verissimum, sine summa justitia rempublicam regi non posse.* I might say, with good reason, that by the words *summa justitia* Cicero means that universal justice which consists in the entire fulfillment of the natural law. But he explains himself elsewhere more in detail on the subject, and he makes it clear enough that he does not limit the mutual duties of men towards one another to the observance of strict justice. "Nothing," he says, "is more conformable to nature, or more capable of affording true satisfaction, than to undertake, after the example of Hercules, even the most painful labors for the preservation and welfare of all nations." *Magis est secundum naturam, pro omnibus gentibus, si fieri possit, conservandis aut juvandis, maximos labores molestiasque suscipere, imitantem Herculem illum, quem hominum fama, beneficiorum memor, in concilium coelestium collocavit; quam vivere in solitudine, non modo sine ullis molestiis, sed etiam in maximis voluptatibus, abundantem omnibus copiis, ut excellas etiam pulchritudine et viribus. Quocirca optimo quisque et splendidissimo ingenio longe illam vitam huic auteponit.* In the same chapter Cicero expressly refutes those who hold that the duties, which they acknowledge with respect to their fellowcitizens, do not extend to aliens. *Qui autem Civium rationem dicunt habendam, externorum negant, hi dirimunt communem humani generis societatem; qua sublata, beneficientia, liberalitas, bonitas, justitia funditus tollitur: quæ qui tollunt, etiam adversus Deos immortales impii judicandi sunt; ab iis enim constitutam inter homines societatem evertunt.*

And why may we not hope still to find among those who govern some wise statesmen who are convinced of the great truth that even for sovereigns and States the path of virtue is the surest way to prosperity and happiness? There is at least one result that may be looked for from the open declaration of sound principles, namely, that they will constrain even those who care least about them to keep within certain bounds lest they altogether disgrace themselves. To fancy that men, and particularly men in power, are going to follow strictly the Laws of Nature, would be grievous self-deception; but to lose all hope of making an impression upon any of them would be to despair of human nature.

Since Nations are bound by the Law of Nature mutually to promote the society of the human race (Introd., § 11), they owe one another all the duties which the safety and welfare of that society require.

The *offices of humanity* consist in the fulfillment of the duty of mutual assistance which men owe to one another because they are men, that is to say, because they are made to live together in society, and are of necessity dependent upon one another's aid for their preservation and happiness, and for the means of a livelihood conformable to their nature. Now, since Nations are not less subject to the laws of nature than are individuals (Introd., § 5), the duties which a man owes to other men, a Nation owes, in its way, to other Nations (Introd., § 10). Such is the foundation of those common duties, those offices of humanity, which Nations mutually owe one another. In general, they consist in doing all in our power for the welfare and happiness of others, as far as is consistent with our duties towards ourselves.

The fact that man, by the very nature of his being, can not be sufficient unto himself, nor continue and develop his existence, nor live happily without the assistance of his fellow-men, makes it clear that it is man's destiny to live in a society where the members give one another mutual aid, and therefore that all men are bound by the very nature of their being to work together for the mutual improvement of their condition in life. The surest means of succeeding in this duty is for each one to labor first for himself and then for others. Hence it follows that whatever we owe to ourselves we owe also to others, as far as they are really in need of our help and we can give it to them without neglecting ourselves. Since, then, one Nation owes, in its way, to another Nation the duties that one man owes to another, we may boldly lay down this general principle: Each State owes to every other State all that it owes to itself, as far as the other is in actual need of its help and such help can be given without the State neglecting its duties towards itself. Such is the eternal and immutable law of Nature. Those who may find it completely subversive of wise statesmanship will be reassured by the two following considerations.

(1) Sovereign States, or the political bodies of which society is composed, are much more self-sufficient than individual men, and mutual assistance is not so necessary among them, nor its practice so frequent. Now, in all matters which a Nation can manage for itself, no help is due it from others.

(2) The duties of a Nation to itself, and especially the care of its own safety, call for

much more circumspection and reserve than an individual need exercise in giving assistance to others. We shall develop this remark presently.

All the duties of a Nation towards itself have for their object the preservation of the Nation and the perfecting both of itself and of the circumstances in which it is placed. The details which we have given in the first book of this treatise will serve to indicate the various matters with respect to which one State can and should assist another. Hence, when the occasion arises, every Nation should give its aid to further the advancement of other Nations and save them from disaster and ruin, so far as it can do so without running too great a risk. Thus, when a neighboring State is attacked unjustly by a powerful enemy which threatens to crush it, if you can defend it without exposing yourself to great danger there is no question but that you should do so. Do not raise the objection that a sovereign has not the right to expose the life of his soldiers for the safety of a foreign Nation with which he has not contracted a defensive alliance. He may happen to have like need to help; and therefore by putting into force the spirit of mutual assistance he is promoting the safety of his own Nation. Statecraft thus goes hand in hand with obligation and duty, for princes have an interest in checking the advance of an ambitious ruler who seeks to increase his power by subduing his neighbors. When the United Provinces were threatened with subjection to the yoke of Louis XIV a powerful league was formed in their behalf. When the Turks laid siege to Vienna the brave Sobieski, King of Poland, saved the House of Austria and perhaps all Germany and his own Kingdom.

For the same reason, if a Nation is suffering from famine, all those who have provisions to spare should assist it in its need, without, however, exposing themselves to scarcity. But if that Nation can pay for the provisions furnished it, they may very properly be sold at a fair price, for there is no duty of giving it what it can obtain for itself, and consequently no obligation of making a present of things which it is able to buy. To give assistance in such dire straits is so instinctive an act of humanity that hardly any civilized Nation is to be found which would refuse absolutely to do so. The great Henry IV could not withhold help even from hardened rebels who sought his destruction.

Whatever be the calamity afflicting a Nation, the same help is due to it. Public collections have been ordered in small States of Switzerland for the relief of certain towns and villages of neighboring States which had been destroyed by fire, and abundant help has been given them without the good work being hindered by differences of religion. The misfortunes of Portugal have given England an opportunity of fulfilling the duties of humanity with the noble generosity characteristic of a great Nation. At the first news of the disaster of Lisbon, Parliament voted the sum of a hundred thousand pounds sterling for the relief of the afflicted people; the King added a considerable amount to the sum; vessels were hastily laden with provisions and articles of every sort which might be needed, and their arrival convinced the Portuguese that differences of religious belief and worship do not deter persons who acknowledge the claims of humanity. On the same occasion the King of Spain manifested his humanity, his generosity, and his sympathy for a close ally.

A Nation should not limit its good offices to the preservation of other States, but in addition it should contribute to their advancement according to its ability and their need of its help. We have already shown (Introd., § 13) that this general obligation is imposed upon it by human society. It is appropriate here to develop that obligation in some detail. A State is more or less perfect according as it is more or less adapted to attain the end of civil society, which consists in procuring for its citizens the necessities, the comforts, and the pleasures of life, and in general their happiness; and in securing to each the peaceful enjoyment of his property and a sure means of obtaining justice, and finally in defending the whole body against all external violence (Book I, § 15). Every Nation should therefore give its aid when the occasion arises, and according to its ability, not only to enable another Nation to enjoy those advantages, but to put it in a way to procure them itself. Thus, if an uncivilized State should desire to improve its condition and should apply to a civilized State for teachers to instruct it, the latter ought not to refuse them. The State which has the happiness of being ruled by wise laws should consider it a duty to impart them to others when the occasion arises. Thus, when the wise and exemplary Romans sent envoys to Greece in search of good laws, the Greeks did not refuse so reasonable and praiseworthy a request.

But while a Nation is bound to further, as far as it can, the advancement of others, it has no right to force them to accept its offer of help. The attempt to do so would be a violation of their natural liberty. Authority is needed if one is to constrain others to receive a benefit, whereas Nations are absolutely free and independent (Introd., § 4). Those ambitious European States which attacked the American Nations and subjected them to their avaricious rule, in order, as they said, to civilize them, and have them instructed in the true religion—those usurpers, I say, justified themselves by a pretext equally unjust and ridiculous. It is surprising to hear the learned and judicious Grotius tell us that a sovereign can

justly take up arms to punish Nations which are guilty of grievous crimes against the natural law, which "treat their parents in an inhuman manner, like the Sogdians, which eat human flesh, like the ancient Gauls," etc. He was led into that mistake from his attributing to every free man, and hence to every sovereign, a certain right to punish crimes in grievous violation of the laws of nature, even when those crimes do not affect his rights or his safety. But we have shown (Book I, § 169) that the right to punish belongs to men solely because of the right to provide for their safety; hence it only exists as against those who have injured them. Did not Grotius perceive that in spite of all the precautions added in the following paragraphs, his view opens the door to all the passions of zealots and fanatics, and gives to ambitious men pretexts without number? Mahomet and his successors laid waste to and subdued Asia to avenge the disbelief in the unity of God; and all those whom they regarded as *associateurs,* or idolaters, were victims of their fanaticism.

Since these duties or offices of humanity should be shown by one Nation to another, according as the one has need of them and the other can reasonably extend them, and since every Nation is free, independent, and sovereign in its acts, it is for each to decide whether it is in a position to ask or to grant anything in that respect. Thus (1) every Nation has a perfect right to ask for assistance and offices of humanity from another if it thinks it has need of them. To prevent it from doing so would be to do it a wrong. If it asks for them without need, it acts contrary to its duty, but its judgment on the point is free from control. It has the right to ask for them, but not to demand them.

For (2) since these offices are only due in a case of need, and from a State which can render them without neglecting its duty to itself, it belongs, on the other hand, to the Nation of whom help is requested to decide whether the case really calls for it, and whether the Nation is in a position to grant it with due regard to its own safety and welfare. For example, if a Nation is in need of grain and seeks to buy it of another, it is for the latter to judge whether, in complying with the request, it will not run the risk of being itself impoverished; and if it refuses to sell, the other must abide by the refusal patiently. Russia has recently given an example of a wise fulfillment of these duties. It has generously assisted Sweden when threatened with a famine; but it has refused to other powers the right to purchase wheat in Livonia, being in need of it itself and having weighty motives of State policy besides.

A Nation has, therefore, only an imperfect right to offices of humanity; it can not force another Nation to perform them. If the other refuses them without good reason it offends against charity, which consists in acknowledging an imperfect right of another; but it does no injury thereby, since injury or injustice results from denying a perfect right.

It is impossible for Nations to fully acquit themselves of their mutual duties if they do not love one another. Offices of humanity should proceed from that pure source, and they will thus retain the character and perfection of it. Then we shall see Nations aid one another with sincerity and true kindness, labor earnestly for their common happiness, and promote peace without jealousy and without distrust.

We shall see a true friendship reign among them, which will consist in mutual affection. Every Nation is bound to cultivate the friendship of other Nations and to avoid carefully whatever might arouse their enmity. Wise and prudent Nations often do so from motives of present and di-

rect interest; a higher interest, more universal and less direct, is too rarely the motive of statesmen. If it is undeniable that men should love one another, as well in response to the designs of nature and in fulfillment of the duties it imposes upon them, as for their own private advantage, can it be doubted that Nations are mutually bound by the same obligation? Is it within the power of men, by dividing into different political groups, to break the bonds of that universal society which nature has established among them?

If a man ought to endeavor to become of service to other men, and a citizen of service to his fellow-citizens, a Nation, in seeking its own advancement, should propose to itself to become thereby more capable of furthering the advancement and happiness of other Nations. It should endeavor to set them good example and avoid any act to the contrary. It is natural to men to imitate others; the virtues of a great Nation are sometimes imitated, and its vices and faults more frequently.

Since its renown is of such importance to a Nation, as we have shown in a special chapter, (*a*) the duty of a Nation towards others includes even a care for their renown. In the first place, it should endeavor, on occasion, to enable them to merit true renown; secondly, it should show them all due honor itself, and endeavor to have others do so, as far as lies in its power; finally, far from increasing the bad effect which certain slight faults of other nations may produce, it should charitably extenuate them.

It is evident from the principles on which we have based the obligation of extending the offices of humanity that it is founded solely upon man's human nature. Hence no Nation may refuse those offices to another Nation under pretext that the latter professes another form of religious belief. No more is needed to merit them than to be one's fellow-man. Conformity of belief and worship may well become a new bond of friendship between Nations, but religious differences should not make men put aside their character as men or the feelings attendant upon that character. We have already related (§ 5) some examples worthy of imitation; let us here do justice to the wise Pontiff who at present occupies the Roman See and has just given a remarkable example in point, which is well worthy of praise. This Prince, learning that there were several Dutch vessels detained at Civita Vecchia through fear of the Algerian corsairs, ordered the Papal frigates to escort them on their way; and the Papal nuncio at Brussels received instructions to signify to the Minister of the States-General that His Holiness made it a rule to protect commerce and to extend the offices of humanity without any regard to religious differences. Such exalted sentiments can not fail to create profound respect for Benedict XIV even among Protestants.

What would be the happiness of the human race if these benevolent precepts of nature were everywhere observed. Nations would mutually exchange their products and their knowledge; profound peace would reign upon the earth and would enrich it with its precious fruits; industry, science, and art would be devoted to promoting our happiness no less than satisfying our needs. Violent means would no longer be used to decide such differences as might arise. They would be terminated by forbearance and by the application of principles of justice and equity. The world would take on the appearance of a great Republic, all men would live together as brothers, and each would be a citizen of the universe. Why should the idea be but a beautiful dream, when it is based upon the very nature of man's being? But the inordinate passions and mistaken self-interest of

men will keep them from ever realizing it. Let us examine, then, the limitations which the actual state of mankind and the ordinary conduct and policy of Nations may put upon the practice of these precepts of nature, in themselves so excellent.

The Law of Nature can not condemn the good to make themselves the prey of the wicked and the victims of their injustice and ingratitude. From sad experience we know that the majority of Nations only seek to strengthen and enrich themselves at the expense of others, to dominate over them, and even to oppress them and subject them to their yoke, should the opportunity present itself. Prudence will never allow us to increase the strength of an enemy or of one in whom we perceive the desire to despoil and oppress us, for the care of our own safety forbids our doing so. We have seen (§ § 3 and foll.) that a Nation only owes to others its assistance and the offices of humanity in so far as it can extend them without failing in its duties to itself. Hence it clearly follows that although a Nation is bound by the universal law of charity to extend at all times and to all persons, even its enemies, such assistance as can only tend to render them more upright and more honorable, because no harm can be feared from granting it, the Nation is not bound to give them any help which might probably be used to its own destruction. It thus happens, (1) that the exceeding importance of trade, not only as a means of supplying the necessities and comforts of life, but also as a source of strength to the State by furnishing it with a means of defense against its enemies, together with the insatiable greed of Nations which seek to draw it all to themselves and take exclusive possession of it—these circumstances, I say, authorize a Nation which is in control of a branch of commerce or which possesses the secret of some important manufacture to keep to itself that source of wealth and, far from imparting it to them, to take measures to prevent them from obtaining possession of it. But where there is question of the necessities or conveniences of life the Nation ought to sell them to others at a just price and not make use of its monopoly as a means of oppression. Commerce is the chief source of the greatness, power, and security of England; who will blame her if she endeavors, by all honest and just means, to keep control of its various branches?

(2) With respect to things which are of more direct and special use in time of war, there is no obligation upon a Nation to share them with others, whom it suspects ever so little, and prudence even forbids it to do so. Thus it was very justly forbidden by law at Rome to communicate to barbarian Nations the art of constructing galleys. So also England has provided by law that the best method of constructing ships should not be made known to foreigners.

This caution should be carried much further with respect to Nations more justly suspected. Thus when the power of the Turks was, so to say, on the ascendant and conquering all before it, all Christian Nations, independently of any religious antagonism, had reason to regard them as enemies; even the most distant Nations, who came in no actual conflict with them, might well break off all commerce with a power which avowedly sought to subdue by force of arms all those who would not recognize the authority of its prophet.

Let us further remark, with special reference to the Prince, that in this matter he may not be unreservedly guided by magnanimous and disinterested sentiments, in which self-interest generously gives way to the good of others; for it is not his own interests that are at stake here, but those of the Nation which has committed itself

to his care. Cicero says that a noble and high-minded soul despises pleasures, riches, and life itself, and accounts them as naught, when there is question of the common welfare. He is right, and such sentiments are worthy of admiration in a private person. But we can not be generous with the property of another. The ruler of a Nation, when dealing with public affairs, may only be generous with moderation, and in so far as may be to the renown of the State and its actual advantage. As to the common welfare of human society, he should have the same care for it as the Nation which he represents would be bound to have if it had itself control of its affairs.

But if the duties of a Nation towards itself limit the obligation of extending the offices of humanity, they can not qualify the prohibition not to do wrong to others or cause them any harm, in a word, to *injure* them, if I may thus render the Latin word *ladere*. To hurt, to offend, to do wrong, to cause harm or prejudice, to wound, have not all precisely the same meaning. To *injure* anyone is, in general, to detract from his personal qualities or to diminish the advantages of his situation in life.

If every man is bound by his very nature to labor for the advancement of others, with much greater reason is he forbidden to diminish the blessings they already enjoy. The same duties are imposed upon Nations (Introd., §§ 5, 6). Hence none of them should do any act tending to deprive the others of their advantages, or to retard their progress, that is to say, to *injure* them. And since the perfection of a Nation consists in its being in a position to attain the end of civil society, and since its circumstances are perfect when it is not wanting in the things needed for that end (Book I, § 14), no State has the right to prevent another from attaining the end of civil society, or to render it incapable of doing so. Upon this general principle it is unlawful for Nations to do any act tending to create trouble in another State, to stir up discord, to corrupt its citizens, to alienate its allies, to stain its renown, or to deprive it of its natural advantages.

However, it will easily be understood that the neglect or even the refusal to fulfill these common duties of humanity is not an *injury*. To neglect or to refuse to further the advancement of a Nation does not constitute an act of aggression.

Moreover, it must be observed that if, in making use of our right or in fulfilling a duty to ourselves or to others, there results from our act some harm to another either in his person or in his circumstances, we are not guilty of doing an *injury*. We are but doing what we have a right to do, or even what we ought to do; the harm which results to another is not intended by us, and is a mere accident, to be imputed to us or not, according to the special circumstances of the case. For example, in a case of lawful self-defense the damage we inflict upon our assailant is not what we aim at; we are acting with a view to our safety and are making use of our right, so that our assailant is alone responsible for the harm he brings on himself.

Nothing is more opposed to the duties of humanity, or more contrary to the social intercourse which should be cultivated by Nations, than *offenses* or acts which are a cause of just displeasure to others. Every Nation should therefore be careful not to give any real cause of offense to another Nation. I say *real*, because if it should happen that, when we are making use of our rights or fulfilling our duties, another takes offense at our conduct, that is his fault, not ours. So much bitterness is caused between Nations by one giving offense to another that they should avoid giving even an ill-founded cause of offense when they can do so without difficulty and without failing in their duties. Certain medals and offensive jests irritated Louis XIV against the United Provinces and brought on his attack upon them in 1672, which proved the destruction of that Republic.

The principles laid down in this chapter, these sacred precepts of nature, were for a long time unknown among Nations. The ancients did not acknowledge any duty towards Nations to which they were not bound by a treaty of friendship. Jews in particular made it a point of patriotism to hate other Nations, and they were in consequence reciprocally hated and despised. Finally the voice of nature came to be heard among civilized Nations, and they realized that all men are brothers. When will the happy time come when they shall act upon their belief?

● ● ●

CHAPTER IV. THE RIGHT OF SELF-PROTECTION AND THE EFFECTS OF THE SOVEREIGNTY AND INDEPENDENCE OF NATIONS.

The duty which nature has imposed upon Nations, as upon individuals, of self-preservation, and of perfecting themselves and the circumstances by which they are surrounded, would be to no effect if they had not at the same time the right to prevent any interference with its fulfillment. A *right* is nothing else than the *moral power to act,* that is to say, the power to do what is morally possible, what is good in itself and conformable to duty. We have, therefore, the general right to do whatever is necessary to the fulfillment of our duties. Hence Nations, as men, have the right to resist any attack upon their existence, or upon the internal or external advantages they enjoy;

that is to say, to protect themselves against all injury (§ 18); and this right is absolute, since it is given for the fulfillment of a natural and indispensable obligation. When force can not be used to cause a right to be respected, the possibility of exercising it effectively is very doubtful. It is this right of securing oneself against all injury which is called the *right of self-protection.*

The safest plan is to prevent evil, where that is possible. A Nation has the right to resist the injury another seeks to inflict upon it, and to use force and every other just means of resistance against the aggressor. It may even anticipate the other's design, being careful, however, not to act upon vague and doubtful suspicions, lest it should run the risk of becoming itself the aggressor.

When the injury has been done the same right of self-protection authorizes the injured party to seek full redress and to use force to obtain it, if necessary.

Finally, the injured party has the right to provide for its security in the future and to punish the offender in such a way as to prevent a recurrence of such attacks and give a warning to any others who may be tempted to make similar attacks. It may even, if circumstances should require the step, disable the aggressor from doing further harm. A Nation is acting within its right in taking such measures if they are called for; and the Nation which brings them upon itself has only its own injustice to blame.

If, then, there should be found a restless and unprincipled Nation, ever ready to do harm to others, to thwart their purposes, and to stir up civil strife among their citizens, there is no doubt that all the others would have the right to unite together to subdue such a Nation, to discipline it, and even to disable it from doing

further harm. Such would be the proper action to take against the policy which Machiavelli praises in Cæsar Borgia. The designs of Philip II of Spain were such as to make all Europe unite against him, and Henry the Great with good reason formed the plan of breaking down a power whose strength was so great and whose policy so destructive.

The principles involved in the three preceding propositions constitute the several grounds upon which a just war may be waged, as we shall show in that connection.

It clearly follows from the liberty and independence of Nations that each has the right to govern itself as it thinks proper, and that no one of them has the least right to interfere in the government of another. Of all the rights possessed by a Nation that of sovereignty is doubtless the most important, and the one which others should most carefully respect if they are desirous not to give cause for offense.

The sovereign is the person to whom the Nation has confided the supreme power and the duty of governing; it has invested him with its rights, and it alone is directly concerned with the manner in which its appointed ruler makes use of his power. No foreign State may inquire into the manner in which a sovereign rules, nor set itself up as judge of his conduct, nor force him to make any change in his administration. If he burdens his subjects with taxes or treats them with severity it is for the Nation to take action; no foreign State is called on to amend his conduct and to force him to follow a wiser and juster course. Prudence will suggest the times when it may interfere to the extent of making friendly representations. The Spaniards acted contrary to all rules when they set themselves up as judges of Inca Atahualpa. If that Prince had violated the Law of Nations in their regard they would have been right in punishing him. But they accused him of having put to death certain of his own subjects, of having had several wives, etc., things for which he was not responsible to them; and, as the crowning point of their injustice, they condemned him by the laws of Spain.

But if a prince, by violating the fundamental laws, gives his subjects a lawful cause for resisting him; if, by his insupportable tyranny, he brings on a national revolt against him, any foreign power may rightfully give assistance to an oppressed people who ask for its aid. The English justly complained of James II. The nobility and the patriotic leaders resolved to put a check upon his policy, which clearly tended to overthrow the Constitution and to destroy the liberties and the religion of the people, and they obtained the help of the United Provinces. Doubtless the authority of the Prince of Orange had an influence in the deliberations of the States-General, but it did not lead them to do an act of injustice. To give help to a brave people who are defending their liberties against an oppressor by force of arms is only the part of justice and generosity. Hence, whenever such dissension reaches the state of civil war, foreign Nations may assist that one of the two parties which seems to have justice on its side. But to assist a detestable tyrant, or to come out in favor of an unjust and rebellious people, would certainly be a violation of duty. When, however, the political bonds between a sovereign and his people are broken, or at least suspended, they may be considered as two distinct parties, and since both are independent of all foreign authority, no one has the right to judge them. Either may be in the right, and those who assist the one or the other may think they are upholding the just cause. Hence, by virtue of the voluntary

Law of Nations (see Introd., § 21), the two parties must be allowed to act as if possessed of equal right, and to be treated accordingly, until the affair is decided.

But this principle should not be made use of so as to authorize criminal designs against the peace of Nations. It is in violation of the Law of Nations to call on subjects to revolt when they are actually obeying their sovereign, although complaining of his rule.

The practice of Nations is in conformity with the principles laid down. When the German Protestants came to the help of the reformed party in France the Court did not attempt to treat them on any other footing than that of belligerents, to whom the laws of war were to be applied. France was at that time giving help to the Netherlands in their revolt against Spain, and expected that its troops should be regarded in the same class as auxiliaries, engaged in regular warfare. But no power would fail to regard other than as a grievous injury any attempt of a foreign Nation, by means of agents, to stir up its subjects to revolt.

As for those monsters who, under the name of sovereigns, act as a scourge and plague of the human race, they are nothing more than wild beasts, of whom every man of courage may justly purge the earth. Hercules was universally praised by the ancients for freeing the world of such monsters as Antæus, Busiris, and Diomedes.

Having shown that foreign Nations have no right to interfere in the government of an independent State, it is not difficult to prove that the latter is justified in resisting such interference. To govern itself after its own good pleasure is the adjunct of its independence. A sovereign State may not be constrained in this respect, except with reference to certain specific rights which others may have acquired by treaty, and which, since a Nation is naturally jealous of interference in its government, can not be extended beyond the clear and express terms of the treaty. Apart from the above case a sovereign has the right to treat as enemies those who undertake to interfere in its domestic affairs otherwise than by their good offices.

• • •

CHAPTER V. THE OBSERVANCE OF JUSTICE BETWEEN NATIONS.

Justice is the foundation of all social life and the secure bond of all civil intercourse. Human society, instead of being an interchange of friendly assistance, would be no more than a vast system of robbery if no respect were shown for the virtue which gives to each his own. Its observance is even more necessary between Nations than between individuals, because injustice between Nations may be followed by the terrible consequences involved in an affray between powerful political bodies, and because it is more difficult to obtain redress. It is easy to prove from the natural law that all men are under the obligation to be just. We presume here that the obligation is sufficiently understood, and we limit ourselves to the observation that not only are Nations not exempt from it (Introd., § 5), but it is even more sacred with respect to them because of the importance of its effects.

Hence there is a strict obligation upon all Nations to promote justice among themselves, to observe it scrupulously in their own conduct, and to refrain carefully from any violation of it. Each should render to the others what belongs to them, respect their rights, and leave them in the peaceful enjoyment of them.

It follows from this indispensable obligation which nature imposes upon Nations as well as from the obligations under which each Nation lies towards itself, that every State has the right to resist any attempt to deprive it of its rights, or of anything which lawfully belongs to it; for in so doing it is only acting in conformity with all its duties, which is the source of its right. (§ 49)

This right is a perfect one; that is, it carries with it the right to use force to make it effective. To what purpose would be the right given us by nature to withstand injustice, and the obligation upon others to do us justice if we could not lawfully constrain them when they refuse to fulfill that duty? The just man would be at the mercy of avaricious and dishonest people, and all his rights would soon be worthless.

From this right there arise, as so many branches, first, the right of lawful self-defense which belongs to every Nation, or the right of resisting by force any attack upon itself or its rights. This is the justification of defensive war.

Secondly, the right to use force to obtain justice, if it can not otherwise be had, or to follow up one's rights by force of arms. This is the justification of offensive war.

An intentional act of injustice is certainly an *injury*. A Nation has, therefore, the right to punish it, as we pointed out above when speaking of injuries in general (§ 52). The right to resist injustice is derived from the right of self-protection.

Let us apply, moreover, to unjust Nations what we said above (§ 53) with respect to a wrong-doer. If a Nation were to make open profession of treading justice under foot by despising and violating the rights of another whenever it had an opportunity of doing so, the safety of the human society at large would warrant all the other Nations in uniting together to subdue and punish such a Nation. We are not overlooking the principle laid down in the Introduction that it does not belong to Nations to set themselves up as judges over one another. In individual cases, where there is any room at all for doubt, it should be presumed that each of the parties may have some justice on its side; it is possible that the injustice of the one in the wrong may be the result of mistake and not of deliberate contempt for justice. But if a Nation, by its accepted principles and uniform policy, shows clearly that it is in that malicious state of mind in which no right is sacred to it, the safety of the human race requires that it be put down. To set up and maintain an unjust claim is an injury merely to the one who is affected by the claim; but to manifest a general contempt for justice is a wrong to all Nations.

Perpetual Peace

(1795)

Immanuel Kant

Immanuel Kant (1724–1804) was born in East Prussia and spent most of his life teaching philosophy in Konigsberg. Kant is generally regarded as the greatest of the modern philosophers.

'THE PERPETUAL PEACE'

A Dutch innkeeper once put this satirical inscription on his signboard, along with the picture of a graveyard. We shall not trouble to ask whether it applies to men in general, or particularly to heads of state (who can never have enough of war), or only to the philosophers who blissfully dream of perpetual peace. The author of the present essay does, however, make one reservation in advance. The practical politician tends to look down with great complacency upon the political theorist as a mere academic. The theorist's abstract ideas, the practitioner believes, cannot endanger the state, since the state must be founded upon principles of experience; it thus seems safe to let him fire off his whole broadside, and the *worldly-wise* statesman need not turn a hair. It thus follows that if the practical politician is to be consistent, he must not claim, in the event of a dispute with the theorist, to scent any danger to the state in the opinions which the theorist has randomly uttered in public. By this saving clause, the author of this essay will consider himself expressly safeguarded, in correct and proper style, against all malicious interpretation.

FIRST SECTION WHICH CONTAINS THE PRELIMINARY ARTICLES OF A PERPETUAL PEACE BETWEEN STATES

1. 'No conclusion of peace shall be considered valid as such if it was made with a secret reservation of the material for a future war.'

For if this were the case, it would be a mere truce, a suspension of hostilities, not a *peace*. Peace means an end to all hostilities, and to attach the adjective 'perpetual' to it is already suspiciously close to pleonasm. A conclusion of peace nullifies all existing reasons for a future war, even if these are not yet known to the contracting parties, and no matter how acutely and carefully they may later be pieced together out of old documents. It is possible that either party may make a mental reservation with a view to reviving its old pretensions in the future. Such reservations will not be mentioned explicitly, since both parties may simply be too exhausted to continue the war, although they may nonetheless possess sufficient ill will to seize the first favourable opportunity of attaining their end. But if we consider such reservations in themselves, they soon appear as Jesuitical casuistry; they are beneath the dignity of a ruler, just as it is beneath the dignity of a minister of state to comply with any reasoning of this kind.

But if, in accordance with 'enlightened' notions of political expediency, we believe that the true glory of a state consists in the constant increase of its power by any means whatsoever, the above judgement will certainly appear academic and pedantic.

2. 'No independently existing state, whether it be large or small, may be acquired by another state by inheritance, exchange, purchase or gift.'

For a state, unlike the ground on which it is based, is not a possession (*patrimonium*). It is a society of men, which no-one other than itself can command or dispose of. Like a tree, it has its own roots, and to graft it on to another state as if it were a shoot is to terminate its existence as a moral personality and make it into a commodity. This contradicts the idea of the original contract, without which the rights of a people are unthinkable.[1] Everyone knows what danger the supposed right of acquiring states in this way, even in our own times, has brought upon Europe (for this practice is unknown in other continents). It has been thought that states can marry one another, and this has provided a new kind of industry by which power can be increased through family alliances, without expenditure of energy, while landed property can be extended at the same time. It is the same thing when the troops of one state are hired to another to fight an enemy who is not common to both; for the subjects are thereby used and misused as objects to be manipulated at will.

3. 'Standing armies (*miles perpetuus*) will gradually be abolished altogether.'

For they constantly threaten other states with war by the very fact that they are always prepared for it. They spur on the states to outdo one another in arming unlimited numbers of soldiers, and since the resultant costs eventually make peace more oppressive than a short war, the armies are themselves the cause of wars of aggression which set out to end burdensome military expenditure. Furthermore, the hiring of men to kill or to be killed seems to mean using them as mere machines and instruments in the hands of someone else (the state), which cannot easily be reconciled with the rights of man in one's own person. It is quite a different matter if the citizens undertake voluntary military training from time to time in order to secure themselves and their fatherland against attacks from outside. But it would be just the same if wealth rather than soldiers were accumulated, for it would be seen by other states as a military threat; it might compel them to mount preventive attacks, for of the three powers within a state—the *power of the army,* the *power of alliance* and the *power of money*—the third is probably the most reliable instrument of war. It would lead more often to wars if it were not so difficult to discover the amount of wealth which another state possesses.

4. 'No national debt shall be contracted in connection with the external affairs of the state.'

There is no cause for suspicion if help for the national economy is sought inside or outside the state (e.g. for improvements to roads, new settlements, storage of foodstuffs for years of famine, etc.). But a credit system, if used by the powers as an instrument of aggression against one another, shows the power of money in its most dangerous form. For while the debts thereby incurred are always secure against present demands (because not all the creditors will demand payment at the same time), these debts go on growing indefinitely. This ingenious system, invented by a commercial people in the present century, provides a military fund which may exceed the resources of all the other states put together. It can only be exhausted by an eventual tax-deficit, which

may be postponed for a considerable time by the commercial stimulus which industry and trade receive through the credit system. This ease in making war, coupled with the warlike inclination of those in power (which seems to be an integral feature of human nature), is thus a great obstacle in the way of perpetual peace. Foreign debts must therefore be prohibited by a preliminary article of such a peace, otherwise national bankruptcy, inevitable in the long run, would necessarily involve various other states in the resultant loss without their having deserved it, thus inflicting upon them a public injury. Other states are therefore justified in allying themselves against such a state and its pretensions.

5. 'No state shall forcibly interfere in the constitution and government of another state.'

For what could justify such interference? Surely not any sense of scandal or offence which a state arouses in the subjects of another state. It should rather serve as a warning to others, as an example of the great evils which a people has incurred by its lawlessness. And a bad example which one free person gives to another (as a *scandalum acceptum*) is not the same as an injury to the latter. But it would be a different matter if a state, through internal discord, were to split into two parts, each of which set itself up as a separate state and claimed authority over the whole. For it could not be reckoned as interference in another state's constitution if an external state were to lend support to one of them, because their condition is one of anarchy. But as long as this internal conflict is not yet decided, the interference of external powers would be a violation of the rights of an independent people which is merely struggling with its internal ills. Such interference would be an active offence and would make the autonomy of all other states insecure.

6. 'No state at war with another shall permit such acts of hostility as would make mutual confidence impossible during a future time of peace. Such acts would include the employment of *assassins (percussores)* or *poisoners (venefici), breach of agreements, the instigation of treason (perduellio)* within the enemy state, etc.

These are dishonourable stratagems. For it must still remain possible, even in wartime, to have some sort of trust in the attitude of the enemy, otherwise peace could not be concluded and the hostilities would turn into a war of extermination (*bellum internecinum*). After all, war is only a regrettable expedient for asserting one's rights by force within a state of nature, where no court of justice is available to judge with legal authority. In such cases, neither party can be declared an unjust enemy, for this would already presuppose a judge's decision; only the *outcome* of the conflict, as in the case of a so-called 'judgement of God', can decide who is in the right. A war of punishment (*bellum punitivum*) between states is inconceivable, since there can be no relationship of superior to inferior among them. It thus follows that a war of extermination, in which both parties and right itself might all be simultaneously annihilated, would allow perpetual peace only on the vast graveyard of the human race. A war of this kind and the employment of all means which might bring it about must thus be absolutely prohibited. But the means listed above would inevitably lead to such a war, because these diabolical arts, be-

sides being intrinsically despicable, would not long be confined to war alone if they were brought into use. This applies, for example, to the employment of spies (*uti exploratoribus*), for it exploits only the dishonesty of others (which can never be completely eliminated). Such practices will be carried over into peacetime and will thus completely vitiate its purpose.

All of the articles listed above, when regarded objectively or in relation to the intentions of those in power, are *prohibitive laws (leges prohibitivae)*. Yet some of them are of the strictest sort (*leges strictae*), being valid irrespective of differing circumstances, and they require that the abuses they prohibit should be abolished *immediately* (Nos. 1, 5, and 6). Others (Nos. 2, 3, and 4), although they are not exceptions to the rule of justice, allow some *subjective* latitude according to the circumstances in which they are applied (*leges latae*). The latter need not necessarily be executed at once, so long as their ultimate purpose (e.g. the *restoration* of freedom to certain states in accordance with the second article) is not lost sight of. But their execution may not be *put off* to a non-existent date (*ad calendas graecas,* as Augustus used to promise), for any delay is permitted only as a means of avoiding a premature implementation which might frustrate the whole purpose of the article. For in the case of the second article, the prohibition relates only to the *mode of acquisition,* which is to be forbidden henceforth, but not to the present *state of political possessions*. For although this present state is not backed up by the requisite legal authority, it was considered lawful in the public opinion of every state at the time of the putative acquisition.[2]

SECOND SECTION WHICH CONTAINS THE DEFINITIVE ARTICLES OF A PERPETUAL PEACE BETWEEN STATES

A state of peace among men living together is not the same as the state of nature, which is rather a state of war. For even if it does not involve active hostilities, it involves a constant threat of their breaking out. Thus the state of peace must be *formally instituted,* for a suspension of hostilities is not in itself a guarantee of peace. And unless one neighbour gives a guarantee to the other at his request (which can happen only in a *lawful* state), the latter may treat him as an enemy.[3]

Notes

1. A hereditary kingdom is not a state which can be inherited by another state. Only the right to rule over it may be bequeathed to another physical person. In this case, the state acquires a ruler, but the ruler as such (i.e. as one who already has another kingdom) does not acquire the state.

2. It has hitherto been doubted, not without justification, whether there can be permissive laws (*leges permissivae*) in addition to preceptive laws (*leges praeceptivae*) and prohibitive laws (*leges prohibitivae*). For all laws embody an element of objective practical necessity as a reason for certain actions, whereas a permission depends only upon practical contingencies. Thus a *permissive law* would be a compulsion to do something which one cannot be compelled to do, and if the object of the law were the same as that of the permission, a contradiction would result. But in the permissive law contained in the second article above, the initial prohibition applies only to the mode of acquiring a right in the future (e.g. by inheritance), whereas the exemption from this prohibition (i.e. the permissive part of the law) applies to the state of political possessions in the present. For in accordance with a permissive law of natural right, this present state can be allowed to remain even although the state of nature has been abandoned for that of civil society. And even if these present possessions are unlawful, they are nevertheless *honest (possessio putativa).* A putative possession is prohibited, however, as soon as it has been recognised as

such, both in the state of nature and after the subsequent transition to civil society (if the mode of acquisition is the same). And continued possession could not be permitted if the supposed acquisition had been made in the state of civil society, for it would then have to end immediately, as an offence against right, as soon as its unlawfulness had been discovered.

My intention here was merely to point out briefly to exponents of natural right the concept of a permissive law, which automatically presents itself within the systematic divisions of reason. It is especially noteworthy since it is frequently used in civil or statutory law, with the one difference that the prohibitive part of the law exists independently, and the permissive part is not included within the law itself as a limiting condition (as it ought to be), but added to cover exceptional cases. Such laws usually state that this or that is prohibited, *except* in cases 1, 2, or 3, and so on *ad infinitum,* for permissive clauses are only added to the law fortuitously, by a random review of particular cases, and not in accordance with any definite principle. Otherwise, the limiting conditions would have had to be included *in the actual formula of the prohibitive law,* whereby it would have become a permissive law in itself. It is therefore to be regretted that the ingenious but unsolved competition question submitted by that wise and clear-sighted gentleman, Count Windischgrätz, was so soon abandoned, for it might have solved the legal difficulty we are at present discussing. For the possibility of finding a universal formula like those of mathematics is the only true test of consistent legislation, and without it, the so-called *ius certum* must remain no more than a pious hope. Otherwise, we shall only have *general* laws (i.e. laws *valid in general*), but no universal laws (i.e. laws which are *generally valid*) such as the concept of a law seems to demand.

3. It is usually assumed that one cannot take hostile action against anyone unless one has already been actively *injured* by them. This is perfectly correct if both parties are living in a *legal civil state.* For the fact that the one has entered such a state gives the required guarantee to the other, since both are subject to the same authority. But man (or an individual people) in a mere state of nature robs me of any such security and injures me by virtue of this very state in which he coexists with me. He may not have injured me actively *(facto),* but he does injure me by the very lawlessness of his state *(statu iniusto),* for he is a permanent threat to me, and I can require him either to enter into a common lawful state along with me or to move away from my

vicinity. Thus the postulate on which all the following articles are based is that all men who can at all influence one another must adhere to some kind of civil constitution. But any legal constitution, as far as the persons who live under it are concerned, will conform to one of the three following types:

(1). a constitution based on the *civil right* of individuals within a nation (*ius civitatis*).

(2). a constitution based on the *international right* of states in their relationships with one another (*ius gentium*).

(3). a constitution based on *cosmopolitan right,* in so far as individuals and states, coexisting in an external relationship of mutual influences, may be regarded as citizens of a universal state of mankind (*ius cosmopoliticum*). This classification, with respect to the idea of a perpetual peace, is not arbitrary, but necessary. For if even one of the parties were able to influence the others physically and yet itself remained in a state of nature, there would be a risk of war, which it is precisely the aim of the above articles to prevent.

On the Art of War

(1832)

Carl von Clausewitz

Carl von Clausewitz (1780–1831) was a Prussian soldier and writer. He played a major role in reforming the Prussian army and served for twelve years as director of the Military Academy in Berlin. His great work on war was published posthumously.

CHAPTER 1 WHAT IS WAR?

1. Introduction

WE propose to consider first the single elements of our subject, then each branch or part, and, last of all, the whole, in all its relations—therefore to advance from the simple to the complex. But it is necessary for us to commence with a glance at the nature of the whole, because it is particularly necessary that in the consideration of any of the parts their relation to the whole should be kept constantly in view.

2. Definition

We shall not enter into any of the abstruse definitions of War used by publicists. We shall keep to the element of the thing itself, to a duel. War is nothing but a duel on an extensive scale. If we would conceive as a unit the countless number of duels which make up a War, we shall do so best by supposing to ourselves two wrestlers. Each strives by physical force to compel the other to submit to his will: each endeavours to throw his adversary, and thus render him incapable of further resistance.

War therefore is an act of violence intended to compel our opponent to fulfil our will.

Violence arms itself with the inventions of Art and Science in order to contend against violence. Self-imposed restrictions, almost imperceptible and hardly worth mentioning, termed usages of International Law, accompany it without essentially impairing its power. Violence, that is to say, physical force (for there is no moral force without the conception of States and Law), is therefore the *means;* the compulsory submission of the enemy to our will is the ultimate *object.* In order to attain this object fully, the enemy must be disarmed, and disarmament becomes therefore the immediate object of hostilities in theory. It takes the place of the final object, and puts it aside as something we can eliminate from our calculations.

3. Utmost use of Force

Now, philanthropists may easily imagine there is a skilful method of disarming and overcoming an enemy without causing great bloodshed, and that this is the proper tendency of the Art of War. However plausible this may appear, still it is an error which must be extirpated; for in such dangerous things as War, the errors which proceed from a spirit of benevolence are the worst. As the use of physical power to the utmost extent by no means excludes the cooperation of the intelligence, it follows that he who uses force unsparingly, without reference to the bloodshed involved, must obtain a superiority if his adversary uses less vigour in its application. The former then dictates the law to the latter, and both proceed to extremities to which the only limitations are those imposed by the amount of counter-acting force on each side.

This is the way in which the matter must be viewed, and it is to no purpose, it is even against one's own interest, to turn away from the consideration of the real nature of the affair because the horror of its elements excites repugnance.

If the Wars of civilized people are less cruel and destructive than those of savages, the difference arises from the social condition both of States in themselves and in their relations to each other. Out of this social condition and its relations War arises, and by it War is subjected to conditions, is controlled and modified. But these things do not belong to War itself; they are only given conditions; and to introduce into the philosophy of War itself a principle of moderation would be an absurdity.

Two motives lead men to War: instinctive hostility and hostile intention. In our definition of War, we have chosen as its characteristic the latter of these elements, because it is the most general. It is impossible to conceive the passion of hatred of the wildest description, bordering on mere instinct, without combining with it the idea of a hostile intention. On the other hand, hostile intentions may often exist without being accompanied by any, or at all events by any extreme, hostility of feeling. Amongst savages views emanating from the feelings, amongst civilized nations those emanating from the understanding, have the predominance; but this difference arises from attendant circumstances, existing institutions, etc., and, therefore, is not to be found necessarily in all cases, although it prevails in the majority. In short, even the most civilized nations may burn with passionate hatred of each other.

We may see from this what a fallacy it would be to refer the War of a civilized nation entirely to an intelligent act on the part of the Government, and to imagine it as continually freeing itself more and more from all feeling of passion in such a way that at last the physical masses of combatants would no longer be required; in reality, their mere relations would suffice—a kind of algebraic action.

Theory was beginning to drift in this direction until the facts of the last War taught it better. If War is an *act* of force, it belongs necessarily also to the feelings. If it does not originate in the feelings, it *reacts,* more or less, upon them, and the extent of this reaction depends not on the degree of civilization, but upon the importance and duration of the interests involved.

Therefore, if we find civilized nations do not put their prisoners to death, do not devastate towns and countries, this is because their intelligence exercises greater influence on their mode of carrying on War, and has taught them more effectual means of applying force than these rude acts of mere instinct. The invention of gunpowder, the constant progress of improvements in the construction of firearms, are sufficient proofs that the tendency to destroy the adversary which lies at the bottom of the conception of War is in no way changed or modified through the progress of civilization.

We therefore repeat our proposition, that War is an act of violence pushed to its utmost bounds; as one side dictates the law to the other, there arises a sort of reciprocal action, which logically must lead to an extreme. This is the first reciprocal action, and the first extreme with which we meet (*first reciprocal action*).

4. The Aim is to Disarm the Enemy

We have already said that the aim of all action in War is to disarm the enemy, and we shall now show that this, theoretically at least, is indispensable.

If our opponent is to be made to comply with our will, we must place him in a situation which is more oppressive to him than the sacrifice which we demand; but the disadvantages of this position must naturally not be of a transitory nature, at least in appearance, otherwise the enemy, instead of yielding, will hold out, in the prospect of a change for the better. Every change in this position which is produced by a continuation of the War should therefore be a change for the worse. The worst condition in which a belligerent can be placed is that of being completely disarmed. If, therefore, the enemy is to be reduced to submission by an act of War, he must either be positively disarmed or placed in such a position that he is threatened with it. From this it follows that the disarming or overthrow of the enemy, whichever we call it, must always be the aim of Warfare. Now War is always the shock of two hostile bodies in collision, not the action of a living power upon an inanimate mass, because an absolute state of endurance would not be making War; therefore, what we have just said as to the aim of action in War applies to both parties. Here, then, is another case of reciprocal action. As long as the enemy is not defeated, he may defeat me; then I shall be no longer my own master; he will dictate the law to me as I did to him. This is the second reciprocal action, and leads to a second extreme (*second reciprocal action*).

5. Utmost Exertion of Powers

If we desire to defeat the enemy, we must proportion our efforts to his powers of resistance. This is expressed by the product of two factors which cannot be separated, namely, *the sum of available means* and *the strength of the Will.* The sum of the available means may be estimated in a measure, as it depends (although not entirely) upon numbers; but the strength of volition is more difficult to determine, and can only be estimated to a certain extent by the strength of the motives. Granted we have obtained in this way an approximation to the strength of the power to be contended with, we can then take a review of our own means, and either increase them so as to obtain a preponderance, or, in case we have not the resources to effect this, then do our best by increasing our means as far as possible. But the adversary does the same; therefore, there is a new mutual enhancement, which, in pure conception, must create a fresh effort towards an extreme. This is the third case of reciprocal action, and a third extreme with which we meet (*third reciprocal action*).

6. Modification in the Reality

Thus reasoning in the abstract, the mind cannot stop short of an extreme, because it has to deal with an extreme, with a conflict of forces left to themselves, and obeying no other but their own inner laws. If we should seek to deduce from the pure conception of War an absolute point for the aim which we shall propose and for the means which we shall apply, this constant reciprocal action would involve us in extremes, which would be nothing but a play of ideas produced by an almost invisible train of logical subtleties. If, adhering closely to the absolute, we try to avoid all difficulties by a stroke of the pen, and insist with logical strictness that in every case the extreme must be the object, and the utmost effort must be exerted in that direction, such a stroke of the pen would be a mere paper law, not by any means adapted to the real world.

Even supposing this extreme tension of forces was an absolute which could easily be ascertained, still we must admit that the human mind would hardly submit itself to this kind of logical chimera. There would be in many cases an unnecessary waste of power, which would be in opposition to other principles of statecraft; an effort of Will would be required disproportioned to the proposed object, which therefore it would be impossible to realize, for the human will does not derive its impulse from logical subtleties.

But everything takes a different shape when we pass from abstractions to reality. In the former, everything must be subject to optimism, and we must imagine the one side as well as the other striving after perfection and even attaining it. Will this ever take place in reality? It will if,

(1) *War becomes a completely isolated act, which arises suddenly, and is in no way connected with the previous history of the combatant States.*

(2) *If it is limited to a single solution, or to several simultaneous solutions.*

(3) *If it contains within itself the solution perfect and complete, free from any reaction upon it, through a calculation beforehand of the political situation which will follow from it.*

7. War is Never an Isolated Act

With regard to the first point, neither of the two opponents is an abstract person to the other, not even as regards that factor in the sum of resistance which does not depend on objective things, viz. the Will. This Will is not an entirely unknown quantity; it indicates what it will be to-morrow by what it is today. War does not spring up quite suddenly, it does not spread to the full in a moment; each of the two opponents can, therefore, form an opinion of the other, in a great measure, from what he is and what he does, instead of judging of him according to what he, strictly speaking, should be or should do. But, now, man with his incomplete organization is always below the line of absolute perfection, and thus these deficiencies, having an influence on both sides, become a modifying principle.

8. War does not Consist of a Single Instantaneous Blow

The second point gives rise to the following considerations:

If War ended in a single solution, or a number of simultaneous ones, then naturally all the preparations for the same would have a tendency to the extreme, for an omission could not in any way be repaired; the utmost, then, that the world of reality could furnish as a guide for us would be the preparations of the enemy, as far as they are known to us; all the rest would fall into the domain of the abstract. But if the result is made up from several successive acts, then naturally that which precedes with all its phases may be taken as a measure for that which will follow, and in this manner the world of reality again takes the place of the abstract, and thus modifies the effort towards the extreme.

Yet every War would necessarily resolve itself into a single solution, or a sum of simultaneous results, if all the means required for the struggle were raised at once, or could be at once raised; for as one adverse result necessarily diminishes the means, then if all the means have been applied in the first, a second cannot properly be supposed. All hostile acts which might follow would belong essentially to the first, and form in reality only its duration.

But we have already seen that even in the preparation for War the real world steps into the place of mere abstract conception—a material standard into the place of the hypotheses of an extreme: that therefore in that way both parties, by the influence of the mutual reaction, remain below the line of extreme effort, and therefore all forces are not at once brought forward.

It lies also in the nature of these forces and their application that they cannot all be brought into activity at the same time. These forces are *the armies actually on foot, the country,* with its superficial extent and its population, *and the allies.*

In point of fact, the country, with its superficial area and the population, besides being the source of all military force, constitutes in itself an integral part of the efficient quantities in War, providing either the theatre of war or exercising a considerable influence on the same.

Now, it is possible to bring all the movable military forces of a country into operation at once, but not all fortresses, rivers, mountains, people, etc.—in short, not the whole country, unless it is so small that it may be completely embraced by the first act of the War. Further, the cooperation of allies does not depend on the Will of the belligerents; and from the nature of the political relations of states to each other, this cooperation is frequently not afforded until after the War has commenced, or it may be increased to restore the balance of power.

That this part of the means of resistance, which cannot at once be brought into activity, in many cases, is a much greater part of the whole than might at first be supposed, and that it often restores the balance of power, seriously affected by the great force of the first decision, will be more fully shown hereafter. Here it is sufficient to show that a complete concentration of all available means in a moment of time is contradictory to the nature of War.

Now this, in itself, furnishes no ground for relaxing our efforts to accumulate strength to gain the first result, because an unfavourable issue is always a disadvantage to which no one would purposely expose himself, and also because the first decision, although not the only one, still will have the more influence on subsequent events, the greater it is in itself.

But the possibility of gaining a later result causes men to take refuge in that expectation, owing to the repugnance in the human mind to making excessive efforts; and therefore forces are not concentrated and measures are not taken for the first decision with that energy which would otherwise be used. Whatever one belligerent omits from weakness, becomes to the other a real objective ground for limiting his own efforts, and thus again, through this reciprocal action, extreme tendencies are brought down to efforts on a limited scale.

9. The Result in War is Never Absolute

Lastly, even the final decision of a whole War is not always to be regarded as absolute. The conquered State often sees in it only a passing evil, which may be repaired in after times by means of political combinations. How much this must modify the degree of tension, and the vigour of the efforts made, is evident in itself.

• • •

21. War is a Game Both Objectively and Subjectively

If we now take a look at the *subjective nature* of War, that is to say, at those conditions under which it is carried on, it will appear to us still more like a game. Primarily the element in which the operations of War are carried on is danger; but which of all the moral qualities is the first in danger? *Courage.* Now certainly courage is quite compatible with prudent calculation, but still they are things of quite a different kind, essentially different qualities of the mind; on the other hand, daring reliance on good fortune, boldness, rashness, are only expressions of courage, and all these propensities of the mind look for the fortuitous (or accidental), because it is their element.

We see, therefore, how, from the commencement, the absolute, the mathematical as it is called, nowhere finds any sure basis in the calculations in the Art of War; and that from the outset there is a play of possibilities, probabilities, good and bad luck, which spreads about with all the coarse and fine threads of its web, and makes War of all branches of human activity the most like a gambling game.

22. How this Accords Best with the Human Mind in General

Although our intellect always feels itself urged towards clearness and certainty, still our mind often feels itself attracted by uncertainty. Instead of threading its way with the understanding along the narrow path of philosophical investigations and logical conclusions, in order, almost unconscious of itself, to arrive in spaces where it feels itself a stranger, and where it seems to part from all well-known objects, it prefers to remain with the imagination in the realms of chance and luck. Instead of living yonder on poor necessity, it revels here in the wealth of possibilities; animated thereby, courage then takes wings to itself, and daring and danger make the element into which it launches itself as a fearless swimmer plunges into the stream.

Shall theory leave it here, and move on, self-satisfied with absolute conclusions and rules? Then it is of no practical use. Theory must also take into account the human element; it must accord a place to courage, to boldness, even to rashness. The Art of War has to deal with living and with moral forces, the consequence of which is that it can never attain the absolute and positive. There is therefore everywhere a margin for the accidental, and just as much in the greatest things as in the smallest. As there is room for this accidental on the one hand, so on the other there must be courage and self-reliance in proportion to the room available. If these qualities are forthcoming in a high degree, the margin left may likewise be great. Courage and self-reliance are, therefore, principles quite essential to War; consequently, theory must only set up such rules as allow ample scope for all degrees and varieties of these necessary and noblest of military virtues. In daring there may still be wisdom, and prudence as well, only they are estimated by a different standard of value.

23. War is Always a Serious Means for a Serious Object. Its more Particular Definition

Such is War; such the Commander who conducts it; such the theory which rules it. But War is no pastime; no mere passion for venturing and winning; no work of a free enthusiasm: it is a serious means for a serious object. All that appearance which it wears from the varying hues of fortune, all that it assimilates into itself of the oscillations of passion, of courage, of imagination, of enthusiasm, are only particular properties of this means.

The War of a community—of whole Nations, and particularly of civilized Nations—always starts from a political condition, and is called forth by a political motive. It is, therefore, a political act. Now if it was a perfect, unrestrained, and absolute expression of force, as we had to deduce it from its mere conception, then the moment it is called forth by policy it would step into the place of policy, and as something quite independent of it would set it aside, and only follow its own laws, just as a mine at the moment of explosion cannot be guided into any other direction than that which has been given to it by preparatory arrangements. This is how the thing has really been viewed hitherto, whenever a want of harmony between policy and the conduct of a War has led to theoretical distinctions of the kind. But it is not so, and the idea is radically false. War in the real world, as we have already seen, is not an extreme thing which expends itself at one single discharge; it is the operation of powers which do not develop themselves completely in the same manner and in the same measure, but which at one time expand sufficiently to overcome the resistance opposed by inertia or friction, while at another they are too weak to produce an effect; it is therefore, in a certain measure, a pulsation of violent force more or less vehement, consequently making its discharges and exhausting its powers more or less quickly—in other words, conducting more or less quickly to the aim, but always lasting long enough to admit of influence being exerted on it in its course, so as to give it this or that direction, in short, to be subject to the will of a guiding intelligence. Now, if we reflect that War has its root in a political object, then naturally this original motive which called it into existence should also continue the first and highest consideration in its conduct. Still, the political object is no despotic lawgiver on that account; it must accommodate itself to the nature of the means, and though changes in these means may involve modification in the political objective, the latter always retains a prior right to consideration. Policy, therefore, is interwoven with the whole action of War, and must exercise a continuous influence upon it, as far as the nature of the forces liberated by it will permit.

24. War is a Mere Continuation of Policy by Other Means

We see, therefore, that War is not merely a political act, but also a real political instrument, a continuation of political commerce, a carrying out of the same by other means. All beyond this which is strictly peculiar to War relates merely to the peculiar nature of the means which it uses. That the tendencies and views of policy shall not be incompatible with these means, the Art of War in general and the Commander in each particular case may demand, and this claim is truly not a trifling one. But however powerfully this may react on political views in particular cases, still it must always be regarded as only a modification of them; for the political view is the object, War is the means, and the means must always include the object in our conception.

On the Duty of Civil Disobedience

(1849)

Henry David Thoreau

Henry David Thoreau (1817–1862) was born in Massachusetts and educated at Harvard. He was a famous recluse and anarchist who spent much of his life living in the wild. His essay on civil disobedience was his best-known work.

I heartily accept the motto,—"That government is best which governs least;" and I should like to see it acted up to more rapidly and systematically. Carried out, it finally amounts to this, which also I believe,—"That government is best which governs not at all;" and when men are prepared for it, that will be the kind of government which they will have. Government is at best but an expedient; but most governments are usually, and all governments are sometimes, inexpedient. The objections which have been brought against a standing army, and they are many and weighty, and deserve to prevail, may also at last be brought against a standing government. The standing army is only an arm of the standing government. The government itself, which is only the mode which the people have chosen to execute their will, is equally liable to be abused and perverted before the people can act through it. Witness the present Mexican war, the work of comparatively a few individuals using the standing government as their tool; for, in the outset, the people would not have consented to this measure.

This American government,—what is it but a tradition, though a recent one, endeavoring to transmit itself unimpaired to posterity, but each instant losing some of its integrity? It has not the vitality and force of a single living man; for a single man can bend it to his will. It is a sort of wooden gun to the people themselves; and, if ever they should use it in earnest as a real one against each other, it will surely split. But it is not the less necessary for this; for the people must have some complicated machinery or other, and hear its din, to satisfy that idea of government which they have. Governments show thus how successfully men can be imposed on, even impose on themselves, for their own advantage. It is excellent, we must all allow; yet this government never of itself furthered any enterprise, but by the alacrity with which it got out of its way. *It* does not keep the country free. *It* does not settle the West. *It* does not educate. The character inherent in the American people has done all that has been accomplished; and it would have done somewhat more, if the government had not sometimes got in its way. For government is an expedient by which men would fain succeed in letting one another alone; and, as has been said, when it is most expedient, the governed are most let alone by it. Trade and commerce, if they were not made of India rubber, would never manage to bounce over the obstacles which legislators are continually putting in their way; and, if one were to judge these men wholly by the effects of their actions, and not partly by their intentions, they would deserve to be classed and punished with those mischievous persons who put obstructions on the railroads.

But, to speak practically and as a citizen, unlike those who call themselves no-government men, I ask for, not at once no government, but *at once* a better government. Let every man make known what kind of government would command his respect, and that will be one step toward obtaining it.

After all, the practical reason why, when the power is once in the hands of the people, a majority are permitted, and for a long period continue, to rule, is not because they are most likely to be in the right, nor because this seems fairest to the minority, but because they are physically the strongest. But a government in which the majority rule in all cases cannot be based on justice, even as far as men understand it. Can there not be a government in which majorities do not virtually decide right and wrong, but conscience?—in which majorities decide only those questions to which the rule of expediency is applicable? Must the citizen ever for a moment, or in the least degree, resign his conscience, to the legislator? Why has every man a conscience, then? I think that we should be men first, and subjects afterward. It is not desirable to cultivate a respect for the law, so much as for the right. The only obligation which I have a right to assume, is to do at any time what I think right. It is truly enough said, that a corporation has no conscience; but a corporation of conscientious men is a corporation *with* a conscience. Law never made men a whit more just; and, by means of their respect for it, even the well-disposed are daily made the agents of injustice. A common and natural result of an undue respect for law is, that you may see a file of soldiers, colonel, captain, corporal, privates, powder-monkeys and all, marching in admirable order over hill and dale to the wars, against their wills, aye, against their common sense and consciences, which makes it very steep marching indeed, and produces a palpitation of the heart. They have no doubt that it is a damnable business in which they are concerned; they are all peaceably inclined. Now, what are they? Men at all? or small moveable forts and magazines, at the service of some unscrupulous man in power? Visit the Navy Yard, and behold a marine, such a man as an American government can make, or such as it can make a man with its black arts, a mere shadow and reminiscence of humanity, a man laid out alive and standing, and already, as one may say, buried under arms with funeral accompaniments, though it may be

> Not a drum was heard, nor a funeral note,
> As his corpse to the ramparts we
>   hurried;
> Not a soldier discharged his farewell shot
> O'er the grave where our hero we buried.

The mass of men serve the State thus, not as men mainly, but as machines, with their bodies. They are the standing army, and the militia, jailers, constables, *posse comitatus,* &c. In most cases there is no free exercise whatever of the judgment or of the moral sense; but they put themselves on a level with wood and earth and stones; and wooden men can perhaps be manufactured that will serve the purpose as well. Such command no more respect than men of straw, or a lump of dirt. They have the same sort of worth only as horses and dogs. Yet such as these even are commonly esteemed good citizens. Others, as most legislators, politicians, lawyers, ministers, and office-holders, serve the State chiefly with their heads; and, as they rarely make any moral distinctions, they are as likely to serve the devil, without intending it, as God. A very few, as heroes, patriots, martyrs, reformers in the great sense, and *men,* serve the State with their consciences also, and so necessarily resist it for the most part; and they are commonly treated by it as enemies. A wise man will only be useful as a man, and will not submit to be "clay," and "stop a hole to keep the wind away," but leave that office to his dust at least:—

> I am too high-born to be propertied,
> To be a secondary at control,
> Or useful serving-man and instrument
> To any sovereign state throughout the
>   world.

He who gives himself entirely to his fellow-men appears to them useless and selfish: but he who gives himself partially to them is pronounced a benefactor and philanthropist.

How does it become a man to behave toward this American government to-day? I answer that he cannot without disgrace be associated with it. I cannot for an instant recognize that political organization as *my* government which is the *slave's* government also.

All men recognize the right of revolution; that is, the right to refuse allegiance to and to resist the government, when its tyranny or its inefficiency are great and unendurable. But almost all say that such is not the case now. But such was the case, they think, in the Revolution of '75. If one were to tell me that this was a bad government because it taxed certain foreign commodities brought to its ports, it is most probable that I should not make an ado about it, for I can do without them: all machines have their friction; and possibly this does enough good to counterbalance the evil. At any rate, it is a great evil to make a stir about it. But when the friction comes to have its machine, and oppression and robbery are organized, I say, let us not have such a machine any longer. In other words, when a sixth of the population of a nation which has undertaken to be the refuge of liberty are slaves, and a whole country is unjustly overrun and conquered by a foreign army, and subjected to military law, I think that it is not too soon for honest men to rebel and revolutionize. What makes this duty the more urgent is the fact, that the country so overrun is not our own, but ours is the invading army.

Paley, a common authority with many on moral questions, in his chapter on the "Duty of Submission to Civil Government," resolves all civil obligation into expediency; and he proceeds to say, "that so long as the interest of the whole society requires it, that is, so long as the established government cannot be resisted or changed without public inconveniency, it is the will of God, that the established government be obeyed, and no longer."— "This principle being admitted, the justice of every particular case of resistance is reduced to a computation of the quantity of the danger and grievance on the one side, and of the probability and expense of redressing it on the other." Of this, he says, every man shall judge for himself. But Paley appears never to have contemplated those cases to which the rule of expediency does not apply, in which a people, as well as an individual, must do justice, cost what it may. If I have unjustly wrested a plank from a drowning man, I must restore it to him though I drown myself. This, according to Paley, would be inconvenient. But he that would save his life, in such a case, shall lose it. This people must cease to hold slaves, and to make war on Mexico, though it cost them their existence as a people.

In their practice, nations agree with Paley; but does any one think that Massachusetts does exactly what is right at the present crisis?

> A drab of state, a cloth-o'-silver slut,
> To have her train borne up, and her soul
>   trail in the dirt.

Practically speaking, the opponents to a reform in Massachusetts are not a hundred thousand politicians at the South, but a hundred thousand merchants and farmers here, who are more interested in commerce and agriculture than they are in humanity, and are not prepared to do justice to the slave and to Mexico, *cost what it may*. I quarrel not with far-off foes, but with those who, near at home, co-operate with, and do the bidding of those far away, and without whom the latter would be harmless. We are accustomed to say, that the mass of men are unprepared; but improvement is slow, because the few are not materially wiser or better than the many. It is not so important that many should be as good as you, as that there be some absolute goodness somewhere; for that will leaven the whole lump. There are thousands who are *in opinion* opposed to slavery and to the war, who yet in effect do nothing to put an end to them; who, esteeming themselves children of Washington and Franklin, sit down with their hands in their pockets, and say that they know not what to do, and do nothing; who even postpone the question of freedom to the question of free-trade, and quietly read the prices-current along with the latest advices from Mexico, after dinner, and, it may be, fall asleep over them both. What is the price-current of an honest man and patriot to-day? They hesitate, and they regret, and sometimes they petition; but they do nothing in earnest and with effect. They will wait, well disposed, for others to remedy the evil, that they may no longer have it to regret. At most, they give only a cheap vote, and a feeble countenance and Godspeed, to the right, as it goes by them. There are nine hundred and ninety-nine patrons of virtue to one virtuous man; but it is easier to deal with the real possessor of a thing than with the temporary guardian of it.

All voting is a sort of gaming, like checquers or backgammon, with a slight moral tinge to it, a playing with right and wrong, with moral questions; and betting naturally accompanies it. The character of the voters is not staked. I cast my vote, perchance, as I think right; but I am not vitally concerned that that right should prevail. I am willing to leave it to the majority. Its obligation, therefore, never exceeds that of expediency. Even voting *for the right* is *doing* nothing for it. It is only expressing to men feebly your desire that it should prevail. A wise man will not leave the right to the mercy of chance, nor wish it to prevail through the power of the majority. There is but little virtue in the action of masses of men. When the majority shall at length vote for the abolition of slavery, it will be because they are indifferent to slavery, or because there is but little slavery left to be abolished by their vote. *They* will then be the only slaves. Only *his* vote can hasten the abolition of slavery who asserts his own freedom by his vote.

I hear of a convention to be held at Baltimore, or elsewhere, for the selection of a candidate for the Presidency, made up chiefly of editors, and men who are politicians by profession; but I think, what is it to any independent, intelligent, and respectable man what decision they may come to, shall we not have the advantage of his wisdom and honesty, nevertheless? Can we not count upon some independent votes? Are there not many individuals in the country who do not attend conventions? But no: I find that the respectable man, so called, has immediately drifted from his position, and despairs of his country, when his country has more reason to despair of him. He forthwith adopts one of the candidates thus selected as the only *available* one, thus proving that he is himself *available* for any purposes of the demagogue. His vote is of no more worth than that of any unprincipled foreigner or hireling native, who may have been bought. Oh for a man who is a *man,* and, as my neighbor says, has a bone in his back which you cannot pass your hand through! Our statistics are at fault: the population has been returned too large. How many *men* are there to a square thousand miles in this country? Hardly one. Does not America offer any inducement for men to settle here? The American has dwindled into an Odd Fellow,—one who may be known by the development of his organ of gregariousness, and a manifest lack of intellect and cheerful self-reliance; whose first and chief concern, on coming into the world, is to see that the almshouses are in good repair; and, before yet he has lawfully donned the virile garb, to collect a fund for the support of the widows and orphans that may be; who, in short, ventures to live only by the aid of the mutual insurance company, which has promised to bury him decently.

It is not a man's duty, as a matter of course, to devote himself to the eradication of any, even the most enormous wrong; he may still properly have other concerns to engage him; but it is his duty, at least, to wash his hands of it, and, if he gives it no thought longer, not to give it practically

"A man cannot govern a nation if he cannot govern a city; he cannot govern a city if he cannot govern a family; he cannot govern a family unless he can govern himself; and he cannot govern himself unless his passions are subject to reason."

...self to other pur-
...I must first see,
...sue them sitting
...ders. I must get
...pursue his con-
...gross inconsis-
...eard some of my
...ke to have them
...wn an insurrec-
...ch to Mexico,—
...these very men
...allegiance, and
...eir money, fur-
...soldier is ap-
...e in an unjust
...fuse to sustain
...ich makes the
...whose own act
...s and sets at
...re penitent to
...e to scourge it
...at degree that
...oment. Thus,
...l civil govern-
...t to pay hom-
...wn meanness.
...mes its indif-
...becomes, as it
...unnecessary
...de.
...evalent error
...ted virtue to
...to which the
...ly liable, the
...: Those who,
...haracter and
...ld to it their
...undoubtedly
...ters, and so
...stacles to re-
...he State to
...d the requi-
...do they not
...ion between

themselves and the State,—and refuse to pay their quota into its treasury? Do not they stand in the same relation to the State, that the State does to the Union? And have not the same reasons prevented the State from resisting the Union, which have prevented them from resisting the State?

How can a man be satisfied to entertain an opinion merely, and enjoy *it?* Is there any enjoyment in it, if his opinion is that he is aggrieved? If you are cheated out of a single dollar by your neighbor, you do not rest satisfied with knowing that you are cheated or with saying that you are cheated, or even with petitioning him to pay you your due; but you take effectual steps at once to obtain the full amount, and see that you are never cheated again. Action from principle,—the perception and the performance of right,—changes things and relations; it is essentially revolutionary, and does not consist wholly with any thing which was. It not only divides states and churches, it divides families, aye, it divides the *individual,* separating the diabolical in him from the divine.

Unjust laws exist; shall we be content to obey them, or shall we endeavor to amend them, and obey them until we have succeeded, or shall we transgress them at once? Men generally, under such a government as this, think that they ought to wait until they have persuaded the majority to alter them. They think that, if they should resist, the remedy would be worse than the evil. But it is the fault of the government itself that the remedy *is* worse than the evil. *It* makes it worse. Why is it not more apt to anticipate and provide for reform? Why does it not cherish its wise minority? Why does it cry and resist before it is hurt? Why does it not encourage its citizens to be on the alert to point out its faults, and *do* better than it would have them? Why does it always crucify Christ, and excommunicate Copernicus and Luther, and pronounce Washington and Franklin rebels?

One would think, that a deliberate and practical denial of its authority, was the only offense never contemplated by government; else, why has it not assigned its definite, its suitable and proportionate penalty? If a man who has no property refuses but once to earn nine shillings for the State, he is put in prison for a period unlimited by any law that I know, and determined only by the discretion of those who placed him there; but if he should steal ninety times nine shillings from the State, he is soon permitted to go at large again.

If the injustice is part of the necessary friction of the machine of government, let it go, let it go; perchance it will wear smooth,—certainly the machine will wear out. If the injustice has a spring, or a pulley, or a rope, or a crank, exclusively for itself, then perhaps you may consider whether the remedy will not be worse than the evil; but if it is of such a nature that it requires you to be the agent of injustice to another, then, I say, break the law. Let your life be a counter friction to stop the machine. What I have to do is to see, at any rate, that I do not lend myself to the wrong which I condemn.

As for adopting the ways which the State has provided for remedying the evil, I know not of such ways. They take too much time, and a man's life will be gone. I have other affairs to attend to. I came into this world, not chiefly to make this a good place to live in, but to live in it, be it good or bad. A man has not every thing to do, but something; and because he cannot do *every thing,* it is not necessary that he should do *something* wrong. It is not my business to

be petitioning the governor or the legislature any more than it is theirs to petition me; and, if they should not hear my petition, what should I do then? But in this case the State has provided no way: its very Constitution is the evil. This may seem to be harsh and stubborn and unconciliatory; but it is to treat with the utmost kindness and consideration the only spirit that can appreciate or deserve it. So is all change for the better, like birth and death which convulse the body.

I do not hesitate to say, that those who call themselves abolitionists should at once effectually withdraw their support, both in person and property, from the government of Massachusetts, and not wait till they constitute a majority of one, before they suffer the right to prevail through them. I think that it is enough if they have God on their side, without waiting for that other one. Moreover, any man more right than his neighbors, constitutes a majority of one already.

• • •

The authority of government, even such as I am willing to submit to,—for I will cheerfully obey those who know and can do better than I, and in many things even those who neither know nor can do so well,—is still an impure one: to be strictly just, it must have the sanction and consent of the governed. It can have no pure right over my person and property but what I concede to it. The progress from an absolute to a limited monarchy, from a limited monarchy to a democracy, is a progress toward a true respect for the individual. Is a democracy, such as we know it, the last improvement possible in government? Is it not possible to take a step further towards recognizing and organizing the rights of man? There will never be a really free and enlightened State, until the

State comes to recognize the individual as a higher and independent power, from which all its own power and authority are derived, and treats him accordingly. I please myself with imagining a State at last which can afford to be just to all men, and to treat the individual with respect as a neighbor; which even would not think it inconsistent with its own repose, if a few were to live aloof from it, not meddling with it, nor embraced by it, who fulfilled all the duties of neighbors and fellow-men. A State which bore this kind of fruit, and suffered it to drop off as fast as it ripened, would prepare the way for a still more perfect and glorious State, which also I have imagined, but not yet anywhere seen.

Vietnam stay in Cambodia → humanity intervention → become responsibility · of humanity paradige

PART II

CONTEMPORARY MORAL FOUNDATIONS

A. Pacifism and the Credibility of the Just War Tradition

War has traditionally meant intentional mass killing, the destruction of property and resources, and forced displacement. As a result, it is crucial to ask at the outset why war would ever be morally justified. Why would not pacifism, generally the refusal to engage in war, morally always be demanded of everyone? Just War theorists must be able to provide an adequate answer to this question. And even if good reasons can be given, Just War theorists must provide a good explanation of the moral conditions that must be met before a state can engage in war. In addition, they must be able to state what kind of war or what kind of conduct in war is morally permissible. Certainly, to be morally justified, not any reason justifies engaging in war and not any type of conduct in war is morally permissible.

We begin this section with William James's article titled "The Moral Equivalent of War." In his article, James attempts to explain what motivates war, and he attempts to provide a substitute for war. In light of the inevitable mass killing and destruction in war, James finds any motivation for war misguided. For James, war is irrational, and the more monstrous and destructive the weapons of war become, the more irrational war is.

Yet, at the same time, James thinks that many people rightly value the sense of duty, pride, good order, and discipline instilled by military institutions and military training. James argues that pacifists need to appropriate and promote these "martial virtues" or these "human goods" that have been associated with military exercises and campaigns. These human goods, according to James, can and should be fostered without war. Instead of military conscription, James posits a conscription of youth "against *Nature*." For James, a martial type of character should be "bred" not from military participation but from forced participation in "civic" projects such as working in "coal and iron mines," "clothes-washing," and "road-building." According to James, "The only thing needed henceforward is to inflame the civic temper as past history has inflamed the military temper."

In his article "Pacifism: A Philosophical Analysis," Jan Narveson argues that pacifism as a moral principle is incoherent. He also claims that while conscientious objectors are not necessarily cowards or traitors, they are confused. For Narveson, these conclusions are based on the fact that pacifists, who are committed to pacifism as a moral principle (rather than as a matter of personal preference), are committed to the conclusion that everyone has a moral duty to refrain from using violence against others. This duty, according to Narveson, entails that everyone has a right not to be harmed by others. And having this right, for Narveson, means that every person is committed to doing what is "enough" to prevent people from being harmed. When aggressors fail to listen to rational persuasion, Narveson concludes that doing what is "enough" means using force.

Narveson also argues that since pacifists could not possibly think that all criminals should be set free, they must think that force can be used for self-protection and the protection of others. For Narveson, pacifists are confused if they think that a state is justified in punishing and confining criminals but that a state is unjustified in using force to repel the combatants of an aggressor state. When states use force against criminals and when states use force to repel the combatants of an aggressor state, the use of force is employed for exactly the same reason: It is necessary to protect citizens.

At least some criticism of Narveson's article might stem from his notion of a right not to be harmed. While a duty to refrain from violence might entail a right not to be harmed, it is not at all clear that this right necessarily leads to the conclusion that one is sometimes justified in participating in war. Is Narveson correct in thinking that a right to use force to prevent harm can be inferred from a right not to be harmed? And, even if this further right is granted Narveson, would not the amount or kind of force allowed be limited by other rights or moral principles? If war itself is immoral or monstrous or an atrocity, then it might not ever be morally acceptable to engage in war to prevent harm. Even if there is a right to use force to protect citizens from criminals, it seems that it could still be argued that war presents a different set of moral concerns that override any right to use force.

Stanley Hauerwas claims that it would be a "philosophical mistake" to try to provide a philosophical foundation for pacifism. In his article, "Pacifism: Some Philosophical Considerations," Hauerwas claims that pacifism is not "intelligible" apart from "the theological convictions that form it." According to Hauerwas, since pacifists are always obligated to resist injustice, the crucial question is *how* they are to resist. Christian pacifists are committed to the claim that attackers are also objects of God's love, and as a result, the Christian pacifist has moral obligations to an attacker. Attackers do not automatically forfeit their right to life, and attacking soldiers are not necessarily guilty.

For Hauerwas, pacifism is not a duty or a strategy for dealing with violence. Rather, it is a way of life. Pacifism is much closer to an ethics of virtue. Hauerwas states that a life committed to nonviolence is an affirmation of the truth or the moral way to live in a world in which evil exists, and its moral and "rational power" depends on the "existence of examples, that is, people who have learned to live nonviolently." While some have thought that a pacifist must be an anarchist, Hauerwas disagrees. Hauerwas argues that being a good citizen means being committed to actions that contribute to the common good of the state, and he concludes that a pacifist is certainly a good citizen in this respect.

The final selection in this section offers a slightly different challenge to the credibility of the Just War tradition. Among other reasons, John Yoder, in *When War is Unjust: Being Honest in Just War Thinking* offers the following three reasons why the Just War tradition in the past has lacked credibility. First, he argues that the condition of "last resort" has not been met. It has not been met because governments have failed to exhaust all available methods of international arbitration and because governments have failed to provide adequate resources, that is, people, training and money, for establishing and implementing nonviolent alternatives to war. Second, Yoder claims that in the past adequate information regarding the conflict or aggression has been lacking and public debate pertaining to the relevant moral conditions and responses has been avoided. Third, Yoder argues that the Just War tradition lacks credibility because Just War theorists have failed to oppose wars for reasons consistent with the tradition. Yoder concludes, "If the tradition which claims that war may be justified does not also admit that in particular cases it may *not* be justified, the affirmation is not morally serious."

The Moral Equivalent of War

(1910)

William James

William James was for many years professor of philosophy at Harvard. He resigned his professorship in 1907 at the age of sixty-five and died in 1910. He wrote and lectured widely on a variety of topics in or related to philosophy. Some of his well-known writings are Principles of Psychology *(1890),* The Varieties of Religious Experience *(1902),* Pragmatism *(1907), and* A Pluralistic Universe *(1909).*

The war against war is going to be no holiday excursion or camping party. The military feelings are too deeply grounded to abdicate their place among our ideals until better substitutes are offered than the glory and shame that come to nations as well as to individuals from the ups and downs of politics and the vicissitudes of trade. There is something highly paradoxical in the modern man's relation to war. Ask all our millions, north and south, whether they would vote now (were such a thing possible) to have our war for the Union expunged from history, and the record of a peaceful transition to the present time substituted for that of its marches and battles, and probably hardly a handful of eccentrics would say yes. Those ancestors, those efforts, those memories and legends, are the most ideal part of what we now own together, a sacred spiritual possession worth more than all the blood poured out. Yet ask those same people whether they would be willing in cold blood to start another civil war now to gain another similar possession, and not one man or woman would vote for the proposition. In modern eyes, precious though wars may be, they must not be waged solely for the sake of the ideal harvest. Only when forced upon one, only when an enemy's injustice leaves us no alternative, is a war now thought permissible.

It was not thus in ancient times. The earlier men were hunting men, and to hunt a neighboring tribe, kill the males, loot the village and possess the females, was the most profitable, as well as the most exciting, way of living. Thus were the more martial tribes selected, and in chiefs and peoples a pure pugnacity and love of glory came to mingle with the more fundamental appetite for plunder.

Modern war is so expensive that we feel trade to be a better avenue to plunder; but modern man inherits all the innate pugnacity and all the love of glory of his ancestors. Showing war's irrationality and horror is of no effect upon him. The horrors make the fascination. War is the *strong* life; it is life *in extremis;* war-taxes are the only ones men never hesitate to pay, as the budgets of all nations show us. . . .

At the present day, civilized opinion is a curious mental mixture. The military instincts and ideals are as strong as ever, but are confronted by reflective criticisms which sorely curb their ancient freedom. Innumerable writers are showing up the bestial side of military service. Pure loot and mastery seem no longer morally avowable motives, and pretexts must be found for attributing them solely to the enemy. England and we, our army and navy authorities repeat without ceasing, arm solely for "peace," Germany and Japan it is who are bent on loot and glory. "Peace" in military mouths today is a synonym for "war expected." The word has become a pure provocative, and no government wishing peace sincerely should allow it ever to be printed in a newspaper. Every up-to-date dictionary should say that "peace" and "war" mean the same thing, now *in posse,* now *in actu.* It may even reasonably be said that the intensely sharp competitive *preparation* for war by the nations *is the real war,* permanent, unceasing; and that the battles are only a sort of public verification of the mastery gained during the "peace" interval.

It is plain that on this subject civilized man has developed a sort of double personality. If we take European nations, no legitimate interest of any one of them would seem to justify the tremendous destructions which a war to compass it would necessarily entail. It would seem as though common sense and reason ought to find a way to reach agreement in every conflict of honest interests. I myself think it our bounden duty to believe in such international rationality as possible. But, as things stand, I see how desperately hard it is to bring the peace-party and the war-party together, and I believe that the difficulty is due to certain deficiencies in the program of pacifism which set the militarist imagination strongly, and to a cer-

tain extent justifiably, against it. In the whole discussion both sides are on imaginative and sentimental ground. It is but one utopia against another, and everything one says must be abstract and hypothetical. Subject to this criticism and caution, I will try to characterize in abstract strokes the opposite imaginative forces, and point out what to my own very fallible mind seems the best utopian hypothesis, the most promising line of conciliation.

In my remarks, pacificist though I am, I will refuse to speak of the bestial side of the war-*regime* (already done justice to by many writers) and consider only the higher aspects of militaristic sentiment. Patriotism no one thinks discreditable; nor does any one deny that war is the romance of history. But inordinate ambitions are the soul of every patriotism, and the possibility of violent death the soul of all romance. The military patriotic and romantic-minded everywhere, and especially the professional military class, refuse to admit for a moment that war may be a transitory phenomenon in social evolution. The notion of a sheep's paradise like that revolts, they say, our higher imagination. Where then would be the steeps of life? If war had ever stopped, we should have to re-invent it, on this view, to redeem life from flat degeneration.

Reflective apologists for war at the present day all take it religiously. It is a sort of sacrament. Its profits are to the vanquished as well as to the victor; and quite apart from any question of profit, it is an absolute good, we are told, for it is human nature at its highest dynamic. Its "horrors" are a cheap price to pay for rescue from the only alternative supposed, of a world of clerks and teachers, of co-education and zo-ophily, of "consumer's leagues" and "associated charities," of industrialism unlimited, and feminism unabashed. No scorn, no hardness, no valor any more! Fie upon such a cattleyard of a planet!

So far as the central essence of this feeling goes, no healthy minded person, it seems to me, can help to some degree partaking of it. Militarism is the great preserver of our ideals of hardihood, and human life with no use for hardihood would be contemptible. Without risks or prizes for the darer, history would be insipid indeed; and there is a type of military character which every one feels that the race should never cease to breed, for every one is sensitive to its superiority. The duty is incumbent on mankind, of keeping military characters in stock—of keeping them, if not for use, then as ends in themselves and as pure pieces of perfection,—so that Roosevelt's weaklings and mollycoddles may not end by making everything else disappear from the face of nature.

This natural sort of feeling forms, I think, the innermost soul of army-writings. Without any exception known to me, militarist authors take a highly mystical view of their subject, and regard war as a biological or sociological necessity, uncontrolled by ordinary psychological checks and motives. When the time of development is ripe the war must come, reason or no reason, for the justifications pleaded are invariably fictitious. War is, in short, a permanent human *obligation*. General Homer Lea, in his recent book "The Valor of Ignorance," plants himself squarely on this ground. Readiness for war is for him the essence of nationality, and ability in it the supreme measure of the health of nations. . . .

Other militarists are more complex and more moral in their considerations. The "Philosophie des Krieges," by S. R. Steinmetz is a good example. . . .

Dr. Steinmetz is a conscientious thinker, and his book, short as it is, takes much into account. Its upshot can, it seems to me, be summed up in Simon Patten's word, that mankind was nursed in pain and fear, and that the transition to a "pleasure-economy" may be fatal to a being wielding no powers of defense against its disintegrative influences. If we speak of the *fear of emancipation from the fear-regime,* we put the whole situation into a single phrase; fear regarding ourselves now taking the place of the ancient fear of the enemy.

Turn the fear over as I will in my mind, it all seems to lead back to two unwillingnesses of the imagination, one aesthetic, and the other moral; unwillingness, first to envisage a future in which army-life, with its many elements of charm, shall be forever impossible, and in which the destinies of peoples shall nevermore be decided quickly, thrillingly, and tragically, by force, but only gradually and insipidly by "evolution"; and, secondly, unwillingness to see the supreme theatre of human strenuousness closed, and the splendid military aptitudes of men doomed to keep always in a state of latency and never show themselves in action. These insistent unwillingnesses, no less than other aesthetic and ethical insistencies, have, it seems to me, to be listened to and respected. One cannot meet them effectively by mere counter-insistency on war's expensiveness and horror. The horror makes the thrill; and when the question is of getting the extremest and supremest out of human nature, talk of expense sounds ignominious. The weakness of so much merely negative criticism is evident—pacifism makes no converts from the military party. The military party denies neither the bestiality nor the horror, nor the expense; it only says that these things tell but half the story. It only says that war is *worth* them; that, taking human nature as a whole, its wars are its best protection against its weaker and more cowardly self, and that mankind cannot *afford* to adopt a peace-economy.

Pacificists ought to enter more deeply into the aesthetical and ethical point of view of their opponents. Do that first in any controversy, says J. J. Chapman, *then move the point,* and your opponent will follow. So long as anti-militarists propose no substitute for war's disciplinary function, no *moral equivalent* of war, analogous, as one might say, to the mechanical equivalent of heat, so long they fail to realize the full inwardness of the situation. And as a rule they do fail. The duties, penalties, and sanctions pictured in the utopias they paint are all too weak and tame to touch the military-minded. Tolstoi's pacificism is the only exception to this rule, for it is profoundly pessimistic as regards all this world's values, and makes the fear of the Lord furnish the moral spur provided elsewhere by the fear of the enemy. But our socialistic peace-advocates all believe absolutely in this world's values; and instead of the fear of the Lord and the fear of the enemy, the only fear they reckon with is the fear of poverty if one be lazy. This weakness pervades all the socialistic literature with which I am acquainted. Even in Lowes Dickinson's exquisite dialogue,[1] high wages and short hours are the only forces invoked for overcoming man's distaste for repulsive kinds of labor. Meanwhile men at large still live as they always have lived, under a pain-and-fear economy—for those of us who live in an ease-economy are but an island in the stormy ocean—and the whole atmosphere of present-day utopian literature tastes mawkish and dish-

watery to people who still keep a sense for life's more bitter flavors. It suggests, in truth, ubiquitous inferiority.

Inferiority is always with us, and merciless scorn of it is the keynote of the military temper. "Dogs, would you live forever?" shouted Frederick the Great. "Yes," say our utopians, "let us live forever, and raise our level gradually." The best thing about our "inferiors" to-day is that they are as tough as nails, and physically and morally almost as insensitive. Utopianism would see them soft and squeamish, while militarism would keep their callousness, but transfigure it into a meritorious characteristic, needed by "the service," and redeemed by that from the suspicion of inferiority. All the qualities of a man acquire dignity when he knows that the service of the collectivity that owns him needs them. If proud of the collectivity, his own pride rises in proportion. No collectivity is like an army for nourishing such pride; but it has to be confessed that the only sentiment which the image of pacific cosmopolitan industrialism is capable of arousing in countless worthy breasts is shame at the idea of belonging to *such* a collectivity. It is obvious that the United States of America as they exist to-day impress a mind like General Lea's as so much human blubber. Where is the sharpness and precipitousness, the contempt for life, whether one's own, or another's? Where is the savage "yes" and "no," the unconditional duty? Where is the conscription? Where is the blood-tax? Where is anything that one feels honored by belonging to?

Having said thus much in preparation, I will now confess my own utopia. I devoutly believe in the reign of peace and in the gradual advent of some sort of a socialistic equilibrium. The fatalistic view of the war-function is to me nonsense, for I know that war-making is due to definite motives and subject to prudential checks and reasonable criticisms, just like any other form of enterprise. And when whole nations are the armies, and the science of destruction vies in intellectual refinement with the sciences of production, I see that war becomes absurd and impossible from its own monstrosity. Extravagant ambitions will have to be replaced by reasonable claims, and nations must make common cause against them. I see no reason why all this should not apply to yellow as well as to white countries, and I look forward to a future when acts of war shall be formally outlawed as between civilized peoples.

All these beliefs of mine put me squarely into the anti-militarist party. But I do not believe that peace either ought to be or will be permanent on this globe, unless the states pacifically organized preserve some of the old elements of army-discipline. A permanently successful peace-economy cannot be a simple pleasure-economy. In the more or less socialistic future towards which mankind seems drifting we must still subject ourselves collectively to those severities which answer to our real position upon this only partly hospitable globe. We must make new energies and hardihoods continue the manliness to which the military mind so faithfully clings. Martial virtues must be the enduring cement; intrepidity, contempt of softness, surrender of private interest, obedience to command, must still remain the rock upon which states are built—unless, indeed, we wish for dangerous reactions against commonwealths fit only for contempt, and liable to invite attack whenever a center of crystallization for military-minded enterprise gets formed anywhere in their neighborhood.

The war-party is assuredly right in affirming and reaffirming that the martial virtues, although originally gained by the race through war, are absolute and permanent human goods. Patriotic pride and ambition in their military form are, after all, only specifications of a more general competitive passion. They are its first form, but that is no reason for supposing them to be its last form. Men now are proud of belonging to a conquering nation, and without a murmur they lay down their persons and their wealth, if by so doing they may fend off subjection. But who can be sure that *other aspects of one's country* may not, with time and education and suggestion enough, come to be regarded with similarly effective feelings of pride and shame? Why should men not some day feel that it is worth a blood-tax to belong to a collectivity superior in *any* ideal respect? Why should they not blush with indignant shame if the community that owns them is vile in any way whatsoever? Individuals, daily more numerous, now feel this civic passion. It is only a question of blowing on the spark till the whole population gets incandescent, and on the ruins of the old morals of military honor, a stable system of morals of civic honor builds itself up. What the whole community comes to believe in grasps the individual as in a vise. The war-function has grasped us so far; but constructive interests may some day seem no less imperative, and impose on the individual a hardly lighter burden.

Let me illustrate my idea more concretely. There is nothing to make one indignant in the mere fact that life is hard, that men should toil and suffer pain. The planetary conditions once for all are such, and we can stand it. But that so many men, by mere accidents of birth and opportunity, should have a life of *nothing else* but toil and pain and hardness and inferiority imposed upon them, should have no vacation, while others natively no more deserving never get any taste of this campaigning life at all,—*this* is capable of arousing indignation in reflective minds. It may end by seeming shameful to all of us that some of us have nothing but campaigning, and others nothing but unmanly ease. If now—and this is my idea—there were, instead of military conscription a conscription of the whole youthful population to form for a certain number of years a part of the army enlisted against *Nature,* the injustice would tend to be evened out, and numerous other goods to the commonwealth would follow. The military ideals of hardihood and discipline would be wrought into the growing fiber of the people; no one would remain blind as the luxurious classes now are blind, to man's relations to the globe he lives on, and to the permanently sour and hard foundations of his higher life. To coal and iron mines, to freight trains, to fishing fleets in December, to dishwashing, clothes-washing, and window-washing, to road-building and tunnel-making, to foundries and stoke-holes, and to the frames of sky-scrapers, would our gilded youths be drafted off, according to their choice, to get the childishness knocked out of them, and to come back into society with healthier sympathies and soberer ideas. They would have paid their blood-tax, done their own part in the immemorial human warfare against nature; they would tread the earth more proudly, the women would value them more highly, they would be better fathers and teachers of the following generation.

Such a conscription, with the state of public opinion that would have required it, and the many moral fruits it would bear, would preserve in the midst of a pacific civilization the manly virtues which the military party is so afraid of seeing disappear in peace. We should get toughness without callousness, authority with as little criminal cruelty as possible, and painful work done cheerily because the duty is temporary, and threatens not, as now, to degrade the whole remainder of one's life. I spoke of the "moral equivalent" of war. So far, war has been the only force that can discipline a whole community, and until an equivalent discipline is organized, I believe that war must have its way. But I have no serious doubt that the ordinary prides and shames of social man, once developed to a certain intensity, are capable of organizing such a moral equivalent as I have sketched, or some other just as effective for preserving manliness of type. It is but a question of time, of skilful propagandism, and of opinion-making men seizing historic opportunities.

The martial type of character can be bred without war. Strenuous honor and disinterestedness abound elsewhere. Priests and medical men are in a fashion educated to it, and we should all feel some degree of it imperative if we were conscious of our work as an obligatory service to the state. We should be *owned,* as soldiers are by the army, and our pride would rise accordingly. We could be poor, then, without humiliation, as army officers now are. The only thing needed henceforward is to inflame the civic temper as past history has inflamed the military temper. H. G. Wells, as usual, sees the center of the situation. "In many ways," he says,

Military organization is the most peaceful of activities. When the contemporary man steps from the street, of clamorous insincere advertisement, push, adulteration, underselling and intermittent employment into the barrack-yard, he steps on to a higher social plane, into an atmosphere of service and cooperation and of infinitely more honorable emulations. Here at least men are not flung out of employment to degenerate because there is no immediate work for them to do. They are fed and drilled and trained for better services. Here at least a man is supposed to win promotion by self-forgetfulness and not by self-seeking. And beside the feeble and irregular endowment of research by commercialism, its little short-sighted snatches at profit by innovation and scientific economy, see how remarkable is the steady and rapid development of method and appliances in naval and military affairs! Nothing is more striking than to compare the progress of civil conveniences which has been left almost entirely to the trader, to the progress in military apparatus during the last few decades. The house-appliances of to-day, for example, are little better than they were fifty years ago. A house of to-day is still almost as ill-ventilated, badly heated by wasteful fires, clumsily arranged and furnished as the house of 1858. Houses a couple of hundred years old are still satisfactory places of residence, so little have our standards risen. But the rifle or battleship of fifty years ago was beyond all comparison inferior to those we possess; in power, in speed, in convenience alike. No one has a use now for such superannuated things.[2]

Wells adds[3] that he thinks that the conceptions of order and discipline, the tradition of service and devotion, of physical fitness, unstinted exertion, and universal responsibility, which universal military duty is now teaching European nations, will remain a permanent acquisition, when the last ammunition has been used in the fireworks that celebrate the final peace. I believe as he does. It would be simply preposterous if the only force that could work ideals of honor and standards of efficiency into English or American natures should be the fear of being killed by the Germans or the Japanese. Great indeed is Fear; but it is not, as our military enthusiasts believe and try to make us believe, the only stimulus known for awakening the higher ranges of men's spiritual energy. The amount of alteration in public opinion which my utopia postulates is vastly less than the difference between the mentality of those black warriors who pursued Stanley's party on the Congo with their cannibal war-cry of "Meat! Meat!" and that of the "general-staff" of any civilized nation. History has seen the latter interval bridged over: the former one can be bridged over much more easily.

Notes

1. "Justice and Liberty," New York, 1909.
2. "First and Last Things," 1908, p. 215.
3. *Ibid.*, p. 226.

Pacifism: A Philosophical Analysis

(1965)

Jan Narveson

Jan Narveson is professor of philosophy at the University of Waterloo in Canada. He is the author of several articles and books in moral and social philosophy, including Morality and Utility *(1967),* Moral Matters *(1999), and* Respecting Persons in Theory and Practice *(2002).*

Several different doctrines have been called "pacifism," and it is impossible to say anything cogent about it without saying which of them one has in mind. I must begin by making it clear, then, that I am limiting the discussion of pacifism to a rather narrow band of doctrines, further distinctions among which will be brought out below. By "pacifism," I do *not* mean the theory that violence is evil. With appropriate restrictions, this is a view that every person with any pretensions to morality doubtless holds: Nobody thinks that we have a right to inflict pain wantonly on other people. The pacifist goes a very long step further. *His* belief is not only that violence is evil but also that it is morally wrong to use force to resist, punish, or prevent violence. This further step makes pacifism a radical moral doctrine. What I shall try to establish below is that it is in fact, more than merely radical—it is actually incoherent because self-contradictory in its fundamental intent. . . .

Pacifism, then, must be the principle that the use of force to meet force is wrong *as such,* that is, that nobody may do so unless he has a special justification.

There is another way in which one might advocate a sort of "pacifism," however, which we must also dispose of before getting to the main point. One might argue that pacifism is desirable as a tactic: that, as a matter of fact, some good end, such as the reduction of violence itself, is to be achieved by "turning the other cheek." For example, if it were the case that turning the other cheek caused the offender to break down and repent, then that would be a very good reason for behaving "pacifistically." If unilateral disarmament causes the other side to disarm, then certainly unilateral disarmament would be a desirable policy. But note that its desirability, if this is the argument, is due to the fact that peace is desirable, a moral position which anybody can take, pacifist or no, plus the purely contingent fact that this policy causes the other side to disarm, that is, it brings about peace.

And, of course, that's the catch. If one attempts to support pacifism because of its probable effects, then one's position depends on what the effects are. Determining what they are is a purely empirical matter, and, consequently, one could not possibly be a pacifist as a matter of pure principle if his reasons for supporting pacifism are merely tactical. One must, in this case, submit one's opinions to the governance of fact.

It is not part of my intention to discuss matters of fact, as such, but it is worthwhile to point out that the general history of the human race certainly offers no support for the supposition that turning the other cheek always produces good effects on the aggressor. Some aggressors, such as the Nazis, were apparently just "egged on" by the "pacifist" attitude of their victims. Some of the S.S. men apparently became curious to see just how much torture the victim would put up with before he began to resist. Furthermore, there is the possibility that, while pacifism might work against some people (one might cite the British, against whom pacifism in India was apparently rather successful—but the British are comparatively nice people), it might fail against others (e.g., the Nazis).

A further point about holding pacifism to be desirable as a tactic is that this could not easily support the position that pacifism is a *duty*. The question whether we have no *right* to fight back can hardly be settled by noting that not to fight back might cause the aggressor to stop fighting. To prove that a policy is a desirable one because it works is not to prove that it is *obligatory* to follow it. We surely need considerations a good deal less tenuous than this to prove such a momentous contention as that we have no *right* to resist.

It appears, then, that to hold the pacifist position as a genuine, full-blooded moral principle is to hold that nobody has a right to fight back when attacked, that fighting back is inherently evil, as such. It means that we are all mistaken in supposing that we have a right of self-protection. And, of course, this is an extreme and extraordinary position in any case. It appears to mean, for instance, that we have no right to punish criminals, that all of our machinery of criminal justice is, in fact, unjust. Robbers, murderers, rapists, and miscellaneous delinquents ought, on this theory, to be let loose.

Now, the pacifist's first move, upon hearing this, will be to claim that he has been misrepresented. He might say that it is only one's *self* that one has no right to defend, and that one may legitimately fight in order to defend other people. This qualification cannot be made by those pacifists who qualify as conscientious objectors, however, for the latter are refusing to defend their fellow citizens and not merely themselves. But this is comparatively trivial when we contemplate the next objection to this amended version of the theory. Let us now ask ourselves what it is about attacks on *other* people which could possibly justify *us* in defending them, while we are not justified in defending ourselves? It cannot be the mere fact that they are other people than ourselves, for, of course, everyone is a different person from everyone else, and if such a consideration could ever of itself justify anything at all it could also justify anything whatever. That mere difference of person, as such, is of no moral importance, is a presupposition of anything that can possibly pretend to be a moral theory.

Instead of such idle nonsense, then, the pacifist would have to mention some specific characteristic which every *other* person has which we lack and which justifies us in defending them. But this, alas, is impossible, for, while there may be some interesting difference between *me,* on the one hand, and everyone else, on the other, the pacifist is not merely addressing himself to me. On the contrary, as we have seen, he has to address himself to everyone. He is claiming that each person has no right to defend himself, although he does have a right to defend other people. And, therefore, what is needed is a characteristic which distinguishes *each* person from everyone else, and not just *me* from everyone else—which is plainly self-contradictory.

If the reader does not yet see why the "characteristic" of being identical with oneself cannot be used to support a moral theory, let him reflect that the proposition "Everyone is identical with himself" is a trivial truth—as clear an example of an analytic proposition as there could possibly be. But a statement of moral principle is not a trivial truth; it is a substantive moral assertion. But non-tautologous statements, as everyone knows, cannot logically be derived from tautologies, and, consequently, the fact that everyone is identical with himself cannot possibly be used to prove a moral position.

Again, then, the pacifist must retreat in order to avoid talking idle nonsense. His next move, now, might be to say that we have a right to defend all those who are not able to defend themselves. Big, grown-up men who are able to defend themselves ought not to do so, but they ought to defend mere helpless children who are unable to defend themselves.

This last, very queer theory could give rise to some amusing logical gymnastics. For instance, what about groups of people? If a group of people who cannot defend themselves singly can defend themselves together, then when it has grown to that size ought it to stop defending itself? If so, then every time a person *can* defend someone else, he would form with the person being defended a "defensive unit" which was able to defend itself, and thus would by his very presence debar himself from making the defense. At this rate, no one will ever get defended, it seems: The defenseless people by definition cannot defend themselves, while those who can defend them would enable the group consisting of the defenders and the defended to defend themselves, and hence they would be obliged not to do so.

Such reflections, however, are merely curious shadows of a much more fundamental and serious logical problem. This arises when we begin to ask: But why should even defenseless people be defended? If resisting violence is inherently evil, then how can it suddenly become permissible when we use it on behalf of other people? The fact that they are defenseless cannot possibly account for this, for it follows from the theory in question, that everyone ought to put himself in the position of people who are defenseless by refusing to defend himself. This type of pacifist, in short, is using the very characteristic (namely, being in a state of not defending oneself) which he wishes to encourage in others as a reason for denying it in the case of those who already have it (namely, the defenseless). This is indeed self-contradictory.

To attempt to be consistent, at least, the pacifist is forced to accept the characterization of him at which we tentatively arrived. He must indeed say that no one ought ever to be defended against attack. The right of self-defense can be denied coherently only if the right of defense, in general, is denied. This in itself is an important conclusion.

It must be borne in mind, by the way, that I have not said anything to take exception to the man who simply does not wish to defend himself. So long as he does not attempt to make his pacifism into a principle, one cannot accuse him of any inconsistency, however much one might wish to say that he is foolish or eccentric. It is solely with moral principles that I am concerned here.

We now come to the last and most fundamental problem of all. If we ask ourselves what the point of pacifism is, what gets it going, so to speak, the answer is, of course, obvious enough: opposition to violence. The pacifist is generally thought of as the man who is so much opposed to violence that he will not even use it to defend himself or anyone else. And it is precisely this characterization which I wish to show is far from being plausible, morally inconsistent.

To begin with, we may note something which at first glance may seem merely to be a matter of fact, albeit one which should worry the pacifist, in our latest characterization of him. I refer to the commonplace observation that, generally speaking, we measure a man's degree of opposition to something by the amount of effort he is willing to put forth against it. A man could hardly be said to be dead set against something if he is not willing to lift a finger to keep it from going on. A person who claims to be completely opposed to something yet does nothing to prevent it would ordinarily be said to be a hypocrite.

As facts, however, we cannot make too much of these. The pacifist could claim to be willing to go to any length, short of violence, to prevent violence. He might, for instance, stand out in the cold all day long handing out leaflets (as I have known some to do), and this would surely argue for the sincerity of his beliefs.

But would it really?

Let us ask ourselves, one final time, what we are claiming when we claim that violence is morally wrong and unjust. We are, in the first place, claiming that a person *has no right* to indulge in it, as such (meaning that he has no right to indulge in it, *unless* he has an overriding justification). But what do we mean when we say that he has no right to indulge in it? Violence, of the type we are considering, is a

two-termed affair: one does violence *to* somebody, one cannot simply "do violence." It might be oneself, of course, but we are not primarily interested in those cases, for what makes it wrong to commit violence is that it harms the people to whom it is done. To say that it is wrong is to say that those to whom it is done have a right *not* to have it done to them. (This must again be qualified by pointing out that this is so only if they have done nothing to merit having that right abridged.)

Yet what could that right to their own security, which people have, possibly consist in, if not a right at least to defend themselves from whatever violence might be offered them? But lest the reader think that this is a gratuitous assumption, note carefully the reason why having a right involves having a right to be defended from breaches of that right. It is because the prevention of infractions of that right is precisely what one has a right to when one has a right at all. A right just *is* a status justifying preventive action. To say that you have a right to *X* but that no one has any justification whatever for preventing people from depriving you of it, is self-contradictory. If you claim a right to *X,* then to describe some action as an act of depriving you of *X,* is logically to imply that its absence is one of the things that you have a right to.

Thus far it does not follow logically that we have a right to use force in our own or anyone's defense. What does follow logically is that one has a right to whatever may be necessary to prevent infringements of his right. One might at first suppose that the universe *could* be so constructed that it is never necessary to use force to prevent people who are bent on getting something from getting it. Yet even this is not so, for when we speak of "force" in the sense in which pacifism is concerned with it, we do not mean merely physical "force." To call an action a use of force is not merely to make a reference to the laws of mechanics. On the contrary, it is to describe whatever is being done as being a means to the infliction on somebody of something (ordinarily physical) which he does not want done to him; and the same is true for "force" in the sense in which it applies to war, assault and battery, and the like.

The proper contrary of "force" in this connection is "rational persuasion." Naturally, one way there *might* be of getting somebody not to do something he has no right to do is to convince him he ought not to do it or that it is not in his interest to do it. But it is inconsistent, I suggest, to argue that rational persuasion is the only morally permissible method of preventing violence. A pragmatic reason for this is easy enough to point to: Violent people are too busy being violent to be reasonable. We cannot engage in rational persuasion unless the enemy is willing to sit down and talk; but what if he isn't? One cannot contend that every human being can be persuaded to sit down and talk before he strikes, for this is not something we can determine just by reasoning: it is a question of observation, certainly. But these points are not strictly relevant anyway, for our question is not the empirical question of whether there is some handy way which can always be used to get a person to sit down and discuss moral philosophy when he is about to murder you. Our question is: *If* force is the only way to prevent violence in a given case, is its use justified *in that case?* This is a purely moral question which we can discuss without any special reference to matters of fact. And, moreover, it is precisely this question which we should have to discuss with the would-be violator. The point is that if a person can be rationally persuaded that he ought not to engage in violence, then precisely what he

would be rationally persuaded of if we were to succeed would be the proposition that the use of force is justifiable to prevent him from doing so. For note that if we were to argue that only rational persuasion is permissible as a means of preventing him, we would have to face the question: Do we mean *attempted* rational persuasion, or *successful* rational persuasion, that is, rational persuasion which really does succeed in preventing him from acting? Attempted rational persuasion might fail (if only because the opponent is unreasonable), and then what? To argue that we have a right to use rational persuasion which also succeeds (i.e., we have a right to its success as well as to its use) is to imply that we have a right to prevent him from performing the act. But this, in turn, means that, if attempts at rational persuasion fail, we have a right to the use of force. Thus what we have a right to, if we ever have a *right* to anything, is not merely the use of rational persuasion to keep people from depriving you of the thing to which you have the right. We do indeed have a right to that, but we also have a right to anything else that might be necessary (other things being equal) to prevent the deprivation from occurring. And it is a logical truth, not merely a contingent one, that what *might* be necessary is *force.* (If merely saying something could miraculously deprive someone of the ability to carry through a course of action, then those speech-acts would be called a type of force, if a very mysterious one. And we could properly begin to oppose their use for precisely the same reasons as we now oppose violence.)

What this all adds up to, then, is that *if* we have any rights at all, we have a right to use force to prevent the deprivation of the thing to which we are said to have a right. But the pacifist, of *all* people, is the one most concerned to insist that we do have some rights, namely, the right not to have violence done to us. This is logically implied in asserting it to be a duty on everyone's part to avoid violence. And this is why the pacifist's position is self-contradictory. In saying that violence is wrong, one is at the same time saying that people have a right to its prevention, by force if necessary. Whether and to what extent it may be necessary is a question of fact, but, since it is a question of fact only, the *moral* right to use force on some possible occasions is established.

We now have an answer to the question. How much force does a given threat of violence justify for preventive purposes? The answer, in a word, is "Enough." That the answer is this simple may at first sight seem implausible. One might suppose that some elaborate equation between the aggressive and the preventive force is needed: the punishment be proportionate to the crime. But this is a misunderstanding. In the first place, prevention and punishment are not the same, even if punishment is thought to be directed mainly toward prevention. The punishment of a particular crime logically cannot prevent *that* instance of the crime, since it presupposes that it has already been performed; and punishment need not involve the use of any violence at all, although law-enforcement officers in some places have a nasty tendency to assume the contrary. But preventive force is another matter. If a man threatens to kill me, it is desirable, of course, for me to try to prevent this by the use of the least amount of force sufficient to do the job. But I am justified even in killing him *if* necessary. This much, I suppose, is obvious to most people. But suppose his threat is much smaller: suppose that he is merely pestering me, which is a very mild form of aggression indeed. Would I be justified in killing him to prevent this, under any circumstances whatever?

Suppose that I call the police and they take out a warrant against him, and suppose that when the police come, he puts up a struggle. He pulls a knife or a gun, let us say, and the police shoot him in the ensuing battle. Has my right to the prevention of his annoying me extended to killing him? Well, not exactly, since the immediate threat in response to which he is killed is a threat to the lives of the policemen. Yet my annoyer may never have contemplated real violence. It is an unfortunate case of unpremeditated escalation. But this is precisely what makes the contention that one is justified in using enough force to do the job, whatever amount that may be, to prevent action which violates a right less alarming than at first sight it seems. For it is difficult to envisage a reason why extreme force is needed to prevent mild threats from realization except by way of escalation, and escalation automatically justifies increased use of preventive force.

The existence of laws, police, courts, and more or less civilized modes of behavior on the part of most of the populace naturally affects the answer to the question of how much force is necessary. One of the purposes of a legal system of justice is surely to make the use of force by individuals very much less necessary than it would otherwise be. If we try to think back to a "state of nature" situation, we shall have much less difficulty envisaging the need for large amounts of force to prevent small threats of violence. Here Hobbes's contention that in such a state every man has a right to the life of every other becomes understandable. He was, I suggest, relying on the same principle as I have argued for here: that one has a right to use as much force as necessary to defend one's rights, which include the right of safety of person.

I have said that the duty to avoid violence is only a duty, other things being equal. We might arrive at the same conclusion as we have above by asking the question: Which "other things" might count as being *un*equal? The answer to this is that whatever else they may be, the purpose of preventing violence from being done is necessarily one of these justifying conditions. That the use of force is never justified to prevent initial violence being done to one logically implies that there is nothing wrong with initial violence. We cannot characterize it as being wrong if preventive violence is not simultaneously being characterized as justifiable.

We often think of pacifists as being gentle and idealistic souls, which in its way is true enough. What I have been concerned to show is that they are also confused. If they attempt to formulate their position using our standard concepts of rights, their position involves a contradiction: Violence is wrong, *and* it is wrong to resist it. But the right to resist is precisely what having a right of safety of person is, if it is anything at all.

Could the position be reformulated with a less "committal" concept of rights? I do not think so. It has been suggested[1] that the pacifist need not talk in terms of this "kind" of rights. He can affirm, according to this suggestion, simply that neither the aggressors nor the defenders "have" rights to what they do, that to affirm their not having them is simply to be against the use of force, without this entailing the readiness to use force if necessary to protect the said rights. But this will not do, I believe. For I have not maintained that having a right, or believing that one has a right, entails a *readiness* to defend that right. One has a perfect right not to resist violence to oneself if one is so inclined. But our question has been whether self-defense is justifiable, and not whether one's belief that violence is wrong entails a willingness or readiness to use it. My contention has been that such a belief does entail the justifiability of using it. If one came upon a community in which no sort of violence was ever resisted and it was claimed in that community that the non-resistance was a matter of conscience, we should have to conclude, I think, not that this was a community of saints, but rather that this community lacked the concept of justice—or perhaps that their nervous systems were oddly different from ours.

The true test of the pacifist comes, of course, when he is called upon to assist in the protection of the safety of other persons and not just of himself. For while he is, as I have said, surely entitled to be pacific about his own person if he is so inclined, he is not entitled to be so about the safety of others. It is here that the test of principles comes out. People have a tendency to brand conscientious objectors as cowards or traitors, but this is not quite fair. They are acting as if they were cowards or traitors, but claiming to do so on principle. It is not surprising if a community should fail to understand such "principles," for the test of adherence to a principle is willingness to act on it, and the appropriate action, if one believes a certain thing to be grossly wrong, is to take steps to prevent or resist it. Thus people who assess conscientious objection as cowardice or worse are taking an understandable step: from an intuitive feeling that the pacifist does not really believe what he is saying they infer that his actions (or inaction) must be due to cowardice. What I am suggesting is that this is not correct: The actions are due, not to cowardice, but to confusion. . . .

Notes

1. I owe this suggestion to my colleague, Leslie Armour.

Pacifism: Some Philosophical Considerations

(1985)

Stanley Hauerwas

Stanley Hauerwas is the Gilbert T. Rowe Professor of Theological Ethics at Duke University Divinity School. He also holds an appointment in Duke Law School. His many books include The Peaceable Kingdom: A Primer in Christian Ethics *(1984),* A Community of Character *(1988),* Dispatches From the Front: Theological Engagements With the Secular *(1995),* Sanctify Them in the Truth: Holiness Exemplified *(1999),* With the Grain of the Universe: The Church's Witness and Natural Theology *(2001), and* Performing the Faith: Bonhoeffer and the Practice of Nonviolence *(2004).*

A pacifist speaking to philosophers faces a temptation that is almost impossible to resist—namely to try to defend pacifism philosophically. Yet I think such a temptation must be resisted, for to try to provide a philosophical foundation for pacifism would be a philosophical mistake. It is the same kind of mistake that those make who try to show that God must have created the universe if he is to be God—i.e. to make a metaphysical necessity out of what must remain contingent relation. I do not wish to be misunderstood, however, as such a claim might be interpreted to suggest that pacifism is a position without relational appeal, being based on theological convictions that cannot stand the light of critical scrutiny. I certainly do not believe that. Rather I am trying to make the simpler point that pacifism, at least the kind of Christian non-resistance to which I am committed, is at the beginning and end a theological position. As such it raises philosophical issues which cannot be avoided, but in and of itself, its integrity is theological.

Given the interest of this group it would be inappropriate for me to try to develop to any great extent my understanding of Christian pacifism. However I must at least try to say enough to substantiate as well as exemplify how it draws on fundamental theological convictions for its intelligibility. The reason I believe Christians have been given the permission, that is, why it is good news for us, to live without resort to violence is that by doing so we live as God lives. Therefore pacifism is not first of all a prohibition, but an affirmation that God wills to rule his creation not through violence and coercion but by love. Moreover he has called us to be part of his rule by calling us into a community that is governed by peace.

Therefore pacifism is not simply one implication among others for Christians. Pacifism is not just another way that some Christians think they should live. Rather pacifism is the form of life that is inherent in the shape of Christian convictions about God and his relation to us. Though it counts individual passages of scripture such as Matthew 5:38–48 important, pacifism does not derive its sole justification from them. Rather pacifism follows from our understanding of God which we believe has been most decisively revealed in the cross of Jesus Christ. Just as God refused to use violence to insure the success of his cause, so must we. Therefore Christian pacifism is not based on any claims about the proximate or ultimate success of non-violent strategies, though we certainly do not try to fail as if failure in and of itself is an indication of the truthfulness of our position. Faithfulness, however, rather than effectiveness, is the ultimate test of Christian pacifism.

Even though for the purposes of this presentation I am willing to be designated a pacifist, I am extremely unhappy with such a description of my position. For to say one is a pacifist gives the impression that pacifism is a position that is intelligible apart from the theological convictions that form it. But that is exactly what I wish to deny. Christians are non-violent not because certain implications may follow from their beliefs, but because the very shape of their beliefs form them to be non-violent. Moreover when the designation, pacifism, is used to describe Christian non-resistance the impression is given that Christians in the face of violence are primarily passive in the face of evil. Yet that is at odds with Jesus' active engagement with the powers. The pacifist is no less obligated to resist injustice, for not to resist means we abandon our brother or sister to their injustice. Pacifists, however, contend the crucial question is *how* we are to resist.

There are obviously many objections that such a position must meet, but I think that for those that are philosophically trained one challenge is particularly interesting—namely, pacifism seems contradictory since in the name of non-violence Christians must abandon their responsibility to care for and protect their neighbor. Christians, it is alleged, are obligated to love those in need and Christian pacifism cannot help but acquiesce in the face of injustice and violence. Therefore we must at times take up the means of violence to prevent greater injustice. This objection is often extremely appealing to philosophers, as it seems to put the issue in conceptual terms that allow for, if not demand, further nuance. The issue is not faithfulness to the figure of Jesus, but how love is to be understood and how its implications are to be displayed when we seem caught between contending values; or why justice is more basic than love, and so on.

However this way of putting the "problem" is a refusal to accept the radical implications of the kind of love Jesus demanded of those who would be part of God's kingdom. For the "problem" presupposes that we should only love the one being attacked unjustly; such an account is far too restrictive. The attacker, who may well be unjust, is no less an object of God's love than the one being attacked. The pacifist, no less than those who support violence in the name of the defense of the innocent, cannot abandon those who are being attacked. But the pacifist refuses to accept any account of what such "help" would look like if it requires us to witness to the one being attacked that they are any less obligated to love the enemy than we. To be sure, we are required to love the attacked, but we are equally obligated to love the attacker. That we are so may surely mean that certain situations may end tragically, but I do not see how those who support the use of violence provide any less tragic "solution."

There is one issue worth highlighting in this respect, as it is often missed by many who assume some form of just-war logic for the legitimation of violence. For it is too often assumed that the logic of the just war position is determined on analogy with self-defense rather than defense of the innocent. But the two are not the same, though admittedly a defense of self can possibly be justified as a defense of the innocent. Yet if just war is defended on analogy of defense of the innocent, then at the very least it would seem that those who use just war to justify resort to violence must not be so quick to assume the legitimacy of a violent response simply because their side is attacked. Or perhaps more accurately put, they need to be much more critical of the assumption that they have a "side."

Much more needs to be said about such matters, but I hope I have said enough to indicate that those that defend just war need to be much more candid about how the basic analogies underwriting just war logic works. They need to show us, for example, how one moves from individual analogies, whether they be of self-defense or defense of the innocent, to underwriting war as a valid response by Christians. Or they need to illumine why just war is better understood as a form of state craft rather than a general theory of the justifiable use of violence. Only when such matters are clarified can we better understand which criteria are to deter-

mine whether a war is justifiable and the priority relations between the criteria.

By raising these kind of issues I am not trying to defend pacifism by showing the incoherence of just war theories. I am simply trying to illumine how many of the challenges brought against pacifism work equally in relation to just war thinking. At this point, however, I think it best not to try to defend pacifism but rather to indicate some of the philosophical issues I think pacifism entails. In other words I want to try to indicate how pacifism may engender some philosophically fruitful problems and perspectives.

For example I think it is interesting that the kind of pacifism I defend does not neatly fit into the current philosophical options for understanding normative ethics. That is, it is neither consequential or deontological even though it may well involve aspects of both. For the emphasis is not on decision or even a set of decisions and their justification. Rather this kind of pacifism forces us to consider the kind of persons we ought to be so that certain kinds of decisions are simply excluded from our lives. Thus pacifism is not so much a strategy for how we should deal with violence as it is a way of life that forces us to live free from violence as an option. The pacifist is someone committed to never facing the question of whether to use or not use violence as a means of securing some good.

Of course that is easier said than done. Nor am I suggesting that such a task is ever over. Indeed I suspect few of us ever "decide" to be a pacifist. It is even not clear to me how anyone could make such a decision since we could hardly know what kind of decision we had made since one no more becomes a pacifist all at once than one becomes a Christian all at once. Rather pacifism is a willingness to accept the slow training necessary to rid the self of the presumption that violence is necessary for living life well.

From this perspective the problem with the just war rationale for violence is that it so seldom places a limit on the use of violence. The just warrior assumes that violence can only be used as a last resort, but the very meaning of "last resort" becomes elastic exactly because it is assumed that if things become rough we can resort to the gun we keep handy for just such emergencies. As a result, we fail to become the kind of people whose very commitment to nonviolence makes it possible for us to live non-violently.

Put in the language of philosophical ethics I am suggesting that pacifism is much closer to an ethics of virtue than to those positions that tend to limit ethics to questions concerning the justification of decisions. For the pacifist does not accept descriptions of situations as constant. Questions of what we are to do are determined by what we are or should be. Virtues of courage, temperance, justice, humility, patience are no less necessary for the pacifist than anyone else. However these virtues assume a different intentionality and priority for those who would be pacifist. For example the pacifist, I suspect, has a much greater stake in the significance of learning to be patient than those who would defend justifiable use of violence. Just to the extent we are patient, moreover, we are forced to redescribe our world—e.g., we must entertain the possibility that our enemy is also one of God's creatures.

I am not suggesting that pacifism and an ethic of virtue rise or fall together, but rather that pacifism forces us to think much harder about an ethic of virtue than has been characteristic of recent philoso-

phy. Indeed I would put the matter more strongly and say philosophers' general assumption or acceptance of violence as legitimate has been one of the reasons they have paid such scant attention to questions of virtue and character. An emphasis on the significance of the virtues does not conceptually require a pacifist position, but such an emphasis might at least make one more receptive to some accounts of pacifism.

The kind of pacifism I am willing to defend, I think, also challenges some of the prevailing assumptions about moral rationality as it has been depicted by contemporary philosophers. For here we have a position that is clearly derived from particularistic convictions; yet I would argue they apply to anyone. The "universality" of these convictions however, is not in their form but in their substance. All people ought to be nonviolent not because of some general truth about humanity, but because all people have been called to be part of the kingdom initiated by Jesus of Nazareth.

This kind of claim cannot help but make philosophers nervous. For it seems that, in order to convince others of the possibility of this position, we must ask them to accept particularistic religious convictions. In such a situation the possibility of argument seems next to impossible and, even worse, moral relativism is threatened. I can say little to assuage fear of such results, but I can at least suggest that the kind of position I hold about pacifism is not without resources to respond to this set of concerns. Yet these resources require the philosopher to accept concepts and language in matters dealing with rationality that they usually wish to avoid.

For example, it means that the philosopher might have to take sin seriously, not simply as a general statement about the human condition, but as a serious claim about our moral and rational capacity. For it is the pacifist claim that our unwillingness to live nonviolently is but an indication of our unwillingness to live in a way appropriate to our being creatures of a good creator. To live rightly, to say nothing of reasoning rightly, requires a transformation of our lives. We can only begin to appreciate the truth of nonviolence when we begin to live nonviolently.

Put differently, the kind of claims Christians make for nonviolence require living representatives if they are to be convincing. The rational power of nonviolence as a morality for anyone depends on the existence of examples, that is, people who have learned to live nonviolently. Such a claim is not peculiar to pacifism, however, but rather denotes how any substantive account of the moral life must work in a world determined by sin. Indeed pacifism in such a world is the very form of moral rationality since it is a pledge that we can come to common agreement on the basis of discussion rather than violence. What the nonviolent witness denies is that such agreement is possible by argument abstracted from the kind of people who have learned that even their enemy may be speaking the truth. We cannot exhaust moral rationality with a formal account of reason in and of itself, though such accounts promise to teach us much, but rather we must attend to the actual process of people who learn to be present to one another without fear. Put simply, what has been missing from most accounts of moral rationality is a consideration of why courage is integral to those that would want to know the truth.

The particularistic convictions that sustain nonviolence, therefore, do not pre-

tend that others already share the same set of convictions that make nonviolence rational. Indeed the fact that we know the world is divided into hostile camps is exactly the reason we believe that nonviolence is true. I do not mean to imply that nonviolence is a strategy for resolution of differences, though I certainly do not think it is without strategic importance. Rather I am suggesting that nonviolence has a strong claim to being true exactly because it helps us understand the nature of our existence without accepting the limits of our world as final. Nonviolence is a pledge, a promise based on the work of Christ, that moral rationality is not just an ideal but a possibility in a world shaped by the sinful illusion that we are people who love the truth.

There is one final set of philosophical issues raised by pacifism that I think must be considered—namely, questions of political obligation. It is often alleged that anyone who holds the kind of absolutist position I do must be an anarchist. Yet I refuse to accept such a characterization, for it seems that the state, in essence, is violent. I do not deny that the rise of the modern state has often been described and/or justified by the claim that the state is that body that claims hegemony over violence in an identifiable geographic area. Yet I see no compelling philosophical reason why that account of the state must be accepted.

Indeed I simply refuse as a pacifist to think I need any account of the state at all. In other words I do not think that one needs a theory of legitimacy in order to determine how one will or will not relate to one's social order or governmental authority. Rather I simply take societies and the state as I find them. As a pacifist I will cooperate in all those activities of the state that contribute to the common good. Put simply, I do not see any in principle reason why I cannot be a good citizen, but much depends on how a particular social order determines what being a citizen entails. If citizenship means that we can only serve others through societal functions if we are willing to kill, then indeed the pacifist cannot be a citizen. But at least that tells us much, for such a state, whether it be democratic or not, must surely deserve to be described as the beast.

When War is Unjust:
Being Honest in Just-War Thinking
(1984)

John Howard Yoder

John Howard Yoder was professor of christian ethics in the Department of Theology and Teaching Fellow at the Joan B. Kroc Institute for International Peace Studies at the University of Notre Dame. He is the author of many books, including The Original Revolution: Essays on Christian Pacifism *(1972),* The Politics of Jesus: Vicit Agnus Noster *(2nd ed., 1994). He died in 1997.*

MAKING THE TRADITION CREDIBLE

The preceding review of the ups and downs of history should have made it clear that the just-war tradition is not a simple formula ready to be applied in a self-evident and univocal way. It is rather a set of very broad assumptions whose implications demand—if they are to be respected as morally honest—that they be spelled out in some detail and then tested for their ability to throw serious light on real situations and on the decisions of persons and institutions regarding those situations. We therefore turn to the effort to itemize the resources that would be needed if such au-

thentic implementation were to become a reality.

Intention

Beginning from the inside, we would need to clarify whether in the minds and the hearts of the people using this language there has been a conscious commitment to make the sacrifices required to apply the doctrine negatively. At some time, if the doctrine is not a farce, there would be cases where an intrinsically just cause would have to go undefended militarily because there would be no authority legitimated to defend it. Or an intrinsically just cause defended by a legitimate authority would have to be forsaken because the only way to defend it would be by unjust means. That would be the setting for testing whether citizens or leaders were able in principle to conceive of the sacrifice of that value as morally imperative. Is it something citizens would press on their leaders? Is it reason for the draftee to refuse to serve, or reason for a statesman to negotiate peace?

There is no strong evidence for believing that most people using just-war language are ready, either psychically or intellectually, for that serious choice. In popular language—which translates "negotiated peace" as "surrender," proclaims that there is "no substitute for victory," and loosely uses the military language of "necessity" to cover almost any infraction of the laws of war—we have seen the evidence not merely of the high value attributed uncritically to one's own nation or to the righteousness of its cause, but also a profound psychodynamic avoidance mechanism. By refusing to face real options, that avoidance makes it highly unlikely that in undesirable situations there will be any chance of making the hard moral choice.

Last Resort

What constitutes a situation of last resort is not something that can be decided only at the last minute or only by one party. What is decisive to determine whether efforts to resolve political conflicts by means less destructive than war have been adequate will largely depend on whether there was any disposition or plan to attempt to use such prior means in the first place.

During the first decade after Hiroshima the United States could count on its nuclear monopoly to enforce its view of peace

around the world; there were not sufficient non-nuclear military means available for effective use in smaller conflicts, so that disproportionate nuclear means threatened to become not the last but the only resort. Similarly, any preoccupation with projecting an image of strength tempts the strong party to leapfrog up the scale past the less destructive recourses.

The United States has been less willing than some other nations to accept in principle the authority of agencies of international arbitration, with the Connally Amendment[1] actually undercutting in a formal way the possibility of recourse to agencies like The Hague International Court of Justice. Even less have we invested in means of conflict resolution on lower levels. We spent forty years sharing with the Soviet Union and China the strategy of escalating local conflicts into surrogates for superpower confrontation, rather than seeking to maximize the authentic independence of non-aligned nations or mediating institutions.

The economic patterns dominating our country have militated against the use of economic and cultural sanctions (positive and negative) to foster international goals, although there have been more efforts (mostly ad hoc, clumsy, and often counterproductive) to use means short of war in some cases.[2] Our international aid agencies hardly have the expertise to administer positive reinforcement in such a way as to diminish recourse to military sanctions without falling prey to new forms of dependency, corruption, and so on. When a government abroad raises any questions about our national interests, we have agencies like the CIA that contribute to escalating rather than diminishing tensions. If we sought to be honest about the restraint on violence implied in the just-war tradition, we would have a nonviolent alternative to the CIA. This would be a creative, non-threatening, information-gathering instrument, which instead of destabilizing regimes it considers un-friendly would find positive means of fos-tering interdependent development.

Strategies of Nonviolence

Recourse to international agencies of arbi-tration and mediation as a factor in evalu-ating when a situation of "last resort" exists is an old idea becoming increasingly pertinent. More attention needs to be given, and has only begun to be given, to a newer development, namely, the rise of ag-gressive nonviolent strategies for social conflict and change. The impact of Gandhi and King is only the tip of the iceberg. Be-sides, beyond, and since them, there have also been:

(a) *Numerous spontaneous phenomena of non-cooperation with injustice, which have achieved sometimes the desired social change and sometimes a more powerful witness of martyrdom than lashing out with firearms would have done*[3];

(b) *A growing circle of leaders, using similar tactics in their most varied circumstances, most notably and recently:*
   - *the change of government in Manila in February 1986;*
   - *changes of government in Eastern Europe in the fall of 1989 and in Madagascar in 1991; sometimes the recourse to nonvio-lence was thought through and sometimes it was spontaneous;*

(c) *A growing body of political science literature projecting the serious possibility of attaining without military violence some of the objec-tives it has previously been claimed could only be attained by war.*[4] *Nonviolent action on behalf of justice is no automatic formula for success, but neither is war. Most people who go to war for some cause they deem worthy are defeated.*[5]

A careful reading of history can find far greater reason than many have previ-ously recognized for expecting nonviolent strategies to be effective. Both anecdotal evidence and social-science analysis have made good beginnings toward projecting and evaluating possible nonmilitary means for defending those values which military means can no longer defend, whether that "no longer" is taken morally or practically.

It is not our task to review that body of literature. If there is available a body of thought and a set of tools of analysis and projection that can respond seriously to the question, How can we defend ourselves if war can no longer do it?, then the situa-tion called last resort cannot be held to obtain. Most of these thinkers are not doc-trinaire pacifists.[6] For their arguments to hold water it suffices to agree that war is not justified when it does not achieve its stated aims and when it does more harm than good.

If there are more nonviolent resources available than people have thought about, and if there would be still more available if they *were* thought about, then the conclu-sion is unavoidable that the notion of last resort—one of the classical criteria of the just-war tradition—must exercise more re-straint than it did before.

Authority

The next logical test of the mental readi-ness of people to live within the limits of honest just-war thinking is at the insti-tutional level. Our government invests millions of staff hours and billions of tax-payers' dollars in developing contingency plans for all possible situations in which the legitimate military prosecution of hos-tilities would be effective. Where is the contingency planning, where are the thought exercises and training maneuvers for continuing the defense of our values in those situations where military means will not be appropriate? In the 1960s Stephen King-Hall projected the case for defense in a nuclear age needing to be, at least in some cases, nonmilitary.[7] Since then many others have spelled out these possibilities. It cannot be said that the failure of military scientists or political ethicists to respond to King-Hall's challenge is due to the author's not being competent and respected or his argument not being cogent. Whether the avoidance mechanisms that refuse to face this challenge are best analyzed in budgetary, psychodynamic, or political terms, they tend to count against the credibility of those who refuse to respond to the practically formulated challenges of King-Hall, Sharp, and the others. Thereby they tend to compromise the credibility of their *pro forma* adherence to the laws of war, and thereby in turn they tend to discredit the coherence of the just-war system itself.

The last few sentences made a backhanded argument. Now I should state the affirmation that corresponds to it. The legitimate authority, which claims the right and the duty to defend the legitimate interests of its citizens (or its allies) by the disciplined and proportionate use of military violence, will be morally credible only when and as it gives evidence of a proportionate investment of creativity and foresight in arrangements to defend those same values by alternate means, in those other contexts in which military means would *not* be morally or legally or technically appropriate. If they are not making those contingency plans, then both their claim that they have the right and duty to use war and their claim that they will do it within the moral limits of the just-war heritage and the legal limits of the laws of war lose credibility.

This awareness that contingency planning for alternative strategies would be a proof of sincerity yields another benefit for our conversation. It tells us that in the measurement of what constitutes last resort, it is not morally sufficient for politicians and strategists to shrug their shoulders and say "we could not think of anything else to do." At least in our times we have the social-science instruments and the intellectual discipline for thinking of alternatives. Last resort can only be claimed when other recourses short of the last have been tested seriously.

Proportion

The reasoning process required by the just-war tradition calls for the evil likely to be caused by warfare to be measured against the evil it hopes to prevent. The critics of the tradition have always wondered what kind of reasoning is going on when one measures various kinds of goods and evils against each other: for example, lives against freedom, or institutions against architecture. We are now trying to wager on the credibility of the tradition. Those who believe that this thought pattern is reliable owe it to their own integrity (and to their potential victims) to possess reliable and verifiable measures of the evil they claim to be warding off and the lesser evil they are willing to commit, albeit reluctantly and without "direct intention."

Such calculation must properly seek to take account not only of specific deeds that one is immediately aware of choosing, but also of the potential for escalation and proliferation which a first step across the threshold of violence can let loose. One would have to factor in the greater or lesser degree of uncertainty with which one can predict both kinds of evils and their causal connection so as to promise just-cause results. Certainly decisions based upon the claimed ability to bring about less evil results, and to do so at the cost of the lives and values of others, need for the sake of one's own integrity to stand up to testing. Such reckoning of proportionality can never be fully certain, but the burden of proof lies with the party who says that it is probable enough to justify intervening by causing some certain lethal evil in order to reduce other projected evils.[8]

Moral Leverage

Thus far I have been describing what institutional instruments would be needed to make the doctrine credible in the sense of applicable. There are however other questions which might come first logically from the perspective of religious moral commitment. Are there people who affirm that their own uncoerced allegiance as believers gives them strength and motivation to honor the restraints of the just-war tradition and to help one another to do so? This might be the only angle from which the development of the needed institutions could be fostered. Would believers commit themselves, and commit themselves to press each other, to be willing to enter the political opposition, or to resign public office, or to espouse selective objection? Does any church teach future soldiers and citizens in such a way that they will know beyond what point they cannot support an unjust war or use an unjust weapon?

Since the capacity to reach an independent judgment concerning the legality and morality of what is being done by one's rulers depends on information, which by the nature of the case must be contested, does the religious community provide alternative resources for gathering and evaluating information concerning the political causes for which their governments demand their violent support? What are the preparations being made to obtain and verify an adequately independent and reliable source of facts and of analytical expertise, enabling honest dissent to be so solidly founded as to be morally convincing? Is every independent thinker on his or her own, or will the churches support agencies to foster dissent when called for?

Neither the pacifist nor the crusader needs to study in depth the facts of politics in order to make a coherent decision. The person claiming to respect just-war rationality must do so, however, and therefore must have a reliable independent source of information. I have stated this as a question about the church, but it also applies to the society. Is there free debate? Are the information media free? Is opposition legitimate? Does the right of conscientious objection have legal recognition?

Are soldiers when assigned a mission given sufficient information to determine whether this is an order they should obey? If a person under orders is convinced he or she must disobey, will the command structure, the society, and the church honor that dissent? It is reported that in the case of the obliteration bombing of Dresden the pilots were not informed that it could hardly be considered a military target. For most of the rest of the just-war criteria factual knowledge is similarly indispensable.

Until today church agencies on any level have invested little effort in literature or other educational means to teach the just-war limitations. The few such efforts one sees are in no way comparable to the way in which the churches teach their young people about other matters concerning which they believe morality is important, such as sexuality. The understanding of the just-war logic that led American young men to refuse to serve in Vietnam came to them not primarily from the ecclesiastical or academic interpreters of the tradition but rather from the notions of fair play presupposed in our popular culture.[9]

A Fair Test

Those who conclude, either deliberately or rapidly, that in a given situation of injustice there are no nonviolent options available, often do so in a way that avoids responsibility for any intensive search for such options. The military option for which they so quickly reach has involved a long lead time in training and equipping the forces. It demands the preparation of a special class of leadership, for which most societies have special schools and learning experiences. It demands costly special resources dependent on abundant government funding, and it demands broad alliances. It includes the willingness to lose lives and to take lives, to sacrifice other cultural values for a generation or more, and the willingness of families to be divided.

Yet the decision that nonviolent means will not work for comparable ends is made without any comparable investment of time or creativity, without comparable readiness to sacrifice, and without serious projection of comparable costs. The American military forces would not "work" if we did not invest billions of dollars in equipping, planning, and training. Why should it be fair to measure the moral claims of an alternative strategy by setting up the debate in such a way that that other strategy should have to promise equivalent results with far less financial investment and less planning on every level? The epigram of the 1960s—People give nonviolence two weeks to solve their problems and then say it has failed; they've gone on with violence for centuries, and it seems never to have failed—is not a pacifist argument. It is a sober self-corrective within just-war reasoning.

In sum, the challenge should be clear. If the tradition which claims that war may be justified does not also admit that in particular cases it may *not* be justified, the affirmation is not morally serious. A Christian who prepares the case for a justifiable war without being equally prepared for the negative case has not soberly weighed the *prima facie* presumption that any violence is wrong until the case for the exception has been made. We honor the moral seriousness of the nonpacifist Christian when we spell out the criteria by which the credibility of that commitment, shaped in the form of the just-war system, must be judged.

Notes

1. In 1946 the United States Senate passed Resolution 196 concerning the submission of United States international affairs to the jurisdiction of the International Court of Justice. Senator Connally's amendment consisted of six words: "as determined by the United States." That is, we get to determine what is domestic and to be controlled by our courts, and what is not domestic and hence controlled by international justice. In 1984–85 the United States ruled that the mining of harbors in Nicaragua was domestic.

2. The cynic observing the reluctance of U.S. legislators and administrators to commit troops in overseas interventions (e.g, Somalia, Bosnia, Haiti) would suggest that it was the product not of just-war scruples but of unwillingness to run

risks where strong economic "national interests" would not be served.

3. Some of these stories are told by Ronald J. Sider, *Nonviolence: The Invincible Weapon?* (Dallas: Word Books, 1989).

4. See John Howard Yoder, "The Power of Nonviolence," available from the Joan B. Kroc Institute for International Peace Studies, Notre Dame, IN 46556 (document 6:WP:2). (See the bibliography on nonviolent alternatives below.)

5. Logically speaking, one side in every war is defeated. Often the "victor" is also worse off than before. The classical just-war criterion of probable success is one of the most difficult to honor; it is one of the points where holy or macho reflexes most easily override rational restraint.

6. See King-Hall, *Defense in a Nuclear Age.* Sir Stephen King-Hall served as instructor in military science in the war colleges of the United Kingdom during World War II. Gene Sharp's numerous publications are based on political realism (see bibliography).

7. King-Hall, *Defense in a Nuclear Age.*

8. "If you have the choice between a real evil and a hypothetical evil, always take the hypothetical one" (Joan Baez, "Three Cheers for Grandma!" *Daybreak* [New York: Dial, 1968] and *Atlantic Monthly* [August 1968], cited in J. Yoder, ed., *What Would You Do?* [Scottdale, Penn.: Herald Press, 1992], 63).

9. Like the morality plays of medieval Europe, the police thriller and the western in our culture are the primary instruments of moral education. That the good guy does not shoot first, that innocents should not be killed, and that the good guy wins in the end even though (or even because) he fights by the rules, are staples of that narrative moral instruction.

B. The Doctrine of Double Effect

Any good discussion of the morality of war will eventually turn to the question of the multiplicity of effects, intended and unintended, that may come from a particular act performed during wartime. If a bomber drops a bomb on a munitions plant in an area populated with civilians, intent only on destroying the plant, is he less morally responsible than a bomber who specifically targets the civilian population in order to dishearten, terrorize, or polarize the enemy population? The doctrine of double effect (referred to here as DDE, but also commonly called the principle of double effect) is one way to explain how intended and unintended effects can be a mitigating factor in the moral evaluation of actions. The DDE is normally understood as a principle of moral reasoning that argues that the pursuit of a good end tends to be less acceptable when a resulting harm is directly intended rather than merely foreseen. The articles in this section explore the history of the doctrine, the views in support of and in opposition to the doctrine, and a very specific application of the doctrine in light of the nature of warfare itself.

Joseph M. Boyle, Jr., opens this section with a primarily historical account of the doctrine, "Toward Understanding the Principle of Double Effect." Boyle begins by exploring the backdrop against which the seminal modern version of the doctrine is formulated, beginning with its genesis in the work of St. Thomas Aquinas.[1] The modern formulation is expressed most clearly by J. P. Gury, who claims that the DDE contains four crucial conditions:

1. The agent's end must be morally acceptable.
2. The cause must be good or indifferent.
3. The good effect must be immediate.
4. There must be a grave reason and sufficient proportionality.

If these four conditions are met, one can be morally exempt from blame for the evil effect(s) of the action performed. Boyle points out the most common applications of the DDE, which include the killing of noncombatants in a justified military action and killing in self-defense, but also points out that the doctrine should not be viewed as a principle of permissibility, but rather as a principle of justification for an otherwise morally questionable act. The doctrine does not say the act, *simpliciter,* is a morally acceptable one, or even that the agent is not responsible for the harm done, but instead that the act, while clearly volitional in some way, is to be considered justified in light of the circumstances surrounding it.

Further, Boyle argues that what is crucial for an appropriate moral account of agency (and from this, responsibility) is a commitment to the claim that it is one's choices and the execution of their choices that are primarily voluntary. This explains why the distinction between the foreseen but unintended and the completely intended is a relevant distinction for the moral evaluation of actions. When viewed as a doctrine of justification in light of this particular view of human moral agency, Boyle argues, the DDE holds up to scrutiny.

Where Boyle's paper is primarily historical in its exploration of the background of the DDE, emphasizing the roots of the doctrine and the moral and metaphysical foundations of the relevant theory of agency, Warren Quinn's project has more of a normative bent. In "Actions, Intentions, and Consequences: The Doctrine of Double Effect," Quinn attempts to perform two crucial tasks: to find a suitable formulation of the doctrine, and to provide a plausible rationale and justification for it. Quinn's focus is not on how the doctrine is formulated or how it is understood, but rather on how it *should* be formulated and understood. He begins by pointing out two major problems with standard understandings of the DDE. The first is that, when formulated too broadly, it would tend to make cases that seem to be troublesome or offensive to most sensibilities seem acceptable. The second problem is that, while the doctrine might be in line with certain pre-theoretical intuitions, it may not connect well with clear moral reasoning.

Quinn's description of the DDE intentionally paints it in an anticonsequentialist light: It argues against the claim that the moral worth of an action is found only in the consequences of that action. Instead, the doctrine seeks a way to distinguish pairs of cases with similar consequences but different sets of motives and intentions in order to provide a different moral evaluation for each case. He provides a series of examples to highlight these sorts of cases, including the Strategic Bomber/Terror Bomber case that serves as the basis for the example we began with at the beginning of this introduction. Quinn leaves fairly wide open the question of what particular theory of agency must be adhered to for the doctrine to function. In his view, the doctrine must be able to be coherent with any theory of intention. The way Quinn attempts to provide this broad reading of intentionality is by making a distinction between direct harms, those in which harm comes to individuals because the harmer had deliberately involved them in order to further his or her purpose, and indirect harms, where the individuals are not deliberately involved by the harmer. It is clear, Quinn argues, under this distinction, that harmful direct agency requires a stronger justification than indirect harmful agency.

Because of the distinction between direct and indirect agency, Quinn is able to find a moral rationale for the grounding of the DDE. When someone commits a direct harm, the harmer must treat the victims of the harm as if they were there for his or her purposes. In Kantian terms, the harmer treats the victims as mere means. Those who are harmed indirectly, on the other hand, are not viewed in this light, although they might be treated with less respect than they deserve. As Quinn puts it, the DDE gives each person some "veto power" over attempts to use them as mere means to make the world a better place. By making an argument against direct harmful agency, the doctrine reflects a Kantian moral program that does meet the requirement of consistency with both pre-theoretical and moral intuitions.

Jonathan Bennett argues for a very different understanding of the DDE in his selection, "Morality and Consequences."[2] He addresses the distinction between the Terror Bomber and the Strategic Bomber, and struggles to find the morally relevant distinction between them. For Bennett, the problem is that we readily bestow moral blame upon the Terror Bomber, who intends to kill ten thousand civilians as a means to lower enemy morale, while we refuse to blame the Strategic Bomber, who intends to destroy a factory while confidently expecting that his bombs will kill ten thousand civilians. Bennett is concerned with the moral significance in the difference in intention between the two cases, and he discusses the standard view of intention (that intentions are explanatory of conduct and indicative of what an agent believes) in light of them.

In examining the two cases, Bennett argues that the civilian deaths are "causally downstream" for the tactical bomber (in which the deaths are a downstream effect from the upstream intended event, the bombing of the munitions plant) and "causally upstream" for the terror bomber (where the deaths are the upstream intended event and the shattering of morale is the downstream effect). The simple fact that the bombing is an upstream or downstream event, however, is irrelevant because Bennett thinks that in the counterfactual situation, in which it is known beforehand that no civilians would be harmed by the bombing, both bombers would continue on their intended mission. The tactical bomber, of course, is going to be happy that no innocent civilians were harmed by the bombing, while the terror bomber also would prefer to achieve his main goal (lowering morale) without harming civilians.

Bennett also offers a challenge to Quinn's Kantian analysis of the doctrine, arguing that while the tactical bomber might not be using his victims as a mere means, he also fails to treat those victims as ends in themselves. The victims are not being treated with the kind respect that one would expect from a Kantian morality. Bennett's challenge to the doctrine, it seems, is rooted in questioning the way that changing an *intention* changes the moral culpability of an *action:* The Terror bomber and the Strategic Bomber are not morally different from each other. Each is willing to put innocent civilians in harm's way in pursuit of their own ends, and what they intend to do seems to do very little to change the relevant moral facts.

The final reading in this section is an excerpt from Michael Walzer's *Just and Unjust Wars,* a seminal analysis of Just War theory and the morality of armed conflict. Walzer begins by examining the convention that, in wartime, noncombatants can never be attacked at any time. Most civilians are injured or killed in armed conflicts not because they have been directly targeted, but instead because they have been incidentally harmed because of their proximity to the field of battle. The issue that Walzer wants to address in this section, then, has to do with the amount of care that soldiers need to take, in the heat of battle, in order not to harm nearby noncombatants. The DDE is one way of reconciling the absolute prohibition against attacking noncombatants with the legitimate ends of a just war.

Walzer provides an analysis of the classic formulation of the doctrine, noting that the weight of the argument is carried by the third condition. For Walzer, the third condition must be understood in the following way: the intention of the actor must be good, meaning that he or she aims only at the acceptable effect and not at the evil effect. The evil effect is not one of the actor's ends, nor is it a means to his or her ends. This condition shows the importance of both taking aim in wartime and of making sure that what one aims at is, in fact, a legitimate target. But the third clause, on its own, is not enough to satisfy the spirit of the prohibition against killing noncombatants in war. Walzer thinks that, in the heat of battle, soldiers tend not to give adequate consideration to the well-being of nearby noncombatants, instead focusing solely on their lives and the lives of the fellow soldiers. More precautions need to be taken, even in the middle of a firefight, to avoid causing harm to those who are not legitimate military targets. We need to show a positive commitment to save human lives, and not rely solely on the claim that we do not *intend* to kill civilians and noncombatants. According to Walzer, the way we can do this, and still support the DDE, is to modify the third clause in such a way that it promotes a *double intention:* both that the good aim be achieved and that the amount of foreseeable evil be reduced as much as possible. This may require additional risks (within limits) to soldiers' lives to protect the lives of civilians and noncombatants, but this is part and parcel to the life of a soldier and the responsibilities that they accept.

Walzer concludes by applying his new conception of double intention to the Free French bombings of occupied France and the Norwegian bombings of the Vemork heavy water plant in occupied Norway during World War II, and finds these cases to be justified under the new description of the DDE, given the military importance of the targets and the likelihood of failure of other methods of attack.

The articles in this section are intended to familiarize the reader with some of the most crucial and interesting arguments for and against the doctrine of double effect. It is left to the reader to decide whether or not the doctrine, in whatever form it may take, is convincing and whether or not it is germane to the discussion of violent armed conflict. These essays only begin to examine this rich and complicated philosophical issue.[3]

Notes

1. Several of the citations to Aquinas's work can be found in the first section of this volume.
2. This is an abbreviated version of a longer paper. For a more detailed depiction of Bennett's arguments against the doctrine, see his book *The Act Itself* (New York: Oxford University Press, 1995): esp. 194–225.
3. A detailed introduction to the DDE, which includes several of the pieces found here, as well as other ethical applications and more detailed discussion on the theory itself, can be found in *The Doctrine of Double Effect*, P.A. Woodward, Ed. (Notre Dame, IN: University of Notre Dame Press, 2001).

Toward Understanding the Principle of Double Effect[1]

(1980)

Joseph M. Boyle, Jr.

Joseph M. Boyle, Jr. is professor of philosophy at the University of Toronto. His research interests include moral philosophy, ethical theory, bioethics, and applied natural law. Along with articles in these areas, he has coauthored Nuclear Deterrence, Morality, and Realism *(Clarendon Press, 1987), with John Finnis and Germain Grisez.*

The Principle of Double Effect (hereafter PDE) has long been a mainstay of Catholic moral thinking.[2] In recent years, however, the use and discussion of this doctrine have not been limited to Catholics or to theologians.[3] The PDE, or propositions closely related to it, have come up for considerable discussion by English-speaking philosophers.[4]

In spite of this discussion, however, the PDE remains something of a mystery. As I hope to show, its purpose, its essential claims, and its presuppositions are not adequately understood. This lack of understanding is due both to the difficulties and ambiguities in traditional formulations of the PDE and to the fact that its central conceptions are either foreign or contrary to much of contemporary ethics and action theory.[5]

The purpose of this paper, therefore, is to state plainly the propositions involved in the PDE and at least some of the propositions concerning intention, action, and moral responsibility which must be true if some version of the PDE is to be defensible and morally relevant. I will not seek to defend or criticize these propositions here. My aim is to state them clearly and thus to make possible a more intelligent and more decisive discussion of the PDE.

The classic modern formulation of the PDE is presented in J. P. Gury's widely used and often revised manual, *Compendium theologiae moralis*: "It is licit to posit a cause which is either good or indifferent from which there follows a twofold effect, one good, the other evil, if a proportionately grave reason is present, and if the end of the agent is honorable—that is, if he does not intend the evil effect.[6] In a clarification of this statement Gury makes it clear that the PDE contains four conditions, all of which together are required for the type of act in question to be licit: (1) the agent's end must be morally acceptable (*honestus*), (2) the cause must be good or at least indifferent, (3) the good effect must be immediate, and (4) there must be a grave reason for positing the cause.[7]

The determination of what constitutes a grave reason is a matter of normative ethics which I will not consider here; moreover it is sufficiently clear that a grave reason is required to bring about an evil state of affairs—one which it would presumably not be licit to bring about except under these conditions.[8] The sense of 'immediate' in the third condition seems to be that the evil effect may not be a *means* to the good effect. This is suggested by Gury's remark that, if the good came about through the evil effect (*mediante pravo effectu*), good would be sought through evil, and this can never be moral.[9] Thus this condition allows that the evil effect should follow from the good effect, or that the evil effect and the good effect should follow independently from the cause, but not that the good effect should follow from the evil effect.

The second condition—that it must be morally permissible to posit the cause—suggests that the cause which brings about both effects can be morally evaluated independently of either of its effects. Thus we may take the first condition to refer to a human undertaking, the executing of a choice, which can be the subject of moral evaluation independent of the good and evil effects which are brought about.

The application of these four conditions to many cases has been widely controverted. But several clear examples show how it is intended to work. The killing of noncombatants in a justified military action is one example used by Gury: the action may be justified—even if it is foreseen that some noncombatants will certainly be killed—if killing them is not a means of achieving one's military objective, since in this case undertaking the action may be presumed to be in itself good, the bringing about of the deaths is not intended, and there is a grave reason for the action. Gury says that the death of the innocents follows *per accidens,* and is not intended but only permitted.

The justification of killing in self-defense is another frequently used but more controversial application of the PDE. According to Saint Thomas, one intends only one's self-defense, the aggressor's death being outside the agent's intention—an effect of one's defensive act and not a means to one's defense.[10]

Discussion of the application of the PDE to cases like this is beyond the scope of this paper. Such a discussion presupposes that the PDE is intelligible. A first step in understanding the PDE is the determination of what it is meant to do. Is it meant to show that certain acts which, except under these conditions, would be morally impermissible, are, if its conditions are met, morally *justified?* Or is the PDE meant to be a principle of excuse—that is, a principle which lessens the imputability of a bad act?[11]

The Catholic moralists who developed this doctrine are none too clear on this point. Gury, for example, in stating the PDE, formulates it as a set of conditions for the *licitness* or permissibility of a certain action. But Gury in other places and other authors in this tradition write in such a way as to suggest that the PDE is a principle of excuse. They say, in effect, that the unintended consequences of one's acts are not imputable to the agent, or they suggest that the imputability is diminished or somehow indirect.[12] This interpretation is reinforced by the fact that most of these authors deal with the PDE in their treatments of the various kinds of voluntary acts and because of the importance of intention in the PDE.

I believe, however, that the PDE should be understood as a principle of *justification,* and that the tradition, even if it is unclear on this point, is most coherently understood in this way.[13] There are two reasons for thinking this. First, the unintended evil effect, the bringing about of which is rendered licit by the PDE, is clearly imputable to the agent: he knowingly and willingly brings it about. The scholastics often say that it is permitted or consented to; one could more clearly say in modern English that it is *accepted.* But permitting, consenting to, and so on, are volitional acts, or at least volitional dispositions, even if they are not volitional in the paradigmatic sense of intentional actions.[14] There might be a difference in the mode of responsibility one has for what one intends to bring about from that which one has for what one does not intend but willingly accepts. In both cases there might be degrees of imputability, but there is no necessary difference in degree between the two types of willing. What one intends and what one permits are both voluntarily brought about, and thus *both* are imputable. If what one permits were not voluntarily brought about, and thus ascribable to the agent, the fourth condition of the PDE would have no use. This condition states a requirement for the permissibility of permitting certain effects which one may not intend to bring about.

My second reason is a historical consideration. Aquinas's view of human action and intention forms the background for the distinctions upon which the PDE is based. The moralists who articulate and use the PDE often refer explicitly to his analysis of killing in self-defense, and some of the ancestors of the PDE are the sixteenth- and seventeenth-century commentaries on Aquinas's theory of action.[15] This is not to say, of course, that modern proponents of the PDE either consistently or clearheadedly develop his action theory.

According to Aquinas, an act is, morally speaking, the kind of act it is in virtue of what is intended.[16] In other words, Aquinas believes that actions are at least in part defined by the intention with which the agent performs them; intention is an act of volition, and it is necessarily the case that one intend whatever functions as an end or goal in one's actions;[17] one must intend not only the more distant and ulterior goals but also the immediate aim one has in undertaking an action. Thus one must intend what Aquinas calls the *formal object* of one's act.[18] In more contemporary language, an action is undertaking to bring about a certain state of affairs. This state of affairs is intrinsic or essential to the act and is necessarily intended.[19]

If this understanding of action is applied to the conditions of the PDE, it becomes clear that the first condition is invoked to determine the moral kind of the act which is at issue. In the first condition it is required that the agent's end be morally acceptable. The end referred to here might be either the immediate object of the act—the state of affairs the bringing about of which defines the act—or it might be a more remote end. In either case, it is among the things one must intend in acting.[20] Moreover, as Gury explicitly states, this condition is meant to exclude the agent's intending the evil effect. If the good effect is intended and the evil effect is not intended, the act will be, morally speaking, a good act. It will be specified by the good effect as a morally good act.

The act-defining character of intention is also relevant for understanding the third condition. If the evil effect is brought about as a *means* to the good effect, then the evil effect must be intended, and the bringing about of the instrumental state of affairs is morally impermissible. The bad effect is intended if it is chosen as a means because it becomes something which the agent is committed to realizing. The bringing about of this instrumental state of affairs is a morally impermissible act because this state of affairs—the bad effect—determines the moral character of the undertaking. Thus, the third condition is implied by the first condition and the definition of a "means." This condition does not assume, therefore, that the causal sequence of the effects is *itself* morally significant, as is often supposed.[21] In most cases in which one chooses a certain means, it is because of one's beliefs about the causal consequences of what one chooses as a means that one chooses it, but what is morally significant about such a choice is the intention and action involved in executing it.[22]

The first condition and the third, therefore, are attempts to determine exactly what one's act is in situations where the causal initiative involved in one's undertaking brings about both good and evil states of affairs. Together with the fourth condition, these conditions constitute a basis for the *justification* of actions having evil effects: such actions are not themselves evil in kind and there is grave reason for performing them.

The foregoing attempt to explain the PDE as a principle of justification by reference to Aquinas's theory of action can also accommodate the second condition of the PDE—namely, that initiating the causal sequence must be morally permissible independently of its good and bad effects. If this "positing of the cause" can be determined to be impermissible independently of the evil effect at issue, or of some other evil end, then one is not justified in initiating the causal sequence.

To the extent that this condition suggests that it is possible to determine the morality of initiating the causal sequence without reference to *any* effect, then it is inconsistent with Aquinas's view of action. But to that extent it is also confused: cause and effect are correlative, and "positing a cause" can be immoral only because it brings about *some* effect which it is impermissible to bring about.

This way of understanding the second condition has the effect of rendering it, strictly speaking, superfluous. If an act is not permissible, then the doing of that act would involve the intention of what is evil, and this is prohibited by the first condition.

By this point my attempt to treat the PDE as a principle of justification may appear to be radically revisionist. The second condition is rendered superfluous, and the third is implied by the first together with the definition of a means.

The redundancy of the traditional formulations of the PDE, however, is understandable if one considers the casuistical purpose for which the PDE was meant to be used and the distinctions the scholastics were accustomed to make. Following Aquinas, the scholastics held that the moral character of an act was determined by the end, the object of the act, and the circumstances in which the act was performed.[23] Thus, the first condition could be taken to exclude acts done for an immoral purpose; the second to exclude acts which are intrinsically immoral—that is, whose object it is impermissible to bring about; and the third to exclude immoral means to good ends—an exclusion which is not always covered by the second condition.

More concretely, the first condition would exclude, for example, giving someone money in order to get him drunk; the second, making oneself drunk in order to give someone a lesson in the value of sobriety; and the third, giving someone money in order to get him drunk in order to teach him a lesson. In the first case, the "positing of the cause" is permissible and there is no evil means to a good end, but the aim is evil. In the second case, the aim is good but the cause posited—getting oneself drunk— is evil. In the third case, the final end of the action is good, as is the positing of the cause, but an intermediate means is evil— namely, getting the person drunk.

The PDE, then, can be understood as a principle of justification. In its briefest form it can be stated in the following way: it is morally permissible to undertake an action when one knows that the undertaking will bring about at least one state of affairs such that, if this state of affairs were intrinsic to the action undertaken, the action would be rendered morally impermissible, if and only if (1) the state of affairs is not intrinsic to the action undertaken— that is, it is not intended—and (2) there is a serious reason for undertaking the action.

This formulation, however, gives rise to further questions. In particular, it gives rise to questions about the distinctions made by the PDE and about the moral significance of these distinctions.

First, the PDE as explained here forces one to draw in an odd way the distinction between the objective considerations about the rightness or wrongness of behavior and the subjective considerations relevant to evaluating the moral quality of the agent. One might expect that the question of rightness or wrongness is a question about behavior and its consequences, whereas questions about the goodness or badness of the agent would consider such things as the agent's motives and intentions as well as factors related to the imputability of his act. The PDE as explained here, however, requires one to regard the

question of rightness or wrongness not simply as a question about behavior but also as a question about actions which contain intentions as an essential part.

Second, the PDE requires the moral significance of a distinction which, according to many, cannot even be drawn. Many modern philosophers regard the difference between what is intended and what is foreseen and "permitted," but not intended, as a merely verbal difference.[24] Moreover, it is certainly not clear what significance this difference has—supposing it can be drawn—for purposes of the moral evaluation of acts. Even if one admits that acts are defined by the agent's intentions and distinguished from foreseen consequences which are merely "permitted," one might wonder why it is that an agent's acts have a moral significance which is different from—and more decisive than—the moral significance of the foreseen consequences of what he does. It is important to recognize that the PDE does not require that the foreseen consequences of acts be in no way relevant to determining the rightness or wrongness of the agent's concrete behavior; they are relevant, but only in a subsidiary way. Thus, if the action is itself morally permissible, and if there is a serious reason for undertaking it, then it may be done morally no matter what the foreseen consequences may be.

The answers to these questions are based on a factor which has been completely overlooked in discussions of the PDE[25]—namely, the view of voluntariness and responsibility which the PDE presupposes.

An account of this view goes something like the following.[26] There are many different types of voluntary acts; in fact, the notion of "voluntariness" is an equivocal one. There is, however, an order in these senses such that one could say with the medievals that voluntariness is an "analogous" notion, or, in more current language, that there are family resemblances between the various senses of "voluntary."

In this ordered set of meanings of "voluntary" one is paradigmatic—namely, that sense in which it is said of an act which is the execution of deliberate, free choice. In this case, the elements which all voluntary acts have in one way or another are preeminently present;[27] no human act is so clearly or properly self-initiated as is an action which executes a free choice. A free choice is a choice in which all the causal factors other than the agent's choosing are not sufficient to bring about the choice.[28] Moreover, in a deliberate choice one knows what one is doing; one considers and reflects upon the options and their various attractions.

By contrast, actions which are voluntary in any other sense of the word involve some diminishing of one or both of these components. Nondeliberate acts—for example, actions done out of passion or fear or under duress—will lack the cognitional component involved in deliberate choices. Similarly, habitual acts, automatic reactions, and the actions of children and of those who are not *compos mentis* are in various ways not self-initiated as free choices are; they are self-initiating but the self is not in control.

Human behavior which carries out deliberate free choices, therefore, is voluntary in the strongest sense of the term.[29] Thus it is not surprising that such behavior is often regarded as the primary subject of moral evaluation.

Such behavior can be understood in the following way: In deliberating one considers various incompatible practical proposals—one's bringing about state of affairs *P* or one's bringing about state of affairs *Q* (where *P* includes non-*Q* and *Q* non-*P*). Choice is one's selection of one's bringing about *P* rather than *Q* or *Q* rather than *P*. The behavior consequent upon a choice is the undertaking to bring about *P* or to bring about *Q*. In other words, the agent acts with the intention of bringing about *P* or with the intention of bringing about *Q*.

Thus, one who, after considering several practical proposals and freely selecting one of them, executes his choice by undertaking to bring about the state of affairs proposed is performing a paradigmatically voluntary act. This performance is, according to this view of voluntariness, a doing of the type that is either right or wrong.

But how is this performance to be understoood? Should the performance be understood in a formal way—as simply bringing about the state of affairs which it was undertaken to bring about? Or should this performance be taken as a kind of individual, a concrete event with many causal connections which bring about many states of affairs? It seems to me that the controverted ontological question of whether actions are individuals of some sort or the bringing about of certain abstract states of affairs can be set aside for present purposes. If an action is a *concretum,* then it will be truly described by a number of propositions. The question relevant here, should such an ontological view be accepted, would be under which of the descriptions the act should be morally evaluated in the first instance.

The proponent of the PDE would hold that the performance should be understood *formally,* since the performance is—insofar as it is the type of voluntary act defined above—the execution of a choice, and the choice is the commitment to bring about a certain definite state of affairs.

In other words, while an agent's performance involves a causal initiative that can have many foreseeable consequences, it is not the performance as a willing causal initiative, together with some set of the effects of that initiative, which is primarily voluntary or the primary subject of moral evaluation.[30] A causal initiative—or at least the willful refraining from such an initiative—is part of the notion of a voluntary act in this paradigmatic sense. But it is part of the act only insofar as it executes the choice and not as a concrete event with an indefinite set of effects.

This is not to say, of course, that the bringing about of the foreseen effects of one's performances is not voluntary. It is, but not in the way in which the executions of choices—regarded just as such—are voluntary. The foreseen consequences of one's potential performances are no doubt a part of what is considered in the deliberation leading to choices. But they are included in this deliberative process in a unique way. Frequently, they do not appear to be of any practical consequence to the person deliberating, and sometimes they are seen to interfere with the achievement of either the state of affairs one is considering bringing about or some further goal with respect to which this state of affairs is taken to be instrumental. In other words, the foreseen consequences of one's bringing about an intended state of affairs are often considered in deliberating, but not as reasons *for* the action—rather, they are sometimes conditions *in spite of which* one acts. It is not for the sake of such conditions that one selects an option; it is not these effects to which one is committed in acting.

If this is correct, the agent in acting has a fundamentally different attitude toward what he intends and toward what he foresees and consents to or accepts but does not intend. The agent who acts with the intention of bringing about a certain state of affairs makes that state of affairs his goal; he sees it as worthwhile or as instrumentally valuable and commits himself to bringing it about. Clearly, what is thus regarded as valuable is not all that one foresees will come about by his initiative. For example, pain involved in undergoing surgery is not regarded as valuable by the patient. He would avoid it if he could.

The agent's attitude toward such consequences as this is entirely different from his attitude toward what he intends. These consequences need not be seen as good or as desirable; there is no commitment to bring them about; in many cases the agent would avoid them if he could. They are not a part of what one chooses to bring about.

This account of voluntary action provides the basis for answering the questions listed above. Given this account of voluntary action, the distinction between factors relevant to determining the rightness of actions and factors relevant to assessing the moral qualities of agents are properly drawn where the PDE requires. The primary object of the moral evaluation of the act is the bringing about of the state of affairs which the agent is committed to realizing. This action includes and is defined by the agent's intention. Moreover, this way of drawing the distinction between factors relevant to determining the imputability of the act and factors relevant to characterizing the act to be evaluated allows for the obvious excusing factors. It allows for questions about whether the agent knows the moral character of his undertaking and questions about whether the agent's choice is free. It does imply, however, that an action will be regarded *as if* it were a voluntary act even if in fact it is not imputable, because it is only as the execution of a choice that behavior can be characterized as morally significant. Thus, for example, if an omission or piece of habitual behavior is regarded as morally wrong, it is because that omission or piece of behavior would be wrong if it embodied the execution of a deliberate choice.

The second question is also resolved by this account of voluntary action; the distinction between what is intended and what is consented to is intelligible in terms of this account. A morally significant act is the execution of a choice. What one chooses is not an indeterminate set of foreseeable results of one's performance but the bringing about of a definite state of affairs regarded as worthwhile or valuable. Thus there is a basis for the distinction between what is intended and what is not intended but consented to, or between actions defined by the state of affairs intended and the consequences of actions defined by what is not intended but consented to.

Moreover, this account of voluntary action shows why the distinction between what is intended and what is foreseen and accepted but not intended is taken to be morally relevant. Since it is one's choices and their execution which are primarily voluntary, it is these which are the primary object of moral evaluation. The states of affairs intended in such acts are what the agent, as it were, sets his or her heart on. It is the commitment to these states of affairs which is the basis upon which a person forms his character and makes himself a certain kind of person. Moreover, if moral demands are regarded as unconditional demands upon one's free choice,[31] then it is by choosing and committing oneself to some such states of affairs that one acts morally or immorally. In

other words, if moral demands are demands upon one's free choice and if free choice is the adopting of a proposal that one bring about a certain state of affairs regarded as valuable or worthwhile, then what moral normativeness primarily bears upon—as far as behavior goes—is human action in the sense defined here.

This account of the view of voluntary action presupposed by the PDE also throws light on the connection between the PDE and the so-called absolutism of traditional Catholic ethics. By "absolutism" I mean the view that there are exceptionless moral proscriptions.

First of all, absolutism is not required by the PDE. The PDE does not explain how one is to come to the normative judgments presupposed by the first three conditions and enjoined by the fourth. The first three conditions, if met, are sufficient to characterize the act in question as a good type of act. But they do not explain how acts of that type are judged to be morally good. Likewise, these conditions require that the "evil effect" would be a bad kind of act if any of the first three is not met, and that there must be a grave reason for accepting such an act, but they do not specify what makes an immoral act immoral. This judgment might well be made on the basis of the view that such an act is proscribed by a general exceptionless proscription, but it need not be so based. Any normative theory which allows that there are kinds of acts which are good and bad could be *consistent* with the PDE and could make use of the PDE.

Furthermore, the PDE is not required by all forms of absolutism. An absolutist system such as Kant's, for example, does not make use of the PDE, and it is possible to use principles other than the PDE to resolve cases of moral perplexity.[32] Moreover, an absolutist might limit his exceptionless proscriptions so that cases dealt with by the PDE are either clearly prohibited or clearly allowed by the relevant rule.

But there is a vital connection between the PDE and the form of "absolutism" with which it is usually associated. This form of absolutism does not depend on a set of intuited or commanded absolutes, or a set of absolutes based on generalizations from particular cases, but on moral rules which direct one to respect basic human goods or values. Specifically moral precepts mandate that these basic goods be promoted whenever possible and that they not be attacked or acted against. This leads to moral norms—including absolute proscriptions—of a very general sort. For example, human life is taken to be a basic human good. The proscription of killing, therefore, will be quite general.[33] Moreover, these goods are the basis for deliberation and choice. They are pursued—in the morally relevant way—by voluntary acts and especially by acts executing free choices. The demand that we respect all the human goods—and especially that we not act against them—is a demand on our free choice.

This normative view does require the PDE, but *not* simply because it is absolutist. This connection is not a matter of straightforward implication. The normative theory in question does imply a part of the theory of human agency presupposed by the PDE. Thus they both imply the same thing. The necessity of the connection between this normative theory and the PDE is established by the facts that (1) the actual world is such that the realization of most human choices is by way of causal initiatives which bring about many states of affairs other than that state of affairs which the agent intends to realize through his performance, and (2) some of

these states of affairs are contrary to one or more basic goods. These facts require that one committed to a normative theory demanding respect for a set of basic goods hold the PDE. Otherwise respecting the goods becomes an impossibility, since any performance can—and many performances do—bring about what is contrary to one or more basic goods.

To sum up: the PDE is a coherent doctrine of justification. But it continues to be misunderstood because the theory of agency which it presupposes is ignored. If this view of human agency is false, then the PDE must be abandoned; but if this theory of agency is true, and if the normative theory which makes use of the PDE can be defended, then the PDE is a long way toward vindication.

Notes

1. The work for this paper was begun while on a College Teachers in Residence Fellowship of the National Endowment for the Humanities. I have profited from discussing the issues taken up here with R. M. Chisholm and Alan Donagan. I thank Germain Grisez for help on several drafts of this paper.

2. See Joseph Mangan, S.J., "An Historical Analysis of the Principle of Double Effect," *Theological Studies* 10 (1949): 41–61; J. Ghoos, "L'Acte a double effet: Etude de théologie positive," *Ephemerides theologicae Louvaniensis* 27 (1951): 30–52; and F. J. Connell, in *The New Catholic Encyclopedia,* s.v. "Principle of Double Effect."

3. E.g., Paul Ramsey, the eminent Methodist theologian, makes extensive use of the PDE; see his *War and the Christian Conscience* (Durham, N.C.: Duke University Press, 1961). For a non-theologian, see G. E. M. Anscombe, "War and Murder," in *War and Morality,* ed. R. Wasserstrom (Belmont, Calif.: Wadsworth Publishing Co., 1970), pp. 50–51.

4. See, e.g., Philippa Foot, "Abortion and the Doctrine of Double Effect," in *Moral Problems,* ed. J. Rachels (New York: Harper & Row, 1971), pp. 28–41; Jonathan Bennett, "Whatever the Consequences," *Analysis* 26 (1966): 83–102 and the ensuing discussion; Alan Donagan, *The Theory of*

Morality (Chicago: University of Chicago Press, 1977), pp. 122–27, 157–64.

5. See Germain Grisez, "Toward a Consistent Natural Law Ethics of Killing," *American Journal of Jurisprudence* 15 (1970): 73–79, for a critique of certain aspects of traditional formulations.

6. J. P. Gury, S.J. (revised by A. Ballerini, S.J.), *Compendium theologiae moralis,* 2d ed. (Rome and Turin, 1869), p. 7. The translation from the Latin is mine. Mangan, pp. 60–61, provides a translation from the fifth German edition of Gury's entire treatment of the PDE.

7. Gury, p. 8.

8. This condition can, but need not, be understood in a consequentialist way. It can be understood as requiring that relevant obligations other than those bearing on the directness or indirectness of the bringing about of the evil effect be considered.

9. Gury, p. 8.

10. *S.T.* II-II,64,7.

11. See J. L. Austin, "A Plea for Excuses," in *Philosophical Papers,* ed. J. O. Urmson and G. J. Warnock, 2d ed. (London: Oxford University Press, 1970), pp. 175–77, for an explanation of the difference between justification and excuse.

12. See, e.g., Arthurus Vermeersch, S.J., *Theologiae moralis: Principia, responsa, consilia* (Rome: Gregorian University Press, 1922), 1:118. Vermeersch, one of the most important Catholic moralists in the early decades of this century, states the PDE as follows: "Effectus malus qui actionem sequi permittitur, *non imputatur,* si diversa est efficientia immediata, et permissio ratione proportionata gravi excusatur" (emphasis mine).

13. See William Conway, "The Act of Two Effects," *Irish Theological Quarterly* 18 (1951): 127–29.

14. See R. G. Frey, "Some Aspects to the Doctrine of Double Effect," *Canadian Journal of Philosophy* 5 (1975): 265.

15. See John of St. Thomas, *Cursus theologicus, tome 6: De bonitate et malitia actuum humanorum,* disputatio 11 (Paris, 1885); and Salmanticenses, *Cursus theologicus,* tome 7, tractatus 13, disputatio 10, dubium 6 (Paris, 1877).

16. *S.T.* II-II,64,7: "Morales autem act us recipiunt speciem secundum id quod intenditur,. . ." See also *S.T.* I-II,72,1.

17. *S.T.* I-II,12,1; *De Veritate* 22,14. For a discussion of these and other relevant texts, see my "Aquinas on *Praeter Intentionem,*" *Thomist* 42 (1978): 649–65.

18. *S.T.* I-II,20,4;I-II,72,3, ad 2;I-II,73,1.

19. See G. H. von Wright, *Norm and Action: A Logical Inquiry* (New York: Humanities Press, 1963), pp. 39–41; *The Varieties of Goodness* (New York: Humanities Press, 1963), pp. 39–41, 123–25.

20. Gury, p. 7.

21. E.g., by Frey, pp. 261, 280–81.

22. See Grisez, pp. 87–89, for a critique of traditional formulations of the PDE on this point.

23. *S.T.* I-II,18,2,3,4.

24. See Henry Sidgwick, *Methods of Ethics,* 7th ed. (New York: Dover Publications, 1966), p. 202; R. M. Chisholm, "The Structure of Intention," *Journal of Philosophy* 67 (1970): 636; for a response and reference to other literature, see Joseph M. Boyle, Jr., and Thomas D. Sullivan, "The Diffusiveness of Intention Principle: A Counter-Example," *Philosophical Studies* 31 (1977): 357–60.

25. For example, by R. A. Duff, "Absolute Principles and Double Effect," *Analysis* 36 (1976): 68–80.

26. The following paragraphs are inspired by *S.T.* I-II,6–21.

27. The notion of "voluntary act" supposed is Aristotle's; see *Nichomachean Ethics* 3.1109b30–1111b3, and esp. 1111a22–23: "The voluntary would seem to be that of which the moving principle is in the agent himself, he being aware of the particular circumstances of the action."

28. Joseph M. Boyle, Jr., Germain Grisez, and Olaf Tollefsen, *Free Choice: A Self-referential Argument* (Notre Dame, Ind.: University of Notre Dame Press, 1976), pp. 11–23.

29. See *S.T.* I-II,6,1: "Whence when a human being most fully [*maxime*] knows the end of his act and moves himself, then is his act most fully [*maxime*] voluntary."

30. See Donagan, pp. 37–52, 112–22, for a contrary view.

31. See Boyle et al., pp. 164–66, for an exposition of this view of moral norms.

32. See Donagan, pp. 149–56.

33. See ibid., pp. 60–65; and Grisez.

Actions, Intentions, and Consequences: The Doctrine of Double Effect[1]

(1989)

Warren S. Quinn

Warren S. Quinn was professor of philosophy at UCLA from 1968 until his tragic death in 1991. He worked in many philosophical areas, including action theory, moral philosophy, metaethics, and metaphysics. Some of his most important work in moral theory and metaethics can be found in Morality and Action *(Cambridge University Press, 1994).*

Situations in which good can be secured for some people only if others suffer harm are of great significance to moral theory.[2] Consequentialists typically hold that the right thing to do in such cases is to maximize overall welfare. But nonconsequentialists think that many other factors matter. Some, for example, think that in situations of conflict it is often more acceptable to let a certain harm befall someone than actively to bring the harm about. I believe that this view, which I call the Doctrine of Doing and Allowing, is correct, and I defend it elsewhere.[3] But there is a different and even better known anticonsequentialist principle in the Doctrine of Double Effect (for short, the DDE).[4] According to one of the common readings of this principle, the pursuit of a good tends to be less acceptable where a resulting harm is intended as a means than where it is merely foreseen.[5] It is this controversial idea that I wish to examine here.

There are two major problems with the DDE. First, there is a difficulty in formulating it so that it succeeds in discriminating between cases that, intuitively speaking, should be distinguished. In particular, I will need to find a formulation that escapes the disturbing objection that under a strict enough interpretation the doctrine fails to rule against many or most of the choices commonly taken to illustrate its negative force. Second, there is a question of rationale. What, apart from its agreeing with our particular intuitions, can be said in favor of the doctrine? Indeed, why should we accept the intuitions that support it? In answer, I shall suggest a rationale with clear Kantian echoes.

I

Like the Doctrine of Doing and Allowing, the DDE discriminates between two kinds of morally problematic agency. It discriminates against agency in which there is some kind of intending of an objectionable outcome as conducive to the agent's end, and it discriminates in favor of agency that involves only foreseeing, but not that kind of intending, of an objectionable outcome. That is, it favors and disfavors these forms of agency in allowing that, *ceteris paribus,* the pursuit of a great enough good might justify one but not the other. The doctrine is meant to capture certain kinds of fairly common moral intuitions about pairs of cases which have the *same* consequential profile—in which agents bring about the same good result at the same cost in lives lost and harm suffered—but in which the character of the intention differs in the indicated way.

One such pair of contrasting cases is drawn from modern warfare: In the Case of the Strategic Bomber (SB), a pilot bombs an enemy factory in order to destroy its productive capacity. But in doing this he foresees that he will kill innocent civilians who live nearby. Many of us see this kind of military action as much easier to justify than that in the Case of the Terror Bomber (TB), who deliberately kills innocent civilians in order to demoralize the enemy. Another pair of cases involves medicine: In both there is a shortage of resources for the investigation and proper treatment of a new, life-threatening disease. In the first scenario doctors decide to cope by selectively treating only those who can be cured most easily, leaving the more stubborn cases untreated. Call this the Direction of Resources Case (DR). In the contrasting and intuitively more problematic example, doctors decide on a crash experimental program in which they deliberately leave the stubborn cases untreated in order to learn more about the nature of the disease. By this strategy they reasonably expect to do as much long-term medical good as they would in DR. Call this the Guinea Pig Case (GP). In neither case do the nontreated know about or consent to the decision against treating them.

Another pair of medical examples is found in most discussions of double effect. In the Craniotomy Case (CC) a woman will die unless the head of the fetus she is trying to deliver is crushed. But the fetus may be safely removed if the mother is allowed to die. In the Hysterectomy Case (HC), a pregnant mother's uterus is cancerous and must be removed if she is to be saved. This will, given the limits of available medical technology, kill the fetus. But if no operation is performed the mother will eventually die after giving birth to a healthy infant. Many people see less of a moral difference between these two cases than between the other pairs. This might be for a variety of reasons extraneous to the doctrine: because the fetus is not yet a person and therefore not yet within the moral framework, because the craniotomy is seen as a way of defending the mother against the fetus, because the fetus's position within the mother's body gives her special rights over it, and so on. But the relative weakness of the intuitive contrast here might also signal something important about the doctrine's central distinction. I shall say more about this later. But for the present it will be useful to include this pair of cases under the DDE, if only because it naturally illustrates the objection mentioned earlier.

According to that objection, the doctor in CC does not intend, at least not strictly speaking, that the fetus actually die.[6] On the contrary, we would expect the doctor to be glad if, by some miracle, it survived unharmed. It is not death itself, or even harm itself, that is strictly intended, but rather an immediately physical effect on the fetus that will allow its removal.[7] That effect will of course be fatal to the fetus, but it is not intended *as* fatal. The intentions in CC are therefore really no different from those in HC.

It might seem that this kind of point cannot be made about the bombing and nontreatment cases. In GP the doctors seem to need the disease to continue so that they can observe its effects. And in TB the pilot seems to need the deaths of the civilians to lower enemy morale. But Jonathan Bennett suggests a way of extending the objection to the bombing case.[8] The terror bomber does not, he argues, need the civilians actually to be dead. He only needs them to be as good as dead and to seem dead until the war ends. If by some miracle they "came back to life" after the war was over, he would not object. And something similar might be said about the doctors in GP. While they need the disease to continue its course, they do not need the victims actually to be harmed by it. If by some miracle the victims developed special ways of withstanding the disease so that they remained comfortable and well-functioning despite its progress, the doctors would be glad.[9]

This line of objection clearly threatens to deprive the doctrine of most of its natural applications. One reply is to say that it surely matters how *close* the connection is between that which is, strictly speaking, intended and the resulting foreseen harm. If the connection is close enough, then the doctrine should treat the harm as if it were strictly intended.[10] And, the reply might go on, the connection is close enough in the cases I have used to illustrate the doctrine's negative force. But what does this idea of closeness amount to? H.L.A. Hart suggests a possible answer by way of the example of someone violently striking a glass just in order to hear the sound of the initial impact. In such a case the further outcome, the shattering of the glass, is "so immediately and invariably" connected with the intended impact that the

connection seems conceptual rather than contingent.[11] The death of the fetus in CC is, arguably, connected with the intended impact on its skull in just this immediate and invariable way. And the deaths, or at lease some harms, in TB and GP seem just as closely connected with what is strictly intended in those cases.

But what of the contrasting cases? Since hysterectomies are rarely performed on pregnant women, they rarely result in the death of a fetus. So we might say that what is strictly intended in HC (that the uterus be removed) is not, in the relevant sense, closely connected with the fetus's death. And we might hope to find something similar to say in SB and DR. But in taking this way of preserving the contrasts, we would be making everything depend on which strictly intended outcomes of the various choices we fasten upon.

This leads to a new problem. For certain things that the doctor in CC strictly intends for the fetus lack an invariable fatal upshot. Indeed, if craniotomies are ever performed on fetuses that are already dead, then a craniotomy is already such a thing. Even more obviously, the doctor in HC might strictly intend something that is invariably fatal to a fetus. Suppose, for example, that hysterectomies performed on patients who are in the early months of pregnancy are distinguished by the use of a special anesthetic that is safer for the patient and, in itself, harmless to the fetus. This peculiarity could hardly make the operation in HC more difficult to justify, but it would imply that the strictly intended medical means were immediately and invariably connected with the death of a fetus.[12] Perhaps similar things can be said about the other cases. A strategic bomber might have as his mission the bombing of automotive factories. This would not make him a terror bomber, for he would still not aim at civilian casualties. But, for obvious reasons, no automobile factories have ever existed completely apart from civilian populations. So the kind of thing the bomber strictly intends immediately and invariably results in some innocent deaths.

Two problems have emerged: First, since more than one thing may be strictly intended in a given choice, the pronouncements of the doctrine may depend on how the choice happens to be described. This relativity is embarrassing. We would like the doctrine to speak with one voice in any given case. Second, if we try to get around this problem by saying that the doctrine discriminates against a choice in which anything that is strictly intended is also closely connected with death or harm, the doctrine will make uninviting moral distinctions. As we have seen, it will speak against HC if hysterectomies performed on pregnant patients have some distinguishing surgical feature. Otherwise it will speak in favor. And it will speak against the strategic bomber's attack on an urban factory if he was looking specifically for an automotive plant but not, perhaps, if he was looking for a strategically important productive facility.[13] Another approach clearly seems called for.

Instead of looking for a way to identify intrinsically bad effects that are 'close enough' to what is intended, we might look instead for a way to identify choices that are intended under some intrinsically negative description. We might then find a way to show that the actions in TB and CC, but not in SB or HC, are intentional *as killings* and that the inaction in GP, but not in DR, is intentional *as a letting die.* Elizabeth Anscombe gives us one such criterion.[14] If we ask a man why he is pushing a mower, he will perhaps say "to cut the grass"; if we ask why he is cutting the grass, he may say "to get things spruced up around here," and so on. The "to. . ." answers, or answers that can be understood in terms of them, give further intentions with which the agent acts. If, his choice being described in a certain way, he accepts the 'why' question and replies with a "to. . ." answer, then his choice is intentional under that description. But if he rejects the question in a certain familiar way, his choice is unintentional. If asked why he is cutting the grass he replies, for example, "I don't care about that, I'm just out to annoy the neighbors" or "Can't be helped—it goes with this terrific form of exercise," his cutting the grass is not, as such, intentional.

This seems to give the desired result when applied to our cases. If we ask the doctor in CC why he is killing the fetus, he will naturally say "to save the mother." If we ask the pilot in TB why he is killing the civilians, he will say "to help with the war." And if we ask the doctors in GP why they withhold treatment, they will say "to observe the progress of the disease." And it might be thought that if we ask similar questions in the other cases, the 'why' question will be rejected in a way that shows the choices to be unintentional. Thus, if asked why he is killing the fetus, the doctor in HC will avoid a "to. . ." answer, saying instead something like "It can't be helped if I am to save the mother."

Actually, this seems not quite right. If the doctors in DR were asked why they weren't treating the group in question, they might naturally reply "*to* save our resources for more easily treated cases." And this, by Anscombe's criterion, would seem to make the nontreatment intentional. But waiving this difficulty, there is another worry. What if the agents in the problematic cases (TB, GP, and CC) become philosophically sophisticated? Perhaps they will then come to reject the 'why' questions in the manner of their counterparts. The terror bomber, for example, might respond by saying, "The actual deaths can't be helped if I am to create the realistic appearance of death and destruction." By giving such answers, he and the others will be opting for a more demanding criterion of the intentional. All aspects of an action or inaction that do not in the strictest sense contribute to an agent's goal will be trimmed away as unintentional. By this criterion, the action in CC is intentional as a crushing and that in TB is intentional as an apparent killing. But neither is intentional as a killing. And in GP the inaction is intentional as way of facilitating medical research, but not as a letting die.

Now it would be very natural to object that the ordinary, more relaxed criterion of the intentional is the right one, and that the stricter criterion is specious. But how is this to be made out? We might try to introduce a form of essentialism here, claiming that the surgery in CC and the bombing in TB are essentially killings or harmings, while the surgery in HC and the bombing in SB are not. But surely the ground of this essentialism would be the prior conviction that the killings in CC and TB are intentional while those in HC and SB are not. The issue about intentionality seems to be the basic one. And what would we say about the inaction in GP—that it was essentially a failure to prevent harm? But then this would also seem true of the inaction in DR.

On the one side we have Anscombe's criterion of the intentional, which pretty well maps our ordinary ways of speaking, while on the other we have a criterion that is structurally similar but stricter. The problem here about intention is reminis-

cent of a problem about causality that arises in connection with the Doctrine of Doing and Allowing. Certain defenses of that doctrine (which discriminates against active harming and in favor of allowing harm) appeal to a familiar conception of causality according to which active harming *causes* harm while inactively allowing harm does not. But opponents counter that according to other, philosophically superior conceptions of causality, inaction can be every bit as much a cause of harm. Now I have argued that if DDA is sound theory, it ought to have force on any plausible conception of causality.[15] And I feel much the same here. If the DDE is sound, its force ought to be capturable on any plausible theory of the intentional, even one that would revise ordinary ways of speaking. So, for purposes of argument, I shall grant opponents of the doctrine the greatest latitude in paring back intentional actions to their indisputably intentional cores.

II

We must therefore find a different reply to the difficulty with which we started. And I think I see a way. For we have been neglecting one striking respect in which members of our contrasting pairs differ. Take TB and SB. In the former case, but not the latter, the bomber undeniably intends in the strictest sense that the civilians be involved in a certain explosion, which he produces, precisely because their involvement in it serves his goal. He may not, if Bennett is right, intend their deaths. But his purpose requires at least this—that they be violently impacted by the explosion of his bombs. That this undeniably intended effect can be specified in a way that does not strictly entail their deaths is, on the view I am proposing, beside the point. What matters is that the effect serves the agent's end precisely because it is an effect *on civilians*. The case with SB is quite different. The bomber in that case intends an explosion, but not in order that any civilians be affected by it. Of course he is well aware that his bombs will kill many of them, and perhaps he cannot honestly say that this effect will be "unintentional" in any standard sense, or that he "does not mean to" kill them. But he can honestly deny that their involvement in the explosion is anything to his purpose.

The same contrast is found in the medical cases. The doctor in CC strictly intends to produce an effect on the fetus so that the mother can be saved by that effect. But the doctor in HC has, as we have seen, no such intention. Even if he cannot deny that, in some ordinary sense, he "intends" the fetus's death, he can rightly insist that the effects on the fetus of his surgery are nothing toward his medical purpose. Similarly, the doctors in GP intend, as something toward their further goal, that the disease in the untreated patients work its course. And this could be true even if, wishing to investigate only the effects of the disease within cells, they had no interest in the pain and loss of function it also causes. But in DR nothing that happens to the untreated patients serves the doctors' further goal.[16]

The important way in which the cases differ should not be obscured by the following complication. We have seen that a doctor in HC might intend to use the special anesthetic "safest for a *pregnant* patient." Would it follow from this allusion to the fetus that the doctor does, after all, strictly intend something for it? No. The medical relevance of the patient's pregnancy does not mean that any of the surgical effects on the fetus are medically useful. Some-

thing similar holds in SB. Suppose the bomber wants, for moral reasons, to target factories in the least populated district of a certain city. If so, the formulation of his strictly intended means contains an indirect reference to the civilians whom he may kill. But this hardly turns him into a terror bomber. The impact of his bombs on those civilians is still nothing to his military purpose.

This clear distinction between the intentional structures of the contrasting cases is the key to a new and better formulation of the doctrine. To put things in the most general way, we should say that it distinguishes between agency in which harm comes to some victims, at least in part, from the agent's deliberately involving them in something in order to further his purpose precisely by way of their being so involved (agency in which they figure as *intentional objects*)[17] and harmful agency in which either nothing is in that way intended for the victims or what is so intended does not contribute to their harm.[18] Let us call the first kind of agency in the production of harm *direct* and the second kind *indirect*. According to this version of the doctrine, we need, *ceteris paribus,* a stronger case to justify harmful direct agency than to justify equally harmful indirect agency.[19] Put this way, the doctrine solves the original problem of showing a genuine difference in the intentional structures of our contrasting cases, even under a strict interpretation of what is intended. And it makes no appeal to the problematic notion of "closeness." For direct agency requires neither that harm itself be useful nor that what is useful be causally connected in some especially close way with the harm it helps bring about.[20] There is another, related advantage. With this version of the doctrine, we can sidestep all potentially controversial questions about whether the agents in our various cases kill or harm intentionally. It is enough that we can identify the things they uncontroversially intend as contributing to their goal.

Our further bit of line-drawing remains. We have not yet defined the difference between the more pronounced moral asymmetry of DR and GP, or SB and TB, and the apparently weaker asymmetry of HC and CC. This difference may partly depend on whether the agent, in his strategy, sees the victim as an advantage or as a difficulty. In CC the doctor wants the fetus removed from the birth canal. Its presence there is the problem. In GP and TB, on the other hand, the availability of potential victims presents an opportunity. By bringing it about that certain things are true of them, the agents positively further their goals. Perhaps it would not be surprising if we regarded fatal or harmful exploitation as more difficult to justify than fatal or harmful elimination. If so, we might say that the doctrine strongly discriminates against direct agency that benefits from the presence of the victim (direct *opportunistic* agency) and more weakly discriminates against direct agency that aims to remove an obstacle or difficulty that the victim presents (direct *eliminative* agency).

III

The DDE, of course, has only prima facie moral force. Special rights may allow us to harm someone's interests by way of direct (and even direct opportunistic) agency. Various rights of competition and the right to punish seem to be examples. Certain other cases may prompt qualifications or special interpretations of the doctrine. Suppose that the doctor in HC needs to alter, harmlessly, the position of the fetus before the womb can be safely removed. Whether the overall surgical procedure would still count as indirect harming seems a matter of interpretation. If we saw the manipulation of the fetus as a partial cause of its later removal, we would presumably count the harming as direct. If we saw the manipulation as a precondition, but not a partial cause, of the removal, we would count the harming as indirect.

Another problematic kind of case involves innocent hostages or other persons who physically get in the way of our otherwise legitimate targets or projects. Does our shooting through or running over them involve a direct intention to affect them? I think not. It is to our purpose, in the kind of case I am imagining, that a bullet or car move through a certain space, but it is not to our purpose that it in fact move through or over someone occupying that space. The victims in such cases are of no use to us and do not constitute empirical obstacles (since they will not deflect the missile or vehicle in question). If we act despite their presence, we act exactly as we would if they were not there. If, on the other hand, we needed to aim at someone in order to hit a target, that person would clearly figure as an intentional object. Another tricky case is one in which we could, and would if we had to, accomplish our end by harmful indirect agency; but it is better, perhaps safer for those to be benefited, to pursue the end by harmful agency that is direct. It seems clear why we might wish to make this kind of case an exception.

Before we turn to the defense of the doctrine, we should briefly consider the way in which it interacts with the distinction, mentioned in connection with the Doctrine of Doing and Allowing, between what is actively brought about and what is merely allowed to happen. I have claimed that DDE, with the exceptions noted, discriminates against harmful direct agency. But, as we have seen, people may figure as intentional objects not only of a choice to act but also of a choice not to act. DDE therefore cuts across the distinction between harming and allowing harm. Sometimes, as in TB and CC, it discriminates against direct agency in which harm is done. And sometimes, as in GP, it discriminates against direct agency in which harm is allowed.

In all of these cases we seem to find an original negative or positive right that, while opposed by other rights, seems to be strengthened by the fact that harm will come via direct agency.[21] Civilians in wartime have negative rights not to be killed. But if their government is waging an unjust war, these rights may conflict with strong rights of self-defense. A sufficiently developed fetus *in utero* might also have some negative right not to be killed. But this right may not prevail, either because the fetus is not yet fully one of us or because its mother has strong rights over her body. In TB and CC, the directness of the threatening agency apparently serves to strengthen these negative rights, perhaps giving them a power to stand against moral forces to which they would otherwise give way. Something similar happens in GP. The untreated people have, presumably, some positive right to medical aid. This right might not be binding if doctors could cure more people by directing aid elsewhere. But it stands against any attempt to maximize medical benefit *by* deliberately letting the people deteriorate. Again, the directness of the intention strengthens the force of the opposing right or claim.

It is interesting to consider whether DDE might also come into play where no independent negative or positive right is present. Suppose, in an act of pure supererogation, I am about to aid you but am checked by the realization that your difficulty can be turned either to my advantage or to that of someone I care more for. Does my change of mind, for that reason, violate any of your rights? I am inclined to think not. It might be bad of me to be checked by such a reason, but its appearance cannot create an obligation where none existed before. Rights not to be caught up, to one's disadvantage, in the direct agency of others seem to exist only where some positive or negative right already applies. Their effect always seems to be that of strengthening some other right.

The effect of the doctrine is therefore to *raise* rather than to lower moral barriers. So we should not expect a proponent of DDE to be more tolerant of harmful indirect agency than those who reject the doctrine but share the rest of his moral outlook. We should rather expect him to be *less* tolerant of harmful direct agency. This point is important. For casual critics of the doctrine sometimes seem to suppose that its defenders must be ready to allow killings or harmings simply on the ground that the agency is indirect. But nothing could be further from the truth. The doctrine in no way lessens the constraining force of any independent moral right or duty.

IV

We must now turn to the question of rationale. At first glance, harmful direct agency might seem harder to justify because it requires that the agent welcome something bad for the victim. The terror bomber, for example, must welcome the news that the innocent civilians are blown up, even if he is not glad that they won't be miraculously resurrected after the war. The trouble is that it also seems the strategic bomber must, in some sense, welcome the same news, since if the civilians had been unharmed the factory would not in fact have been destroyed.[22] Of course the news is good for different reasons. It is good news for the terror bomber because it announces the very thing that he intended, while it is good news for the strategic bomber because it announces the thing that he foresaw would be evidence of what he intended. But this difference does little more than register what we already knew—that the terror bomber strictly intended the deaths while the strategic bomber merely foresaw them as necessary costs. So it is hard to see how it could be used to explain the moral difference between direct and indirect agency.

Nor is it the case that harms of direct agency need be worse than those of indirect agency. If someone threatened by a terror bomber and someone equally threatened by a strategic bomber both needed rescuing, the former would not seem to have the stronger claim to help. Indeed, there would seem to be no reason to rescue either in preference to someone threatened by purely natural causes.[23] And if we sometimes think that the first rescue must have priority, it seems to be only because we are tempted to regard the violation of a special right against harmful direct agency as a distinctive and additional kind of moral evil. But then it would be circular simply to appeal to the evil in order to explain the existence or force of the right.

Perhaps the following rationale is more promising. Someone who unwillingly suffers because of what we intend for him as a way of getting our larger goal seems to fall under our power and control in a distinctive way. And there may be some-

thing morally problematic in this special relation—something over and above what is morally objectionable in the simpler relation of bringing about or not preventing harm. If this is right, then harmful direct agency must have two things against it, while equally harmful indirect agency need have only one. This additional negative element can be seen most clearly in the contrast between the doctors' attitudes in GP and DR. In the former, but not the latter, they show a shocking failure of respect for the persons who are harmed; they treat their victims as they would treat laboratory animals. DDE might therefore seem to rest on special duties of respect for persons, duties over and above any duty not to harm or to prevent harm.

While this is surely on the right track, we must proceed with caution. For there is also a kind of disrespect in typical cases of wrongful indirect agency. A strategic bomber who ought to have refrained from destroying a rather unimportant target because of likely civilian casualties has failed to treat his victims with the consideration that they and their interests deserve. So we must look for a kind of disrespect that is peculiar to wrongful direct agency—a kind different from that shown in wrongly giving a victim's interests too little weight.

What seems specifically amiss in relations of direct harmful agency is the particular way in which victims enter into an agent's strategic thinking. An indirect agent may be certain that his pursuit of a goal will leave victims in its wake. But this is not because their involvement in what he does or does not do will be useful to his end. The agent of direct harm, on the other hand, has something in mind for his victims—he proposes to involve them in some circumstance that will be useful to him precisely because it involves them. He sees them as material to be strategically shaped or framed by his agency.

Someone who harms by direct agency must therefore take up a distinctive attitude toward his victims. He must treat them as if they were then and there *for* his purposes. But indirect harming is different. Those who simply stand unwillingly to be harmed by a strategy—those who will be incidentally rather than usefully affected—are not viewed strategically at all and therefore not treated as for the agent's purposes rather than their own. They may, it is true, be treated as beings whose harm or death does not much matter—at least not as much as the achievement of the agent's goals. And that presumption is morally questionable. But in a counterpart case of direct agency there is the *additional* presumption that the victim may be cast in some role that serves the agent's goal.

The civilians in TB serve the bomber's goal by becoming casualties, and the infected people in GP serve the doctors' goal by becoming guinea pigs. If things were different, the victims might become these things only voluntarily. Suppose, for example, the civilians had effective bomb shelters and the sick people medicines of their own. Then the bomber or doctors could succeed only with the cooperation of the victims. The service exacted would then be voluntary. But in cases of indirect agency the victims make *no* contribution. If the civilians in SB had shelters and if the sick people in DR had medicines, the bomber and the doctors would see no point in their refusing to use them.

The DDE rests on the strong moral presumption that those who can be usefully involved in the promotion of a goal only at the cost of something protected by their independent moral rights (such as their life, their bodily integrity, or their freedom) ought, prima facie, to serve the goal only voluntarily.[24] The chief exceptions to this strong presumption are cases in which people have or would have strong moral obligations to give themselves to the service of a goal even at such personal costs—especially cases in which it would be indecent of them to refuse. But surely there is not, or may not be, any such obligation in the cases we have been considering: noncombatants (even those on the wrong side) are not morally obligated to serve the right side by accepting the role of demoralizing civilian casualties, victims of dangerous diseases are not typically obligated to become guinea pigs for the sake of others, and I suppose it is at least open to question whether the fetus in CC, if it could grasp its predicament, would have to accept, for the sake of its mother, the sacrifice of its life.

In these cases, but not in their indirect counterparts, the victims are made to play a role in the service of the agent's goal that is not (or may not be) morally required of them. And this aspect of direct agency adds its own negative moral force—a force over and above that provided by the fact of harming or failing to prevent harm.[25] This additional force seems intuitively clearest in direct opportunistic agency, such as TB and GP, where unwilling victims are not only harmed but, in some sense, used. And this must be why the doctrine seems most plausible when it discriminates against opportunistic direct agency. It must also help explain why some of the most perverse forms of opportunistic agency, like torture, can seem absolutely unjustifiable.

It is less plausible, on the other hand, to think of the victims of direct eliminative agency as used. This may be why the doctrine seems to discriminate against eliminative agency less forcefully. And it may therefore help explain why some people feel that the direct agency of CC is not much harder to justify than the indirect agency of HC. But something of the questionable character of direct opportunistic agency also seems present in direct eliminative agency. Someone who gets in your way presents a strategic problem—a causal obstacle whose removal will be a service to your goals. And this is quite unlike what we find in harmful indirect agency, where victims can be obstacles only in a moral sense.

In discriminating to some extent against both forms of direct agency, the doctrine reflects a Kantian ideal of human community and interaction.[26] Each person is to be treated, so far as possible, as existing only for purposes that he can share. This ideal is given one natural expression in the language of rights. People have a strong prima facie right not to be sacrificed in strategic roles over which they have no say. They have a right not to be pressed, in apparent violation of their prior rights, into the service of other people's purposes. Sometimes these additional rights may be justifiably infringed, especially when the prior right is not terribly important and the harm is limited, but in all cases they add their own burden to the opposing moral argument.

The Doctrine of Double Effect thus gives each person some veto power over a certain kind of attempt to make the world a better place at his expense. This would be absurd if the entire point of morality were to maximize overall happiness or welfare. But that is not its entire point. An equally urgent basic task is to define the forms of respect that we owe to one another, and the resulting limits that we may not presume to exceed. The doctrine embodies our sense that certain forms of forced strategic subordination are especially inappropriate among free and equal agents.

Notes

1. I am grateful for very helpful suggestions from Rogers Albritton, Philippa Foot, Matthew Hanser, and many others; and for criticism from audiences at New York University, the University of California at Irvine, and Princeton University.
2. Harm is meant in a very broad sense that includes the loss of life, rightful property, privacy, and so on. In my examples, the relevant harm will usually be the loss of life.
3. Warren S. Quinn, "Actions, Intentions, and Consequences: The Doctrine of Doing and Allowing," *Philosophical Review,* July 1989, pp. 287–312.
4. The doctrine, which is usually traced to Thomas Aquinas, *Summa Theologiae,* II-II, Q. 64, art. 7, is typically put as a set of necessary conditions on morally permissible agency in which a morally questionable bad upshot is foreseen: (a) the intended final end must be good, (b) the intended means to it must be morally acceptable, (c) the foreseen bad upshot must *not* itself be willed (that is, must not be, in some sense, intended), and (d) the good end must be proportionate to the bad upshot (that is, must be important enough to justify the bad upshot). The principle that follows in the text, which I henceforth treat as if it were itself the doctrine, is really what I find most important and plausible in its first three conditions. I ignore the fourth condition both because it is probably best understood in a way that makes it noncontroversial and because I am concerned here not so much with how choices with a 'second effect' can be justified as with whether, *ceteris paribus,* the structure of intention makes a justificatory difference. That seems to me the fundamental question.
5. The principle is sometimes put in terms of the difference between a harmful *result* that is "directly" intended and one that is "indirectly" (or "obliquely") intended. But it also might be put in terms of the difference between a directly and an indirectly intended *act* of harming. In either variant, the point of calling the merely foreseen result or action "indirectly *intended*" is to mark a species of linguistic impropriety in an agent's asserting, with a completely straight face, that a clearly foreseen harm or harming is quite *un*intended. If I have no desire to wake you but simply do not care that my fiddling will have that effect, I cannot say that your waking or my waking you is purely unintentional. Whether

there is any natural sense in which they are intentional is a debated point. In the final analysis, I shall sidestep this controversy, concerning myself with a species of intention that an agent clearly does not have toward a merely foreseen result of his agency—namely, the intention that the result occur, or that he bring it about, as a means of achieving his purpose.

6. See Herbert L. A. Hart, "Intention and Punishment," in *Punishment and Responsibility* (Oxford: Clarendon Press, 1968), p. 123. Hart finds the intentions in CC and HC to be parallel. But he does not argue, and does not seem to think, that a similar point can be made about most other cases that the doctrine might seem to distinguish. Nancy Davis finds more general problems along these lines in "The Doctrine of Double Effect: Problems of Interpretation," *Pacific Philosophical Quarterly* 65 (1984): 107–23.

7. If the miracle happened, and after its removal the fetus were quickly restored to its previous healthy condition, we would say that the craniotomy had done no real harm. In the actual case, the harm done to the fetus by the craniotomy consists in the *combination* of the desired immediate effect on it (which permits its removal) and the further natural effects that flow from that first effect. Since these further effects are not strictly intended, the objection holds that the harm itself is not strictly intended. See Jonathan Bennett, *Morality and Consequences*, The Tanner Lectures on Human Values II (Salt Lake City: University of Utah Press, 1981), pp. 110–11.

8. Ibid., p. 111.

9. Perhaps then it would not really be, at least in these people, a disease. But then it might be said that the doctors don't really need it to be a disease in *them*. It would be good enough if, due to their special powers of compensation, it is for them a harmless condition very much like a disease in others.

10. Philippa Foot perhaps suggests this kind of reply in "The Problem of Abortion and the Doctrine of the Double Effect," in *Virtues and Vices and Others Essays* (Berkeley and Los Angeles: University of California Press, 1978), pp. 21–22.

11. Hart, "Intention and Punishment," p. 120.

12. Of course this special operation could, however inappropriately, be performed on patients who were not pregnant. And this might lead someone to speculate that the doctrine speaks against a strictly intended and invariably harmful kind of action or omission only if the harm is an empirically necessary consequence. But this cannot be right. Suppose there is some good that will arise immediately upon your being injected with a certain fatal poison. The good does not require that you actually die. But that is what will happen, since the very real and naturally abundant

antidote that could save you has not been, and in fact never will be, discovered. In such a case, the doctrine should certainly speak against my poisoning you. But the directly and invariably connected harm would not follow of empirical necessity.

13. If the latter intention sometimes gets fulfilled, for example, by bombing electric power facilities built into remote and isolated dams.

14. G.M.A. Anscombe, *Intention,* 2d ed. (Oxford: Blackwell, 1963), sec. 25, pp. 41–45.

15. See Quinn, "Actions, Intentions, and Consequences: The Doctrine of Doing and Allowing," pp. 293–94.

16. Not even, I would argue, the fact of their not receiving the treatment. What really furthers the goal is the treatment received by the other, more tractable cases. The nontreatment of the first group contributes, at most, in an odd and secondary sense. This point applies, I think, to a wide range of intentional expressions. Suppose we decide to combat a disease by spending our limited resources on education rather than on inoculation. Education, and not noninoculation, will then be our *means* of combat; and the *way* we fight the disease will be by educating, not by not inoculating.

17. I might instead have said "agency in which harm comes to victims . . . from the agent's deliberately producing some *effect on them* in order to further his purpose precisely by way of their being so affected." But there is a certain kind of ingenious case, attributed to David Lewis, that such a formulation might seem to miss. Suppose that another terror bomber wishes to demoralize enemy leaders by bombing a major center of population, and suppose he knows that these leaders will be convinced that the city is destroyed by seeing, from afar, the explosion of his bombs over it. The explosion occurs an instant before the fatal effects below. So in this case the bomber does not, strictly speaking, intend to blow up the civilians, or produce any *physical* effects on them, as a means to his end. Yet the case seems, morally speaking, to be like TB rather than SB. But notice that while such a strategy does not aim at *physically* affecting its victims, it does strictly aim at exploding bombs in their vicinity. Whether or not this change in their situation could be counted as an effect on them, as I think it could, the bomber strictly intends to involve them in something (to make his bombs explode over them) in order to further his purpose precisely by way of their being involved.

18. This way of drawing the distinction excludes a pair of cases sometimes used to illustrate double effect: in one we give powerful analgesics to lessen the terrible pain of a dying patient, where we foresee that he will die as a side effect. In the other we relieve his suffering by intentionally

killing him with the same or other drugs. In both cases we are to suppose that life is no longer a good and that we act with his explicit or correctly presumed consent. So we cannot see ourselves as infringing, justifiably or unjustifiably, any of his moral rights. For this reason I see these cases as really quite different from the others, in which there is conflict between the moral claims of different people. Indeed, I think that the doctrine is misapplied in nonconflict cases. I see, for example, no difference between amputating someone's leg to save him and proceeding with some life-saving treatment that, as a side effect, results in the loss of the limb. And by parity of reasoning it seems to me that if stopping pain is urgent enough from the patient's perspective to make death acceptable as a side effect, it ought to make death acceptable as a means.

19. A terminological point: Something counts as 'harmful direct agency' only insofar as harm comes to the very people who are deliberately affected by the agency. Insofar as harm comes to others, the agency also counts as 'indirectly harmful'. A single act or omission can thus be both directly and indirectly harmful.

20. Nor, of course, does it require that the agent have *particular* victims in mind. It is enough, as in the case of a terrorist's car bomb, that he intends something for someone or other.

21. Positive rights are rights to aid while negative rights are rights to noninterference. While borrowed originally from the law, these terms are here used in a moral sense.

22. See Bennett, *Morality and Consequences,* pp. 102–3.

23. Samuel Scheffler makes a similar point in *The Rejection of Consequentialism* (Oxford: Clarendon Press, 1982), p. 109.

24. I am deliberately not considering cases where the sacrifice is financial. What to think in such cases partly depends on the sorts of moral rights people really have to keep money or property that is legally or conventionally theirs when others have more pressing material needs. It is quite consistent with everything I say here to deny that the doctrine speaks against liberal schemes of redistributing wealth.

25. Although it is, as we have seen, a kind of negative moral force that is activated only when other rights are present.

26. But there is a way in which the rationale I have provided is not Kantian. For it draws a sharp moral line between adversely affecting someone in the pursuit of an end that he does not share (not treating him as an end in itself) and adversely affecting someone because his being so affected is strategically important to achieving an end that he does not share (very roughly, treating him as a means). Neither the terror nor the strategic bomber treats his victims as ends in themselves, but only the former treats them as something like means. And I have argued that this difference is significant—that morality erects an extra barrier against the strategic posture of harmful direct agency. Kant might disagree, focused as he is on the alleged status of people as ends in themselves. But I have difficulty attaching any sense to that idea except via intuitions that certain forms of treatment are unacceptably disrespectful of rational beings. And the intuition that it is more disrespectful, all other things being equal, to treat someone as if he existed for purposes he does not share than simply not to be constrained by his purposes, seems to me plausible enough to be worth incorporating in a proper idea of what it means for persons to be ends in themselves. On this conception, one aspect of being an end in itself would be to have, *ceteris paribus,* a stronger right against directly harmful agency than against indirectly harmful agency.

Morality and Consequences

(1981)

Jonathan Bennett

Jonathan Bennett has been a lecturer in moral science at the University of Cambridge and professor of philosophy at Syracuse University. His most recent works include the two-volume Learning from Six Philosophers: Descartes, Spinoza, Leibniz, Locke, Berkeley, Hume *(Oxford University Press, 2003) and the* Philosophical Guide to Conditionals *(Oxford University Press, 2003).*

In this lecture I shall exhibit some difficulties about a certain distinction which is thought important by many moralists—namely that between what you intend to come about as a means to your end and what you do not intend although you foresee that it will come about as a by-product of your means to your end. This has a role in most defences of *the Doctrine of Double Effect,* and is one source for the view that terror bombing is never permissible though tactical bombing may sometimes be—i.e., that it is never right to kill civilians as a means to demoralizing the enemy country, though it may sometimes be right to destroy a munitions factory as a means to reducing the enemy's military strength, knowing that the raid will also kill civilians. In the former case—so the story goes—the civilian deaths are intended as a means; in the latter they are not intended but merely foreseen as an inevitable by-product of the means; and that is supposed to make a moral difference, even if the probabilities are the same, the number of civilian deaths the same, and so on.

First, let us look at two kinds of causal structure:

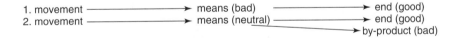

The item on the left is the movement the person makes—the 'basic action' whose upshots are in question. The other terms name particular events, and I add evaluations of them as a reminder of why these structures are supposed to be of moral interest.

Some moralists say that a type 1 situation is worse than a type 2 one, but they are hard put to it to give reasons for this. A vague impression of reasons is sometimes conveyed by saying that in type 1 situations the bad is "directly" produced while in type 2 ones it is not; but there is no good sense in which that is true. A type 2 case must admittedly have at least one event between the basic action and the bad event; but a type 1 case could also have an intermediate event, or a dozen of them for that matter. There is no essential difference between the two types in respect of what leads up to the bad event: the essential difference is in what flows from it; and it seems absurd to express that difference by saying that in one case but not the other the production of the bad event is "direct." Anyway, think for a moment about the claim that the tactical bomber in dropping live bombs onto the heads of the civilians does not "directly" kill them!

A more usual position amongst those who morally contrast the two types of situation is not that type 1 is inherently worse than type 2 but that it is worse to intend to bring about a type 1 situation than to intend to bring about a type 2 one. I am interested in this only if it is maintained even when the degrees of good and bad are the same, and the probabilities are the same. It is the thesis that the terror bomber is in a worse frame of mind in intending to kill ten thousand civilians as a means to lowering enemy morale than the tactical bomber is in when he intends to destroy a factory and confidently expects his raid to have the side effect of killing ten thousand civilians. Some writers take examples where the numbers of deaths, or the levels of probability, are different; but I shall filter out such differences as those and look for the moral significance of the difference in intention, taken on its own.

Let us see what truth there is in the statement that the terror bomber does, while the tactical bomber does not, intend to produce something bad—specifically, to produce the deaths of civilians. It must be a weaker sense of "intend" than that given by "pursue as an end" i.e., as something sought for its own sake; for neither of our bombers need regard civilian deaths as intrinsically desirable. But it must be

stronger than "foresee as an inevitable upshot of one's conduct;" for both of our bombers foresee the civilian deaths.

The only way I can see of driving a wedge between the two is by invoking the view of intentions which is found in G. E. M. Anscombe's book: this is now the dominant opinion in the relevant parts of philosophy, and I am sure it is correct.[1] The core of it is the idea that intentions are explanatory of conduct: what you intend is determined by which of your beliefs explain or give your reasons for your behaviour. That immediately distinguishes our two bombers, for the terror bomber is in some way motivated by his expectation that his raid will produce civilian deaths, while the tactical bomber, though having similar expectations, is in no way motivated by them.

But let us not too rapidly draw any moral conclusions. That there is a moral difference between the states of mind of the two bombers is *not* automatically established just by the fact that one of them intends something bad which the other does not intend.

There is moral significance in what a man intends as an end, what he pursues for its own sake. It would be a bad man who wanted civilian deaths for their own sakes; but neither of our bombers is like that. This is a *sufficient* condition for intending something, and neither bomber satisfies it.

There is also moral significance in what a man is prepared knowingly to bring about. As Aquinas said, in effect: "If a man wills a bombing raid from which he knows civilian deaths will result, it follows that he wills those deaths. Although perhaps he does not intend the deaths in themselves, nevertheless he rather wishes that the civilians die than that the raid be called off." And that is highly morally significant. But this is only a *necessary* condition of intention, and it applies not just to the terror bomber who intends the deaths but also to the tactical one who does not. The tactical bomber would rather have civilian deaths than not have his raid, and that is something for which he needs a pretty good excuse. So our question is left standing: is the tactical bomber easier to excuse than the terror one? If so, it must be for a reason which stems from the difference in what they intend, but it is not handed to us on a plate just by the fact that the word "intend" fits in one case but not in the other. So we shall have to dig for it. Let us try to be more precise about what the difference in intention amounts to.

If intentions are determined by which of the person's beliefs motivate his action, then we should be able to get at them by asking how the behaviour would have differed if the beliefs had differed in given ways. The difference between our two men should show up in their answers to the test question:

> If you had believed that there would be no civilian deaths, would you have been less likely to go through with the raid?

Specifically, the difference should show up in the terror bomber's answering Yes and the tactical bomber's answering No. I am not saying that an intention is just a disposition to be moved by certain beliefs, merely that the difference between these two intentional states is equivalent to the difference between two dispositions to be moved by beliefs. Even that is doubtless only an approximation, but I do not think its inaccuracies matter for present purposes.

The test question is a counterfactual one, and there are different ways of interpreting it. Each man is asked: Would you have been likely to behave differently if . . .? If what? What is the possible state of himself which he is asked to entertain, telling us how he would have behaved if he had been in that state? We know that it is to include his thinking his raid will not lead to civilian deaths; and it had better also involve whatever follows from that by virtue of his working logic, so that it won't also include his believing, for instance, that the raid *will* cause civilian deaths. Now, how else is his supposed state to differ from the frame of mind he was actually in when he launched his raid? There are three possible interpretations.

1. His supposed state is to differ from his actual one *only* in respect of the belief that there would be no civilian deaths and its logical accompaniments—in no other way. In that case, we are leaving the terror man with his belief that his raid will lower morale, and the tactical man with his belief that his raid will destroy the factory. Each of them, then, if faced with the question "Would you in that case have called off your raid?", will answer No. So this version of the test question does not separate them.

2. His supposed state is to differ from his actual one in the belief that there would be no civilian deaths together with whatever follows from that by virtue of his causal beliefs. On that reading of the test question, the terror bomber will answer that Yes, in that case he would have cancelled his bombing raid, for he is supposing himself to believe that there would be no civilian deaths and thus no lowering of morale—for he has the causal belief that morale can't be lowered without killing civilians. But the tactical bomber will also answer that Yes, he too would have called off his raid, for he is supposing himself to

believe that there would be no civilian deaths and thus no destruction of the factory—for he has the causal belief that the factory can't be destroyed without killing civilians.

Of those readings of the test question, the first supposes too little change in the antecedent state, the second too much. We need something in between, and it is not hard to see what it is.

3. The bomber's supposed state is to differ from his actual one in the belief that no civilian deaths would be caused, together with whatever follows from that, by virtue of his causal beliefs, through a causally *downstream* inference. That is, the adjustments are to concern what results, not what is causally prerequired. So the terror bomber is being supposed to think that there will be no civilian deaths and therefore no lowering of enemy morale; while the tactical bomber is being supposed to think that there will be no civilian deaths, but not to think that the factory will survive—since the factory's fate is not causally downstream from the deaths of the civilians. So the terror bomber will answer Yes, while the tactical bomber will answer No, to the test question.

That is the best I can do to clarify the difference between the two states of mind. That third reading of the test question confers reasonable clarity and undeniable truth on the statement that one man does and the other does not intend to produce civilian deaths. But it doesn't add plausibility to the claim that this makes a moral difference. Neither bomber would call off his raid if his beliefs changed only in not including the belief that it would kill civilians. Each would call it off if they changed in that way and in every way that causally follows from it. To get them apart we had to specify what causally follows down-

stream and not what causally follows upstream, and I cannot see why anyone should knowingly attach moral significance to that difference as it appears here.

There is obviously great moral significance in the difference between upstream and downstream from one's own conduct. From the facts about the surgeon's behaviour it is causally inferable that there is a wounding upstream from it (he is stitching up the wound); and that is no ground for complaint against him as it would be if one could infer that there was a wounding downstream from his behaviour (because he was causing it). But that is irrelevant to our question, for in each raid the civilian deaths are downstream from the bomber's basic action.

It has been suggested that there is a difference in respect of what the two men are hoping for, or what they would in the circumstances *welcome*. The terror bomber, even if he does not want civilian deaths for themselves, still wants them—is in a frame of mind where the news of the civilian deaths would be *good* news—whereas the tactical bomber does not want the deaths: he merely thinks they will occur.

There is truth in that, but we must pick carefully if we are to retrieve it without bringing along falsehood as well. The terror bomber will indeed be glad when he hears that many civilians have died, because he needs their deaths for his ultimate aim. But the tactical bomber will also be glad when he hears that many civilians have died, because their deaths are evidence that something has happened which he needs for his ultimate aim. Because the raid will inevitably kill many civilians if it destroys the factory, it would be bad news for the tactical bomber if he heard that few civilians had died, for that would show that something had gone wrong—his bombs had not exploded, or had fallen in open countryside. Something which contradicts that bad news is good news.

There is a difference between the two welcomes of the news of civilian deaths: one man is glad because of what will flow from the deaths, the other is glad because of what will flow from what must have preceded them; one is downstream glad, so to speak, while the other is upstream and then downstream glad. But there need be no difference in how greatly glad they will be; and so, as far as I can see, there need be no difference which creates a moral difference.

It is true that the tactical bomber's wish for the civilian deaths is a reluctant one: if he could, he would destroy the factory without killing civilians. But the terror bomber too, if he could, would drop his bombs in such a way as to lower morale without killing civilians. So there is nothing in that.

It may occur to you that there is some chance of bombing the factory without killing civilians, whereas there is none that the terror raid will lower morale unless civilians are killed by it. This goes with the thought that the tactical man's regret at killing civilians could generate a sane, practical desire for more precise bombing or for a wonderful coincidence in which all the civilians happen to be out of town at the time of the raid; whereas the terror man's regret at killing civilians could only lead to a sigh for a miracle. That is all true, but only because of a difference in probability which is an accident of this example; the difference between intending as a means and foreseeing as a by-product is not systematically linked to a difference in probability.

Here is another reason which has been offered as making a moral difference between the two men. Suppose for simplicity's sake that each case involves only the death of a single civilian—*you.* The tactical bomber expects his raid to kill you; but if it doesn't, and he sees you staggering to your feet amidst the rubble of the factory, he may rejoice. On the other hand, if the terror bomber sees that you have survived his raid, he has reason to drop another bomb on you, since his purpose will be defeated if you survive. This suggests a difference in how hostile they are: if the terror bomber's plans go awry, he will use his flexibility and ingenuity in ducking and weaving his way *right up to your death;* but not so the tactical bomber.

From your point of view the two cases feel different. But that difference in feeling is hard to justify unless it reflects a difference in the probability of your death; which difference exists only if there is some chance that each bomber's expectations will turn out to be wrong. But the moral doctrine I am examining is supposed to hold even when the relevant upshots are perfectly certain, so that the question doesn't even arise of the agent's using his ingenuity to deal with breakdowns in his plans.

Anyway, why should the difference in how it feels to you reflect a moral difference between the two men? Each of them is prepared to maneuver towards your death: the tactical bomber may work to overcome political resistance to his raid, evade the defences which try to keep him away from you, solve the mechanical problem with the bomb-aiming equipment, and so on, using all his skill and ingenuity and plasticity to keep on a path which has your death on it. It is true that eventually the path to your death forks away from the path to his goal, and his ingenuity goes with the latter and not the former. But he has in common with the terror bomber that he relentlessly and ingeniously pursues, *for as long as he has any reason to,* a path with your death on it. The moral difference eludes me.

It is sometimes implied that the terror bomber is *using* people as a *means* to his end whereas the tactical bomber is not. I shan't take time to sort out that tangle. As a start on it, consider whether the tactical bomber, who is supposed not to be treating people as means, is treating them as ends!

Some writers who think there is moral significance in the distinction between doing or causing on the one hand and allowing or letting on the other believe that this invests our present distinction also with moral significance. I disagree with their premise, but even if it were true, it would not do this work, as I shall now show.

If it were to do this work, the difference between what is intended and what is foreseen would have to contain or involve the difference between what you do or cause or make to happen and what you merely let or allow to happen. Some writers seem to assume that there is not merely an involvement or intertwining but a downright equivalence between these two distinctions. I have found a moral theologian clearly implying that "the distinction between rendering someone unconscious at the risk of killing him and killing him to render him unconscious" is the same as the distinction be-

tween "allowing to die and killing." Another moralist slides smoothly in the reverse direction, starting with a mention of "what we do, rather than what we allow to happen" and moving on, as though with no change of topic, to a mention of "what we intend, and not the whole range of things which come about as a result of what we do intentionally."

I submit that this is a mistake. Given that you do something, or actively bring it about or make it happen, it is a further question whether you intend it as a means to your end or merely foresee it as a by-product of your means; and that further question could be asked, though a bit less happily, about something which you don't do or bring about but merely allow to happen. The two distinctions cut right across one another; the belief that they are somehow aligned or intertwined seems to me to have no truth in it whatsoever.

If you are not convinced about this, consider whether you are willing to say that the tactical bomber in dropping bombs right onto people does not kill them but merely allows them to die.

Notes

1. G. E. M. Anscombe, *Intention* (Oxford: Blackwell, 1957).

Double Effect and Double Intention

(1977)

Michael Walzer

Michael Walzer is the UPS Foundation Professor at the Institute for Advanced Study at Princeton University. He has written on a broad variety of topics in political theory and moral philosophy, including political obligation, war, nationalism and ethnicity, and economic justice. His books include Just and Unjust Wars *(Basic Books, 1977),* Spheres of Justice *(Basic Books, 1983), and* On Toleration *(Yale University Press, 1997).*

The second principle of the war convention is that noncombatants cannot be attacked at any time. They can never be the objects or the targets of military activity. But as the *Laconia* affair suggests, noncombatants are often endangered not because anyone sets out to attack them, but only because of their proximity to a battle that is being fought against someone else. I have tried to argue that what is then required is not that the battle be stopped, but that some degree of care be taken not to harm civilians—which means, very simply, that we recognize their rights as best we can within the context of war. But what degree of care should be taken? And at what cost to the individual soldiers who are involved? The laws of war say nothing about such matters; they leave the cruelest decisions to be made by the men on the spot with reference only to their ordinary moral notions or the military traditions of the army in which they serve. Occasionally one of these soldiers will write about his own decisions, and that can be like a light going on in a dark place. Here is an incident from Frank Richards' memoir of the First World War, one of the few accounts by a man from the ranks.[1]

> When bombing dug-outs or cellars, it was always wise to throw the bombs into them first and have a look around them after. But we had to be very careful in this village as there were civilians in some of the cellars. We shouted down to them to make sure. Another man and I shouted down one cellar twice and receiving no reply were just about to pull the pins out of our bombs when we heard a woman's voice and a young lady came up the cellar steps . . . She and the members of her family . . . had not left [the cellar] for some days. They guessed an attack was being made and when we first shouted down had been too frightened to answer. If the young lady had not cried out when she did, we would have innocently murdered them all.

Innocently murdered, because they had shouted first; but if they had not shouted, and then killed the French family, it would have been, Richards believed, murder simply. And yet he was accepting a certain risk in shouting, for had there been German soldiers in the cellar, they might have scrambled out, firing as they came. It would have been more prudent to throw the bombs without warning, which means that military necessity would have justified him in doing so. Indeed, he would have been justified on other grounds, too, as we shall see. And yet he shouted.

The moral doctrine most often invoked in such cases is the principle of double effect. First worked out by Catholic casuists in the Middle Ages, double effect is a complex notion, but it is at the same time closely related to our ordinary ways of thinking about moral life. I have often found it being used in military and political debates. Officers will tend to speak in its terms, knowingly or unknowingly, whenever the activity they are planning is likely to injure noncombatants. Catholic writers themselves frequently use military examples; it is one of their purposes to suggest what we ought to think when "a soldier in firing at the enemy foresees that he will shoot some civilians who are nearby."[2] Such foresight is common enough in war; soldiers could probably not fight at all, except in the desert and at sea, without endangering nearby civilians. And yet it is not proximity but only some contribution to the fighting that makes a civilian liable to attack. Double effect is a way of reconciling the absolute prohibition against attacking noncombatants with the legitimate conduct of military activity. I shall want to argue, following the example of Frank Richards, that the reconciliation comes too easily, but first we must see exactly how it is worked out.

The argument goes this way: it is permitted to perform an act likely to have evil consequences (the killing of noncombatants) provided the following four conditions hold.[3]

(1) *The act is good in itself or at least indifferent, which means, for our purposes, that it is a legitimate act of war.*

(2) *The direct effect is morally acceptable—the destruction of military supplies, for example, or the killing of enemy soldiers.*

(3) *The intention of the actor is good, that is, he aims only at the acceptable effect; the evil effect is not one of his ends, nor is it a means to his ends.*

(4) *The good effect is sufficiently good to compensate for allowing the evil effect; it must be justifiable under Sidgwick's proportionality rule.*

The burden of the argument is carried by the third clause. The "good" and evil effects that come together, the killing of soldiers and nearby civilians, are to be defended only insofar as they are the product of a single intention, directed at the first and not the second. The argument suggests the great importance of taking aim in wartime, and it correctly restricts the targets at which one can aim. But we have to worry, I think, about all those unintended but foreseeable deaths, for their number can be large; and subject only to the proportionality rule—a weak constraint—double effect provides a blanket justification. The principle for that reason invites an angry or a cynical response: what difference does it make whether civilian deaths are a direct or an indirect effect of my actions? It can hardly matter to the dead civilians, and if I know in advance that I am likely to kill so many innocent people and go ahead anyway, how can I be blameless?[4]

We can ask the question in a more concrete way. Would Frank Richards have been blameless if he had thrown his bombs without warning? The principle of double effect would have permitted him to do so. He was engaged in a legitimate military activity, for many cellars were in fact being used by enemy soldiers. The effects of making "bomb without warning" his general policy would have been to reduce the risks of his being killed or disabled and to speed up the capture of the village, and these are "good" effects. Moreover, they were clearly the only ones he intended; civilian deaths would have served no purpose of his own. And finally, over an extended period of time, the proportions would probably have worked out favorably or at least not unfavorably; the mischief done would, let us assume, be balanced by the contribution to victory. And yet Richards was surely doing the right thing when he shouted his warning. He was acting as a moral man ought to act; his is not an example of fighting heroically, above and beyond the call of duty, but simply of fighting well. It is what we expect of soldiers. Before trying to state that expectation more precisely, however, I want to see how it works in more complex combat situations.

BOMBARDMENT IN KOREA

I am going to follow here a British journalist's account of the way the American army waged war in Korea. Whether it is an entirely just account I do not know, but I am more interested in the moral issues it raises than in its historical accuracy. This, then, was a "typical" encounter on the road to Pyongyang. A battalion of American troops advanced slowly, without opposition, under the shadow of low hills. "We were well into the valley now, halfway down the straight . . . strung out along the open road, when it came, the harsh stutter of automatic fire sputtering the dust around us."[5] The troops stopped and dove for cover. Three tanks moved up, "pounding their shells into the . . . hillside and shattering the air with their machine guns. It was impossible in this remarkable

inferno of sound to detect the enemy, or to assess his fire." Within fifteen minutes, several fighter planes arrived, "diving down upon the hillside with their rockets." This is the new technique of warfare, writes the British journalist, "born of immense productive and material might": "the cautious advance, the enemy small arms fire, the halt, the close support air strike, artillery, the cautious advance, and so on." It is designed to save the lives of soldiers, and it may or may not have that effect. "It is certain that it kills civilian men, women, and children, indiscriminately and in great numbers, and destroys all that they have."

Now there is another way to fight, though it is only open to soldiers who have had a "soldierly" training and who are not "roadbound" in their habits. A patrol can be sent forward to outflank the enemy position. In the end, it often comes to that anyway, as it did in this case, for the tanks and planes failed to hit the North Korean machine gunners. "At last, after more than an hour . . . a platoon from Baker Company began working their way through the scrub just under the ridge of the hill." But the first reliance was always on bombardment. "Every enemy shot released a deluge of destruction." And the bombardment had, or sometimes had, its characteristic double effect: enemy soldiers were killed, and so were any civilians who happened to be nearby. It was not the intention of the officers who called in the artillery and planes to kill civilians; they were acting out of a concern for their own men. And that is a legitimate concern. No one would want to be commanded in wartime by an officer who did not value the lives of his soldiers. But he must also value civilian lives, and so must his soldiers. He cannot save them, because they cannot save themselves, by killing innocent people. It is not just that they can't kill a lot of innocent people. Even if the proportions work out favorably, in particular cases or over a period of time, we would still want to say, I think, that the patrol must be sent out, the risk accepted, before the big guns are brought to bear. The soldiers sent on patrol can plausibly argue that they never chose to make war in Korea; they are soldiers nevertheless; there are obligations that go with their war rights, and the first of these is the obligation to attend to the rights of civilians—more precisely, of those civilians whose lives they themselves endanger.

The principle of double effect, then, stands in need of correction. Double effect is defensible, I want to argue, only when the two outcomes are the product of a *double intention:* first, that the "good" be achieved; second, that the foreseeable evil be reduced as far as possible. So the third of the conditions listed above can be restated:

(3) *The intention of the actor is good, that is, he aims narrowly at the acceptable effect; the evil effect is not one of his ends, nor is it a means to his ends, and, aware of the evil involved, he seeks to minimize it, accepting costs to himself.*

Simply not to intend the death of civilians is too easy; most often, under battle conditions, the intentions of soldiers are focused narrowly on the enemy. What we look for in such cases is some sign of a positive commitment to save civilian lives. Not merely to apply the proportionality rule and kill no more civilians than is militarily necessary—that rule applies to soldiers as well; no one can be killed for trivial purposes. Civilians have a right to something more. And if saving civilian lives means risking soldier's lives, the risk must be accepted. But there is a limit to the risks

that we require. These are, after all, unintended deaths and legitimate military operations, and the absolute rule against attacking civilians does not apply. War necessarily places civilians in danger; that is another aspect of its hellishness. We can only ask soldiers to minimize the dangers they impose.

Exactly how far they must go in doing that is hard to say, and for that reason it may seem odd to claim that civilians have rights in such matters. What can this mean? Do civilians have a right not only not to be attacked but also not to be put at risk to such and such a degree, so that imposing a one-in-ten chance of death on them is justified, while imposing a three-in-ten chance is unjustified? In fact, the degree of risk that is permissible is going to vary with the nature of the target, the urgency of the moment, the available technology, and so on. It is best, I think, to say simply that civilians have a right that "due care" be taken.[6]* The case is the same in domestic society: when the gas company works on the lines that run under my street, I have a right that its workmen observe very strict safety standards. But if the work is urgently required by the imminent danger of an explosion on a neighboring street, the standards may be relaxed

---

*Since judgments of "due care" involve calculations of relative value, urgency, and so on, it has to be said that utilitarian arguments and rights arguments (relative at least to indirect effects) are not wholly distinct. Nevertheless, the calculations required by the proportionality principle and those required by "due care" are not the same. Even after the highest possible standards of care have been accepted, the probable civilian losses may still be disproportionate to the value of the target; then the attack must be called off. Or, more often, military planners may decide that the losses entailed by the attack, even if it is carried out at minimal risk to the attackers, are not disproportionate to the value of the target: then "due care" is an additional requirement.

and my rights not violated. Now, military necessity works exactly like civil emergency, except that in war the standards with which we are familiar in domestic society are always relaxed. That is not to say, however, that there are no standards at all, and no rights involved. Whenever there is likely to be a second effect, a second intention is morally required. We can move some way toward defining the limits of that second intention if we consider two more wartime examples.

THE BOMBING OF OCCUPIED FRANCE AND THE VEMORK RAID

During World War II, the Free French air force carried out bombing raids against military targets in occupied France. Inevitably, their bombs killed Frenchmen working (under coercion) for the German war effort; inevitably too, they killed Frenchmen who simply happened to live in the vicinity of the factories under attack. This posed a cruel dilemma for the pilots, which they resolved not by giving up the raids or asking someone else to carry them out, but by accepting greater risks for themselves. "It was . . . this persistent question of bombing France itself," says Pierre Mendes-France, who served in the air force after his escape from a German prison, "which led us to specialize more and more in precision bombing—that is, flying at a very low altitude. It was more risky, but it also permitted greater precision . . ."[7] The same factories, of course, could have been (perhaps should have been) attacked by squads of partisans or commandos carrying explosives; their aim would have been perfect, not merely more precise, and no civilians except those

working in the factories would have been endangered. But such raids would have been extremely dangerous and the chances of success, and especially of reiterated success, very slim. Risks of that sort were more than the French expected, even of their own soldiers. The limits of risk are fixed, then, roughly at that point where any further risk-taking would almost certainly doom the military venture or make it so costly that it could not be repeated.

There is obviously leeway for military judgment here: strategists and planners will for reasons of their own weigh the importance of their target against the importance of their soldiers' lives. But even if the target is very important, and the number of innocent people threatened relatively small, they must risk soldiers before they kill civilians. Consider, for example, the one case I have found from the Second World War where a commando raid was tried instead of an air attack. In 1943, the heavy water plant at Vemork in occupied Norway was destroyed by Norwegian commandos operating on behalf of the British S.O.E. (Special Operations Executive). It was vitally important to stop the production of heavy water so as to delay the development of an atomic bomb by German scientists. British and Norwegian officials debated whether to make the attempt from the air or on the ground and chose the latter approach because it was less likely to injure civilians.[8] But it was very dangerous for the commandos. The first attempt failed, and thirty-four men were killed in its course; the second attempt, by a smaller number of men, succeeded without casualties—to the surprise of everyone involved, including the commandos. It was possible to accept such risks for a single operation that would not, it was thought, have to be repeated. For a "battle" that extended over time, consisting of many separate incidents, it would not have been possible.

Later in the war, after production was resumed at Vemork and security considerably tightened, the plant was bombed from the air by American planes. The bombing was successful, but it resulted in the deaths of twenty-two Norwegian civilians. At this point, double effect seems to work, justifying the air attack. Indeed, in its unrevised from it would have worked sooner. The importance of the military aim and the actual casualty figures (foreseeable in advance, let us assume) would have justified a bombing raid in the first place. But the special value we attach to civilian lives precluded it.

Now, the same value attaches to the lives of German as to those of French or Norwegian civilians. There are, of course, additional moral as well as emotional reasons for paying that respect and accepting its costs in the case of one's own people or one's allies (and it is no accident that my two examples involve attacks on occupied territory). Soldiers have direct obligations to the civilians they leave behind, which have to do with the very purpose of soldiering and with their own political allegiance. But the structure of rights stands independently of political allegiance; it establishes obligations that are owed, so to speak, to humanity itself and to particular human beings and not merely to one's fellow citizens. The rights of German civilians—who did no fighting and were not engaged in supplying the armed forces with the means of fighting—were no different from those of their French counterparts, just as the war rights of German soldiers were no different from those of French soldiers, whatever we think of their war.

The case of occupied France (or Norway) is, however, complex in another way. Even if the French pilots had reduced their risks and flown at high altitudes, we would not hold them solely responsible for the additional civilian deaths they caused. They would have shared that responsibility with the Germans—in part because the Germans had attacked and conquered France, but also (and more importantly for our immediate purposes) because they had mobilized the French economy for their own strategic ends, forcing French workers to serve the German war machine, turning French factories into legitimate military targets, and putting the adjacent residential areas in danger. The question of direct and indirect effect is complicated by the question of coercion. When we judge the unintended killing of civilians, we need to know how those civilians came to be in a battle zone in the first place. This is, perhaps, only another way of asking who put them at risk and what positive efforts were made to save them. But it raises issues that I have not yet addressed and that are most dramatically visible when we turn to another, and a much older, kind of warfare.

Notes

1. *Old Soldiers Never Die* (New York, 1966), p. 198.
2. Kenneth Dougherty, *General Ethics: An Introduction to the Basic Principles of the Moral Life According to St. Thomas Aquinas* (Peekskill, N.Y., 1959), p. 64.
3. Dougherty, pp. 65–66; cf. John C. Ford, S. J. "The Morality of Obliteration Bombing," in *War and Morality*, ed. Richard Wasserstrom (Belmont, California, 1970). I cannot make any effort here to review the philisophical controversies over double effect. Dougherty provides a (very simple) text book description, Ford a careful (and courageous) application.
4. For a philosophical version of the argument that it cannot make a difference whether the killing

of innocent people is direct or indirect, see Jonathan Bennett, "Whatever the Consequences," *Ethics,* ed. Judith Jarvis Thomson and Gerald Dworkin (New York, 1968).

5. Reginald Thompson, *Cry Korea* (London, 1951), pp. 54, 142–43.

6. I have been helped in thinking about these questions by Charles Fried's discussion of "Imposing Risks on Others," *An Anatomy of Values: Problems of Personal and Social Choice* (Cambridge, Mass., 1970), ch. XI.

7. Quoted from the published text of Marcel Ophuls' documentary film, *The Sorrow and the Pity* (New York, 1972), p. 131.

8. Thomas Gallagher, *Assault in Norway* (New York, 1975), pp. 19–20, 50.

C. Absolutists and Consequentialists

In this section, we provide four selections that provide insight into the moral justification for conduct in war. The first three selections specifically address the question of whether noncombatants or "innocents" can be intentionally killed in war. The last article addresses the moral justification for the rules of war more generally. In general, this section presents a debate on whether there are any absolute prohibitions on conduct in war. Is some conduct, e.g., torture, in war morally "off limits," even if this conduct would likely hasten the end of the war and avoid suffering and death for thousands, possibly millions, of people?

On one side of this debate are the absolutists. Regarding the absolute prohibition on the intentional killing of noncombatants, absolutists have been termed "immunity theorists." Immunity theorists hold that it is always morally impermissible to intentionally kill noncombatants in war. Noncombatants are "innocent" and thus immune from attack. For absolutists, this moral prohibition is not convention-dependent. Also, this prohibition continues to be in place even if one party to the war fails to adhere to it. For instance, according to absolutists, the fact that Germany bombed London during World War II does not morally justify the British and American bombings of Hamburg. Whatever the circumstances presented by war, for absolutists, it is not morally acceptable to kill noncombatants intentionally.

On the other side of the debate are consequentialists. Consequentialists believe that actions in war can be morally justified depending on the end or aim of the action. If it is morally sufficient, the end can justify the means. For consequentialists, when all available actions appear to be evils, the action that results in the lesser evil is morally justified. From this perspective, consequentialists, unlike absolutists, can morally justify the intentional killing of noncombatants or "innocents" in war. A controversial example addressed in this debate is the bombing of Hiroshima and Nagasaki in World War II. Consequentialists can morally justify these bombings. Absolutists, however, contend that these bombings were immoral because these bombings targeted noncombatants.

We start this section with Elizabeth Anscombe's article titled "War and Murder." Anscombe believes that while the intentional killing of combatants in war is morally justified, the intentional killing of "innocents" is murder. For Anscombe, some examples of "innocents" are those who grow crops and make clothes, the sick, the elderly, and children. Anscombe argues that these people are innocent, or not guilty, because they are not "engaged in an objectively unjust proceeding." In her article, Anscombe specifically criticizes both pacifism and past interpretations of the "principle of double effect" for creating confusion about the moral status of innocents. Though there may be some difficulty in determining exactly who is "innocent," in her article, Anscombe adamantly rejects common arguments that have been used in the past to justify the intentional killing of innocents.

In the next article, "Conventions and the Morality of War," George Mavrodes argues that some moral restrictions in war, e.g., the prohibition on the intentional killing of noncombatants, are not absolute. Rather, they are convention-dependent. For Mavrodes, conventions can provide a moral basis for making moral distinctions and placing moral restrictions on conduct in war. If the states participating in war agree to abide by certain distinctions and rules that make war "better," then this agreement provides the moral justification for these distinctions and rules.

Unlike Anscombe, Mavrodes thinks that absent some type of convention it is difficult or impossible to make sense, both practically and morally, of the distinction between combatants and noncombatants and the prohibition on killing noncombatants. According to Mavrodes, however, it is not difficult to ascertain that war would be worse without this distinction and prohibition. As a result, Mavrodes concludes that if states can agree to abide by this distinction and prohibition, then this agreement creates a moral duty to abide by them.

Mavrodes makes it clear that he does not think that all conventions are moral and not all restrictions in war need be convention-dependent. Rather, he states that some are, and some should be followed because war is "better" with them. Also, Mavrodes concludes that it is not the case that "anything goes" if any of the parties to the war fail to adhere to the conventions. Instead, conduct in war should always accord with fundamental moral principles, e.g., justice and proportionality. According to Mavrodes, states should always choose what is morally "better" over what is worse. Yet, sometimes conventions create moral obligations because they specify restrictions that have been agreed upon and allow states to do what is morally "better."

Thomas Nagel disagrees with Mavrodes that the prohibition against intentionally killing noncombatants is convention-dependent. Nagel is an absolutist. In "War and Massacre," Nagel, like Anscombe, contends that it is always morally impermissible to kill noncombatants intentionally. Nagel, however, disagrees with Anscombe that noncombatants are innocent in that they are free from guilt. Rather, Nagel believes that noncombatants are innocent because they do not pose an immediate threat to the person or persons being attacked.

In his article, Nagel contrasts absolutism with utilitarianism. Nagel states that utilitarianism is concerned with what will happen, while absolutism is principally concerned with what one is doing. Like other critics of consequentialist moral theories, Nagel is concerned that if one puts one's absolutist intuitions aside, then justification could be given for many horrific and murderous acts. Unlike utilitarians who can morally justify acting in accordance with the lesser of two evils, Nagel holds that evil, e.g., torture, is never morally justified. Regarding the lesser of two evils, Nagel contends that sometimes the world presents us with "situations in which there is no honorable or moral course for a man to take, no course free of guilt and responsibility for evil."

Nagel's article presents a formidable challenge to consequentialists. He emphasizes that conduct in war is always conduct between persons. Nagel claims that "Hostility is a personal relation," and some "hostile treatment" between persons is always morally impermissible, even for persons defending their lives against an attacker. To illustrate this point, he argues that it is never morally permissible, even in self-defense, for a soldier to kill the spouse and children (who pose no immediate threat to the soldier) of an attacker to thwart the attacker. Killing the spouse and children would be using them merely as a means. For Nagel, any morally justified defense must be aimed at the attacker, the immediate threat, and all defensive hostility "must be suited to its target." Nagel argues that all persons engaged in war are subject to these same moral requirements.

In "Utilitarianism and the Rules of War," Richard Brandt disagrees with Nagel. Brandt offers a *contractual* rule-utilitarian reply. He argues that all morally justified rules of war are justified because they are impartial and are preferred by rational people. Brandt argues that morally justified rules of war are rules which rational people behind a "veil of ignorance" would prefer if they thought that they would be involved in a war at some time. Also, he argues that these rational people behind a "veil of ignorance" would choose rules that "would maximize expectable utility."

What type of rules does Brandt think maximize expectable utility? The following is an example of one: "substantial destruction of the lives and property of enemy civilians is permissible only when there is good evidence that it will significantly enhance the prospect of victory." For the most part, Brandt's rules are general and contingent and purposely so to adjust to the circumstances presented by war. Also, they are general enough to be accepted. Brandt argues that no one would agree to restrictions in war that seriously impair one's ability to be victorious. For Brandt, the rules of war provide considerable benefits but do not give either party to a war an advantage in victory. They are rules that force those in war to make moral judgments based on proportionality, what is necessary, and what is foreseeable. And though general and contingent, the rules of war are still useful in delineating moral conduct. Evidence can be provided to show that certain actions violated the rules of war, and thus those actions were not morally justified. Brandt points out that many of the current rules of war are consistent with the kind of rules that would be generated by his contractual rule-utilitarian theory.

War and Murder

(1961)

G. E. M. Anscombe

G. E. M. Anscombe was professor of philosophy at the University of Cambridge. Her publications include Intention *(1957),* An Introduction to Wittgenstein's Tractatus *(1959), and three volumes of her* Collected Papers *(1981). She died in 2001 at the age of eighty-one.*

THE USE OF VIOLENCE BY RULERS

Since there are always thieves and frauds and men who commit violent attacks on their neighbours and murderers, and since without law backed by adequate force there are usually gangs of bandits; and since there are in most places laws administered by people who command violence to enforce the laws against law-breakers; the question arises: what is a just attitude to this exercise of violent coercive power on the part of rulers and their subordinate officers?

Two attitudes are possible: one, that the world is an absolute jungle and that the exercise of coercive power by rulers is only a manifestation of this; and the other, that it is both necessary and right that there should be this exercise of power, that through it the world is much less of a jungle than it could possibly be without it, so that one should in principle be glad of the existence of such power, and only take exception to its unjust exercise.

It is so clear that the world is less of a jungle because of rulers and laws, and that the exercise of coercive power is essential to these institutions as they are now—all this is so obvious, that probably only Tennysonian conceptions of progress enable people who do not wish to separate themselves from the world to think that nevertheless such violence is objectionable, that some day, in this present dispensation, we shall do without it, and that the pacifist is the man who sees and tries to follow the ideal course, which future civilization must one day pursue. It is an illusion, which would be fantastic if it were not so familiar.

In a peaceful and law abiding country such as England, it may not be immediately obvious that the rulers need to command violence to the point of fighting to the death those that would oppose it; but brief reflection shews that this is so. For those who oppose the force that backs law will not always stop short of fighting to the death and cannot always be put down short of fighting to the death.

Then only if it is in itself evil violently to coerce resistant wills, can the exercise of coercive power by rulers be bad as such. Against such a conception, if it were true, the necessity and advantage of the exercise of such power would indeed be a useless plea. But that conception is one that makes no sense unless it is accompanied by a theory of withdrawal from the world as man's only salvation; and it is in any case a false one. We are taught that God retains the evil will of the devil within limits by violence: we are not given a picture of God permitting to the devil all that he is capable of. There is current a conception of Christianity as having revealed that the defeat of evil must always be by pure love without coercion; this at least is shewn to be false by the foregoing consideration. And without the alleged revelation there could be no reason to believe such a thing.

To think that society's coercive authority is evil is akin to thinking the flesh evil and family life evil. These things belong to the present constitution of mankind; and if the exercise of coercive power is a manifestation of evil, and not the just means of restraining it, then human nature is totally depraved in a manner never taught by Christianity. For society is essential to human good; and society without coercive power is generally impossible.

The same authority which puts down internal dissension, which promulgates laws and restrains those who break them if it can, must equally oppose external enemies. These do not merely comprise those who attack the borders of the people ruled by the authority; but also, for example, pirates and desert bandits, and, generally, those beyond the confines of the country ruled whose activities are viciously harmful to it. The Romans, once their rule in Gaul was established, were eminently justified in attacking Britain, where were nurtured the Druids whose pupils infested northern Gaul and whose practices struck the Romans themselves as "dira immani-

tas." Further, there being such a thing as the common good of mankind, and visible criminality against it, how can we doubt the excellence of such a proceeding as that violent suppression of the man-stealing business[1] which the British government took it into its head to engage in under Palmerston? The present-day conception of "aggression," like so many strongly influential conceptions, is a bad one. Why *must* it be wrong to strike the first blow in a struggle? The only question is, who is in the right.

Here, however, human pride, malice and cruelty are so usual that it is true to say that wars have mostly been mere wickedness on both sides. Just as an individual will constantly think himself in the right, whatever he does, and yet there is still such a thing as being in the right, so nations will constantly wrongly think themselves to be in the right—and yet there is still such a thing as their being in the right. Palmerston doubtless had no doubts in prosecuting the opium war against China, which was diabolical; just as he exulted in putting down the slavers. But there is no question but that he was a monster in the one thing, and a just man in the other.

The probability is that warfare is injustice, that a life of military service is a bad life "militia or rather malitia," as St. Anselm called it. This probability is greater than the probability (which also exists) that membership of a police force will involve malice, because of the character of warfare: the extraordinary occasions it offers for viciously unjust proceedings on the part of military commanders and warring governments, which at the time attract praise and not blame from their people. It is equally the case that the life of a ruler is usually a vicious life: but that does not shew that ruling is as such a vicious activity.

The principal wickedness which is a temptation to those engaged in warfare is the killing of the innocent, which may often be done with impunity and even to the glory of those who do it. In many places and times it has been taken for granted as a natural part of waging war: the commander, and especially the conqueror, massacres people by the thousand, either because this is part of his glory, or as a terrorizing measure, or as part of his tactics.

INNOCENCE AND THE RIGHT TO KILL INTENTIONALLY

It is necessary to dwell on the notion of non-innocence here employed. Innocence is a legal notion; but here, the accused is not pronounced guilty under an existing code of law, under which he has been tried by an impartial judge, and therefore made the target of attack. There is hardly a possibility of this; for the administration of justice is something that takes place under the aegis of a sovereign authority; but in warfare—or the putting down by violence of civil disturbance—the sovereign authority is itself engaged as a party to the dispute and is not subject to a further earthly and temporal authority which can judge the issue and pronounce against the accused. The stabler the society, the rarer it will be for the sovereign authority to have to do anything but apprehend its internal enemy and have him tried: but even in the stablest society there are occasions when the authority has to fight its internal enemy to the point of killing, as happens in the struggle with external belligerent forces in international warfare; and then the characterization of its enemy as non-innocent has not been ratified by legal process.

This, however, does not mean that the notion of innocence fails in this situation. What is required, for the people attacked to be non-innocent in the relevant sense, is that they should themselves be engaged in an objectively unjust proceeding which the attacker has the right to make his concern; or—the commonest case—should be unjustly attacking him. Then he can attack them with a view to stopping them; and also their supply lines and armament factories. But people whose mere existence and activity supporting existence by growing crops, making clothes, etc. constitute an impediment to him—such people are innocent and it is murderous to attack them, or make them a target for an attack which he judges will help him towards victory. For murder is the deliberate killing of the innocent, whether for its own sake or as a means to some further end.

The right to attack with a view to killing is something that belongs only to rulers and those whom they command to do it. I have argued that it does belong to rulers precisely because of that threat of violent coercion exercised by those in authority which is essential to the existence of human societies. It ought not to be pretended that rulers and their subordinates do not choose[2] the killing of their enemies as a means, when it has come to fighting in which they are determined to win and their enemies resist to the point of killing: this holds even in internal disturbances.

When a private man struggles with an enemy he has no right to aim to kill him, unless in the circumstances of the attack on him he can be considered as endowed with the authority of the law and the struggle comes to that point. By a "private" man, I mean a man in a society; I am not speaking of men on their own, without government, in remote places; for such men are neither public servants nor "private." The plea of self-defence (or the defence of someone else) made by a private man who has killed someone else must in conscience—even if not in law—be a plea that the death of the other was not intended, but was a side effect of the measures taken to ward off the attack. To shoot to kill, to set lethal man-traps, or, say, to lay poison for someone from whom one's life is in danger, are forbidden. The deliberate choice of inflicting death in a struggle is the right only of ruling authorities and their subordinates.

In saying that a private man may not choose to kill, we are touching on the principle of "double effect." The denial of this has been the corruption of non-Catholic thought, and its abuse the corruption of Catholic thought. Both have disastrous consequences which we shall see. This principle is not accepted in English law: the law is said to allow no distinction between the foreseen and the intended consequences of an action. Thus, if I push a man over a cliff when he is menacing my life, his death is considered as intended by me, but the intention to be justifiable for the sake of self-defence. Yet the lawyers would hardly find the laying of poison tolerable as an act of self-defence, but only killing by a violent action in a moment of violence. Christian moral theologians have taught that even here one may not seek the death of the assailant, but may in default of other ways of self-defence use such violence as will in fact result in his death. The distinction is evidently a fine one in some cases: what, it may be asked, can the intention be, if it can be said to be absent in this case, except a mere wish or desire?

And yet in other cases the distinction is very clear. If I go to prison rather than perform some action, no reasonable person will call the incidental consequences of my refusal—the loss of my job, for example—intentional just because I knew they must happen. And in the case of the administration of a pain-relieving drug in mortal illness, where the doctor knows the drug may very well kill the patient if the illness does not do so first, the distinction is evident; the lack of it has led an English judge to talk nonsense about the administration of the drug's not having *really* been the cause of death in such a case, even though a post mortem shews it was. For everyone understands that it is a very different thing so to administer a drug, and to administer it with the intention of killing. However, the principle of double effect has more important applications in warfare, and I shall return to it later.

THE INFLUENCE OF PACIFISM

Pacifism has existed as a considerable movement in English speaking countries ever since the first world war. I take the doctrine of pacifism to be that it is *eo ipso* wrong to fight in wars, not the doctrine that it is wrong to be compelled to, or that any man, or some men, may refuse; and I think it false for the reasons that I have given. But I now want to consider the very remarkable effects it has had: for I believe its influence to have been enormous, far exceeding its influence on its own adherents.

We should note first that pacifism has as its background conscription and enforced military service for all men. Without conscription, pacifism is a private opinion that will keep those who hold it out of armies, which they are in any case not obliged to join. Now universal conscription, except for the most extraordinary reasons, i.e. as a regular habit among most nations, is such a horrid evil that the refusal of it automatically commands a certain amount of respect and sympathy.

We are not here concerned with the pacifism of some peculiar sect which in any case draws apart from the world to a certain extent, but with a pacifism of people in the world, who do not want to be withdrawn from it. For some of these, pacifism is prevented from being a merely theoretical attitude because they are liable to, and so are prepared to resist conscription; or are able directly to effect the attitude of some who are so liable.

A powerful ingredient in this pacifism is the prevailing image of Christianity. This image commands a sentimental respect among people who have no belief in Christianity, that is to say, in Christian dogmas; yet do have a certain belief in an ideal which they conceive to be part of "true Christianity." It is therefore important to understand this image of Christianity and to know how false it is. Such understanding is relevant, not merely to those who wish to believe Christianity, but to all who, without the least wish to believe, are yet profoundly influenced by this image of it.

According to this image, Christianity is an ideal and beautiful religion, impracticable except for a few rare characters. It preaches a God of love whom there is no reason to fear; it marks an escape from the conception presented in the Old Testament, of a vindictive and jealous God who will terribly punish his enemies. The "Christian" God is a *roi fainéant,* whose only triumph is in the Cross; his appeal is to goodness and unselfishness, and to follow him is to act according to the Sermon on the Mount—to turn the other cheek and to offer no resistance to evil. In this account some of the evangelical counsels are chosen as containing the whole of Christian ethics: that is, they are made into precepts. (Only some of them; it is not likely that someone who deduces the *duty* of pacifism from the Sermon on the Mount and the rebuke to Peter, will agree to take "Give to him that asks of you" equally as a universally binding precept.)

The turning of counsels into precepts results in high-sounding principles. Principles that are mistakenly high and strict are a trap; they may easily lead in the end directly or indirectly to the justification of monstrous things. Thus if the evangelical counsel about poverty were turned into a precept forbidding property owning, people would pay lip service to it as the ideal, while in practice they went in for swindling. "Absolute honesty!" it would be said: "I can respect that—but of course that means having no property; and while I respect those who follow that course, I have to compromise with the sordid world myself." If then one must "compromise with evil" by owning property and engaging in trade, then the amount of swindling one does will depend on convenience. This imaginary case is paralleled by what is so commonly said: absolute pacifism is an ideal; unable to follow that, and committed to "compromise with evil," one must go the whole hog and wage war *à outrance.*

The truth about Christianity is that it is a severe and practicable religion, not a beautifully ideal but impracticable one. Its moral precepts, (except for the stricter laws about marriage that Christ enacted, abrogating some of the permissions of the Old Law) are those of the Old Testament; and its God is the God of Israel.

It is ignorance of the New Testament that hides this from people. It is characteristic of pacifism to denigrate the Old Testament and exalt the New: something quite contrary to the teaching of the New Testament itself, which always looks back to and leans upon the Old. How typical it is that the words of Christ "You have heard it said, an eye for an eye and a tooth for a tooth, but I say to you . . ." are taken as a repudiation of the ethic of the Old Testament! People seldom look up the occurrence of this phrase in the juridical code of the Old Testament, where it belongs, and is the admirable principle of law for the punishment of certain crimes, such as procuring the wrongful punishment of another by perjury. People often enough *now* cite the phrase to justify private revenge; no doubt this was as often "heard said" when Christ spoke of it. But no justification for this exists in the personal ethic taught by the Old Testament. On the contrary. What do we find? "Seek no revenge," (Leviticus xix, 18), and "If you find your enemy's ox or ass going astray, take it back to him; if you see the ass of someone who hates you lying under his burden, and would forbear to help him; you must help him" (Exodus xxiii, 4–5). And "If your enemy is hungry, give him food, if thirsty, give him drink" (Proverbs xxv, 21).

This is only one example; given space, it would be easy to shew how false is the conception of Christ's teaching as *correcting* the religion of the ancient Israelites, and substituting a higher and more "spiritual" religion for theirs. Now the false picture I have described plays an important part in the pacifist ethic and in the ethic of the many people who are not pacifists but are influenced by pacifism.

To extract a pacifist doctrine—i.e. a condemnation of the use of force by the ruling authorities, and of soldiering as a profession—from the evangelical counsels and the rebuke to Peter, is to disregard what else is in the New Testament. It is to forget St. John's direction to soldiers: "do not blackmail people; be content with your pay"; and Christ's commendation of the centurion, who compared his authority over his men to Christ's. On a pacifist view, this must be much as if a madam in a brothel had said: "I know what authority is, I tell this girl to do this, and she does it . . ." and Christ had commended her faith. A centurion was the first Gentile to be baptized; there is no suggestion in the New Testament that soldiering was regarded as incompatible with Christianity. The martyrology contains many names of soldiers whose occasion for martyrdom was not any objection to soldiering, but a refusal to perform idolatrous acts.

Now, it is one of the most vehement and repeated teachings of the Judaeo-Christian tradition that the shedding of innocent blood is forbidden by the divine law. No man may be punished except for his own crime, and those "whose feet are swift to shed innocent blood" are always represented as God's enemies.

For a long time the main outlines of this teaching have seemed to be merely obvious morality: hence, for example, I have read a passage by Ronald Knox complaining of the "endless moralizing," interspersed in records of meanness, cowardice, spite, cruelty, treachery and murder, which forms so much of the Old Testament. And indeed, that it is terrible to kill the innocent is very obvious; the morality that so stringently forbids it must make a great appeal to mankind, especially to the poor threatened victims. Why should it need the thunder of Sinai and the suffering and preaching of the prophets to promulgate such a law? But human pride and malice are everywhere so strong that now, with the fading of Christianity from the mind of the West, this morality once more stands out as a demand which strikes pride- and fear-ridden people as too intransigent. For Knox, it seemed so obvious as to be dull; and he failed to recognize the bloody and beastly records that it accompanies for the dry truthfulness about human beings that so characterizes the Old Testament.[3]

Now pacifism teaches people to make no distinction between the shedding of innocent blood and the shedding of any human blood. And in this way pacifism has corrupted enormous numbers of people who will not act according to its tenets. They become convinced that a number of things are wicked which are not; hence, seeing no way of avoiding "wickedness," they set no limits to it. How endlessly pacifists argue that all war must be *à outrance!* that those who wage war must go as far as technological advance permits in the destruction of the enemy's people. As if the Napoleonic wars were perforce fuller of massacres than the French war of Henry V of England. It is not true: the reverse took place. Nor is technological advance particularly relevant; it is mere squeamishness that deters people who would consent to area bombing from the enormous massacres *by hand* that used once to be committed.

The policy of obliterating cities was adopted by the Allies in the last war; they need not have taken that step, and it was taken largely out of a villainous hatred, and as corollary to the policy, now universally denigrated, of seeking "unconditional surrender." (That policy itself was visibly wicked, and could be and was judged so at the time; it is not surprising that it led to disastrous consequences, even if no one was clever and detached enough to foresee this at the time.)

Pacifism and the respect for pacifism is not the only thing that has led to a universal forgetfulness of the law against killing the innocent; but it has had a great share in it.

The Principle of Double Effect

Catholics, however, can hardly avoid paying at least lip-service to that law. So we must ask: how is it that there has been so comparatively little conscience exercised on the subject among them? The answer is: double-think about double effect.

The distinction between the intended, and the merely foreseen, effects of a voluntary action is indeed absolutely essential to Christian ethics. For Christianity forbids a number of things as being bad in themselves. But if I am answerable for the foreseen consequences of an action or refusal, as much as for the action itself, then these prohibitions will break down. If someone innocent will die unless I do a wicked thing, then on this view I am his murderer in refusing: so all that is left to me is to weigh up evils. Here the theologian steps in with the principle of double effect and says: "No, you are no murderer, if the man's death was neither your aim nor your chosen means, and if you had to act in the way that led to it or else do something absolutely forbidden." Without understanding of this principle, anything can be—and is wont to be—justified, and the Christian teaching that in no circumstances may one commit murder, adultery, apostasy (to give a few examples) goes by the board. These absolute prohibitions of Christianity by no means exhaust its ethic; there is a large area where what is just is determined partly by a prudent weighing up of consequences. But the prohibitions are bedrock, and without them the Christian ethic goes to pieces. Hence the necessity of the notion of double effect.

At the same time, the principle has been repeatedly abused from the seventeenth century up till now. The causes lie in the history of philosophy. From the seventeenth century till now what may be called Cartesian psychology has dominated the thought of philosophers and theologians. According to this psychology, an intention was an interior act of the mind which could be produced at will. Now if intention is all important—as it is—in determining the goodness or badness of an action, then, on this theory of what intention is, a marvellous way offered itself of making any action lawful. You only had to "direct your intention" in a suitable way. In practice, this means making a little speech to yourself: "What I mean to be doing is. . . ."

This perverse doctrine has occasioned repeated condemnations by the Holy See from the seventeenth century to the present day. Some examples will suffice to shew how the thing goes. Typical doctrines from the seventeenth century were that it is all right for a servant to hold the ladder for his criminous master so long as he is merely avoiding the sack by doing so; or that a man might wish for and rejoice at his parent's death so long as what he had in mind was the gain to himself; or that it is not simony to offer money, not *as a price* for the spiritual benefit, but only *as an in-*

ducement to give it. A condemned doctrine from the present day is that the practice of *coitus reservatus* is permissible: such a doctrine could only arise in connexion with that "direction of intention" which sets everything right no matter what one does. A man makes a practice of withdrawing, telling himself that he *intends* not to ejaculate; of course (if that is his practice) he usually does so, but then the event is "accidental" and *praeter intentionem:* it is, in short, a case of "double effect."

This same doctrine is used to prevent any doubts about the obliteration bombing of a city. The devout Catholic bomber secures by a "direction of intention" that any shedding of innocent blood that occurs is "accidental." I know a Catholic boy who was puzzled at being told by his schoolmaster that it was an *accident* that the people of Hiroshima and Nagasaki were there to be killed; in fact, however absurd it seems, such thoughts are common among priests who know that they are forbidden by the divine law to justify the direct killing of the innocent.

It is nonsense to pretend that you do not intend to do what is the means you take to your chosen end. Otherwise there is absolutely no substance to the Pauline teaching that we may not do evil that good may come.

SOME COMMONLY HEARD ARGUMENTS

There are a number of sophistical arguments, often or sometimes used on these topics, which need answering.

Where do you draw the line? As Dr. Johnson said, the fact of twilight does not mean you cannot tell day from night. There are borderline cases, where it is difficult to distinguish, in what is done, between means and what is incidental to, yet in the circumstances inseparable from, those means. The obliteration bombing of a city is not a borderline case.

The old "conditions for a just war" are irrelevant to the conditions of modern warfare, so that must be condemned out of hand. People who say this always envisage only major wars between the Great Powers, which Powers are indeed now "in blood stepp'd in so far" that it is unimaginable for there to be a war between them which is not a set of enormous massacres of civil populations. But these are not the only wars. Why is Finland so far free? At least partly because of the "posture of military preparedness" which, considering the character of the country, would have made subjugating the Finns a difficult and unrewarding task. The offensive of the Israelis against the Egyptians in 1956 involved no plan of making civil populations the target of military attack.

In a modern war the distinction between combatants and non-combatants is meaningless, so an attack on anyone on the enemy side is justified. This is pure nonsense; even in war, a very large number of the enemy population are just engaged in maintaining the life of the country, or are sick, or aged, or children.

It must be legitimate to maintain an opinion—viz. that the destruction of cities by bombing is lawful—if this is argued by competent theologians and the Holy See has not pronounced. The argument from the silence of the Holy See has itself been condemned by the Holy See (Denzinger, 28th Edition, 1127). How could this be a sane doctrine in view of the endless twistiness of the human mind?

Whether a war is just or not is not for the private man to judge: he must obey his government. Sometimes, this may be, especially as far as concerns causes of war. But the individual who joins in destroying a city, like a Nazi massacring the inhabitants of a village, is too obviously marked out as an enemy of the human race, to shelter behind such a plea.

Finally, horrible as it is to have to notice this, we must notice that even the arguments about double effect—which at least show that a man is not willing openly to justify the killing of the innocent—are now beginning to look old-fashioned. Some Catholics are not scrupling to say that *anything* is justified in defence of the continued existence and liberty of the Church in the West. A terrible fear of communism drives people to say this sort of thing. "Our Lord told us to fear those who can destroy body and soul, not to fear the destruction of the body" was blasphemously said to a friend of mine; meaning: "so, we must fear Russian domination more than the destruction of people's bodies by obliteration bombing."

But whom did Our Lord tell us to fear, when he said: "I will tell you whom you shall fear" and "Fear not them that can destroy the body, but fear him who can destroy body and soul in hell"? He told us to fear God the Father, who can and will destroy the unrepentant disobedient, body and soul, in hell.

A Catholic who is tempted to think on the lines I have described should remember that the Church is the spiritual Israel: that is, that Catholics are what the ancient Jews were, salt for the earth and the people of God—and that what was true of some devout Jews of ancient times can equally well be true of us now: "You compass land and sea to make a convert, and when you have done so, you make him twice as much a child of hell as yourselves." Do Catholics sometimes think that they are immune from such a possibility? That the Pharisees—who sat in the seat of Moses and who were so zealous for the true religion—were bad in ways in which we cannot be bad if we are zealous? I believe they do. But our faith teaches no such immunity, it teaches the opposite. "We are in danger all our lives long." So we have to fear God and keep his commandments, and calculate what is for the best only within the limits of that obedience, knowing that the future is in God's power and that no one can snatch away those whom the Father has given to Christ.

It is not a vague faith in the triumph of "the spirit" over force (there is little enough warrant for that), but a definite faith in the divine promises, that makes us believe that the Church cannot fail. Those, therefore, who think they must be prepared to wage a war with Russia involving the deliberate massacre of cities, must be prepared to say to God: "We had to break your law, lest your Church fail. We could not obey your commandments, for we did not believe your promises."

Notes

1. It is ignorance to suppose that it takes modern liberalism to hate and condemn this. It is cursed and subject to the death penalty in the Mosaic law. Under the code, too, runaway slaves of all nations had asylum in Israel.
2. The idea that they may lawfully do what they do, but should not *intend* the death of those they attack, has been put forward and, when suitably expressed, may seem high-minded. But someone who can fool himself into this twist of thought will fool himself into justifying anything, however atrocious, by means of it.
3. It is perhaps necessary to remark that I am not here adverting to the total extermination of certain named tribes of Canaan that is said by the Old Testament to have been commanded by God. That is something quite outside the provisions of the Mosaic Law for dealings in war.

Conventions and the Morality of War

(1972)

George I. Mavrodes

George Mavrodes is Professor Emeritus of Philosophy at the University of Michigan. He works primarily in the philosophy of religion and social philosophy. His books include Belief in God: A Study in the Epistemology of Religion *(1970),* The Rationality of Belief in God *(editor, 1970), and* Revelation In Religious Belief *(1988), along with numerous articles in journals and edited collections.*

The point of this paper is to introduce a distinction into our thinking about warfare, and to explore the moral implications of this distinction. I shall make two major assumptions. First, I shall assume without discussion that under some circumstances and for some ends warfare is morally justified. These conditions I shall lump together under such terms as "justice" and "just cause," and say no more about them. I shall also assume that in warfare some means, including some killing, are morally justified. I sometimes call such means "proportionate," and in general I say rather little about them. These assumptions, incidentally, are common to all of the philosophers whom I criticize here.

The distinction which I introduce can be thought of either as dividing wars into two classes, or else as distinguishing wars from certain other international combats. I have no great preference for one of these ways of speaking over the other, but I shall generally adopt the latter alternative. I am particularly interested in the moral significance of this distinction, and I shall explore in some detail its bearing on one moral question associated with warfare, that of the intentional killing of noncombatants.

My paper has two main parts. In the first I examine three closely related treatments of this moral question: the arguments of Elizabeth Anscombe, John C. Ford, and Paul Ramsey. These treatments seem to ignore the distinction which I will propose. I argue that on their own terms, and without reference to that distinction, they must be counted as unsatisfactory.

In the second part of the paper I propose and explain my distinction. I then explore what I take to be some of its moral implications, especially with reference to the alleged immunity of noncombatants, and I argue that it supplies what was missing or defective in the treatments previously criticized.

I. THE IMMUNITY THEORISTS

A number of philosophers have held that a large portion of the population of warring nations have a special moral status. This is the *non-combatant* segment of the population, and they have a moral immunity from being intentionally killed. This view seems to have been especially congenial to philosophers who have tried to apply Christian ethics to the problems of warfare. Among the philosophers who have held this view are Elizabeth Anscombe, John C. Ford, and Paul Ramsey. I shall refer to this trio of thinkers as the *immunity theorists.*

Perhaps we should indicate a little more in detail just what the immunity theorists appear to hold, specifying just what segment of the population is being discussed and just what their immunity consists in. The immunity theorists commonly admit that there is some difficulty in specifying exactly who are the noncombatants.[1] Roughly, they are those people who are not engaged in military operations and whose activity is not immediately and directly related to the war effort. Perhaps we could say that if a person is engaged only in the sort of activities which would be carried on even if the nation were not at war (or preparing for war) then that person is a noncombatant. So generally farmers, teachers, nurses, firemen, sales people, housewives, poets, children, etc. are noncombatants.[2] There are, of course, difficult cases, ranging from the high civilian official of the government to the truck driver (either military or civilian) who hauls vegetables toward the front lines. But despite the hard cases it is held that warring nations contain large numbers of readily identifiable people who are clearly non-combatants.

What of their immunity? The writers whom I consider here make use of the "principle of double-effect."[3] This involves dividing the consequences of an act (at least the foreseeable consequences) into two classes. Into the first class go those consequences which constitute the goal or purpose of the act, what the act is done for, and also those consequences which are means to those ends. Into the other class go those consequences which are neither the sought-after ends nor the means to those ends. So, for example, the bombing of a rail yard may have among its many consequences the following: the flow of supplies toward the front is disrupted, several locomotives are damaged, and a lot of smoke, dust, etc. is discharged into the air. The disruption of transport may well be the end sought by this action, and perhaps the damage to locomotives is sought as a means of disrupting transport. If so, these consequences belong in the first class, a class which I shall generally mark by using the words "intentional" or "intended." The smoke, on the other hand, though as surely foreseeable as the other effects, may be neither means nor end in this situation. It is a side-effect, and belongs in the second class (which I shall sometimes call "unintentional" or "unintended").

Now, the moral immunity of noncombatants consists, according to these writers, in the fact that their death can never, morally, be made the intended consequence of a military operation. Or to put it

another way, any military operation which seeks the death of noncombatants either as an end or a means is immoral, regardless of the total good which it might accomplish.

The *unintended* death of noncombatants, on the other hand, is not absolutely forbidden. A military operation which will foreseeably result in such deaths, neither as means nor ends but as side effects, may be morally acceptable according to these writers. It will be morally acceptable if the good end which it may be expected to attain is of sufficient weight to overbalance the evil of these noncombatant deaths (as well as any other evils involved in it). This principle, sometimes called the principle of proportionality, apparently applies to foreseen but unintended noncombatant deaths in just the same way as it applies to the intended death of combatants, the destruction of resources, and so on. In all of these cases it is held to be immoral to cause many deaths, much pain, etc., in order to achieve minor goals. Here combatant and noncombatant stand on the same moral ground, and their deaths are weighed in the same balances. But when the slaying of noncombatants is envisioned as an end or, more commonly, as a means—perhaps in order to reduce the production of foodstuffs or to damage the morale of troops— then there is an unqualified judgment that the projected operation is flatly immoral. The intentional slaying of combatants, on the other hand, faces no such prohibition. This, then, is the place where the moral status of combatant and noncombatant differ sharply.

Now, if a scheme such as this is not to appear simply arbitrary it looks as though we must find some morally relevant basis for the distinction. It is perhaps worthwhile to notice that in this context the immunity of noncombatants cannot be supported by reference to the sanctity or value of human life, nor by reference to a duty not to kill our brothers, etc. For these authors recognize the moral permissibility, even perhaps the duty, of killing under certain circumstances. What must be sought is the ground of a distinction, and not merely a consideration against killing.

Such a ground, however, seems very hard to find, perhaps unexpectedly so. The crucial argument proposed by the immunity theorists turns on the notions of guilt and innocence. Anscombe, for example, says:

> Now, it is one of the most vehement and repeated teachings of the Judaeo-Christian tradition that the shedding of innocent blood is forbidden by the divine law. No man may be punished except for his own crime, and those "whose feet are swift to shed innocent blood" are always represented as God's enemies.[4]

Earlier on she says, "The principal wickedness which is a temptation to those engaged in warfare is the killing of the innocent,"[5] and she has titled one of the sections of her paper, "Innocence and the Right to Kill Intentionally." Clearly enough the notion of innocence plays a large role in her thinking on this topic. Just what that role is, or should be, will be considered shortly. Ford, in the article cited earlier, repeatedly couples the word "innocent" with "civilian" and "noncombatant." His clearest statement, however, is in another essay. There he says:

> Catholic teaching has been unanimous for long centuries in declaring that it is never permitted to kill directly noncombatants in wartime. Why? Because they are innocent. That is, they are innocent of the violent and destructive action of war, or of any close participation in the violent and destructive action of war. It is such participation *alone* that would make them legitimate targets of violent repression themselves.[6]

Here we have explicitly a promising candidate for the basis of the moral distinction between combatants and noncombatants. It is promising because innocence itself seems to be a moral property. Hence, if we could see that noncombatants were innocent while combatants were not it would be plausible to suppose that this fact made it morally proper to treat them in different ways.

If we are to succeed along this line of thought, then we must meet at least two conditions. First, we must find some one sense of "innocence" such that all noncombatants are innocent and all combatants are guilty. Second, this sense must be morally relevant, a point of the greatest importance. We are seeking to ground a moral distinction, and the facts to which we refer must therefore be morally relevant. The use of a morally tinged word, such as "innocent," does not of itself guarantee such relevance.

Well, is there a suitable sense for "innocent"? Ford said that noncombatants "are innocent of the violent and destructive action of war." Anscombe, writing of the people who can properly be attacked with deadly force, says, "What is required, for the people attacked to be noninnocent in the relevant sense, is that they themselves be engaged in an objectively unjust proceeding which the attacker has the right to make his concern; or—the commonest case—should be unjustly attacking him." On the other hand, she speaks of "people whose mere existence and activity supporting existence by growing crops, making clothes, etc.," might contribute to the war effort, and she says, "such people are innocent and it is murderous to attack them, or make them a target for an attack which he judges will help him towards victory."[7] These passages contain, I think, the best clues we have as to the sense of "innocent" in these authors.

It is probably evident enough that this sense of "innocent" is vague in a way parallel to the vagueness of "noncombatant." It will leave us with troublesome borderline cases. In itself, that does not seem to me a crucial defect. But perhaps it is a clue to an important failing. For I suspect that there is this parallel vagueness because "innocent" here is just a synonym for "noncombatant."

What can Ford mean by saying that some people are "innocent of the violent and destructive action of war" except that those people are not engaged in the violence of war? Must not Anscombe mean essentially the same thing when she says that the noninnocent are those who are themselves "engaged in an objectively unjust proceeding"? But we need not rely wholly on these rhetorical questions. Ramsey makes this point explicitly. He first distinguishes between close and remote cooperation in military operations, and then he alludes to the distinction between the "guilty" and the "innocent." Of this distinction he says, "These are very misleading terms, since their meaning is exhaustively stated under the first contrast, and is reducible to degrees of actual participation in hostile force."[8] In this judgment Ramsey certainly seems to me to be right.

Now, we should notice carefully that a person may be an enthusiastic supporter of the unjust war and its unjust aims, he may give to it his voice and his vote, he may have done everything in his power to procure it when it was yet but a prospect, now that it is in progress he may contribute to it both his savings and the work which he knows best how to do, and he may avidly hope to share in the unjust gains which will follow if the war is successful. But such a person may clearly be a noncombatant, and (in the sense of the immunity theorists) unquestionably "innocent" of the war. On the other hand, a young man of limited mental ability and almost no education may be drafted, put into uniform, trained for a few weeks, and sent to the front as a replacement in a low-grade unit. He may have no understanding of what the war is about, and no heart for it. He might want nothing more than to go back to his town and the life he led before. But he is "engaged," carrying ammunition, perhaps, or stringing telephone wire or even banging away ineffectually with his rifle. He is without doubt a combatant, and "guilty," a fit subject for intentional slaughter. Is it not clear that "innocence," as used here, leaves out entirely all of the relevant moral considerations—that it has no moral content at all? Anscombe suggests that intentional killing during warfare should be construed on the model of punishing people for their crimes, and we must see to it, if we are to be moral, that we punish someone only for his own crime and not for someone else's. But if we construe the criminality involved in an unjust war in any reasonable moral sense then it must either be the case that many noncombatants are guilty of that criminality or else many combatants are innocent. In fact, it will probably be the case that *both* of these things are true. Only if we were to divest "crime" of its moral bearings could we make it fit the combatant/noncombatant distinction in modern wars.

The fact that both Anscombe and Ramsey[9] use the analogy of the criminal in discussing this topic suggests that there is an important fact about warfare which is easily overlooked. And that is that warfare, unlike ordinary criminal activity, is not an activity in which individuals engage qua individuals or as members of voluntary associations. They enter into war as members of nations. It is more proper to say that the nation is at war than that its soldiers are at war. This does not, of course, entail that individuals have no moral responsibility for their acts in war. But it does suggest that moral responsibility may not be distributed between combatant and noncombatant in the same way as between a criminal and his children. Many of the men who are soldiers, perhaps most of them, would not be engaged in military operations at all if they did not happen to be citizens of a warring nation. But noncombatants are citizens of warring nations in exactly the same sense as are soldiers. However these facts are to be analyzed they should warn us not to rely too heavily on the analogy with ordinary criminality.

We seem, then, to be caught in a dilemma. We can perhaps find some sense for notions such as *innocence* and *criminality* which will make them fit the distinction in which we are interested. But the price of doing so seems to be that of divesting these notions of the moral significance which they require if they are to justify the moral import of the distinction itself. In the ordinary senses, on the other hand, these notions do have the required moral bearings. But in their ordinary senses they do not fit the desired distinction. In neither way, therefore, can the argument from innocence be made to work, and the alleged moral immunity of noncombatants seems to be left as an arbitrary claim.

II. CONVENTION-DEPENDENT MORALITY

Despite the failure of these arguments I have recently come to think that there may be something of importance in this distinction after all, and even that it may have an important moral bearing. How might this be?

Imagine a statesman reflecting on the costliness of war, its cost in human life and human suffering. He observes that these costs are normally very high, sometimes staggering. Furthermore, he accepts the principle of proportionality. A consequence of this is that he sometimes envisions a just war for a just cause, but nevertheless decides not to prosecute that war even though he believes it could be won. For the cost of winning would be so high as to outweigh the good which would be attained. So he must sometimes let oppression flourish and injustice hold sway. And even in those wars which can be prosecuted the costs eat very seriously into the benefits.

Then he has an idea. Suppose—just suppose—that one could replace warfare with a less costly substitute. Suppose, for example, that one could introduce a convention—and actually get it accepted and followed by the nations—a convention which replaced warfare with single combat. Under this convention, when two nations arrived at an impasse which would otherwise have resulted in war they would instead choose, each of them, a single champion (doubtless a volunteer). These two men would then meet in mortal combat, and whoever won, killing his opponent or driving him from the field, would win for his nation. To that nation would then be ceded whatever territory, influence, or other prize would have been sought in the war, and the nation whose champion was defeated would lose correspondingly.

Suppose, too, that the statesman believes that if such a convention were to come into force his own nation could expect to win and lose such combats in about the same proportion as it could now expect to win and lose ordinary wars. The same types of questions would be settled by such combats as would otherwise be settled by war (though perhaps more questions would be submitted to combat than would be submitted to war), and approximately the same resolutions would be arrived at. The costs, however—human death and suffering—would be reduced by several orders of magnitude. Would that not be an attractive prospect? I think it would.

While the prospect may seem attractive it may also strike us as hopelessly utopian, hardly to be given a serious thought. There seems to be some evidence, however, that exactly this substitution was actually attempted in ancient times. Ancient literature contains at least two references to such attempts. One is in the Bible, I Samuel 17, the combat between David and Goliath. The other is in the *Iliad,* book 3, where it is proposed to settle the seige of Troy in the very beginning by single combat between Menelaus and Paris. It may be significant that neither of these attempts appears to have been successful. The single combats were followed by bloodier and more general fighting. Perhaps this substitute for warfare is too cheap; it cannot be made practical, and nations just will not consent in the end to

abide by this convention. But consider, on the one hand, warfare which is limited only by the moral requirements that the ends sought should be just and that the means used should be proportionate, and, on the other hand, the convention of single combat as a substitute for warfare. Between these extremes there lie a vast number of other possible conventions which might be canvassed in the search for a less costly substitute for war. I suggest that the long struggle, in the western world at least, to limit military operations to "counter-forces" strategies, thus sparing civilian populations, is just such an attempt.

If I am right about this, then the moral aspects of the matter must be approached in a way rather different from that of the immunity theorists. Some, but not all, of their conclusions can be accepted, and somewhat different grounds must be given for them. These thinkers have construed the immunity of noncombatants as though it were a moral fact which was independent of any actual or envisioned convention or practice. And they have consequently sought to support this immunity by argument which makes no reference to convention. I have already argued that their attempts were failures. What I suggest now is that all such attempts *must* be failures, for they mistake the sort of moral requirement which is under consideration. Let me try to make this clearer.

I find it plausible to suppose that I have a moral obligation to refrain from wantonly murdering my neighbors. And it also seems plausible to discuss this, perhaps in utilitarian terms, or in terms of the will of God, or of natural law, or in terms of a rock-bottom deontological requirement, but in any case without essential reference to the laws and customs of our nation. We might, indeed, easily imagine our laws and customs to be other than they are with respect to murder. But we would then judge the moral adequacy and value of such alternative laws and customs by reference to the moral obligation I have mentioned and not vice versa. On the other hand, I may also have a moral obligation to pay a property tax or to drive on the right side of the street. It does not seem plausible to suppose, however, that one can discuss these duties without immediately referring to our laws and customs. And it seems likely that different laws would have generated different moral duties, e.g. driving on the left. These latter are examples of "convention-dependent" moral obligations. More formally, I will say that a given moral obligation is convention-dependent if and only if (1) given that a certain convention, law, custom, etc., is actually in force one really does have an obligation to act in conformity with that convention, and (2) there is an alternative law, custom, etc. (or lack thereof) such that if that had been in force one would not have had the former obligation.

At this point, before developing the way in which it may apply to warfare, let me forestall some possible misunderstandings by a series of brief comments on this notion. I am not claiming, nor do I believe, that all laws, customs, etc., generate corresponding moral obligations. But some do. I am not denying that one may seek, and perhaps find, some more general moral law, perhaps independent of convention, which explains why this convention generates the more specific obligation. I claim only that one cannot account for the specific obligation apart from the convention. Finally, I am not denying that one might have an obligation, perhaps independent of convention, to try to change a convention of this sort. For I think it possible that one might simultaneously have a moral obligation to conform to a certain convention and also a moral obligation to replace that convention, and thus to eliminate the first obligation.

Now, the core of my suggestion with respect to the immunity of noncombatants is this. The immunity of noncombatants is best thought of as a convention-dependent obligation related to a convention which substitutes for warfare a certain form of limited combat. How does this bear on some of the questions which we have been discussing?

To begin with, we might observe that the convention itself is presumably to be justified by its expectable results. (Perhaps we can refer to some moral rule to the effect that we should minimize social costs such as death and injury.) It seems plausible to suppose that the counter-forces convention, if followed, will reduce the pain and death involved in combat—will reduce it, that is, compared to unlimited warfare. There are surely other possible conventions which, if followed, would reduce those costs still more, e.g. the substitution of single combat. Single combat, however, is probably not a live contender because there is almost no chance that such a convention would actually be followed. It is possible, however, that there is some practical convention which is preferable to the present counter-forces convention. If so, the fact that it is preferable is a strong reason in favor of supposing that there is a moral obligation to promote its adoption.

It does not follow, however, that we now have a duty to act in conformity with this other possible convention. For the results of acting in conformity with a preferable convention which is not widely observed may be much worse than the results of acting in conformity with a less desirable convention which is widely observed. We might, for example, discover that a "left-hand" pattern of traffic flow would be preferable to the present system of "right-hand" rules, in that it would result in fewer accidents, etc. The difference might be so significant that we really would be morally derelict if we did not try to institute a change in our laws. We would be acquiescing in a very costly procedure when a more economical one was at hand. But it would be a disaster, and, I suspect, positively immoral, for a few of us to begin driving on the left before the convention was changed. In cases of convention-dependent obligations the question of what convention is actually in force is one of considerable moral import. That one is reminded to take this question seriously is one of the important differences between this approach and that of the immunity theorists.

Perhaps the counter-forces convention is not really operative now in a substantial way. I do not know. Doubtless, it suffered a severe blow in World War II, not least from British and American bombing strategies. Traffic rules are embedded in a broad, massive, comparatively stable social structure which makes their status comparatively resistant to erosion by infraction. Not so, however, for a convention of warfare. It has little status except in its actual observance, and depends greatly on the mutual trust of the belligerents; hence it is especially vulnerable to abrogation by a few contrary acts. Here arises a related difference with the immunity theorists. Taking the obligation to be convention-independent they reject argument based on

the fact that "the enemy did it first," etc.[10] If the obligation were independent they would be correct in this. But for convention-dependent obligations, what one's opponent does, what "everyone is doing," etc., are facts of great moral importance. Such facts help to determine within what convention, if any, one is operating, and thus they help one to discover what his moral duties are.

If we were to decide that the counter-forces convention was dead at present, or, indeed, that no convention at all with respect to warfare was operative now, it would not follow that warfare was immoral. Nor, on the other hand, would it follow that warfare was beyond all moral rules, an area in which "anything goes." Instead, we would simply go back to warfare per se, limited only by independent moral requirements, such as those of justice and proportionality. That would, on the whole, probably be a more costly way of handling such problems. But if we live in a time when the preferable substitutes are not available, then we must either forgo the goods or bear the higher costs. If we had no traffic laws or customs, traffic would be even more dangerous and costly than it is now. Traveling, however, might still be justified, if the reason for traveling were sufficiently important.

In such a case, of course, there would be no obligation to drive on the right, or in any regular manner, nor would there be any benefit in it. Probably the best thing would be to drive in a completely ad hoc way, seeking the best maneuver in each situation as it arose. More generally, and ignoring for the moment a final consideration which will be discussed below, there is no obligation and no benefit associated with the unilateral observance of a convention. If one's cause is unjust then one ought not to kill noncombatants. But that is because of the independent moral prohibition against prosecuting such a war at all, and has nothing to do with any special immunity of noncombatants. If one's cause is just, but the slaying of noncombatants will not advance it to any marked degree, then one ought not to slay them. But this is just the requirement of proportionality, and applies equally and in the same way to combatants. If one's cause is just and the slaying of noncombatants would advance it—if, in other words, one is not prevented by considerations of justice and proportionality—this is the crucial case. If one refrains unilaterally in this situation then he seems to choose the greater of two evils (or the lesser of two goods). By hypothesis, the good achieved, i.e. the lives spared, is not as weighty as the evil which he allows in damage to the prospects for justice or in the even more costly alternative measures, e.g. the slaying of a larger number of combatants, which he must undertake. Now, if the relevant convention were operative, then his refraining from counter-population strategies here would be related to his enemy's similar restraint, and indeed it would be related to the strategies which would be used in future wars. These larger considerations might well tip the balance in the other direction. But by hypothesis we are considering the case in which there is no such convention, and so these larger considerations do not arise. One acts unilaterally. In such a situation it certainly appears that one would have chosen the worse of the two alternatives. It is hard to suppose that one is morally obligated to do so.

I said above that we were ignoring for the moment one relevant consideration. It should not be ignored forever. I have already called attention to the fact that conventions of warfare are not, like traffic rules, embedded in a more massive social structure. This makes them especially precarious, as we have noted. But it also bears on the way in which they may be adopted. One such way, perhaps a rather important way, is for one party to the hostilities to signal his willingness to abide by such a convention by undertaking some unilateral restraint on his own part. If the opponent does not reciprocate, then the offer has failed and it goes no further. If the opponent does reciprocate, however, then the area of restraint may be broadened, and a kind of mutual respect and confidence may grow up between the belligerents. Each comes to rely on the other to keep the (perhaps unspoken) agreement, and therefore each is willing to forgo the immediate advantage which might accrue to him from breaking it. If this happens, then a new convention has begun its precarious life. This may be an event well worth seeking.

Not only may it be worth seeking, it may be worth paying something for it. For a significant increase in the likelihood that a worthwhile convention will be adopted it may be worth accepting an increased risk or a higher immediate cost in lives and suffering. So there may be some justification in unilateral restraint after all, even in the absence of a convention. But this justification is prospective and finite. It envisions the possibility that such a convention may arise in the future as a result of this restraint. Consequently, the justification should be proportioned to some judgment as to the likelihood of that event, and it should be reevaluated as future events unfold.

III. CONVENTION VS. MORALITY

I began by examining some attempts to defend a certain alleged moral rule of war, the immunity of noncombatants. These defenses have in common the fact that they construe this moral rule as independent of any human law, custom, etc. I then argued that these defenses fail because they leave a certain distinction without moral support, and yet the distinction is essential to the rule. Turning then to the task of construction rather than criticism, I suggested that the immunity of noncombatants is not an independent moral rule but rather a part of a convention which sets up a morally desirable alternative to war. I argued then that some conventions, including this one, generate special moral obligations which cannot be satisfactorily explained and defended without reference to the convention. And in the final pages I explored some of the special features of the obligation at hand and of the arguments which are relevant to it.

The distinction I have drawn is that between warfare per se on the one hand, and, on the other hand, international combats which are limited by convention and custom. But the point of the distinction is to clarify our thinking about the *morality* of such wars and combats. That is where its value must be tested.

Notes

1. Elizabeth Anscombe, "War and Murder," *War and Morality* ed. Richard A. Wasserstrom (Belmont, Calif., 1970), p. 52; John C. Ford, "The Morality of Obliteration Bombing," ibid., pp. 19–23; Paul Ramsey, *The Just War* (New York, 1968), pp. 157, 158.
2. Ford gives a list of over 100 occupations whose practitioners he considers to be "almost without exception" noncombatants.
3. Anscombe, pp. 46, 50, 51; Ford, pp. 26–28; Ramsey, pp. 347–358.
4. Anscombe, p. 49.
5. Ibid., p. 44.
6. John C. Ford, "The Hydrogen Bombing of Cities," *Morality and Modern Warfare* ed. William J. Nagle (Baltimore: Helicon Press, 1960), p. 98.
7. Anscombe, p. 45.
8. Ramsey, p. 153.
9. Ibid., p. 144.
10. For example, Ford, "The Morality of Obliteration Bombing," pp. 20, 33.

War and Massacre

(1972)

Thomas Nagel[1]

Thomas Nagel is professor of philosophy, University Professor, and Fiorello La Guardia Professor of Law at New York University. He specializes in political philosophy, ethics, epistemology, and philosophy of mind. Among his many books are The Possibility of Altruism *(1970),* Mortal Questions *(1979), and* The View From Nowhere *(1986).*

From the apathetic reaction to atrocities committed in Vietnam by the United States and its allies, one may conclude that moral restrictions on the conduct of war command almost as little sympathy among the general public as they do among those charged with the formation of U.S. military policy. Even when restrictions on the conduct of warfare are defended, it is usually on legal grounds alone: their moral basis is often poorly understood. I wish to argue that certain restrictions are neither arbitrary nor merely conventional, and that their validity does not depend simply on their usefulness. There is, in other words, a moral basis for the rules of war, even though the conventions now officially in force are far from giving it perfect expression. . . .

I

I propose to discuss the most general moral problem raised by the conduct of warfare: the problem of means and ends. In one view, there are limits on what may be done even in the service of an end worth pursuing—and even when adherence to the restriction may be very costly. A person who acknowledges the force of such restrictions can find himself in acute moral dilemmas. He may believe, for example, that by torturing a prisoner he can obtain information necessary to prevent a disaster, or that by obliterating one village with bombs he can halt a campaign of terrorism. If he believes that the gains from a certain measure will clearly outweigh its costs, yet still suspects that he ought not to adopt it, then he is in a dilemma produced by the conflict between two disparate categories of moral reason: categories that may be called *utilitarian* and *absolutist*.

Utilitarianism gives primacy to a concern with what will *happen*. Absolutism gives primacy to a concern with what one is *doing*. The conflict between them arises because the alternatives we face are rarely just choices between *total outcomes*: they are also choices between alternative pathways or measures to be taken. When one of the choices is to do terrible things to another person, the problem is altered fundamentally; it is no longer merely a question of which outcome would be worse.

Few of us are completely immune to either of these types of moral intuition, though in some people, either naturally or for doctrinal reasons, one type will be dominant and the other suppressed or weak. But it is perfectly possible to feel the force of both types of reason very strongly; in that case the moral dilemma in certain situations of crisis will be acute, and it may appear that every possible course of action or inaction is unacceptable for one reason or another.

II

Although it is this dilemma that I propose to explore, most of the discussion will be devoted to its absolutist component. The utilitarian component is straightforward by comparison, and has a natural appeal to anyone who is not a complete skeptic about ethics. Utilitarianism says that one should try, either individually or through institutions, to maximize good and minimize evil (the definition of these categories need not enter into the schematic formulation of the view), and that if faced with the possibility of preventing a great evil by producing a lesser, one should choose the lesser evil. There are certainly problems about the formulation of utilitarianism, and much has been written about it, but its intent is morally transparent. Nevertheless, despite the addition of various refinements, it continues to leave large portions of ethics unaccounted for. I do not suggest that some form of absolutism can account for them all, only that an examination of absolutism will lead us to see the complexity, and perhaps the incoherence, of our moral ideas.

Utilitarianism certainly justifies *some* restrictions on the conduct of warfare. There are strong utilitarian reasons for adhering to any limitation which seems natural to most people—particularly if the limitation is widely accepted already. An exceptional measure which seems to be justified by its results in a particular conflict may create a precedent with disastrous long-term effects.[2] It may even be argued that war involves violence on such a scale that it is never justified on utilitarian grounds—the consequences of refusing to go to war will never be as bad as the war itself would be, even if atrocities were not committed. Or in a more sophisticated vein it might be claimed that a uniform policy of never resorting to military force would do less harm in the long run, if followed consistently, than a policy of deciding each case on utilitarian grounds (even though on occasion particular applications of the pacifist policy might have worse results than a specific utilitarian decision). But I shall not consider these arguments, for my concern is with reasons of a different kind, which may remain when reasons of utility and interest fail.[3]

In the final analysis, I believe that the dilemma cannot always be resolved. While not every conflict between absolutism and utilitarianism creates an insoluble dilemma, and while it is certainly right to adhere to absolutist restrictions unless the utilitarian considerations favoring violation are overpoweringly weighty and extremely certain—nevertheless, when that special condition is met, it may become impossible to adhere to an absolutist position. What I shall offer, therefore, is a somewhat qualified defense of absolutism. I believe it underlies a valid and fundamental type of moral judgment—which cannot be reduced to or overridden by other principles. And while there may be other principles just as fundamental, it is particularly important not to lose confidence in our absolutist intuitions, for they are often the only barrier before the abyss of utilitarian apologetics for large-scale murder.

III

One absolutist position that creates no problems of interpretation is pacifism: the view that one may not kill another person under any circumstances, no matter what good would be achieved or evil averted thereby. The type of absolutist position that I am going to discuss is different. Pacifism draws the conflict with utilitarian considerations very starkly. But there are other views according to which violence may be undertaken, even on a large scale, in a clearly just cause, so long as certain absolute restrictions on the character and direction of that violence are observed. The line is drawn somewhat closer to the bone, but it exists. . . .

The policy of attacking the civilian population in order to induce an enemy to surrender, or to damage his morale, seems to have been widely accepted in the civilized world, and seems to be accepted still, at least if the stakes are high enough. It gives evidence of a moral conviction that the deliberate killing of noncombatants— women, children, old people—is permissible if enough can be gained by it. This follows from the more general position that any means can in principle be justified if it leads to a sufficiently worthy end. Such an attitude is evident not only in the more spectacular current weapons systems but also in the day-to-day conduct of the nonglobal war in Indochina: the indiscriminate destructiveness of antipersonnel weapons, napalm, and aerial bombardment; cruelty to prisoners; massive relocation of civilians; destruction of crops; and so forth. An absolutist position opposes to this the view that certain acts cannot be justified no matter what the consequences. Among those acts is murder—the deliberate killing of the harmless: civilians, prisoners of war, and medical personnel.

In the present war such measures are sometimes said to be regrettable, but they are generally defended by reference to military necessity and the importance of the long-term consequences of success or failure in the war. I shall pass over the inadequacy of this consequentialist defense in its own terms. (That is the dominant form of moral criticism of the war, for it is part of what people mean when they ask, "Is it worth it?") I am concerned rather to account for the inappropriateness of offering any defense of that kind for such actions.

Many people feel, without being able to say much more about it, that something has gone seriously wrong when certain measures are admitted into consideration in the first place. The fundamental mistake is made there, rather than at the point where the overall benefit of some monstrous measure is judged to outweigh its disadvantages, and it is adopted. An account of absolutism might help us to understand this. If it is not allowable to *do* certain things, such as killing unarmed prisoners or civilians, then no argument about what will happen if one doesn't do them can show that doing them would be all right.

Absolutism does not, of course, require one to ignore the consequences of one's acts. It operates as a limitation on utilitarian reasoning, not as a substitute for it. An absolutist can be expected to try to maximize good and minimize evil, so long as this does not require him to transgress an absolute prohibition like that against murder. But when such a conflict occurs, the prohibition takes complete precedence over any consideration of consequences. Some of the results of this view are clear enough. It requires us to forgo certain potentially useful military measures, such as the slaughter of hostages and prisoners or indiscriminate attempts to reduce the enemy civilian population by starvation, epidemic infectious diseases like anthrax and bubonic plague, or mass incineration. It means that we cannot deliberate on whether such measures are justified by the fact that they will avert still greater evils, for as intentional measures they cannot be justified in terms of any consequences whatever.

Someone unfamiliar with the events of this century might imagine that utilitarian arguments, or arguments of national interest, would suffice to deter measures of this sort. But it has become evident tha such considerations are insufficient to prevent the adoption and employment of enormous antipopulation weapons once their use is considered a serious moral possibility. The same is true of the piecemeal wiping out of rural civilian populations in airborne antiguerrilla warfare. Once the door is opened to calculations of utility and national interest, the usual speculations about the future of freedom, peace, and economic prosperity can be brought to bear to ease the consciences of those responsible for a certain number of charred babies.

For this reason alone it is important to decide what is wrong with the frame of mind which allows such arguments to begin. But it is also important to understand absolutism in the cases where it genuinely conflicts with utility. Despite its appeal, it is a paradoxical position, for it can require that one refrain from choosing the lesser of two evils when that is the only choice one has. And it is additionally paradoxical because, unlike pacifism, it permits one to do horrible things to people in some circumstances but not in others.

IV

Before going on to say what, if anything, lies behind the position, there remain a few relatively technical matters which are best discussed at this point.

First, it is important to specify as clearly as possible the kind of thing to which absolutist prohibitions can apply. We must take seriously the proviso that they concern what we deliberately do to people. There could not, for example, without incoherence, be an absolute prohibition against *bringing about* the death of an innocent person. For one may find oneself in a situation in which, no matter what one does, some innocent people will die as a result. I do not mean just that there are cases in which someone will die no matter

what one does, because one is not in a position to affect the outcome one way or the other. That, it is to be hoped, is one's relation to the deaths of most innocent people. I have in mind, rather, a case in which someone is bound to die, but who it is will depend on what one does. Sometimes these situations have natural causes, as when too few resources (medicine, lifeboats) are available to rescue everyone threatened with a certain catastrophe. Sometimes the situations are manmade, as when the only way to control a campaign of terrorism is to employ terrorist tactics against the community from which it has arisen. Whatever one does in cases such as these, some innocent people will die as a result. If the absolutist prohibition forbade doing what would result in the deaths of innocent people, it would have the consequence that in such cases nothing one could do would be morally permissible.

This problem is avoided, however, because what absolutism forbids is *doing* certain things to people, rather than bringing about certain *results*. Not everything that happens to others as a result of what one does is something that one has *done* to them. . . .

The second technical point to take up concerns a possible misinterpretation of this feature of the position. The absolutist focus on actions rather than outcomes does not merely introduce a new, outstanding item into the catalogue of evils. That is, it does not say that the worst thing in the world is the deliberate murder of an innocent person. For if that were all, then one could presumably justify one such murder on the ground that it would prevent several others, or ten thousand on the ground that they would prevent a hundred thousand more. That is a familiar argument. But if this is allowable, then there is no absolute prohibition against murder after all.

Absolutism requires that we *avoid* murder at all costs, not that we *prevent* it at all costs.[4]

• • •

V

It is easier to dispose of false explanations of absolutism than to produce a true one. A positive account of the matter must begin with the observation that war, conflict, and aggression are relations between persons. The view that it can be wrong to consider merely the overall effect of one's actions on the general welfare comes into prominence when those actions involve relations with others. A man's acts usually affect more people than he deals with directly, and those effects must naturally be considered in his decisions. But if there are special principles governing the manner in which he should *treat* people, that will require special attention to the particular persons toward whom the act is directed, rather than just to its total effect.

Absolutist restrictions in warfare appear to be of two types: restrictions on the class of persons at whom aggression or violence may be directed and restrictions on the manner of attack, given that the object falls within that class. These can be combined, however, under the principle that hostile treatment of any person must be justified in terms of something *about that person* which makes the treatment appropriate. Hostility is a personal relation, and it must be suited to its target. One consequence of this condition will be that certain persons may not be subjected to hostile treatment in war at all, since nothing about them justifies such treatment. Others will be proper objects of hostility only in certain circumstances, or when they are engaged in certain pursuits. And

the appropriate manner and extent of hostile treatment will depend on what is justified by the particular case.

A coherent view of this type will hold that extremely hostile behavior toward another is compatible with treating him as a person—even perhaps as an end in himself. This is possible only if one has not automatically stopped treating him as a person as soon as one starts to fight with him. If hostile, aggressive, or combative treatment of others always violated the condition that they be treated as human beings, it would be difficult to make further distinctions on that score *within* the class of hostile actions. That point of view, on the level of international relations, leads to the position that if complete pacifism is not accepted, no holds need be barred at all, and we may slaughter and massacre to our hearts' content, if it seems advisable. Such a position is often expressed in discussions of war crimes.

But the fact is that ordinary people do not believe this about conflicts, physical or otherwise, between individuals, and there is no more reason why it should be true of conflicts between nations. There seems to be a perfectly natural conception of the distinction between fighting clean and fighting dirty. To fight dirty is to direct one's hostility or aggression not at its proper object, but at a peripheral target which may be more vulnerable, and through which the proper object can be attacked indirectly. This applies in a fist fight, an election campaign, a duel, or a philosophical argument. If the concept is general enough to apply to all these matters, it should apply to war—both to the conduct of individual soldiers and to the conduct of nations.

Suppose that you are a candidate for public office, convinced that the election of your opponent would be a disaster, that he is an unscrupulous demagogue who will serve a narrow range of interests and seriously infringe the rights of those who disagree with him; and suppose you are convinced that you cannot defeat him by conventional means. Now imagine that various unconventional means present themselves as possibilities: you possess information about his sex life which would scandalize the electorate if made public; or you learn that his wife is an alcoholic or that in his youth he was associated for a brief period with a proscribed political party, and you believe that this information could be used to blackmail him into withdrawing his candidacy; or you can have a team of your supporters flatten the tires of a crucial subset of his supporters on election day; or you are in a position to stuff the ballot boxes; or, more simply, you can have him assassinated. What is wrong with these methods, given that they will achieve an overwhelmingly desirable result?

There are, of course, many things wrong with them: some are against the law; some infringe the procedures of an electoral process to which you are presumably committed by taking part in it; very importantly, some may backfire, and it is in the interest of all political candidates to adhere to an unspoken agreement not to allow certain personal matters to intrude into a campaign. But that is not all. We have in addition the feeling that these measures, these methods of attack are *irrelevant* to the issue between you and your opponent, that in taking them up you would not be directing yourself to that which makes him an object of your opposition. You would be directing your attack not at the true target of your hostility, but at peripheral targets that happen to be vulnerable.

The same is true of a fight or argument outside the framework of any system

of regulations or law. In an altercation with a taxi driver over an excessive fare, it is inappropriate to taunt him about his accent, flatten one of his tires, or smear chewing gum on his windshield; and it remains inappropriate even if he casts aspersions on your race, politics, or religion, or dumps the contents of your suitcase into the street.[5]

The importance of such restrictions may vary with the seriousness of the case; and what is unjustifiable in one case may be justified in a more extreme one. But they all derive from a single principle: that hostility or aggression should be directed at its true object. This means both that it should be directed at the person or persons who provoke it and that it should aim more specifically at what is provocative about them. The second condition will determine what form the hostility may appropriately take.

It is evident that some idea of the relation in which one should stand to other people underlies this principle, but the idea is difficult to state. I believe it is roughly this: whatever one does to another person intentionally must be aimed at him as a subject, with the intention that he receive it as a subject. It should manifest an attitude to *him* rather than just to the situation, and he should be able to recognize it and identify himself as its object. The procedures by which such an attitude is manifested need not be addressed to the person directly. Surgery, for example, is not a form of personal confrontation but part of a medical treatment that can be offered to a patient face to face and received by him as a response to his needs and the natural outcome of an attitude toward *him.*

Hostile treatment, unlike surgery, is already addressed *to* a person, and does not take its interpersonal meaning from a wider context. But hostile acts can serve as the expression or implementation of only a limited range of attitudes to the person who is attacked. Those attitudes in turn have as objects certain real or presumed characteristics or activities of the person which are thought to justify them. When this background is absent, hostile or aggressive behavior can no longer be intended for the reception of the victim as a subject. Instead it takes on the character of a purely bureaucratic operation. This occurs when one attacks someone who is not the true object of one's hostility—the true object may be someone else, who can be attacked through the victim; or one may not be manifesting a hostile attitude toward anyone, but merely using the easiest available path to some desired goal. One finds oneself not facing or addressing the victim at all, but operating on him—without the larger context of personal interaction that surrounds a surgical operation.

If absolutism is to defend its claim to priority over considerations of utility, it must hold that the maintenance of a direct interpersonal response to the people one deals with is a requirement which no advantages can justify one in abandoning. The requirement is absolute only if it rules out any calculation of what would justify its violation. I have said earlier that there may be circumstances so extreme that they render an absolutist position untenable. One may find then that one has no choice but to do something terrible. Nevertheless, even in such cases absolutism retains its force in that one cannot claim *justification* for the violation. It does not become *all right*.

As a tentative effort to explain this, let me try to connect absolutist limitations with the possibility of justifying *to the victim* what is being done to him. If one abandons a person in the course of rescuing several others from a fire or a sinking ship, one *could* say to him, "You understand, I have to leave you to save the others." Similarly, if one subjects an unwilling child to a painful surgical procedure, one can say to him, "If you could understand, you would realize that I am doing this to help you." One could *even* say, as one bayonets an enemy soldier, "It's either you or me." But one cannot really say while torturing a prisoner, "You understand, I have to pull out your fingernails because it is absolutely essential that we have the names of your confederates"; nor can one say to the victims of Hiroshima, "You understand, we have to incinerate you to provide the Japanese government with an incentive to surrender."

This does not take us very far, of course, since a utilitarian would presumably be willing to offer justifications of the latter sort to his victims, in cases where he thought they were sufficient. They are really justifications to the world at large, which the victim, as a reasonable man, would be expected to appreciate. However, there seems to me something wrong with this view, for it ignores the possibility that to treat someone else horribly puts you in a special relation to him, which may have to be defended in terms of other features of your relation to him. The suggestion needs much more development; but it may help us to understand how there may be requirements which are absolute in the sense that there can be no justification for violating them. If the justification for what one did to another person had to be such that it could be offered to him specifically, rather than just to the world at large, that would be a significant source of restraint.

If the account is to be deepened, I would hope for some results along the following lines. Absolutism is associated with a view of oneself as a small being interacting with others in a large world. The justifications it requires are primarily interpersonal. Utilitarianism is associated with a view of oneself as a benevolent bureaucrat distributing such benefits as one can control to countless other beings, with whom one may have various relations or none. The justifications it requires are primarily administrative. The argument between the two moral attitudes may depend on the relative priority of these two conceptions.[6]

VI

Some of the restrictions on methods of warfare which have been adhered to from time to time are to be explained by the mutual interests of the involved parties: restrictions on weaponry, treatment of prisoners, etc. But that is not all there is to it. The conditions of directness and relevance which I have argued apply to relations of conflict and aggression apply to war as well. I have said that there are two types of absolutist restrictions on the conduct of war: those that limit the legitimate targets of hostility and those that limit its character, even when the target is acceptable. I shall say something about each of these. As will become clear, the principle I have sketched does not yield an unambiguous answer in every case.

First let us see how it implies that attacks on some people are allowed, but not attacks on others. It may seem paradoxical to assert that to fire a machine gun at someone who is throwing hand grenades at your emplacement is to treat him as a human being. Yet the relation with him is direct and straightforward.[7] The attack is aimed specifically against the threat presented by a dangerous adversary, and not against a peripheral target through which

he happens to be vulnerable but which has nothing to do with that threat. For example, you might stop him by machine-gunning his wife and children, who are standing nearby, thus distracting him from his aim of blowing you up and enabling you to capture him. But if his wife and children are not threatening your life, that would be to treat them as means with a vengeance.

This, however, is just Hiroshima on a smaller scale. One objection to weapons of mass annihilation—nuclear, thermonuclear, biological, or chemical—is that their indiscriminateness disqualifies them as direct instruments for the expression of hostile relations. In attacking the civilian population, one treats neither the military enemy nor the civilians with that minimal respect which is owed to them as human beings. This is clearly true of the direct attack on people who present no threat at all. But it is also true of the character of the attack on those who *are* threatening you, viz., the government and military forces of the enemy. Your aggression is directed against an area of vulnerability quite distinct from any threat presented by them which you may be justified in meeting. You are taking aim at them through the mundane life and survival of their countrymen, instead of aiming at the destruction of their military capacity. And of course it does not require hydrogen bombs to commit such crimes.

This way of looking at the matter also helps us to understand the importance of the distinction between combatants and noncombatants, and the irrelevance of much of the criticism offered against its intelligibility and moral significance. According to an absolutist position, deliberate killing of the innocent is murder, and in warfare the role of the innocent is filled by noncombatants. This has been thought to raise two sorts of problems: first, the widely imagined difficulty of making a division, in modern warfare, between combatants and noncombatants; second, problems deriving from the connotation of the word "innocence."

Let me take up the latter question first.[8] In the absolutist position, the operative notion of innocence is not moral innocence, and it is not opposed to moral guilt. If it were, then we would be justified in killing a wicked but noncombatant hairdresser in an enemy city who supported the evil policies of his government, and unjustified in killing a morally pure conscript who was driving a tank toward us with the profoundest regrets and nothing but love in his heart. But moral innocence has very little to do with it, for in the definition of murder "innocent" means "currently harmless," and it is opposed not to "guilty" but to "doing harm." It should be noted that such an analysis has the consequence that in war we may often be justified in killing people who do not deserve to die, and unjustified in killing people who do deserve to die, if anyone does.

So we must distinguish combatants from noncombatants on the basis of their immediate threat or harmfulness. I do not claim that the line is a sharp one, but it is not so difficult as is often supposed to place individuals on one side of it or the other. Children are not combatants even though they may join the armed forces if they are allowed to grow up. Women are not combatants just because they bear children or offer comfort to the soldiers. More problematic are the supporting personnel, whether in or out of uniform, from drivers of munitions trucks and army cooks to civilian munitions workers and farmers. I believe they can be plausibly classified by applying the condition that the prosecution of conflict must direct itself to the cause of danger, and not to what is peripheral. The threat presented by an army and its members does not consist merely in the fact that they are men, but in the fact that they are armed and are using their arms in the pursuit of certain objectives. Contributions to their arms and logistics are contributions to this threat; contributions to their mere existence as men are not. It is therefore wrong to direct an attack against those who merely serve the combatants' needs as human beings, such as farmers and food suppliers, even though survival as a human being is a necessary condition of efficient functioning as a soldier.

This brings us to the second group of restrictions: those that limit what may be done even to combatants. These limits are harder to explain clearly. Some of them may be arbitrary or conventional, and some may have to be derived from other sources; but I believe that the condition of directness and relevance in hostile relations accounts for them to a considerable extent.

Consider first a case which involves both a protected class of noncombatants and a restriction on the measures that may be used against combatants. One provision of the rules of war which is universally recognized, though it seems to be turning into a dead letter in Vietnam, is the special status of medical personnel and the wounded in warfare. It might be more efficient to shoot medical officers on sight and to let the enemy wounded die rather than be patched up to fight another day. But someone with medical insignia is supposed to be left alone and permitted to tend and retrieve the wounded. I believe this is because medical attention is a species of attention to completely general human needs, not specifically the needs of a combat soldier, and our conflict with the soldier is not with his existence as a human being.

By extending the application of this idea, one can justify prohibitions against certain particularly cruel weapons: starvation, poisoning, infectious diseases (supposing they could be inflicted on combatants only), weapons designed to maim or disfigure or torture the opponent rather than merely to stop him. It is not, I think, mere casuistry to claim that such weapons attack the men, not the soldiers. The effect of dum-dum bullets, for example, is much more extended than necessary to cope with the combat situation in which they are used. They abandon any attempt to discriminate in their effects between the combatant and the human being. For this reason the use of flamethrowers and napalm is an atrocity in all circumstances that I can imagine, whoever the target may be. Burns are both extremely painful and extremely disfiguring—far more than any other category of wound. That this well-known fact plays no (inhibiting) part in the determination of U.S. weapons policy suggests that moral sensitivity among public officials has not increased markedly since the Spanish Inquisition.[9]

Finally, the same condition of appropriateness to the true object of hostility should limit the scope of attacks on an enemy country: its economy, agriculture, transportation system, and so forth. Even if the parties to a military conflict are considered to be not armies or governments but entire nations (which is usually a grave error), that does not justify one nation in warring against every aspect or element of another nation. That is not justified in a conflict between individuals,

and nations are even more complex than individuals, so the same reasons apply. Like a human being, a nation is engaged in countless other pursuits while waging war, and it is not in those respects that it is an enemy.

The burden of the argument has been that absolutism about murder has a foundation in principles governing all one's relations to other persons, whether aggressive or amiable, and that these principles, and that absolutism, apply to warfare as well, with the result that certain measures are impermissible no matter what the consequences.[10] I do not mean to romanticize war. It is sufficiently utopian to suggest that when nations conflict they might rise to the level of limited barbarity that typically characterizes violent conflict between individuals, rather than wallowing in the moral pit where they appear to have settled, surrounded by enormous arsenals.

VII

Having described the elements of the absolutist position, we must now return to the conflict between it and utilitarianism. Even if certain types of dirty tactics become acceptable when the stakes are high enough, the most serious of the prohibited acts, like murder and torture, are not just supposed to require unusually strong justification. They are supposed *never* to be done, because no quantity of resulting benefit is thought capable of *justifying* such treatment of a person.

The fact remains that when an absolutist knows or believes that the utilitarian cost of refusing to adopt a prohibited course will be very high, he may hold to his refusal to adopt it, but he will find it difficult to feel that a moral dilemma has been satisfactorily resolved. The same may be true of someone who rejects an absolutist requirement and adopts instead the course yielding the most acceptable consequences. In either case, it is possible to feel that one has acted for reasons insufficient to justify violation of the opposing principle. In situations of deadly conflict, particularly where a weaker party is threatened with annihilation or enslavement by a stronger one, the argument for resorting to atrocities can be powerful, and the dilemma acute.

There may exist principles, not yet codified, which would enable us to resolve such dilemmas. But then again there may not. We must face the pessimistic alternative that these two forms of moral intuition are not capable of being brought together into a single, coherent moral system, and that the world can present us with situations in which there is no honorable or moral course for a man to take, no course free of guilt and responsibility for evil.

The idea of a moral blind alley is a perfectly intelligible one. It is possible to get into such a situation by one's own fault, and people do it all the time. If, for example, one makes two incompatible promises or commitments—becomes engaged to two people, for example—then there is no course one can take which is not wrong, for one must break one's promise to at least one of them. Making a clean breast of the whole thing will not be enough to remove one's reprehensibility. The existence of such cases is not morally disturbing, however, because we feel that the situation was not unavoidable: one had to do something wrong in the first place to get into it. But what if the world itself, or someone else's actions, could face a previously innocent person with a choice between morally abominable courses

of action, and leave him no way to escape with his honor? Our intuitions rebel at the idea, for we feel that the constructibility of such a case must show a contradiction in our moral views. But it is not in itself a contradiction to say that someone can do X or not do X, and that for him to take either course would be wrong. It merely contradicts the supposition that *ought* implies *can*—since presumably one ought to refrain from what is wrong, and in such a case it is impossible to do so.[11] Given the limitations on human action, it is naïve to suppose that there is a solution to every moral problem with which the world can face us. We have always known that the world is a bad place. It appears that it may be an evil place as well.

Notes

1. This paper grew out of discussions at the Society for Ethical and Legal Philosophy, and I am indebted to my fellow members for their help.
2. Straightforward considerations of national interest often tend in the same direction: the inadvisability of using nuclear weapons seems to be overdetermined in this way.
3. These reasons, moreover, have special importance in that they are available even to one who denies the appropriateness of utilitarian considerations in international matters. He may acknowledge limitations on what may be done to the soldiers and civilians of other countries in pursuit of his nation's military objectives, while denying that one country should in general consider the interests of nationals of other countries in determining its policies.
4. Someone might of course acknowledge the *moral relevance* of the distinction between deliberate and nondeliberate killing, without being an absolutist. That is, he might believe simply that it was *worse* to bring about a death deliberately than as a secondary effect. But that would be merely a special assignment of value, and not an absolute prohibition.
5. Why, on the other hand, does it seem appropriate, rather than irrelevant, to punch someone in the mouth if he insults you? The answer is that

in our culture it is an insult to punch someone in the mouth, and not just an injury. This reveals, by the way, a perfectly unobjectionable sense in which convention may play a part in determining exactly what falls under an absolutist restriction and what does not. I am indebted to Robert Fogelin for this point.

6. Finally, I should mention a different possibility, suggested by Robert Nozick: that there is a strong general presumption against benefiting from the calamity of another, whether or not it has been deliberately inflicted for that or any other reason. This broader principle may well lend its force to the absolutist position.

7. It has been remarked that according to my view, shooting at someone establishes an I-thou relationship.

8. What I say on this subject derives from Anscombe.

9. Beyond this I feel uncertain. Ordinary bullets, after all, can cause death, and nothing is more permanent than that. I am not at all sure why we are justified in trying to kill those who are trying to kill us (rather than merely in trying to stop them with force which may also result in their deaths). It is often argued that incapacitating gases are a relatively humane weapon (when not used, as in Vietnam, merely to make people easier to shoot). Perhaps the legitimacy of restrictions against them must depend on the dangers of escalation, and the great utility of maintaining *any* conventional category of restriction so long as nations are willing to adhere to it.

Let me make clear that I do not regard my argument as a defense of the moral immutability of the Hague and Geneva Conventions. Rather, I believe that they rest partly on a moral foundation, and that modifications of them should also be assessed on moral grounds.

But even this connection with the actual laws of war is not essential to my claims about what is permissible and what is not. Since completing this paper I have read an essay by Richard Wasserstrom entitled "The Laws of War" (forthcoming in *The Monist*), which argues that the existing laws and conventions do not even attempt to embody a decent moral position: that their provisions have been determined by other interests, that they are in fact immoral in substance, and that it is a grave mistake to refer to them as standards in forming moral judgments about warfare. This possibility deserves serious consideration, and I am not sure what to say about it, but it does not affect my view of the moral issues.

10. It is possible to draw a more radical conclusion, which I shall not pursue here. Perhaps the technology and organization of modern war are such as to make it impossible to wage as an acceptable form of interpersonal or even international hostility. Perhaps it is too impersonal and large-scale for that. If so, then absolutism would in practice imply pacifism, given the present state of things. On the other hand, I am skeptical about the unstated assumption that a technology dictates its own use.

11. This was first pointed out to me by Christopher Boorse.

Utilitarianism and the Rules of War

(1972)

Richard B. Brandt

Richard Brandt was Roy Wood Sellars Distinguished College Professor of Philosophy at the University of Michigan. His books include Hopi Ethics *(1954),* Ethical Theory *(1959), and* The Theory of the Good and the Right *(1979). He died in 1997 at age eighty-six.*

The topic of the present symposium is roughly the moral proscriptions and prescriptions that should govern the treatment by a belligerent, and in particular by its armed forces, of the nationals of an enemy, both combatants and noncombatants. In addressing myself to it, the central question I shall try to answer is: What, from a moral point of view, ought to be the rules of war? But this question, taken as an indication of what I shall be discussing, is both too broad and too narrow. Too broad because the rules of war include many topics like the rights and duties of neutral countries and the proprieties pertaining to an armistice. And too narrow because a full view of the topic requires me to consider, as I shall, such questions as: Is it ever morally right for a person to infringe "ideal" rules of war?

I shall aim to illuminate our topic by discussing it from the point of view of a rule-utilitarianism of the "contractual" variety (to use a term employed by John Rawls in his book *A Theory of Justice*).[1] What this point of view is has of course to be explained, as do the special problems raised by the fact that the rules are to apply to nations at war. I believe it will become clear that the rule-utilitarian viewpoint is a very helpful one for thinking of rules of warfare, and I believe reflection on its implications will confirm us both in conclusions about certain normative rules and in a conviction that a contractual utilitarian view of such matters is essentially sound. Needless to say, I shall be led to express some disagreement with Professor Nagel.[2] . . .

In view of Nagel's tentativeness, I think it fair to disassociate him from the positive view I wish to criticize, although I am *calling* it Nagel's "absolutism." This positive view is, however, the only definite proposal he puts forward, and if I am to consider critically any positive antiutilitarian view in connection with Nagel's essay, it has to be this one. At any rate, this view is one that somebody *might* hold, and is well worth discussing.

The first point I wish to make is that a rule-utilitarian may quite well agree with Nagel that certain kinds of action are morally out of bounds absolutely and no matter what the circumstances. Take, for instance, some of the rules of warfare recognized by the United States Army:

> It is especially forbidden . . . to declare that no quarter will be given. . . . It is especially forbidden . . . to kill or wound an enemy who, having laid down his arms, or having no longer means of defense, has surrendered at discretion. . . .
>
> It is especially forbidden . . . to employ arms, projectiles, or material calculated to cause unnecessary suffering. . . .
>
> The pillage of a town or place, even when taken by assault, is prohibited. . . .
>
> A commander may not put his prisoners to death because their presence retards his movements or diminishes his power of resistance by necessitating a large guard, or by reason of their consuming supplies, or because it appears certain that they will regain their liberty through the impending success of their forces. It is likewise unlawful for a commander to kill his prisoners on grounds of self-preservation, even in the case of airborne or commando operations, although the circumstances of the operation may make necessary rigorous supervision of and restraint upon the movement of prisoners of war.[3]

A rule-utilitarian is certainly in a position to say that utilitarian considerations cannot morally justify a departure from these rules; in that sense they are absolute. But he will of course also say that the moral justification of these rules lies in the fact that their acceptance and enforcement will make an important contribution to long-range utility. The rule-utilitarian, then, may take a two-level view: that in justifying the rules, utilitarian considerations are in order and nothing else is; whereas in making decisions about what to do in concrete circumstances, the rules are absolutely binding. In the rule-utilitarian view, immediate expediency is not a moral justification for infringing the rules.[4]

It is not clear that Nagel recognizes this sort of absolutism about "ideal" rules of war as a possible utilitarian view, but he seems to disagree with it when he claims that some moral prohibitions are entirely independent of utilitarian considerations.

What absolute rule, then, does Nagel propose? . . .

The absolutist principle that Nagel espouses as the basic restriction on legitimate targets and weapons is this: "hostility or aggression should be directed at its true object. This means both that it should be directed at the person or persons who provoke it and that it should aim more specifically at which is provocative about them. The second condition will determine what form the hostility may appropriately take." Now, while I find this principle reasonably clear in its application to simple two-person cases discussed by him, I find it difficult to apply in the identification of morally acceptable military operations. With some trepidation I suggest that Nagel intends it to be construed to assert something like the following for the case of military operations: "Persons may be attacked 'deliberately' only if their presence or their position prevents overpowering the military forces of the enemy in some way; and they may be attacked only in a manner that is reasonably related to the objective of disarming or disabling them." If this is what he has in mind it is still rather vague, since it does not make clear whether attacks on

munitions factories are legitimate, or whether attacks on persons involved in supporting services, say, the provisioning of the army, are acceptable. . . .

MORALLY JUSTIFIABLE RULES AS RULES IMPARTIALLY PREFERABLE

I shall now proceed to a positive account of the rules of war and of their justification. We shall have to consider several distinct questions, but the central question will be: Which of the possible rules of war are morally justifiable? . . .

I have said that I shall offer a utilitarian answer to the question which rules of war (in the above sense) are morally justifiable. But I have also said that I shall be offering what I (following Rawls) call a *contractual* utilitarian answer. What I mean by that (the term "contractual" may be a bit misleading) is this. I accept the utilitarian answer to the question which rules of war are morally justifiable because utilitarian rules of war are the ones *rational, impartial persons would choose* (the ones they would be willing to put themselves under a contract to obey). The more basic question is, then: Which rules of war would people universally prefer to have accorded authoritative status among nations if the people deciding were rational, believed they might be involved in a war at some time, and were impartial in the sense that they were choosing behind a veil of ignorance? (It is understood that their ignorance is to be such as to prevent them from making a choice that would give them or their nation a special advantage; it would, for instance, prevent them from knowing what weaponry their country would possess were it to be at war, and from knowing whether, were war to occur, they would be on the front lines, in a factory, or in the general staff office.) In other words, the more fundamental question is: What rules would rational, impartial people, who expected their country at some time to be at war, want to have as the authoritative rules of war—particularly with respect to the permitted targets and method of attack? I suggest that the rules of war which rational, impartial persons would choose are the rules that would maximize long-range expectable utility for nations at war. In saying this I am offering a contractual utilitarian answer to the question what rules of war are morally justifiable. I am saying, then: (1) that rational, impartial persons would choose certain rules of war; (2) that I take as a basic premise ("analytic" in some sense, if you like) that a rule of war is morally justified if and only if it would be chosen by rational, impartial persons; and (3) that the rules rational, impartial persons would choose are ones which will maximize expectable long-range utility for nations at war.[5]

Nagel objects to utilitarianism and hence presumably would object to (3), but he might be agreeable to both (1) and (2). At least he seems close to these principles, since he seems to hold that an action is justified if one can justify to its victim what is being done to him. For instance, he implies that if you were to say to a prisoner, "You understand, I have to pull out your fingernails because it is absolutely essential that we have the name of your confederates" and the prisoner agreed to this as following from principles he accepts, then the torture would be justified. Nagel rather assumes that the prisoner would not agree, in an appropriate sense. In this connection we must be clearly aware of an important distinction. A judge who sentences a criminal might also be

unable to persuade the criminal to want the sentence to be carried out; and if persuading him to want this were necessary for a moral justification of the criminal law, then the system of criminal justice would also be morally objectionable. We must distinguish between persuading a person to whom something horrible is about to be done to want this thing to happen or to consent to its happening at that very time and something quite different— getting him to accept, when he is rational and choosing in ignorance of his own future prospects, some general principles from which it would follow that this horrible thing should or might be done to a person in his present circumstances. I think Nagel must mean, or ought to mean, that a set of rules of war must be such as to command the assent of rational people choosing behind a veil of ignorance, *not* that a person must be got to assent at the time to his fingernails being pulled out in order to get information, if that act is to be justified. It may be, however, that Nagel does not agree with this distinction, since he hints at the end of his discussion that something more may be required for moral justification than I have suggested, without indicating what the addition might be.

We should notice that the question which rules of war would be preferred by rational persons choosing behind a veil of ignorance is roughly the question that bodies like the Hague Conventions tried to answer. . . .

THE RATIONAL, IMPARTIAL CHOICE: UTILITARIAN RULES

I wish now to explain in a few words why I think rational, impartial persons would choose rules of war that would maximize expectable utility. Then—and this will occupy almost all of the present section—I shall classify the rules of war into several types, and try to show that representative rules of each type would be utility-maximizing and therefore chosen. I shall hope (although I shall not say anything explicitly about this) that the ideal rules of war, identified in this way, will coincide with the reflective intuitions of the reader. If so, I assume that this fact will commend to him the whole of what I am arguing.

I have suggested that rational persons, choosing behind a veil of ignorance but believing that their country may well be involved in a war at some time, would prefer rules of war that would maximize expectable utility, *in the circumstance that two nations are at war.* Why would they prefer such rules? About this I shall say only that if they are self-interested they will choose rules which will maximize expectable utility generally, for then their chance of coming out best will be greatest (and they do not know how especially to favor themselves); and that if they are altruistic they will again choose that set of rules, for they will want to choose rules which will maximize expectable utility generally. The rules of war, then, subject to the restriction that the rules of war may not prevent a belligerent from using all the power necessary to overcome the enemy, will be ones whose authorization will serve to maximize welfare.

It is worth noting that a preamble to the U.S. Army Manual offers an at least partially utilitarian theory of the rules of war (I say "at least partially" because of doubts about the interpretation of clause *b*). This preamble states that the law of land warfare "is inspired by the desire to diminish the evils of war by: *a*. Protecting both combatants and noncombatants from unnecessary suffering; *b*. Safeguarding

certain fundamental human rights of persons who fall into the hands of the enemy, particularly prisoners of war, the wounded and sick, and civilians; and *c*. Facilitating the restoration of peace" (p. 3).

Which rules, then, would maximize expectable utility for nations at war? (I shall later discuss briefly whether the ideal rules would altogether forbid war as an instrument of national policy.)

First, however, we must understand why the above-mentioned restriction, guaranteeing that the rules of war will not prevent a belligerent from using all the force necessary to overcome the enemy, must be placed on the utility-maximizing rules of war. The reason for this restriction is to be found in the nature of a serious war. There are, of course, many different kinds of war. Wars differ in magnitude, in the technologies they employ, in the degree to which they mobilize resources, in the type of issue the belligerents believe to be at stake, and in many other ways as well. The difference between the Trojan War and World War II is obviously enormous. The former was a simple, small-scale affair, and the issues at stake might well have been settled by a duel between Paris and Menelaus, or Hector and Achilles, and the belligerents might not have been seriously dissatisfied with the outcome. In the case of World War II, the British thought that Hitler's Germany and its policies threatened the very basis of civilized society. The destruction of Hitler's power seemed so important to the British that they were willing to stake their existence as a nation on bringing it about. Wars have been fought for many lesser reasons: to spread a political or religious creed, to acquire territory or wealth, to obtain an outlet to the sea, or to become established as a world power. Wars may be fought with mercenaries, or primarily by the contribution of equipment and munitions; such wars make relatively little difference to the domestic life of a belligerent.

It is possible that the rules which would maximize expectable utility might vary from one type of war to another. I shall ignore this possibility for the most part, and merely note that practical difficulties are involved in equipping military handbooks with different sets of rules and establishing judicial bodies to identify the proper classification of a given war. I shall take the position of Britain in World War II as typical of that of a belligerent in a serious war.

The position of a nation in a serious war is such, then, that it considers overpowering the enemy to be absolutely vital to its interests (and possibly to those of civilized society generally)—so vital, indeed, that it is willing to risk its very existence to that end. It is doubtful that both sides can be well justified in such an appraisal of the state of affairs. But we may assume that in fact they do make this appraisal. In this situation, we must simply take as a fact that neither side will consent to or follow rules of war which seriously impair the possibility of bringing the war to a victorious conclusion. This fact accounts for the restriction within which I suggested a choice of the rules of war must take place. We may notice that the recognized rules of war do observe this limitation: they are framed in such a way as not to place any serious obstacle in the way of a nation's using any available force, if necessary, to destroy the ability of another to resist. As Oppenheim has observed, one of the assumptions underlying the recognized rules of war is that "a belligerent is justified in applying any amount and any kind of force which is necessary for . . . the overpowering of the opponent."[6] This limitation, however, leaves a good deal of

room for rules of war which will maximize expectable long range utility for all parties.

This restriction, incidentally, itself manifests utilitarian considerations, for a nation is limited to the use of means *necessary* to overcome an opponent. Clearly it is contrary to the general utility that any amount or manner of force be employed when it is *not* necessary for victory.

It will be convenient to divide the rules restricting military operation, especially the targets and weapons of attack, into three types. (I do not claim that these are exhaustive.)

1. *Humanitarian Restrictions of No Cost to Military Operation.* There are some things that troops may be tempted to do which are at best of negligible utility to their nation but which cause serious loss to enemy civilians, although not affecting the enemy's power to win the war. Such behavior will naturally be forbidden by rules designed to maximize expectable utility within the understood restriction. Consider, for example, rules against the murder or ill-treatment of prisoners of war. A rule forbidding wanton murder of prisoners hardly needs discussion. Such murder does not advance the war effort of the captors: indeed, news of its occurrence only stiffens resistance and invites retaliation. Moreover, there is an advantage in returning troops having been encouraged to respect the lives of others. A strict prohibition of wanton murder of prisoners therefore has the clear support of utilitarian considerations. Much the same may be said for a rule forbidding ill-treatment of prisoners. . . .

Again, much the same may be said of the treatment of civilians and of civilian property in occupied territories. There is no military advantage, at least for an affluent nation, in the plunder of private or public property. And the rape of women or the ill-treatment of populations of occupied countries serves no military purpose. On the contrary, such behavior arouses hatred and resentment and constitutes a military liability. So utility is maximized, within our indicated basic limitations, by a strict rule calling for good treatment of the civilian population of an occupied territory. And the same can be said more generally for the condemnation of the wanton destruction of cities, towns, or villages, or devastation not justified by military necessity, set forth in the charter of the Nuremburg tribunal.

Obviously these rules, which the maximization of expectable utility calls for, are rules that command our intuitive assent.

2. *Humanitarian Restrictions Possibly Costly to Military Victory.* Let us turn now to rules pertaining to actions in somewhat more complex situations. There are some actions which fall into neither of the classes so far discussed. They are not actions which must be permitted because they are judged necessary or sufficient for victory, and hence actions on which no party to a major war would accept restrictions. Nor are they actions which morally justified rules of war definitely prohibit, as being actions which cause injury to enemy nations but serve no military purpose. It is this large class of actions neither clearly permitted nor definitely prohibited, for reasons already discussed, that I now wish to consider. I want to ask which rules of war are morally justified, because utility-maximizing, for actions of this kind. In what follows I shall be distinguishing several kinds of actions and suggesting appropriate rules for them. The first type is this: doing something which will result in widespread destruction of civilian life and property and at the same time will add (possibly by that very destruction) to the *probability* of victory but will not definitely decide the war. Some uses of atomic weapons, and area bombing of the kind practiced at Hamburg, illustrate this sort of case.

A proper (not ideally precise) rule for such operations might be: substantial destruction of lives and property of enemy civilians is permissible only when there is good evidence that it will significantly enhance the prospect of victory. Application of the terms "good evidence" and "significantly enhance" requires judgment, but the rule could be a useful guideline all the same. For instance, we now know that the destruction of Hamburg did not significantly enhance the prospect of victory; in fact, it worked in the wrong direction, since it both outraged the population and freed workers formerly in non-war-supporting industries to be moved into industry directly contributing to the German war effort. The generals surely did not have good evidence that this bombing would significantly enhance the prospect of victory.

This rule is one which parties to a war might be expected to accept in advance, since following it could be expected to minimize the human cost of war on both sides, and since it does not involve a significant compromise of the goal of victory. The proposed rule, incidentally, has some similarities to the accepted rule cited above from the U.S. Army Manual, that "loss of life and damage to property must not be out of proportion to the military advantage to be gained."

This rule, which I am suggesting only for wars like World War II, where the stakes are very high, may become clearer if seen in the perspective of a more general rule that would also be suitable for wars in which the stakes are much lower. I pointed out above that what is at stake in a war may be no more than a tiny strip of land or national prestige. (The utility of these, may, however, be considered very great by a nation.) Now, it is clear that a risk of defeat which may properly be taken when the stakes are enormous might quite properly be run when the stakes are small. So if the above-suggested rule is plausible for serious wars, in which the stakes are great, a somewhat different rule will be plausible in the case of wars of lesser importance—one that will require more in the way of "good evidence" and will require that the actions more "significantly enhance" the prospect of victory than is necessary when the stakes are much higher. These thoughts suggest the following general principle, applicable to all types of war: a military action (e.g., a bombing raid) is permissible only if the utility (broadly conceived, so that the maintenance of treaty obligations of international law could count as a utility) of victory to all concerned, multiplied by the increase in its probability if the action is executed, on the evidence (when the evidence is reasonably solid, considering the stakes), is greater than the possible disutility of the action to both sides multiplied by its probability. The rule for serious wars suggested above could then be regarded as a special case, one in which the utility of victory is virtually set at infinity—so that the only question is whether there is reasonably solid evidence that the action will increase the probability of victory. The more general rule obviously involves difficult judgments; there is a question, therefore, as to how it could be applied. It is conceivable that tough-minded civilian review boards would be beneficial, but we can hardly expect very reliable judgment even from them.[7]

These rules are at least very different from a blanket permission for anything the military thinks might conceivably improve the chances of victory, irrespective of any human cost to the enemy. In practice, it must be expected that each party to a war is likely to estimate the stakes of victory quite high, so that the rule which has the best chance of being respected is probably the first one mentioned, and not any modification of it that would be suggested to an impartial observer by the second, more general principle. . . .

It may be objected that the rules suggested are far too imprecise to be of practical utility. To this I would reply that there is no reason why judgment may not be required in staff decisions about major operations. Furthermore, the U.S. Army Manual already contains several rules the application of which requires judgment. For example:

> Absolute good faith with the enemy must be observed as a rule of conduct. . . . In general, a belligerent may resort to those measures for mystifying or misleading the enemy against which the enemy ought to take measures to protect himself.
>
> The measure of permissible devastation is found in the strict necessities of war. Devastation as an end in itself or as a separate measure of war is not sanctioned by the law of war. There must be some reasonably close connection between the destruction of property and the overcoming of the enemy's army. . . .
>
> The punishment imposed for a violation of the law of war must be proportionate to the gravity of the offense. The death penalty may be imposed for grave breaches of the law. . . . Punishments should be deterrent. (pp 22, 23–24, 182).

It has sometimes been argued, for instance by Winston Churchill, that obliteration bombing is justified as retaliation. It has been said that since the Germans destroyed Amsterdam and Coventry, the British had a right to destroy Hamburg. And it is true that the Hague Conventions are sometimes regarded as a contract, the breach of which by one side released the other from its obligations. It is also true that a government which has itself ordered obliteration bombing is hardly in a position to complain if the same tactic is employed by the enemy. But maximizing utility permits obliteration bombing only as a measure of deterrence or deterrent reprisal. This rule, incidentally, is recognized by the army manual as a principle governing all reprisals: "Reprisals are acts of retaliation . . . for the purpose of enforcing future compliance with the recognized rules of civilized warfare. . . . Other means of securing compliance with the law of war should normally be exhausted before the resort is had to reprisals. . . . Even when appeal to the enemy for redress has failed, it may be a matter of policy to consider, before resorting to reprisals, whether the opposing forces are not more likely to be influenced by a steady adherence to the law of war on the part of the adversary" (p. 177). Purposes of retaliation, then, do not permit bombing in contravention of the suggested general principles.

Special notice should be taken that widespread civilian bombing might be defended by arguing that a significant deterioration in civilian morale could bring an end to a war by producing internal revolution. Our principle does not exclude the possibility of such reasoning, in the presence of serious evidence about civilian morale, when the stakes of victory are high. But we know enough about how bombing affects civilian morale to know that such bombing could be justified only rarely, if at all. The U.S. Army seems to go further than this; its rule asserts that any attack on civilians "for the sole purpose of terrorizing the civilian population is also forbidden."[8] It may be, however, that in actual practice this rule is interpreted in such a way that it is identical with the less stringent rule which is as much as utilitarian considerations can justify; if not, I fear we have to say that at this point the army's theory has gone somewhat too far.

3. *Acceptance of Military Losses for Humanitarian Reasons.* Let us now turn to some rules which have to do with what we might call the *economics* of warfare, when the ultimate outcome is not involved, either because the outcome is already clear or because the action is fairly local and its outcome will not have significant repercussions. What damage may one inflict on the enemy in order to cut down one's own losses? For instance, may one destroy a city in order to relieve a besieged platoon, or in order to avoid prolonging a war with consequent casualties? (The use of atom bombs in Japan may be an instance of this type of situation.) It is convenient to deal with two types of cases separately.

First, when may one inflict large losses on the enemy in order to avoid smaller losses for oneself, given that the issue of the war is not in doubt? A complicating fact is that when the issue is no longer in doubt it would seem that the enemy ought to concede, thereby avoiding losses to both sides. Why fight on when victory is impossible? (Perhaps to get better terms of peace.) But suppose the prospective loser is recalcitrant. May the prospective victor then unleash any horrors whatever in order to terminate the war quickly or reduce his losses? It is clear that the superior power should show utmost patience and not make the terms of peace so severe as to encourage further resistance. On the other hand, long-range utility is not served if the rules of war are framed in such a way as to provide an umbrella for the indefinite continuation of a struggle by an

inferior power. So it must be possible to inflict losses heavy enough to produce capitulation but not so heavy as to be out of
proportion to the estimated cost of further
struggle to both sides. This condition is especially important in view of the fact that
in practice there will almost always be
other pressures that can be brought to
bear. The application of such a rule requires difficult judgments, but some such
rule appears called for by long-range utilitarian considerations.

The second question is: Should there
be restrictions on the treatment of an
enemy in the case of local actions which
could hardly affect the outcome of the war,
when these may cause significant losses?
Rules of the army manual forbid killing of
prisoners when their presence retards
one's movements, reduces the number of
men available for combat, uses up the food
supply, and in general is inimical to the integrity of one's troops. Again, the Second
Hague Convention forbids forcing civilians
in occupied territory to give information
about the enemy, and it forbids reprisals
against the general civilian population "on
account of the acts of individuals for which
they cannot be regarded as jointly and sev-
erally responsible."[9] The taking of hostages
is prohibited (U.S. Army Manual, p. 107).

All these rules prescribe that a belligerent be prepared to accept certain military disadvantages for the sake of the lives
and welfare of civilians and prisoners. The
disadvantages in question are not, however, losses that could be so serious as to
affect the outcome of a war. Furthermore,
the military gains and losses are ones
which are likely to be evenly distributed,
so that neither side stands to gain a long-
term advantage if the rules are observed
by both. So, without affecting the outcome
of the war and without giving either side

an unfair advantage, a considerable benefit can come to both belligerents in the
form of the welfare of their imprisoned and
occupied populations. Thus the long-run
advantage of both parties is most probably
served if they accept forms of self-restraint
which can work out to be costly in occa-
sional instances. Such rules will naturally
be accepted by rational, impartial people
in view of their long-range benefits.

RULES OF WAR AND MORALITY

. . . It is obvious that there may well be discrepancies between what a person morally
may do in wartime and what is permitted
by morally justified rules of war, just as
there are discrepancies between what is
morally permitted and what is permitted
by morally justifiable rules of the criminal
law. For one thing, the rules of war, like the
criminal law, must be formulated in such a
way that it is decidable whether a person
has violated them; it must be possible to
produce evidence that determines the
question and removes it from the realm of
speculation. More important, just as there
are subtle interpersonal relations—such
as justice and self-restraint in a family—
which it is undesirable for the criminal
law to attempt to regulate but which may
be matters of moral obligation, so there
may well be moral obligations controlling
relations between members of belligerent
armies which the rules of war cannot
reach. For instance, one might be morally
obligated to go to some trouble or even
take a certain risk in order to give aid to a
wounded enemy, but the rules of war could
hardly prescribe doing so. I am unable to
think of a case in which moral principles
require a person to do what is forbidden by
morally justifiable rules of war; I suppose

this is possible. But it is easy to think of cases in which moral principles forbid a person to injure an enemy, or require him to aid an enemy, when morally justifiable rules of war do not prescribe accordingly and when the military law even forbids the morally required behavior. (Consider, for instance, the fact that, according to the manual, the U.S. Army permits severe punishment for anyone who "without proper authority, knowingly harbors or protects or gives intelligence to, or communicates or corresponds with or holds any intercourse with the enemy, either directly or indirectly." [p. 33])

The possible contrast between morally justifiable rules of war and what is morally permitted will seem quite clear to persons with firm moral intuitions. It may be helpful, however, to draw the contrast by indicating what it would be, at least for one kind of rule-utilitarian theory of moral principles. A rule-utilitarian theory of morality might say that what is morally permissible is any action that would not be forbidden by the kind of conscience which would maximize long-range expectable utility were it built into people as an internal regulator of their relations with other sentient beings, as contrasted with other kinds of conscience or not having a conscience at all. Then justifiable rules of war (with the standing described above) would be one thing; what is morally permissible, in view of ideal rules of conscience, might be another. Rational, impartial persons, understanding that their country may be involved in a war, might want one set of rules as rules of war, whereas rational, impartial persons choosing among types of conscience might want a different and discrepant set of rules as rules of conscience. In the same way there may be a discrepancy between a morally justified system of criminal law and morally justified rules of conscience. And just as, consequently, there may occasionally be a situation in which it is one's moral duty to violate the criminal law, so there may occasionally be a situation in which it is one's moral duty to violate morally unjustifiable rules of war.

It might be asked whether a person who subscribed to sound moral principles would, if given the choice, opt for a system of rules of war; and if so, whether he would opt for a set that would maximize expectable utility for the situation of nations at war. I suggest that he would do so; that such a person would realize that international law, like the criminal law, has its place in human society, that not all decisions can simply be left to the moral intuitions of the agent, and that the rules of war and military justice are bound to be somewhat crude. He would opt for that type of system which will do the most good, given that the nations will sometimes go to war. I am, however, only *suggesting* that he would; in order to show that he would, one would have to identify the sound moral principles which would be relevant to such a decision. . . .

Notes

1. Cambridge, Mass., 1971.
2. Thomas Nagel, "War and Massacre."
3. Department of the Army Field Manual PM 27-10, *The Law of Land Warfare* (Department of the Army, July 1956), pp. 17, 18, 21, 35. The Manual specifically states that the rules of war may not be disregarded on grounds of "military necessity" (p. 4), since considerations of military necessity were fully taken into account in framing the rules. (All page numbers in the text refer to this publication, hereafter called the Army Manual.)

Other valuable discussions of contemporary rules of warfare are to be found in L. Oppenheim, *International Law*, ed. H. Lauterpacht, 7th ed. (New York, 1952) and in Margorie M. Whiteman, *Digest of International Law*, esp. Vol. 10 (U.S. Department of State, 1963).

4. It is conceivable that ideal rules of war would include one rule to the effect that anything is allowable, if necessary to prevent absolute catastrophe. As Oppenheim remarks, it may be that if the basic values of society are threatened nations are possibly released from all the restrictions in order to do what "they deem to be decisive for the ultimate vindication of the law of nations" (*International Law,* p. 351).

5. This summary statement needs much explanation, e.g., regarding the meaning of "rational." It is only a close approximation to the view I would defend, since I think it is better to substitute a more complex notion for that of impartiality or a veil of ignorance.

6. *International Law,* p. 226.

7. If we assume that both sides in a major struggle somehow manage to be persuaded that their cause is just, we shall have to expect that each will assign a net positive utility to its being the victor. For this reason it makes very little difference whether the more general principle uses the concept of the utility of victory by one side for everyone concerned, or the utility for that side only.

One might propose that the general restriction on rules of war, to the effect that in a serious war the use of any force necessary or sufficient for victory must be permitted, might be derived from the above principle if the utility of victory is set virtually at infinity, and the probability of a certain action affecting the outcome is set near one. I believe this is correct, if we assume, as just suggested, that each side in a serious war will set a very high positive utility on *its* being the victor, despite the fact that both sides cannot possibly be correct in such an assessment. The reason for this principle as stated in the text, however, seems to me more realistic and simple. There is no reason, as far as I can see, why *both* lines of reasoning may not be used in support of the claim that the principle (or restriction) in question is a part of a morally justifiable system of rules of war.

8. Whiteman, *Digest of International Law* 10, 135.

9. Article 50.

D. Self-Defense

Currently, self-defense is the only internationally accepted uncontroversial reason to engage in war. There are at least the following three reasons for the wide acceptance of a right of state self-defense. First, at the international level, it is often thought that states interact with other states, and at this level, states have rights similar to the rights held by the citizens within states. This is commonly known as the *domestic analogy*. Second, it is thought that a right of state self-defense is grounded in the personal right of self-defense held by the citizens of a state. This has been termed the *reductive strategy*. According to the *reductive strategy,* a state (and its resources) is an instrument to be used by citizens to exercise their personal right of self-defense. Third, it is thought that a right of state self-defense deters aggression, and as a result, states (or their representatives) agree to have this right because it helps protect citizens, and it helps advance the goal of international peace and security.

In *Just and Unjust Wars,* Michael Walzer accepts the *domestic analogy.* He accepts the view that states, like people, have a right of self-defense. Walzer points out that the analogy is not a perfect one. On the domestic level, law enforcement officers aid citizens in defending themselves and in obtaining restitution for harms committed. Because these same resources do not exist at the international level, a right of state self-defense permits actions that a personal right of self-defense does not. For instance, at the domestic level, a right of self-defense often requires a victim to retreat when possible to avoid harm. At the international level, however, there is no duty to retreat. Also, at the domestic level, generally one cannot kill a robber who is only attempting to steal one's property. At the international level, however, killing the soldiers of an aggressor state who are only attempting to take over a piece of land belonging to a victim state is commonly thought to be justified on grounds of self-defense.

Walzer's article begins by presenting what he terms the *legalist paradigm.* He argues that this paradigm provides a "baseline" that is to be used in analyzing and justifying aggression between states. After presenting the *legalist paradigm,* Walzer offers a revision. Walzer's revision concerns the ability of states to use defensive force prior to actually being attacked. Walzer asks his reader to imagine an "anticipation spectrum." At one end of the spectrum is preventive war. Preventive war is, for Walzer, unjustified because it is based on fear, not on an actual threat of harm. On the other end of the spectrum are mere reflexive actions to imminent physical threats. For Walzer, the use of force in response to imminent threats is obviously justified, but it often fails to provide an adequate defense. Since preventative war is unjustified and states often need to respond to threats before they are imminent, Walzer concludes that states may use force when there is a "sufficient threat." Walzer admits that the phrase "sufficient threat" is vague. However, he provides examples and criteria to help illustrate what he means by a sufficient threat. In support of his position, Walzer claims that "a state under threat is like an individual hunted by an enemy who has announced his intention of killing or injuring him. Surely, such a person may surprise the hunter, if he is able to do so."

In *War and Self-Defense*, David Rodin argues that both the *domestic analogy* and the *reductive strategy* fail to provide a normative foundation for a right of state self-defense (which he terms "national-defense"). Regarding the *domestic analogy*, Rodin argues that if the *domestic analogy* justifies a right of state self-defense, it will be because all states, like all people, have some inherent normative value that is worth defending. For Rodin, all rights are substantially grounded in their end or aim. Although it is often assumed that states have a value or end worth defending, Rodin concludes that they actually do not have a distinct value or end that justifies a right of state self-defense.

One such end offered by Rodin is the fact that states consist of a distinctive community or a "common way of life" that has value and a right to self-determination. Rodin, however, thinks that it is a myth that states consist of a single distinctive community. Rodin claims that "No community is ever fully integrated within a particular state and no territory ever nurtures but a single community." Also, he contends that if a "common way of life" were the end of the right of self-defense, then communities, not states, would be justified in using force. In fact, when they conflict, communities could invoke a right of self-defense to justify using force against states.

The version of the *reductive strategy* that Rodin rejects is the claim that states have a duty to protect their citizens similar to the duty that parents have to protect their children. For Rodin, this strategy is reductive in the sense that the right of state self-defense is ultimately grounded in each citizen's right to defend himself or herself from harm.

Rodin argues that this *reductive strategy* fails to provide a normative foundation for a right of state self-defense for the following two reasons. First, if accepted, this strategy would justify humanitarian intervention. Since the end or goal of this strategy is to protect citizens, Rodin argues that states that fail to protect their citizens could no longer invoke a right of self-defense. In fact, it might be possible for the intervening state to invoke a right of self-defense because it is the intervening state that is attempting to protect the citizens of the failing state. According to Rodin, this result "flies in the face of common sense as well as the law and the moral theory of national-defense." A right of state self-defense is normally thought to further a state's "sovereign rights," not permit breaches of those sovereign rights. Second, Rodin argues that in cases of "bloodless invasion" or acts of aggression that do not threaten the lives of any citizens, a victim state could not invoke a right of self-defense to repel this invasion. For Rodin, it follows from the *reductive strategy* that if there is no threat of harm to any citizens, then there is no right to use force in defense.

Like Rodin, David Luban is critical of the Just War theorist's reliance on self-defense and state sovereignty to justify engaging in war. In "Just War and Human Rights," Luban argues that the Just War tradition, by focusing on self-defense and sovereignty, provides the wrong starting point for analyzing whether a war is just. Rather than self-defense, Luban argues that the moral starting point should be an inquiry into whether a state is providing all, or subverting any, *socially basic human rights*. A right is socially basic, according to Luban, if it is necessary to satisfy any other rights. Some examples are the rights to food, clothing, and shelter.

According to Luban, all states are morally obligated to provide these basic human rights, as well as refrain from subverting any of them. For Luban, waging war against an aggressor state is not justified because it is an act of self-defense. Rather, it is justified because such aggression attacks human rights. Also, on Luban's account, military intervention to bring humanitarian relief to the citizens of a state that fails to provide a socially basic human right is justified. States that fail to provide basic human rights are not morally justified in preventing such military intervention, and in fact, it is "morally urgent" that other states provide such relief.

Luban's approach then is reductive. War is justified because all people, or all citizens, have human rights and states are morally obligated to satisfy these human rights. States are merely instruments to be used by their citizens. For Luban, states have "privileges," not "rights." By grounding just war in human rights, Luban challenges traditional conceptions (like Walzer's legalist paradigm) used to determine when it is permissible to engage in war. Luban states that before engaging in war, a state should compare the violations of socially basic human rights likely to occur from engaging in war with the violations of socially basic human rights that provide the impetus for engaging in war. This comparison between human rights violations is supposed to help discern whether a state would be justified in engaging in war.

The previous three selections of this section concerned self-defense and *jus ad bellum*. The last selection of this section is concerned with self-defense and *jus in bello*. In "Justification or Excuse: Saving Soldiers at the Expense of Civilians," Paul Woodruff analyzes whether soldiers are ever justified in killing civilians based on their personal right of self-defense. This issue arises because in war soldiers are often ordered to participate in missions in which it is difficult to tell whether they are being attacked, who the attacker is, and where the attack is coming from. On these difficult missions, it is foreseeable that soldiers will kill some civilians in seeking to preserve their own lives. Though Woodruff offers an example from Vietnam, a current example might be the killing of civilians that fail to yield at checkpoints on roads controlled by the United States military in Iraq. Ultimately, Woodruff concludes that soldiers cannot *justify* killing civilians based on self-defense. However, soldiers sometimes can be *excused* for killing civilians. For Woodruff, then, there is a moral distinction between justification and excuse. Roughly, this distinction consists in the fact that an action that is justified is not wrong, while an action that is excused is still wrong but not blameworthy.

Are there good reasons for making this moral distinction between justification and excuse? Among others, Woodruff provides the following three reasons. First, Woodruff claims that making this distinction best explains what happens when one chooses the lesser of two evils. Choosing the lesser evil is still doing evil, though it sometimes may be reasonably excused. Second, this distinction assists in determining when actions are no longer morally reasonable or when excuse no longer works. Woodruff argues that the more times a person allows himself or herself to be put in situations in which it is likely that person will kill civilians, the less likely he or she can be excused for killing civilians.

Third, according to Woodruff, this distinction shifts much (and sometimes all) of the moral blame to commanders who place subordinates in situations where it is likely that subordinates will kill civilians to preserve their own lives. Woodruff contends that since commanders are better situated to change future military operations according to information gathered from past missions, commanders are morally obligated to consider the likelihood of soldiers killing civilians when planning future operations. And, Woodruff concludes, when they continue to put soldiers in these difficult situations, commanders can be held morally responsible. In contrast, it is unreasonable to expect subordinates to refuse orders to participate in what would appear to be a legal mission. Regarding the subordinate, Woodruff concludes, "Neither the courts nor the public would accept [his] plea that the danger to civilians made void his oath to obey."

Just and Unjust Wars

(1977)

Michael Walzer

Michael Walzer is the UPS Foundation Professor at the Institute for Advanced Study at Princeton University. He has written on a broad variety of topics in political theory and moral philosophy, including political obligation, war, nationalism and ethnicity, and economic justice. His books include Spheres of Justice: A Defense of Pluralism and Equality *(1984),* On Toleration *(1997), and* Just and Unjust Wars *(3rd ed., 2000).*

The Legalist Paradigm

If states actually do possess rights more or less as individuals do, then it is possible to imagine a society among them more or less like the society of individuals. The comparison of international to civil order is crucial to the theory of aggression. I have already been making it regularly. Every reference to aggression as the international equivalent of armed robbery or murder, and every comparison of home and country or of personal liberty and political independence, relies upon what is called the *domestic analogy.*[1] Our primary perceptions and judgments of aggression are the products of analogical reasoning. When the analogy is made explicit, as it often is among the lawyers, the world of states takes on the shape of a political society the character of which is entirely accessible through such notions as crime and punishment, self-defense, law enforcement, and so on.

These notions, I should stress, are not incompatible with the fact that international society as it exists today is a radically imperfect structure. As we experience it, that society might be likened to a defective building, founded on rights; its superstructure raised, like that of the state itself, through political conflict, cooperative activity, and commercial exchange; the whole thing shaky and unstable because it lacks the rivets of authority. It is like domestic society in that men and women live at peace within it (sometimes), determining the conditions of their own existence, negotiating and bargaining with their neighbors. It is unlike domestic society in that every conflict threatens the structure as a whole with collapse. Aggression challenges it directly and is much more dangerous than domestic crime, because there are no policemen. But that only means that the "citizens" of international society must rely on themselves and on one another. Police powers are distributed among all the members. And these members have not done enough in the exercise of their powers if they merely contain the aggression or bring it to a speedy end—as if the police should stop a murderer after he has killed only one or two people and send him on his way. The rights of the member states must be vindicated, for it is only by virtue of those rights that there is a society at all. If they cannot be upheld (at least sometimes), international society collapses into a state of war or is transformed into a universal tyranny. . . .

The theory of aggression first takes shape under the aegis of the domestic analogy. I am going to call that primary form of the theory the *legalist paradigm,* since it consistently reflects the conventions of law and order. It does not necessarily reflect the arguments of the lawyers, though legal as well as moral debate has its starting point here.[2] Later on, I will suggest that our judgments about the justice and injustice of particular wars are not entirely determined by the paradigm. The complex realities of international society drive us toward a revisionist perspective, and the revisions will be significant ones. But the paradigm must first be viewed in its unrevised form; it is our baseline, our model, the fundamental structure for the moral comprehension of war. We begin with the familiar world of individuals and rights, of crimes and punishments. The theory of aggression can then be summed up in six propositions.

1. *There exists an international society of independent states.* States are the members of this society, not private men and women. In the absence of an universal state, men and women are protected and their interests represented only by their own governments. Though states are founded for the sake of life and liberty, they cannot be challenged in the name of life and liberty by any other states. Hence the principle of non-intervention, which I will analyze later on. The rights of private persons

can be recognized in international society, as in the UN Charter of Human Rights, but they cannot be enforced without calling into question the dominant values of that society: the survival and independence of the separate political communities.

2. *This international society has a law that establishes the rights of its members— above all, the rights of territorial integrity and political sovereignty.* Once again, these two rest ultimately on the right of men and women to build a common life and to risk their individual lives only when they freely choose to do so. But the relevant law refers only to states, and its details are fixed by the intercourse of states, through complex processes of conflict and consent. Since these processes are continuous, international society has no natural shape; nor are rights within it ever finally or exactly determined. At any given moment, however, one can distinguish the territory of one people from that of another and say something about the scope and limits of sovereignty.

3. *Any use of force or imminent threat of force by one state against the political sovereignty or territorial integrity of another constitutes aggression and is a criminal act.* As with domestic crime, the argument here focuses narrowly on actual or imminent boundary crossings: invasions and physical assaults. Otherwise, it is feared, the notion of resistance to aggression would have no determinate meaning. A state cannot be said to be forced to fight unless the necessity is both obvious and urgent.

4. *Aggression justifies two kinds of violent response: a war of self-defense by the victim and a war of law enforcement by the victim and any other member of international society.* Anyone can come to the aid of a victim, use necessary force against an aggressor, and even make whatever is the

international equivalent of a "citizen's arrest." As in domestic society, the obligations of bystanders are not easy to make out, but it is the tendency of the theory to undermine the right of neutrality and to require widespread participation in the business of law enforcement. In the Korean War, this participation was authorized by the United Nations, but even in such cases the actual decision to join the fighting remains a unilateral one, best understood by analogy to the decision of a private citizen who rushes to help a man or woman attacked on the street.

5. *Nothing but aggression can justify war.* The central purpose of the theory is to limit the occasions for war. "There is a single and only just cause for commencing a war," wrote Vitoria, "namely, a wrong received."[3] There must actually have been a wrong, and it must actually have been received (or its receipt must be, as it were, only minutes away). Nothing else warrants the use of force in international society— above all, not any difference of religion or politics. Domestic heresy and injustice are never actionable in the world of states: hence, again, the principle of non-intervention.

6. *Once the aggressor state has been militarily repulsed, it can also be punished.* The conception of just war as an act of punishment is very old, though neither the procedures nor the forms of punishment have ever been firmly established in customary or positive international law. Nor are its purposes entirely clear: to exact retribution, to deter other states, to restrain or reform this one? All three figure largely in the literature, though it is probably fair to say that deterrence and restraint are most commonly accepted. When people talk of fighting a war against war, this is usually what they have in mind. The domestic maxim is, punish crime to prevent violence; its international analogue is, punish aggression to prevent war. Whether the state as a whole or only particular persons are the proper objects of punishment is a harder question, for reasons I will consider later on. But the implication of the paradigm is clear: if states are members of international society, the subjects of rights, they must also be (somehow) the objects of punishment.

ANTICIPATIONS

The first questions asked when states go to war are also the easiest to answer: who started the shooting? who sent troops across the border? These are questions of fact, not of judgment, and if the answers are disputed, it is only because of the lies that governments tell. The lies don't, in any case, detain us long; the truth comes out soon enough. Governments lie so as to absolve themselves from the charge of aggression. But it is not on the answers to questions such as these that our final judgments about aggression depend. There are further arguments to make, justifications to offer, lies to tell, before the moral issue is directly confronted. For aggression often begins without shots being fired or borders crossed.

Both individuals and states can rightfully defend themselves against violence that is imminent but not actual; they can fire the first shots if they know themselves about to be attacked. This is a right recognized in domestic law and also in the legalist paradigm for international society. In most legal accounts, however, it is severely restricted. Indeed, once one has stated the restrictions, it is no longer clear whether the right has any substance at all. Thus the argument of Secretary of State Daniel Webster in the *Caroline* case of 1842 (the details of which need not concern us here): in order to justify pre-emptive violence, Webster wrote, there must be shown "a necessity of self-defense . . . instant, overwhelming, leaving no choice of means, and no moment for deliberation."[4] That would permit us to do little more than respond to an attack *once we had seen it coming* but before we had felt its impact. Preemption on this view is like a reflex action, a throwing up of one's arms at the very last minute. But it hardly requires much of a "showing" to justify a movement of that sort. Even the most presumptuous aggressor is not likely to insist, as a matter of right, that his victims stand still until he lands the first blow. Webster's formula seems to be the favored one among students of international law, but I don't believe that it addresses itself usefully to the experience of imminent war. There is often plenty of time for deliberation, agonizing hours, days, even weeks of deliberation, when one doubts that war can be avoided and wonders whether or not to strike first. The debate is couched, I suppose, in strategic more than in moral terms. But the decision is judged morally, and the expectation of that judgment, of the effects it will have in allied and neutral states and among one's own people, is itself a strategic factor. So it is important to get the terms of the judgment right, and that requires some revision of the legalist paradigm. For the paradigm is more restrictive than the judgments we actually make. We are disposed to sympathize with potential victims even before they confront an instant and overwhelming necessity.

Imagine a spectrum of anticipation: at one end is Webster's reflex, necessary and determined; at the other end is preventive war, an attack that responds to a distant danger, a matter of foresight and free choice. I want to begin at the far end of the spectrum, where danger is a matter of judgment and political decision is unconstrained, and then edge my way along to the point where we currently draw the line between justified and unjustified attacks. What is involved at that point is something very different from Webster's reflex; it is still possible to make choices, to begin the fighting or to arm oneself and wait. Hence the decision to begin at least resembles the decision to fight a preventive war, and it is important to distinguish the criteria by which it is defended from those that were once thought to justify prevention. Why not draw the line at the far end of the spectrum? The reasons are central to an understanding of the position we now hold.

Preventive War and the Balance of Power

Preventive war presupposes some standard against which danger is to be measured. That standard does not exist, as it were, on the ground; it has nothing to do with the immediate security of boundaries. It exists in the mind's eye, in the idea of a balance of power, probably the dominant idea in international politics from the seventeenth century to the present day. A preventive war is a war fought to maintain the balance, to stop what is thought to be an even distribution of power from shifting into a relation of dominance and inferiority. The balance is often talked about as if it were the key to peace among states. But it cannot be that, else it would not need to be defended so often by force of arms. "The balance of power, the pride of modern policy . . . invented to preserve the general peace as well as the freedom of Europe," wrote Edmund Burke in 1760, "has only preserved its liberty. It has been the original of innumerable and fruitless wars."[5] In fact, of course, the wars to which Burke is referring are easily numbered. Whether or not they were fruitless depends upon how one views the connection between preventive war and the preservation of liberty. Eighteenth century British statesmen and their intellectual supporters obviously thought the connection very close. A radically unbalanced system, they recognized, would more likely make for peace, but they were "alarmed by the danger of universal monarchy."* When they went to war on behalf of the balance, they thought they were defending, not national interest alone, but an international order that made liberty possible throughout Europe.

That is the classic argument for prevention. It requires of the rulers of states, as Francis Bacon had argued a century earlier, that they "keep due sentinel, that none of their neighbors do overgrow so (by increase of territory, by embracing of trade, by approaches, or the like) as they become more able to annoy them, than they were."[6] And if their neighbors do "overgrow," then they must be fought, sooner rather than later, and without waiting for the first blow. "Neither is the opinion of some of the Schoolmen to be received: that a war cannot justly be made, but upon a precedent injury or provocation. For there is no question, but a just fear of an imminent danger, though no blow be given, is a lawful cause of war." Imminence here is not a matter of hours or days. The sentinels stare into temporal as well as geographic distance as they watch the growth of their neighbor's power. They will fear that growth as soon as it tips or seems likely to tip the balance. War is justified (as in Hobbes' philosophy) by fear alone and not by anything other states actually do or any signs they give of their malign intentions. Prudent rulers assume malign intentions.

The argument is utilitarian in form; it can be summed up in two propositions: (1) that the balance of power actually does preserve the liberties of Europe (perhaps also the happiness of Europeans) and is therefore worth defending even at some cost, and (2) that to fight early, before the balance tips in any decisive way, greatly reduces the cost of the defense, while waiting doesn't mean avoiding war (unless one also gives up liberty) but only fighting on a larger scale and at worse odds. The argument is plausible enough, but it is possible to imagine a second-level utilitarian response: (3) that the acceptance of propositions (1) and (2) is dangerous (not useful) and certain to lead to "innumerable and fruitless wars" whenever shifts in power relations occur; but increments and losses

---

*The line is from David Hume's essay "Of the Balance of Power," where Hume describes three British wars on behalf of the balance as having been "begun with justice, and even, perhaps, from necessity." I would have considered his argument at length had I found it possible to place it within his philosophy. But in his *Enquiry Concerning the Principles of Morals* (Section III, Part I), Hume writes: "The rage and violence of public war: what is it but a suspension of justice among the warring parties, who perceive that this virtue is now no longer of any *use* or advantage to them?" Nor is it possible, according to Hume, that this suspension itself be just or unjust; it is entirely a matter of necessity, as in the (Hobbist) state of nature where individuals "consult the dictates of self-preservation alone." That standards of justice exist alongside the pressures of necessity is a discovery of the *Essays*. This is another example, perhaps, of the impossibility of carrying over certain philosophical positions into ordinary moral discourse. In any case, the three wars Hume discusses were none of them necessary to the preservation of Britain. He may have thought them just because he thought the balance generally useful.

of power are a constant feature of international politics, and perfect equilibrium, like perfect security, is a utopian dream; therefore it is best to fall back upon the legalist paradigm or some similar rule and wait until the overgrowth of power is put to some overbearing use. This is also plausible enough, but it is important to stress that the position to which we are asked to fall back is not a prepared position, that is, it does not itself rest on any utilitarian calculation. Given the radical uncertainties of power politics, there probably is no practical way of making out that position—deciding when to fight and when not—on utilitarian principles. Think of what one would have to know to perform the calculations, of the experiments one would have to conduct, the wars one would have to fight—and leave unfought! In any case, we mark off moral lines on the anticipation spectrum in an entirely different way.

It isn't really prudent to assume the malign intent of one's neighbors; it is merely cynical, an example of the worldly wisdom which no one lives by or could live by. We need to make judgments about our neighbor's intentions, and if such judgments are to be possible we must stipulate certain acts or sets of acts that will count as evidence of malignity. These stipulations are not arbitrary; they are generated, I think, when we reflect upon what it means *to be threatened*. Not merely *to be afraid,* though rational men and women may well respond fearfully to a genuine threat, and their subjective experience is not an unimportant part of the argument for anticipation. But we also need an objective standard, as Bacon's phrase "just fear" suggests. That standard must refer to the threatening acts of some neighboring state, for (leaving aside the dangers of natural disaster) I can only be threatened by

someone who is threatening me, where "threaten" means what the dictionary says it means: "to hold out or offer (some injury) by way of a threat, to declare one's intention of inflicting injury."[7] It is with some such notion as this that we must judge the wars fought for the sake of the balance of power. Consider, then, the Spanish Succession, regarded in the eighteenth century as a paradigmatic case for preventive war, and yet, I think, a negative example of threatening behavior.

The War of the Spanish Succession

Writing in the 1750s, the Swiss jurist Vattel suggested the following criteria for legitimate prevention: "Whenever a state has given signs of injustice, rapacity, pride, ambition, or of an imperious thirst of rule, it becomes a suspicious neighbor to be guarded against: and at a juncture when it is on the point of receiving a formidable augmentation of power, securities may be asked, and on its making any difficulty to give them, its designs may be prevented by force of arms."[8] These criteria were formulated with explicit reference to the events of 1700 and 1701, when the King of Spain, last of his line, lay ill and dying. Long before those years, Louis XIV had given Europe evident signs of injustice, rapacity, pride, and so on. His foreign policy was openly expansionist and aggressive (which is not to say that justifications were not offered, ancient claims and titles uncovered, for every intended territorial acquisition). In 1700, he seemed about to receive a "formidable augmentation of power"—his grandson, the Duke of Anjou, was offered the Spanish throne. With his usual arrogance, Louis refused to provide any assurances or guarantees to his fellow monarchs. Most importantly, he refused to bar Anjou from the French succession, thus holding open the possibility of a unified and powerful Franco-Spanish state. And then, an alliance of European powers, led by Great Britain, went to war against what they assumed was Louis' "design" to dominate Europe. Having drawn his criteria so closely to his case, however, Vattel concludes on a sobering note: "it has since appeared that the policy [of the Allies] was too suspicious." That is wisdom after the fact, of course, but still wisdom, and one would expect some effort to restate the criteria in its light.

The mere augmentation of power, it seems to me, cannot be a warrant for war or even the beginning of warrant, and for much the same reason that Bacon's commercial expansion ("embracing of trade") is also and even more obviously insufficient. For both of these suggest developments that may not be politically designed at all and hence cannot be taken as evidence of intent. As Vattel says, Anjou had been invited to his throne "by the [Spanish] nation, conformably to the will of its last sovereign"—that is, though there can be no question here of democratic decision-making, he had been invited for Spanish and not for French reasons. "Have not these two Realms," asked Jonathan Swift in a pamphlet opposing the British war, "their separate maxims of Policy . . .?"[9] Nor is Louis' refusal to make promises relating to some future time to be taken as evidence of design—only, perhaps, of hope. If Anjou's succession made immediately for a closer alliance between Spain and France, the appropriate answer would seem to have been a closer alliance between Britain and Austria. Then one could wait and judge anew the intentions of Louis.

But there is a deeper issue here. When we stipulate threatening acts, we are looking not only for indications of intent, but also for rights of response. To characterize certain acts as threats is to characterize them in a moral way, and in a way that makes a military response morally comprehensible. The utilitarian arguments for prevention don't do that, not because the wars they generate are too frequent, but because they are too common in another sense: *too ordinary*. Like Clausewitz's description of war as the continuation of policy by other means, they radically underestimate the importance of the shift from diplomacy to force. They don't recognize the problem that killing and being killed poses. Perhaps the recognition depends upon a certain way of valuing human life, which was not the way of eighteenth-century statesmen. (How many of the British soldiers who shipped to the continent with Marlborough ever returned? Did anyone bother to count?) But the point is an important one anyway, for it suggests why people have come to feel uneasy about preventive war. We don't want to fight until we are threatened, because only then can we rightly fight. It is a question of moral security. That is why Vattel's concluding remark about the War of the Spanish Succession, and Burke's general argument about the fruitlessness of such wars, is so worrying. It is inevitable, of course, that political calculations will sometimes go wrong; so will moral choices; there is no such thing as perfect security. But there is a great difference, nonetheless, between killing and being killed by soldiers who can plausibly be described as the present instruments of an aggressive intention, and killing and being killed by soldiers who may or may not represent a distant danger to our country. In the first case, we confront an army recognizably hostile, ready for war, fixed in a posture of attack. In the second, the hostility is prospective and imaginary, and it will always be a charge against us that we have made war upon soldiers who were themselves engaged in entirely legitimate (nonthreatening) activities. Hence the moral necessity of rejecting any attack that is merely preventive in character, that does not wait upon and respond to the willful acts of an adversary.

Pre-emptive Strikes

Now, what acts are to count, what acts do count as threats sufficiently serious to justify war? It is not possible to put together a list, because state action, like human action generally, takes on significance from its context. But there are some negative points worth making. The boastful ranting to which political leaders are often prone isn't in itself threatening; injury must be "offered" in some material sense as well. Nor does the kind of military preparation that is a feature of the classic arms race count as a threat, unless it violates some formally or tacitly agreed-upon limit. What the lawyers call "hostile acts short of war," even if these involve violence, are not too quickly to be taken as signs of an intent to make war; they may represent an essay in restraint, an offer to quarrel within limits. Finally, provocations are not the same as threats. "Injury and provocation" are commonly linked by Scholastic writers as the two causes of just war. But the Schoolmen were too accepting of contemporary notions about the honor of states and, more importantly, of sovereigns.[10] The moral significance of such ideas is dubious at best. Insults are not occasions for wars, any more than they are (these days) occasions for duels.

For the rest, military alliances, mobilizations, troop movements, border incursions, naval blockades—all these, with or without verbal menace, sometimes count and sometimes do not count as sufficient indications of hostile intent. But it is, at least, these sorts of actions with which we are concerned. We move along the anticipation spectrum in search, as it were, of enemies: not possible or potential enemies, not merely present ill-wishers, but states and nations that are already, to use a phrase I shall use again with reference to the distinction of combatants and noncombatants, *engaged in harming us* (and who have already harmed us, by their threats, even if they have not yet inflicted any physical injury). And this search, though it carries us beyond preventive war, clearly brings us up short of Webster's pre-emption. The line between legitimate and illegitimate first strikes is not going to be drawn at the point of imminent attack but at the point of sufficient threat. That phrase is necessarily vague. I mean it to cover three things: a manifest intent to injure, a degree of active preparation that makes that intent a positive danger, and a general situation in which waiting, or doing anything other than fighting, greatly magnifies the risk. The argument may be made more clear if I compare these criteria to Vattel's. Instead of previous signs of rapacity and ambition, current and particular signs are required; instead of an "augmentation of power," actual preparation for war; instead of the refusal of future securities, the intensification of present dangers. Preventive war looks to the past and future, Webster's reflex action to the immediate moment, while the idea of being under a threat focuses on what we had best call simply *the present*. I cannot specify a time span; it is a span within which one can still make choices, and within which it is possible to feel straitened.[11]

What such a time is like is best revealed concretely. We can study it in the three weeks that preceded the Six Day War of 1967. Here is a case as crucial for an understanding of anticipation in the twentieth century as the War of the Spanish Succession was for the eighteenth, and one suggesting that the shift from dynastic to national politics, the costs of which have so often been stressed, has also brought some moral gains. For nations, especially democratic nations, are less likely to fight preventive wars than dynasties are.

The Six Day War

Actual fighting between Israel and Egypt began on June 5, 1967, with an Israeli first strike. In the early hours of the war, the Israelis did not acknowledge that they had sought the advantages of surprise, but the deception was not maintained. In fact, they believed themselves justified in attacking first by the dramatic events of the previous weeks. So we must focus on those events and their moral significance. It would be possible, of course, to look further back still, to the whole course of the Arab-Jewish conflict in the Middle East. Wars undoubtedly have long political and moral pre-histories. But anticipation needs to be understood within a narrower frame. The Egyptians believed that the founding of Israel in 1948 had been unjust, that the state had no rightful existence, and hence that it could be attacked at any time. It follows from this that Israel had no right of anticipation since it had no right of self-defense. But self-defense seems the primary and indisputable right of any political community, merely because

it is *there* and whatever the circumstances under which it achieved statehood.* Perhaps this is why the Egyptians fell back in their more formal arguments upon the claim that a state of war already existed between Egypt and Israel and that this condition justified the military moves they undertook in May 1967.[12] But the same condition would justify Israel's first strike. It is best to assume, I think, that the existing cease-fire between the two countries was at least a near-peace and that the outbreak of the war requires a moral explanation—the burden falling on the Israelis, who began the fighting.

The crisis apparently had its origins in reports, circulated by Soviet officials in mid-May, that Israel was massing its forces on the Syrian border. The falsity of these reports was almost immediately vouched for by United Nations observers on the scene. Nevertheless, on May 14, the Egyptian government put its armed forces on "maximum alert" and began a major buildup of its troops in the Sinai. Four days later, Egypt expelled the United Nations Emergency Force from the Sinai and the Gaza Strip; its withdrawal began immediately, though I do not think that its title had been intended to suggest that it would depart so quickly in event of emergency. The Egyptian military buildup continued, and on May 22, President Nasser announced that the Straits of Tiran would henceforth be closed to Israeli shipping.

---

*The only limitation on this right has to do with internal, not external legitimacy: a state (or government) established against the will of its own people, ruling violently, may well forfeit its right to defend itself even against a foreign invasion. I will take up some of the issues raised by this possibility in the next chapter.

In the aftermath of the Suez War of 1956, the Straits had been recognized by the world community as an international waterway. That meant that their closing would constitute a *casus belli,* and the Israelis had stated at that time, and on many occasions since, that they would so regard it. The war might then be dated from May 22, and the Israeli attack of June 5 described simply as its first military incident: wars often begin before the fighting of them does. But the fact is that after May 22, the Israeli cabinet was still debating whether or not to go to war. And, in any case, the actual initiation of violence is a crucial moral event. If it can sometimes be justified by reference to previous events, it nevertheless has to be justified. In a major speech on May 29, Nasser made that justification much easier by announcing that if war came the Egyptian goal would be nothing less than the destruction of Israel. On May 30, King Hussein of Jordan flew to Cairo to sign a treaty placing the Jordanian army under Egyptian command in event of war, thus associating himself with the Egyptian purpose. Syria already had agreed to such an arrangement, and several days later Iraq joined the alliance. The Israelis struck on the day after the Iraqi announcement.

For all the excitement and fear that their actions generated, it is unlikely that the Egyptians intended to begin the war themselves. After the fighting was over, Israel published documents, captured in its course, that included plans for an invasion of the Negev; but these were probably plans for a counter-attack, once an Israeli offensive had spent itself in the Sinai, or for a first strike at some later time. Nasser would almost certainly have regarded it as a great victory if he could have closed the Straits and maintained his army on Israel's borders without war. Indeed, it would have been a great victory, not only because of the economic blockade it would have established, but also because of the strain it would have placed on the Israeli defense system. "There was a basic assymetry in the structure of forces: the Egyptians could deploy . . . their large army of long-term regulars on the Israeli border and keep it there indefinitely; the Israelis could only counter their deployment by mobilizing reserve formations, and reservists could not be kept in uniform for very long . . . Egypt could therefore stay on the defensive while Israel would have to attack unless the crisis was defused diplomatically."[13] *Would have to attack:* the necessity cannot be called instant and overwhelming; nor, however, would an Israeli decision to allow Nasser his victory have meant nothing more than a shift in the balance of power posing possible dangers at some future time. It would have opened Israel to attack at any time. It would have represented a drastic erosion of Israeli security such as only a determined enemy would hope to bring about.

The initial Israeli response was not similarly determined but, for domestic political reasons having to do in part with the democratic character of the state, hesitant and confused. Israel's leaders sought a political resolution of the crisis—the opening of the Straits and a demobilization of forces on both sides—which they did not have the political strength or support to effect. A flurry of diplomatic activity ensued, serving only to reveal what might have been predicted in advance: the unwillingness of the Western powers to pressure or coerce the Egyptians. One always wants to see diplomacy tried before the resort to war, so that we are sure that war is the last resort. But it would be difficult in this case to make an argument for its necessity. Day by day, diplomatic efforts seemed only to intensify Israel's isolation.

Meanwhile, "an intense fear spread in the country." The extraordinary Israeli triumph, once fighting began, makes it difficult to recall the preceding weeks of anxiety. Egypt was in the grip of a war fever, familiar enough from European history, a celebration in advance of expected victories. The Israeli mood was very different, suggesting what it means to live under threat: rumors of coming disasters were endlessly repeated; frightened men and women raided food shops, buying up their entire stock, despite government announcements that there were ample reserves; thousands of graves were dug in the military cemeteries; Israel's political and military leaders lived on the edge of nervous exhaustion.[14] I have already argued that fear by itself establishes no right of anticipation. But Israeli anxiety during those weeks seems an almost classical example of "just fear"—first, because Israel really was in danger (as foreign observers readily agreed), and second, because it was Nasser's intention to put it in danger. He said this often enough, but it is also and more importantly true that his military moves served no other, more limited goal.

The Israeli first strike is, I think, a clear case of legitimate anticipation. To say that, however, is to suggest a major revision of the legalist paradigm. For it means that aggression can be made out not only in the absence of a military attack or invasion but in the (probable) absence of any immediate intention to launch such an attack or invasion. The general formula must go something like this: states may use military force

in the face of threats of war, whenever the failure to do so would seriously risk their territorial integrity or political independence. Under such circumstances it can fairly be said that they have been forced to fight and that they are the victims of aggression. Since there are no police upon whom they can call, the moment at which states are forced to fight probably comes sooner than it would for individuals in a settled domestic society. But if we imagine an unstable society, like the "wild west" of American fiction, the analogy can be restated: a state under threat is like an individual hunted by an enemy who has announced his intention of killing or injuring him. Surely such a person may surprise his hunter, if he is able to do so.

The formula is permissive, but it implies restrictions that can usefully be unpacked only with reference to particular cases. It is obvious, for example, that measures short of war are preferable to war itself whenever they hold out the hope of similar or nearly similar effectiveness. But what those measures might be, or how long they must be tried, cannot be a matter of *a priori* stipulation. In the case of the Six Day War, the "asymmetry in the structure of forces" set a time limit on diplomatic efforts that would have no relevance to conflicts involving other sorts of states and armies. A general rule containing words like "seriously" opens a broad path for human judgment—which it is, no doubt, the purpose of the legalist paradigm to narrow or block altogether. But it is a fact of our moral life that political leaders make such judgments, and that once they are made the rest of us do not uniformly condemn them. Rather, we weigh and evaluate their actions on the basis of criteria like those I have tried to describe. When we do that we are acknowledging that there are threats with which no nation can be expected to live. And that acknowledgment is an important part of our understanding of aggression.

Notes

1. For a critique of this analogy, see the two essays by Hedley Bull, "Society and Anarchy in International Relations," and "The Grotian Conception of International Society," in *Diplomatic Investigations,* chs. 2 and 3.
2. It is worth noting that the United Nations' recently adopted definition of aggression closely follows the paradigm: see the *Report of the Special Committee on the Question of Defining Aggression* (1974), General Assembly Official Records, 29th session, supplement no. 19 (A/9619), pp. 10–13. The definition is reprinted and analyzed in Yehuda Melzer, *Concepts of Just War* (Leyden, 1975), pp. 26ff.
3. Vitoria *On the Law of War,* trans. John Pawley Bate, p. 170.
4. D. W. Bowett, *Self-Defense in International Law* (New York, 1958), p. 59. My own position has been influenced by Julius Stone's critique of the legalist argument: *Aggression and World Order* (Berkeley, 1968).
5. Quoted from the *Annual Register,* in H. Butterfield, "The Balance of Power," *Diplomatic Investigations,* (Cambridge, Mass., 1996) pp. 144–45.
6. Francis Bacon, *Essays* ("Of Empire"): see also his treatise *Considerations Touching a War With Spain* (1624), in *The Works of Francis Bacon,* ed. James Spedding *et al.* (London, 1874), XIV, pp. 469–505.
7. *Oxford English Dictionary,* "threaten."
8. M. D. Vattel, *The Law of Nations* (Northampton, Mass., 1805), Bk. III, ch. III, paras. 42–44, pp. 357–78. Cf. John Westlake, *Chapters on the Principles of International Law* (Cambridge, England, 1894), p. 120.
9. Jonathan Swift, *The Conduct of the Allies and of the Late Ministry in Beginning and Carrying on the Present War* (1711), in *Prose Works,* ed. Temple Scott (London, 1901), V, 116.
10. As late as the eighteenth century, Vattel still argued that a prince "has a right to demand, even by force of arms, the reparation of an insult." *Law of Nations,* Bk. II, ch. IV, para. 48, p. 216.
11. Compare the argument of Hugo Grotius: "The danger . . . must be immediate and imminent in point of time. I admit, to be sure, that if the assailant seizes weapons in such a way that his intent to kill is manifest, the crime can be forestalled; for in morals as in material things a point is not to be found which does not have a certain breadth." *The Law of War and Peace,* trans. Francis W. Kelsey (Indianapolis, n.d.), Bk. II, ch. I, section V, p. 173.
12. Walter Laquer, *The Road to War: The Origin and Aftermath of the Arab-Israeli Conflict,* 1967–8 (Baltimore, 1969), p. 110.
13. Edward Luttwak and Dan Horowitz, *The Israeli Army* (New York, 1975), p. 212.
14. Luttwak and Horowitz, p. 224.

War and Self-Defense

(2002)

David Rodin

David Rodin is Director of Research at the Centre for Applied Ethics, University of Oxford. His research covers a broad range of issues in moral and political philosophy. He is the author of War and Self-Defense *(2002).*

THE TWO LEVELS OF WAR

Michael Walzer argues that war should be viewed not as a relation between individual persons, but between states: 'The war itself isn't a relation between persons, but between political entities and their human instruments'.[1] This view is shared by Ian Clark: 'The conscript in the opposing trench is at the very-least relegated to the role of representative of the enemy'.[2] Thomas Nagel, on the other hand, premises his moral investigation of war on precisely the opposite assumption: 'A positive account of the matter must begin with the observation that war, conflict, and aggression are relations between persons'.[3] David Luban concurs with this judgement: 'Wars are not fought by states, but by men and women.'[4]

It seems to me that there is a profound issue here, and one which underlies a great deal of what is morally most difficult about war. For the phenomenon of war may be accessed on two distinct levels each suggesting a distinctive moral point of view: that of the rights and responsibilities of individual persons and that of the rights and responsibilities of states or other 'political entities'. War can at once be viewed as a relation between persons and as a relation between super-personal collective entities. Every military action is ascribable to some kind of collective entity, but it is at the same time constituted by actions ascribable to particular persons.

But both sets of entities—the collective and the individual—are conceived as moral agents, the bearers of rights and the subjects of duties. Which, if either, is the most basic or fundamental level for the moral analysis of war? In our moral investigation of national-defense, should we follow Walzer and Clark in giving primacy to the moral relation between states, or follow Nagel and Luban in insisting on the primacy of the moral relations between individual persons?

These questions are of the utmost importance for us, for they suggest two possible ways forward in the project of providing a moral vindication of the right of national-defense. At the same time they indicate the great difficulties that any such account will have to overcome. The crux of the analogical argument for national-defense is succinctly summarized by Douglas Lackey: 'The notions of self-defence and of just war are commonly linked: just wars are said to be defensive wars, and the justice of defensive wars is inferred from the right of personal self-defence.'[5] But if there is an inference from self-defense to national-defense, what form does the inference take? The two levels of war suggest two broad strategies for answering this question. The first is to give primacy to war as a relation between individuals and attempt to explain national-defense reductively at the level of personal rights. Thus one might attempt to show that national-defense can be derived from, or analysed in terms of, the personal defensive rights of citizens. The second strategy is to take the notion of state rights seriously and try to give moral content to them as independent from, yet analogous to, the rights of personal self-defense. These two broad strategies will provide the basic framework for my investigation of national-defense. . . .

THE REDUCTIVE STRATEGY

Though a proper understanding of the right of national-defense cannot be purely reductive, it is possible that it can be construed in such a way that we continue to see the end of national-defense in personal terms even if the subject and perhaps also the object of the right must be seen as super-personal. This leads us to the second way we might understand the suggestion that national-defense is the 'collective form' of self-defense. It may be argued that the state has an obligation (and therefore a right) to defend its citizens in much the same way that a parent has the right to defend his or her child. This view was expressed, for instance, by the American Roman Catholic Bishops in their well-known Pastoral Letter of 1983 which asserted that: 'Governments threatened by armed unjust aggression must defend their people'.[6] The same idea surfaces also in Walzer: 'the government is bound to its citizens to defend them against foreigners'[7] and also in the lawyer Fernando Tesón: 'a war in response to aggression is justified as *governmental action to defend the rights of its subjects, that is, the rights of individuals as victims of foreign aggression*'. . . .[8]

This view takes us some way closer to a satisfactory account of national-defense since we need no longer restrict ourselves to the unpromising task of attempting to build up a moral picture of war as a composite of individual acts of defense. However, in so far as these models assume that the right of national-defense is grounded in the end of defending the lives of individual citizens, it too must fail as an account of national-defense. I shall bring forward two arguments to show this: the first I shall call the argument from humanitarian intervention, the second I shall call the argument from bloodless invasion.

A standard definition of humanitarian intervention is: 'Military intervention in a state, without the approval of its authori- ties, and with the purpose of preventing widespread suffering or death among the inhabitants'.[9] Common sense tells us that humanitarian intervention is a very differ- ent creature to national-defense. They are different and indeed antagonistic because one is directed towards the maintenance of state sovereignty while the other involves an explicit permission to violate it. Yet if national-defense were a right of defense whose end is protecting the lives of individual citizens then not only would na- tional-defense and humanitarian interven- tion share an underlying moral structure but the latter right could be derived from the former by this simple argument: according to the account under considera- tion, if the citizens of state *A* are threat- ened by aggressive actions of state *B*, then state *A* has the right to engage in a defen- sive war against *B* in order to protect its (*A*'s) citizens. Similarly any third party, state *C*, has the right to engage in war against *B* (and hence intervene in that state without the approval of its authori- ties) with the end of protecting the citizens of *A*. But now it would seem that humani- tarian intervention is simply the applica- tion of this general principle with respect to third party intervention on the assump- tion that states *A* and *B* are the same state. To put the point another way, if a particular military action of state *C* is jus- tified by the fact that it defends the endan- gered lives of the citizens of *A,* then it should make no difference to the morality of *C*'s action whether the citizens of *A* are threatened by their own state or a third party.

But, of course, such a result flies in the face of common sense as well as the law and the moral theory of national-defense. Humanitarian intervention is no instance of the right of national-defense; it is rather a moral consideration which is in deep tension with it. When a state intervenes in another state on humanitarian grounds, one of the moral considerations weighed against this action is the defensive rights of the subject of the intervention. Thus the United Nations condemned Vietnam's 1978 invasion of Democratic Kampuchea (now Cambodia) as a breach of that state's sovereign rights, even though the intervention succeeded in bringing to a halt the murderous campaign of violence conducted by the Kampuchean state against its own people.[10] Without endorsing the UN's position, what the example clearly brings into focus is the fact that if there is a right to humanitarian intervention, then it is because the moral basis of the right of national-defense can in certain circumstances be justly overridden, not because the right of humanitarian intervention is, in some sense, an application of those moral considerations. Just as an adequate understanding of national-defense must recognize that there is a potential tension between the right of national-defense and the maintenance of international peace and security (as we saw in the last chapter), so it must recognize that there is a potential tension between national-defense and the protection of endangered citizens. It is precisely such a distinction which an account grounding national-defense in the end of protecting the lives of citizens is incapable of making.

The argument from humanitarian intervention shows that having the end of defending the lives of persons is not sufficient to bring a proportionate and necessary military action within the purview of the right of national-defense. The argument from bloodless invasion is designed to show that defending the lives of citizens is not a necessary condition for national-defense. This argument begins from the observation that the right of national-defense, as defined in international law and in the just war tradition, can be effective in the face of acts of aggression which threaten the lives of no citizens of the victim state. Such a situation may arise in a number of ways. An aggressive act may violate the territorial integrity and political independence of the victim state only by annexing or intervening in a remote and uninhabited piece of territory, or by making an illegal armed incursion into a state's air space or territorial waters where no citizen is threatened. Secondly, an aggressor may invade with such an overwhelming show of force that the victim state declines to resist and the intervention is accomplished with no loss of life.

The right of national-defense is effective in international law in the face of attacks against a state's 'territorial integrity or political independence', but this condition is both logically and factually independent of the question of whether the lives of individual citizens within the state are threatened. As Montesquieu reminds us: 'The state is the association of men, not the men themselves; the citizen may perish and the man remain'.[11] If this is correct, if, in other words, there are acts of international aggression which generate a legal and moral right of national-defense and yet which threaten the lives of no citizens, then the attempt to ground national-defense in the end of defending the lives of citizens must fail. . . .

ANALOGICAL STRATEGY

In the last chapter I identified two fundamental strategies for providing an account of national-defense. The first was to attempt to explain national-defense reductively at the level of personal rights. This was the approach explored in the last chapter. The second is what we might call the 'analogical strategy'. This approach takes seriously the notion of national-defense as a right held by states and attempts to give moral content to that right as one analogous to the personal right of self-defense. It is this idea that I will examine in the current chapter. Once again I understand the challenge principally to be one about providing an effective account of the end of the right.

The way I propose to address this challenge is by exploring the purposely broad conception of what is often called the 'common life' of a community. I take the common life to consist in the set of interconnected social structures which emerge when people live together in a community. Thus understood, the common life has a character and identity over time, it grows and develops, and it is shaped, both consciously and unconsciously, by those who live within it. It is also something which may be disrupted, irreparably altered, or even destroyed. For all of these reasons the designation collective or common 'life', though metaphorical (for a society is not literally an organism), seems appropriate. The suggestion that I shall now consider is that national-defense is a right held by states and grounded principally in the end, not of defending the lives of individual citizens, but of defending the common life of the community.

How are we to understand the idea of the common life in light of the argument about national-defense? I think that it is possible to discern three viable interpretations of the common life as a potential end of national-defense. The first interpretation would be to seek an understanding of the value of the common life in an account of state legitimacy. The second would be to see the common life as the embodiment of a particular cultural and historical heritage. The third interpretation sees the common life as the arena of collective self-determination and autonomy. My intention is to investigate whether any of these conceptions is capable of identifying a value sufficient to ground the right of national-defense as a right analogous to self-defense. . . [*Ed. Note:* Rodin's arguments against the "third interpretation" are presented below.]

COMMUNAL INTEGRITY AND SELF-DETERMINATION

The last two sections set up what I take to be the basic problematic of explaining how the common life can function as an appropriate end of national-defense. The value which grounds national-defense must be particular in the sense that it provides a reason for defending one form of common life against another, but its value cannot be so particular as to be simply subjective. Our first interpretation of the value of the common life sought an explanation in terms of state legitimacy, but the value of political association understood through the Hobbesian social contract or similarly minimal theory of legitimation could provide no reason to defend a particular order against others. Our second attempt focused on the particular character of communities, but this provided us with a reason for defending a particular common life only at the cost of relativizing those reasons themselves. What we require is a value that is both objective and particular—it must be objective and recognizable as valid across cultures, yet still provide a reason for defending a particular state or community.

Freedom, autonomy, and self-determination are objective transcultural goods in this way. I do not mean by this that persons in all societies could agree on some substantive political conception of freedom or self-determination. Rather I mean that in so far as each person pursues projects which they are committed to regarding as good, they are also committed to regarding the freedom necessary to the attainment of those projects as a good. Humans cannot flourish or obtain full well-being, without the ability to shape their own lives in accordance with their own conception of the good.

Michael Walzer, drawing heavily on an essay by John Stuart Mill, has fashioned from this observation a vigorous defense of the moral importance of state sovereignty.[12] Both authors begin from the premise that in addition to the familiar individual or personal form of autonomy, there is an important realm of self-determination which is necessarily collective. When a community shapes its common life and political institutions, it exercises a valuable form of autonomy which cannot be realized outside the communal sphere. As Walzer says: 'In the individual case we mark out a certain area for individual choice; in the communal case we fix a certain area for political choice. Unless these areas are clearly marked out and protected, both sorts of choices are likely to become problematic.'[13] It is the process of collective self-determination which foreign intervention disturbs and disrupts. Intervention is always wrong, even if it is directed towards assisting or liberating citizens of an oppressive state, because it

violates the rights of peoples to determine collectively the form and nature of their own common life. This collective self-determination is, according to Walzer, a value sufficient to make proportionate the use of lethal force in defense.

This idea would seem to overcome the dilemma generated in the last two sections. Unlike the value of order embodied in the Hobbesian political association, collective self-determination can provide us with a reason to defend a particular form of common life. Unlike the purported value of the character of particular common lives, it does not lead us to a form of relativism, for we can recognize the objective value of a community's right to choose, even if this requires us to accept that the agents in question will sometimes choose badly. Thus it could be argued that even a common life whose form we find strange or morally distasteful has an integrity which can be viewed as a value. For what deserves respect and protection is not its form or character as such, but the process of collective choosing which lies behind it. Moreover, the idea has affinities with an attractive account of the value of human life. Richard Norman has argued that what informs the moral presumption against killing people is not simply the fact that they are alive, but that they *have* a life. By this he means that humans have a capacity to shape a meaningful life as a distinctive ongoing project.[14] What Walzer and Mill both assume is that communities are similarly capable of shaping themselves as ongoing meaningful projects, and that it is the value represented by this process that underlies the rightfulness of their engaging in acts of national-defense.

In order to assess this view, the notion of communal self-determination must be probed further. One objection to this line of argument is to claim that although collective self-determination is indeed an important good, it is something that is only realized with the establishment of democratic rights. Only in a democratic society can persons in a community be said to freely shape their common life and enjoy the good of collective self-determination. If this were the case then we would find ourselves in the embarrassing situation of excluding non-democratic regimes (a substantial proportion of the world's states) from enjoyment of the right of national-defense. Clearly such a view could not form the basis of an apology for the right of national-defense as it is currently conceived in the Just War Theory and enshrined in international law.

This objection, however, misses the substance of Walzer's thesis. The kind of collective self-determination that he has in mind is not wholly captured by the exercise of democratic rights; 'self-determination and political freedom are not equivalent terms' says Walzer.[15] As he sees it, an important part of collective self-determination is the capacity to choose a political system commensurate with one's national culture, even if this results in an illiberal and authoritarian regime. Collective self-determination is the right of people 'to express their inherited culture through political forms worked out amongst themselves'.[16]

But here the account becomes strained: what exactly does this process of 'working out' consist of, if not the exercise of democratic processes? Walzer's response is that it is an eminently political process. It involves the manoeuvring of interest groups, the mobilizing of social and economic forces, and, in its most extreme form, civil

war. A crucial aspect of the kind of self-determination Walzer has in mind is the right of citizens to rebel against their government if the state is not representing and defending their common life—if there is no 'fit' between the common life and the state.[17] Walzer says that civil war is a clear example of the phenomenon he has in mind when he talks of collective self-determination. This is why he insists that it is always illegitimate for foreign powers to intervene in favour of one faction in a civil war.[18]

There are, however, deep problems here, for Walzer seems to be reducing collective self-determination ultimately to coercion and the balance of force.[19] Walzer seeks to avoid this result by making the assumption, that, in a civil war, the faction with greatest normative legitimacy (i.e. greatest 'fit' with the intrinsic common life of the population) will in general be victorious. The reason for this, he says, is that victory in civil war reflects the support of the majority of the people: 'Armies and police forces are social institutions; soldiers and policemen come from families, villages, neighbourhoods, classes. They will not fight cohesively, with discipline, or at length unless the regime for which they are fighting has some degree of social support.'[20]

But this position is clearly unacceptable. The outcome of a civil war reflects far more than the support of a majority of the population. It reflects, among much else, access to armaments and military training at the commencement of the conflict and the preparedness to use brutality and terror, all too often against members of the civilian population. It seems facile to suppose that a military outcome can serve as an accurate proxy for a normative process such as self-determination and normative judgements such as legitimacy. Walzer's account remains deeply problematic to the extent that it depends on such implausible assumptions.

THE MYTH OF DISCRETE COMMUNITIES

These difficulties arise for Walzer because he has retreated from a straightforwardly political conception of collective self-determination as consisting in the exercise of democratic rights, and replaced it with a looser account in which collective self-determination arises out of the undisturbed operation of organic social processes of contention and dispute. But the approach has two problems. The immediate problem is that it is highly doubtful whether such processes can be viewed as embodying a form of autonomous decision-making, when they so often involve or depend upon patterns of political, social, and military coercion. The more fundamental difficulty is that the position depends upon highly dubious assumptions about the organic unity of national communities and the nature of their relationship to states.

As we have already seen, the right of national-defense as it is defined in international law is a right possessed by states. Yet it will be noted that in the last two sections the ground of the right of national-defense has been sought, not in an account of the value of the state as such, but in the value of the communities or nations associated with states. In Walzer's view, for example, the state's right of national-defense derives from the rights of communities to integrity and autonomy. In the preceding section the value of the particular charac-

ter of a community was held to underlie the right of national-defense. Now both approaches are vulnerable to a number of serious objections, the most fundamental of which is that human communities do not coincide with the boundaries of states. No community is ever fully integrated within a particular state and no territory ever nurtures but a single community. This is an obvious point, but it is one with significant consequences. The discontinuity between communities and states substantially undermines the attempt to ground the right of national-defense on an account of the rights of communities.

The discontinuity between communities or nations on the one hand and states on the other takes different forms and can be approached in different ways. On the political level, the mismatch between states and nations is evident in the existence of multinational states such as the United Kingdom and in nations which exist across the boundaries of several states, for example the Kurds. On the sociological level, the problem stems from the fact that communal life is far richer and more varied than the simple division into sovereign states would suggest. Social life is not broken into discrete units which might potentially coincide with the boundaries of states. Rather, it consists of an intersecting network of communal affiliations, each of which defines a form of common life and contributes to individual identity. Communities are nested within others—the so-called 'Russian doll effect'. I am a member of the community defined by my family, my neighbourhood, my city, my national region, my country, my international region, and perhaps also the global community of mankind. In different contexts any one of these communal associations may be most important to me and each plays a significant role in defining my identity. The situation is yet more complicated still, for cutting across these vertically nested communities are numerous horizontally ordered communities and affiliations: social classes, ethnic and racial groups, churches, clubs, professional associations, trade unions, colleges, and so on. Our lives are embedded within an indefinite number of common lives, many of which criss-cross national boundaries, each of which possesses an ongoing character, and each of which constitutes a value for those who participate in it.

The problem for an account of national-defense is clear. If it is the value of communities (or the realm of collective autonomy that they make possible) which serves as the end of national-defense, then it is unclear why those rights should be attributed to states, whose relationship to these communities is often one of ambivalence and sometimes one of antagonism. The problem has two aspects. The first is that there are circumstances in which the end of protecting a community can directly conflict with a state's right to national-defense. This situation will arise most clearly in cases of humanitarian intervention in which an international agent violates the sovereignty of a state for the declared purpose of protecting the rights of a specific minority or community. Humanitarian intervention of this kind provides a clear example in which the rights of communities to autonomy and integrity do not underlie and support the defensive rights of states but rather stand in direct conflict with them.

The second aspect of the problem is that an explanation is needed of why the right to use collective violence should be limited to states and not attributed also to communities which are not sovereign states. The right to defend communal integrity with lethal force has been asserted not only by proto-states such as national liberation movements, but also by more marginal communities such as extremist religious sects, cults, and anti-government militias. Marxists, employing the notion of class war, view social class, not sovereign states, as the primary focus for the application of justified collective force. Such claims are not recognized by current international law and the dominant interpretation of the Just War Theory. But because the present account locates the grounding of the right of national-defense in the existence of a genuine community capable of exercising a form of collective autonomy, it is difficult to see why such groups should be denied an analogous right to defend their integrity with force.

The Just War Theorist may respond that the state is justified in defending itself whereas other communal entities are not, because historically it has been the state which has been able to command military allegiance. But this argument puts the cart before the horse. People are evidently increasingly prepared to die and kill for non-state community affiliations. What is more, the historic importance of national identity in our social consciousness stems, to a large extent, from the nation state's conventional ability to command legitimate military defense. Once this presumption in favour of legitimate military defense is established, the state is able to bring into play a series of powerful coercive and propaganda devices to bolster the importance of national identity in the eyes of its citizens.

A further problem with grounding the right of national-defense in the rights of communities is that it implausibly assumes that communities are discrete entities with clear criteria of identity and individuation. But, unlike states whose existence can be defined in reasonably clear legal terms, no plausible and determinate criteria exist for the identity and individuation of communities. This issue is of great importance for Walzer and Mill because their theory requires that we be able to determine with the highest degree of certainty whether a given conflict is occurring between different communities or within a single community. It is on this basis that they seek to determine when it is legitimate for an external power to intervene in the conflict. Military intervention is legitimate if the conflict is one between different communities, but it is illegitimate if the conflict is one within a single community, because in that case the war is to be regarded as a form of communal self-determination which must be protected from outside interference.[21]

The view, therefore, requires identity and individuation criteria of the strongest kind, for we must suppose that even when a community is so factionalized that it has divided into warring parties, it is still possible to identify a single continuing common-life whose rights of collective self-determination must be respected. But it is difficult to see what grounds we could ever have for making such a judgement. Notoriously, the concepts typically employed in this context, for example, the concept of a 'nationhood', have proved stubbornly resistant to analysis. As one observer says: 'Historically speaking, most nations have always been culturally and ethnically diverse, problematic, protean and artificial constructs that take shape very quickly and come apart just as fast'.[22]

Two conditions would have to be fulfilled if an account of the value of communities were to provide an effective underpinning for the right of national-defense as that right is defined in international law and in the Just War Theory. First, we would need clear criteria for settling the identity and individuation of communities. Secondly, the communities thus identified would have to be substantially co-extensive with the states. Neither condition is satisfied in the real world and it is difficult to imagine how they ever could be, given the realities of human communal life. It would seem, therefore, that the task of grounding national-defense in an account of the value of the common life is as problematic as the attempt to ground it in the end of protecting individual persons was seen to be in the previous chapter. The analogical strategy has proved as problematic and unpersuasive as the reductive strategy.

The argument which draws a connection between personal self-defense and national-defense is at once beguilingly simple and intuitively appealing. It has informed moral and philosophical thinking on warfare since at least the time of the Christian Fathers and has had a powerful influence on the development of modern international law. But I have argued that the analogy cannot be philosophically sustained. National-defense cannot be reduced to a collective application of personal rights of self-defense, and it cannot be explained as a state-held right analogous to personal self-defense. Because the right of national-defense has always been the central 'just cause' for war within the Just War Theory, and because the analogy with self-defense has always been its central justification, this result must be seen as a serious challenge to the traditional Just War doctrine of international morality.

I take this to be a surprising and disconcerting result, one which challenges us to revisit some of the basic normative conceptions of international relations. If the defensive rights of states cannot be simply modelled on the rights of persons, then we must work to develop new or amended conceptions for dealing with the problems of war, conflict, and aggression.

Notes

1. Walzer, M., *Just and Unjust Wars,* New York: Basic Books, 1977: 36.
2. Clark, I., *Waging War: A Philosophical Introduction,* Oxford: Clarendon Press, 1990: 17.
3. Nagel, T., 'War and Massacre', in *Mortal Questions,* Cambridge: Cambridge University Press, 1979: 64.
4. Luban, D., 'Just War and Human Rights', *Philosophy and Public Affairs,* 94 (1980), 160–81, at 166.
5. Lackey, D., *The Ethics of War and Peace,* Englewood Cliffs, NJ: Prentice Hall, 1989: 18.
6. National Conference of Catholic Bishops, *The Challenge of Peace,* Washington, DC, 1983, para. 75.
7. Walzer, 'The Moral Standing of States: A Response to Four Critiques,' Philosophy and Public Affairs (1980), 211.
8. Tesón, F., *Humanitarian Intervention, an Inquiry into Law and Morality,* New York: Transnational Publishers Inc., 1997: 113 (emphasis in original).
9. Roberts, A., 'Intervention and Human Rights', *International Affairs,* 691 (1993), 429–49, at 429.
10. See Weisburd, A. M., *Use of Force, the Practice of States since World War II,* Pennsylvania: The

Pennsylvania State University Press, 1997: 40–2.
11. Baron de Montesquieu, *The Spirit of the Laws,* Nugent, T. (trans.), Berkeley: University of California Press, 1977, bk. X, ch. 3: 192.
12. See Mill, J. S., 'A Few Words on Non-Intervention', in *Dissertations and Discussions Vol. III,* London: Longman Green Reader and Dyer, 1875. Walzer spells out his views in Walzer, *Just and Unjust Wars,* ch. 6. and especially in id., 'The Moral Standing of States: A Response to Four Critiques', *Philosophy and Public Affairs* (1980), 209–29.
13. ibid. 224.
14. See Norman, R., *Ethics, Killing and War,* Cambridge: Cambridge University Press, 1995, ch. 2.
15. Walzer, *Just and Unjust Wars,* 87.
16. Walzer, 'The Moral Standing of States', 211.
17. ibid. 214.
18. The sole exception being an intervention which balances, but does no more than balance, the prior intervention of another foreign power.
19. Gerald Doppelt makes this point: 'Walzer's Theory of Morality in International Relations,' *Philosophy and Public Affairs,* 8 (1978), 3–26, at 13.
20. Walzer, 'The Moral Standing of States', 221.
21. See Walzer, *Just and Unjust Wars,* ch. 6; id., 'The Moral Standing of States', 209–29. Interestingly, the Ancient Greeks had something of a composite conception of the conflicts that occurred between Greek city states. While those wars were clearly seen as intercommunal, they were also, in so far as they consisted in hostilities between Greeks, viewed as intra-communal. Thus different and stricter regulations pertained to conflicts between Greeks than to wars against non-Greek 'barbarians'. See Draper, G. I. A. D., 'Grotius' Place in the Development of Legal Ideas about War', in Bull, H., Kingsbury, B., and Roberts A. (eds.), *Hugo Grotius and International Relations,* Oxford: Clarendon Press, 1992: 177.
22. Linda Colley quoted in Franck, T., 'Clan and Superclan: Loyalty, Identity and Community in Law and Practice', *American Journal of International Law,* 90 (1996), 359–83, at 365.

...ghts

Davi...   ...d Philosophy at Georgetown
Univ...   ...le works in legal ethics, inter-
nati...   ...idence, among other topics. He
has ...   ...s and several books, including
Lawyers and Justice...   ...dernism *(1994)* and (with Deborah Rhode) Legal Ethics *(3rd ea., 2...*

Doctrines of just war have been formulated mainly by theologians and jurists in order to provide a canon applicable to a variety of practical situations. No doubt these doctrines originate in a moral understanding of violent conflict. The danger exists, however, that when the concepts of the theory are adopted into the usage of politics and diplomacy their moral content is replaced by definitions which are merely convenient. If that is so, the concepts of the traditional theory of just war could be exactly the wrong starting point for an attempt to come to grips with the relevant moral issues.

This is the case, I wish to argue, with the moral assessment of the justice of war (*jus ad bellum*).[1] My argument is in four parts. First I show that the dominant definition in international law is insensitive to one morally crucial dimension of politics. Secondly, I connect this argument with classical social contract theory. Thirdly, I propose an alternative definition which attempts to base itself more firmly on the moral theory of human rights. And finally, I apply this definition to two hard cases.

I

Unjust War as Aggression

International law does not speak of just or unjust war as such, but rather of legal or illegal war. For the purpose of the present discussion I shall assume that the latter distinction expresses a theory of just war and treat the two distinctions as equivalent. The alternative would be to claim that international law is simply irrelevant to the theory of just war, a claim which is both implausible and question-begging.

Several characterizations of illegal war exist in international law. The Kellogg-Briand Pact of 1928, for example, condemns any use of war as an instrument of national policy except in the case of self-defense; and Brierly maintained that it did not lapse among it signers.[2] It is a very wide criterion for unjust war—wider, it may at first appear, than the United Nations Charter, which reads:

> All members shall refrain in their international relations from the threat or use of force against the territorial integrity or political independence of any State, or in any other manner inconsistent with the purposes of the United Nations.[3]

Presumably an act of war could exist which violated neither the political independence nor the territorial integrity of any state—say, a limited sea war. Or, to take another example, two states could agree to settle an issue by fighting a series of prearranged battles with prior agreements protecting their political independence and territorial integrity. Such acts would be barred by the Kellogg-Briand Pact; whether they are prohibited by Article 2(4) depends on how one reads the phrase "inconsistent with the purposes of the United Nations." I believe that on the most plausible reading, they would be prohibited.[4] Moreover, they would most likely constitute violations of the *jus cogens,* the overriding principles of general international law.[5] Thus, Article 2(4) is in fact roughly equivalent to the Kellogg-Briand Pact.

In any case, the provisions of Article 2(4) are subsumed under the definition of aggression adopted by the UN General Assembly in 1974. It includes the clause:

> Aggression is the use of armed force by a State against the sovereignty, territorial integrity or political independence of another State, or in any other manner incon-

sistent with the Charter of the United Nations.[6]

That this is a characterization of unjust war may be seen from the fact that it terms aggression "the most serious and dangerous form of the illegal use of force."[7] The definition of aggression differs from Article 2(4) in that it includes a reference to sovereignty not present in the latter. This does not, however, mean that it is a wider characterization of unjust war than Article 2(4), for an armed attack on a state's sovereignty would be barred by the latter's catchall phrase "inconsistent with the purposes of the United Nations." Thus, the definition of aggression is not really an emendation of Article 2(4). Rather, it should be viewed as an attempt to conceptualize and label the offense at issue in Article 2(4). It attempts to give a sharp statement of principle.

Matters are further complicated by the fact that the General Assembly in 1946 adopted the Charter of the Nuremberg Tribunal as UN policy. Article 6 of this Charter includes among the crimes against peace "waging of a war of aggression or a war in violation of international treaties, agreements, or assurances. . . ."[8] This appears to be wider in scope than the definition of aggression, in that a war of aggression is only one type of criminal war. However, an argument similar to the one just given can be made here. Wars in violation of international treaties, agreements, or assurances are without question "inconsistent with the Charter of the United Nations," and hence fall under the definition of aggression; the Nuremberg Charter and the definition of aggression are thus extensionally equivalent.

It appears, then, that the definition of aggression captures what is essential in the Kellogg-Briand Pact, Article 2(4) of the UN Charter, and the relevant clause in the Nuremberg Charter. Thus, we may say that the UN position boils down to this:

(1) *A war is unjust if and only if it is aggressive.*

This gives us a characterization of unjust war, which is half of what we want. The other half emerges from Article 51 of the UN Charter:

> Nothing in the present Charter shall impair the inherent right of individual or collective self-defense if an armed attack occurs against a member of the United Nations. . . .[9]

This tells us, at least in part, what a just war is. Thus, we have

(2) *A war is just if it is a war of self-defense (against aggression).*

We note that "just" and "unjust" do not, logically speaking, exhaust the possibilities, since it is (just barely) possible that a war which is not fought in self-defense also does not threaten the sovereignty, territorial integrity, or political independence of any state, nor violate international treaties, agreements, or assurances. Now the expression "just war" suggests "permissible war" rather than "righteous war"; if so, then any war which is not specifically proscribed should be just. It is perhaps better, then, to make the two characterizations exhaustive of the possibilities. This can be done in two ways. Either (1) can be expanded to

(1′)*A war is unjust if and only if it is not just, used in conjunction with (2), or (2) can be relaxed to*

(2′)*A war is just if and only if it is not unjust, used in conjunction with (1). Overall, it appears that the conjunction of (1′) and (2), which makes every war except a war of self-defense unjust, is more in the spirit of the UN Charter than the more permissive conjunction of (1) and (2′).*

Thus, (1′) and (2) capture pretty much what we want, namely the extant conception of *jus ad bellum*. In what follows I will refer to the conjunction of (1′) and (2) as "the UN definition," although it must be emphasized that it is not formulated in these words in any United Nations document . . .

II

[Ed. Note: Most of Part II has been omitted]

The Modern Moral Reality of War

Modern international law is coeval with the rise of the European nation-state in the seventeenth and eighteenth centuries. As the term suggests, it is within the historical context of nation-states that a theory will work whose tendency is to equate the rights of nations with the rights of states. It is plausible to suggest that an attack on the French state amounts to an attack on the French nation (although even here some doubts are possible: a Paris Communard in 1871 would hardly have agreed). But when nations and states do not characteristically coincide, a theory of *jus ad bellum* which equates unjust war with aggression, and aggression with violations of state sovereignty, removes itself from the historical reality of war.

World politics in our era is marked by two phenomena: a breakup of European hegemony in the Third World which is the heritage of nineteenth-century imperialism; and maneuvering for hegemony by the (neo-imperialist) superpowers, perhaps including China. The result of this process is a political configuration in the Third World in which states and state boundaries are to an unprecedented extent the result of historical accident (how the European colonial powers parceled up their holdings) and political convenience (how the contending superpowers come to terms with each other). In the Third World the nation-state is the exception rather than the rule. Moreover, a large number of governments possess little or no claim to legitimacy. As a result of these phenomena, war in our time seems most often to be revolutionary war, war of liberation, civil war, border war between newly established states, or even tribal war, which is in fact a war of nations provoked largely by the noncongruence of nation and state.

In such circumstances a conception of *jus ad bellum* like the one embodied in the UN definition fails to address the moral reality of war. It reflects a theory that speaks to the realities of a bygone era. The result is predictable. United Nations debates—mostly ineffectual in resolving conflicts—and discussions couched in terms of aggression and defense, have deteriorated into cynical and hypocritical rhetoric and are widely recognized as such. Nor is this simply one more instance of the well-known fact that politicians lie in order to dress up their crimes in sanctimonious language. For frequently these wars are fought for reasons which are recognizably moral. It is just that their morality cannot be assessed in terms of the categories of the UN definition; it must be twisted and

distorted to fit a conceptual Procrustes' bed.

III

Human Rights and the New Definition

What, then, are the terms according to which the morality of war is to be assessed? In order to answer this question, let me return to my criticism of the contractarian derivation of the rights of states from the rights of individuals. States—patriots and Rousseau to the contrary—are not to be loved, and seldom to be trusted. They are, by and large, composed of men and women enamored of the exercise of power, men and women whose interests are consequently at least slightly at variance with those of the rest of us. When we talk of the rights of a state, we are talking of rights—"privileges" is a more accurate word—which those men and women possess over and above the general rights of man; and this is why they demand a special justification.

I have not, however, questioned the framework of individual rights as an adequate language for moral discourse. It is from this framework that we may hope to discover the answer to our question. Although I accept the vocabulary of individual rights for the purpose of the present discussion, I do not mean to suggest that its propriety cannot be questioned. Nevertheless, talk of individual rights does capture much of the moral reality of contemporary politics, as talk of sovereignty and states' rights does not. This is a powerful pragmatic reason for adopting the framework.

To begin, let me draw a few elementary distinctions. Although rights do not necessarily derive from social relations, we do not have rights apart from them, for rights are always claims on other people. If I catch pneumonia and die, my right to life has not been violated unless other humans were directly or indirectly responsible for my infection or death. To put this point in syntactic terms, a right is not to be thought of as a one-place predicate, but rather a two-place predicate whose arguments range over the class of beneficiaries and the class of obligors. A human right, then, will be a right whose beneficiaries are all humans and whose obligors are all humans in a position to effect the right. (The extension of this latter class will vary depending on the particular beneficiary.)[10] Human rights are the demands of all of humanity on all of humanity. This distinguishes human rights from, for example, civil rights, where the beneficiaries and obligors are specified by law.

By a *socially basic human right* I mean a right whose satisfaction is necessary to the enjoyment of any other rights.[11] Such rights deserve to be called "basic" because, while they are neither intrinsically more valuable nor more enjoyable than other human rights, they are means to the satisfaction of all rights, and thus they must be satisfied even at the expense of socially non-basic human rights if that is necessary. In Shue's words, "Socially basic human rights are everyone's minimum reasonable demands upon the rest of humanity." He goes on to argue that socially basic human rights include security rights—the right not to be subject to killing, torture, assault, and so on—and subsistence rights, which include the rights to healthy air and water, and adequate food, clothing, and shelter.[12]

Such rights are worth fighting for. They are worth fighting for not only by those to whom they are denied but, if we take seriously the obligation which is indicated when we speak of human rights, by the rest of us as well (although how strictly this obligation is binding on "neutrals" is open to dispute). This does not mean that any infringement of socially basic human rights is a *casus belli:* here as elsewhere in the theory of just war the doctrine of proportionality applies. But keeping this reservation in mind we may formulate the following, to be referred to henceforth as the "new definition":

(3) *A just war is (i) a war in defense of socially basic human rights (subject to proportionality); or (ii) a war of self-defense against an unjust war.*

(4) *An unjust war is (i) a war subversive of human rights, whether socially basic or not, which is also (ii) not a war in defense of socially basic human rights.*

I shall explain. The intuition here is that any proportional struggle for socially basic human rights is justified, even one which attacks the non-basic rights of others. An attack on human rights is an unjust war *unless* it is such a struggle. This is why clause (4) (ii) is necessary: without it a war could be both just and unjust. Clause (3) (ii) is meant to capture the moral core of the principle of self-defense, formulated above as (2). And it is worth noting that clause (4) (i) is an attempt to reformulate the concept of aggression as a crime against people rather than states; an aggressive war is a war against human rights. Since the rights of nations may be human rights (I shall not argue the pros or cons of this here), this notion of aggression may cover ordinary cases of aggression against nations.

Let me emphasize that (3) and (4) refer to *jus ad bellum*, not *jus in bello*. When we consider the *manner* in which wars are fought, of course, we shall always find violations of socially basic human rights. One might well wonder, in that case, whether a war can ever be justified. Nor is this wonder misplaced, for it addresses the fundamental horror of war. The answer, if there is to be one, must emerge from the doctrine of proportionality; and here I wish to suggest that the new definition is able to make sense of this doctrine in a way which the UN definition is not.[13] For the UN definition would have us measure the rights of states against socially basic human rights, and this may well be a comparison of incommensurables. Under the new definition, on the other hand, we are asked only to compare the violations of socially basic human rights likely to result from the fighting of a war with those which it intends to rectify. Now this comparison, like the calculus of utilities, might be Benthamite pie-in-the-sky; but if it is nonsense, then proportionality under the UN definition is what Bentham once called the theory of human rights: "nonsense on stilts."

IV

Two Hard Cases

The new definition differs in extension from the UN definition in two ways: on the one hand, an aggressive war may be intended to defend socially basic human rights, and thus be just according to (3); on the other, a war of self-defense may be fought in order to preserve a status quo which subverts human rights, and thus be unjust according to (4). But, I suggest, this is no objection, because (3) and (4) accord more with the moral reality of war in our time than do (1) or (1') and (2).

There are two situations which are of particular interest for the theory of *jus ad bellum* because they exhibit marked differences between the UN definition and the new definition. The first concerns a type of economic war, the second an armed intervention in a state's internal affairs.

What I have in mind in the first case is a war for subsistence. Consider this example: *A* and *B* are neighboring countries of approximately the same military capability, separated by a mountain range. *A* is bordered by the ocean and receives plentiful rainfall; however, the mountains prevent rain clouds from crossing over to *B*, which is consequently semi-arid. One year the lack of rain causes a famine in *B* which threatens millions of lives. *A,* on the other hand, has a large food surplus; but for a variety of cultural, historical, and economic reasons it makes none of this food available to *B.* Can *B* go to war with *A* to procure food?

According to the UN definition such a war would constitute an aggression, and consequently be unjust; but according to (3), since the war would be an attempt to procure socially basic human rights for *B*'s people, it would be just. Indeed, *A* is morally obligated to give food to *B,* and assuming that *B*'s sole purpose in fighting is to procure food, a defense by *A* would be an unjust war.

This, I suggest, is a position fully in accord with moral decency. Indeed, it is interesting to note that Walzer adopts a similar position, despite the fact that it runs counter to his basic argument concerning the criminality of aggression. Discussing the case of barbarian tribes who, driven west by invaders, demanded land from the Roman Empire on which to settle, Walzer quotes Hobbes with approval: "he that shall oppose himself against [those doing what they must do to preserve their own lives], for things superfluous, is guilty of the war that thereupon is to follow."[14] A fight for life is a just fight.

An important qualification must be made to this argument, however. If *A* itself has a food shortage it cannot be obligated to provide food to *B*, for its own socially basic human rights are in jeopardy. Thus *B* loses its claim against *A*. And if a third nation, *C*, can supply food to *A* or *B* but not both, it is unclear who has a right to it. Socially basic human rights can conflict, and in such cases the new definition of just war will not yield clear-cut answers. Nor, however, do we have reason to expect that clear-cut answers might exist.

There are less clear examples. What about a fight against impoverishment? In the 1960s and 1970s Great Britain and Iceland were repeatedly embroiled in a conflict over fishing grounds. This resulted in an act of war on the part of Iceland, namely, a sea attack on British ships. Of course, Iceland's belligerence may have been merely theatrical; moreover, on Iceland's interpretation of the limits of fisheries jurisdiction, she was simply defending her own right, since the British vessels were within the two-hundred mile fisheries zone claimed by Iceland. But the moral issue had to do with the fact that Iceland's economy is built around the fishing industry, and thus a threat to this industry presented a threat of impoverishment. Now no socially basic human rights are at issue here: impoverishment is not starvation. Nevertheless, there is a certain moral plausibility to the Icelanders' position, and it clearly resembles the position of country *B* in our previous example. But if we weaken the definition of unjust war to include struggles against economic collapse, the door is opened to allowing any

economic war. For example, do industrialized countries have a right to go to war for OPEC oil?

One way to handle this would be to claim that while nations have no socially basic right to any given economic level beyond subsistence, they do possess a socially basic right not to have their economic position worsened at a catastrophic rate. There is a certain plausibility to this suggestion, inasmuch as a collapsing economy will undoubtedly cause social disruption sufficient to prevent the enjoyment of other rights. The point is nevertheless debatable. Without pretending to settle it, I would, however, claim that we are now on the right moral ground for carrying out the debate, whereas a discussion couched in terms of aggression and sovereignty would miss the point completely.

The other case I wish to discuss concerns foreign intervention into a country's internal affairs. The point is that if such an intervention is on behalf of socially basic human rights it is justified according to the new definition.

Here again it will be useful to look at Walzer's position. He begins by endorsing an argument of Mill's which is based on the right of national self-determination. Mill's point is that this is a right of nations to set their own house in order *or fail to* without outside interference. If a people struggles against a dictatorship but loses, it is still self-determining; whereas if it wins due to the intervention of an outside power, its right to self-determination has been violated. Walzer admits only three exceptions: (i) a secession, when there are two or more distinct political communities contending within the same national boundary; (ii) a situation in which another foreign power has already intervened; and (iii) a situation in which human rights violations of great magnitude—massacres or enslavements—are occurring. Only in these cases may intervention be justified.[15]

Now Mill's argument employs a somewhat Pickwickian conception of self-determination. A self-determining people, it suggests, fights its own battles, even if it loses them. But then one might infer that a self-determining people fights its own wars as well, even if it loses them. Thus, a nation's conquest by a foreign power would become an instance of its self-determination.[16] Surely the fact that it is a foreign rather than a domestic oppressor is not a morally relevant factor, for that would imply that oppressions can be sorted on moral grounds according to the race or nationality of the oppressor. Yet something is clearly wrong with an argument which leads to this doublethink concept of self-determination.[17]

The problem with Mill's position is that it takes the legitimacy of states too much at face value. "Mill generally writes as if he believes that citizens get the government they deserve. . . ."[18] That is, somehow oppression of domestic vintage carries a prima facie claim to legitimacy which is not there in the case of foreign conquest. It seems that Mill suspects that the state would not be there if the people did not secretly want it. This seems to me to be an absurd, and at times even obscene view, uncomfortably reminiscent of the view that women are raped because secretly they want to be. The only argument for Mill's case, I believe, is the improbable claim that the fact that people are not engaged in active struggle against their state shows tacit consent. Even granting this, however, there remains one case in which Mill's position is unacceptable on its own terms. That is when there is overwhelming evidence that the state enjoys no legitimacy—when there is active and virtually universal struggle against it. Such struggles do not always succeed, and after each bloody suppression the possibility of another uprising grows less. Heart and flesh can bear only so much. In such a case an argument against intervention based on the people's right of self-determination is merely perverse. It makes the "self" in "self-determination" mean "other"; it reverses the role of people and state. One thinks of Brecht's poem "Die Lösung," written after the rebellion of East German workers in 1953: "After the rebellion of the seventeenth of June . . . one could read that the people had forfeited the government's confidence and could regain it only by redoubling their work efforts. Would it not be simpler for the government to dissolve the people and elect another one?"[19] I might add that in fact Walzer grants the point: "a state (or government) established against the will of its own people, ruling violently, may well forfeit its right to defend itself even against a foreign invasion."[20] Thus, it would appear that in such a case intervention is morally justified, even in the absence of massacres and slavery.

And, to make a long story short, the new definition will endorse this view. For the kind of evidence which demonstrates a government's illegitimacy must consist of highly visible signs that it does not enjoy consent, for example, open insurrection or plain repression. And this necessitates violations of security rights, which are socially basic human rights. Obedience which is not based on consent is based on coercion; thus the more obvious it is that a government is illegitimate, the more gross and widespread will its violations of security rights be, reaching even those who do not actively oppose it. This is akin to a law of nature. And thus an intervention becomes morally justified, or even morally urgent.

No definition of just war is likely to address all of the difficult cases adequately—and there is no realm of human affairs in which difficult cases are more common. Seat-of-the-pants practical judgment is a necessary supplement to one's principles in such matters: in this respect I fully agree with Walzer that "The proper method of practical morality is casuistic in character."[21] Thus, while I do not doubt that troubling examples may be brought against the new definition, it seems to me that if it corresponds with our moral judgments in a large number of actual cases, and can be casuistically stretched to address others, it serves its purpose. My claim is that, whatever its deficiencies, the new definition of *jus ad bellum* offered in (3) and (4) is superior to the existing one in this respect.

Notes

1. I follow the traditional distinction between the justice of war, that is, which side is in the right with respect to the issues over which they are fighting, and justice in war (*jus in bello*), which pertains to the way the war is fought.
2. J. L. Brierly, *The Law of Nations,* 6th ed., ed. Humphrey Waldock (Oxford: Oxford University Press, 1963), p. 409.
3. Article 2(4), quoted in Brierly, p. 415.
4. This is Brierly's claim, p. 409. The relevant Article of the Charter is I(I).
5. This point was suggested to me by Professor Boleslaw Boczek.
6. Quoted in Yehuda Melzer, *Concepts of Just War* (Leyden: A. W. Sijthoff, 1975), pp. 28–29.
7. Ibid.
8. Quoted in Ian Brownlie, *Principles of Public International Law,* 2nd ed. (Oxford: Clarendon Press, 1973), p. 545.
9. Quoted in Melzer, *Concepts of Just War,* p. 18. I have omitted a clause which does not bear on the present argument.
10. Other analyses of the concept of "human right" are possible. Walzer, for example, makes the interesting suggestion that the beneficiary of human rights is not a person but humanity itself (*Just and Unjust Wars,* p. 158). Such an analysis has much to recommend it, but it does not concern us here, for humanity will still enjoy its rights through particular men and women.
11. I take this concept from Henry Shue, "Foundations for a Balanced U.S. Policy on Human Rights: The Significance of Subsistence Rights" (College Park, Maryland: Center for Philosophy and Public Policy Working Paper HRFP-1, 1977), pp. 3–4. Shue discusses it in detail in *Basic Rights: Subsistence, Affluence, and U.S. Foreign Policy* (Princeton: Princeton University Press, in press), chap. I.
12. Ibid., pp. 3, 6–12.
13. The new definition also allows us to make sense of an interesting and plausible suggestion by Melzer, namely that a just war (in the sense of *jus ad bellum*) conducted in an unjust way (*jus in bello*) becomes unjust (*jus ad bellum*), in other words, that the *jus ad bellum* is "anchored" in the *jus in bello*. On the new definition this would follow from the fact that a war conducted in a sufficiently unjust way would violate proportionality. See Melzer, pp. 87–93.
14. Walzer, *Just and Unjust Wars,* (New York: Basic Books, 1977), p. 57. See also Charles R. Beitz, *Political Theory in International Relations* (Princeton: Princeton University Press, 1979), pp. 175–176.
15. Walzer, *Just and Unjust Wars,* pp. 87–91.
16. As Walzer expressly denies, p. 94.
17. I take Doppelt to be making a similar point when he suggests that a people can be "aggressed" against by its own state as well as by a foreign state, "Walzer's Theory," p. 8. My argument in this section is quite in sympathy with Doppelt's, pp. 10–13. Gerald Doppelt, "Walzer's Theory of Morality in International Relations," *Philosophy & Public Affairs* 8, no. 1 (Fall 1978).
18. Walzer, p. 88.
19. Quoted by Hannah Arendt, *Men in Dark Times* (New York: Harcourt, Brace and World, 1968), p. 213.
20. Walzer, *Just and Unjust Wars,* p. 82 n.
21. Ibid., p. xvi.

Justification or Excuse:
Saving Soldiers at the Expense of Civilians
(1982)

Paul Woodruff

Paul Woodruff is Darrell K. Royal Professor in Ethics and American Society at the University of Texas at Austin, where he has taught since 1973. He is known for his work on Socrates and Plato and on the "Greek Enlightenment" movement. His recent publications include On Justice, Power, and Human Nature: The Essence of Thucydides' History of the Peloponnesian War *(1993),* Early Greek Political Thought from Homer to the Sophists *(edited with Michael Gagarin, 1995), and* Reverence: Renewing a Forgotten Virtue *(2002).*

1. INTRODUCTION

When soldiers find it morally comfortable to kill civilians and the public accepts such actions easily, philosophers are inclined to ask whether their comfort and acceptance rests on a misunderstanding. If it does, then philosophy could save lives by clearing up the problem. But most recent discussion has been about the wrong issue— *whether* killing non-combatants is wrong, and if so, *why*.[1] That is all beside the point. Soldiers who kill civilians, in my experience, believe already that it is a bad thing to do. That they consider their actions at least prima facie wrong is evident from their readiness with excuses and justifications. Indeed, many of them take care to silence their consciences in advance with arguments of self-exoneration for the

wrongs they are about to commit. We may reasonably hope that these soldiers would find it harder to kill civilians without those arguments to relieve their anticipated guilt. The others, the ones who have no qualms about killing civilians, are not likely to be restrained by arguments of any kind. So a practical moral discussion of the problem should study the arguments soldiers of good character use to prepare themselves for killing civilians. The important issue is whether those arguments are sound. If they are not, so much the better. But if some of them are sound, we will need to ask what practical consequences follow from the sound ones—whether soldiers are morally free to kill civilians in certain circumstances, or whether the situation is more complicated. It may turn out, for example, that one soldier may clear himself by shifting blame to another. If so, the other may be surprised to find that he carries the burden of exoneration.

This essay addresses the following specific question: can a soldier at war clear himself of blame for killing civilians on the grounds that he does so to save his own life? Soldiers who say they can do that usually invoke the principle of self-defense, the familiar rule that justifies killing an attacker in private life under certain conditions. If they do so correctly, then their actions against civilians would be justified and therefore morally right in the last analysis. But on close examination we find that the common principle of self-defense does not apply, because the civilians in question cannot be counted as attackers under the principle. What makes the soldiers' argument persuasive is not the principle of self-defense but another very different sort of rule, the excuse of self-preservation. This has the effect of shifting moral blame from the killers to their commander, whether or not he ordered or condoned the killings, as we shall see. So the soldiers' argument succeeds as an *excuse* but not as a *justification,* and the killing of civilians in a soldier's self-defense is wrong in the final analysis. Someone, though not necessarily the killer, is to blame for it, and someone is morally obliged to prevent it.

The basis for this conclusion is a strong distinction between *justification* (which makes an action right) and *excuse* (which reduces blame for an action that is wrong). The distinction allows us to make more sophisticated final evaluations than 'right' and 'wrong.' We can say also 'wrong but excusable,' a useful epithet for actions like those atrocities of war that strike us as evil necessities, actions whose particular agents we have no wish to blame, but

actions we would nevertheless like to prevent. The practical power of this distinction, which has been neglected by philosophers, is illustrated by the result of this essay—an argument for evaluating operations orders in the light of the excuses they make available to the soldiers they govern.

A number of issues are easily confused with the one at stake here, and should be dismissed at once. (1) The argument does not help decide what should be done with soldiers who have already committed atrocities against civilians. Its interesting results are for choices about how to wage war in future. (2) It does not treat the *laws* of war or the legal definition of a war crime. (3) The argument is independent of wider moral questions about the overall justification of wars. I do not ask whether wars themselves may be justified in defense of nations, nor whether any action necessary to the defense of a nation is *ipso facto* justified. My concern is with the moral evaluation of actions taken in a war *not known to be just.* I impose that limitation because I suspect that few wars are *known* to be just.

2. INTRODUCING MILES ATROX

I shall examine the arguments of a specimen of *Miles Atrox* whom I call Miles. Let us assume Miles has certain common and highly plausible moral beliefs: (1) Killing people is ordinarily wrong, but (2) there is nothing wrong with killing (if you must) someone who attacks you. In other words (and he acknowledges this formulation as well), you have the right to kill anyone who attacks you if you must to survive his attack, but killing people in other cases violates their rights. (3) War, he thinks, is often necessary, but a very bad thing, and the less of it the better. (4) Civilians should be spared the horrors of war, in his opinion, and not harmed unless they take active part in combat. Miles adheres to these beliefs absolutely, and will not abandon them whatever the consequences. In particular, Miles' moral beliefs are the same in war as they are in other circumstances. Nevertheless, Miles would not blame a soldier in combat harshly for breaking his moral rules. It is hard, he thinks, to blame anyone for what he does in fear of his life.

Miles has massacred thousands of civilians, and is confident he has done no wrong. How can this be? It is not that Miles holds a false theory of ethics. Indeed, he knows no theory whatever about the basis of right and wrong, but like most of us draws practical consequences from unsystematic moral beliefs that are, as far as they go, unexceptionable. Where Miles goes wrong, if he goes wrong, is in applying his beliefs. It is not that he loses his head in a tight situation. Far from it. Miles is an experienced officer, cool under fire, and always has reasons for what he does. I want to consider a case in which his reason for killing civilians is the defense of himself and his unit. Miles argues that his action is justified by the principle of self-defense.

I shall argue that this is an improper use of the principle as it is commonly understood. In my argument I appeal freely to common language, common sense, and common law. I do this without apology to Miles, since his is clearly meant to be the common principle of defense, the rule that permits killing attackers but not innocent persons. I shall take 'innocent' here to mean 'not an attacker' and devote the core of this paper to an explication of the relevant sense of 'attacker.' It turns out that the civilians Miles killed were not attack-

ers in the sense required by the principle of defense.

3. THE SITUATION

Miles is pilot and aircraft commander of an armed reconnaissance helicopter ('hunter-killer'). His mission is to search for and destroy enemy units moving at night, and to defend his aircraft and crew against all attacks. He is instructed to fly low over areas in which the enemy operates, so as to draw fire and thereby to locate the enemy. He is also instructed to return fire immediately when fired upon.

Miles often kills harmless civilians while carrying out his mission. Here is a typical case. Flying low at night over an area densely populated by civilians known to be neutral or friendly (and in either case harmless), he thinks he sees tracer ammunition coming towards him from the ground. Believing that he is under fire, he smothers the ground beneath him with incendiary rockets. It turns out that the ground is a village guarded by friendly militia, and that he has burned the village, killing or maiming a number of civilians. Subsequent investigation fails to determine who fired the offending shot or why he fired it, and does not confirm Miles' contention that he was under fire. If there was an attack, it appears the village was not involved.[2]

Miles argues that he has done no wrong. He acted in self-defense against what appeared to be an attack. If he had not countered immediately, he might have been shot down. It was not safe to take evasive action, or to wait to ascertain his location or the origin of the fire threatening him. He could not tell in the darkness whether the shots came from the forest or the village, and even if he could have told the difference, he could not be absolutely sure that the village did not harbor an enemy. Miles is not sorry about the civilian casualties. They were unavoidable accidents of war. They may even have a salutory effect, in deterring civilians from letting people shoot at helicopters from their village.

Miles' argument raises these questions about the principle of self-defense:

(a) *Does the principle justify killing non-attacking bystanders to repel an attack?*

(b) *Does the principle justify killing persons to deter an attack?*

(c) *If one places oneself in danger of an attack, by inviting or provoking it, does the principle justify killing the attacker in order to survive that attack?*

To answer these questions we need to examine the common views—to which Miles subscribes—about the rights and wrongs of repelling attacks. Under examination, Miles reveals two deep-seated convictions:

(1) *It is not wrong to kill someone who attacks you, if you must do so to save your life from that attack.*

(2) *It is wrong to blame a person fully for anything he must do to save his own life.*

I shall distinguish these convictions by calling them the principles of self-defense and self-preservation respectively. They represent different kinds of exculpation, and we shall need to persuade Miles not to confuse them.

4. TWO KINDS OF EXCULPATION[3]

Miles' acknowledged beliefs presuppose a distinction. Though (as he thinks) killing human beings is generally wrong, there are two sorts of circumstances in which he would withhold blame from a killer:

Justification. Sometimes, Miles thinks the killer had a right to kill (as in self-defense), and so did nothing wrong in killing.

Excuse. In other cases Miles thinks that the killing was wrong, but does not blame the killer for it (or reduces the blame due him) for such reasons as these: (1) He may sympathize with him, thinking his action natural in the circumstances (if the killer were in a state of panic, for example). (2) He may hold someone else responsible for the killing (as when someone is forced to kill by an evil master). An excuse must be in proportion to the wrong it is supposed to cover; he thinks of the circumstances cited in the excuse as balancing the wrong. The distinction Miles presupposes is rooted in common usage and reflected in common law. It is, however, often blurred, so we must state it clearly.

The chief difference between justification and excuse is this: You cannot be excused for an action unless there is something wrong with it; but if an action is justified, in the final analysis there is *nothing* wrong with it, though we would not justify an action unless it seemed wrong or belonged to a type that is generally wrong. A successful excuse for wrongdoing shows that an agent should not be blamed for what he did; the justification of an action shows that, appearances to the contrary, it is right. Of course, an action may be justified and still not be the best thing to do in the circumstances. It is faint praise to say of someone that he was within his rights; and there is a sort of blame reserved for those whose actions are justified but not, for example, generous or merciful. But we are not concerned in this essay with that sort of blame. Principles of justification do not discriminate between actions presumed to be right; similarly, it is not a principle of justification that tells us to choose the better of two actions presumed to be wrong. For even a lesser wrong cannot be chosen with justification. A justification does not, strictly speaking, admit that there is anything wrong in the final analysis with what it justifies. Suppose a wicked tyrant orders you to murder a man who has not attacked anyone. If you fail, he threatens, he will kill a family of five. Suppose that you attribute to such persons the right to life. Then you would be mistaken if you argued that the family's danger *justified* your murder of the one; for neither the tyrant's threat, nor the family's need, vitiates that man's right to life. If you kill him, however, you are a candidate for excuse. If the threatened family is your wife and children, then your excuse might exonerate you completely. Of course, you will think differently if you deny the man's right to life in these circumstances. But that has two unfortunate consequences. First, after the killing we will have little with which to reproach the tyrant if the victim's rights were not violated. Second, tyrants will have the power by issuing such threats to negative a person's moral rights. Since Miles has no wish to deny the right to life of such a person, we need not argue the point anyway.

Miles may not agree that I have correctly stated the distinction he presupposes. He might argue that if you are fully excused for an action, your action is not wrong. It means nothing, he might say, to call an action wrong unless you are prepared to blame the person who did it. But there are excellent reasons for speaking as I do about excuses. If you repeat an action covered by an excuse, you may wear out your excuse. But it is not so with justification. For example, it is an excuse that you acted to save your life. But the more people you kill under that excuse, the worse; so it must have been wrong on the first occasion. On the other hand, you are justified in killing your attacker to save your life, and that goes for any number of attackers. So it is important to keep in mind that a fully excusable act remains wrong.

Miles' argument confuses justification with excuse by applying simultaneously the principles of defense and self-preservation to the same case. His amalgam of the two principles lets him think he can justify killing civilians when he is under attack by someone else. But we shall see that the principle of defense does not apply at all to Miles' situation, and that the principle of self-preservation does not *justify* Miles' action. However, the weaker principle yields a surprising result—it shifts the burden of argument from Miles to his superior.

5. DEFENSE

We must not let Miles' tendency to excuse acts of self-preservation obscure his other principles: that it is ordinarily wrong to kill human beings, but that it is not wrong to do so when you are under attack and have good reason to think you can survive only by killing your attacker. Miles' belief on this point is common, and is represented in the common law.

We have been calling this the principle of *self*-defense, but it is merely a special case of the more general principle of defense. To defend under the wider rule, you do not need to be under attack yourself. The violent defense of any innocent victim is justified if it is necessary to save the victim's life. This also is generally recognized in law and morality.

The principle of defense is not a special case of the excuse of self-preservation. (1) The principle of defense is stronger, in that it claims to exculpate completely in every case to which it applies. Like all excuses, the excuse of self-preservation carries more weight in some of the situations in which it applies than it does in others. (2) The principle of defense does not discriminate among victims; but the excuse of self-preservation draws some of its force from the idea that saving one*self* from danger is naturally irresistable. (3) The principle of defense depends on a distinction that makes no difference to the principle of self-preservation—the distinction between attacker and innocent person. The principle of defense is good only for acts against *attackers,* whereas the principle of self-preservation applies indifferently to acts reasonably deemed necessary for the survival of the agent, and so may extend to acts against the innocent. (If you must kill innocent persons to survive an attack, your attacker is responsible, as we shall see. . . . But you are not *justified* in doing so. And it would be better [though supererogatory] for you not to kill the innocent persons in the first place.[4])

To describe the moral difference between innocent and attacker, it helps to translate 'wrong' as 'violation of a moral claim.' Then, since it is usually wrong to kill people, we can say that humans usually have moral claims over one another that their lives be respected. Unless he attacks you, a person generally keeps intact his claim on you. To kill an innocent (non-attacking) person, therefore, would be to transgress a moral claim and could not be justified. For nothing wrong is justifiable. But when an attacker attacks, he cuts the ground from under his claims over the person he attacks in so far as he makes it necessary for that person to kill him to survive.

Whether this is really so, and why it is so if it is, are questions we need not an-

swer here. Our question is whether the principle of defense warrants Miles' conclusion. To answer that, we need to say what it is to be an attacker; for our purposes that is to say what it is to endanger someone's life in such a way as to give him the right to kill you. Is an attacker anyone who endangers another's life? Or must one be guilty of something to be an attacker?

Clearly, an attacker endangers his victim's life by performing an act. Can we stop there, or must we go on to ask whether the victim has good reason to believe that the supposed attacker is *responsible* for endangering the victim's life? Suppose I induce my enemy under hypnosis to attack me, in the hope that I may kill him with the justification of self-defense. Or suppose I booby-trap my room for the same purpose, so that his turning a light switch would kill me. In neither case would it be justifiable for me to kill my enemy in self-defense, apparently because *I* am responsible, not he, for the danger to my life. So we cannot escape the issue of responsibility for endangerment.

On the other hand, you are not required to find your attacker *guilty* before you kill him. If you were, you would not be justified in saving yourself from attacks by a lunatic, or a child, or by a person who thought you were someone else. Killing in self-defense is not justified as punishment; if it were you would be justified in killing your attacker whether or not it were necessary to save your life. But according to the principle of defense, you may kill your attacker *only* if you have good reason to believe it necessary to do so to save your life from his attack. So the attacker does not need to satisfy the conditions that justify punishment; he need not be guilty of anything. However, he must be causally responsible by some act for endangering your life. To understand the principle of defense, we need a sense of 'causally responsible' not so narrow as 'guilty,' but narrow enough to exclude such innocent attackers as the one hyponotized by his victim.

A person is causally responsible by an act for anything caused by that act, unless another's responsibility supervenes. We need to distinguish between an attack and an innocent act necessary to the success of someone else's attack. Consider the case of the devious attacker. He leads you to a crowded field where an Olympic competition is in progress. At the crucial moment he pushes you into the path of a pole-vaulter. You are hemmed in by the crowd and will surely be impaled and killed unless you stop the jumper, who is so intent on his goal that he does not see you. You can stop him by shooting him with a heavy pistol. But would you be justified? Surely not on the grounds that he had attacked you. In such a case it will do you no good to kill your devious attacker. The jumper seems not to be an attacker at all; between you and him occur conditions that warrant no more than the excuse of self-preservation. In such a situation a pair of people, through no fault of either, face a danger that no more than one of them can survive. Of course, if you *do* shoot the jumper, your devious attacker will be responsible, in as much as your shooting is a natural response to his putting you in danger. His being responsible is a powerful excuse for you, but it does not put you in the right; it does not undercut the jumper's claim on you that you respect his life. That claim you would violate, and so you would do wrong in circumstances that incline us to excuse you. It is worse if you put yourself in danger. Then you make the excuse of self-preservation hollow indeed. Suppose you trip and fall in the jumper's path, or suppose you arrive at that point while

crossing the field in a straight line as part of your initiation into a secret society. In those cases you alone are causally responsible for your plight; no one has by endangering you given up his claim that you respect his life.

Your attacker by the principle of defense, then, is any person who performs an act necessary to your being in danger *unless:*

(i) The supposed attacker puts you in danger without knowledge or intent *and* there is another person who has acted or is acting with the intent to put you in that danger, the latter act being necessary for that danger to you. (This excludes as innocent anyone whose acts are, without his knowledge, part of a devious plan of attack.)

(ii) The supposed attacker puts you in danger without knowledge or intent, and you put yourself into that danger with or without knowledge or intent. (So no one who unintentionally contributed to your endangering yourself counts as your attacker. Of course, he may still be answerable to you for damages, if he is negligent for example; but that is another matter.)

These two exclusions reflect the general principle that the chain of responsibility linking a person with unintended or unforeseen consequences of his actions is cut if someone else intervenes (with knowledge and intent) to bring about those consequences.[5] The same consideration is part of the grounds for the last exclusion:

(iii) You knowingly and intentionally put yourself in danger, whether or not the supposed attacker acts with knowledge or intent, *unless* you do so as a necessary response to his attack on a person (or perhaps on a person's rights). This excludes from attacker status, for example, anyone who joins you in a dangerous fight you helped to start. Obviously you cannot acquire the *right* to kill your enemy by starting or even joining with him in mortal combat, unless you do so in defense of someone, or perhaps of someone's rights. Much hangs on what it is to put yourself in danger. Acting routinely or exercising one's rights in the face of an unusual threat should not count as putting yourself in danger.

More conditions are necessary for a complete account of what it is to be an attacker. We want to exclude one who endangers another by accident, and not to admit without qualification one who does so by negligence. But precision on those matters is beyond the scope of this paper.

We are now able to make clear the intuitive distinction between *attacker* and *innocent* needed for the principle of defense. In those terms the distinction is misleading, for 'innocent' would seem to mean either 'guiltless' or 'harmless.' But the attacker need not be guilty (he could be a child) and the non-attacker need not be harmless (he could be like the pole-vaulter). In fact, 'innocent' in this context means 'not-an-attacker' in the sense of 'attacker' just elucidated. . . .

A surprising consequence of this is that it is a confusion to justify killing enemy soldiers generally in a war *simply* by citing the principle of defense. You need to show, for that justification, not only that the enemies bring your life into danger, but also that you yourself are not causally responsible for that danger. If you provoke or invite an attack by being dangerous to the enemy (and most soldiers are dangerous to their enemies at war[6]) then by Condition (iii) . . . you are not entitled to justify your defense under the principle we have discussed. So the principle of defense cannot ground the moral distinction between soldiers (who may be killed) and civilians (who may not). My argument is thus open to the objection that it undercuts the very moral distinction it seeks to uphold. . . .

Now that we know roughly what Miles' principle of defense says, we can turn to the question of whether it warrants his conclusion. Let us consider the three practical questions his argument raised.

(a) *Does the principle of defense justify killing non-attacking bystanders to repel an attack?*

Obviously not. The principle commits Miles to considering attackers in a special light. If he does that, he cannot use the principle to justify killing villagers who attacked no one. . . . An attack involves action of some kind, and the villagers took no action in connection with the attack on Miles. True, they failed to prevent the attack. But that does not appear to be an action. If they had (contrary to the hypothesis) invited the attackers to work from their village, then they would seem to be attackers as well.[7]

(b) *Does the principle justify killing persons to deter an attack?*

Miles supposes that other villagers will be frightened by the example of the innocents he has killed, and take care in the future that no attacks be made from their village on aircraft such as Miles'. So far, Miles is right. But he tries to justify his killing of innocents on the grounds that he has the right to defend himself against attack by any means necessary, and that deterrence is necessary to his defense.

The principle of defense cannot be stretched so far. It justifies only so much killing of attackers as is necessary for survival from their attack. But a principle licensing deterrence would justify any amount of killing; and of innocents as well as attackers. So that could not be the principle of defense.

(c) *If one places himself in danger of an attack, by inviting it or provoking it, can he justify killing the attacker by the principle of defense?*

Again, the answer is negative. Miles flew an armed aircraft within range of his enemy in order to search them out and kill them. If the enemy responded with a pre-emptive attack, Miles is responsible for his own plight, and cannot consider the enemy his attacker under the principle of defense. If he really cared to avoid danger he would have refused the mission, or flown at a safe altitude. . . .

But Miles is not completely in the wrong. Though his plea of self-defense does him no good as such, it points to a sound excuse he may make for himself: that he acted to save his own life. That excuse is really what gave an air of plausibility to his initial plea. We need to explicate the principle of self-preservation to see how much good it does him, and whether it has practical consequences for us.

6. SELF-PRESERVATION

The desire to go on living is strong in us, so strong that under great pressure we find ourselves trying to survive in ways that are not compatible with the principles we cling to in ordinary circumstances. This is so familiar a fact about human character that the common law counts acts of self-preservation among those natural occurrences that do *not* negative responsibility when they come between another person's act and its consequences.[8] For example, if you put me in a small boat with a valuable cargo and cast me adrift in heavy seas, and I must jettison the cargo to survive, you are responsible for the loss of the cargo and I am excused. My action (though voluntary in a sense) does not break the causal chain between you and the loss of the cargo.

It is another matter if you cast me adrift with a third person, and I must jettison her to survive. For me to take a life to save mine is bad and selfish; nevertheless you are responsible for the drowning of whichever of us drowns, and the blame due the survivor is reduced accordingly. (From fear of sanctioning homicide, we hesitate to say how far the survivor's blame is reduced.) This variation in the example illustrates the point that there is a limit to how far an excuse can be stretched. I can expect to be excused for drowning a cargo, and to be partially excused for drowning a person. But if I drown every passenger of the Queen Elizabeth to survive, I must expect to be considered a monster of selfishness. Of course I may undercut the excuse by my own action. If *I* set out in heavy seas with the cargo, and I am forced to jettison it, then I am responsible for its loss. The same goes for the case of the drowned person. I cannot reduce the blame due me for drowning him by causing a situation in which I must drown him to survive.

To see how the principle applies to Miles we must disentangle the web of responsibility for Miles' being in a situation in which he had reason to believe that he had to kill civilians in order to survive. Miles knew that such a situation was likely to occur if he carried out his mission. Yet he did so voluntarily; so it would seem that he has undercut his excuse.

But on this charge Miles can appeal to the further excuse that he was acting under orders which he was bound to obey. We can expect him to refuse to obey direct orders to commit obvious atrocities; but it is not fair to expect him to refuse a legal recon mission. Neither the courts nor the public would accept Miles' plea that the danger to civilians made void his oath to obey. So Miles' excuse passes responsibility for his atrocities on to whoever decided to give him the dangerous mission. Miles' commander bears the blame not because he ordered Miles to kill civilians (he did not)—but because he sent Miles on a mission in which civilian casualties were quite likely to follow from Miles' natural attempts to save his own life.

7. CONSEQUENCES: THE BURDEN OF PREVENTION

If Miles' excuse is sound, then the burden of preventing such incidents would fall on Miles' commander. To see why this is reasonable, imagine that the surviving villagers gather on the morning after the disaster to petition against further destruction of their village. To whom should they go?

To Miles? But surely they cannot expect him to break his oath and ruin his career by not carrying out plainly legal orders for recon missions. Nor can they expect him to give up his life on the chance that there are civilians below him.

To the commander of the troops opposing Miles? If a member of his command had fired at Miles, he must share the blame for the burning of the village. The enemy commander can insure that attacks on aircraft are not made from villages, and he has a responsibility to do so. But the present case could have occurred without enemy action, for we do not know who, if anyone, fired the shot Miles reported. So although it is worthwhile asking the enemy commander, his action alone cannot save the village from people like Miles.

To Miles' commander? That is the best course. He can and should alter Miles' orders in such a way that he will not court attack from populated areas, by cancelling the mission or forbidding Miles to fly below a safe altitude. He should have known the cost of the orders he gave Miles in burnt villages, and so must bear part of the blame, and apparently *keep* it, for none of the excuses we accept from Miles apply to his case. He was not in danger, nor was he acting under direct orders. If he can defend his conduct at all, he must do so by pleading the military utility of Miles' mission. He might make a case that he cannot win the war without such tactics, and argue that what justifies the war justifies whatever must be done to win it. But that sort of argument is incompatible with Miles' absolute position on homicide, and we need not discuss it here.[9]

Our conclusion was that though killing the civilians was wrong (because not a true case of self-defense), Miles was to be excused for doing it, and the blame passed on to his commander. It follows that unless the commander can defend his practice in some way not envisaged, he is morally obliged to stop sending his troops on missions that endanger civilians in the way Miles' reconnaissance did. That is a significant result; if the commander held Miles' mistaken view about self-defense, he would not think the killing was wrong, and consequently could not consider himself responsible for any wrongdoing. If he recognized that the principle of defense did not apply to Miles' sort of case, we can hope he would act differently in future. So although we have found nothing helpful to tell Miles himself, we have identified a mistake about self-defense, a mistake that has no doubt contributed to civilian casualties in war.

Notes

1. The chief contributions of this kind are: G.E.M. Anscombe, 'War and Murder,' in *Nuclear Weapons: A Catholic Response,* ed. Walter Stein (New York 1961); Thomas Nagel, 'War and Massacre,' *Philosophy and Public Affairs* **1** (1971–72) 123–44; the discussions of Nagel's essay by R. B. Brandt (ibid., 145–65) and R.M. Hare (ibid., 166–81); and George I. Mavrodes, 'Conventions and the Morality of War,' *Philosophy and Public Affairs* **4** (1974–75) 117–31.

    Recently there has been a debate over whether the rule against killing civilians can be based on the principle of self-defense: Robert K. Fullinwider, 'War and Innocence,' *Philosophy and Public Affairs* **5** (1975–76), 90–7; and Lawrence A. Alexander, 'Self-Defense and the Killing of Noncombatants: A Reply to Fullinwider,' *Philosophy and Public Affairs* **5** (1975–76) 408–15.

    In this essay I use 'civilians' as a synonym for 'non-combatants,' and make no effort to solve the problem of saying exactly what it is to be a civilian, since, in the sort of case I discuss, no one would question the civilian status of the victims.

2. Based loosely on a case investigated by the author in Chau Doc Province in 1970.

3. The distinction I make here entered philosophical discussion with J.L. Austin's 'A Plea for Excuses,' *Proceedings of the Aristotelian Society,* **57** (1956–57) 1–30. I do not fully agree with Austin's use of the relevant terms, but there is not space here to discuss my disagreement.

4. Lawrence Alexander's principle of self-defense is an ingenious combination of the principles of defense and preservation. It permits you to kill anyone (attacker or not) whom you must to save your life, but enjoins you (in effect) to prefer killing attackers over innocents. This is probably good advice but not the principle of defense, for that has always been held to apply only in cases of attack. However much, for example, a fetus endangers the life of the woman who carries it, the woman cannot justify destroying the fetus by the principle of defense. For she is not under attack by the fetus. I owe the point to Baruch A. Brody, 'Abortion and the Sanctity of Human Life,' *American Philosophical quarterly,* **10** (1973) 133–40.

5. Cf. H.L.A. Hart and A.M. Honoré, *Causation in the Law* (Oxford: Clarendon Press 1959) 128ff.

6. See Appendix, note 13. Genuine cases of self-defense certainly do occur in combat, and justify both carrying weapons and using them. The point is that they are not sufficiently the rule to allow the principle of defense to generate our conventional soldier-civilian distinction.

7. The not-quite-innocent bystander presents us with a practical paradox, however, which cannot be resolved by the principle of defense. See my article, 'The Bystander Paradox,' *Analysis,* **37** (1977) 74–8.

8. See Hart and Honoré, 135 and 296, where they classify acts of self-preservation as non-voluntary conduct that does not negative causal connection either in criminal law or in the law of torts.

9. Historical note: after a number of actions like Miles' against Chau Doc Province, Vietnam, in 1970, local authorities made representations to both sides. To the credit of all concerned, in one instance the enemy ceased to launch attacks from villages, and in the other the U.S. commander ordered missions such as Miles' to be flown at a higher, safer altitude.

PART III
RECENT APPLICATIONS

A. Terrorism

To paraphrase the Supreme Court's discussion of pornography, while we might not be able to provide a clear definition of terrorism, we know it when we see it. Or, at least we *seem* to know it. Terrorism has been on the minds of people around the world for decades, if not centuries, but has become of utmost concern for Americans following the events of September 11th, 2001. While the use of the term terrorism has its historical origins in the French Revolution as a description of the actions of the French government against its own people, it has been primarily used in the recent past to describe the violent activities of labor organizations, anarchists, nationalist groups, minority political organizations, and religious movements. At the turn of the century, terrorism most frequently referred to the acts of non-state agents (individually or collectively) acting against another group, be it a government, a multinational corporation, or a dominant religious hierarchy. But the practical problems of providing an appropriate definition of terrorism are precisely the sort of crucial philosophical issues that are on the table. The articles in this section tackle some of the crucial questions present in philosophical discussions of terrorism, including how to define terrorist acts, whether terrorism can ever be practiced in light of a Just War framework, and whether terrorists, by definition, are indiscriminate in their choice of targets.

In "Terrorism: A Critique of Excuses," Michael Walzer characterizes terrorists as people who attack individuals who belong to a certain group, attempting to make public a larger social or political message by bringing terror to the larger populace. These attacks are indiscriminate in that they broadly target a certain class or group. For Walzer, terrorism is wrong because it involves an attack on innocent parties, it is deliberate, and the terrorists are rational in their choice of targets. The advocates of terrorism can offer, at best, only unconvincing excuses for their actions: It is a last resort; it is the only option when facing far more powerful states; it is the most effective method available; or that it is simply the method secretly adopted by all states and, as such, is a universally recognized form of response. Walzer argues that terrorism must be resisted at all costs, but its opponents must not use terrorism as a method of resistance. All retaliation must be aimed at the terrorists themselves, and not at the people they claim to represent. And, despite the terrorist's methods, if the terrorists do draw attention to genuine cases of oppression, the opponents of terrorism should work diligently to eliminate this oppression wherever it occurs.

Contrary to Walzer's claims, Robert Fullinwider argues in "Understanding Terrorism" that terrorists are often quite discriminating in their choice of targets. They do not consider the groups they target to be innocent noncombatants, as Walzer does. So, says Fullinwider, either Walzer's simple definition begs the question of terrorism or more work needs to be done to show that the actions of specific terrorist groups are indiscriminate and aimed at the innocent. The problem with Walzer's definition seems to be that it has failed to do the required work to show that the actions of terrorists are, in fact, morally wrong. Fullinwider points out that in many cases, terrorists are not acting *immorally* in resorting to what he calls the "irregular justice" of terrorism, but are instead appealing to the highest level of justice, to morality itself. While we might not want to see this sort of freelance justice on a regular basis, Fullinwider points out that we often sympathize with those whose moral concerns are so intense that they would lead a person to take drastic and violent action in the name of justice. Ultimately, Fullinwider thinks that Walzer's blanket condemnation of terrorism deliberately refuses to understand the terrorist mind. Terrorists can attempt to defend their actions in light of an existing unjust system of law or social practice, or in view of a broader notion of "guilt" and "innocence." We are free, of course, to challenge these, and other, defenses of terrorism, but we must take the time to consider them *as defenses* (rather than as excuses, as Walzer argues) before we can make our final moral evaluation of terrorism.

Andrew Valls tackles the issue of terrorism by more directly addressing the standard criteria for *jus ad bellum* (who carries out the terrorist act and why) and how the acts might be evaluated in light of the Just War tradition. He begins by challenging Walzer's claims in *Just and Unjust Wars* that the bombing of German cities (and the intentional targeting of German civilians) was justified, while a similar act performed by a non-state actor (e.g., a member of a stateless nation) would be unjustified.[1] This distinction strikes Valls as a double standard, giving certain liberties to nations or states while withholding them from non-state actors, and Valls thinks that consistency must be demanded in all evaluation of violent action. If the criteria for the deliberate Allied bombing of German civilians can be defended, then we must be able to apply those same criteria to non-state actors in similar situations. As such, Valls provides a definition of terrorism that focuses on the non-state actors by saying that terrorism is "violence committed by non-state actors against persons or property for political purposes." He then moves through the standard criteria for a Just War; just cause, legitimate authority, right intention, last resort, probability of success, and proportionality, and argues that some acts of terrorism, even under his stipulated definition can meet all of the criteria of *jus ad bellum.* He then moves on to the greater challenge of showing that terrorism can also meet the requirements of *jus in bello,* or how the armed action is carried out. Valls argues that terrorism can meet the challenges of proportionality and discrimination by invoking the doctrine of double effect and making explicit the claim that innocents may be killed so long as they are not *the targets* of the terrorist attacks. He concludes by noting that most terrorist acts do not satisfy all of the Just War criteria and should therefore be morally condemned, but his view allows at least the possibility of a justified terrorist attack under the rubric of Just War Theory.

Joseph Boyle's contribution to this section, "Just War Doctrine and the Military Response to Terrorism," also approaches terrorism from the perspective of what he calls "traditional" Just War Theory, but his argument is aimed in a different direction: Where Valls argues for the possibility of a justified terrorist action, Boyle argues for the right of a polity to defend itself against terrorist attack by groups that are usually not polities themselves. For Boyle, a "war on terrorism" is a perfectly coherent statement.

Boyle begins by offering his own definition of terrorism. Where a more traditional military action seeks to overwhelm and displace an enemy by overpowering force, terrorism is the use of violent action that is intended to influence decisions, to cause fear and demoralize the population, and to lead to changes in policy rather than changes in polity. Mere acts of destruction for its own sake with no attempt to influence decision making may cause terror, but these are not the core cases of terrorism with which Boyle is concerned. For Boyle, terrorism is wrong because those agents who perform the terrorist acts seek to affect the decision making of others by directly or indirectly harming individuals whom they have no right to harm. For the most part, the targets of the terrorist actions are, in the relevant sense, "innocent." Even if non-innocents (the leaders if the oppressive enemy regime, for instance) are killed in terrorist attacks, there is no justification to be offered: Members of the oppressive regime may be killed in defense but never merely as a means of causing fear and influencing the sentiments of the public. When persons intentionally harm someone that they have no right to harm in order to enable a change in policy or public opinion, they have performed an act of terrorism.

Boyle then moves through a discussion of the conditions for *jus ad bellum* with an emphasis on what he calls "the traditional just war theory." He explores the requirements of proper authority, just cause, and right intention, and gives a clear explication of how these requirements are met in most cases of a just war. He then moves on to apply these requirements to the very specific case of a polity responding to terrorist attacks against its own people. Although there are difficulties for each of the requirements, including the problem of making war against a frequently stateless enemy, the problem of national sovereignty involved in crossing borders to apprehend or eliminate terrorists, and the problem of making certain the response to terrorism is rightly intended (and not simply a matter of payback or vengeance), Boyle thinks the *jus ad bellum* requirements can be met by a polity in some cases as a response to terrorism.

All four of the essays in this section highlight the various difficulties involved in the moral evaluation of terrorism, including the problem of definition, the challenge of fitting acts of terrorism into the Just War tradition, and the difficulties of battling an enemy that may not be a sovereign nation. Given the realities of the post-9/11 world, a world of color-coded terror warnings and armed marshals on airliners, it seems that getting a firm philosophical grip on the morality of terrorism is necessary and crucial.

Note

1. Michael Walzer, *Just and Unjust Wars: A Moral Argument with Historical Illustrations* (2nd ed.) (New York: Basic Books, 1992).

Terrorism: A Critique of Excuses

(1988)

Michael Walzer

Michael Walzer is the UPS Foundation Professor in the Institute for Advanced Study at Princeton University. He has written on a broad variety of topics in political theory and moral philosophy, including political obligation, war, nationalism and ethnicity, and economic justice. His books include Just and Unjust Wars *(Basic Books, 1977),* Spheres of Justice *(Basic Books, 1983), and* On Toleration *(Yale University Press, 1997).*

No one these days advocates terrorism, not even those who regularly practice it. The practice is indefensible now that it has been recognized, like rape and murder, as an attack upon the innocent. In a sense, indeed, terrorism is worse than rape and murder commonly are, for in the latter cases the victim has been chosen for a purpose; he or she is the direct object of attack, and the attack has some reason, however twisted or ugly it may be. The victims of a terrorist attack are third parties, innocent bystanders; there is no special reason for attacking them; anyone else within a large class of (unrelated) people will do as well. The attack is directed indiscriminately against the entire class. Terrorists are like killers on a rampage, except that their rampage is not just expressive of rage or madness; the rage is purposeful and programmatic. It aims at a general vulnerability: Kill these people in order to terrify those. A relatively small number of dead victims makes for a very large number of living and frightened hostages.

This, then, is the peculiar evil of terrorism—not only the killing of innocent people but also the intrusion of fear into everyday life, the violation of private purposes, the insecurity of public spaces, the endless coerciveness of precaution. A crime wave might, I suppose, produce similar effects, but no one plans a crime wave; it is the work of a thousand individual decisionmakers, each one independent of the others, brought together only by the invisible hand. Terrorism is the work of visible hands; it is an organizational project, a strategic choice, a conspiracy to murder and intimidate . . . you and me. No wonder the conspirators have difficulty defending, in public, the strategy they have chosen.

The moral difficulty is the same, obviously, when the conspiracy is directed not against you and me but against *them*—Protestants, say, not Catholics; Israelis, not Italians or Germans; blacks, not whites. These "limits" rarely hold for long; the logic of terrorism steadily expands the range of vulnerability. The more hostages they hold, the stronger the terrorists are. No one is safe once whole populations have been put at risk. Even if the risk were contained, however, the evil would be no different. So far as individual Protestants or

297

Israelis or blacks are concerned, terrorism is random, degrading, and frightening. That is its hallmark, and that, again, is why it cannot be defended.

But when moral justification is ruled out, the way is opened for ideological excuse and apology. We live today in a political culture of excuses. This is far better than a political culture in which terrorism is openly defended and justified, for the excuse at least acknowledges the evil. But the improvement is precarious, hard won, and difficult to sustain. It is not the case, even in this better world, that terrorist organizations are without supporters. The support is indirect but by no means ineffective. It takes the form of apologetic descriptions and explanations, a litany of excuses that steadily undercuts our knowledge of the evil. Today that knowledge is insufficient unless it is supplemented and reinforced by a systematic critique of excuses. That is my purpose in this chapter. I take the principle for granted: that every act of terrorism is a wrongful act. The wrongfulness of the excuses, however, cannot be taken for granted; it has to be argued. The excuses themselves are familiar enough, the stuff of contemporary political debate. I shall state them in stereotypical form. There is no need to attribute them to this or that writer, publicist, or commentator; my readers can make their own attributions.[1]

THE EXCUSES FOR TERRORISM

The most common excuse for terrorism is that it is a last resort, chosen only when all else fails. The image is of people who have literally run out of options. One by one, they have tried every legitimate form of political and military action, exhausted every possibility, failed everywhere, until no alternative remains but the evil of terrorism. They must be terrorists or do nothing at all. The easy response is to insist that, given this description of their case, they should do nothing at all; they have indeed exhausted their possibilities. But this response simply reaffirms the principle, ignores the excuse; this response does not attend to the terrorists' desperation. Whatever the cause to which they are committed, we have to recognize that, given the commitment, the one thing they cannot do is "nothing at all."

But the case is badly described. It is not so easy to reach the "last resort." To get there, one must indeed try everything (which is a lot of things) and not just once, as if a political party might organize a single demonstration, fail to win immediate victory, and claim that it was now justified in moving on to murder. Politics is an art of repetition. Activists and citizens learn from experience, that is, by doing the same thing over and over again. It is by no means clear when they run out of options, but even under conditions of oppression and war, citizens have a good run short of that. The same argument applies to state officials who claim that they have tried "everything" and are now compelled to kill hostages or bomb peasant villages. Imagine such people called before a judicial tribunal and required to answer the question, What exactly did you try? Does anyone believe that they could come up with a plausible list? "Last resort" has only a notional finality; the resort to terror is ideologically last, not last in an actual series of actions, just last for the sake of the excuse. In fact, most state officials and movement militants who recommend a policy of terrorism recommend it as a first resort; they are for it from the beginning, although they may not get their way at the beginning. If they are honest, then, they must make other excuses and give up the pretense of the last resort.

The second excuse is designed for national liberation movements struggling against established and powerful states. Now the claim is that nothing else is possible, that no other strategy is available except terrorism. This is different from the first excuse because it does not require would-be terrorists to run through all the available options. Or, the second excuse requires terrorists to run through all the options in their heads, not in the world; notional finality is enough. Movement strategists consider their options and conclude that they have no alternative to terrorism. They think that they do not have the political strength to try anything else, and thus they do not try anything else. Weakness is their excuse.

But two very different kinds of weakness are commonly confused here: the weakness of the movement vis-à-vis the opposing state and the movement's weakness vis-à-vis its own people. This second kind of weakness, the inability of the movement to mobilize the nation, makes terrorism the "only" option because it effectively rules out all the others: nonviolent resistance, general strikes, mass demonstrations, unconventional warfare, and so on.

These options are only rarely ruled out by the sheer power of the state, by the pervasiveness and intensity of oppression. Totalitarian states may be immune to nonviolent or guerrilla resistance, but all the evidence suggests that they are also immune to terrorism. Or, more exactly, in totalitarian states state terror dominates every other sort. Where terrorism is a possible strategy for the oppositional movement (in liberal and democratic states, most obviously), other strategies are also

possible if the movement has some significant degree of popular support. In the absence of popular support, terrorism may indeed be the one available strategy, but it is hard to see how its evils can then be excused. For it is not weakness alone that makes the excuse, but the claim of the terrorists to represent the weak; and the particular form of weakness that makes terrorism the only option calls that claim into question.

One might avoid this difficulty with a stronger insistence on the actual effectiveness of terrorism. The third excuse is simply that terrorism works (and nothing else does); it achieves the ends of the oppressed even without their participation. "When the act accuses, the result excuses."[2] This is a consequentialist argument, and given a strict understanding of consequentialism, this argument amounts to a justification rather than an excuse. In practice, however, the argument is rarely pushed so far. More often, the argument begins with an acknowledgment of the terrorists' wrongdoing. Their hands are dirty, but we must make a kind of peace with them because they have acted effectively for the sake of people who could not act for themselves. But, in fact, have the terrorists' actions been effective? I doubt that terrorism has ever achieved national liberation—no nation that I know of owes its freedom to a campaign of random murder—although terrorism undoubtedly increases the power of the terrorists within the national liberation movement. Perhaps terrorism is also conducive to the survival and notoriety (the two go together) of the movement, which is now dominated by terrorists. But even if we were to grant some means-end relationship between terror and national liberation, the third excuse does not work unless it can meet the further requirements of a consequentialist argument. It must be possible to say that the desired end could not have been achieved through any other, less wrongful, means. The third excuse depends, then, on the success of the first or second, and neither of these look likely to be successful.

The fourth excuse avoids this crippling dependency. This excuse does not require the apologist to defend either of the improbable claims that terrorism is the last resort or that it is the only possible resort. The fourth excuse is simply that terrorism is the universal resort. All politics is (really) terrorism. The appearance of innocence and decency is always a piece of deception, more or less convincing in accordance with the relative power of the deceivers. The terrorist who does not bother with appearances is only doing openly what everyone else does secretly.

This argument has the same form as the maxim "All's fair in love and war." Love is always fraudulent, war is always brutal, and political action is always terrorist in character. Political action works (as Thomas Hobbes long ago argued) only by generating fear in innocent men and women. Terrorism is the politics of state officials and movement militants alike. This argument does not justify either the officials or the militants, but it does excuse them all. We hardly can be harsh with people who act the way everyone else acts. Only saints are likely to act differently, and sainthood in politics is supererogatory, a matter of grace, not obligation.

But this fourth excuse relies too heavily on our cynicism about political life, and cynicism only sometimes answers well to experience. In fact, legitimate states do not need to terrorize their citizens, and strongly based movements do not need to terrorize their opponents. Officials and militants who live, as it were, on the margins of legitimacy and strength sometimes

choose terrorism and sometimes do not. Living in terror is not a universal experience. The world the terrorists create has its entrances and exits.

If we want to understand the choice of terror, the choice that forces the rest of us through the door, we have to imagine what in fact always occurs, although we often have no satisfactory record of the occurrence: A group of men and women, officials or militants, sits around a table and argues about whether or not to adopt a terrorist strategy. Later on, the litany of excuses obscures the argument. But at the time, around the table, it would have been no use for defenders of terrorism to say, "Everybody does it," because there they would be face to face with people proposing to do something else. Nor is it historically the case that the members of this last group, the opponents of terrorism, always lose the argument. They can win, however, and still not be able to prevent a terrorist campaign; the would-be terrorists (it does not take very many) can always split the movement and go their own way. Or, they can split the bureaucracy or the police or officer corps and act in the shadow of state power. Indeed, terrorism often has its origin in such splits. The first victims are the terrorists' former comrades or colleagues. What reason can we possibly have, then, for equating the two? If we value the politics of the men and women who oppose terrorism, we must reject the excuses of their murderers. Cynicism at such a time is unfair to the victims.

The fourth excuse can also take, often does take, a more restricted form. Oppression, rather than political rule more generally, is always terroristic in character, and thus, we must always excuse the opponents of oppression. When they choose terrorism, they are only reacting to someone else's previous choice, repaying in kind the treatment they have long received. Of course, their terrorism repeats the evil—innocent people are killed, who were never themselves oppressors—but repetition is not the same as initiation. The oppressors set the terms of the struggle. But if the struggle is fought on the oppressors' terms, then the oppressors are likely to win. Or, at least, oppression is likely to win, even if it takes on a new face. The whole point of a liberation movement or a popular mobilization is to change the terms. We have no reason to excuse the terrorism reactively adopted by opponents of oppression unless we are confident of the sincerity of their opposition, the seriousness of their commitment to a nonoppressive politics. But the choice of terrorism undermines that confidence.

We are often asked to distinguish the terrorism of the oppressed from the terrorism of the oppressors. What is it, however, that makes the difference? The message of the terrorist is the same in both cases: a denial of the peoplehood and humanity of the groups among whom he or she finds victims. Terrorism anticipates, when it does not actually enforce, political domination. Does it matter if one dominated group is replaced by another? Imagine a slave revolt whose protagonists dream only of enslaving in their turn the children of their masters. The dream is understandable, but the fervent desire of the children that the revolt be repressed is equally understandable. In neither case does understanding make for excuse—not, at least, after a politics of universal freedom has become possible. Nor does an understanding of oppression excuse the terrorism of the oppressed, once we have grasped the meaning of "liberation."

These are the four general excuses for terror, and each of them fails. They depend upon statements about the world that are false, historical arguments for which there is no evidence, moral claims that turn out to be hollow or dishonest. This is not to say that there might not be more particular excuses that have greater plausibility, extenuating circumstances in particular cases that we would feel compelled to recognize. As with murder, we can tell a story (like the story that Richard Wright tells in *Native Son,* for example) that might lead us, not to justify terrorism, but to excuse this or that individual terrorist. We can provide a personal history, a psychological study, of compassion destroyed by fear, moral reason by hatred and rage, social inhibition by unending violence—the product, an individual driven to kill or readily set on a killing course by his or her political leaders.[3] But the force of this story will not depend on any of the four general excuses, all of which grant what the storyteller will have to deny: that terrorism is the deliberate choice of rational men and women. Whether they conceive it to be one option among others or the only one available, they nevertheless argue and choose. Whether they are acting or reacting, they have made a decision. The human instruments they subsequently find to plant the bomb or shoot the gun may act under some psychological compulsion, but the men and women who choose terror as a policy act "freely." They could not act in any other way, or accept any other description of their action, and still pretend to be the leaders of the movement or the state. We ought never to excuse such leaders.

THE RESPONSE TO TERRORISM

What follows from the critique of excuses? There is still a great deal of room for argument about the best way of responding to terrorism. Certainly, terrorists should be resisted, and it is not likely that a purely defensive resistance will ever be sufficient. In this sort of struggle, the offense is always ahead. The technology of terror is simple; the weapons are readily produced and easy to deliver. It is virtually impossible to protect people against random and indiscriminate attack. Thus, resistance will have to be supplemented by some combination of repression and retaliation. This is a dangerous business because repression and retaliation so often take terroristic forms and there are a host of apologists ready with excuses that sound remarkably like those of the terrorists themselves. It should be clear by now, however, that counterterrorism cannot be excused merely because it is reactive. Every new actor, terrorist or counterterrorist, claims to be reacting to someone else, standing in a circle and just passing the evil along. But the circle is ideological in character; in fact, every actor is a moral agent and makes an independent decision.

Therefore, repression and retaliation must not repeat the wrongs of terrorism, which is to say that repression and retaliation must be aimed systematically at the terrorists themselves, never at the people for whom the terrorists claim to be acting. That claim is in any case doubtful, even when it is honestly made. The people do not authorize the terrorists to act in their name. Only a tiny number actually participate in terrorist activities; they are far more likely to suffer than to benefit from the terrorist program. Even if they supported the program and hoped to benefit from it, however, they would still be immune from attack—exactly as civilians in time of war who support the war effort but are not themselves part of it are subject to the same immunity. Civilians may be put at risk by attacks on military targets, as by attacks on terrorist targets, but the risk must be kept to a minimum, even at some cost to the attackers. The refusal to make ordinary people into targets, whatever their nationality or even their politics, is the only way to say no to terrorism. Every act of repression and retaliation has to be measured by this standard.

But what if the "only way" to defeat the terrorists is to intimidate their actual or potential supporters? It is important to deny the premise of this question: that terrorism is a politics dependent on mass support. In fact, it is always the politics of an elite, whose members are dedicated and fanatical and more than ready to endure, or to watch others endure, the devastations of a counterterrorist campaign. Indeed, terrorists will welcome counterterrorism; it makes the terrorists' excuses more plausible and is sure to bring them, however many people are killed or wounded, however many are terrorized, the small number of recruits needed to sustain the terrorist activities.

Repression and retaliation are legitimate responses to terrorism only when they are constrained by the same moral principles that rule out terrorism itself. But there is an alternative response that seeks to avoid the violence that these two entail. The alternative is to address directly, ourselves, the oppression the terrorists claim to oppose. Oppression, they say, is the cause of terrorism. But that is merely one more excuse. The real cause of terrorism is the decision to launch a terrorist campaign, a decision made by that group of people sitting around a table whose deliberations I have already described. However, terrorists do exploit oppression, injustice, and human misery generally and look to these at least for their excuses. There can hardly be any doubt that oppression strengthens their hand. Is that a reason for us to come to the defense of the oppressed? It seems to me that we have our own reasons to do that, and do not need this one, or should not, to prod us into action. We might imitate those movement militants who argue against the adoption of a terrorist strategy—although not, as the terrorists say, because these militants are prepared to tolerate oppression. They already are opposed to oppression and now add to that opposition, perhaps for the same reasons, a refusal of terror. So should we have been opposed before, and we should now make the same addition.

But there is an argument, put with some insistence these days, that we should refuse to acknowledge any link at all between terrorism and oppression—as if any defense of oppressed men and women, once a terrorist campaign has been launched, would concede the effectiveness of the campaign. Or, at least, a defense of oppression would give terrorism the appearance of effectiveness and so increase the likelihood of terrorist campaigns in the future. Here we have the reverse side of the litany of excuses; we have turned over the record. First oppression is made into an excuse for terrorism, and then terrorism is made into an excuse for oppression. The first is the excuse of the far left; the second is the excuse of the neoconservative right.[4] I doubt that genuine conservatives would think it a good reason for defending the status quo that it is under terrorist attack; they would have independent reasons and would be prepared to defend the status quo against any attack. Similarly, those of us who think that the status quo urgently requires change have our own reasons for thinking so and need not be intimidated by terrorists or, for that matter, antiterrorists.

If one criticizes the first excuse, one should not neglect the second. But I need to state the second more precisely. It is not so much an excuse for oppression as an excuse for doing nothing (now) about oppression. The claim is that the campaign against terrorism has priority over every other political activity. If the people who take the lead in this campaign are the old oppressors, then we must make a kind of peace with them—temporarily, of course, until the terrorists have been beaten. This is a strategy that denies the possibility of a two-front war. So long as the men and women who pretend to lead the fight against oppression are terrorists, we can concede nothing to their demands. Nor can we oppose their opponents.

But why not? It is not likely in any case that terrorists would claim victory in the face of a serious effort to deal with the oppression of the people they claim to be defending. The effort would merely expose the hollowness of their claim, and the nearer it came to success, the more they would escalate their terrorism. They would still have to be defeated, for what they are after is not a solution to the problem but rather the power to impose their own solution. No decent end to the conflict in Ireland, say, or in Lebanon, or in the Middle East generally, is going to look like a victory for terrorism—if only because the different groups of terrorists are each committed, by the strategy they have adopted, to an indecent end.[5] By working for our own ends, we expose the indecency.

OPPRESSION AND TERRORISM

It is worth considering at greater length the link between oppression and terror. To pretend that there is no link at all is to ignore the historical record, but the record is more complex than any of the excuses acknowledge. The first thing to be read out of it, however, is simple enough: Oppression is not so much the cause of terrorism as terrorism is one of the primary means of oppression. This was true in ancient times, as Aristotle recognized, and it is still true today. Tyrants rule by terrorizing their subjects; unjust and illegitimate regimes are upheld through a combination of carefully aimed and random violence.[6] If this method works in the state, there is no reason to think that it will not work, or that it does not work, in the liberation movement. Wherever we see terrorism, we should look for tyranny and oppression. Authoritarian states, especially in the moment of their founding, need a terrorist apparatus—secret police with unlimited power, secret prisons into which citizens disappear, death squads in unmarked cars. Even democracies may use terror, not against their own citizens, but at the margins, in their colonies, for example, where colonizers also are likely to rule tyrannically. Oppression is sometimes maintained by a steady and discriminate pressure, sometimes by intermittent and random violence—what we might think of as terrorist melodrama—designed to render the subject population fearful and passive.

This latter policy, especially if it seems successful, invites imitation by opponents of the state. But terrorism does not spread only when it is imitated. If it can be invented by state officials, it can also be invented by movement militants. Neither one need take lessons from the other; the circle has no single or necessary starting point. Wherever it starts, terrorism in the movement is tyrannical and oppressive in exactly the same way as is terrorism in the state. The terrorists aim to rule, and murder is their method. They have their own internal police, death squads, disappearances. They begin by killing-or intimidating those comrades who stand in their way, and they proceed to do the same, if they can, among the people they claim to represent. If terrorists are successful, they rule tyrannically, and their people bear, without consent, the costs of the terrorists' rule. (If the terrorists are only partly successful, the costs to the people may be even greater: What they have to bear now is a war between rival terrorist gangs.) But terrorists cannot win the ultimate victory they seek without challenging the established regime or colonial power and the people it claims to represent, and when terrorists do that, they themselves invite imitation. The regime may then respond with its own campaign of aimed and random violence. Terrorist tracks terrorist, each claiming the other as an excuse.

The same violence can also spread to countries where it has not yet been experienced; now terror is reproduced not through temporal succession but through ideological adaptation. State terrorists wage bloody wars against largely imaginary enemies: army colonels, say, hunting down the representatives of "international communism." Or movement terrorists wage bloody wars against enemies with whom, but for the ideology, they could readily negotiate and compromise: nationalist fanatics committed to a permanent irredentism. These wars, even if they are without precedents, are likely enough to become precedents, to start the circle of terror and counterterror, which is endlessly oppressive for the ordinary men and women whom the state calls its citizens and the movement its "people."

The only way to break out of the circle is to refuse to play the terrorist game.

Terrorists in the state and the movement warn us, with equal vehemence, that any such refusal is a sign of softness and naiveté. The self-portrait of the terrorists is always the same. They are tough-minded and realistic; they know their enemies (or privately invent them for ideological purposes); and they are ready to do what must be done for victory. Why then do terrorists turn around and around in the same circle? It is true: Movement terrorists win support because they pretend to deal energetically and effectively with the brutality of the state. It also is true: State terrorists win support because they pretend to deal energetically and effectively with the brutality of the movement. Both feed on the fears of brutalized and oppressed people. But there is no way of overcoming brutality with terror. At most, the burden is shifted from these people to those; more likely, new burdens are added for everyone. Genuine liberation can come only through a politics that mobilizes the victims of brutality and takes careful aim at its agents, or by a politics that surrenders the hope of victory and domination and deliberately seeks a compromise settlement. In either case, once tyranny is repudiated, terrorism is no longer an option.

For what lies behind all the excuses, of officials and militants alike, is the predilection for a tyrannical politics.

Notes

1. I cannot resist a few examples: Edward Said, "The Terrorism Scam," *The Nation,* June 14, 1986; and (more intelligent and circumspect) Richard Falk, "Thinking About Terrorism," *The Nation,* June 28, 1986.
2. Machiavelli, *The Discourses* I:ix. As yet, however, there have been no results that would constitute a Machiavellian excuse.
3. See, for example, Daniel Goleman, "The Roots of Terrorism Are Found in Brutality of Shattered Childhood," *New York Times,* September 2, 1986, pp. C1, 8. Goleman discusses the psychic and social history of particular terrorists, not the roots of terrorism.
4. The neoconservative position is represented, although not as explicitly as I have stated it here, in Benjamin Netanyahu, ed., *Terrorism: How the West Can Win* (New York: Farrar, Straus & Giroux, 1986).
5. The reason the terrorist strategy, however indecent in itself, cannot be instrumental to some decent political purpose is because any decent purpose must somehow accommodate the people against whom the terrorism is aimed, and what terrorism expresses is precisely the refusal of such an accommodation, the radical devaluing of the Other. See my argument in *Just and Unjust Wars* (New York: Basic Books, 1977), pp. 197–206, especially 203.
6. Aristotle, *The Politics* 1313-1314a.

Understanding Terrorism[1]

(1988)

Robert Fullinwider

Robert Fullinwider is Senior Research Scholar in the University of Maryland School of Public Affairs. He works primarily in issues of philosophy and public policy, including education and affirmative action. His book, The Reverse Discrimination Controversy *(Rowman and Littlefield, 1980), was published as a selection of the Lawyer's Literary Guild.*

I hold that a little rebellion now and then is a good thing, & as necessary in the political world as storms in the physical.

What signify a few lives lost in a century or two? The tree of liberty must be refreshed from time to time with the blood of patriots & tyrants. It is its natural manure.

—*Thomas Jefferson*

It belongs to men to judge the law at the risk of being judged by it.

—*Maurice Merleau-Ponty*

"No one these days advocates terrorism," writes Michael Walzer, "not even those who regularly practice it." This is because there is no moral defense available to the terrorist, no justification. Terrorism is worse than murder and rape, and no one can justify *them*. The only thing we can do with terrorists is excuse them. But the standard excuses we might offer are themselves lame and unpersuasive. So Walzer begins his analysis.

It is a puzzling analysis. First, there is no precise characterization of the terrorist. We do not know exactly who it is that is beyond justification, and so we remain un-

clear as to why. Second, and more puzzling, Walzer does not talk about excuses at all. The arguments he criticizes are all defenses of terrorism.

Consider the second point first. The avowed aim of the chapter is to examine excuses made for terrorism. According to Walzer, there are basically four of them: Terrorism is an act of last resort; terrorism is a tool of the weak; terrorism is the only effective tool the weak have; everybody practices terrorism. But these are not excuses, strictly speaking.

We excuse people by arguing that they acted in ignorance or under compulsion.[2] This is not what the apologists of terrorism say about terrorists. As Walzer himself points out, the four "excuses" he discusses acknowledge that terrorism is the deliberate choice of rational men and women. The apologists for terrorism do not offer an *apology* but an *apologia*. They put forward arguments that say the terrorist, all things considered, did not act wrongly.

So it is puzzling to find half of Walzer's chapter attacking defenses of terrorism when he begins by saying that no defense is available, that he will simply take for granted that every act of terrorism is a wrongful act. To reintroduce the first point: This puzzlement is compounded by the lack of a clear account in the chapter of who the terrorist is. Walzer pictures the terrorist as attacking "innocent bystanders," as killing or harming "indiscriminately." This is not a picture likely to enlist our sympathetic ear to the terrorist's case. We are going to take it for granted, too, that the terrorist is wrong. But some of Walzer's own later observations belie his initial description. Terrorists are often very discriminate in their targets.

I press these points because the outrage we feel for terrorist acts too easily prompts us to make and support blanket condemnations of terrorism by resort to equivocation or word play.[3] Therefore, it is important not to be vague about who the terrorist is and not to blur distinctions or relevant questions.

Who are terrorists? Here is a list: Basque separatists, factions of the PLO, the IRA, the Red Brigades, Croation nationalists, the Tupamaros, the Puerto Rican National Liberation Front, the Baader-Meinhof Gang, Black September, Shining Path, Posse Comitatus, South Moluccan nationalists, Armenian revanchists, the Symbionese Liberation Army. Why is there no defense for what they do? Why are they beyond justification? It must be because (1) they make no claims and arguments at all or in terms we can understand or (2) they make claims and arguments so flimsy that it is a waste of energy to go through the exercise of answering them.

Benzion Netanyahu takes the first path by diabolizing the terrorist. "The terrorist," he claims, "represents a new breed of man which takes humanity back to prehistoric times, to the times when morality was not yet born. Divested of any moral principle, he has no moral sense, no moral controls, and is therefore capable of committing any crime, like a killing machine, without shame or remorse."[4] If this is the terrorist, then he or she is so alien from our own moral experience that there is no ground for understanding him or her. There are no moral claims and arguments to answer.

Even Walzer's characterization of terrorists as indiscriminate killers of the innocent puts terrorists and their cause beyond the pale. What recognizable moral view could these killers possibly employ? What arguments could there be for us to take seriously? Walzer, in fact, uneasily straddles the line between the first and second paths. There *are* arguments, although Walzer puts them not in the mouths of terrorists—what could indiscriminate killers say?—but in the mouth of the apologist for terrorism. These arguments are "excuses" too incomplete or shallow to be taken very seriously.

The slaughter of Jewish worshippers in the Neve Shalom Synagogue in Istanbul last year exemplifies the mad and indiscriminate terrorism that Walzer obviously has in mind. During services, two terrorists entered the synagogue, barred the doors, and machine-gunned twenty-two people to death before exploding grenades to destroy themselves and all identity of who they were.[5] The worshippers in Istanbul met their deaths because they were Jews and because their attackers were willing to target Jews as such in the former's "war against Zionism." The slaughter was so horrible and revolting that it may strike us as too morally grotesque to understand, from their point of view, the goals and the values that animated the slaughterers.

But the Turkish synagogue episode is less typical of terrorism during the last one hundred years—or even the past twenty years—than is, for example, the kidnapping and murder of Aldo Moro in 1978. The Red Brigades abducted Moro, probably the most respected political leader in Italy, subjected him to a "trial" for his "crimes" (as representative and principal agent of the "rotten" and "repressive" Italian state), and "executed" him. The abduction had been planned over several months and followed a period of kidnappings and kneecappings of industrialists and lesser political figures. There was nothing indiscriminate about the taking of Aldo Moro.

Are the *brigatisti,* too, morally beyond the pale, subhuman throwbacks to a prehistoric time, divided from us by some moral chasm, their aims not worth a charitable understanding? It is, unfortunately, too easy to foreclose questions of justification here by definitional sleights of hand. Benjamin Netanyahu agrees with Walzer that "terrorism is always unjustifiable."[6] This seems to follow from Netanyahu's definition ("Terrorism is the deliberate and systematic murder, maiming, and menacing of the innocent to inspire fear for political ends"[7]) and from the fact that deliberately killing innocents is wrong. But Netanyahu gets the kidnappers of Aldo Moro under his proscription only by sliding over to a characterization of terrorists as attackers of *civilians,* implicitly equating "innocents" and "civilians."[8] According to the Netanyahu definition—and under Walzer's characterization—the Red Brigades' kidnapping of Aldo Moro does not qualify as terrorism unless we characterize Moro as an *innocent* civilian, but

that just begs the question against the Red Brigades. They chose Moro because he was *not* innocent (by their lights).

Italy was convulsed by the Aldo Moro kidnapping not because the actions of the Red Brigades were incomprehensible but because the actions were fully comprehensible in moral terms. Everybody understands crime and punishment. The arguments of the Red Brigades were so understandable, in fact, that the Italian establishment feared they might even seduce many Italian citizens.

The political parties of Italy from the onset of the Moro crisis locked themselves into a rigid position: No negotiations for Moro's release. The parties did not take this position because they thought the arguments of the Red Brigades had no credibility. If the Red Brigades had defended their kidnapping of Moro on the grounds that he was guilty of secretly poisoning all the water in Italy with fluorides, or that he had betrayed the planet earth to galactic enemies, the Italian government would not have felt that negotiations for Moro's life risked giving the kidnappers widespread legitimacy among the populace. It was precisely because the Red Brigades' arguments had enough facial credibility to start with that the government saw any concessions as undermining its own legitimacy.[9] Its policy on Moro amounted to an argument-by-deed addressed to the Italian public that there was no truth to the charge that the state was rotten, repressive, and illegitimate.

Thus, not only were the arguments of the Red Brigades comprehensible; they had to be answered. The answers were not, and are not, transparent. They have to be worked at, especially if they are not to beg the central questions. Simply taking for granted that every act of terrorism is wrong may allow us to make short work of the Red Brigades, but not honest work. Pushing aside the question of justification as pointless is more likely to impede rather than advance our understanding of terrorism.

THE APPEAL TO MORALITY VERSUS THE APPEAL TO LAW

Benzion Netanyahu gets the matter exactly backward: Terrorists are not throwbacks to a prehistoric time "when morality was not yet born." If anything, terrorists are throwbacks to a "time" when morality was not yet under control. What is often scary about terrorists is that they appeal to morality without appealing to the law. Let me explain.

Political theorists tell a story about the "state of nature" to explain and defend government. The state of nature proves to be intolerable for its inhabitants, whose lives are "solitary, poore, nasty, brutish, and short."[10] Contrary to common impressions, however, the problem in the state of nature is not that people are so immoral—so selfish and rapacious that they persistently endanger each other. The problem is that people are so moral—so determined to vindicate rights or to uphold honor at any costs that they become a menace to one another.

The distinctive feature of the state of nature, as John Locke points out, is not the absence of morality but the absence of law. It is a circumstance in which "the law of nature"—the moral law—must be enforced by each person. Each is responsible for vindicating his or her own rights and the rights of others. All prosecution of crime and injustice in the state of nature is freelance. Such a situation is the inevitable

spawning ground of the neverending chain of retaliation and counter-retaliation of the blood feud. "For every one in that state being both Judge and Executioner of the Law of Nature, Men being partial to themselves, Passion and Revenge is very apt to carry them too far, and with too much heat, in their own Cases; as well as negligence, and unconcernedness, to make them too remiss, in other Mens."[11]

Even if persons were not biased in their own favor, the problems of enforcing justice in the state of nature would remain deadly. How would crime be defined? How would evidence for its commission be gathered? Who is to be punished, and in what manner? Nothing about the state of nature ensures any common understanding about these questions. The contrary is the case. Private understanding pitted against private understanding produces an escalation of response and counter-response that lets violence erupt and feed on itself.

The solution, of course, is "an establish'd, settled, known *Law,* received and allowed by common consent to be the Standard of Right and Wrong, and the common measure to decide all Controversies" and "a known and indifferent Judge, with Authority to determine all differences according to the established Law."[12] Conventions, established standards, and enforced rulings keep the peace, and when they exist by "common consent," they do justice as well.

"Consent of the governed" is the ideal that underlies democratic regimes, at least in Anglo-American cultures. It is an attractive ideal. When a regime of law is "chosen" by "free and rational persons," the "strains of commitment" will be minimal.[13] That is to say, there will be widespread willingness to obey the law and accept its rulings.

But in the real governments we live under—even the best of them—the strains of commitment often are severe. Impatience with the existing procedures of law can, and does, lead people to resort to "irregular justice," including political violence. Such "irregular justice," even when it is violent and rebellious, need not repudiate the existing rule of law. Irregular justice may be directed only at egregious failures of the law or at illegality tolerated as law.

Ordinary political violence can itself have all the earmarks of terrorism. The Molly Maguires—a secret band of Irish miners in mid-nineteenth century Pennsylvania—carried on a decade-long labor "war" with mine owners and police. Emerging from violent resistance among Pennsylvania Irish to the Civil War draft, the Molly Maguires had their own way of dealing with the labor strife of the time. They resorted to arson, beatings, and murder, directed against mine foremen, superintendents, policemen, and others against whom the Molly Maguires had grievances. The violence was meant to intimidate (targeted foremen, for example, often left the community after receiving threats) for political ends.[14] The Molly Maguires resorted to war because they perceived both the law and its enforcers to be in the pockets of owners and bankers.

A less remote situation is the bombing and burning of scores of abortion facilities in the United States during the last decade. The aim of the attackers is to stop or impede abortions, and these attackers resort to "irregular justice" because the law fails to protect the unborn. They appeal to a "higher law," to morality itself.[15]

Our responses to political violence of this kind are ambivalent. In general we do not want free-lance justice; we do not want people arrogating to themselves decisions the law should make. But in particular cases, our sympathies often are enlisted on the side of the violent, even if we go through pro forma condemnations of their actions. We as often romanticize the Molly Maguires of our history as vilify them.

This is not surprising because it is a part of U.S. political tradition that we may be forced, in Merleau-Ponty's words, "to judge the law at the risk of being judged by it."[16] "I like a little rebellion now and then," wrote Thomas Jefferson to Abigail Adams. "The spirit of resistance to government is so valuable on certain occasions, that I wish it to be always kept alive. It will often be exercised when wrong, but better so than not to be exercised at all."[17] Political violence serves the useful function of shaking government out of its unresponsiveness to the rights and interests of some of its citizens.[18] The violence strains but does not rupture the rule of law because the appeal to morality made by the rebels draws from the same principles embodied in the law.

It is not Jeffersonian rebellions and outbreaks that truly frighten and disturb us, but revolutionary violence directed against a whole existing regime of law, including its underlying principles. The kidnapping and trial of Aldo Moro were an assault against the very idea of capitalist and bourgeois legality. They were acts of war on behalf of a new social order that would emerge from the ruins of "rotten" Italy.

Political violence that strikes against the very regime itself is doubly disturbing. For one thing, such violence is more frightening than ordinary dissidence or rebellion because the underlying common allegiance to the principles of the law that we expect to moderate or contain the violence of the dissident or rebel is absent. It is false to say that the revolutionary terrorist has no moral limits; but it is true that he or she repudiates the conventional boundaries that guide our own actions.

More importantly for our purposes, revolutionary violence is more frustrating because it is hard to answer the challenge of revolutionaries without begging the question against them. We can condemn ordinary political violence, including ordinary terrorism, by appealing to the "constitution," that is, the basic ideas of legality upon which our political, economic, and cultural institutions rest. Revolutionaries repudiate the "constitution." They do so in the name of recognizable moral ideas: creating a just or humane society, ending oppression and misery. But "just," "humane," and so on are abstractions that we typically fill in by reference to the principles and practices of our existing social order. If we cannot resort to this strategy in answering revolutionaries, then how do we convincingly repudiate their claims of justice? How do we show their violence to be condemned rather than supported by morality?

I do not mean we have to answer these questions for the satisfaction of revolutionaries. They have already pulled a gun. It is for our own satisfaction that we would like to give an intellectually honest answer to revolutionaries' rejectionism. We appeal to the law; they reject our law and appeal to morality. We claim morality, too, but then notice we have filled it up with our law.

ATTACKING THE INNOCENT

The ease with which we beg the question against revolutionaries is illustrated by Walzer's depiction of terrorists as killers of the innocent. How are we to understand "innocence"? Aldo Moro was clearly innocent in one sense: He had never been convicted of any wrong by a duly authorized judge or jury of any state or officially recognized international agency. But this sense of innocence is not terribly helpful for condemning the Red Brigades. Many instances of political violence that any of us would endorse are directed against innocents in this respect. Was Moro innocent in a deeper sense: not causally or morally responsible for the "crimes" of Italy, not an accessory, not complicit?

If we accept that the Italian state is a "criminal" enterprise, a repressive and unjust system, then it was clearly reasonable directly to connect Moro with it and its "crimes." Few other figures in Italy were so centrally involved in maintaining the rule of Christian democratic governments since World War II. Other targets of the Red Brigades were similarly connected in some important way to the political, military, or economic functioning of the state. If we *grant* the premises of the Red Brigades, then the charge that they killed innocent people is not so readily sustainable.

But aren't there some lines to be drawn that are independent of point of view, lines that everyone must acknowledge? Perhaps so, but finding an institutionally contextless conception of innocence will not be easy.[19] Consider the infamous massacre of the Israeli athletes at the 1972 Munich Olympics. Weren't they uncontroversially innocent? Yet a case can be made, from the point of view of their attackers, that these athletes were legitimate targets. They were willing and knowing representatives of their state to an international affair in which their presence and participation would lend yet further international credibility and legitimacy to Israel. Thus, from the point of view of their attackers, the athletes were active and informed accessories in a continuing "crime"—the support of the "criminal" state of Israel.

Of course, by international convention, unarmed athletes participating in the Olympics *are* "innocent." The willingness of terrorists to violate this convention burdens their defense. A great deal can be said in favor of such a convention; even terrorists are unlikely to prefer a world in which every "criminal" is an open target. Nevertheless, the circumstances, as the terrorists saw them, may have justified "irregular justice." Like the Molly Maguires, the terrorists saw themselves as attacking fair targets that current conventions protect. Such terrorists concede that they attack the "conventionally innocent," but not that they attack the "really innocent."

What about the victims of the slaughter at Neve Shalom Synagogue in Istanbul? Surely *they* cannot be connected to "crimes" of any sort. Their only connection to "Zionist imperialism" was that they were Jews; and if that is enough of a connection to make them fair targets, then "immunity of the innocent" is emptied as a moral notion and there will be no one who is "really innocent."

There is, doubtless, some point of view from which the slaughter in Istanbul makes sense, but it is a point of view that comes close to being too alien for us to comprehend or even credit as a moral point of view. Here the claims of Walzer and the rhetoric of Netanyahu seem appropriate. But I say "comes close" because the rationalization of the Istanbul massacre may be less alien than we expect.

Walzer's response to terrorism, or the terrorism I am describing now, flows from a conception of universal human rights.[20] Every human individual has an inviolability and dignity *just as a human being*. Independently of any feature of his or her social environment or historical circumstance, a person has a claim to our moral concern, a claim expressed in the possession of basic human rights. The "immunity thesis"—that innocent persons cannot be made the targets of violent assault—describes one of those rights.

An alternative view denies the moral individualism and universalism underlying the human rights approach. This view claims that the value of a person is wholly exhausted in his or her class or group membership. There is no transgroup or extraclass "humanity" that creates moral pull. Moral universalism is false.

Stated so starkly, perhaps this is a view not subscribed to by anyone. But there clearly are views that show considerable kinship. For example, at least some forms of Marxism imply, in present historical circumstances, that a person's rights and duties are wholly a function of his or her class.[21] Moreover, parochial moralities that see the universe from the point of view of God's, or history's, chosen people are not hard to imagine or even to find in history.

Another alternative conception sees the modern world as so dehumanized, so devoid of value, that it is perverse to agonize over the protection of innocents, to erect conventions, make law, and pass judgments as if current humanity itself had any value. Modern humans are deracinated and deformed, a mockery of what a fully realized humanity could be. That such beings are incidentally slaughtered, maimed, and terrorized in the upheaval of a revolution for a transformed social order is of no importance. What will their deaths signify in a century or two, from the perspective of a new order and a new humanity?[22]

Thus, two basic ideas compete against the idea of universal human rights. One measures the worth of people according to their group membership. The other measures the worth of people against an ideal of humanity. These measures are not alien and incomprehensible to us. In attenuated and confined forms, they are a part of the moral armory of even those of us who, like Walzer, subscribe to universal human rights. We value community and cherish special relations of affinity and kinship. We hold ideals and strive for collective reform and improvement.

We thus can comprehend the role of these ideas for those who acknowledge no limits on their force. Even the maddest terrorism shows a familiar face. Moreover, within our own philosophical culture, we cannot say with confidence that the intellectual foundations of human rights are clear or that they are universally acknowledged. The reigning fashions in the academy today include various attacks on "liberal individualism." In contrast to the "atomistic" individual supposedly subscribed to by liberalism, current critics offer pictures of individuals "essentially connected" to others in community, individuals whose identities are "constituted by community."[23]

The ideas of essence and constitution in these pictures are not made clear; these ideas may turn out to be innocuous enough and hardly at odds with anything except a caricature of individualism. But lurking within them are possible interpretations that would make the grounds of moral universalism obscure. To say that people are *essentially related* to community may mean they have no value outside *some* community or other; or it may mean they have no value outside their own community. "Community" may encompass the loosest human associations and the most casual forms of sociability, or it may mean

a highly structured group bound by corporate values. Out of these options there can emerge interpretations that render the view that human beings have a worth and dignity independently of *any* of their relations a proposition too abstract and empty to hold.

Perhaps other grounds of universalism are available; or perhaps a conception of human rights can be erected on nonuniversalist views. But our intellectual house is not in such good order that rationally irrefutable barriers are in place against an extreme extension of the quest for community or the quest for ideals—both of which can lead us to discount rather sharply the value of some humans. Then the rationalization of Neve Shalom is not so far away.

To understand terrorists and to take their self-justification seriously is not to acquiesce in the terrorists' deeds or concede them any measure of right. Rather, the point is to see the full spectrum of political violence realistically, without demonization, for our *own* sake, not the sake of terrorists. Because revolutionary terrorists repudiate so much of what is settled and in place, we struggle to make sense of the meaning they give to the moral notions they deploy. But they invite us to see how rotten the existing system is and to trust that in destroying it a new and morally preferable society will emerge. If terrorists war on us, we can war on them without compunction, but that does not answer their invitation. To do that, we have to say why the existing rule of law deserves allegiance.

Terrorists typically appeal to history for vindication. We can appeal to history, too, in defense of the conventions and practices terrorists revolt against or violate. Some terrorism we can condemn by appeal to those very conventions, some we can condemn by appeal to abstract principle, but most we must condemn because we judge the terrorists grotesquely mistaken in their understanding of historical possibilities. The Red Brigades deluded themselves into thinking the kidnapping of Aldo Moro would bring on the revolution. The Molly Maguires might have thought their violence was an effective—or the only—way to bring justice for the miners. Walzer's discussion of the four "excuses" eloquently shows the burden of proof that terrorism, ordinary or revolutionary, seldom meets. But this failure is contingent, not necessary. We cannot define terrorism into a moral corner where we do not have to worry any more about justification.

Notes

1. I am grateful to Steven Luper-Foy and to my colleagues at the Center for Philosophy and Public Policy, especially Claudia Mills, for comments on an earlier draft of this chapter.
2. See J. L. Austin, "A Plea for Excuses," *Philosophical Papers,* 2nd ed. (London: Oxford University Press, 1970), p. 176: "In the one defence [i.e., justifying], briefly, we accept responsibility but deny [of the conduct] that it was bad. In the other [i.e., excusing], we admit [of the conduct] that it was bad don't accept full, or any, responsibility." In subsequent correspondence, Michael Walzer writes that what he is talking about *are* excuses because they "have this construction: 'of course it is wrong to kill innocent people, but. . . .'" This construction, however, is ambiguous between "of course it is *ordinarily* wrong to kill innocent people, but there are special circumstances in this case to justify it," and "of course it is wrong to kill innocent people and *it was wrong in this case,* but there are special circumstances that excuse it," the special circumstances in this second construction being the presence of responsibility-relieving factors. Because Walzer acknowledges that the apologist for terrorism does not deny the terrorists' responsibility, I take the apologies to have the form of the first rather than the second construction and thus to be justificatory in nature. In any case, I do not want to make too much of the difference between excusing and justifying or of the way I draw the distinction.
3. I have benefited, on this point, from reading Judith Lichtenberg's unpublished essay, "Beneath the Rhetoric of Terrorism."
4. Benzion Netanyahu, "Terrorists and Freedom Fighters," in Benjamin Netanyahu, ed., *Terrorism: How the West Can Win* (New York: Farrar, Straus, Giroux, 1986), pp. 29–30.
5. See the account by Judith Miller, "The Istanbul Synagogue Massacre: An Investigation," *New York Times Magazine,* January 4, 1987, pp. 14–18.
6. "Defining Terrorism," in Netanyahu, *Terrorism,* p. 12.
7. Ibid., p. 9.
8. Ibid., p. 10. Netanyahu explicitly refers to the Red Brigades. Walzer's writings are usually rich with examples and cases but in the present case, we never meet any real examples of terrorism. Part of the initial puzzlement I express at the beginning of this chapter derived from uncertainty about whether Walzer's initial characterization of terrorists as indiscriminate killers was meant as a *description* of those individuals and groups most frequently referred to as terrorists (and this would include the Red Brigades) or was meant as a *stipulative definition,* marking off as terrorists only those who engage in indiscriminate murder. In subsequent correspondence, Walzer writes, "I do not believe that the kidnapping of Aldo Moro was a terrorist act . . . [and] I don't think that it unduly restricts the idea of terrorism to insist on its randomness: the carpet bombing of cities, the bomb in the pub, cafe, bus station, supermarket—all this is common enough, and awful enough, to deserve a name."
9. Nations also resist negotiating with terrorists in order not to encourage future terrorism. This was a secondary consideration in the present case. On the Italian policy of no-negotiations, and on the Moro kidnapping generally, see Robin Erica Wagner-Pacifici, *The Moro Morality Play: Terrorism as Social Drama* (Chicago: University of Chicago Press, 1986), pp. 47–163; and Robert Katz, *Days of Wrath: The Ordeal of Aldo Moro* (Garden City, N.Y.: Doubleday, 1980), p. 70ff.
10. Thomas Hobbes, *Leviathan* (Baltimore, Md.: Penguin Books, 1968), p. 186.
11. John Locke, *Two Treatises of Government* (New York: New American Library, 1965), pp. 395–396.
12. Ibid., p. 396.
13. John Rawls, *A Theory of Justice* (Cambridge, Mass.: Harvard University Press, 1971), pp. 175–183.
14. The Molly Maguires clearly count as terrorists on some definitions. See, for example, C.A.J. Coady, "The Morality of Terrorism," *Philosophy* 60 (January 1985):52.

15. "Perhaps it *is* terrorism to use violence to intimidate. But which is the greater terror: the destruction of two dozen buildings without loss of life in 1984, or the destruction of 1.5 million human beings because they were inconvenient to the mothers who carried them?" Patrick Buchanan, *Washington Times,* January 4, 1985, p. C1.

16. Maurice Merleau-Ponty, *Humanism and Terror* (Boston: Beacon Press, 1969), p. xxxix.

17. Thomas Jefferson, *Writings* (New York: Library of America, 1984), pp. 889–890. For the quotations at the beginning of this chapter, see p. 882 (letter to James Madison, January 1787), and p. 911 (letter to William Smith, November 1787).

18. Shay's Rebellion, which was the occasion for Jefferson's comments, is a case in point. To a certain extent we owe our Constitution to this insurrection of desperate farmers in western Massachusetts (but it apparently would have failed Walzer's strictures about last resort). A few lives were lost in the affair. See Marion L. Starkey, *A Little Rebellion* (New York: Knopf, 1955).

19. Less easy, perhaps, than I supposed in R. Fullinwider, "War and Innocence," *Philosophy & Public Affairs* 5 (Fall 1975):90–97.

20. See Michael Walzer, *Just and Unjust Wars* (New York: Basic Books, 1977), pp. 134–135. See also his *Spheres of Justice* (New York: Basic Books, 1983), p. xv.

21. "The correct basis for what is morally good, what one's duty is, what the right thing to do is, what is fair to do . . . is one's place in one's society. The correct basis is not the human person taken in isolation. Rather, the focus is on the groups in society to which a person belongs. . . . The right thing to do is determined by a consideration of what ultimately, in view of the primacy of class, advances the realization of the tendencies of one's class." Milton Fisk, *Ethics and Society: A Marxist Interpretation of Value* (New York: New York University Press, 1980), pp. xiii, xvi.

"Whoever does not care to return to Moses, Christ, or Mohammed; whoever is not satisfied with eclectic *hodge-podges* must acknowledge that morality is a product of social development; that there is nothing immutable about it; that it serves social interests; that these interests are contradictory; that morality more than any other form of ideology has a class character.

"But do not elementary moral precepts exist, worked out in the development of humanity as a whole and indispensable for the existence of every collective body? Undoubtedly such precepts exist but the extent of their action is extremely limited and unstable. Norms 'obligatory upon all' become the less forceful the sharper the character assumed by the class struggle. The highest form of the class struggle is civil war, which explodes into midair all moral ties between the hostile classes." Leon Trotsky, *Their Morals and Ours* (New York: Pathfinder Press, 1973), p. 21.

22. For a discussion of views that find the modern world generally worthless, see Bernard Yack, *The Longing for Total Revolution: Philosophic Sources of Social Discontent from Rousseau to Marx and Nietzsche* (Princeton, N.J.: Princeton University Press, 1986).

23. For a typical recent attack on "liberal individualism," see Suzanna Sherry, "Civic Virtue and the Feminine Voice in Constitutional Adjudication," *Virginia Law Review* 72 (April 1986):546ff, and her citations of Alasdair MacIntyre, Michael Sandel, Carol Gilligan, and so forth.

Can Terrorism Be Justified?

(2000)

Andrew Valls

Andrew Valls is assistant professor of political science at Oregon State University. He works in political theory and has edited volumes on Race and Racism in Modern Philosophy *(Cornell University Press, 2004) and* Ethics in International Affairs *(Rowman and Littlefield, 2000).*

. . . In the public and scholarly reactions to political violence, a double standard often is at work. When violence is committed by states, our assessment tends to be quite permissive, giving states a great benefit of the doubt about the propriety of their violent acts. However, when the violence is committed by nonstate actors, we often react with horror, and the condemnations cannot come fast enough. Hence, terrorism is almost universally condemned, whereas violence by states, even when war has not been declared, is seen as legitimate, if not always fully justified. This difference in assessments remains when innocent civilians are killed in both cases and sometimes when such killing is deliberate. Even as thoughtful a commentator as Michael Walzer, for example, seems to employ this double standard. In his *Just and Unjust Wars,* Walzer considers whether "soldiers and statesmen [can] override the rights of innocent people for the sake of their own political community" and answers "affirmatively, though not without hesitation and worry" (1992, 254). Walzer goes on to discuss a case in point, the Allied bombing of German cities during World War II, arguing that, despite the many civilians who

deliberately were killed, the bombing was justified. However, later in the book, Walzer rejects out of hand the possibility that terrorism might sometimes be justified, on the grounds that it involves the deliberate killing of innocents (1992, chapter 12). He never considers the possibility that stateless communities might confront the same "supreme emergency" that justified, in his view, the bombing of innocent German civilians. I will have more to say about Walzer's position below, but for now I wish to point out that, on the face of it at least, his position seems quite inconsistent.

From a philosophical point of view, this double standard cannot be sustained. As Coady (1985) argues, consistency requires that we apply the same standards to both kinds of political violence, state and nonstate. Of course, it may turn out that there are simply some criteria that states can satisfy that nonstate actors cannot, so that the same standard applied to both inevitably leads to different conclusions. There may be morally relevant features of states that make their use of violence legitimate and its use by others illegitimate. However, I will argue that this is not the case. I argue that, on the most plausible account of just war theory, taking into account the ultimate moral basis of its criteria, violence undertaken by nonstate actors can, in principle, satisfy the requirements of a just war.

To advance this view, I examine each criterion of just war theory in turn, arguing in each case that terrorism committed by nonstate actors can satisfy the criterion. The most controversial parts of my argument will no doubt be those regarding just cause, legitimate authority, and discrimination, so I devote more attention to these than to the others. I argue that, once we properly understand the moral basis for each of these criteria, it is clear that some nonstate groups may have the same right as states to commit violence and that they are just as capable of committing that violence within the constraints imposed by just war theory. My conclusion, then, is that if just war theory can justify violence committed by states, then terrorism committed by nonstate actors can also, under certain circumstances, be justified by it as well. But before commencing the substantive argument, I must attend to some preliminary matters concerning the definition of *terrorism*.

DEFINITIONAL ISSUES

There is little agreement on the question of how *terrorism* is best defined. In the political arena, of course, the word is used by political actors for political purposes, usually to paint their opponents as monsters. Scholars, on the other hand, have at least attempted to arrive at a more detached position, seeking a definition that captures the essence of terrorism. However, there is reason, in addition to the lack of consensus, to doubt whether much progress has been made.

Most definitions of terrorism suffer from at least one of two difficulties. First, they often define terrorism as murder or otherwise characterize it as intrinsically wrong and unjustifiable. The trouble with this approach is that it prejudges the substantive moral issue by a definitional consideration. I agree with Teichman, who writes that "we ought not to begin by *defining* terrorism as a bad thing" (1989, 507). Moral conclusions should follow from moral reasoning, grappling with the moral issues themselves. To decide a normative issue by definitional considerations, then, ends the discussion before it begins.

The second shortcoming that many definitions of terrorism exhibit is being too revisionist of its meaning in ordinary language. As I have noted, the word is often used as a political weapon, so ordinary language will not settle the issue. Teichman (1989, 505) again is correct that any definition will necessarily be stipulative to some extent. But ordinary language does, nevertheless, impose some constraints on the stipulative definition that we can accept. For example, Carl Wellman defines *terrorism* as "the use or attempted use of terror as a means of coercion" (1979, 251) and draws the conclusion that when he instills terror in his students with threats of grade penalties on late papers, he commits terrorism. Clearly this is not what most of us have in mind when we speak of terrorism, so Wellman's definition, even if taken as stipulative, is difficult to accept.

Some definitions of terrorism suffer from both of these shortcomings to some degree. For example, those that maintain that terrorism is necessarily random or indiscriminate seem both to depart markedly from ordinary usage—there are lots of acts we call terrorist that specifically target military facilities and personnel—and thereby to prejudge the moral issue. (I will argue below that terrorism need not be indiscriminate at all.) The same can be said of definitions that insist that the aim of terrorism must be to terrorize, that it targets some to threaten many more (see, for example, Khatchadourian 1998). As Virginia Held has argued, "We should probably not construe either the intention to spread fear or the intention to kill noncombatants as necessary for an act of political violence to be an act of terrorism" (1991, 64). Annette Baier adds that "the terrorist may be ill named" because what she sometimes wants is not to terrorize but "the shocked attention of her audience population" (1994, 205).

With all of this disagreement, it would perhaps be desirable to avoid the use of the term *terrorism* altogether and simply to speak instead of political violence. I would be sympathetic to this position were it not for the fact that *terrorism* is already too much a part of our political vocabulary to be avoided. Still, we can with great plausibility simply define *terrorism* as a form of political violence, as Held does: "I [see] terrorism as a form of violence to achieve political goals, where creating fear is usually high among the intended effects" (1991, 64). This is a promising approach, though I would drop as nonessential the stipulation that terrorism is usually intended to spread fear. In addition, I would make two stipulations of my own. First, "violence" can include damage to property as well as harm to people. Blowing up a power plant can surely be an act of terrorism, even if no one is injured. Second, for the purposes of this chapter, I am interested in violence committed by nonstate actors. I do not thereby deny the existence of state terrorism. Indeed, I endorse Gordon and Lopez's discussion of it in their chapter in this volume. However,

for the purposes of my present argument, I assume that when a state commits terrorism against its own citizens, this is a matter for domestic justice, and that when it commits violence outside of its own borders, just war theory can, fairly easily, be extended to cover these cases. The problem for international ethics that I wish to address here is whether just war theory can be extended to nonstate actors. So my stipulative definition of *terrorism* in this chapter is simply that it is violence committed by nonstate actors against persons or property for political purposes. This definition appears to leave open the normative issues involved and to be reasonably consistent with ordinary language.

JUS AD BELLUM

It is somewhat misleading to speak of just war *theory,* for it is not a single theory but, rather, a tradition within which there is a range of interpretation. That is, just war theory is best thought of as providing a framework for discussion about whether a war is just, rather than as providing a set of unambiguous criteria that are easily applied. In what follows I rely on what I believe is the most plausible and normatively appealing version of just war theory, one that is essentially the same as the one articulated and developed by the preceding chapters. I begin with the *jus ad bellum* criteria, concerning the justice of going to war, and then turn to *jus in bello* criteria, which apply to the conduct of the war.

Just Cause

A just cause for a war is usually a defensive one. That is, a state is taken to have a just cause when it defends itself against aggression, where *aggression* means the violation or the imminent threat of the violation of its territorial integrity or political independence (Walzer 1992). So the just cause provision of just war theory holds, roughly, that the state has a right to defend itself against the aggression of other states.

But on what is this right of the state based? Most students of international ethics maintain that any right that a state enjoys is ultimately based on the rights of its citizens. States in and of themselves have value only to the extent that they serve some good for the latter. The moral status of the state is therefore derivative, not foundational, and it is derivative of the rights of the individuals within it. This, it seems, is the dominant (liberal) view, and only an exceedingly statist perspective would dispute it (Beitz 1979b; Walzer 1992).

The right that is usually cited as being the ground for the state's right to defend itself is the right of self-determination. The state is the manifestation of, as well as the arena for, the right of a people to determine itself. It is because aggression threatens the common life of the people within a state, as well as threatening other goods they hold dear, that the state can defend its territory and independence. This is clear, for example, from Walzer's (1992, chapter 6) discussion of intervention. Drawing on John Stuart Mill (1984), Walzer argues that states generally ought not to intervene in the affairs of other states because to do so would be to violate the right of self-determination of the community within the state. However, once the right of self-determination is recognized, its implications go beyond a right against intervention or a right of defense. Walzer makes this clear as well, as his discussion of Mill's argument for nonintervention is followed immediately by exceptions to the rule, one of which is secession. When a secessionist movement has demonstrated that it represents the will of its people, other states may intervene to aid the secession because, in this case, secession reflects the self-determination of that people . . .

For the purposes of my present argument, I need not enter this important debate but only point out that any one of these views can support the weak claim I wish to make. The claim is that under some circumstances, some groups enjoy a right to self-determination. The circumstances may include—or, following Buchanan, even be limited to—cases of injustice toward the group, or, in a more permissive view, it may not. This right may be enjoyed only by nations or by any group within a territory. It may be that the right of self-determination does not automatically ground a right to political independence, but if some form of self-determination cannot be realized within an existing state, then it can, under these circumstances, ground such a right. For the sake of simplicity, in the discussion that follows I refer to nations or peoples as having a right of self-determination, but this does not commit me to the view that other kinds of groups do not enjoy this right. Similarly, I will sometimes fail to distinguish between a right of self-determination and a right to a state, despite realizing that the former does not necessarily entail the latter. I will assume that in some cases— say, when a federal arrangement cannot be worked out—one can ground the right to a state on the right to self-determination.

My conclusion about the just cause requirement is obvious. Groups other than those constituted by the state in which they live can have a just cause to defend their right of self-determination. While just war theory relies on the rights of the citizens to ground the right of a state to defend itself, other communities within a state may have that same right. When the communal life of a nation is seriously threatened by a state, that nation has a just cause to defend itself. In the case in which the whole nation is within a single state this can justify secession. In a case in which the community is stateless, as with colonial rule, it is probably less accurate to speak of secession than national liberation.

This is not a radical conclusion. Indeed, it is recognized and endorsed by the United Nations, as Khatchadourian points out: "The UN definition of 'just cause' recognizes the rights of peoples as well as states," and in Article 7 of the definition of *aggression,* the United Nations refers to "the right to self-determination, freedom, and independence, as derived from the Charter, of *peoples* forcibly deprived of that right" (1998, 41). So both morally and legally, "peoples" or "nations" enjoy a right to self-determination. When that right is frustrated, such peoples, I have argued, have the same just cause that states have when the self-determination of their citizens is threatened.

Legitimate Authority

The legitimate authority requirement is usually interpreted to mean that only states can go to war justly. It rules out private groups waging private wars and claiming them to be just. The state has a monopoly on the legitimate use of force, so it is a necessary condition for a just war that it be undertaken by the entity that is uniquely authorized to wield the sword. To allow other entities, groups, or agencies to undertake violence would be to invite chaos. Such violence is seen as merely private violence, crime.

The equation of legitimate authority with states has, however, been criticized by a number of philosophers—and with good reason. Gilbert has argued that "the equation of proper authority with a lawful claim to it should be resisted" (1994, 29). Tony Coates (1997, chapter 5) has argued at some length and quite persuasively that to equate legitimate authority with state sovereignty is to rob the requirement of the moral force that it historically has had. The result is that the principle has become too permissive by assuming that any de facto state may wage war. This requirement, then, is too easily and quickly "checked off": If a war is waged by a state, this requirement is satisfied. This interpretation has meant that "the criterion of legitimate authority has become the most neglected of all the criteria that have been traditionally employed in the moral assessment of war" (Coates 1997, 123). Contrary to this tendency in recent just war thinking, Coates argues that we must subject to close scrutiny a given state's claim to represent the interests and rights of its people.

When we reject the view that all states are legitimate authorities, we may also ask if some nonstates may be legitimate authorities. The considerations just adduced suggest that being a state is not sufficient for being a legitimate authority. Perhaps it is not necessary either. What matters is the plausibility of the claim to represent the interests and rights of a people. I would like to argue that some nonstate entities or organizations may present a very plausible case for being a people's representative. Surely it is sufficient for this that the organization is widely seen as their representative by the members of the nation itself. If an organization claims to act on behalf of a people and is widely seen by that people as legitimately doing so, then the rest of us should look on that organization as the legitimate authority of the people for the purposes of assessing its entitlement to engage in violence on their behalf.

The alternative view, that only states may be legitimate authorities, "leads to political quietism [and is] conservative and uncritical" (Coates 1997, 128). Once we acknowledge that stateless peoples may have the right to self-determination, it would render that right otiose to deny that the right could be defended and vindicated by some nonstate entity. As Dugard (1982, 83) has pointed out, in the case of colonial domination, there is no victim state, though there is a victim people. If we are to grant that a colonized people has a right to self-determination, it seems that we must grant that a nonstate organization— a would-be state, perhaps—can act as a legitimate authority and justly engage in violence on behalf of the people. Examples are not difficult to find. Coates cites the Kurds and the Marsh Arabs in Iraq and asks, "Must such persecuted communities be denied the right of collective self-defense simply because, through some historical accident, they lack the formal character of states?" (1997, 128).

It must be emphasized that the position advocated here requires that the organization not only claim representative status but be perceived to enjoy that status by the people it claims to represent. This is a rather conservative requirement because it rules out "vanguard" organizations that claim representative status despite lack of support among the people themselves. The position defended here is also more stringent than that suggested by Wilkins, who writes that it might "be enough for a terrorist movement simply to claim to represent the aspirations or the moral rights of a people" (1992, 71). While I agree that "moral authority may be all that matters" (Wilkins 1992, 72). I would argue that moral authority requires not merely claiming to represent a people but also being seen by the people themselves as their representative.

How do we know whether this is the case? No single answer can be given here. Certainly the standard should not be higher than that used for states. In the case of states, for example, elections are not required for legitimacy, as understood in just war theory. There are many members of the international community in good standing that are not democratic regimes, authorized by elections. In the case of nonstate entities, no doubt a number of factors will weigh in, either for or against the claim to representativeness, and, in the absence of legal procedures (or public opinion polls), we may have to make an all-things-considered judgment. No doubt there will be some disagreement in particular cases, but all that is required for the present argument is that, in principle, nonstate organizations may enjoy the moral status of legitimate authorities.

Right Intention

If a national group can have a just cause, and if a nonstate entity can be a legitimate authority to engage in violence on behalf of that group, it seems unproblematic that those engaging in violence can be rightly motivated by that just cause. Hence, if just cause and legitimate authority can be satisfied, there seems to be no reason to think that the requirement of right intention cannot be satisfied. This is not to say, of course, that if the first two are satisfied, the latter is as well, but only that if the first two requirements are met, the latter can be. All that it requires is that the relevant actors be motivated by the just cause and not some other end.

Last Resort

Can terrorist violence, undertaken by the representatives of a stateless nation to vindicate their right of self-determination, be a last resort? Some have doubted that it can. For example, Walzer refers to the claim of last resort as one of the "excuses" sometimes offered for terrorism. He suggests that terrorism is usually a first resort, not a last one, and that to truly be a last resort, "one must indeed try everything (which is a lot of things), and not just once. . . . Politics is an art of repetition" (1988, 239). Terrorists, according to Walzer, often claim that their resort to violence is a last resort but in fact it never is and never can be.

Two problems arise concerning Walzer's position. First, related to the definitional issues discussed above and taken up again below when discrimination is treated, Walzer takes terrorism to be "an attack upon the innocent," and he "take[s] the principle for granted: that every act of terrorism is a wrongful act" (1988, 238). Given the understanding of terrorism as murder, it can never be a justified last resort. But as Fullinwider (1988) argues in his response to Walzer, it is puzzling both that Walzer construes terrorism this way, for not all terrorism is random murder, and that Walzer simply takes it for granted that nothing can justify terrorism. Walzer's position is undermined by a prejudicial definition of *terrorism* that begs the substantive moral questions, reflected in the fact that he characterizes arguments in defense of terrorism as mere "excuses."

The second problem is that again Walzer appears to use a double standard. While he does not say so explicitly in the paper under discussion, Walzer elsewhere clearly endorses the resort to war by states. Here, however, he argues that, because "politics is an art of repetition," the last resort is never arrived at for nonstate actors contemplating violence. But why is it that the territorial integrity and political independence of, say, Britain, justify the resort to violence—even violence that targets civilians—but the right of self-determination of a stateless nation never does? Why can states arrive at last resort, while stateless nations cannot? Walzer never provides an answer to this question.

The fact is that judgment is called for by all political actors contemplating violence, and among the judgments that must be made is whether last resort has been. This is a judgment about whether all reasonable nonviolent measures have been tried, been tried a reasonable number of times, and been given a reasonable amount of time to work. There will always be room for argument about what *reasonable* means here, what it requires in a particular case, but I see no justification for employing a double standard for what it means, one for states, another for nonstate actors. If states may reach the point of deciding that all nonviolent measures have failed, then so too can nonstate actors.

Probability of Success

Whether terrorism ever has any probability of success, or enough probability of success to justify embarking on a terrorist campaign, depends on a number of factors, including the time horizon one has in mind. Whether one considers the case of state actors deciding to embark on a war or nonstate actors embarking on terrorism, a prospective judgment is required, and prospective judgments are liable to miscalculations and incorrect estimations of many factors. Still, one must make a judgment, and if one judges that the end has little chance of being achieved through violence, the probability of success criterion requires that the violence not be commenced.

Does terrorism ever have any probability of success? There are differing views of the historical record on this question. For example, Walzer thinks not. He writes, "No nation that I know of owes its freedom to a campaign of random murder" (1988, 240). Again, we find that Walzer's analysis is hindered by his conception of what terrorism is, and so it is of little help to us here. To those who have a less loaded notion of terrorism, the evidence appears more ambiguous. Held provides a brief, well-balanced discussion of the issue. She cites authors who have argued on both sides of the question, including one who uses the bombing of the U.S. Marines' barracks in Beirut in 1982 (which prompted an American withdrawal) as an example of a successful terrorist attack. Held concludes that "it may be impossible to predict whether an act of terrorism will in fact have its intended effect" but notes that in this it is no different from other prospective judgments (1991, 71). Similarly, Teichman concludes that the historical evidence on the effectiveness of terrorism is "both ambiguous and incomplete" (1989, 517). And Baier suggests that, at the least, "the prospects for the success of a cause do not seem in the past to have been reduced by resort to unauthorized force, by violent demonstrations that cost some innocent lives" (1994, 208). Finally, Wilkins (1992, 39) believes that some terrorist campaigns

have indeed accomplished their goal of national independence and cites Algeria and Kenya as examples.

I am not in a position to judge all of the historical evidence that may be relevant to this issue. However, it seems clear that we cannot say that it is never the case that terrorism has some prospect of success. Perhaps in most cases—the vast majority of them, even—there is little hope of success. Still, we cannot rule out that terrorism can satisfy the probability of success criterion.

Proportionality

The proportionality criterion within *jus ad bellum* also requires a prospective judgments—whether the overall costs of the violent conflict will be outweighed by the overall benefits. In addition to the difficulties inherent in prospective judgments, this criterion is problematic in that it seems to require us to measure the value of costs and benefits that may not be amenable to measurement and seems to assume that all goods are commensurable, that their value can be compared. As a result, there is probably no way to make these kinds of judgments with any great degree of precision.

Still, it seems clear that terrorism can satisfy this criterion at least as well as conventional war. Given the large scale of destruction that often characterizes modern warfare, and given that some very destructive wars are almost universally considered just, it appears that just war theory can countenance a great deal of violence if the end is of sufficient value. If modern warfare is sometimes justified, terrorism, in which the violence is usually on a far smaller scale, can be justified as well. This is especially clear if the end of the violence is the same or similar in both cases, such as when a nation wishes to vindicate its right to self-determination.

JUS IN BELLO

Even if terrorism can meet all the criteria of *jus ad bellum,* it may not be able to meet those of *jus in bello,* for terrorism is often condemned, not so much for who carries it out and why but for how it is carried out. Arguing that it can satisfy the requirements of *jus in bello,* then, may be the greatest challenge facing my argument.

Proportionality

The challenge, however, does not come from the proportionality requirement of *jus in bello.* Like its counterpart in *jus ad bellum,* the criterion requires proportionality between the costs of an action and the benefits to be achieved, but now the requirement is applied to particular acts within the war. It forbids, then, conducting the war in such a way that it involves inordinate costs, costs that are disproportionate to the gains.

Again, there seems to be no reason to believe that terrorist acts could not satisfy this requirement. Given that the scale of the death and destruction usually involved in terrorist acts pales in comparison with that involved in wars commonly thought to be just, it would seem that terrorism would satisfy this requirement more easily than war (assuming that the goods to be achieved are not dissimilar). So if the means of terrorism is what places it beyond the moral pale for many people, it is probably not because of its disproportionality.

Discrimination

The principle of discrimination holds that in waging a war we must distinguish between legitimate and illegitimate targets of attack. The usual way of making this distinction is to classify persons according to their status as combatants and noncombatants and to maintain that only combatants may be attacked. However, there is some disagreement as to the moral basis of this distinction, which creates disagreement as to where exactly this line should be drawn. While usually based on the notion of moral innocence, noncombatant status, it can be argued, has little to do with innocence, for often combatants are conscripts, while those truly responsible for aggression are usually not liable (practically, not morally) to attack. Moreover, many who provide essential support to the war effort are not combatants.

For the moment, though, let us accept the conventional view that discrimination requires that violence be directed at military targets. Assuming the line can be clearly drawn, two points can be made about terrorism and discrimination. The first is that, a priori, it is possible for terrorism to discriminate and still be terrorism. This follows from the argument presented above that, as a matter of definition, it is implausible to define terrorism as intrinsically indiscriminate. Those who define terrorism as random or indiscriminate will disagree and maintain that "discriminate terrorism" is an oxymoron, a conceptual impossibility. Here I can only repeat that this position departs substantially from ordinary language and does so in a way that prejudges the moral issues involved. However, if my argument above does not convince on this question, there is little more to be said here.

Luckily, the issue is not a purely a priori one. The fact is that terrorists, or at least those called terrorists by almost everyone, in fact do often discriminate. One example, cited above, is the bombing of the barracks in Beirut, which killed some 240 American soldiers. Whatever one wants to say to condemn the attack, one cannot say that it was indiscriminate. . . .

. . . All of this is consistent with the assumption that a clear line can be drawn between combatants and noncombatants. However, the more reasonable view may be that combatancy status, and therefore liability to attack, are matters of degree. This is suggested by Holmes (1989, 187), and though Holmes writes as a pacifist critic of just war theory, his suggestion is one that just war theorists may nevertheless want to endorse. Holmes conceives of a spectrum along which we can place classes of individuals, according to their degree of responsibility for an aggressive war. At one end he would place political leaders who undertake the aggression, followed by soldiers, contributors to the war, supporters, and, finally, at the other end of the spectrum, noncontributors and nonsupporters. This view does indeed better capture our moral intuitions about liability to attack and avoids debates (which are probably not resolvable) about where the absolute line between combatants and noncombatants is to be drawn.

If correct, this view further complicates the question of whether and when terrorism discriminates. It means we must speak of more and less discriminate violence, and it forces us to ask questions like, To what *extent* were the targets of violence implicated in unjust aggression? Children, for example, would be clearly off-limits, but nonmilitary adults who actively take part in frustrating a people's right to self-determination may not be. With terrorism, as with war, the question to ask may not be, Was the act discriminate, yes or no? but, rather, How discriminate was the violence? Our judgment on this matter, and hence our moral appraisal of the violence, is likely to be more nuanced if we ask the latter question than if we assume that a simple yes or no settles the matter. After all, is our judgment really the same—and ought it be—when a school bus is attacked as when gun-toting citizens are attacked? Terrorism, it seems, can be more discriminate or less so, and our judgments ought to reflect the important matters of degree involved.

One final issue is worth mentioning, if only briefly. Even if one were to grant that terrorism necessarily involves the killing of innocents, this alone does not place it beyond the scope of just war theory, for innocents may be killed in a just war. All that just war theory requires is that innocents not be *targeted*. The basis for this position is the principle of double effect, which holds, roughly, that innocents may be killed as long as their deaths are not the intended effects of violence but, rather, the unintended (though perhaps fully foreseen) side effects of violence. So the most that can be said against my position, even granting that terrorism involves the killing of innocents, is that the difference between (just) war and terrorism is that in the former innocents are not targeted but (routinely) killed while in the latter they are targeted and killed. Whether this is a crucial distinction is a question that would require us to go too far afield at this point. Perhaps it is enough to say that if there are reasons to reject the principle of double effect, such as those offered by Holmes (1989, 193–200), there is all the more basis to think that terrorism and war are not so morally different from each other.

CONCLUSION

I have argued that terrorism, understood as political violence committed by nonstate actors, can be assessed from the point of view of just war theory and that terrorist acts can indeed satisfy the theory's criteria. Though stateless, some groups can nevertheless have a just cause when their right to self-determination is frustrated. Under such circumstances, a representative organization can be a morally legitimate authority to carry out violence as a last resort to defend the group's rights. Such violence must conform to the other criteria, especially discrimination, but terrorism, I have argued, can do so. . . .

. . . It is important to be clear about what I have not argued here. I have not defended terrorism in general, nor certainly have I defended any particular act of violence. It follows from my argument not that terrorism can be justified but that if war can be justified, then terrorism can be as well. I wish to emphasize the conditional nature of the conclusion. I have not established just war theory as the best or the only framework within which to think about the moral issues raised by political violence. Instead I have relied on it because it is the most developed and widely used in thinking about violence carried out by states. I have done so because the double standard that is often used in assessing violence committed by states and nonstate actors seems indefensible. Applying just war theory to both, I believe, is a plausible way to bring both kinds of violence under one standard. . . .

I have little doubt that most terrorist acts do not satisfy all of the criteria of just war theory and that many of them fall far short. In such cases we are well justified in condemning them. But the condemnation must follow, not precede, examination of the case and is not settled by calling the act terrorism and its perpetrators terrorists. I agree with Fullinwider that, while terrorism often fails to be morally justified, "this failure is contingent, not neces-

sary. We cannot define terrorism into a moral corner where we do not have to worry any more about justification" (1988, 257). Furthermore, failure to satisfy the requirements of just war theory is not unique to acts of terrorism. The same could be said of wars themselves. How many wars, after all, are undertaken and waged within the constraints imposed by the theory?

The conditional nature of the conclusion, if the above argument is sound, forces a choice. Either both interstate war and terrorism can be justified or neither can be. For my part, I must confess to being sorely tempted by the latter position, that neither war nor terrorism can be justified. This temptation is bolstered by pacifist arguments, such as that presented by Holmes (1989, chapter 6), that the killing of innocents is a perfectly predictable effect of modern warfare, the implication of which is that no modern war can be just. That is, even if we can imagine a modern just war, it is not a realistic possibility. Though the pacifist position is tempting, it also seems clear that some evils are great enough to require a response, even a violent response. And once we grant that states may respond violently, there seems no principled reason to deny that same right to certain nonstate groups that enjoy a right to self-determination.

References

Baier, Annette. 1994. "Violent Demonstrations." In *Moral Prejudices: Essays on Ethics*. Cambridge, MA: Harvard University Press.

Beitz, Charles R. 1979. *Political Theory and International Relations*. Princeton: Princeton University Press.

Coady, C.A.J. 1985. "The Morality of Terrorism." *Philosophy* 60: 47–69.

Coates, Anthony J. 1997. *The Ethics of War*. Manchester: Manchester University Press.

Dugard, John. 1982. "International Terrorism and the Just War." In *The Morality of Terrorism: Reli-*

gious and Secular Justifications, ed. David C. Rapoport and Yonah Alexander. New York: Pergamon Books.

Fullinwider, Robert K. 1988. "Understanding Terrorism." In *Problems of International Justice,* ed. Steven Luper-Foy. Boulder: Westview Press.

Gilbert, Paul. 1994. *Terrorism, Security and Nationality: An Introductory Study in Applied Political Philosophy.* New York: Routledge.

Held, Virginia. 1991. "Terrorism, Rights, and Political Goals." In *Violence, Terrorism, and Justice,* ed. R.G. Frey and Christopher W. Morris. Cambridge: Cambridge University Press.

Holmes, Robert L. 1989. *On War and Morality.* Princeton: Princeton University Press.

Khatchadourian, Haig. 1998. *The Morality of Terrorism.* New York: Peter Lang.

Mill, John Stuart. 1984 [1859]. "A Few Words on Non-Intervention." In *Essays On Equality, Law, and Education: Collected Works of John Stuart Mill,* Volume 21, ed. John Robson. Toronto: University of Toronto Press.

Teichman. Jenny. 1989. "How To Define Terrorism." *Philosophy* 64: 505–517.

Walzer, Michael. 1988. "Terrorism: A Critique of Excuses." In *Problems of International Justice,* ed. Steven Luper-Foy. Boulder: Westview Press.

Walzer, Michael. 1992 [1979]. *Just and Unjust Wars: A Moral Argument With Historical Illustrations.* 2nd Edition. New York: Basic Books.

Wellman, Carl. 1979. "On Terrorism Itself." *Journal of Value Inquiry* 13: 250–258.

Wilkins, Burleigh Taylor. 1992. *Terrorism and Collective Responsibility.* New York: Routledge.

Just War Doctrine and the Military Response to Terrorism

(2003)

Joseph M. Boyle, Jr.

Joseph M. Boyle, Jr., is professor of philosophy at the University of Toronto. His research interests include moral philosophy, ethical theory, bioethics, and applied natural law. Along with articles in these areas, he has coauthored Nuclear Deterrence, Morality, and Realism *(Clarendon Press, 1987) with John Finnis and Germain Grisez.*

I. DEFINING TERMS AND FORMULATING ISSUES

In this article, I will articulate a traditional version of just war theory and apply it to the case of a polity's response to terrorist actions by groups that are not themselves polities. I will argue that, according to just war theory, defending against this sort of terrorism is a just cause; that within significant constraints sovereign political authorities can have authority to undertake military actions for the sake of this just cause, notwithstanding the nature of organization of the terrorists; and that a political community can pursue such a cause with right intention, even though in the world as it is military efforts to defend against terrorism may well not meet this condition.

In this introduction I will define key terms; in the second section I will provide a formulation of just war theory, and in the last section I will apply its conditions for the permissibility of waging war to the case of responding to terrorism by groups that are not states.

Traditional just war theory has some potential to illumine issues raised by the response to terrorism because, on the one hand, it is related historically and conceptually to the forms of just war thinking embedded in international law, and on the other, it is rooted in a normatively richer and distinctive conception of practical life than is current just war doctrine. The difference pointed to by my distinguishing current from traditional just war doctrine is in the rationale for the judgments made within each. There will certainly be disagreements about theory and particular judgments in both; but in current just war theory, the project of seeking agreement within the common moral world by careful casuistry from broadly acceptable paradigms, often embodied in international law and agreements, is central. By contrast, in traditional just war doctrine, the consensus is not so central, and the project of determining a war's justice by application of a conception of morally good social living to the bellicose circumstances is central. In particular, the conception of social action and authority provides a distinctive rationale for and limitation of the authority to wage war, and the requirement that the intention in making war be peaceful and focused strictly on war aims satisfying the just cause both excludes appealing to abstractly just causes to justify unwarranted violence, and highlights the moral perplexity caused by the conjunction of the politi-

cal obligation to defend against terrorism and the refusal of those having this obligation to desist from wrongs which make genuine peace impossible. Traditional just war theory, therefore, is likely to be more controversial than current just war theory, but also more illuminating, particularly when issues to be settled fall outside the consensus and its logical extension in casuistry.

The response to terrorism since September 11, 2001 provides the motivation for much current interest in the topics discussed here. But I shall take a step back from the controversial details of current events and focus on the ethical analysis.

A. Just War Theory

The just war doctrine that I will discuss is reasonably named "traditional just war theory." By this expression I refer to the doctrine and rationale concerning the moral permissibility of engaging in warfare that was developed by medieval canonists and moral theologians chiefly from the work of St. Augustine, and articulated by St. Thomas Aquinas in a pithy summary that has become its classic formulation.

. . . An important component of the concept of war in the just war tradition is that waging war is a group action—something individuals cannot do acting alone, but only in concert with others. Therefore, it requires the coordination of individuals' contributing actions by means of social authority. The authority directs and coordinates the multiplicity of actions that comprise making war towards a common goal, and thereby unifies them into a single social act of the community. This does not imply that individuals can surrender responsibility for their own part in a war.[1]

It does imply as a condition for a war's permissibility that the authority coordinating the bellicose action be of the right kind.

The form of war to be discussed is a polity's military response to terrorist actions directed against it, its citizens or allies by groups that are not polities. Military action is the use of force outside the framework of domestic and international criminal law enforced by police and the criminal justice system.

Responding to terrorist activities is reasonably understood to presuppose that those activities actually exist, that is, that they are not simply actions projected in planning, or actions a group has capability and reason to undertake. So, I am not addressing preventive war against terrorists, but only defensive and punitive responses to terrorism. Setting aside preventive war against terrorism does not assume that there is a clear and easily recognized distinction between preventive war and defensive or punitive war. For preemption against bellicose actions begun but not fully executed can be defensive or punitive. The distinction emerges only through casuistry on a case-by-case basis.

B. Terrorism

The notion of terrorism at work in current discussions of international relations is difficult to characterize with precision. I will, therefore, try to specify a core idea of a terrorist action, recognizing that there will be actions having only some of its defining features, and that terrorist actions will usually have other morally relevant features as well.

I begin by distinguishing the terrorist actions I will discuss from those military actions in which one group seeks to overwhelm an enemy by force, or simply to destroy or displace a population by genocide or ethnic cleansing. In such cases the intended goals are achieved—or could be—completely by force. Except incidentally, they involve no effort to persuade the targeted enemy, but only efforts to overwhelm or destroy it. Thus, if an army going down to military defeat decides on surrender in the face of the prospect of an enemy's continued battlefield victories, that decision could be no more than a response to the prospect of being overwhelmed. This decision might be ignored by the powerful opponent, who might also accept it only as completely shaped by the weaker opponent's prospect of destruction.

By contrast, terrorist actions fall within the category of violent actions that do not include the intent to displace decision-making by violence; they are violent acts intended to influence decisions. Terrorist actions are undertaken to cause fear and demoralization, and thereby to lead to changes in policy on the part of the terrorized party. Vengeful, destructive acts having no further purpose than destruction certainly cause terror in those being destroyed, but these are not the core cases of terrorism.

Terrorist acts are like deterrence, which is undertaken to affect the decision-making of the deterred party by threatening to bring about what the deterred party does not want if it acts in ways the deterring party wants to prevent.

Plainly, there are important differences between terrorism and deterrence. Terrorist actions are not as such threats, although terrorist undertakings ordinarily involve the threat of further terrorism. Moreover, the very idea of deterrence does not connote something morally wrong or questionable, as the idea of terrorism surely does. For it is possible to deter by threatening only what one may rightfully do, as happens in the formation and execution of provisions of the criminal law, at least partially for the sake of deterring future criminal acts.

But one can also threaten precisely terrorist action to deter, as seems to have been the case in the nuclear deterrence by the great powers during the Cold War. This possibility suggests that the designation of an action as terrorist, and so as generally morally suspect, is triggered not by the persuasive or political structure terrorist actions share with deterrence and many other actions involving violence, but by the particular ways in which violence is used. What is it that makes an action terrorist and so wrongful, or at least presumptively so?

It seems that terrorist actions are wrong because those who do them seek to affect others' behavior and decisions by directly or indirectly harming people whom they have no right to harm. The bad means whose use defines actions as terrorist are the intentional harms inflicted on some people to cause fear (often on the part of others than those harmed). Those harms are wrongs because the targets of the terrorist harms are in the relevant sense "innocent." Even if some are oppressors who may be attacked, they may not be killed by terrorist acts because these are acts seeking to cause politically effective fear, and so do not kill the oppressor to defend but as a means of causing fear, and most such acts are "indiscriminate" in a strong sense: anyone who can be harmed and whose harming will cause the hoped-for fear is a reasonable target, and so those who might be harmed only as a side effect of other actions are harmed intentionally in terrorist actions.

Any person or group performs a terrorist act, therefore, when he, she or they in-

tentionally harm someone they have no right to harm to get a person or group to choose differently than she or they otherwise would.

There will, of course, be borderline cases in which it is unclear independently of careful inquiry whether the harms are intentionally inflicted and whether those on whom they are inflicted should be immune from such harm. For example, freedom fighters in a justified war of independence need not terrorize the group with whom they contend. However, freedom fighters can, and may be tempted to, use terrorism. In many cases they seek to persuade those who oppress them, instead of achieving military victory by overwhelming force. In such situations, some actions will likely appear terrorist, and the temptation to use terrorism may be strong. In such situations, actions that are impermissible by the traditional *in bello* conditions for carrying out warfare justly are likely to be terrorist. Strategies that involve indiscriminately harming those who are not carrying out the oppression fought, intentionally harming them, and so on ordinarily contribute to the persuasion of the oppressors only in virtue of the terror they cause.

Terrorist actions, as I have defined them, can be performed by individuals or groups and their targets can be individuals or groups. For example, a person could terrorize a neighbor by wronging someone she cares about (although this would likely provoke a response from police if the matter were serious), a criminal gang can terrorize a neighborhood by killing or maiming some of its residents, a nation can terrorize another by bombing some of its cities. For simplicity, however, I will use the expressions "terrorism" and "terrorist actions" to refer to terrorist actions as the action of a group that is not organized as a polity. Al-Qaeda seems to be a clear example of such an agent; other terrorist groups in the Middle East, and perhaps the IRA, appear to be somewhat more closely connected to political communities, even if these groups do not have, or do not clearly have, responsibility for the common goods of these communities.

II. THE CONDITIONS FOR THE PERMISSIBILITY OF WAGING WAR

Thomas Aquinas gathered the teachings of Augustine on the morality of war, by his day widely interpreted and incorporated into canon law, and in a short, clear statement provided what is probably the classic statement of traditional just war theory. This treatment is in Aquinas' best known and most mature work, the *Summa Theologiae*, in the second part of the second part, which deals with moral problems. The discussion falls within the sins against the virtue of charity, since war is presumptively a sin against charity.[2]

Aquinas maintains that a war can be morally justified if and only if three conditions are met. Those conditions are proper authority, just cause and right intent. His concern is plainly with conditions for what came to be called *jus ad bellum,* the moral permissibility of going to war (or continuing in fighting a war already begun).[3] The *jus in bello* norms for the conduct of war, which have been the center of just war concern about 20th century warfare, were not explicit until Vitoria's work, but the normative outlook already shaped what Aquinas said. Most importantly, it is reasonable to think that he assumes in this discussion that the absolute prohibition against murder—intentionally or wantonly killing innocents—applies in warfare just as robustly as the prohibition against lying, which he explicitly holds as applying in warfare. For, as Aquinas made plain in the discussion of killing, no one can be authorized to intentionally kill innocents.[4]

But since the main issue in this article is the moral permissibility of undertaking warfare to defend against or punish terrorists, Aquinas' focus on the conditions for going to or continuing in warfare is more helpful than the recent just war concern about how war is executed.

A. Proper Authority

The first of Aquinas' conditions is proper authority; that is, only the head of a polity (*princeps,* often translated as "sovereign"), can properly command the waging of war. Two reasons are given: first, private persons have no business waging war and other lesser political leaders can appeal to higher authority to settle disputes and to remedy injustices. Second, only the head of the polity is authorized to bring together the community to fight.

What grounds the sovereign's authority in both these relationships is the fact that the care of the republic is entrusted to the sovereign, who has the responsibility to look after the welfare of the city, province or kingdom. This responsibility includes authority to use force not only internally against domestic criminals but against outsiders who harm the polity.

Augustine and, following him, Aquinas clearly make an inference here from the domestic situation in which the magistrate is justified in using force for the common good to the international situation in which the sovereign is justified in using force to respond to externally based wrongs. This inference is required because the biblical text cited by Augustine is understood as referring to the domestic authority of leaders.[5] But the inference is passed over as if straightforward. This inference seems justified, and it can be construed as an analogy from the domestic to the international sphere. It is not, however, an analogy from a private right of self-defense to a national right of self-defense, but from authority exercised within a polity to that same authority exercised against outsiders, for the same reason as it is exercised internally. Indeed, Augustine was suspicious of a private right of self-defense, and this suspicion led Aquinas to develop his complex story about killing in self-defense, an account which provided the elements for the later doctrine of double effect.[6]

In short, war waged without public authority is not permissible. And not any kind of public authority qualifies. Only the authority of one who has the final say for the welfare of a political community may rightly take it to war; by implicit definition a leader has "final say" when there is no higher authority capable of and authorized to deal with the harm to the polity without commanding and carrying out violent action. The idea seems to be that the welfare of a political community, which includes the just protection of its subjects' liberties and other aspects of its common good, requires care and protection; and that care sometimes requires violent action. Those who are in charge of the community's welfare are the legitimate primary agents of this violent action. Those leaders who can invoke higher authority within the community are not in this ultimate way in charge of its welfare. . . .

My point here is only that the proper authority of the sovereign in undertaking war, which Aquinas took to be a necessary

condition for a permissible war, now belongs to the leaders of a polity, not to leaders of transnational organizations. If a transnational organization developed the capacity to coordinate the actions of all in the world for a global common good, and if such leaders had the capacity to protect the common goods of the various political communities around the world, then such a government would have the essential features of sovereignty and there would always be this final court of appeal. Until these conditions obtain some residue of the right of a polity to respond to unjust attacks from beyond its borders must remain. Still, that authority may be qualified by treaty, vested in an international authority or rightly limited by the development of a renewed *jus gentium*. On just war grounds such limitations can be significant.[7]

B. Just Cause

Aquinas' second necessary condition for the permissibility of a war is that there be a just cause. He gives little justification for what he rightly takes to be an obvious ethical condition; that any action should be done only for a good purpose is for him a fundamental requirement of moral life. Nor does he provide a list or a set of examples of just reasons for undertaking warfare; such a list shows up only later in Vitoria.

But Aquinas does provide something more than the obvious moral requirement. He specifies the just cause needed for a permissible war as arising only in the face of the wrongdoing of outsiders, and further specifies it as being essentially punitive. He thus goes beyond the self-evident ethical point that a just cause is necessary, and beyond the intuitive requirement that a just war responds to wrongdoing, and adds the punitive understanding of that response, bolstering his claim with a reference to Augustine's authority.

He says that those who are rightly attacked must deserve it on account of some wrong they have done. Augustine's text makes plain that this response to wrongdoing is understood to be punitive: "We usually describe a just war as one that avenges wrongs, that is, when a nation or state has to be punished either for refusing to make amends for outrages done by its subjects or to restore what has been seized injuriously."

. . . The relationships between punishment, the common good of a polity, and the authority of the leaders who serve it are such that the punitive conception of just cause is not justifiable; in a word, leaders lack the authority to punish outsiders.

The reasoning is as follows: political leaders have authority over their subjects and authority to punish malefactors. That authority is rooted in the common good of the polity and the special role of service which political leaders have to that good. The care for that good sometimes requires the use of force to stop and deter domestic criminals, those who share in the life of a political community but violate its just regulations. This reasonably includes the right to punish them as a means of restoring justice, which also enhances the fulfillment of the deterrent and defensive responsibilities of leaders.

For the same reason, political leaders also have authority to lead and command defensive measures against externally based threats to the welfare of the polity. Defending subjects from injuries inflicted by outsiders plainly is a responsibility of those entrusted with the care of a polity's common good. That defensive action is for the sake of that common good.

What is needed at this point is a justification of the authority of the leaders of a polity not simply to command and organize defense from outside attack but precisely to punish those who are not its citizens or voluntary residents, namely, other polities and the subjects of other polities. For those who are resisted in defense do not thereby become subjects of the defending state. The condition of hostility does not make individual enemies participants in the common lives of the opposing communities, but only mutual external threats to those lives; similarly, the state of war does not collapse the common goods of the belligerents into one, or the authority of leaders into a kind of bloody election. A sign of the abiding political distinction among belligerent states and their citizens is the presumptive injustice of the victors lacking the impartiality of judges needed fairly to put the vanquished on trial.

Yet that status of citizenship, that participation in the life of a community, is necessary if those who punish are to have the authority to do so. This is so because the authority to organize and command defense is not the stronger authority to punish, which involves imposing further burdens on those against whom defense is mounted than defense itself implies.

Punishment can be a means to defense, insofar as it deters some from actions for which punishments are prescribed, and sometimes prevents the punished persons from continuing in their criminal activity. But it is possible to choose to defend without choosing to inflict any further harm on the attacker that might constitute punishment. The negative effects on those against whom one defends can perhaps be understood as punishment, but that sort of injury to the attacker is an unavoidable aspect of defense. Just as a private self-defender may ward off an attack with no punitive authority and no interest in punishing, so may a community.

The stronger authority to punish is rooted in the leaders' coordination of the actions of community members for common action for the sake of a community's common good. That basis sets its limits. They may punish those over whom they have authority, not outsiders against whom they may authoritatively organize and defend. Consequently, the only ground for extending this authority beyond community members is instrumental.

But, given the difference between punishment and defense, a justification of defense is not thereby a justification of punishment instrumental to it. Even the necessity of punishment for defense in some situations does not justify it, since plainly some forms of defense are wrongful, and, in the face of a lack of authority, more is needed than an instrumental justification of extending the authority to punish.[8]

This is not to affirm that the relationship between attacker and defender is simply a matter of power. It is true that attackers sometimes suffer the ill effects of the violent, defensive action of the polity they injure. And when the attacker acts wrongfully, there is more to the forceful defense than simply its power; just as any fair-minded observer could address the attacker in moral terms, so too can those who are injured. But this appeal to general moral norms—"You are out of line in attacking and we are within our rights in defending"—is not sufficient to render the attacker part of the community in a way that justifies anything like legal punishment. The truth of that moral judgment does not imply the cooperative relationship of membership in a common polity.

To sum up this line of reasoning: the defensive rather than punitive understanding of just cause which has developed in just war thinking in the 20th century is a proper development of traditional just war doctrine.

Reflecting on this development makes clear that the authority to make war is constrained in important ways, and plainly the exact shape of these limitations will be important for assessing the permissibility of responding to terrorist actions by groups that are not organized as a polity.

C. Right Intention

Aquinas argues that waging war can be wrong even if there is proper authority and just cause because a community can wage war with a perverse intention. The citations from Augustine make clear that the kind of bad motives Aquinas has in mind are hatred, revenge, a desire to dominate and so on. The idea seems to be that the presence of a just cause must not be a pretext for fighting for other morally questionable purposes, but rather the just cause must function as the practical principle of the bellicose action. The normative ground for this exclusion can be inferred from the Augustinian texts cited by Aquinas: war is presumptively immoral; its evils can be justified only on the narrow grounds that war justly serves peace, and any hostile action not completely controlled by that objective falls under the presumptive immorality of war. . . .

Right intention, therefore, gives concrete shape to the condition of just cause. If there is a just cause, and if that is the reason for making war—not a pretext— then there will be war aims, concrete goals, namely, a just state of affairs which can be produced by the military action, and which satisfies the just cause. That concrete goal, in turn, strictly controls the actions for its sake; violence for other goals or destructive in ways not required by the war aims is excluded.

Any action to serve a further goal remains unjustified, and that plainly includes the other legitimate interests a state might have within the international community. To pursue them by war is wrong.

The limitation of legitimate warfare to actions taken for and required by goals in which the just cause is realized does not mean that the war aims must be pursued as ends in themselves insofar as they realize the just cause. A just war aims at peace, as Aquinas, quoting Augustine, holds.[9] Surely, therefore, the intrinsic benefit of the fair and friendly relationships definitive of genuine peace, and the further advantages that come from peace may be hoped for as a result of succeeding in achieving morally defensible war aims. But peace is a good which war is never alone sufficient to achieve, and which war cannot rightly advance, except by seeking to bring about the just state of affairs satisfying the just cause.

This further horizon of human purposes that can be served by war in a limited way raises further questions about right intent and just cause. Since warfare undertaken for a just cause and fought with right intent must aim for peace, even though warfare is not sufficient for realizing this good, it is possible that a polity's warfare can fail to meet the condition of right intention because of its failure properly to pursue peace. This could happen if a state pursued policies incompatible with the peace achievable by the successful realization of just war aims, for example, a polity might continue its own unjust policies that provoke terrorist responses while making otherwise justified defensive war on the terrorists. . . .

III. APPLYING JUST WAR CONDITIONS TO WARFARE RESPONSIVE TO TERRORISM

A. Is There Legitimate Authority to Make War on Terrorists?

Plainly, the leaders of a sovereign political community have the responsibility and so the authority to respond in some way to terrorist acts against their community, its subjects or its allies. Since terrorist actions harm innocent people in ways serious enough to create fear in them or others that is sufficient to change their behavior and policies, such actions profoundly harm the common good of the affected community. Both the wrongs to innocents and the use of the fear these wrongs create for political purposes are of profound public concern. Those responsible for the welfare of the community are duty-bound to respond.

Depending upon the seriousness of the terrorist action and the capacity of police action, domestic and international, to provide a realistic response to terrorism, leaders may exercise this responsibility by commanding or requesting appropriate police action. Such action seems essential in dealing with terrorist acts having global reach by groups that are not polities. But where police action is insufficient to respond to terrorism, and military action likely to be effective, it appears to fall within the legitimate authority of political leaders.

This legitimacy has limitations. There are treaties and international law that may prohibit or constrain a state from taking unilateral military action in response to terrorism, or may require UN approval or action instead. Traditional just war theory assumes that treaties are solemn promises to be kept, and that procedures and prohibitions that are widely agreed upon internationally should be followed. Consequently, there likely exists a presumption against a state's taking unilateral military action without appropriate international approval.

These limitations on the legitimacy of a state's authority to respond to terrorism appear to allow that there is some proper authority to wage war against terrorism. For if the UN can rightly approve waging war against terrorists who are not organized as a polity, then the needed authority exists. And if it is states, not the UN, that are sovereign polities, the source of that authority is the common good of the state involved, even though it may be wrong to exercise that authority because of treaties and custom.

Since what gives authority to command and wage war to political leaders is the welfare of the polity they serve, that authority is not inherently limited by the character of an enemy's social organization. Whether or not contending militarily with terrorists who do not form a political community qualifies as a war in international law, a state so contending is bound by the requirements of just war. And there is no basis in just war theory for thinking that the fact that a state contends with a non-political group removes its authority to wage war.

But other complications abound. In particular, making war on terrorists ordinarily involves crossing the borders of other countries, presumptively, the crime of aggression unless invited. Border crossings without the consent of the country entered will be aggression, unless approved by the UN, or unless the state invaded can be justly invaded to make war on the terrorists, in other words, if the refusal to consent is itself rightly understood to be a just cause for war. Thus, for example, the Taliban rulers of Afghanistan may have been so involved in al-Qaeda activities that there was just cause for the USA and its allies to cross Afghanistan's borders and attack Taliban soldiers and assets. But the condition seems exceptional and, consequently, permission of states in whose territory military action is conducted is a general limit on the authority of leaders to make war on terrorists.

B. Is Responding to Terrorism a Just Cause?

According to Aquinas' conception of just cause, military actions to defend against terrorism are for the sake of a just cause. According to the 20th century limitation of just cause, military actions for the sake of punishing terrorists for their action, or for preventing terrorism not actually under way are not for the sake of a just cause.

The justice of military defense against terrorism arises from the wrongfulness of the terrorist actions. As noted above, this is not only the wrongfulness of harming innocents but also the political wrong of using the terror this causes to change a polity's behavior and policy.

Two other wrong-making factors exist in the kind of terrorism under consideration: first, that terrorists do not act for a just cause; and second, that the leaders of the terrorist organizations lack the proper authority to wage war. Terrorists may act in response to wrongs on the part of other groups; for example, they may be acting in response to unjust oppression by powerful countries. But that is not sufficient for a just cause, since that is defined not simply by the wrong addressed but includes what the group means to do about it. This requires that the goal for which bellicose action is taken be just and terrorist goals are not. Similarly, terrorist leaders are not the persons finally responsible for the common good of a political society, and seem to have such authority as they do only within the terrorist group. They have recourse to higher courts of appeal. Of course, leaders of a community engaged in a civil war or succession may have proper authority, even if not formally recognized as leaders of a polity; their tolerance of or use of terrorism would not be flawed in this way.

The idea of defending from terrorism, when that excludes punishing terrorists or preventing their acts, needs some explaining. A definite terrorist act, once carried out, cannot be the object of defense. It seems that all that can be done here is to prevent or to punish. The response is that the social act of a terrorist group directed against a polity is not ordinarily a single discreet terrorist action but a coordinated set of actions, since a single act of terrorism, understood as such by terrorists and their victims, could hardly cause the fear needed to change a polity's behavior. So, the terrorist action ordinarily is not a single discreet performance but a complex, interlocked set of behaviors unified by the intention of a common goal—at least the goal of causing the change in policy the terrorist action seeks.

It is possible to defend against actions such as this. One can do this by preventing those who are engaged in the action from carrying out their part in it, by apprehending or incapacitating them, by destroying the assets needed and so on. This is certainly prevention, but not prevention of the kind modern just war and international law theory finds morally questionable. For in this case, one is defending against an ongoing social act by preventing the carrying out of some of its elements. This is different from preventing a group from what they may have the capacity or motive or plans to do but are not evidently doing.

Analogous observations apply in the case of punishment: the effects of defense on terrorists are likely to be bad, and likely to be seen by them as punishments. But if the defensive actions are designed only to thwart ongoing terrorism, punishing by them is not part of the rationale for waging war against terrorists. This is not to deny that terrorists can be punished and should be. The internationally organized criminal justice system can rightly do that, if they are apprehended in war or by police action. But that is distinct from war being waged to punish or to allow for later punishment.

C. Can a State Respond to Terrorism with Right Intent?

This condition is difficult to apply to defending against terrorism, and raises the most difficult questions about it from a just war perspective. Recall that this condition addresses not the individual motives of soldiers and leaders in making war but the intention involved in the social act of making war. That intention, as noted above in Section II, is revealed in the war aims a state adopts, the relation of its bellicose actions to those war aims, and, ultimately, by whether the state removes obstacles to peace that are of its own making.

There are war aims that would reasonably satisfy the just cause of defending against terrorism, and would reveal the war effort as defensive but not punitive, vengeful or inappropriately preventive. The state of affairs in which the prospect of terrorist activity is not a serious threat to people's conduct of their lives but part of the disagreeable but acceptable risks of modern life is a reasonable public goal in relationship to terrorism generally, as it is in relation to criminal activity more generally. A more ambitious goal for dealing with terrorism seems utopian, and seems motivated by punitive intent or vengeance against terrorists who have been successful in prior actions.

Much of the effort to put the prospect of terrorism within acceptable levels of risk will be carried out by police work and by addressing the conditions and grievances that give rise to terrorism. But if military action is called for to defend against an ongoing terrorist campaign, there will be a component of this larger public goal that military action can aim to secure. That component will be the war aim of reasonable military defense against terrorist action. Consequently, the war aim must be concrete—the violence is justified only by an ongoing terrorist initiative. Stopping that is what is justified—not anything so grand as ridding the world of terrorism. And only the violence needed for precisely that defensive effort is justified. Such things as the destruction of the command and control system of a terrorist group by focused bombing, or capture or isolation of leaders and soldiers are perhaps not by themselves sufficient to define the war aims of a defense against terrorism, but some list of such things consid-

ered in the light of what military action can do to defend against terrorism without itself turning to punishment, vengeance or terror certainly seems to specify the kind of war aim that can rightly be sought. War aims including greater destruction of terrorists than such as these, for example, killing them all, appear vengeful.

. . . any polity must do what it can to protect its members going lawfully about their ordinary, daily business. Since most terrorist activities aim at harming people in going about living their lives and to get terrorist results from the fear that induces, there seems to be a straightforward responsibility for leaders to deal with such actions. That responsibility seems basic for political leaders, and appears to exist independently of their foreign policy.

At the same time, leaders create for themselves and their subjects a moral dilemma if they refuse to take steps to remove the blocks to peace that exist because of their own national commitments. The dilemma arises from this refusal, and so that must be abandoned. In short, this is not a case of strict moral perplexity but of one created by wrongdoing. Here, as elsewhere, desisting from the wrongdoing is likely to be difficult but is morally required not only because any wrong should be repented, but because persisting in it makes immoral the carrying out of the basic responsibility to protect citizens lawfully going about their business.

Of course, many leaders will not recognize the moral ambiguity of their situations. They can recognize, however, that others see their carrying out of their social responsibilities as maintaining a status quo wrongful to them. That recognition perhaps will lead to a very strict application of the defensive conception of waging war to fight terrorism.

Notes

1. The question of the personal responsibility of members of a society for its warfare is complex, and there is much in traditional just war theory to criticize on this score, as David Rodin, *War and Self-Defense* (Oxford: Oxford University Press), pp. 165–73, indicates. These complexities can be sorted out in a traditional way; for example, see John Finnis et al., *Nuclear Deterrence, Morality and Realism* (Oxford: Oxford University Press, 1987), pp. 342–60, for the responsibilities of various parties holding various beliefs in the context of Cold War deterrence.

2. Thomas Aquinas, *Summa Theologiae,* 2–2 (second part of the second part), q. 40, a. 1. All editions and translations of Aquinas' work follow this form of citation. There are four articles in question 40: (1) whether some war is licit; (2) whether it is licit for clerics to fight in a war; (3) whether it is licit to lay traps (*uti insidiis*) in war; and (4) whether it is licit to fight on feast days. My focus is on article 1, but the set of concerns addressed is important for our subject. Article 3 prohibits lying to enemies in war.

3. The exposition and interpretation of Aquinas in this section follow closely that of my "Traditional Just War and Humanitarian Intervention," presented at the annual meeting of the Association for Political and Legal Philosophy, Boston, August 30, 2002.

4. *Summa Theologiae,* 2–2, q. 64.

5. *Romans* 13, 4.

6. See *Summa Theologiae* 2–2, q. 64, a. 7. If I read traditional just war theory correctly, it does not involve the domestic analogy between private and national self-defense or the reduction of the latter to the former, which Rodin, *War and Self-Defense,* subjects to withering criticism. Aquinas' discussion of war makes no reference to a private right of self-defense. His discussion of homicide suggests that the right to defend oneself by actions having lethal side effects exists only when public authority is unavailable to protect life. This is not to suggest that Rodin's challenge to the defensive conception of just war lacks application to traditional just war theory. I will not undertake a response here since seeing what traditional just war theory has to say about terrorism is a different undertaking than defending its controversial premises.

7. Some within the Catholic just war tradition think this limitation should go very far indeed. See Vatican Council II, Constitution on the Church in the Modern World (*Gaudium et Spes*), paragraph 82: "It is our clear duty then to strain every muscle as we work for the time when all war can be completely outlawed by international agreement. This goal undoubtedly requires the establishment of some universal public authority acknowledged as such by all and endowed with effective power to safeguard on behalf of all, security, regard for justice and respect for rights."

8. Rodin, *Self-Defense and War,* pp. 173–9, criticizes two other efforts to justify state authority to punish outsiders. His reasoning is in the service of a further conclusion contrary to mine. He thinks that nations cannot rightly punish their enemies, and that since self-defense is no justification, there must be a transnational organization for international law enforcement or punishment. While I accept the claim that such an organization could judge impartially, it is clear from the little I have said about it that in the natural law conception of society underlying traditional just war theory impartiality is not sufficient for the authority legally to punish. Although mine is a different argument, I think it is compatible with holding that impartiality is necessary for just punishment.

9. See John Finnis, "The ethics of war and peace in the catholic just war tradition," *The Ethics of War and Peace: Religious and Secular Perspectives,* ed. T. Nardin (Princeton, N.J.: Princeton University Press, 1996), pp. 15–17 for more on the relationship between war and peace in traditional just war theory.

B. Humanitarian Intervention and the Just War

Many of the central problems and puzzles that arise in the moral evaluation of war are related, at least tangentially, to issues of national sovereignty and the adherence to existing national borders. The invasion of one's homeland by aggressors from another state is often considered just cause for armed retaliation, for defense of one's own people. A difficulty arises with the self-defense argument, however, when the defenders are not the denizens of the invaded or oppressed polity, but are instead concerned neighbors or bystanders, and their defense involves crossing national borders. The difficulty is compounded when the humanitarian intervention comes not from any one particular national source, but from a collection of members from disparate nations. International aid groups, nongovernmental organizations (NGOs), humanitarian medical aid groups, and the United Nations all serve as representative cases of the advanced version of the problem: When can one group violate the sovereign national borders of another nation or state for humanitarian reasons? The following essays explore this question, along with other, related, problems of humanitarian intervention.

We begin with a brief, but seminal, paper by David Luban, "The Romance of the Nation-State." Luban's argument rests on what he calls the "cosmopolitan nature of human rights," rights of security and subsistence that are universal and know no political or national boundaries. These rights, which all humans hold simply in virtue of being human, require a universalist or cosmopolitan politics (one that is to consider all human beings as members of a world community, with certain inherent rights and duties *qua* human being) to be implemented properly, in light of the failure of some nations to respect them. Luban defends his cosmpolitanism by challenging the assumptions of nationalism, an ideology that is "drenched in blood." Nationalists, in direct contrast with cosmopolitans, are willing to accept that partiality towards members of one's own community (be it a nation, a state, a neighborhood, or a club) is both acceptable and appropriate.

He points to Walzer's controversial thesis, that states which oppress their people may be considered legitimate by international society unless they violate specific rules of disregard, as an example of the failure of the nationalist project. It is reprehensible, says Luban, to think that a state which oppresses its own people, and violates their human rights, should be considered legitimate merely because of conditions of history and geography. Cases like these clearly explain the presumption that universal human rights, and not the sovereignty of national borders, should shoulder the burden of proof in situations of intervention. What Walzer fails to recognize, according to Luban, is that human beings have universal human rights regardless of what country they live in and regardless of the long-standing history and traditions of any sovereign nation. To respect national borders when rights violations are going on inside of them, according to Luban, is simply to miss the point of human rights entirely. Luban finds there to be an entitlement to intervene when socially basic human rights are being violated, despite the fact that the intervention might seem to violate sovereignty.

Fernando Teson picks up on the fundamental ideas present in Luban's paper, most notably the fundamental nature of human rights and the secondary importance of borders and states. He puts forward a liberal argument for humanitarian intervention when there are serious violations of human rights occurring in a state. The value of state sovereignty is merely instrumental, given that states exist, according to Teson, solely to secure and protect human rights. The existence of human rights, as with the existence of any other right, entails certain consequences for other people: the obligation to respect those rights, the obligation to promote respect for rights, and, in some cases, the duty to rescue those whose rights are being violated when the cost to oneself is not too great. In this way, Teson offers a self-consciously Kantian account of the *raison d'etre* of states and the nature of rights.

For Teson, humanitarian intervention is defined as the "proportionate international use or threat of force, undertaken in principle by a liberal government or alliance, aimed at ending tyranny or anarchy, welcomed by the victims, and consistent with the doctrine of double effect." Moreover, human rights not only give states the *right* to intervene but also an *obligation* to rectify violations of rights that are presently occurring. As with Luban, Teson worries that national borders and national sovereignty are being used as excuses to avoid correcting serious abuses of human rights. He also defends his view against the objection from relativism, the claim that, because some groups reject liberal principles, those principles cannot be used as the foundation for a moral or political theory. Teson accepts that humanitarian intervention can lead to the death or injury of innocent people; this is just a fact about how interventions work. His claim is that it is permissible for humanitarian interveners to cause the deaths or injury of innocents if, by doing so, they prevent a much greater harm *and* if the deaths or injuries were unintentional. Teson's view, at its most basic, is that the doctrine of non-intervention can, and must, be trumped by the protection of human rights. State sovereignty, the obligation to obey existing international laws, and concerns about the "world order" will never trump the crucial social goal of protecting human rights.

Burleigh Wilkins offers a challenge to views like Teson's in his selection, "Humanitarian Intervention: Some Doubts." He begins by pointing out that, in some circumstances (when the rights to life, liberty, and property are being violated), revolution, terrorism, and secession may be justified. He then moves on to examine whether humanitarian intervention to redress human rights violations can ever be justified. Even though humanitarian intervention isn't exactly like traditional warfare, it is enough *like* traditional warfare to warrant consideration from a Just War perspective.

Wilkins offers two reasons why intervention may not result in the protection of human rights. In the face of intervention, an oppressive regime may become *more* oppressive or, after the intervention, the opposition group may become even more militant and destructive. These concerns, along with the difficulty of settling on good "real world" examples of justification, seem to show that while almost everyone agrees that humanitarian intervention might be justified in some cases, these cases seem hard to pinpoint.

Wilkins also takes on the argument that non-intervention is an *absolute* duty. Instead, Wilkins argues that the duty of non-intervention (or, put another way, the duty to respect state sovereignty) is a *prima facie* duty, a duty that can be overridden in the face of compelling reasons to do otherwise. For Wilkins, the duty of non-intervention is then a *prima facie* moral duty that is binding on all states. However, all states also have a moral duty to respect human rights, and the violation of this duty leads to conflict between the duty of one state not to intervene in the domestic affairs of one state and the duty not to allow human rights violations to occur (or continue). For Wilkins, this is a troubling conflict, and the best way it can be resolved is by a unified codification in existing international law. An amendment to the UN Charter on humanitarian intervention should be decided by the members of the United Nations. According to Wilkins, even if the member nations refuse to allow any humanitarian intervention at all, it will be better than the piecemeal procedures that currently exist. If they choose to allow intervention, they must also present appropriate conditions and guidelines for such acts, to alleviate future confusion.

In the final article in this section, George R. Lucas, Jr. evaluates humanitarian intervention in light of the just war tradition. The rise in interventions (Bosnia and Kosovo) and the failure to intervene in other situations (Somalia and Rwanda) have shown us that humanitarian intervention is not a topic that can be passed over in the current, global age. But there are no clear criteria available by which we can evaluate whether or not any one act of humanitarian intervention is justified or not, and Lucas' project is to develop the appropriate criteria for keeping peace and order, a *jus ad pacem* rather than a *jus ad bellum*.

The reason for an alternate theory stems from the very obvious differences between uses of military force for traditional war and those for humanitarian wars, which are much more like the use of force in domestic law enforcement and peacekeeping. Because of these differences, the restrictions will be much more stringent for interveners than for normal military forces. These differences, along with the very nature of humanitarian intervention, lead Lucas to develop his new set of criteria to justify intervention. Basing his criteria on two versions of a "universal maxim" of intervention, as proposed by Stanley Hoffman, Lucas examines the central problems of intervention (namely, the violation of sovereignty that usually follows an intervention, and the problem of whether interveners hold "legitimate authority"). These are to be evaluated in light of the standard requirements of just-war theory: just cause, proper authority, right intention, last resort, likelihood of success, and the proportionality of both ends and means. He admits that all legitimate humanitarian intervention must be subject to multilateral debate and discussion, and must "reflect the collective will of the international community." But, even when this is so, we must follow certain guidelines in performing humanitarian interventions, many of which have connections to traditional *jus in bello,* but others of which are exclusive to these specific cases, including sending prisoners of war to the appropriate international tribunal, and avoiding the direct allocation of harm to noncombatants. A simple statement of the rule of intervention is given by Lucas near the end of his piece: "In humanitarian interventions, as in domestic law enforcement, we cannot and do not forsake our laws and moral principles in order to enforce and protect them." Keeping this in mind, we can *and should* develop and apply appropriate principles of justice to humanitarian interventions, and begin to create a sense of order in the chaotic current world order.

These articles elucidate many of the same central issues, including sovereignty, legitimacy, justification, and the nature of human rights. While the authors come to different conclusions on the relevance and value of national borders and state sovereignty, all of them share a desire to maintain a sense of a peaceful world order, support the existing human rights of people around the globe, and foster the development of a more safe and secure world. We leave it to the reader to decide which of these views (or which parts of various views) is best suited to achieve these goals.

The Romance of the Nation-State

(1980)

David Luban

David Luban is the Frederick Haas Professor of Law and Philosophy at Georgetown University's Law Center and Department of Philosophy. He works in legal ethics, international criminal law, human rights theory, and jurisprudence, among other topics. His books include Lawyers and Justice: An Ethical Study *(Princeton University Press, 1988),* Legal Modernism *(University of Michigan Press, 1994), and (with Deborah Rhode)* Legal Ethics *(3rd ed, Foundation Press, 2001).*

The theory I espoused in "Just War and Human Rights" entitles nations to wage war to enforce basic human rights.[1] This entitlement stems from the cosmopolitan nature of human rights. The rights of security and subsistence, with which I was concerned, are necessary for the enjoyment of any other rights at all; no one can do without them. Basic rights, therefore, are universal. They are no respecters of political boundaries, and require a universalist politics to implement them, even when this means breaching the wall of state sovereignty.

Since the time of the French Revolution, which linked the Rights of Man with the demand for national sovereignty, cosmopolitan theories have been criticized by appealing to the ideology of nationalism. National sovereignty, it was thought, gives people their most important entitlement: a state that expresses their traditions, history and unity—their "national soul.[2] Attack the state, and you attack the soul of its people. The cosmopolitan vision of humanity is really a flattening universalism, a philosopher's conceit. As Herder says,

"Every nation has its own core of happiness just as every sphere has its center of gravity! . . . Philosopher in a northern valley, with the infant's scales of your century in your hand, do you know better than Province?[3]

Nationalism may have originated as an ideology of liberation and tolerance; in our century it is drenched in blood. What Mazzini began, Il Duce ended; other examples are equally obvious and equally painful. The violence of modern nationalism and its indifference to basic human rights arises, I believe, from the conviction that the only right which matters politically is the right to a unified nation-state. Its picture of the nation-state, however, is a myth. It emphasizes a nation's commonality, affinity, shared language and traditions and history, what Mazzini called "unanimity of mind."[4] The picture glosses over intramural class conflict, turmoil, violence, and repression; these it represents as the reflection of inscrutable processes akin to national destiny.[5] This view I shall call the Romance of the Nation-State. In place of respect for people it sets respect

344

for peoples; in place of universalism, relativism.

What disturbs me about Walzer's essay is its acceptance of the premises of nationalism.[6] Walzer embodies his anticosmopolitanism in five theses: (1) that nations are comparatively self-enclosed (p. 227); (2) that "the state is constituted by the union of people and government" (p. 212); (3) that the political and moral status of a nation is aptly characterized by the metaphor of the social contract; (4) that "the only global community is . . . a community of nations, not of humanity" (p. 226); and (5) that the main moral principle of international politics is "pluralism": respect for the integrity of nations and their states; in particular, respect for their right to choose political forms which from our point of view are morally deficient.

This is a molecular theory of world politics, in which self-contained nation-states are the units of moral regard: molecular, because each is bound together from within and presents itself as a unit from without. The fourth and fifth theses yield the anti-cosmopolitan international morality that underlies Walzer's theory of *jus ad bellum;* these theses depend, however, on the first three, which represent the Romance of the Nation-State.

The social contract metaphor is central to this myth. It suggests reciprocity, coincident interests, mutual obligation, formal equality of the parties. But the presence of these features is not a conceptual truth about the nation-state, nor, I think, a factual one. The metaphor and the myth, I shall argue, lead Walzer to a deficient account of human rights and a blindness to the threat physical repression poses to political processes.

The controversial thesis of Walzer's essay is this: he believes that states which oppress their people may, nevertheless, be considered legitimate in international society, as long as they do not fall under what he calls the "rules of disregard." Intervention is allowable in a nation when a national minority is seceding from it; when a foreign power has intervened in a civil war it is fighting; or when it is massacring, enslaving, or expelling large numbers of people. In these instances, Walzer argues, "the absence of 'fit' between the government and community is radically apparent" (p., 214). The rest of the time we are obliged to act *as if* states are legitimate. Walzer calls this "the politics of *as if*" (p. 216); its leading principle is "a morally necessary presumption: that there exists a certain 'fit' between the community and its government and that the state is 'legitimate'" (p. 212). Hard as it is for liberal democrats to believe, foreigners may want their tyranny—there may be a "fit" between government and people.

What supports this presumption? According to Walzer, foreigners just can't judge an alien culture's fit with its government. "They don't know enough about its history, and they have no direct experience, and can form no concrete judgments of the conflicts and harmonies, the historical choices and cultural affinities, the loyalties and resentments, that underlie it" (p. 212).

I find no plausibility in this. True, *if* we don't know enough about a foreign culture to judge its "fit" with its government, we should give it the benefit of the doubt and presume the fit is there. But why presume we are ignorant? We aren't, usually. There are, after all, experts, experienced travelers, expatriates, scholars, and spies; libraries have been written about the most remote cultures. Bafflingly, Walzer does not mention the obvious sources of information even to dismiss them. He seems to take as an a priori truth—it is part of the Romance of the Nation-State—that without "direct experience" a member of one culture cannot, ultimately, know what it's really like to be a member of another. But this is of a piece with "no man can really know what it's like to be a woman" or "you can't know what it's really like to be me": even granting their validity, we don't assume that such considerations preclude making true judgments about other people. That is more like solipsism than pluralism, and if it were true it would spell the end, not the principle, of politics.

Of course Walzer is right that the lack of fit between government and people should be "radically apparent" to justify intervening, because intervention based on a misperception is horribly wrong. But what does it take to make things radically apparent? In my view, Walzer's rules of disregard set the threshold too high; what he calls "ordinary oppression" can make the lack of fit apparent enough. Let us look at ordinary oppression in a medium-size dictatorship. Each year there are a few score executions, a few hundred tortures, a few thousand political imprisonments, a few million people behaving cautiously because they know that a single slip will bring the police. The police and army believe that if the government falls they are dead men; it is the bargain they accepted to escape the poverty of their villages. They take their foreign-made fighters, small arms, and pepper gas and hope for the best.

If this is a "union of people and government," why are the jails so full? Surely all those strapped to the torture table are not misfits in their own culture. I think we should aim at a more common-sense explanation than Walzer's of why people put up with the regime, such as the idea that they

are afraid of being "disappeared" (to use a phrase current in Argentina and the Philippines). The government fits the people the way the sole of a boot fits a human face: after a while the patterns of indentation match with uncanny precision.

It was central to my argument in "Just War and Human Rights" that under ordinary oppression peoples' socially basic human rights are violated—not, to be sure, on the scale envisioned in Walzer's third rule of disregard, which refers to what the Nuremberg court called "crimes against humanity," but systematically enough to define the state's political physiognomy and justify intervention. Walzer's theory of intervention as aggression is also based on individual rights, but those that control are the rights emphasized by nationalism: to fight for the homeland and to live under institutions formed by one's fellow-nationals. They are rights to a nation-state, not claims against it.

This difference is illustrated by Walzer's analysis of the recent Nicaraguan revolution. He emphasizes the fact that in the wake of their initial defeat the *Sandinistas* were forced to clarify their program and solidify their political base. This is indeed an instance of self-determination, and if Walzer's position is that, other things being equal, it is better that it should happen than not, he is undoubtedly right. Let us not forget, though, that other things were not equal. Fifty thousand people were killed in the second round of revolution, Nicaragua's productive capacity was ravaged, and Somoza's followers had an additional year to strip the country of everything they could crate. Because of this, the new government has been forced to make a number of deals that have weakened its political base. Neither should we dismiss as unimportant the fact that

Nicaraguans had to live under an oppressive regime one year longer. We cannot ignore, as Walzer's theory does, the cost in blood, the bottom line in an account that makes socially basic human rights its guiding concept.

The problem with Walzer's argument is this. Human rights accrue to people no matter what country they live in and regardless of history and traditions. If human rights exist at all, they set a moral limit to pluralism. For this reason Walzer's appeal to pluralism begs the question, for making pluralism the overriding value is incompatible from the outset with a theory that grants universal human rights.

Rights, moreover, are crucial values for us—as Walzer points out, they are deeply connected with our notions of personality and moral agency. Thus, when murders, tortures, imprisonments go unchecked, more so when their perpetrators (the worst people in the world) are treated *as if* they are legitimate, the common humanity of all of us is stained. In this way, the politics of *as if,* in which we acknowledge rights but turn our backs on their enforcement (p. 226), fails to take our values seriously. It raises politics above moral theory.

Walzer sees it differently. He claims that he is defending politics while his critics are expressing "the traditional philosophical dislike for politics." This, he says, is because we are unwilling to tolerate unwanted outcomes of "the political process itself, with all its messiness and uncertainty, its inevitable compromises, and its frequent brutality"; we would restrict the outcomes by force of arms (p. 31).

But why is this less political than standing by while an uprising against a repressive regime is crushed by force of arms? Repression is itself an attempt to restrict, or rather, to eliminate the political process. It subjects politics to the essentially apolitical technology of violence, the "great unequalizer." Intervention, when it is just, should restore self-determination, not deny it. In this respect it is similar to counter-intervention of the sort countenanced by Walzer's second rule of disregard—an analogy which is particularly apposite in view of the fact that military technology is usually provided to repressive regimes by foreign powers.

Walzer dismisses the ability of sheer force to stifle the political process because force cannot prevail against the united community, while if the community is not united intervention would be wrong. But a united community is a rare political achievement, particularly under conditions of class oppression and terror, and I think it is wrong to make it the yardstick of politics—doing so is another metamorphosis of the Romance of the Nation-State. One might doubt whether in a civil war an intervener can know which side to support. But the entitlement to intervene derives from the cosmopolitan character of human rights; one intervenes, then, on behalf of socially basic human rights, for it is these which enable people to enjoy their political rights. Walzer's hands-off approach, on the other hand, waiting for the day when the nation unites, simply yields to guns and tanks.

Notes

1. See *Philosophy & Public Affairs* 9, no. 2 (Winter 1980): 160–181.
2. See Hannah Arendt, *The Origins of Totalitarianism,* rev. ed. (New York: Meridian, 1958), pp. 230–231.
3. "Auch eine Philosophie der Geschichte zur Bildung der Menschheit," *Werke,* ed. Suphan, vol. 5, pp. 501 ff.; quoted in Ernst Cassirer, *The Philosophy of the Enlightenment,* trans. Koelln and Pettegrove (Princeton: Princeton University

Press, 1951), pp. 232–233. See also Cassirer, *The Myth of the State* (New Haven: Yale University Press, 1946), pp. 176–186; Isaiah Berlin, *Against the Current* (New York: Viking, 1979), chaps. 1, 13; and Berlin, *Vico and Herder* (New York: Viking, 1976).

4. For this citation, together with a short survey of nineteenth-century nationalist ideology, see Victor Alba, *Nationalists Without Nations* (New York: Praeger, 1968), pp. 5–17.

5. Even Mill seems to subscribe to this, for according to Walzer it is his idea "that citizens get the government they deserve, or, at least, the government for which they are 'fit,'" *Just and Unjust Wars* (New York: Basic Books, 1977), p. 88.

6. Parenthetical references in the text are to Walzer, "The Moral Standing of States: A Response to Four Critics," *Philosophy & Public Affairs* 9, no. 3 (Spring 1980).

The Liberal Case for Humanitarian Intervention[1]

(2003)

Fernando Teson

Fernando Teson is Tobias Simon Eminent Scholar in the College of Law at Florida State University. His work has focused on relating political philosophy to international law and on defending human rights and humanitarian intervention. He is the author of A Philosophy of International Law *(Westview Press, 1998) and* Humanitarian Intervention: An Inquiry into Law and Morality *(2nd ed., Transnational, 1997).*

INTRODUCTION

In this chapter I argue that humanitarian intervention is morally justified in appropriate cases. The argument centrally rests on a standard assumption of liberal political philosophy: a major purpose of states and governments is to protect and secure human rights, that is, rights that all persons have by virtue of personhood alone.[2] Governments and others in power who seriously violate those rights undermine the one reason that justifies their political power, and thus should not be protected by international law. A corollary of the argument is that, to the extent that state sovereignty is a value, it is an instrumental, not an intrinsic, value.[3] Sovereignty serves valuable human ends, and those who grossly assault them should not be allowed to shield themselves behind the sovereignty principle.[4] Tyranny and anarchy cause the moral collapse of sovereignty.[5]

I supplement this argument with further moral assumptions. The fact that persons are right-holders has normative consequences for others. We all have (1) the obligation to *respect* those rights; (2) the obligation to *promote* such respect for all persons; (3) depending on the circumstances, the obligation to *rescue* victims of tyranny or anarchy, if we can do so at a reasonable cost to ourselves. The obligation in (3) analytically entails, under appropriate circumstances, the *right* to rescue such victims—the right of humanitarian intervention. Because human rights are rights held by individuals by virtue of their personhood, they are independent of history, culture, or national borders.

I define permissible humanitarian intervention as the *proportionate international use or threat of military force, undertaken in principle by a liberal government or alliance, aimed at ending tyranny or anarchy, welcomed by the victims, and consistent with the doctrine of double effect.*

I present the argument in the next section. In subsequent sections I consider and reject possible objections: the relativist objection; the argument that humanitarian intervention violates communal integrity or some similar moral status of national borders; the view that governments should refrain from intervening out of respect for international law; and the view that humanitarian intervention undermines global stability. A further section addresses the difficult question of the moral status of acts and omissions. I discuss the conceptual structure of the liberal argument and respond to the objection that humanitarian intervention is wrong because it causes the deaths of innocent persons. I also evaluate the moral status of the failure to intervene and conclude that, depending on the circumstances, it can be morally culpable. I then examine the internal legitimacy of humanitarian intervention. I conclude with a few critical reflections about the non-intervention doctrine.

The liberal argument for humanitarian intervention has two components. The first is the quite obvious judgment that the exercise of governmental tyranny and the behavior that typically takes place in situations of extreme anarchy are serious forms of injustice towards persons. The second is the judgment that, subject to important constraints, external intervention is (at least) morally permissible to end that injustice. I suggest below that the first part of the argument is uncontroversial. For the most part, critics of humanitarian intervention do not disagree with the judgment that the situations that (according to interventionists) call for intervention are morally abhorrent. The situations that trigger humanitarian intervention are acts such as crimes against humanity, serious war crimes, mass murder, genocide, widespread torture, and the Hobbesian state of nature (war of all against all) caused by the collapse of social order.[6] Rather, the disagreement between supporters and opponents of humanitarian intervention concerns the second part of the argument: interventionists claim that foreigners may help stop the injustices; non-interventionists claim they may not. The related claims from political and moral philosophy that I make (that sovereignty is dependent on justice and that we have a right to assist victims of injustice) concern this second part of the argument. If a situation is morally abhorrent (as non-interventionists, I expect, will concede) then neither the sanctity of national borders nor a general prohibition against war should by themselves preclude humanitarian intervention.

This discussion concerns *forcible* intervention to protect human rights. I address here the use and the threat of military force (what I have elsewhere called hard intervention)[7] for humanitarian purposes. However, the justification for the international protection of human rights is best analyzed as part of a continuum of international behavior. Most of the reasons that justify humanitarian intervention are extensions of the general reasons that justify interference[8] with agents in order to help victims of their unjust behavior. Interference and intervention in other societies to protect human rights are special cases of our duty to assist victims of injustice. However, many people disagree that humanitarian intervention is part of a continuum: they treat war as a special case of violence, as a unique case, and not simply as a more violent and destructive form of human behavior that can nonetheless be sometimes justified. They do not regard war as part of a continuum of state action; and do not agree with Clausewitz that war is the continuation of politics (*politik*) by other means. Intuitively, there is something particularly terrible, or awesome, about war. It is the ultimate form of human violence. That is why many people who are committed to human rights nonetheless oppose humanitarian intervention. To them, war is a crime, the most hideous form of destruction of human life, and so it cannot be right to support war, even for the benign purpose of saving people's lives. Good liberals should not support war in any of its forms.

I am, of course, in sympathy with that view. Who would not be? If there is an obvious proposition in international ethics, it has to be that war is a terrible thing. Yet the deeply ingrained view that war is always immoral regardless of cause is mistaken. Sometimes it is morally permissible to fight; occasionally, fighting is even mandatory. The uncritical opposition to all wars begs the question about the justification of violence generally.[9] Proponents of humanitarian intervention simply argue that humanitarian intervention in some instances (rare ones, to be sure) is morally justified, while agreeing of course that war is generally a bad thing. But it is worth emphasizing here that critics of humanitarian intervention are *not* pacifists. They support the use of force in self-defense and (generally) in performance of actions duly authorized by the Security Council. So their hostility to humanitarian intervention cannot be grounded on a general rejection of war. Part of the task of this chapter is to examine those other reasons.

THE LIBERAL ARGUMENT

As I indicated, the liberal case for humanitarian intervention relies on principles of political and moral philosophy. Political philosophy addresses the justification of political power, and hence the justification of the state. Most liberal accounts of the state rely on social contract theory of some kind to explain and justify the state. Here I follow a Kantian account of the state. States are justified as institutions created by ethical agents, that is, by autonomous persons. The liberal state centrally includes a constitution that defines the powers of governments in a manner consistent with respect for individual autonomy. This Kantian conception of the state is the liberal solution to the dilemmas of anarchy and tyranny. Anarchy and tyranny are the two extremes in a continuum of political coercion. Anarchy is the complete absence of social order, which inevitably leads to a Hobbesian war of all against all. The exigencies of survival compel persons in the state of nature to lead a brutal existence marked by massive assaults on human dignity. This is a case of too little government, as it were. At the other extreme, the perpetration of tyranny[10] is not simply an obvious assault on the dignity of persons: it is a betrayal of the very purpose for which government exists. It is a case of abuse of government—of too much government, as it were. Humanitarian intervention is one tool to help move the quantum of political freedom in the continuum of political coercion to the Kantian center of that continuum away, on the one hand, from the extreme lack of order (anarchy), and, on the other, from governmental suppression of individual freedom (tyranny). Anarchical conditions prevent persons, by reason of the total collapse of social order, from conducting meaningful life in common or pursuing individual plans of life. Tyrannical conditions (the misuse of social coercion) prevent the victims, by the overuse of state coercion, from pursuing their autonomous projects. If human beings are denied basic human rights and are, for that reason, deprived of their capacity to pursue their autonomous projects, then others have a prima facie duty to help them.[11] The serious violation of fundamental civil and political rights generates obligations on others. Outsiders (foreign persons, governments, international organizations) have a duty not only to respect those rights themselves but also to help ensure that governments respect them.[12] Like justified revolutions, interventions are sometimes needed to secure a modicum of individual autonomy and dignity. Persons trapped in such situations deserve to be rescued, and sometimes the rescue can only be accomplished by force. We have a general duty to assist persons in grave danger if we can do it at reasonable cost to ourselves. If this is true, we have, by definition, a *right* to do so. The right to intervene thus stems from a general duty to assist victims of grievous injustice. I do not think that the critic of humanitarian intervention necessarily disagrees with this in a general sense. Rather, his opposition to humanitarian intervention relies on the supposed moral

significance of state sovereignty and national borders.

There has been considerable debate about whether or not the concept of a legitimate state requires a thick liberal account. David Copp and John Rawls, among others, have argued that it does not.[13] They claim, in only slightly different ways, that legitimacy is unrelated to the duty of obedience, and that liberals generally must respect non-liberal states that fulfill some minimal functions.[14] They want to say that there is a layer of legitimacy (presumably banning foreign intervention) stemming from the fact that the government in question fulfills those functions. This is true even if the government does not fare well under liberal principles and thus cannot legitimately command the citizens' allegiance.

That discussion, important as it is for other purposes, is largely irrelevant to the present question.[15] The argument in this chapter is concerned with the conditions for the legitimacy of forcible humanitarian intervention, not with the related but distinct question of which states and governments are members in good standing of the international community. These authors seem at times to conflate these two issues. The collapse of state legitimacy is a necessary but not a sufficient condition of humanitarian intervention. The issue of the justification of humanitarian intervention, therefore, is narrower than the general issue of how liberal governments should treat non-liberal regimes. It is perfectly possible to say (*contra* Rawls and Copp) that a non-liberal government should *not* be treated as a member in good standing of the international community while acknowledging (with Rawls and Copp) that it would be wrong to intervene in those states to force liberal reforms. The situations that qualify for forcible intervention are best described as "beyond the pale" situations. Only outlaw regimes (to use Rawls's terminology) are morally vulnerable to humanitarian intervention. Because I differ with these writers on the question of legitimacy of non-liberal (but not "beyond the pale") regimes, I believe that *non-forcible* interference to increase human rights observance in those societies is morally justified—a view they reject.[16] All regimes that are morally vulnerable to humanitarian intervention are of course illegitimate, but the reverse is not true. For many reasons, it may be wrong to intervene by force in many regimes that are objectionable from a liberal standpoint. Humanitarian intervention is reserved for the more serious cases—those that I have defined as tyranny and anarchy. Again, the illegitimacy of the government is a necessary, not a sufficient, condition for the permissibility of humanitarian intervention.[17]

But if this is correct, it does require amending my original argument. It is no longer possible to ground the legitimacy of humanitarian intervention *solely* on the question of the moral legitimacy of the regime, because there are many cases where the collapse of political legitimacy will not be enough to justify intervention. Still, there are several consequences to the finding of illegitimacy. First, intervention against legitimate regimes is always banned. Second, it may well be that in a particular case it would be wrong to intervene, but the reason will never be the need to respect the *sovereignty* of the target state. Third, the liberal conception of state legitimacy will guide the correct behavior by the intervenor. He must abide by the general duty to promote, create, or restore institutions and practices under which the dignity of persons will be preserved.

I indicated that critics of humanitarian intervention are not pacifists. They object to *this kind* of war, a war to protect human rights. They do not object to wars, say, in defense of territory. This position is somewhat anomalous because it requires separate justifications for different kinds of wars. In contrast, the liberal argument offers a unified justification of war. War is justified if, and only if, it is in defense of persons and complies with the requirements of proportionality and the doctrine of double effect.[18] Take the use of force in self-defense. What can possibly be its moral justification? Very plausibly, this: that the aggressor is assaulting the rights of persons in the state that is attacked. The government of the attacked state, then, has a right to muster the resources of the state to defend its citizens' lives and property against the aggressor. The defense of states is justified *qua* defense of persons. There is no defense of the *state* as such that is not parasitic on the rights and interests of individuals. If this is correct, any moral distinction between self-defense and humanitarian intervention, that is, any judgment that self-defense is justified while humanitarian intervention is not, has to rely on something above and beyond the general rationale of defense of persons.

THE RELATIVIST OBJECTION

Some object to the very project of using liberal political theory to address humanitarian intervention—or indeed any international question. The argument goes something like this. The world is ideologically and culturally too diverse to apply any one philosophy to a problem that concerns all persons in the globe. Because many people reject liberal principles, attempts to use liberal philosophy are unduly biased.[19] One would have to draw on different ethical traditions in order to analyze international problems. The outcome of liberal analysis might be good for someone who already accepts liberal principles, but not for those who do not. In other words, it might be necessary to do some comparative ethics before addressing these problems in order to identify which, if any, is the content of a global "overlapping consensus."

I have a general answer and a specific answer to this criticism of the liberal case for humanitarian intervention. I have never been able to see merit in relativism as a general philosophical view.[20] If, say, our philosophical judgment that all persons have rights is sound, then it is universally sound. It does not really matter if the *historical origin* of that judgment is Western or something else. Those who object to liberal principles on the grounds that they are Western commit the genetic fallacy. They confuse the problem of the *origin* of a political theory with the problem of its *justification*. The truth (moral or empirical) of a proposition is logically independent of its origin. The liberal can concede that the views he defends are Western, and still maintain that they are the better views. Another way of putting this is that the effort to find a justification for the exercise of political power is not an effort to *describe* the way Westerners think. Philosophical analysis is critical and normative, not descriptive. Of course, liberal views may be right or wrong, but they cannot possibly be right for some and wrong for others. Conversely, if *illiberal* views of politics are correct, then that has to be shown by rational argument, not by merely recognizing that some people, or other people, or many people, believe in

them. To be sure, any philosophical justification of political power relies on assumptions, and critics may challenge the liberal justification of political power by challenging the assumptions. But that, of course, is philosophical argument. Perhaps the illiberal assumptions are as plausible as the liberal ones, but that will not be because, say, many people in illiberal societies believe in them. If many persons endorse liberal assumptions and many other people endorse inconsistent illiberal assumptions, both sides cannot be right. Liberal analysis must assume that liberal assumptions (such as the importance of individual autonomy) are the better ones, universally. The liberal conception I defend is thus cosmopolitan, and as such rejects attempts at locating political morality in overlapping consensus, or other forms of majority validation. It rejects arguments *ad populum*.

Second, that objection does not seem to reach the first part of the argument: that the situations that warrant intervention—tyranny and anarchy—are morally abhorrent forms of political injustice. I believe that all reasonable religious and ethical theories converge in the judgment that those situations (mass murder, widespread torture, crimes against humanity, serious war crimes) are morally abhorrent. We are not dealing here with differences in conceptions of the good, or with various ways to realize human and collective excellence, or with the place of religion, civic deliberation, or free markets in political life. We are confronting governments that perpetrate atrocities against people, and situations of anarchy and breakdown of social order of such magnitude that no reasonable ethical or political theory could reasonably condone them. And, of course, if there are political theories that condone those situations, too bad for them: they cease to be reasonable or plausible. I do not believe, however, that the critic of humanitarian intervention wants to rely on a moral theory that justifies grievous human rights violations. I hope that I do not need deep studies in comparative ethics and religion to say that under any religious or ethical system the kind of situation that warrants humanitarian intervention is morally intolerable. For example, I doubt that someone who endorses religious or political doctrines that advance communal values and reject liberal reliance on individual autonomy will treat the extreme examples of tyranny or anarchy that warrant humanitarian intervention as morally tolerable or justified.[21]

On the other hand, the *second* part of the argument requires a reliance on conceptions about the justification of states, governments, and borders. As indicated above, I want to say that certain situations are morally abhorrent under any plausible ethical theory, *and* that those situations sometimes justify humanitarian intervention under a liberal conception of politics. Someone may agree with the first proposition but not with the second. He might agree that the situations are morally abhorrent but maintain that humanitarian intervention is still not justified: it is not for foreigners to remedy those wrongs. These other theories might hold particular views about the sanctity of borders, or about the moral centrality of communities, or about the moral relevance of distinctions between nationals and foreigners. Here again, all I can do is offer arguments to reject those views in favor of a more cosmopolitan approach. My point is rather this: to the objection that supporting humanitarian intervention presupposes a (biased) liberal commitment to human rights, the liberal can respond, "But surely you're

not saying that under your (non-liberal) view these atrocities are justified. Whatever it is that you value, it cannot be this." The non-liberal critic can then make the following move: "I agree that this is morally abhorrent under my non-liberal principles as well, but those same principles, unlike yours, bar foreign interventions." Thus, non-interventionist views of international ethics attempt to *sever* (unconvincingly, I contend) domestic from international legitimacy. But if the non-liberal agrees that the situation is abhorrent, then the liberal interventionist cannot be biased because he thinks just that. The non-liberal needs reasons beyond his skepticism about rights and autonomy in order to question the legitimacy of humanitarian intervention in cases where he would agree with the liberal that the situation is morally abhorrent. He needs a theory of sovereignty under which foreigners are morally precluded from saving victims of extreme injustice.

THE MORAL RELEVANCE OF NATIONAL BORDERS: COMMUNAL INTEGRITY

If the non-interventionist accepts that tyranny and anarchy are morally abhorrent, he might resort to theses of international ethics that place decisive value on sovereignty and national borders. Consider the following case. The provincial government in a federal state is committing atrocities against an ethnic group. Moreover, the provincial army is prepared to resist the federal army, so that a civil war will take place if the federal government tries to stop the massacre. Non-interventionists (like everyone else) will no doubt regret that a civil war will erupt, but surely will not object in principle to the *internal* intervention by federal troops aimed at stopping the massacre. In fact, they will likely praise the intervention.

Yet they will object if those same troops cross an *international* border to stop similar atrocities committed by a sovereign government in a neighboring state. For them, national borders mysteriously operate a *change in the description* of the act of humanitarian rescue: it is no longer humanitarian rescue, but war. (Why aren't massive human rights violations also called war, for example a war of the government against its people? Is it because usually part of the population is an accomplice in the perpetration?) The argument for this distinction has to rely on the moral significance of national borders as a corollary of the principle of sovereignty. But national borders can hardly have moral significance *in this context*. For one thing, national borders are the serendipitous result of past violence and other kinds of morally objectionable or irrelevant historical facts. More generally, a great deal of suffering and injustice in the world derives from the exaggerated importance that people assign to national borders. From ethnic cleansing to discrimination against immigrants, from prohibitions to speak foreign languages to trade protections that only benefit special interests, the ideas of nation, state, and borders have been consistently used to justify all kinds of harm to persons.

In spite of all that, there are surely reasons for respecting national borders, at least as long as one believes that a world of separate states is a desirable thing.[22] Those reasons are, in my view, two, and neither invalidates humanitarian intervention in appropriate cases. The first and most important has to do with the legitimacy of the social contract, as it were.

Kant famously wrote, "No state having an independent existence, whether it be small or great, may be acquired by another state through inheritance, exchange, purchase, or gift."[23] The idea here is that a state that is somehow the result of the free consent by autonomous individuals in civil society must be respected. Violating those borders would amount, then, to treating the state and its citizens "as things."[24] This is the liberal premise defended here, that the sovereignty of the state and the inviolability of its borders are parasitic on the legitimacy of the social contract, and thus sovereignty and borders, too, serve the liberal ends of respecting freedom and human rights. Where half the population of the state is murdering the other half, or where the government is committing massive atrocities against its own citizens, national borders have lost most of their moral strength.[25] At the very least, they are morally impotent to contain foreign acts aimed at stopping the massacres.

Michael Walzer offers the best-known defense of the moral aptitude of national borders to ban humanitarian intervention.[26] According to Walzer, there is a crucial distinction between domestic and international legitimacy. A government may be illegitimate internally, but that does not mean that foreign armies are entitled to intervene to restore legitimacy. Walzer claims that in most cases there is enough "fit" between people and government to make injustice a purely domestic matter from which foreigners are excluded. Only the citizens themselves may overthrow their tyrant. It is only when the lack of fit is *radically* apparent, says Walzer, that intervention can be allowed. That will only occur in cases of genocide, enslavement, or mass deportation. He supports this thesis by communal considerations: nations have histories and loyalties that define their political process, and that process should be protected as such, even if some of its outcomes are repulsive to liberal philosophers. Walzer calls this "communal integrity."

As a preliminary matter, Walzer (unlike other non-interventionists) allows humanitarian intervention in important classes of cases. Yet his rationale for not allowing humanitarian intervention in other cases of tyranny and anarchy is, I believe, deeply wrong. By pointing out that dictators come from the society itself, from its families and neighborhoods, Walzer insinuates that tyranny and anarchy come naturally, as it were; that in some sense the victims are responsible for the horrors they suffer. It also presupposes that there is something morally valuable ("self-determination") in the fortuitous balance of existing political forces in a society.[27] But political processes are not valuable per se. Their value depends on their being minimally consistent with the imperative to respect persons.[28] It is even grotesque to describe the kinds of cases that warrant humanitarian intervention as "processes of self-determination" and suggest, as Walzer does, that unless there is genocide, there is a necessary fit between government and people. David Luban put it best: "The government fits the people the way the sole of a boot fits a human face: After a while the patterns of indentation fit with uncanny precision."[29]

Having said that, there is a kernel of truth in a possible reading of Walzer's argument, best put by John Stuart Mill.[30] Mill argued that humanitarian intervention is always wrong because freedom has no value unless the victims themselves fight for their liberation. People cannot really be free if foreigners do the fighting for them. While this argument is problematic (why isn't freedom valuable if someone else helps us achieve it?), it does make an important point. Citizens of the state ruled by a tyrant (or victimized by warlords in a failed state) have a responsibility to help put an end to their plight. The intervenor has a right to expect their reasonable cooperation in putting an end to tyranny, in shouldering the moral and material costs of intervention, and in building democratic institutions. It is their government, their society. Foreign efforts to help them depend on their cooperation and willingness to build or restore those institutions.

One corollary of Mill's point is the requirement that the victims of tyranny or anarchy welcome the intervention. Walzer and other critics of humanitarian intervention say that in most cases the victims do not really want to be liberated by foreigners, that they would rather put up with their tyrants than see their homeland invaded. This is a view influenced by communitarianism. Communitarians contend that persons not only have liberty interests: they also, and more importantly, have communal interests, those that define their membership in a group or community—their social identity. Indeed, for communitarians, liberty interests are parasitic on communal interests or values. On this view, the average citizen in any country (including those ruled by tyrannical regimes) will be wounded in his self-respect if foreigners intervene, even if it is for a good purpose, because such intervention strikes at the heart of his social identity. The corollary seems to be that the average citizen in an oppressive regime *prefers* to remain oppressed than to be freed by foreigners.

I believe that while this situation is empirically possible, it is highly unlikely to occur. For one thing, there is no valid community interest of the citizen who *col-*

laborates with the abusers. In a society afflicted by tyranny there is a group (sometimes the minority, sometimes the majority) that benefits from the government's persecution of others. These are the rent-seekers of the worst kind, those who capture the machine of horror for their own purposes. To describe this as "community interest" is grotesque. It is also wrong to presume that victims oppose liberating intervention. I would think that the evidence supports the opposite presumption: that victims of serious oppression will welcome rather than oppose outside help. This was seemingly the case in the interventions in Grenada, Iraq, Rwanda, Haiti, and Kosovo, among others.

The only persons whose consent deserves consideration are those who oppose both the regime *and* foreign intervention for moral reasons. They might say that the regime is murderous but that foreign invasion of their homeland is unacceptable, even if undertaken for the purpose of ending the ongoing killings. Should their refusal be decisive? Should prospective intervenors treat the veto by political and civic leaders who oppose the regime as a decisive reason for not intervening? I do not think so, for the following reason: I very much doubt that you can cite *your* communal interests validly to oppose aid to *me,* when *I* am strapped to the torture chamber, even if you are not complicitous.[31] Only *I* (the torture victim) can waive my right to seek aid; only my consent counts for that purpose. So, to summarize: in a tyrannical regime the population can be divided into the following groups: the victims; the accomplices and collaborators; and the bystanders. The last group can in turn be subdivided into those who support the regime and those who oppose it. Of these groups, only the first, the victims, have (arguably) a right

to refuse aid. The accomplices and bystanders who support the regime are excluded for obvious reasons. Their opposition to intervention does not count. And the bystanders who oppose the regime cannot validly refuse foreign aid on behalf of the victims.

Democratic leaders must make sure before intervening that they have the support of the very persons they want to assist, the victims. Yet the view (suggested by Walzer)[32] that a *majority* of the population must support the intervention is wrong, because the majority may be complicitous in the human rights violations. Suppose the government of a multi-ethnic state tries to exterminate a minority ethnic group. Let us further assume that a history of ethnic animosity leads the majority group to support the genocide. Humanitarian intervention is justified even if the majority of the population of the state opposes it. An intervenor must abide by the duty to restore the rights of persons threatened by tyranny or anarchy. Whether or not these goals will be advanced cannot be decided by simply taking opinion polls in the population of the tyrannical or anarchical society.

Another reason to respect national borders is that they may help secure the stability of social interaction, that is, the mutual expectations of individuals who interact within and across demarcations of political jurisdictions. The reasons for having national borders, then, are analogous to the reasons for respecting the demarcations of property rights. Property owners should be allowed to exclude trespassers because that facilitates the internalization of externalities and thus maximizes the efficiency in the use of resources.[33] Similarly, it might be argued that states must be allowed to exclude foreign "trespassers" who attempt to free ride on the cooperative efforts of the citizens of the state. Giving the state exclusive jurisdiction over its territory maximizes global gains, just as giving farmers exclusive property rights over their land maximizes aggregate wealth. These efficiency considerations become particularly relevant in the aftermath of the intervention. Successful intervenors, unlike internal victors, have little incentive to treat the target country as something that is theirs—they lack long-term property rights over the territory.[34] Likewise, internal victors (such as the current ruling group in Afghanistan) in an intervention have a greater incentive to restore the political fabric of their society than do external victors. These reasons point to the need to assign *some* instrumental importance to national borders and counsel prudence on the part of the intervenor. Consequentialist considerations are also crucial for planning the post-intervention stage in order to achieve lasting success in terms of the moral values that justified the intervention.[35]

However, these considerations do not exclude the legitimacy of humanitarian intervention, because the kinds of situations that warrant intervention are of such gravity that they cannot possibly be trumped by the pragmatic considerations just discussed. The protection of national borders is necessary, under this argument, to preserve the glue that binds international society, and as such re-emerges in the post-intervention phase. Yet allowing the atrocities to continue is a much worse dissolver of that glue than the infringement of borders.

I conclude, then, that the right of humanitarian intervention in appropriate cases is unaffected by the existence of national borders. The latter owe their importance to considerations of justice and efficiency. Where these values are grossly assaulted by tyranny and anarchy, invoking the sanctity of borders to protect tyranny and anarchy is, on reflection, self-defeating.

• • •

CONCLUDING COMMENT

Non-interventionism is a doctrine of the past. It feeds on illiberal intellectual traditions (relativism, communitarianism, nationalism, and statism) that are objectionable for various reasons and that, where implemented, have caused grievous harm to persons. Neither the assumptions nor the consequences of non-interventionism are defensible from a liberal stand-point. The very structure of the non-interventionist argument belies the spurious pedigree of the doctrine. We are supposed to outlaw humanitarian intervention because that is what most governments say we should do. But, of course, those who wield or seek power over their fellow citizens (incumbent governments and would-be rulers) have an obvious incentive to support non-intervention. We know that governments (even the better ones) will think about international law and institutions with their priorities in mind, that is, presupposing and affirming state values. But we like to think that we are not victims of such a perverse structure of incentives. We have the choice to think about international law and institutions with human values in mind. Non-interventionists deceptively present their doctrine as one that protects communal values and self-government, yet even a cursory look at history unmasks non-intervention as the one doctrine whose origin, design, and effect is to protect established political power and render persons defenseless against the worst forms of human evil. The principle of non-intervention denies victims of tyranny and anarchy the possibility of appealing to people other than their tormentors. It condemns them to fight unaided or die. Rescuing others will always be onerous, but if we deny the moral duty and legal right to do so, we deny not only the centrality of justice in political affairs, but also the common humanity that binds us all.

Notes

1. I am indebted to the authors of this volume for comments and criticisms on earlier drafts. I especially thank Bob Keohane, Jeff Holzgrefe, Elizabeth Kiss, Allen Buchanan, and Guido Pincione.
2. I first made the argument in Fernando R. Tesón, *Humanitarian Intervention: An Inquiry into Law and Morality* (2nd edn, Transnational Publishers, Dobbs Ferry, 1997) (hereinafter *Humanitarian Intervention*). In this chapter I expand and refine this argument.
3. For an extended analysis of this idea, see Fernando R. Tesón, *A Philosophy of International Law* (Westview Press, Boulder, 1998) (hereinafter *Philosophy of International Law*), ch. 2.
4. Most proponents of humanitarian intervention endorse this claim. See Simon Caney, "Humanitarian Intervention and State Sovereignty," in Andrew Walls ed, *Ethics in International Affairs* (Rowman & Littlefield, Oxford, 2000), pp. 117, 120–21, and authors cited therein. For a more guarded version of the same argument, see Michael Smith, "Humanitarian Intervention: An Overview of the Ethical Issues," 12 *Ethics and International Affairs* (1998), 63, 75–79.
5. As Saint Augustine said: "In the absence of justice, what is sovereignty but organized brigandage? For what are bands of brigands but petty kingdoms?" *The City of God*, cited by R. Phillips, "The Ethics of Humanitarian Intervention," in R. L. Phillips and D. L. Cady eds., *Humanitarian Intervention: Just War v. Pacifism* (Rowman & Littlefield, London, 1996), pp. 1, 6.
6. I believe that forcible intervention to restore democracy may be justified, not on general moral grounds, but on specific grounds such as agreement or the existence of regional norms to

that effect—as is the case, I believe, in Europe and the Americas.
7. See my *Humanitarian Intervention,* pp. 133–36.
8. For terminological convenience, I use the term "intervention" to refer to forcible action. I refer to other forms of action to protect human rights, ranging from regular diplomacy to economic and other sanctions, as "interference."
9. The only philosophically coherent (although counterintuitive) argument against humanitarian intervention is the pacifist position, one that opposes all violence. For a spirited defense of that view, see Robert Holmes, *On War and Morality* (Princeton University Press, Princeton, 1989).
10. I use the term "tyranny" as shorthand for gross and widespread human rights abuses. I use the term "anarchy" as shorthand for massive breakup of social order.
11. See the discussion in Nancy Sherman, "Empathy, Respect, and Humanitarian Intervention," 12 *Ethics and International Affairs* (1998), 103.
12. See Thomas Pogge, "Cosmopolitanism and Sovereignty," in C. Brown ed., *Political Restructuring in Europe: Ethical Perspectives* (Routledge, London, 1994), p. 89; and Caney, "Humanitarian Intervention and State Sovereignty," p. 121.
13. See David Copp, "The Idea of a Legitimate State," 28 *Philosophy and Public Affairs* (1999), 1; John Rawls, *The Law of Peoples* (Harvard University Press, Cambridge, Mass., 1999).
14. For Copp, a state is legitimate when it fulfills certain "societal needs": "Idea of a Legitimate State," pp. 36–45. For Rawls, states might be morally objectionable from a liberal standpoint but still legitimate because they are "decent." See Rawls, *Law of Peoples,* pp. 35–44, 59–82.
15. I believe that the account of international legitimacy offered by Rawls (and, for the same reasons, by Copp) is mistaken, for reasons I have explained elsewhere at length. See my *Philosophy of International Law,* ch. 4.
16. In my view, non-liberal yet "within the pale" regimes should be treated as if they were "on probation" on their way either to joining the liberal alliance or collapsing into extreme tyrannies. For a view of international legitimacy similar to the one I defend, see Allen Buchanan, "Recognitional Legitimacy and the State System," 28 *Philosophy and Public Affairs* (1999), 46.
17. I should have made this point clearer in *Humanitarian Intervention*. I was concerned with refuting the non-interventionist argument from sovereignty, and thus paid insufficient attention to other reasons that might bar humanitarian intervention against illegitimate regimes. In this chapter I attempt, among other things, to remedy that omission.

18. See below for a discussion of the doctrine of double effect.

19. See, for example, Bhikhu Parekh, "Rethinking Humanitarian Intervention," 18 *International Political Science Review* (1997), 49, 54–55.

20. See Fernando R. Tesón, "Human Rights and Cultural Relativism," 25 *Virginia Journal of International Law* (1985), 869.

21. For the view that there is a considerable overlap on humanitarian intervention among different religious traditions, see Oliver Ramsbotham, "Islam, Christianity, and Forcible Humanitarian Intervention," 12 *Ethics and International Affairs* (1998), 81.

22. Separate states might be desirable in order to maximize freedom. See my *Philosophy of International Law,* pp. 17–19.

23. Immanuel Kant, "Perpetual Peace: A Philosophical Sketch" (1795), in Hans Reiss ed., *Kant: Political Writings* (Cambridge University Press, Cambridge, 1970), p. 94.

24. Ibid.

25. They have not lost all their moral strength, though, because tyranny and anarchy do not mean open season for foreigners to invade at will. The guiding liberal principle here is the duty to respect persons. Tyranny and anarchy authorize foreigners to cross national borders to restore respect for persons, not for other purposes. But this will be true in the purely domestic example as well.

26. See Michael Walzer, "The Moral Standing of States: A Response to Four Critics," 9 *Philosophy and Public Affairs* (1980), 209–29. I criticize his argument at length in *Humanitarian Intervention,* pp. 92–99. See also the discussion (in basic agreement with the view in the text) in Caney, "Humanitarian Intervention and State Sovereignty," pp. 122–23; and Jeff McMahan, "The Ethics of International Intervention," in Anthony Ellis ed., *Ethics and International Relations* (Manchester University Press, Manchester, 1986), pp. 36–49.

27. See Gerald Doppelt, "Walzer's Theory of Morality in International Relations," 8 *Philosophy and Public Affairs* (1978), 3.

28. The point I make in the text applies to regimes against whom humanitarian intervention presumably would *not* have been justified on other (mostly consequentialist) grounds. Would anyone say now, for example, that there was anything valuable in the "self-determination" of East Germany, a state created and maintained by terror and violence? Yet at the time most people (academics included) bowed to the realities of political power and proclaimed East Germany a legitimate state, entitled as such to all the privileges and prerogatives associated with statehood. Traditional views of international law, on this as in other matters, suffer, at the very least, from moral blindness.

29. David Luban, "The Romance of the Nation-State," 9 *Philosophy and Public Affairs* (1980), 395–96.

30. See John Stuart Mill, "A Few Words on Non-Intervention," in John Stuart Mill, *Dissertations and Discussions* (Spencer, Boston, 1867), vol. III, pp. 171–76.

31. In the same sense, see McMahan, "Ethics of International Intervention," p. 41. This is the appropriate response to relativist critics of the US–British efforts in Afghanistan aimed at liberating women. The male Muslim believer, even if innocent, has no standing to object to efforts aimed at saving others.

32. See Walzer, "Moral Standing of States."

33. See the classic discussion in Harold Demsetz, "Toward a Theory of Property Rights," 57 *American Economic Review Papers* (1967), 347–59.

34. Robert O. Keohane, personal communication (on file with the author).

35. See Robert O. Keohane, "Political Authority after Intervention: Gradations in Sovereignty," ch. 8 in this volume.

Humanitarian Intervention: Some Doubts

(2003)

Burleigh Wilkins

Burleigh Wilkins is professor of philosophy at the University of California at Santa Barbara. His work is in the analytic philosophy of history and political philosophy and his publications include The Problems of Burke's Political Philosophy *(Oxford University Press, 1967),* Hegel's Philosophy of History *(Cornell University Press, 1974), and* Terrorism and Collective Responsibility *(Routledge, 1992).*

If Locke was correct, and I think he was, revolution is justified when there is systematic violation of the rights to life, liberty, and property with no peaceful redress in sight. I believe that secession and even terrorism are also justified when these conditions obtain. But what about humanitarian intervention? Is it also justified in such a situation? Many of us hesitate when confronted by this question, but why? Is it because humanitarian intervention involves military action by some state or states against another state? Is it because it may raise questions about the legitimacy of a state's sovereignty, questions which even the most secure liberal democracy may feel uncomfortable in addressing? Are even more egregious violations of human rights required in the case of humanitarian intervention than in the cases of revolution, secession, and terrorism? Of course, attempted justifications of humanitarian intervention may focus upon issues other than human rights violations, such as the need to establish or reestablish a democracy or to put an end to a vicious civil war, but these issues, although separate from the issue of human rights viola-tions, may nevertheless be related to it. For purposes of this chapter, I shall be concerned only with human rights violations as a possible ground for humanitarian intervention.

Although it involves the violation of a state's independence and territorial integrity, humanitarian intervention is usually distinguished from war on the ground that the loss of independence and territorial integrity is limited in time and scope. Also it is regarded as a means and not an end, with the end being not conquest or the acquisition of land but the restoration or establishment of protection for basic human rights. But how long before a temporary incursion becomes an occupation? And does not the protection of human rights necessitate at times a change of government, as part of what is sometimes called "a comprehensive settlement"? And what, if anything, can the intervening power(s) do about the culture or way of life which may underlie a government's violation of human rights?

International law seems committed to respect for the sovereignty of states, to the protection of human rights, and to the maintenance of peaceful relations among states. In an ideal world where, say, all states are liberal democracies, all three of these commitments would presumably be honored. There is Michael Doyle's "law" that no democracies ever fight one another, but is this a law or just a trend? In any event, in the real world it may be impossible to provide equal protection for sovereignty, human rights, and peaceful co-existence among states. Here we can note the temptation to treat human rights violations in one state as a threat to the peace and security of all states, or at least of neighboring states, and to use this as a justification for the violation of a nation's sovereignty, although this may in some cases seem farfetched and even disingenuous.

Perhaps humanitarian intervention isn't war, but is it enough like war that the doctrine of just war—with its requirements that a war be fought for a just cause and in a just manner, with an expectation of success, and with a respect for proportionality between the means being employed and the end being sought—can be applied? Would a little fine-tuning help? Justice can be cashed in terms of human rights, with the stipulation that the intervention will not become an all-out war and that it will not last too long. *Jus ad interventionem.* It has a fine ring to it! And the numbers are simply appalling: four times as many deaths in the twentieth century at the hands of the victims' own government or as a result of civil strife than from all the wars between states.[1]

Is the model of Good Samaritan intervention by an individual person(s) to assist an individual under attack by another at all helpful here? But these interventions, in those jurisdictions where they are legally mandated, are called for only in cases where the convenience and not the lives of third-party interveners is at risk.

Here the law seems to follow common morality: if an individual chooses to risk his or her life to come to the aid of another, this is not considered a duty but a supererogatory act. Does this help explain the cautious manner in which political philosophers speak only of a right of intervention and the silence of philosophers such as Walzer and Rawls on whether humanitarian intervention may be a duty.[2] Make no mistake: humanitarian intervention involves a high probability that the intervening party will take casualties. Sometimes the mere presence of troops may lead to casualties, as "mission creep" is a fact of geopolitical life. This is what happened in Somalia where American troops who were initially dispatched to protect humanitarian aid supplies for a starving populace got caught in a struggle between rival warlords.

However, consider the case where an intervening party takes no casualties, as for example the US-NATO intervention in Kosovo which relied entirely upon high altitude bombings to achieve its objectives. This kind of attack, which critics have likened to shooting fish in a barrel, raises fundamental questions of fairness in how an intervention is conducted.

Might not humanitarian intervention sometimes yield just the opposite effect where the protection of human rights is concerned? There are two real possibilities. An oppressive government may be prompted to become even more oppressive in response to an intervention, with confidence that its supporters and even some of its previous critics will "rally round the flag." Or, once intervention occurs, the leadership of an opposition group may become more militant and disrespectful of the rights of others, or the leadership may pass into the hands of a more militant faction with even less respect for human rights than the oppressive regime with which we started out.

Almost everyone agrees that humanitarian intervention might be justified in some cases, but real world examples may prove troublesome. Take the example of the persecution of Jews in Nazi Germany. When would humanitarian intervention have been justified? Before or after *Kristallnacht?* Or only after the Holocaust had begun? By then the West was already at war with Germany for other reasons. What this example shows is the difficulty in pointing to the time when intervention would have become justified, and the certainty that early intervention would have inevitably escalated into an all-out war that the West was not prepared, militarily or psychologically, to fight. The same is true today when we raise the question of what to do about Tibet or Chechnya. The answer is that we can do very little with powers that have nuclear weapons at their disposal. And, of course, we would not pressure allies such as Turkey over its mistreatment of the Kurds as much as we would pressure non-allies over less severe mistreatment of some of their citizens.

Michael J. Smith in a defense of humanitarian intervention candidly admits that there "simply won't be consistency" in our reactions to human rights violations, but he asks, "Is it more ethical to say that, since I cannot do everything everywhere consistently, I should do nothing?"[3] Smith proposes that we adopt a scale of evil where human rights abuses are concerned; on this scale Virginia's frequent use of the death penalty would rank far below the massacres in Rwanda and Cambodia since "few disinterested observers would urge or welcome the forcible landing of an international military force to prevent Virginia's next execution." Smith seems to believe that there is nothing problematic about

how rankings on a scale of evil would be determined. This might be true if the executions in Virginia and the massacres in Rwanda and Cambodia were placed at opposite ends of the scale, but other cases might prove more difficult to rank.

There are, as Smith points out, a few success stories for humanitarian intervention, such as India's intervention in East Pakistan and Tanzania's intervention in Uganda. But India's role in the liberation of Bangladesh, according to some observers, only made matters worse, and, given the history of India-Pakistan relations, it may be that India's intervention was not driven mainly by humanitarian concerns. This leaves us with Tanzania's overthrow of the monstrous Idi Amin in Uganda. Such a small success can hardly lend much support to the principle of humanitarian intervention, and large successes are not to be expected. Undoubtedly, as Smith reminds us, there are moral evils far greater than inconsistency, and to do nothing in the face of evil may well be one of them. It is not, however, the problem of consistency per se that concerns me but the problem of how targets for humanitarian intervention get selected.

Scholars agree that there are no instances of purely humanitarian intervention, and, given what we know about the complexity of human motivation and of the relations among states, this is scarcely surprising. Of course, some cases of allegedly humanitarian intervention are clearly bogus, e.g., Hitler's invasion of Czechoslovakia on the ground of protecting the human rights of the German minority. We all know that for Hitler human rights stopped with German rights, but other cases are more subtle. Sometimes humanitarian intervention may be used in part to settle old grudges, as was alleged against Boutros Boutros-Ghali where Somalia was concerned, or humanitarian intervention may be used against states which have previously fallen upon disfavor in our eyes. Serbia needs to be taught a lesson, as the American Secretary of State put it during the US-NATO intervention in Kosovo. Intervention may also be used in restoring a state's moral standing in the eyes of others. For example, American intervention in Bosnia was undoubtedly influenced by the desire to overcome anti-American sentiments in the Muslim world arising from the Gulf War and to restore the American "reputation" for fairness and evenhandedness. One thing we can be sure of is that humanitarian intervention will not occur if there is a risk of a major conflict in which the intervening power(s) can be expected to take significant casualties. It may be possible to devise a scale of evil, as Smith believes, but there already is a scale of power, and no one seriously believes that evils of great magnitude will trump considerations of relative power.

Because of my doubts about humanitarian intervention I shall not explore in any detail the crucial question of who might best decide whether humanitarian intervention is warranted and who should carry out the intervention. Unilateral intervention by a single state has the advantage of swiftness but runs the risk of partiality and of appearing to be a species of "gunboat diplomacy." Regional organizations should be better at filtering out biases, but they may be dominated by a single great power. The UN may take too long in its decision-making, but it is less likely to be biased and has enjoyed, at least until recently, great moral stature. The UN seems to be the best organization for making a decision about intervention, but the problem of consensus is troubling. Kofi Annan in his report on the tragedy of Srebrenica took responsibility for the UN

and the part it played. But politicians and bureaucrats are adroit at taking responsibility in such a way as to shift responsibility. In the "lessons" to be learned from the tragedy, Annan ranked the lack of a common "political will" high on his list of causes which will need to be addressed to avoid future Srebrenicas.[4] However, the lack of a common political will has not been present in all of the activities of the UN as, for example, in the Gulf War which turned on the conquest of one state by another. In cases where there is no common political will, is doing nothing not preferable to the kind of bungling which contributes to disasters like Srebrenica?

The lack of a common political will is, of course, not necessarily confined to the international arena. Domestic support in a state for humanitarian intervention may ebb and flow, depending on the strength of opposed political parties and upon their commitment to a particular humanitarian intervention. One concern I have is the following: once it has been decided that humanitarian intervention is warranted in a particular situation, crucial steps that a more patient diplomacy might pursue may be skipped. An example of this is the haste with which the US and NATO decided to attack Serbia before negotiations were given a real chance—negotiations which were, in fact, a form of ultimatum. There is also the danger of self-righteousness which may lead the UN or other state to make demands which no self-respecting state could possibly accept, such as permitting foreign troops to travel at will throughout its territory or the holding of a plebiscite concerning independence for a contested region.

The current international situation can be characterized as follows. Friends and foes alike are nervous over the US-

NATO intervention in Kosovo. How long will troops continue to be deployed there? What will count as a successful termination of the mission? Does it set a precedent for future interventions elsewhere in the name of human rights? Whatever happened to the duty of non-intervention, and what kind of duty is it anyway?

One possible reading of the duty of non-intervention is that it is an absolute duty, and various UN agreements including the Charter appear to support this interpretation. However, many moral philosophers would deny that a duty—or a right—can be absolute, that is, obtaining under all circumstances. Perhaps we should try to move in one of two other directions. We could say that the duty of non-intervention is *prima facie,* that is, that there is a strong presumption against intervention but one that can be overridden when there are compelling reasons to do so. Or we could try to write out a list of exceptions and make this list an explicit part of the formulation of the duty of non-intervention. What are some of these exceptions? Cases where we are invited to intervene by the legitimate government of a state? Cases where we can prevent or suppress systematic violations of human rights? Cases where we can assist in struggles for "national liberation"? But, except for the case where the intervention is invited, all other cases will be controversial and will call for further elaboration or refinement. The question still remains of whether these elaborations and refinements would be stated as explicit parts of the duty of non-intervention. For various reasons the project of a definitive list of exceptions to any duty—including that of non-intervention—seems doomed to failure. Seeing the duty of non-intervention as *prima facie* becomes a more attractive alternative if only by default. However, it might still be argued that the duty of non-intervention is absolute and that we only need add "except in the case of an emergency." All deontological rules, it is sometimes argued, are properly construed in this way, and the emergency exception would be difficult to satisfy. This may be part of the problem: although some non-emergency but justifiable reasons for intervention may be compelling, <u>one person's emergency may be another person's difficulty which can be resolved short of intervention.</u>

A final possibility is an openly purposive or teleological reading of the duty of non-intervention: it is to be respected except when intervention serves an end or purpose deemed morally justifiable, in accordance with, for example, utilitarianism or Marxism. However, where international law is concerned this purposive or teleological reading of the duty of non-intervention would strain the associative model of the UN and other forms of cooperation among states, as described by Terry Nardin.[5] What is to prevent the protection and especially the promotion of human rights from becoming as divisive as any other teleological reading of the duty of non-intervention? The protection and promotion of human rights might be divisive not only between states that champion human rights and those that do not, but also among states that support human rights but fail to agree on the appropriateness of particular interventions. Consider, for example, the controversies surrounding the Reagan administration's policies in Nicaragua and especially that administration's refusal to acknowledge that the American bombing of Nicaragua's harbors fell under the jurisdiction of the International Court of Justice.

I admit to having grown weary, or at least wary, of disjunctions between doing something and doing nothing. In the present case there are many things which can be done to advance the cause of human rights which fall short of humanitarian intervention. One way to ameliorate conflicts between liberal and decent societies on the one hand and outlaw states on the other is, simply put, trade. There is Thomas Friedman's "law" that no two countries with McDonalds have ever gone to war with one another. Where human rights issues are concerned the strategy, which sounds simple in the abstract, is to link trading privileges with the acceptance of human rights covenants, as, for example, was the case with the European Council when it granted trading privileges to Russia. In the eighteenth century, the Chinese Emperor wrote to the emissary of King George III that he did not wish to trade with the British since the Chinese had no interest in Britain's clever gadgets. Fortunately for us, and the prospects of a stable world order, all the world seems mad to have the US's clever gadgets. The question of how to take this market for American goods and use it to promote the cause of human rights is, however, a question of statecraft to which, as a philosopher, I have nothing to contribute beyond counsels of prudence. However, in the remainder of this paper I shall explore some conceptual matters which may help clarify the connections between morality and international law.

One possible way to approach this problem is to underscore the moral content of international law and to see it as being in itself an ethical tradition. Of course, this interpretation of international law runs counter to the "realist" school of thought, which reduces all relations among states

to questions of national interest. Treaties are made to be broken, according to the realist, whenever one side sees an advantage in doing so, and states are expected to spy not only upon their enemies but upon their friends as well. Trust no one, and promote national self-interest by whatever means are judged to be necessary. Against this bleak picture of the relations among states, which, of course, is not entirely mistaken, it is possible to think of international law as an ethical tradition in its own right similar to natural law theory, Kantianism, utilitarianism, Marxism, etc. This is Terry Nardin's position: ethical traditions evolve over time, and they involve judgments about the application of principles to particular situations.[6] Certainly Nardin is right, since one would be hard pressed to articulate a sharp distinction between legal and moral principles and the ways in which they are applied to particular cases. In what follows, however, I shall be concerned with international law not as an ethical tradition but with the moral obligations to which it gives rise where the conduct of states is concerned.

I begin this final portion of my paper with a confession about international law. I find it to be a perplexing mixture of treaties among states, customary practices among states, the charters and instruments of the United Nations and several regional organizations, the decisions of various international tribunals, and even the writings of international lawyers. International law is so complex and in such a state of change that it cannot, according to some scholars, readily be codified. Then, of course, there is the problem of sanctions or enforcement, a problem so important some commentators have concluded that, strictly speaking, international law is not law at all. Thus, there is something very tentative in what I say when I speak of international law as a legal system.

A municipal legal system differs from mere orders and commands in that it imposes moral duties and obligations upon all members of a society, and there is a general recognition, not limited to legal philosophers, that there is a moral obligation to obey all the laws of a municipal legal system. You cannot pick and choose which laws you will obey. Transposing this picture to international law results in the following: all states are morally bound to respect the provisions of international law, just as individuals are morally bound to respect the provisions of municipal law. But are states the kinds of things that can have moral duties and obligations? Why not, provided we see them as organized groups of individuals bound together by common rules? At the very least it is coherent to say that organized groups of individuals can undertake or enter into agreements with other organized groups of individuals. In fact, this seems to be what actually happens on a daily basis where, for example, the transactions of business corporations are concerned. Where international law is concerned, the agreements between organized groups can be understood in terms of treaties and even customary practices among states.

It is noteworthy that the principles governing the relations among peoples which we find in John Rawls's *The Law of Peoples* are themselves taken from international law. According to Rawls, these principles are: peoples are to observe a duty of non-intervention, peoples are to honor human rights, peoples are to observe treaties and undertakings, and peoples are equal and are parties to the agreements that bind them. Rawls writes that "These familiar and largely tradi-

tional principles I take from the history and usage of international law and practice. The parties are not given a menu of alternative principles and ideals from which to select, as they are in *Political Liberalism* or in *A Theory of Justice*. Rather, the representatives of well-ordered peoples simply reflect on the advantages of these principles of equality among peoples and see no reason to depart from them or to propose alternatives."[7] In Rawls's second Original Position, the representatives of liberal and decent hierarchical peoples select principles that are binding upon all peoples, including outlaw states. (Could there ever be an outlaw people for Rawls? Perhaps not, given, for example, the careful way in which he tries to distinguish the Nazi state from the German people. Here he disagrees with David Goldhagen's position in *Hitler's Willing Executioners*. The possibility that a coercive demonic political leadership could in time produce a demonic people merits careful consideration.)[8] If I am correct, both Rawls's account of the principles governing the relations of peoples and international law as *it already is* presuppose the idea of international law conceived of as a legal system.

The duty of non-intervention is on my interpretation a moral duty binding upon all states, and it is one of many such duties. Here we should note once more the importance of our conceiving of international law as a legal system. It would be nonsensical to speak of a moral obligation to obey a single principle or to abide by a single agreement standing in isolation from a system of principles or agreements. (There is an analog here, I think, with science where scientific laws are seen as part of a system.) All states are morally bound not to intervene in the domestic affairs of other states. Of course all states are also bound to respect human rights; this would be especially true of the member states of the UN and even more so of those states which have signed the two UN Human Rights Covenants. However there are no provisions in the UN Charter or in these covenants for humanitarian intervention in the domestic affairs of states that do not respect human rights. In the past any such intervention clearly would have been illegal, but now things seem less certain. Perhaps in some circumstances humanitarian intervention may trump the obligation of states not to interfere in the domestic affairs of other states. In this connection it is regrettable, though understandable, that the International Court of Justice refused to rule on the legality of US-NATO intervention in Kosovo. At the risk of sounding like a democratic populist in international law when I am emphatically not a democratic populist where American domestic law is concerned, I think humanitarian intervention gives rise to such complex issues that it should be referred to the legislature. Let the member states of the UN address directly the question of whether humanitarian intervention is permissible, and if need be let us amend the Charter. Let us vote humanitarian intervention up or down, but let us not leave it to be decided on a case-by-case basis. Law, ideally, should satisfy the requirements of justice, but at the very least states no less than individuals need to know what the legal consequences of certain courses of conduct may be.[9]

I want to conclude on a cautiously optimistic note, which I think is consistent with the interpretation of international law as a legal system. According to *Political Liberalism*,[10] John Rawls's history of how the West evolved in a liberal and tolerant direction, two variables were highlighted as important. First was luck, and second was a growing appreciation on the part of individuals with different belief systems of the mutual advantages arising from limited *modus vivendi* agreements. From this it was a short step, historically speaking, to the moral quest for fair rules of social cooperation. Where relations among states are concerned, the world today has an additional advantage in international law, conceived of as a legal system that gives rise to moral obligations among states. However the question of humanitarian intervention is resolved, whether or not it is seen as a right or even as a duty, all states—not just liberal or decent states—are under an obligation to abide by international law.

Notes

1. See Sean O. Murphy, *Humanitarian Intervention* (Philadelphia: University of Pennsylvania Press, 1996).
2. Michael Walzer, *Just and Unjust Wars* (New York: Basic Books, 1997). John Rawls, *The Law of Peoples* (Cambridge, MA: Harvard University Press, 1999) 81, 93–94n. Stanley Hoffmann in *The Ethics and Politics of Intervention* (Notre Dame, IN: University of Notre Dame Press, 1996) 12–39, claims that he is more Kantian than Rawls because he believes there is a duty of intervention, but both are more Kantian than Kant who did not believe in intervention.
3. Michael J. Smith, "Humanitarian Intervention: An Overview of the Ethical Issues," *Ethics and International Affairs* 12 (1998): 78.
4. Report of the Secretary General Pursuant to General Assembly Resolution 53/35 (1998).
5. Terry Nardin, *Law, Morality, and the Relations of States* (Princeton, NJ: Princeton University Press, 1983).
6. Terry Nardin, "Ethical Traditions in International Affairs." *Traditions of International Ethics,* ed. Terry Nardin and David R. Mapels (Cambridge: Cambridge University Press, 1992) 1–23.
7. Rawls 41.
8. Rawls 100–01n.
9. Anthony Ellis thinks the small states in the UN would probably defeat any amendment permit-

ting humanitarian intervention. I am not sure this is so, but, if it is, this would reflect a failure by the UN to respect the moral equality of all member states, a failure which could perhaps be alleviated by other changes in the way the UN

operates, for example, by changes in the veto powers of the permanent members of the Security Council.

10. John Rawls, *Political Liberalism* (New York: Columbia University Press, 1993).

From *Jus ad Bellum* to *Jus ad Pacem:* Re-thinking Just-War Criteria for the Use of Military Force for Humanitarian Ends

(2003)

George R. Lucas, Jr.

George R. Lucas, Jr., is professor of philosophy and associate chair of the department of leadership, ethics, and law at the United States Naval Academy. He is the editor of SUNY's newly established book series "Ethics and the Military Profession" and is the author of Perspectives on Military Intervention *(University of California Press, 2001), as well as several articles on justifiable uses of military force for the purposes of international law enforcement.*

During the decade prior to September 11, 2001, many analysts in ethics and international relations had begun to envision a post–Cold War era in which the principal need for military force would come to be the rendering of international humanitarian assistance. Humanitarian tragedies in Somalia and Rwanda, and at least partially successful military interventions to prevent or halt atrocities in Bosnia and Kosovo, had prompted this significant new attention to the problem of using military

force for humanitarian purposes in international relations.

The events of that day served as grim reminder that, humanitarian causes notwithstanding, nations equip and support military forces primarily for the purpose of defending their own borders and protecting their own citizens from unprovoked attacks from abroad. It is nonetheless a sign of the growing importance of this relatively new-found interest in the humanitarian use of military force that military intervention by the United States and Great Britain in Afghanistan (ostensibly to seek out and punish terrorists and destroy their paramilitary organizations) swiftly came to be represented to the world as a humanitarian intervention as well. The recent Afghan campaign was characterized in broad and quite plausible terms as an effort to liberate citizens from an oppressive and unrepresentative regime, restore human rights (primarily to women who had egregiously been denied them), and prevent some of the worst effects of poverty and starvation in a troubled and long-suffering region of the world.

Notwithstanding all this attention to the problem, the criteria governing the justifiable use of military force for humanitarian purposes remain quite vague. Of those analysts who have attempted to address this issue, some, like James Turner Johnson and Paul Christopher,[1] represent humanitarian interventions as an extension of traditional just-war theory because they still involve the use of military force for coercive purposes. Others, like Michael Walzer,[2] have long argued that various caveats and qualifications need to be added to the baseline legalist paradigm in international relations in order to cover extenuating or emergency situations, including massive violations of human rights within what we are now coming to call "failed states." Still others, like Stanley Hoffman, have argued that the humanitarian use of military force represents an emerging new paradigm in international relations that calls into question some of the basic assumptions regarding the sovereignty of nations, thus requiring a set of justifications all its own.[3]

I will suggest that the attempt simply to assimilate or subsume humanitarian uses of military force under traditional just war criteria fails because the use of military force in humanitarian cases is far closer to the use of force in domestic law enforcement and peacekeeping, and so subject to far more stringent restrictions in certain respects than traditional *jus in bello* normally entails. It is not, for example, sufficient that humanitarian military forces (any more than domestic police forces) simply refrain from excessive collateral damage, or merely refrain from the deliberate targeting of non-combatants. In fact, the very nature of intervention suggests that the international military "police-like" forces (like actual police forces) must incur considerable additional risk, even from suspected guilty parties, in order to uphold and enforce the law without themselves engaging in violations of the law.

The second strategy for encompassing humanitarian use of military force is represented in Michael Walzer's longstanding attempts to revise and reform our understanding of international law in lieu of relying on the vagaries of moral reasoning alone. This strategy, however, does not address the underlying conceptual incoherence involved in making the autonomous nation-state the unit of analysis in international law. Humanitarian interventions are not undertaken to address solely the political problems of "failed" states (of which Rwanda and Somalia are examples), nor only to contain or discipline the behavior of "rogue" states (such as Yugoslavia and Iraq). Instead, such interventions are necessary even more frequently to address the substantial pressures placed upon the international community by the behaviors of what might be termed "inept" states (of which Afghanistan, Congo, the Sudan, and many others are examples). "Inept" states are those nations with recognizable but ineffective governments unable to provide for the security and welfare of citizens, secure the normal functioning of the institutions of civil society, or maintain secure borders sufficient to control the operations of criminal elements in their midst. None of Walzer's earliest qualifications of the baseline legalist paradigm in *Just and Unjust Wars* (1977), let alone his more recent elaborations of his reformed legalist paradigm,[4] addresses this dilemma successfully, or explains whether we have either the right or responsibility to do (for example) what the United States and Britain are currently doing in Afghanistan. As mentioned, this current exercise includes not only pursuing and destroying international terrorist networks and apprehending international criminals, but assisting in liberating—and in providing food, humanitarian assistance, and political support in nation-building—for the multi-ethnic citizens of a country held for years in virtual slavery by their own, internationally-recognized government, the Taliban. In what follows, I propose to address the unique and problematic features of *jus ad pacem* and *jus in pace,* by spelling out specific criteria and explanations and justifications for each.

BACKGROUND: "ON THE VERY IDEA OF *JUS AD PACEM* AND *JUS IN PACE*"

Jus ad pacem (or *jus ad interventionem*) refers to the justification of the use of force for humanitarian or peaceful ends.[5] The concept of this use of military force has been much discussed as incidents of it have proliferated since 1990. The discussions of justification, however, have focused mainly upon legitimacy (legality) and legitimate authority: that is, upon

analysis of the sorts of entities that might theoretically have the right to use force across established national boundaries in order to restore peace, maintain order, respond to natural disasters, prevent humanitarian tragedies, or attempt to rebuild so-called "failed" states.[6] Political legitimacy or "legitimate authority" was originally the paramount criterion of just war doctrine as explicated by Aquinas. It has once again been restored to its pre-eminent status[7] as nations cope with the havoc wreaked by semi-autonomous "non-state entities" (organizations like Hamas and Al Qaeda), as well as to the attempts by such entities to justify their alleged right to violate time-honored principles of *jus in bello* by targeting non-combatants who dwell in regions of the world far removed from their spheres of concern, and who are utterly innocent of any kind of involvement in the political affairs with which they claim to express grievances.

Given the extent of the interest in this topic, and the increasing demands made on military forces for this purpose, from Somalia and Rwanda to Bosnia, Kosovo, and arguably now even Afghanistan, these discussions and resulting analyses have been surprisingly unfocused, inchoate, and inconclusive. Many authors seem to treat the use of military force for humanitarian purposes as a novel development of the post-Cold War era, when in fact this use of the military has a long and noble history.[8] Other writers and analysts, suspicious of the use of military force for any purpose whatever, have been reluctant to re-consider their selective anti-military bias (forged in the aftermath of the Vietnam war), let alone embrace the emerging notion that national militaries do now, and will, for the foreseeable future, continue to have a positive and important role to play in enforcing justice, protecting individual liberty, and defending fundamental human rights, as well as in performing their more traditional role of defending national borders and protecting the welfare of their own citizens.

What is often overlooked is that *the prospective need for humanitarian military interventions is rapidly becoming the principal justification for raising, equipping, training and deploying a nation's military force.* What we might call the "interventionist imperative" lies at the core of the policy first officially formulated by former Secretary of State Madeline K. Albright in a speech at the US Naval Academy early in 1997. Secretary Albright's position at the time seemed to assert the following moral principle: "When a clearly recognizable injustice is in progress, and when we as international bystanders are in a position to intervene to prevent it, then it follows that we are under a *prima facie* obligation to do so . . . in Kantian terminology, [the interventionist imperative] amounts to an "imperfect duty" of beneficence: we have a duty to prevent harm and injustice when we are able and in a position to do so, but what actions we choose to perform or strategies we choose to devise to carry out this imperative, and the beneficiaries of our protection, are not specified."[9] . . .

Stanley Hoffman has proposed two versions of what he terms a "universal maxim" of *jus ad interventionem:*

(1) collective intervention is justified whenever a nation-state's condition or behavior results in grave threats to other states' and other peoples' peace and security, and in grave and massive violations of human rights;
(2) sovereignty may be overridden whenever the behavior of the state in question, even within its own territory, threatens the existence of elementary

human rights abroad, and whenever the protection of the rights of its own members can be assured only from the outside.[10]

These proposals deserve careful consideration, not only on account of the distinguished credentials of their author, but because this two-part proposal constitutes the only substantive criterion thus far put forward to guide and clarify the justification for humanitarian military actions. The first version seems designed to define something akin to "just cause" in classical just-war theory, and applies to events ranging from the Holocaust to the genocidal acts in Bosnia, Kosovo, and Rwanda. The wording, however, appears to tie "threats to other states' and other peoples' peace and security" with "grave and massive violations of human rights" (presumably occurring within the affected nation's borders and not necessarily constituting an external threat). The first clause represents the traditional perspective on a state's behavior within the nation-state system; the second adds an additional provision, similar to Walzer's concern for behavior that "shocks the conscience of humanity." Simply replacing the final "and" with "or" would clarify that one or the other objectionable behavior, and not both simultaneously, are sufficient to invoke justification for armed intervention.

In the second version of his "universal maxim," Hoffman addresses the sovereignty problem explicitly. He seems to be attempting to address at least partially the notion of "legitimate authority." Both versions of the maxim seem to imply that legitimate authority in humanitarian interventions is restricted to "the international community" or to collectivities of some sort.

This raises in turn the most vexing aspect of intervention. Why should not a country (India, or Tanzania, or Vietnam, for example) be empowered to "invade" a neighbor (East Pakistan, Uganda, or Cambodia, respectively) engaged in massive violations of human rights carried out against its own citizens? And why should the "international community" be obliged to wait to prevent what Walzer also describes as "gross and massive" violations of human rights like this until some perceived threat to other states' freedom and security is detected? Hoffman's phrasing of (2) accurately reflects current agreements and UN policies on collective security, but for those who found the UN debacles in Bosnia and Rwanda less than satisfying, it is worth reminding ourselves that these collective humanitarian actions were carried out under the constraints imposed by such existing agreements and conventions.[11]

At present, the criterion of "legitimate authority" appears to be largely taken for granted: all legitimate humanitarian interventions, it would appear, should come about through multilateral debate and decision, and should reflect the collective will of the international community. Unilateral interventions should be prohibited. Does this, however, mean that the international community cannot appoint a single nation to act as its agent (and perhaps should have in the cases cited above)? Likewise, the role of regional security organizations, like NATO, needs to be more carefully explored as a possible legitimate agency. Interventions carried out by such regional security collectivities would neither be unilateral (and so not strictly proscribed) nor sufficiently multi-lateral to qualify as legitimate authorities under conventional understandings of that concept. Perhaps language should be included within any new *jus ad pacem* rubric to address problems, like Bosnia and Kosovo, that seem to fall as responsibilities primarily to a region (that is, Western Europe) rather than to the international community as a whole, permitting the affected region's security and cooperation organization to act as the legitimate authority in such a case.

These questions and problems suggest that it is high time to formulate a more complete list of *jus ad pacem* or *jus ad interventionem* (including some preliminary provisions for restrictions on battlefield conduct, or *jus in pace*), sufficient to govern involvement in humanitarian exercises. While there is no compelling need to require that such criteria perfectly match the seven conventional provisions of just-war doctrine, it will help guide our discussion and ensure a full and comprehensive treatment of the problem if we use the traditional provisions as guideposts for our proposed new formulations.

Justifiable Cause for Intervention

Let us begin with the humanitarian equivalent of "just cause":

> Humanitarian intervention is justified whenever a nation-state's behavior results in grave and massive violations of human rights.

From my comments above, it is apparent that this needs to be understood in two senses:

(a) *intervention is justified when these behaviors result in grave threats to the peace and security of other states and other peoples,* and

(b) *intervention need not be restricted to such cases, but may be justified when the threats to human rights are wholly contained within the borders of the state in question.*

Legitimate Authority

We must ask what, if anything, gives the interventionists the right to ignore international borders and nation-state sovereignty in order to respond to the clear humanitarian emergencies cited in the first provision pertaining to "just cause."

> Sovereignty may be overridden whenever the protection of the rights of that states' own citizens can be assured only from the outside.

Hoffman's formulation above contains two additional clarifications:

(a) *sovereignty may be overridden whenever the behavior of the state in question, even within its own territory, threatens the existence of elementary human rights abroad;*
(b) *sovereignty may be overridden even when there is no threat to human rights outside the borders of the state in question, providing the threat to that state's own citizens are real and immediate.*

This still leaves the question of "who" is to determine whether such threats are "real and immediate?" Here I propose a second clause that seems to capture widespread concern on the part of most commentators on this problem that such judgments should be collective rather than unilateral, in order to ensure "right intentions" (see below) and exclude ulterior, self-interested motives.

> The decision to override sovereignty and intervene must be made by an appropriate collective international body.

This does not, however, mean that the intervention itself must constitute a collective military action, although there are ample grounds for finding that preferable. Instead, in light of our recent experience and the analysis above, this legitimacy provision seems to entail:

(a) *The* decision *to intervene can never be undertaken unilaterally; however*
(b) *a unilateral agent of intervention may be authorized by an appropriate international tribunal; and also*

(c) *a regional security organization may be authorized by an appropriate international tribunal to undertake a military intervention for humanitarian purposes.*

Right Intention

Much of the concern over multi-lateralism and collective action concerns the possibility of conflicted and self-interested motives. Paul Christopher notes that Hugo Grotius originally licensed military interventions for clear humanitarian purposes (such as the prevention of cannibalism, rape, abuse of the elderly, and piracy), and simultaneously warned against the likelihood of hidden and less noble agendas, such as greed, religious and cultural differences, and national self-interest, poisoning the presumptive humanitarian and disinterested motivations.[12] These considerations lead straightforwardly to the following restrictions on the use of force for humanitarian purposes:

> The intention in using force must be restricted without exception to purely humanitarian concerns, such as the restoration of law and order in the face of natural disaster, or to the protection of the rights and liberties of vulnerable peoples (as defined in the United Nations Charter and the Universal Declaration of Human Rights).

Furthermore, the intentions must be publicly proclaimed and clearly evident without conflict of interest to the international community. Intervening nations and their militaries should possess no financial, political or material interests in the outcome of the intervention, other than the publicly proclaimed humanitarian ends described above, nor should they stand to gain in any way from the outcome of the intervention, other than from the general welfare sustained by having justice served, innocent peoples protected from harm, and peace and order restored. A useful protection against abuse of this provision is for the intervening powers not only to state clearly and publicly their humanitarian ends, but also to set forth a set of conditions under which the need for intervention will have been satisfied, together with a reasonable timetable for achieving their humanitarian goals. Suspicion of possible ulterior motives might be further allayed not only by ensuring the trans-national character of the intervention, but by providing (in the publicly stated proposal to undertake it) for periodic rotation, where feasible, of the specific nationalities involved in carrying out the action.[13]

Last Resort

> Military intervention may be resorted to for humanitarian purposes only when all other options have been exhausted.

What this means is that good faith efforts by the international community must be made to avert humanitarian disasters within the borders of a sovereign state through diplomatic negotiation, economic sanction, United Nations censure, and other non-military means as appropriate. In practice, this is easier said than done, and could result (as in Rwanda and Bosnia) in delaying necessary deployment of force to prevent a humanitarian tragedy while the "international community" wrings its collective hands ineffectually, worrying whether all other available options have been satisfied. Paul Christopher's sensible proposal from the standpoint of just war theory, applied to humanitarian cases, is that "[this] condition is met when reasonable nonviolent efforts have been unsuccessful and there is

no indication that future attempts will fare any better."[14]

Likelihood of Success

Johnson and Christopher tend to collapse or blend their concerns for the criterion of likely success into others treating everything from last resort and legitimate authority to the proportionality of war to its stated ends. I favor keeping this criterion distinct, as providing a unique and important constraint on the decision to deploy force for humanitarian reasons.

> Military force may be utilized for humanitarian purposes only when there is a reasonable likelihood that the application of force will meet with success in averting a humanitarian tragedy.

This seemingly obvious provision in fact imposes something like Weinberger Doctrine constraints on those whose moral outrage or righteous zeal might tempt them into military adventures for which the intervening powers are ill-prepared and unsuited, or which might make an already-bad situation even worse. Specifically:

(a) *a resort to military force may not be invoked when there is a real probability that the use of such force will prove ineffective, or may actually worsen the prospects for a peaceful resolution of the crisis; and*

(b) *military force may not be employed, even for humanitarian ends, when the international community is unable to define or determine straightforward and feasible goals to be achieved by the application of force.*

These Weinberger-like constraints are also important as reassurances to those political representatives of that camp who have been extremely reluctant to embrace what otherwise appears to be an international moral obligation to render humanitarian assistance or prevent avoidable tragedies when we as bystanders are in a position to do so (the "interventionist imperative").

General Anthony Zinni, speaking of his experiences in Somalia,[15] warns us that this traditional criterion limiting military force has a special urgency and ambiguity in the humanitarian instance. Militaries, including the American military, are not primarily oriented or necessarily well-suited to carry out the varieties of tasks a true humanitarian exercise may require. It is difficult in advance to predict just what sorts of activities these may comprise, but they certainly transcend the straightforward projection of lethal force to include also civil engineering, police and law enforcement, and other functions of a stable civil society. In some instances, military experts on hand may perform, say, civil engineering functions (such as water purification, distribution of food rations, or bridge and road construction) as or even more readily and ably than civilian counterparts. In other instances, as occurred in Somalia, the need to resurrect a moribund legal system and to re-establish police, courts, and a working prison system may push the intervening forces into roles they are ill-prepared and ill-equipped to play, with disastrous consequences. Yet, as Zinni notes, any attempt to avoid engaging in these necessary nation-building exercises is likely to doom the humanitarian mission to failure.

Proportionality of Ends

It is not sufficient, however, to demand that military intervention be successful, or that it merely refrain from worsening a bad situation. The NATO air campaign in Kosovo satisfied both constraints, but concerns abound regarding the consequences of the aforementioned doctrine of force protection, and the resulting civilian casualties sustained (for example, from height restrictions imposed on attacking aircraft).

> The lives, welfare, rights and liberties to be protected must bear some reasonable proportion to the risks of harm incurred, and the damage one might reasonably expect to inflict in pursuit of humanitarian ends.

In the end, the debates over this aspect of the Kosovo air campaign come down to this provision, although the question of whether to engage in that intervention initially focused on what amounted to discussion of the likelihood of success, as outlined above. Post-mortems and continuing analysis of the results of that intervention now routinely raise the question of whether the damage inflicted in an effort to stop the threatened genocide by Serbian troops against Kosovars (as a result of force-protection measures imposed, including the unwillingness to commit ground troops to the exercise) was, in the end, unduly large.[16]

It is at this stage that discussions of justifiable military intervention for humanitarian ends shift from the actual discussion of the justification of such intervention, to discussions, similar in some respects to traditional law of armed combat (*jus in bello*), governing the manner in which intervening forces may operate and conduct themselves. The Kosovo debate illustrates this ambiguity clearly. Given what was known of Serbian intentions within the province of Kosovo, based upon substantial prior experience elsewhere in the region (in Bosnia and Herzegovina, for example), there was every reason to expect that the anticipated casualties to be suffered by innocents in the absence of armed intervention of whatever sort would vastly outweigh any foreseeable "collateral damage" that the intervening forces might inadvertently inflict themselves. While any attempt to engage in such calculus is necessarily fraught with difficulty, it seems that most observers agree that this condition (taken as a constraint to be satisfied in the initial decision to deploy military force) was amply satisfied.

What is being debated after the fact, then, is no longer the initial justification of the intervention, but the manner in which it was ultimately carried out. *Jus ad pacem* demands that a reasonable evaluation of the likely overall outcomes (including necessary forms of military deployment and conduct during the intervention) be undertaken before deciding whether to undertake the mission. By contrast, what is now being debated is whether, during a justifiable humanitarian mission, reasonable resulting constraints on the conduct of military forces during the humanitarian mission were violated in selected instances.

Just Means, Moral Means (or, Proportionality of Means)

The concern that remains unaddressed is something equivalent to the traditional *jus ad bellum* requirement that justifiable wars must be prosecuted by just means. There are a variety of ways of capturing this essential insight, which may well be the most important and difficult provision to achieve in practice for otherwise justifiable, if not downright obligatory, military interventions. This would not be surprising, as strict compliance with *jus in bello,* particularly the principle of discrimination between combatants and non-combatants, remains the most elusive component of just-war theory generally.[17]

The morality of the means employed to carry out a humanitarian intervention, or to achieve its stated goals, must be commensurate with, or proportional to, the morality of the cause or ends for the sake of which the intervention is conducted. Transparently, a military intervention conducted for the sake of protecting human rights or averting a humanitarian tragedy cannot itself rely upon military means of intervention or modes of conduct by military personnel which themselves violate the very rights the interventionists sought to protect, or which provoke a humanitarian tragedy of dimensions similar to the original impending tragedy the interventionists sought to avert.

The last phrase in particular captures the concerns of critics of the NATO bombing strategy, and the concomitant decision against using low-flying Apache combat helicopters or ground forces, for the sake of force protection and the minimization of allied combat casualties in Kosovo. The critics, both military and civilian, are not quibbling about proportionality with the advantage of hindsight, so much as calling attention to this paradoxical feature of the use of deadly force for humanitarian purposes, the details of which I have collectively labeled *jus in pace* or *jus in interventione.*

> Humanitarian intervention can never be pursued via military means that themselves are deemed illegal or immoral.

As I have suggested throughout this essay, the provisions and restrictions upon the conduct of military forces that this final provision imposes are not well understood, but are certainly more, rather than less, constraining than traditional *jus in bello* or law of armed combat, while including those tradition provisions as well. Specifically:

(a) *captured belligerents must be treated as prisoners of war according to established international conventions, and may not be mistreated or subject to trial or sentence by the intervening forces;*

(b) *prisoners of war accused of humanitarian crimes and abuses may be bound over for trial by an appropriate international tribunal;*

(c) *civilian non-combatants must never be deliberately targeted during a humanitarian military operation;*[18]

(d) *military necessity during humanitarian operations can never excuse the use of weapons, or pursuit of battlefield tactics, already proscribed as illegal under established international treaties and conventional law of armed combat;*

(e) *finally, military necessity during humanitarian operations cannot excuse tactics or policies, such as "force protection," that knowingly, deliberately, and disproportionately reallocate risk of harm from the peace keeping forces and belligerents to non-combatants. It is not sufficient that humanitarian military forces simply refrain from excessive collateral damage, or merely refrain from the deliberate targeting of non-combatants. The very nature of intervention suggests that the international military forces (like domestic law enforcement personnel) must incur considerable additional risk, even from suspected guilty parties, in order to uphold and enforce the law without themselves engaging in violations of the law.*

Paragraphs (a) and (c), and (d) capture the conventional constraints characteristic of *jus in bello*. Paragraph (b), however, begins to suggest the character of law enforcement that humanitarian interventions may entail. Paragraph (b) implies that the intervening forces are not, in the name of protecting or minimizing casualties among their own personnel, permitted to turn a blind eye toward international criminals operating in their midst, but have the same obligations to apprehend criminals and enforce justice that their domestic peacekeeping counterparts do. Moreover, it explicitly states that if, during the course of an armed intervention or afterwards, an apparent perpetrator of criminal actions such as Slobodan Milosevic or Osama bin Laden is apprehended, then (as with conventional domestic criminals) the duty of the intervening forces is to ensure that the accused is properly treated and bound over for trial in a legal manner.

Why do I suggest this? Let me hasten to say that it is not because I believe that murderous Yogoslavian thugs or spoiled, vain, and destructive miscreants like bin Laden are somehow especially entitled to avail themselves of the protections of the law which they have otherwise scorned. Instead, there is an important practical element at work in this provision. It properly classifies terrorism and its proponents as "criminals" carrying out "crimes against humanity," rather than dignifying their actions as quasi-legitimate acts of "war," or otherwise conferring upon their perpetrators and their shadowy, non-state organizations the status of statehood. The important domestic analogy is the continuing struggle to avoid "romanticizing" the activities of organized crime or dissident factions within a nation-state with a quasi-cultural status as "acts of war," lest we seem to be sanctioning or excusing the resulting violence and threats to legitimate and established order. No matter how legitimate the *grievances* of such individuals and organizations may otherwise be found to be, it is vital not to permit them or ourselves to fall into the fatal trap of somehow legitimating *criminal actions* (whether of Timothy McVeigh or Osama bin Laden) as if these were some sort of populist redress of grievance or otherwise-justifiable protest against the injustices they purport to cite.

It is precisely this recognition of the radically different moral status of these criminals, and of the international society against which they have set their faces and directed their actions, that imposes special burdens and responsibilities on the decorum and behavior of intervening forces, sent to enforce and uphold the law. Paragraph (e) thus directly enjoins the as-yet-unresolved paradox posed by the increasing tendency toward force protection in the course of carrying out humanitarian interventions. I suggested in the preceding pages that such tactics evolve as a result of thinking dictated by conventional just-war theory and international relations, according to which national sovereignty and national interests are the primary units of analysis. These serve to define the nature of the limitations placed upon an individual's self-sacrifice during wartime, as described in Walzer's "war convention." Since these provisions are almost always lacking in truly justifiable humanitarian interventions, the concerns they engender, while understandable, are seriously misplaced.

What we require of the intervening forces is not merely that their controlling interests and command structures lack any personal conflicts of interest in the enforcement of justice, protection of rights, and establishment of peace, but that they be willing to incur risk and put themselves in harm's way for the sake of these moral ideals, and with an end of securing (and certainly not themselves threatening or destroying) the blessings of rights and liberty to the vulnerable and endangered victims whose desperate plight initially prompts the international call for military intervention. This is not an imposition of lofty moral idealism, but a simple requirement for consistency of purpose that civilized society routinely imposes upon itself, and particularly upon those who choose to uphold and defend civilization's highest ideals and most essential governing principles. *In humanitarian interventions, as in domestic law enforcement, we cannot and we do not forsake our laws and moral principles in order to enforce and protect them.*

These *jus in pace* criteria, and especially this final provision, are not as strange, stringent, or unreasonable as they may at first seem, since we ask precisely these same commitments of any domestic law enforcement agency or authority. It is, I have argued, in the nature of humanitarian intervention that it not only restores a legitimate role to morality in foreign policy, but that it begins to import some of the more cherished securities and civilizing protections of domestic civil society into the international arena precisely to supplant the anarchy, ruthlessness, and terror that still too often flourish in the darker regions of our new global order.

Notes

1. James Turner Johnson, *Morality and Contemporary Warfare* (New Haven, CT: Yale University Press, 1999); and "The Just-War Idea and the Ethics of Intervention," in *The Leader's Imperative: Ethics, Integrity and Responsibility,* ed. J. Carl Ficarrotta (Lafayette, IN: Purdue University Press, 2001); Paul Christopher, *The Ethics of War and Peace,* 2nd edition (Upper Saddle River, NJ: Prentice-Hall, 1999). Hereafter cited as EWP.
2. *Just and Unjust Wars,* 3rd edition (New York: Basic Books, 2000), ch. 6.
3. Stanley Hoffman, *The Ethics and Politics of Humanitarian Intervention* (Notre Dame, IN: Notre Dame University Press, 1996). Hereafter cited as EPHI.
4. "The Politics of Rescue," *Dissent* 42, no. 1 (1995), 35–41; "Emergency Ethics," in J. Carl Ficarrotta, *The Leader's Imperative,* pp. 126–39, and *Nation*

and Universe. "The Tanner Lectures on Human Values, Volume XI" (Lake City, UT: University of Utah Press, 1990).

5. George R. Lucas, Jr., *Perspectives on Humanitarian Military Intervention* (Berkeley, CA: University of California/Public Policy Press, 2001), pp. 4ff.

6. A state "fails" when its ability to guarantee basic rights and liberties, provide fundamental essential services that constitute a civil society (such as basic medical care, education, banking, commerce, agriculture, and a dependable food supply), and enforce the rule of law *completely evaporates*. This contrasts with the behavior of viable but criminal states ("rogue" states) and what I am calling "inept" states. See Robert S. Litwak, *Rogue States and US Foreign Policy* (Baltimore, MD: The Johns Hopkins University Press, 2000) for an analysis of the former. An inept or incompetent state is one which does a poor or incompetent job in any or several of these categories of essential human needs.

7. In Thomas Aquinas' discussion of the morality of war in *Summa Theologica,* legitimate authority is listed as the first criterion (ahead of "just cause") to be fulfilled. It is Hugo Grotius who first reverses this priority and gives pride of place to "just cause" (specifically eliminating religious wars as eligible categories). Johnson explores this history in *The Holy War Idea in Western and Islamic Traditions* (University Park, PA: Penn State University Press, 1998).

8. Martha Finnemore, "Constructing Norms of Humanitarian Intervention." *The Culture of National Security,* ed. Peter J. Katzenstein (NY: Columbia University Press, 1996), pp. 153–85. See also Paul Christopher's discussion of Grotius on the rationale for humanitarian military intervention as early as the seventeenth century, EWP, p. 192.

9. See *Perspectives on Humanitarian Military Intervention,* p. 10. See also Julia Driver, "The Ethics of Intervention," *Philosophy and Phenomenological Research* 57, no. 4 (December, 1997), 851–70; more recently John W. Lango, "Is Armed Humanitarian Intervention to Stop Mass Killing Morally Obligatory," *Public Affairs Quarterly* (July 2001), 173–92, who argue in favor of such

an imperative. It is important to recognize that imperfect duties are no less stringent than perfect duties. The term "imperfect" refers not to their stringency but their lack of specificity: such obligations do not precisely specify the nature of actions taken to fulfill the obligation ("what sort of good acts should I undertake?") nor do they always specify an obligee ("whom should I choose as beneficiary of my good actions?"). Assuming that interventionism is a species of "good Samaritanism," the obligees are specified, but the precise actions undertaken in their defense are not. . . .

10. EPHI, 23.

11. Paul Christopher appears to agree that suitable collective bodies should be able to authorize or otherwise post facto legitimate unilateral interventions with clear humanitarian intent: see EWP, 193, 198.

12. EWP, 199.

13. This proposal is suggested by James Turner Johnson (see Ficarrotta, *The Leader's Imperative,* p. 122), but given the extraordinary logistical difficulties of coalition operations to begin with, this additional provision might add an insuperable burden to interventions justifiable on other grounds.

14. EWP, 201.

15. Lucas, *Perspectives,* pp. 53–63; note that this is an eloquent defense and rejoinder to the charges of "mission creep" that were made against that operation initially as the putative cause of its failure.

16. See, for example, Gen. Wesley K. Clark, *Waging Modern War: Bosnia, Kosovo, and the Future of Combat* (New York: Public Affairs Press, 2001) for a discussion of the differences between US and European military and civilian leadership on these questions.

17. Douglas P. Lackey, *The Ethics of War and Peace* (Upper Saddle River, NJ: Prentice-Hall, 1989), pp. 58–97.

18. For a discussion of how this standard convention plays out in humanitarian intervention, see James Turner Johnson, "Maintaining the Protection of Noncombatants," *Journal of Peace Research 37,* no. 4 (July 2000), 421–48.

C. Recent Armed Conflicts

As is often the case in collections like these, the reader can become easily overwhelmed by the intricate nature of the arguments and the historical distance from much of the foundational material. Michael Walzer recognized this problem quite clearly: The subtitle of his classic study of the Just War tradition points out that *Just and Unjust Wars* is "a moral argument with historical illustrations." When putting this collection together, it seemed prudent to include articles on some of the most recent armed conflicts, in an attempt to connect the more abstract theory to the "real world" and to make the history seem somewhat less distant. In this section, you will find pieces on the humanitarian intervention in Kosovo (which ties in nicely to our section on interventionism), the second Gulf War, and the "war on terror." Given space constraints, we were not able to include articles on other recent conflicts, such as the first Gulf War, Somalia, and Rwanda, but all of these campaigns have been the subject of intense philosophical, legal, and political scrutiny, and can easily be used to augment these particular cases.

We begin with Georg Meggle's "Is This War Good? An Ethical Commentary." The ethnic conflict in Yugoslavia is complicated and detailed: As with almost any armed conflict, the background conditions are important for understanding the full scope of the situation. However, for the sake of its place in this collection, the important details lie mostly in the fact that the NATO intervention in Kosovo was intended to stop the genocide of innocents in the region, that is, to prevent a "second Auschwitz."

Meggle offers a set of necessary (and jointly sufficient) conditions that must be met for a humanitarian intervention to be justified, focusing on the proportionality of the intervention: A humanitarian intervention must be the only possible way of preventing massive crimes against humanity (Meggle calls these kinds of crimes "The Kosovo Dimension"), the amount of harm must be achieved with the least possible harm, the threat to external parties and to the intervener must be minimized, and the intervention itself must not involve massive crimes against humanity. Meggle also downplays the role of motives in interventions, arguing that the assistance is the most relevant factor, and not the motives behind the intervention. One condition that is intentionally left out by Meggle is the requirement that the intervention be sanctioned by international law and, more specifically, by a UN Security Council resolution. He leaves this condition out primarily because he thinks that international law is not sufficiently developed to meet these goals at the present time, and the UN Security Council's resolution procedure is also deficient at the present time.

Meggle leaves the question posed by his title unanswered, for the most part, because of the lack of clear facts about the situation in Kosovo. It is important, in evaluating any conflict, to have as many of the crucial facts available to us as possible, and the Kosovo conflict is no exception. With a dearth of appropriate information available to us, Meggle claims, we must leave the question "is this war good?" open until all of the relevant facts become available.

The conflict that has become known as the Second Gulf War was formally begun in August of 2002, when Vice President Dick Cheney presented the argument that Saddam Hussein was stockpiling weapons of mass destruction: chemical, biological, and nuclear weapons. The antecedents of the war are well-known, including the failed attempt to oust Hussein by George H. Bush in the early 1990s, the alleged connections between Hussein and Osama bin Laden, and the ongoing human rights violations occurring during Hussein's reign of terror. What was unique about this particular case was the preemptive nature of the conflict: The threats posed by "shadowy networks of individuals [who] can bring great chaos and suffering to our shores" are enough to justify a full-scale assault on Iraq *before* any attack were perpetrated by Iraq on the United States. In most of the standard Just War scenarios, the threat of an attack must be imminent to justify an offensive strike: The enemy must be amassing on the borders before a strike can be justified. With Iraq, it remains open to interpretation whether or not there was sufficient evidence that attacks on the United States were imminent. The Bush administration described this new approach to warfare as "preemptive," although Miriam Sapiro argues it is better described as "preventative," as it generally is not aimed to preempt any specific, imminent threats.

Sapiro's essay, "Iraq: The Shifting Sands of Preemptive Self-Defense" examines the foundations of the new preemptive war as proposed by the Bush administration in light of existing international law. Sapiro points out that Article 51 of the UN Charter allows for self-defense *if an attack occurs,* but not in cases of threat or imminence of attack. While the United States has offered no official position on preemptive war prior to the September 2002 release of the *National Security Strategy,* the Bush administration offered support for their view in the history of international law, including the work of Grotius and Vattel. Sapiro finds the international law arguments supporting preemptive war to be unconvincing, and turns instead to other grounds to determine the validity of the claims. She considers several options, including the argument from the humanitarian intervention perspective, the argument from the perspective of the changing nature of international threats (and the need for changes in the respective laws), and the argument from the perspective of changing nature of military technology. Sapiro sees the conflict between the United States and Iraq as presenting a good argument for a wider acceptance of anticipatory self-defense, but she is cautious of any attempt to widen the scope of preemptive warfare. Instead, she says, the United States needs to consider narrowing the scope of the *Strategy,* albeit quietly.

William Galston also tackles the dilemma of preemptive war with Iraq, arguing that most of the considerations made by politicians in defense of the war have been made on *prudential* grounds, while they should have been made on grounds of *principle*. One of the strong considerations of principle that comes into play here is the nearly unilateral nature of the actions of the United States. By invading Iraq preemptively, Galston argues, the United States "would act as a law unto itself, creating new rules of international engagements without the consent of other nations," and this is not in the long-term interest of the United States. Further, international law seems also to cause difficulties for the preemptive attack on Iraq: It seems to go well beyond the accepted bounds of self-defense. Galston states that, if the United States fails to make its case clearly, the world will see our preemptive attack as an "international hunting license."

Galston explores the preemptive war under the rubric of Just War Theory, citing Walzer's claim that anticipatory strikes can occasionally be justified if there is "sufficient threat." While Iraq might have posed a danger to its neighbors, Galston finds no credence in the claim that it was a threat to the United States. For Galston, the preemptive attack on Iraq by the United States does not meet the Just War criteria, and fails as a justified case of anticipatory warfare. Yet Galston accepts the importance of the desire of the United States to safeguard its own security. Before a preemptive war, however, it is imperative that the United States exhausts all other reasonable options and provide a public rationale for its actions that eliminates the appearance of unilateral or punitive military action.

Connected to the war on Iraq, at least according to much of the rhetoric of the Bush administration, are the actions of terrorists and terror networks. One of the central justifications for the preemptive assault on Iraq was the concern that chemical, biological, and nuclear weapons would be distributed to terrorists and terrorist networks to be used against the United States and other targets. Following the tragic events of September 11th, 2001, the Bush administration declared a "war on terrorism." As is made painfully obvious by even a cursory glance at the philosophical literature on terrorism, the problem with a war on terrorism is identifying the targets of such a war: Terrorists generally don't wear uniforms and don't advertise their presence on the battlefield. This makes the target(s) of a war on terrorism very difficult to identify, indeed.

The final selection in the section deals with the war on terrorism, and offers a pessimistic analysis of the policies of the United States government. In "The War on Terrorism and the End of Human Rights," David Luban argues that the war on terror is demarcated by a new model of state action, a hybrid war-law model, which suppresses human rights in such a way that it puts the very existence of those rights at risk.

The "hybrid model," according to Luban, views the terrorist not only as a military adversary, but also as a criminal and conspirator. While, in war, the enemy has the right to shoot back in self-defense, under the law model, criminals don't hold that same right. Those who do attempt to shoot back ("American Taliban" John Walker Lindh, for instance) are committing a federal crime. Under the hybrid model, suspected terrorists seem to be damned if they do and damned if they don't. This model will lead to some shocking and terrifying cases of "rightlessness": Jose Padilla and Yasser Esam Hamdi may be placed in open-ended custody with no mandatory trial, though no proof has been offered that they are, in fact, guilty of the crimes of which they are accused.

Luban argues that the case against the hybrid model is clear: The United States has simply chosen the most useful parts from the doctrines of war and from international law for its interests, abandoning the rest for convenience and expediency. The result of this "cherry-picking" from law and war is the abolition of the rights of potential enemies for no other reason than the fact that it is more convenient and less risky to the United States for these parties to have no rights. Any swelling of the hybrid model, or any further application of these "wartime" standards in questionable (non-wartime) situations, pushes us further down a slippery slope that we have already begun to traverse: the postponement, revocation, or destruction of universal human rights. These rights, which are granted to all of us solely by virtue of our humanity, cannot be taken away from those who hold them regardless of their status as potential terrorists. The hybrid model, Luban argues, may lead us to further transgress on other fundamental human rights, including the right not to be tortured. The war on terrorism, if played out to its extreme, might justify the torture of prisoners of war in the interest of national security, and this is an unacceptable violation of universal human rights. This sort of thing is just the tip of the iceberg, says Luban, and quite possibly the beginning of the end of the era of human rights.

The reader might be left with a sense of doom and gloom from these essays, but it is our sincere hope that detailed philosophical exploration of these, and other military conflicts, will begin to impact both common thought on warfare and public policy about armed military action. If we are able to learn lessons from the past, and avoid repeating its mistakes, there is a sense of hope that the future will see a reduction or elimination in future warfare. Pacifists, realists, absolutists, consequentialists, and others should all share this sense of hope for a peaceful world order.

Is This War [in Kosovo] Good?
An Ethical Commentary[1,2]

(2003)

Georg Meggle

Georg Meggle is professor of philosophy at the University of Leipzig, working in the philosophical bases of anthropology and the cognitive sciences. He has published in action theory, communication theory, ethics, philosophy of mind departments, and social philosophy. He is the author of Fundamental Ideas of Communication *(De Gruyter, 1981) and (with Manfred Beetz) of* Interpretation Theory and Interpretation Practice *(Kronberg, 1976). He has also edited several anthologies, including* Social Facts and Collective Intentionality *(Dr. Hansel-Hohenhausen, 2002).*

The almost unanimous approval in Germany of NATO's war against Yugoslavia is attributable to what is called its "humanitarian aim." The goal of our humanitarian intervention is to stop genocide—or, as it is sometimes described, to prevent "a second Auschwitz." Those who are against Auschwitz must approve of this war. This is the heaviest piece of moral artillery to be wheeled out on our side during our moral war. It is certainly the most effective form of artillery, universally appealing right across the political spectrum, including former pacifists. But is this argument valid? Is this war good? Is this war really *morally* good?

I believe this question, at least the fundamental problem itself, can be answered relatively simply. It is certainly simpler than many other moral questions. Nevertheless, many of us find it very difficult to come up with a genuinely well-founded opinion on the ethical legitimacy of NATO's war against Yugoslavia—assuming we actually try to reach an opinion in the first place. I do not want to deny anyone the right to make up their own mind, but perhaps my comments will make it easier for some people to decide. I therefore invite you to consider with me step-by-step the fundamental moral decisions and the factual assumptions on which our moral assessment of NATO's intervention depends. Even if you still waver in your final opinion, as long as now you at least know why you do, I will have achieved my aim.

SELF-DEFENSE AND EMERGENCY ASSISTANCE

Let us start by taking the customary tack of self-defense and assistance in an emergency. If someone makes an attempt on my life and I cannot ward off his attack in any other way, I may defend myself by killing him before he kills me. Note the use of "may"—I am under no compulsion to do so. I might not value my life so much that I am prepared even to kill in order to save it. Self-defense is a right, not an obligation.

By contrast, whenever emergency assistance is concerned, it is not my life which is at stake but that of at least one other person. Say a murderer wants to kill a defenseless child. If there is no other way of saving the child's life, may I try and kill the murderer? Of course I may. Indeed, it is probably my duty to do so. Although I may choose to relinquish my own life, I may not be able to refrain from saving the child's. In other words, we have a right both to self-defense and to grant assistance in an emergency—but the latter might also be an obligation. (Whether and the extent to which we are duty-bound to assist depends not only on the scale of the threat but also on what sort of risk can reasonably be expected of me in view of my own right to life. Moreover, the risk I am prepared to take doubtless also depends on just how important the victim's life is to me.)

This approach based on reference to cases of self-defense and emergency assistance is almost always chosen when weighing up the moral justification of a license or even a duty to kill. It is also used in other cases—including those in which war is involved. It is used to justify not only recruitment, but also waging war itself. After all, the general assumption goes, states are individuals too. And any individual, be it a single person or a collective of people organized in the form of a state, may defend its existence, even if this might mean the end of the attacking individual. Wars of defense are nothing more than cases of a state's self-defense, and wars of assistance (regardless of whether they are fought within the framework of a defense pact) are nothing more than cases of international emergency aid. Hence, according to the main argument, they are morally justified. And consequently; as far as the right to join wars (the *jus ad bellum*) is concerned, these wars are described as "just wars." So far, so good—perhaps.

But at this point a problem occurs. States themselves consist of individuals and thus of groups of individuals. Although the chief aim of a state is supposed to be to protect its citizens, not every state actually serves this purpose. What about cases in which the state apparatus turns against its own citizens, or against individual groups of its citizens? Do they too have a corresponding right to self-defense if things vital to them (existence and human living conditions) are threatened? Of course they do. This is the famous right of resistance—a moral right that the threatened group has *vis-à-vis* its own state, even if such a right is not enshrined in the state's laws or is actually ruled out in them. Consequently, external parties have the right to provide assistance in an emergency in such cases if the group under threat is unable to help itself.

However, groups—for example, political parties, ethnic or religious groups, etc.—may be threatened not only by states but also by other groups. The respective state is responsible for countering such threats in line with its main aim, its role of protector. However, this role still leaves much to be desired in some cases; moreover, the repression, expulsion, or destruction of one group by at least one other group sometimes suits those in power, and as well as concealing it they might even encourage or initiate it. In this case, too, if the state ignores its responsibility, outsiders may come to the aid of those not sufficiently able to defend themselves.

Let me ask you a question: did you find it as easy to swallow the justification of self-defense and emergency assistance in the last two cases as the previous ones? If so, you have already crossed a critical boundary—the frontier of the state concerned. Those who concur with the principle that we may come to the aid of a group or population under threat in the last two cases evidently believe that the provision of assistance itself is more important than the source of this help, be it domestic or foreign.

And rightly so. If Hitler had not embarked upon foreign conquest and had only maintained concentration camps in Germany, should the rest of the world have stood idly by because his policy of extermination was kept local? Well, the world might have done so, but under no circumstances would this have been acceptable behavior. This is where pacifism becomes a crime, and the view that "No more Auschwitz!" outweighs "No more war" is correct.

One of the moral premises most frequently used at present is also correct: if a second Auschwitz can be prevented, it must be prevented, regardless of its location. This can be easily generalized: violations of human rights are not domestic affairs. Compared to the violation of human rights, the violation of national borders is the lesser evil and, in fact, is no evil at all in the event of violations on the scale of Auschwitz. State sovereignty is not the highest good.

If we reply that people as such have a right to organize themselves in the form of states—in other words, if we say that the question of states is itself a human rights issue—we have to bear in mind that there are serious and less serious human rights. The right to live on this or that side of the Bavarian border is certainly less serious than the right to life itself.

HUMANITARIAN INTERVENTION: THE CONCEPT

Let us get down to business. Interventions by outside states can be justified in precisely this manner. We are not talking just about sending aid parcels and supplying weapons but also about military operation in the narrow sense, that is, those in which the various armed services deploy the various means at their disposal. The so-called "humanitarian interventions" can at least be justified in this way, as long as this term is used to mean interventions which closely fit the above justification strategy. The following definition fits best of all:

> (HI) An intervention on the part of a state or a group of states X in another state Y to benefit Z (certain individuals or groups) is a *humanitarian intervention* iff X undertakes this intervention with the intention of preventing, ending, or at least reducing current serious violations of human rights *vis-à-vis* Z (certain individuals or groups) which are caused, supported, or at least not prevented by Y on the territory of Y.

Whether the conditions ought to include the stipulation that the members of the threatened group Z are citizens of Y (or at least were previously citizens of Y) is a moot point. Should a rescue operation in which the state X tries by means of military action to rescue *its own* citizens from a crisis area in Y be termed humanitarian intervention? Let us not go into this at the moment. In the following I am going to deal only with the current case in which those on whose behalf the intervention was started are citizens of *another* state. Using the symbol Y is thus rather fitting.

According to (HI), humanitarian interventions are actions directed towards a particular purpose. They have an aim: the action subject X intends by his intervention in Y to protect the group Z from the serious violations of human rights with which it is threatened. It is this *humanitarian intention* which makes the intervention humanitarian, or rather, which is supposed to make it humanitarian. Although according to (HI) the intervening X (the "intervention subject") believes and hopes that the intervention will also actually achieve the proclaimed aim, whether this hope is indeed fulfilled depends on more than just the strength of his belief and perhaps on completely different matters. Even if the intervention subject is naturally banking on the success of his intervention, everyone knows that not every purposeful action is successful, and interventions are no exception.

We would therefore do well to draw a distinction between interventions in the sense of *attempts* and *successful interventions*. An intervention is successful if it actually achieves its aim in the way intended, i.e., by means of the intervention. Unless otherwise stated, "interventions" shall in the following be taken to mean only attempted interventions. Of course, it is not the intervention itself which is being attempted; instead, an attempt is made to achieve the proclaimed aim. Humanitarian interventions are special salvation attempts, attempts which, if they succeed, mean salvation for the group threatened.

Furthermore, we have to distinguish between a subjective and an objective interpretation of the definition above. According to the *subjective interpretation,* a humanitarian intervention only applies if the intervention subject X *believes that Z is threatened* and that this threat must be countered by means of intervention.

Humanitarian interventions in this sense need not be reactions to actual threats; it would be enough if they were reactions to merely supposed attacks. Thus, under certain circumstances such interventions could be regarded as humanitarian without a hair of anybody's head being harmed prior to the intervention. According to this interpretation, an intervention is humanitarian iff the intervention subject itself regards it as such.

On the other hand, many will already have understood the above definition—and this corresponds to the *objective interpretation*—to mean that a humanitarian intervention only applies if *Z is actually threatened,* and X believes he is able to counter this threat by means of intervention. X thus does not merely *believe* that Z is threatened, but actually *knows* this to be the case. In this interpretation, therefore, humanitarian intervention is supplemented by the objective components of the actual threat. X then performs the intervention not merely with the intention of countering an emergency (perhaps merely assumed by X) suffered by the victim; the emergency actually exists—and X pursues with his intervention the aim of providing the victim with emergency assistance.

Those performing humanitarian intervention naturally believe that the threat they have assumed actually does exist. From the viewpoint of the intervention subject, humanitarian intervention is always objective. Whether this view is correct is, of course, quite a different matter.

Humanitarian interventions must (in order to be such) be associated with appropriate humanitarian intentions (of emergency assistance); according to the subjective interpretation, humanitarian interventions are such merely by virtue of their intentions. This is not the case regarding acts of self-defense and emergency assistance, at least as far as criminal law is concerned. According to criminal law, these actions are exclusively defined by reference to objective characteristics of a situation of self-defense substantiated by a present illegal attack. According to Section 32, paragraph 2, of the German Criminal Code, "self-defense" constitutes the defense required to protect oneself or another person from such an attack. Moreover, pursuant to paragraph 1 of Section 32, those who perform such an act are not acting illegally. No mention is made of intentions. They only become involved in supposed acts of self-defense, that is, when somebody wrongly assumes a need for self-defense to exist.

This difference between acts of self-defense or emergency assistance on the one hand and humanitarian interventions as a special (perhaps merely supposed) case thereof cannot be emphasized too strongly. What makes an action an act of self-defense is exclusively defined by objective characteristics of the situation; the action subject's viewpoint and the intention he has is irrelevant to whether what he is doing constitutes self-defense or not. In short, self-defense is something objective. By contrast, humanitarian interventions are (at least also) subjective. An intervention is humanitarian (assuming the group Z is suffering an emergency situation) if it is connected with the right humanitarian intention.

Having sorted out the concept of humanitarian intervention, let us now turn to the question of moral justification.

JUSTIFYING HUMANITARIAN INTERVENTIONS

In order to be morally justified by analogy with emergency assistance, humanitarian interventions must also correspond to their self-perception as cases of emergency assistance. Hence, among the group to be protected by the intervention there must prevail a situation of emergency, that is, a situation that corresponds to the scale of assistance. The threatened group must be suffering or directly threatened by serious violations of human rights. This condition is not fulfilled trivially in the case of humanitarian interventions.

Furthermore, the intervention must also be the final means available that can avert the danger or at least reduce the threat to Z. An intervention is thus only morally permissible if this danger cannot be prevented without intervention. Let us sum up these two points of view as follows:

> An HI is morally permissible only if
> (1) serious violations of human rights cannot be prevented in any other way.

Any violation of human rights does not necessarily provide permissible grounds for intervention, otherwise a war of humanitarian intervention could be waged against countries like the US. After all, the US's use of the death penalty constitutes a clear violation of human rights in Amnesty International's view. This raises the extremely difficult question of how serious violations of human rights need to be in order to justify an intervention. I suggest that *pro argumento* we do something for the time being which we otherwise should not: let us settle the argument about where violations of human rights cross the boundary at which intervention is deemed necessary by definition. Let us say, for instance, that massive crimes must have been carried out against humanity on the scale we have been made to believe caused NATO to intervene in the Kosovo crisis, that is, involving all the massacres, systematic rape, mass expulsion, etc., which have been cited by the US and other states as reasons for intervention. In the following, we shall refer to the scale of crimes contained in these reports as the *Kosovo Dimension (KD)*. Then, our first stipulation reads as follows:

> An HI is morally permissible only if
> (1) massive crimes against humanity (KD) cannot be prevented in any other way.

In addition to sparing me the trouble of exact quantification, this rough stipulation also saves me the certainly much more painstaking task of verification. (As soon as we start drawing up opinions about the specific case, it will of course be impossible to avoid these painstaking tasks.) Although the Kosovo Dimension is fortunately somewhat lower down the scale of everything represented by Auschwitz, it—and this is exactly what my stipulation is driving at—ought to be sufficiently terrible in order to allow it to be considered a reason for humanitarian intervention. In other words, the Kosovo Dimension should be a genuine *reason* for humanitarian intervention.

The fact that a means is required to achieve an aim does not yet mean that the usage of this means also makes sense. Not every necessary means is also a *useful*

means. To take a very trivial example, if you want to catch fish in a pond, you must cast a line or set fish traps, etc. But none of these necessary, alternative means is any good if there are no fish in the pond in the first place. Or, to use an example closer to home, to make yourself comfortable in your freezing house you have to light the fire. However, this is not going to do a lot for the comfort factor if you have a house full of gelignite which will blow up as soon as the first sparks waft around. The fact that a means is necessary is not sufficient; it must be an expedient means which will help the aim to be achieved. This demand should also hold for humanitarian interventions and their moral permissibility.

> An HI is morally permissible only if
> (2) the type of intervention (a) is expedient to the aim of intervention.

This stipulation takes us into an examination of the conditions dealt with in theories of just warfare under the category of justice *in* war (of *ius in bello*). The first condition dealt with what it takes to make the launch of an intervention morally right; now we are concerned with the moral limitations surrounding the intervention as a means to an end.

These limitations do not come out of the blue. They result from the corresponding moral limitations for general actions of self-defense and emergency assistance. Even in a situation of self-defense, the victim and those coming to his aid may not resort to any action whatsoever merely because such a situation has arisen. We state that the action must be "required," meaning that apart from the expedience mentioned above, the *counteraction* taken must be *the mildest possible in the circumstances*. To return to our example with the defenseless child threatened by a murderer, of course I may (if I have to) neutralize the killer, but not for instance by cutting his throat *if* I am sufficiently skilled in karate to knock him out with a couple of blows until the police arrive—and if by not resorting to my knife I do not put my own life at much greater risk than by using it.

As (in the case of military interventions), referring to "the mildest possible counteraction" could sound cynical, I shall formulate the new condition (b) as follows:

> An HI is morally permissible only if
> (2) the type of intervention (b) enables the aim of intervention to be achieved with the least possible harm to the intervention precipitator.

This translation is strictly geared towards the previous consideration, which only mentions that the party against whom the emergency assistance is directed must not be harmed more than necessary. Accordingly, the new condition (b) is also aimed only at the harm done to the party who provided the reason for intervention—in short, at the enemy against whom (or to be more accurate: against whose massive crimes against humanity) the intervention is directed, the "intervention precipitator."

The harm befalling the intervention precipitator is not the only—and not the most important—damage that must be considered in the moral assessment of interventions. Those threatening those providing emergency assistance were just mentioned. Let us leave them aside for the time being. Those who in the course of normal self-defense or emergency assistance may not be harmed are clearly identified by the criminal regulations reserved for such cases: self-defense or emergency assistance. may only be directed against the

aggressor, not against *outsiders' legal interests*. The well-aimed sniper's bullet against the terrorist holding hostages, if this really is the last chance of saving the hostages, may be justified under criminal law, yet ceases to be so as soon as another innocent person is jeopardized by this bullet.

This ban is thoroughly acceptable within the framework of criminal law. Within moral consideration (our activity here) however, it will be impossible to maintain it under all circumstances. At this point we ought to embark upon a process of weighing-up similar to that acted out for or against utilitarianism in any introductory seminar course. To borrow one of the most common exercises, let us assume that a terrorist has taken 20 hostages, and let us assume we are all absolutely certain that, as his demands have not been met, he will blow himself up together with all the hostages in the next few seconds. Should the SAS marksman who already has his sights trained on the terrorist be allowed to fire, even if he cannot completely rule out the chance of hitting an innocent passer-by who suddenly appears and strays into his line of fire? If you hesitate to answer yes, would you do the same if the terrorist had taken 50 hostages? Or what about 200? Or 1,000? These reflection games are terrible, but ethics is not supposed to be a barrel of laughs.

The Kosovo Dimension easily outweighs all bank-robber scenarios. Those who in view of this scale of difference accept humanitarian intervention as I have defined it as a *prima facie* option have already made up their minds. For moral reasons they are willing to overstep the bounds of what (in related contexts) is permissible under criminal law. We are thus entering a field where what is forbidden by criminal law is morally allowed. Military interventions that do not put external parties at risk simply do not exist. Even military interventions with the highest of humanitarian intentions are no exception. It is impossible to approve of humanitarian interventions and at the same time rule out others being put at risk.

This certainly does not mean that this hazard can be neglected in future. On the contrary: whenever during an operation a threat to external parties cannot be ruled out, everything must be done to ensure that this threat is minimized. This means in particular:

> An HI is morally permissible only if (2) the type of intervention (c) minimizes the threat to external parties.

Whosoever these external parties just mentioned might be, they certainly include neither those who precipitated the intervention and against whom the intervention is ultimately directed (in order to put a stop to their crimes), nor the intervention subject himself. Stipulation (b) dealt with the intervention precipitators; the intervention subject has so far been neglected by the previous stipulations. This omission is filled by condition (d):

> An HI is morally permissible only if (2) the type of intervention (d) minimizes the harm or threat to the intervening party himself.

Just to cite the extreme case, for example, this stipulation prevents an intervening state from simply using its own citizens as cannon-fodder to make intervention successful. The concept of harm or danger naturally encompasses a little more than the loss of human life. Not to be killed is not the only human value.

Stipulations (a) to (d) listed under (2) cover the core of what is often also described as the demand to *keep things in proportion*. I cannot go into the tricky question here of whether our above stipulations cover every aspect of proportion—and if they do not, how we could do justice to these outstanding points of view. This is not a great loss, as the necessary conditions outlined so far are perfectly adequate to judge NATO's intervention.

To be on the safe side, however, and to make sure that nobody regards the sum of these conditions as sufficient merely for the purpose of experimentation, I would like to include a safeguarding clause (even though many might believe it to be a matter of course):

> An HI is morally permissible as long as (3) it does not itself involve massive crimes against humanity.

This means that a humanitarian intervention is morally justified only if it does not involve the same things it is supposed to be combating and from which the entire *raison d'être* of humanitarian interventions stems. Humanitarian interventions that, in comparison to the crimes they are supposed to prevent, themselves constitute massive crimes against humanity, cannot be morally permissible. Humanitarian interventions may not for their part provide grounds for morally justified humanitarian counter-interventions.

HUMANITARIAN INTERVENTIONS AND INTERNATIONAL LAW

One stipulation for the moral permissibility of humanitarian interventions is still lacking from our necessary conditions— namely, one whose necessity has been the subject of the greatest controversy in the whole debate so far about the war in Kosovo:

> An HI is morally permissible only if
> (? —4— ?) the intervention is sanctioned
> by (a) international law and (b) in particular by a resolution passed by the UN Security Council.

Why is this demand lacking? Quite simply because the world is not yet ready for this stipulation to make sense *now*. International law is not sufficiently developed, and the Security Council's resolution procedure still has a long way to go.

The situation in Kosovo was (as we should have known before the start of the war) an extremely precarious situation. It concerned the relationship between law and morality. Moral questions are very closely linked to legal questions—and this is precisely why we must draw a sharp distinction between the two so that this close connection cannot lead to any confusion. If something is legally necessary, it is generally morally necessary too. Note the "generally": it is not always so (otherwise, there would be no need whatsoever to discuss the moral justification of legal regulations). Isolated cases are conceivable in which it is not merely morally permissible but even morally necessary to violate existing laws, in which case what is legally necessary could even be morally forbidden. Of course, solid reasons are always going to be needed for such exceptions in view of the moral value (which cannot be assessed too highly) of binding legal norms, and these reasons probably exist only in very rare cases.

This potential difference between law and morality occurs in all areas of law, including current international law. Cases *are* conceivable in which violation of the international laws presently in force is not only morally allowed but may in fact be morally imperative. Such a case would be my fictitious Auschwitz scenario above: Auschwitz and all the other concentration camps exist in Germany alone, at a time of no German wars of aggression. Moreover, if it is also assumed that this Nazi Germany is a member of the Security Council with the power of veto, show me those who, in response to this situation, would be prepared to demand what at present many seem willing to blindly sign petitions for: respect for international law *whatever the consequences*. If the world complied with current international law, the consequence would be that the world would be forced to stand by and watch. Yet morality demands precisely the opposite. The Auschwitz Dimension cries out for humanitarian intervention even in contravention of valid international law and, obviously, even without the Security Council's approval (which anyway would not be forthcoming in the above situation owing to Nazi Germany's veto). In order to make this questionable stipulation concerning international law a necessary condition, international law must be changed so that, in the case of this fictitious Auschwitz scenario, the morally necessary humanitarian intervention would no longer be blocked despite the veto of a member of the Security Council.

In order to make myself clear, I would now like to add a few points.

(1) *The Kosovo Dimension is, as mentioned above, not identical with the Auschwitz Dimension.*

(2) *Yugoslavia is not Nazi Germany. Neither is Serbia.*

(3) *Yugoslavia is not a member of the Security Council. In view of the Kosovo Dimension, merely invoking Auschwitz is not enough to reach the same conclusion for the actual Kosovo crisis as for the above fictitious Auschwitz crisis.*

Another aspect has so far been neglected in the debate surrounding the validation of the war in Kosovo under international law. This debate assumes that if in addition to NATO the UN was also in favor of this war, everything would be fine. This is at present legally correct, but in moral terms potentially wrong. It takes more than UN support for an intervention (even a humanitarian intervention) to be morally acceptable. As we have seen above, a few other conditions have to be met as well. And these could then be violated, even with the approval of the Security Council.

This discussion so far constitutes a brilliant victory for the renowned German tradition of hermeneutics. Its domains are the diverse relations between wording and deeper sense. If the *letter* of international law really is opposed to the war, how can its *spirit* be determined so that the *essence* of international law can be reconciled with our humanitarian consciousness and traditions? This is the question which humanitarian writers, intervention ministers, and other experts on international law argued while NATO flew over 20,000 missions over the former Yugoslavia. Let us postpone the apologetic exegesis of international law until tomorrow. Today's question is: is this war morally good?

IS THIS WAR GOOD?
THE RELEVANT QUESTIONS

Is this war good? Is NATO's intervention in Yugoslavia morally justified? Now that the central concepts have been explained and the most relevant moral demands are known, "all" we now need to answer this question is the facts. As usual, these can be divided into three categories: the clear facts, the less clear ones, and those we do not yet know. We should try to support our case on the first category, the clear facts, but unfortunately it is this group which is the smallest—which is probably always the case as far as relevant facts during times of war are concerned. Therefore, at such times one has to make do with the less clear facts, making the resulting moral judgment less solid.

Is our intervention in Yugoslavia morally permissible? This question can now be formulated more precisely. Have all the requirements which need to be met for such an intervention to be morally legitimate actually been met? We know what these requirements are, so let us subject the current NATO intervention—from now on I will often just say *the intervention* for short—to the test of these demands.

The intervention covers a great deal. It can stand for the decision to intervene militarily, the launch of the intervention, the manner of the intervention (e.g., air raids instead of ground troops), the same thing but in more detail (e.g., only bombs dropped from a great height, thus magnifying the risk of collateral damage), the manner of the intervention today, etc. These are very different things. And similarly, moral judgment of these different things can also differ. However, it should always be clear what these and other things mean when we are talking about *the intervention*.

We must ask ourselves the following questions:

(1) *Was or is the intervention really necessary to eliminate the reason for the intervention?*
(2) *Is the manner of the intervention actually beneficial for its aim?*
(3) *Is the intervention being carried out such that for the intervening agents themselves the damage and the threat caused is kept to a minimum?*
(4) *Is the intervention taking place such that it is accompanied by the least damage re-*

quired to achieve the aim of intervention being inflicted on the intervention precipitator?

(5) *Is the intervention being carried out such that the risk to outside parties is minimized?*

(6) *Is the intervention on our part connected with massive crimes against humanity?*

An assessment of the intervention requires answering this list of questions as a whole. What "least possible damage" is supposed to mean in the three areas of damage to be taken into account (intervention subject, intervention precipitator, outside parties) can only be more closely identified by considering the minimization of the overall damage. In doing so, we will not be able to dodge morally weighting the various damage minimization requirements. Do moral reasons not make us devote priority to minimizing damage to third parties over minimizing damage to the intervention precipitator—and over minimizing damage suffered by the intervention subject? It certainly cannot be said that the less harm suffered by the intervening party (at the cost of third parties), the more moral the intervention.

We are dealing with the moral evaluation of a concrete intervention—with the assessment of an *action,* not of an *actor.* Thus what counts for this intervention assessment is primarily its *consequences,* not the (supposed or actual) *intentions* linked to it. Do we really have to remember that these are two different things? And that history contains enough examples of how the best intentions can lead to the most appalling consequences? And vice versa, that even the worst intentions can sometimes result in good? We primarily take intentions into account when we are assessing the actor (the person, the acting institution); we study the consequences when we want to judge the act itself.

This distinction has a clear application: The mere fact that an intervention is humanitarian (i.e., it is associated with a humanitarian intention) does not by itself make an intervention good—not by a long chalk. The reason for this was stated above: the conditions for the moral justification of a humanitarian intervention are not merely fulfilled by virtue of the existence of a humanitarian intention.

This separation between assessing an intention and assessing the consequences takes much of the alleged moral point out of the speculation about the true intentions of the intervening party. What really counts when somebody is in an emergency is for them to receive genuine assistance—not the motives behind the act bringing about this help (or not). These intentions and motives at most become relevant if we analyze reasons for equivalent behavior in future cases.

During moral evaluations, one often falls into the *fictitious da capo trap.* You married the wrong woman, you are in a right mess, and you wonder what the best thing is for everyone, including the kids. The last thing that is going to help is, "I told you so"—as if you could simply slip out of the current situation and leap back to before you got together and then take the right decision this time. The relevant question is: what should be done now?

All well-meaning advice concerning what the various sides should or should not have done beforehand so that the question "Intervention—yes or no?" would not have had to be asked in the first place are equally irrelevant for a moral assessment of the intervention. Being wise after the event should be put to good use in managing similar situations better *in future;* it is no good for a moral assessment of the *current* situation, which we evidently did not manage better. Reference to the genesis of the current situation helps us to understand it; it does not solve the moral problems which only emerge once we are in the middle of it.

Notes

1. This is the English version of a talk I gave at several universities in Germany when NATO attacked Yugoslavia in spring 1999. For the original German version see: *1st dieser Krieg gut? Ein ethischer Kommentar, Der Kosovo-Krieg und das Völkerrecht,* ed. Reinhard Merkel (Frankfurt/M.: Edition Suhrkamp, 2000).

2. For Georg Henrik von Wright and Sarah Rebecca Meggle. My title stems from talks I gave in early May 1999 in Leipzig, Münster, and Frankfurt am Main. Apart from Georg Henrik von Wright and my daughter, I would also like to express my grateful thanks for the help received from Jovan Babic, Kurt Bayertz, Lutz Eckensberger, Günther Grewendorf, Franz von Kutschera, Wolfgang Lenzen, Weyma Lübbe, Matthias Lutz-Bachmann, Thomas Metzinger, Richard Raatzsch, Veronika Reiss, Sabine Rieckhoff, Peter Rohs, Mark Siebel, and my right hand throughout this time, Christian Plunze.

Iraq: The Shifting Sands of Preemptive Self-Defense

(2003)

Miriam Sapiro

Miriam Sapiro is the founder of Summit Strategies International, a consulting firm specializing in Internet policy, electronic commerce, and international issues. She is also an adjunct professor of law at New York University School of Law and has served on the National Security Council and in the State Department. She was a member of the team that negotiated the 1995 Bosnia Peace Accords.

The United States articulated a new concept of preventive self-defense last fall that is designed to preclude emerging threats from endangering the country.[1] Rising like a phoenix from the ashes of the September 11 terrorist attacks, the preventive approach to national security is intended to respond to new threats posed by "shadowy networks of individuals [who] can bring great chaos and suffering to our shores for less than it costs to purchase a single tank."[2] The Bush administration wisely concluded that it could not rely solely upon a reactive security posture, due to the difficulty in deterring potential attacks by those determined to challenge the United States and the magnitude of harm that could occur from weapons of mass destruction falling into the wrong hands. Although the administration has characterized its new approach as "preemptive," it is more accurate to describe it as "preventive" self-defense. Rather than trying to preempt specific, imminent threats, the goal is to prevent more generalized threats from materializing.

There is no question that the nature of threats to security for the United States and other countries has changed dramatically since the founding of the United Nations in 1945. The major impetus behind the creation of a collective security organization, with its ambitious assumption that the use of military power by states could be constrained and even outlawed, developed from the debacle of World War II. Then, as now, those nations that had been attacked were determined not to be lulled into a vulnerable complacency again. But the administration's willingness to use force to address "emerging threats before they are fully formed"[3] takes the already controversial doctrine of anticipatory self-defense a step further into the realm of subjectivity and potential danger. The concept of prevention is an elusive one, with vague criteria that could be employed to justify uses of force from the Korean peninsula to the Taiwan straits, to Kashmir and beyond.

The war in Iraq represents the first time the administration has acted on the basis of a doctrine of preventive war.[4] Indeed, the concept provided the main political justification for its decision to resort to force. This essay considers the extent to which such a doctrine is compatible with international law. To the extent the doctrine appears inconsistent with such norms, I will review whether it is defensible on other grounds. If both its legality and defensibility turn out to be dubious, the issue becomes what, if anything, can be done to reduce the gap between a security posture that is problematic and one

that is not. This is a critical question with implications far beyond Iraq, both for the United States and for other states that may find utility in adopting a concept of preventive self-defense.[5]

I. CONSIDERATIONS OF LEGALITY

The administration issued the *National Security Strategy* (the Strategy) in September 2002 just after the first anniversary of the September 11 attacks. It was released with little fanfare and did not elicit much public debate. At the time, President Bush was focused on trying to build domestic and international support for a final effort to disarm and dislodge Saddam Hussein. Just a week before, he had kicked off diplomatic efforts to draft a tough Security Council resolution with a challenge to the United Nations to show strength or risk irrelevance.[6] On the day the president signed the *Strategy,* the White House Press Office gave greater attention to release of a timeline detailing "Saddam Hussein's Deception and Defiance," which described a dozen instances before 1998 when Baghdad had accepted inspections but then demanded conditions.[7] The preoccupation with Iraq was clearly a driving force in trying to develop a doctrine that could serve two purposes—one immediate and another longer term. Initially, it could provide a political justification for forceful action to remove a regime deemed threatening to the United States, particularly that of Saddam Hussein. Over time, it might enable the United States to shift the benchmarks that define the parameters of legitimate self-defense.

The administration sought to ground its new approach to using force in international law.[8] Indeed, the doctrine of "anticipatory self-defense" (sometimes referred to as "preemptive self-defense"),[9] which enables a state to act under certain circumstances before it is attacked, is not novel. It has historical roots in the early writings of Grotius, Vattel, and other scholars.[10] The *Caroline* dispute, which arose in 1837 between the United States and Great Britain, is the case cited most often for the proposition that a state has the right to resort to force when it faces an imminent threat that is otherwise unavoidable. After the British destroyed the *Caroline* steamer being used by American sympathizers of a Canadian rebellion against the Crown, anger on the U.S. side ran high.[11] Secretary of State Daniel Webster challenged his British counterpart to show "a necessity of self-defence, instant, overwhelming, leaving no choice of means, and no moment for deliberation" and further, that such action was "limited by that necessity."[12] Along with the traditional requirement that an exercise of self-defense be proportional, both imminence and necessity have become critical factors in assessing claims of anticipatory self-defense.

The *Strategy* describes the state of international law correctly, but only insofar as it existed prior to 1945. The analysis neglects to note a rather pivotal event that year—adoption of the UN Charter—which changed the parameters governing the use of force. While the Charter has at times been honored in the breach, its rules represent the only internationally agreed norms regarding when states may resort to force. Article 2(4) imposes a broad prohibition, explicitly requiring countries to "refrain in their international relations from the threat or use of force against the territorial integrity or political independence of any state." There is an exception, of course, in Article 51, which permits the exercise of "the inherent right of individual or collec-

tive self-defense *if an armed attack occurs* . . . until the Security Council has taken measures necessary to maintain international peace and security" (emphasis added).[13]

Article 51 has stirred much debate over the continuing validity of anticipatory self-defense under the Charter in the absence of an "armed attack."[14] Three events are often cited as demonstrating the legitimacy of anticipatory self-defense notwithstanding adoption of the Charter. In none of these cases, however, did a country successfully justify force solely on that basis.[15]

In 1962, during the Cuban missile crisis, President Kennedy recognized that "[w]e no longer live in a world where only the actual firing of weapons represents a sufficient challenge to a nation's security to constitute maximum peril."[16] His administration, however, sought to justify quarantine of Cuba not on the basis of preemptive self-defense under Article 51, but pursuant to a regional call for action from the Organization of American States. Of particular relevance to this analysis, President Kennedy rejected more forceful options, such as a surgical strike or a full-scale invasion.[17]

In 1967, Israel launched an attack on the Egyptian army massing on its borders. Although this action is frequently cited as the classic modern case of legitimate anticipatory self-defense, Israel also sought to justify its strike on the basis that Arab preparations for war constituted an "armed attack."

In 1981, Israel did try to justify its attack on Iraq's nuclear facility at Osirak on the basis of anticipatory self-defense, arguing that such action was vital to its national security. The United States, represented by Ambassador Jeane Kirkpatrick, did not indicate a position on the existence of such a right, but voted for

Security Council censure on the ground that Israel had unnecessarily jeopardized regional security and failed to exhaust peaceful measures.[18]

The better argument in the debate appears to support a cautious view of anticipatory self-defense, with recognition that the concept must be interpreted consistently with the Charter's goal of limiting force. The alternative of leaving the words of Article 51 frozen in an earlier era, which was characterized by different adversaries and weapons systems, could quickly reduce the obligations—and the system of collective security they underpin—to irrelevance. Today it is more likely to be foolish, if not suicidal, for a state that believed its fundamental security interests were at risk to wait until the first attack. This is not to suggest that the Charter's language should be stretched beyond its intended principles and purposes, or that provisions may be selectively disregarded. It is simply to recognize that the meaning of a document meant to be universally accepted and to remain relevant must also be flexible enough to adapt to changed circumstances.

Prior to release of the *Strategy,* the United States has said little publicly on the legitimacy of anticipatory self-defense since adoption of the Charter. Nevertheless, the *Strategy* states that the "United States has long maintained the option of preemptive actions to counter a sufficient threat to our national security." Presumably, this is a reference to the use of anticipatory self-defense, although no post-1945 examples of situations in which the United States has defended the use of force—by itself or others—on this basis are offered.[19]

Continuing debate over the legitimacy of anticipatory self-defense has not deterred the administration from arguing that the time has come to adopt a murkier concept, that of preventive self-defense. The *Strategy* states that the "greater the threat, the greater is the risk of inaction— and the more compelling the case for taking anticipatory action to defend ourselves, *even if uncertainty remains as to the time and place of the enemy's attack.*"[20] The uncertainties inherent in such an analysis are acknowledged, but the consequences of lowering the threshold for resorting to force are not addressed.

Two months after release of the *Strategy,* the Department of State's legal adviser articulated a somewhat narrower view of the doctrine in a memorandum on preemption, which returned to the criteria of imminence and necessity associated with anticipatory self-defense. The legal adviser wrote that

> [t]he President's National Security Strategy relies upon the same legal framework applied to the British in *Caroline* and to Israel in 1981 . . . After the exhaustion of peaceful remedies and a careful, deliberate consideration of the consequences, *in the face of overwhelming evidence of an imminent threat,* a nation may take preemptive action to defend its nationals from unimaginable harm.[21]

This position is somewhat reassuring to those concerned about a legal framework more arbitrary and subjective than anticipatory self-defense. Of course, these words by themselves do not narrow the broader concept embraced in the president's formal *Strategy.*[22] With debate still surrounding whether there exists a right to the more limited doctrine of anticipatory self-defense, the legality of a concept of preventive war remains difficult to defend.

Iraq was the first test of the administration's doctrine of preventive war. In issuing his ultimatum to Saddam Hussein, President Bush stated: "[i]n 1 year, or

5 years, the power of Iraq to inflict harm on all free nations would be multiplied many times over. . . . We choose to meet that threat now, where it arises, before it can appear suddenly in our skies and cities."[23] Despite the grave danger that Iraq's development of weapons of mass destruction would have posed to the United States, the administration would have been hard pressed to justify the invasion as traditional self-defense in the absence of an "armed attack" attributable to Iraq. Nonetheless, at the start of the war the president alluded to the United States' "sovereign authority to use force in assuring its own national security."[24] A few days later, the legal adviser made a similarly oblique reference to self-defense in remarks to the National Association of Attorneys General. Discussing the legal basis for the attack, he described the authority largely in terms of Security Council Resolutions 678, 687, and 1441. But in closing he added, without elaboration, that the president of the United States "may also, of course, always use force under international law in self-defense."[25]

It would also have been difficult to justify the invasion of Iraq as an exercise of classic anticipatory self-defense. As the legal adviser wrote in his memorandum on preemption, "[w]ithin the traditional framework of self-defense, a preemptive use of proportional force is justified only out of necessity. The concept of necessity includes both a credible, imminent threat and the exhaustion of peaceful remedies."[26] Despite the magnitude of its intelligence capabilities, the United States could not pinpoint an imminent threat. An Qaeda connection or evidence of nascent nuclear capability were the strongest ways to link Iraq to an imminent threat to the United States, but intelligence on both points was, at

best, inconclusive.[27] While the administration devoted significant resources to developing a credible case that Iraq had hidden chemical and biological weapons in violation of its disarmament obligations under Security Council Resolution 687, it was unable, for a variety of reasons, to persuade the Council or international public opinion. It also could not convince other permanent members of the Council that remedies short of force had run their course.

Preventive war therefore became the primary political justification the United States used to explain its action against Iraq, despite the absence of support in international law and the risk that preventive war could lead to an unraveling of the constraints governing force. Although the law can be interpreted to permit defensive action in the face of an imminent threat, it is difficult—and dangerous—to stretch it farther. The question remains whether a doctrine of preventive war is defensible on other grounds.

II. ASSESSING DEFENSIBILITY

Could it be argued that, notwithstanding inconsistency with current international law, a doctrine of preventive war ought to be justifiable on other grounds? Might, for example, the brutality of Saddam Hussein's regime constitute a case where the ends justify the means, irrespective of legality?[28] Or perhaps the Iraqi situation presents a compelling case where the law ought to develop in a different direction, one that permits the use of force to deal preventively with grave threats before they become imminent, when it might be too late?

The argument that worthy goals could justify an outcome that might not be legally consistent presents some obvious problems, particularly with respect to subjectivity and proclivity for abuse. It has been suggested that the Clinton administration faced a similar dilemma in Kosovo in 1999. Some have argued that while the law did not expressly authorize NATO's intervention, the action was defensible on humanitarian grounds.[29] In the case of Iraq, there is no question that Saddam Hussein's regime used chemical weapons against its neighbors and its own people. There is also evidence that it had the scientific expertise to do so again, if it so chose. And more evidence of its actual ability to constitute chemical, biological, or even nuclear weapons before the war began may still be discovered in Iraq. These factors, combined with Baghdad's grim record of mass executions, torture, repression, and support for terrorist causes, would certainly make a compelling case. But the difficulty of fashioning a doctrine of humanitarian intervention that would avoid the potential for significant abuse, as well as mounting pressure to intervene against other governments engaged in similarly reprehensible practices, is presumably why neither the current nor previous administration elected to justify its actions on the basis of humanitarian intervention.

Alternatively, could Iraq be a situation that cries out for the law to adapt? This is the main argument the administration puts forth in explaining why it believes it is necessary to adopt a more proactive posture. As the president explained succinctly on the eve of the war, the "people of the United States and our friends and allies will not live at the mercy of an outlaw regime that threatens the peace with weapons of mass murder.[30] It is clear that threats to security have changed drastically since the Charter was drafted more than fifty years ago, and even more so since the *Caroline* standard emerged a century before that.[31] Ought the potentially deadly combination of wider availability of nuclear, biological, and chemical weapons, and new adversaries not constrained by legal niceties, justify expanding the doctrine of anticipatory self-defense to embrace a concept of preventive war? Answering this question affirmatively would mean that the criteria of imminence, necessity, and near certainty that limit reliance on anticipatory self-defense would no longer operate as significant constraints. It would also require that the benefits of such a sweeping change clearly outweigh the risks.

In discussing the *Strategy* last October, the national security adviser noted that "new technology requires new thinking about when a threat actually becomes 'imminent.'"[32] The legal adviser's memorandum on preemption posed the right question: "short of an actual armed attack, how long does a State have to wait before preemptive measures can be taken to prevent serious harm?"[33] It is of course difficult to address this issue in the abstract. The requirement of imminence should mean that there is no time for deliberation, and no time to choose an alternative course of action. Today it may not be possible to see a threat materialize as clearly as in the past, with an enemy ship heading towards its target, or a hostile army amassing on the intended victim's border. But the danger should be imminent in that it can be identified credibly, specifically, and with a high degree of certainty. Further, the requirement of necessity should continue to mean that time has run out because peaceful efforts to avoid a resort to force have been exhausted. Ideally, this requirement would include an appeal to the Security Council to resolve the problem, although there may be cases where the urgency of the threat makes resort to the Council impractical.

The dilemma Iraq posed presents a strong argument for wider acceptance of anticipatory self-defense, but not a more expansive doctrine. The kinds of threats the United States and other countries face today from the lethal combination of new enemies—including nonstate actors—and new technologies undermine the idea of waiting for an actual armed attack to occur. At the same time, there are ways to improve the chances of dealing effectively with threats that are not yet fully formed, including increasingly better methods of intelligence collection and analysis, and closer cooperation between the major players on fighting proliferation and terrorism. We also have a UN system better equipped to act as a collective security organization than during the Cold War era.

This is fortunate, for the risks inherent in adopting a doctrine of preventive war appear significant.[34] Taking Iraq as a case study, we have already seen positive and negative developments. Removal of the Saddam regime is beyond question a tremendous boon on several grounds, including enforcement of the country's disarmament obligations and the promise of a better life for Iraqi citizens. But it is unclear whether the "great threat" that was the catalyst for intervention existed and if so, whether it has been neutralized. It remains to be seen whether Iraq possessed the nuclear, chemical, or biological capabilities that were the impetus for the attack. If so, it is not yet clear if the weapons were secured, or now represent an even greater threat because they have already made their way into the wrong hands. At the

same time, U.S. casualties are rising, and the administration clearly faces the prospect of having to keep forces in Iraq for the foreseeable future. Another negative factor is the political cost of waging a war that was so divisive to both the Security Council and U.S. relations with its closest allies, and that now hampers international cooperation on military stabilization and civilian reconstruction. These considerations are in addition to serious concern that intervention has undermined internationally accepted restraints on the use of force.

Looking beyond Iraq, it has been suggested that there is nothing wrong with elevating to public pronouncement what is always a theoretical option for a state that believes its vital security interests are threatened.[35] But being so open and direct about the propensity to use force can be destabilizing. First, it creates certain expectations that the United States will react in a particular way, which may become a self-fulfilling prophecy because it will be harder to avoid force if diplomatic efforts fail to produce a quick solution. Second, it fuels international animosity towards the United States around the world, particularly in the Muslim world,[36] and can unintentionally breed a new generation of terrorists. Finally, it enables other countries to use the precedent to deal with situations they perceive as endangering their security, with disastrous effect. Pakistan, India, North Korea, and China are examples of countries that could find utility in adopting a doctrine of preventive war to assure their security, with potentially catastrophic consequences.

A doctrine of preventive war may put adversaries on notice that the United States means business. That tactic, however, did not work with Iraq. Now that there is little doubt the United States is willing to back its strategy with force, will such a doctrine deter other adversaries? If so, there is not yet evidence of a more conciliatory posture from Iran or North Korea, the remaining members of what President Bush called the "axis of evil" that appear to pose greater threats than Iraq did with respect to nuclear proliferation and terrorism. At the same time, there is heightened fear emanating from many corners, particularly Europe and the Arab world, about American willingness to rely on force to address these kinds of challenges.

A paradigmatic shift to a new doctrine fraught with questions and uncertainties may be unnecessary. First, the criteria of anticipatory self-defense already permit a state to assume a proactive stance with respect to threats that are imminent, and backed by credibility and a high degree of certainty. Second, there are other ways to deal with the kinds of threats the United States now faces, which may be more effective and stop short of using force. These range from intrusive inspection regimes to counterproliferation actions. The *National Strategy to Combat Weapons of Mass Destruction* and the *National Strategy for Combating Terrorism* set the framework for better domestic coordination and closer global cooperation in this regard.[37] In a welcome sign, the G-8 meeting in Evian agreed on the need for tighter controls on sensitive technologies and weapons, including radioactive sources that could build "dirty bombs" and shoulder-launched missiles that could threaten civil aviation.[38]

Finally, as a practical matter, a state always has the option of using forceful measures to protect what it deems to be vital interests, and then face the consequences if world opinion disagrees. While the extent of repercussions depends on the offender, even a superpower can be susceptible to sustained criticism.

III. WHAT NEXT?

A government that believes its country is threatened with catastrophic consequences will take action quickly rather than run the risk of not acting. Does this indicate that the Charter's prohibition on using force in all but exceptional circumstances should be thrown out? No, violating a rule does not necessarily mean that the problem is with the rule itself, and eliminating it would simply reward the transgressor. But the dilemma should attract support for a more balanced way to deal with threats that lie somewhere on the spectrum between "no action" and "premature action," but that fall short of an actual armed attack. Such a balance was struck in the *Caroline* case, which, despite its very different factual context, has proven to be an enduring standard by which to judge threats of imminent attack.

It is too soon to tell whether U.S. intervention in Iraq will ultimately be destabilizing, or instead become the foundation for a more peaceful Middle East. What is clear is that creating a doctrine of preventive war as set forth in the *Strategy* would expand the already controversial justification of anticipatory self-defense beyond the point where it would be consistent with international law today. It would also seem unwise given the political risks inherent in the concept, as illustrated by the uncertainties raised by the invasion of Iraq and the inflammatory precedent such a doctrine can set.

It is not too late to forestall further development of a doctrine of preventive war. The United States should find opportunities to narrow the scope of the *Strategy* quietly in the months ahead. Such a move need not be a dramatic or explicit repudiation of a document that otherwise contains many sound elements for engagement. Further statements on the importance of the traditional criteria for anticipatory self-defense in determining whether a resort to force is justified, such as those in the legal adviser's memorandum on preemption, would be useful from a legal perspective. Politically, it would be beneficial to reinforce some limitations on the use of force, as the G-8 Declaration on Nonproliferation that places the possibility of using force in the category of "if necessary other measures in accordance with international law" began to do.[39]

Such a change in approach would elicit expressions of relief from several quarters, including key allies, other Security Council members, and the UN Secretariat, and could intensify international efforts to defuse the more dangerous threats emanating from Korea and Iran. It would make the *Strategy* more consistent with international norms by narrowing the gap between accepted rules and recent practice. Ultimately, these rules are far more useful to, than constraining of, U.S. interests. While it may be tempting to select which international rules of the road the United States wants to see upheld, forsaking them will have the unintended consequence of making it harder to invoke them against others. Perhaps Iraq will be the case that highlights the risks of adopting a new doctrine of preventive war, while persuading skeptics that the constraints governing the more traditional justification of anticipatory self-defense make sense. Although the war in Iraq would not have fit the criteria of anticipatory self-defense, it helps demonstrate why these constraints represent the right balance between addressing new threats to security and avoiding the pitfalls of an expansive new doctrine.

Notes

1. *See* Section V of THE NATIONAL SECURITY STRATEGY OF THE UNITED STATES OF AMERICA (Sept. 2002), *available at* <http://whitehouse.gov/nsc/nss.pdf> [hereinafter NSS].
2. *Id.* (President George W. Bush's Introduction).
3. *Id.*
4. Administration officials have claimed that the concept of preventive self-defense is not a significant development or departure from past practice. Deputy Secretary of State Richard Armitage dismissed the idea that the administration favors force as the primary way to resolve disputes. "What people remember," he said, "is that preemption doctrine, instead of the umpteen chapters [in the *National Security Strategy*] on the need for bilateral and multilateral cooperation." Steven R. Weisman, *What Rift? Top Aides Deny State Dept.-Pentagon Chasm* N.Y. TIMES, May 31, 2003, at A1. National Security Adviser Condoleezza Rice suggested that the doctrine does not represent a break with the Clinton administration, citing the 1994 North Korean crisis as affirming a right of anticipatory self-defense. *Dr. Condoleezza Rice Discusses President's National Security Strategy* (Oct. 1, 2002), *available at* <http://www.whitehouse.gov/news/releases/2002/10/20021001-6.html>. But there is a qualitative difference between quietly considering the option of preventive action in a particular case, and publicly embracing it as a doctrine potentially applicable to all adversaries.
5. This essay does not address whether the United States had sufficient legal basis for its actions in Iraq on the basis of existing Security Council resolutions, which is covered elsewhere in this Agora.
6. Address to the United Nations General Assembly in New York City, Sept. 12, 2002, 38 WEEKLY COMP. PRES. DOC. 1529–33 (Sept. 16, 2002).
7. *See* White House Background Paper: A Decade of Deception and Defiance (Sept. 12, 2002), *available at* <http://www.whitehouse.gov/infocus/iraq/iraq_archive.html?static>; <http://usinfo.state.gov/regional/nea/iraq/text/>.
8. The *National Security Strategy* states that "[f]or centuries, international law recognized that nations need not suffer an attack before they can lawfully take action to defend themselves against forces that *present an imminent danger of attack.*" NSS, *supra* note 1, at 15 (emphasis added).

9. The doctrine of anticipatory self-defense is sometimes also called "preemptive self-defense," which should not be confused with the broader notion the administration is trying to advance under the same name. As noted, it is more accurate to describe the administration's approach as "preventive self-defense."

10. 1 HUGO GROTIUS, DE JURE BELLI AC PACIS LIBRI TRES 173 (Francis W. Kelsey trans., 1925) (danger "must be immediate and imminent in point of time . . . [b]ut those who accept fear of any sort as justifying anticipatory slaying are themselves greatly deceived, and deceive other"); EMMERICH DE VATTEL, THE LAW OF NATIONS 243 (Charles G. Fenwick trans., 1916) (a nation has "the right to prevent an injury when it sees itself threatened with one").

11. An excellent summary of the dispute is found in Abraham D. Sofaer, *On the Necessity of Pre-emption,* 14 EUR.J.INT'L L. 209 (2003).

12. Letter from Daniel Webster to Lord Ashburton (Aug. 6, 1842), *quoted in* 2 JOHN BASSETT MOORE, A DIGEST OF INTERNATIONAL LAW 412 (1906).

13. The French version of the Charter, which is equally authentic, uses the term "agression armée" ("armed aggression") for "armed attack." Although "agression armée" could be interpreted as encompassing a broader range of actions, the barrier is still rather high.

14. *See, e.g.,* THOMAS M. FRANCK, RECOURSE TO FORCE 97–108 (2002); YORAM DINSTEIN, WAR, AGGRESSION AND SELF-DEFENCE 165–69 (2001); CHRISTINE GRAY, INTERNATIONAL LAW AND THE USE OF FORCE 111–15 (2000). In the aftermath of two world wars and an impotent League of Nations, the Charter was intended to create a stricter standard by outlawing force, except in the most narrow of circumstances. Some have argued that the explicit reference to an "armed attack" therefore means a state must wait for such an unfortunate event to occur before it may justify a resort to force. Others contend that the Charter's language does not supplant a state's inherent right of self-defense as defined by customary international law, or require that it await a possibly devastating attack before acting, particularly in an era where ever more destructive weapons may be delivered ever more rapidly. The International Court of Justice sidestepped the issue in its Nicaragua decision, *see* Military and Paramilitary Activities in and Against Nicaragua (Nicar. v. U.S.), Merits, 1986 ICJ REP. 14, 94 (June 27). Judge Schwebel made his views known in his famous dissent, *see id.,* at 337–38 (disagreeing with a reading of Article 51 that would mean "if, and only if, an armed attack occurs").

15. *See generally* FRANCK, *supra* note 14, at 99–107; GRAY, *supra* note 14, at 112–15.

16. Radio and Television Report to the American People on the Soviet Arms Buildup in Cuba, 485 PUB. PAPERS 806, 807 (Oct. 22, 1962).

17. In discussing the Kennedy administration's reluctance to cite Article 51 as a basis for the quarantine, Professor Chayes noted that

> it is a very different matter to expand [Article 51] to include threatening deployments or demonstrations that do not have imminent attack as their purpose or probable outcome . . . There is simply no standard against which [such a] decision could be judged. Whenever a nation believed that interests, which in the heat and pressure of a crisis it is prepared to characterize as vital, were threatened, its use of force in response would become permissible.

ABRAM CHAYES, THE CUBAN MISSILE CRISIS: INTERNATIONAL CRISES AND THE ROLE OF LAW 65 (1974).

18. SC Res. 487 (June 19, 1981).

19. One is left to conclude that in the past the "option of preemptive actions" may have been more theoretical than operational. The national security advisor subsequently cited the 1962 Cuban missile crisis and the 1994 Korean missile crisis as evidence that the United States has long affirmed the right of anticipatory self-defense, but these two cases do not clearly stand for that proposition. *See* note 4 and text at notes 16 and 17 *supra*.

20. NSS, *supra* note 1, at 15.

21. William H. Taft IV, Legal Adviser, Department of State, *The Legal Basis for Preemption,* Nov. 18, 2002, *available at* <http://www.cfr.org/publication.php?id=5250> (memorandum to American Society of International Law-Council on Foreign Relations Roundtable on Old Rules, New Threats) (emphasis added).

22. The legal adviser circulated his memorandum after release of the *National Security Strategy,* but the memorandum was prepared for a study group and lacks the status of a formal document. Most important, it is unclear whether it represents the view of the administration as a whole.

23. Address to the Nation on Iraq, Mar. 17, 2003, 39 WEEKLY COMP. PRES. DOC. 338, 340 (Mar. 24, 2003).

24. *Id.* at 339.

25. *Remarks of the Honorable William Howard Taft, IV, Legal Adviser, U.S. Department of State, Before the National Association of Attorneys General* (Mar. 20, 2003), *available at* <http://usinfo.state.gov/regional/nea/iraq/text2003/032129taft.htm>. The legal justification put forward by the British government did not mention self-defense, but cited only the Security Council resolu-

tions. *See* Lord Goldsmith, *Legal Basis for Use of Force Against Iraq* (Mar. 17, 2003) (statement by UK attorney general in answer to a parliamentary question), *available at* <http://www.labour .org.uk/legalbasis>.

26. Taft, *supra* note 21.

27. *See* Nicholas D. Kristof, *Save our Spooks,* N.Y. TIMES, May 30, 2003, at A27.

28. *See* Franck, *supra* note 14 at 174–91, for discussion of whether the concept of mitigation might narrow a chasm between law and morality.

29. *See generally* Editorial Comments, *NATO's Kosovo Intervention,* 93 AJIL 824 (1999).

30. Address to the Nation on Iraq, Mar. 18, 2003, 39 WEEKLY COMP. PRES. DOC. 342, 343 (Mar. 24, 2003).

31. *See, e.g.,* W. Michael Reisman, *Assessing Claims to Revise the Laws of War,* 97 AJIL 82 (2003).

32. Rice, *supra* note 4.

33. Taft, *supra* note 21.

34. *See generally* G. John Ikenberry, *America's Imperial Ambition,* FOREIGN AFF., Sept./Oct. 2002, at 44.

35. Rice, *supra* note 4 ("Some have criticized this frankness as impolitic. But surely clarity is a virtue here.").

36. *See* The Pew Global Attitudes Project, *Views of a Changing World* (June 2003), *available at* <http://people-press.org/reports/display.php3 ?ReportID=185> (finding that the Iraq war has widened the rift between Americans and Western Europeans, further inflamed the Muslim world, softened support for the war on terrorism, and significantly weakened global public support for the United Nations and NATO); *see also* Michael Dobbs, *Arab Hostility Toward U.S. Growing, Poll Finds,* WASH. POST, June 4, 2003, at A18.

37. *See* NATIONAL STRATEGY TO COMBAT WEAPONS OF MASS DESTRUCTION (Dec. 2002), *available at* <http://www.whitehouse.gov/news/releases/2002/ 12/WMDStrategy.pdf> and NATIONAL STRATEGY FOR COMBATING TERRORISM (Feb. 2003), *available*

at <http://www.whitehouse.gov/news/ releases/2003/02/counter_terrorism/counter_ terrorism_strategy.pdf>. *See also* the "Proliferation Security Initiative" launched by President Bush during his May visit to Europe, which calls for partners to develop agreement on ways to interrupt the flow of WMD material, Remarks by the President to the People of Poland at Wawel Royal Castle, Krakow, Poland (May 31, 2003), *available at* <http://www.whitehouse.gov/news/ releases/2003/05/20030531-3.html>.

38. *See* David Sanger, *Bush Presses Case on Iran and Korea at Economic Talks,* N.Y. TIMES, June 2, 2003, at A1; G-8 Declaration on Nonproliferation of Weapons of Mass Destruction (June 3, 2003), *available at* <http://www.g8.fr>, which states that

> We have a range of tools available to tackle this threat: international treaty regimes; inspection mechanisms such as those of the International Atomic Energy Agency (IAEA) and Organization for the Prohibition of Chemical Weapons; initiatives to eliminate WMD stocks such as the G8 Global Partnership; national and internationally-co-ordinated export controls; international co-operation and diplomatic efforts; and if necessary other measures in accordance with international law.

The G-8 countries are Canada, France, Italy, Germany, Japan, Russia, the United Kingdom and the United States.

39. G-8 Declaration, *supra* note 38. *See also* U.S.-European Union Joint Statement on Proliferation of Weapons of Mass Destruction (June 25, 2003), *available at* <http://www.whitehouse.gov/news/ releases/2003/06/20030625-17.html> ("[w]e recognize that, if necessary, other measures in accordance with international law may be needed to combat proliferation").

The Perils of Preemptive War

(2002)

William Galston

William Galston is Saul Stern Professor of Civic Engagement and Director of the Institute for Philosophy and Public Policy in the School of Public Affairs at the University of Maryland. He is a political theorist who both studies and participates in American politics and domestic policy. He has served as Deputy Assistant to the President for Domestic Policy and as Executive Director of the National Commission on Civic Renewal. His books include Liberal Purposes: Goods, Virtues, and Diversity in the Liberal State *(Cambridge University Press, 1991) and* Liberal Pluralism: The Implications of Value Pluralism for Political Theory and Practice *(Cambridge University Press, 2002).*

INTRODUCTION

On June 1, 2002 at West Point, President George W. Bush set forth a new doctrine for US security policy. The successful strategies of the Cold War era, he declared, are ill suited to national defense in the twenty-first century. Deterrence means nothing against terrorist networks; containment will not thwart unbalanced dictators possessing weapons of mass destruction. We cannot afford to wait until we are attacked. In today's circumstances, Americans must be ready to take "preemptive action" to defend our lives and liberties.

On August 26, 2002, Vice President Dick Cheney forcefully applied this new doctrine to Iraq. Saddam Hussein, he stated, is bolstering the country's chemical and biological capabilities and is aggressively pursuing nuclear weapons. "What we must not do in the face of a mortal threat," he declared, "is to give in to wishful thinking or willful blindness . . . Deliverable weapons of mass destruction in the hands of a terror network or murderous dictator or the two working together constitutes as grave a threat as can be imagined. The risks of inaction are far greater than the risks of action."

After an ominous silence lasting much of the summer, a debate about US policy toward Iraq has finally begun. Remarkably, Democratic elected officials are not party to it. Some agree with Bush administration hawks; others have been intimidated into acquiescence or silence. The Senate Foreign Relations Committee hearings yielded questions rather than answers and failed to prod Democratic leaders into declaring their position. Meanwhile, Democratic political consultants are advising their clients to avoid foreign policy and to wage their campaigns on the more hospitable turf of corporate fraud and prescription drugs. The memory of the Gulf War a decade ago, when the vast majority of Democrats ended up on the wrong side of the debate, deters many from reentering the fray today.

The Democratic Party's abdication has left the field to Republican combatants—unilateralists versus multilateralists, ideologues versus "realists." The resulting debate has been intense but narrow, focused primarily on issues of prudence rather than principle.

ARGUMENTS FROM PRUDENCE

This is not to suggest that the prudential issues are unimportant, or that the intra-Republican discord has been less than illuminating. Glib analogies between Iraq and Afghanistan and cocky talk about a military cakewalk have given way to more sober assessments. President Bush's oft-repeated goal of "regime change" would likely require 150,000 to 200,000 US troops, allies in the region willing to allow us to pre-position and supply those forces and bloody street battles in downtown Baghdad. With little left to lose, Saddam Hussein might carry out a "Samson scenario" by equipping his Scud missiles with chemical or biological agents and firing them at Tel Aviv. Senior Israeli military and intelligence officials doubt that Israeli Prime Minister Ariel Sharon would defer to US calls for restraint, as Yitzhak Shamir's government did during the Gulf War. Israeli retaliation could spark a wider regional conflagration.

Assume that we can surmount these difficulties. The Bush administration's goal of regime change is the equivalent of our World War II aim of unconditional surrender, and it would have similar postwar consequences. We would assume total responsibility for Iraq's territorial integrity, for the security and basic needs of its pop-

ulation, and for the reconstruction of its system of governance and political culture. This would require an occupation measured in years or even decades. Whatever our intentions, nations in the region (and elsewhere) would view our continuing presence through the historical prism of colonialism. *The Economist,* which favors a US invasion of Iraq, nonetheless speaks of the "imperial flavour" of such a potential occupation.

But the risks would not end there. The Bush administration and its supporters argue that the overthrow of Saddam Hussein would shift the political balance in our favor throughout the Middle East (including among the Palestinians). Henry Kissinger is not alone in arguing that the road to solving the Israeli-Palestinian conflict leads through Baghdad, not the other way around. More broadly, say the optimists, governments in the region would see that opposing the United States carries serious risk, and that there is more to be gained from cooperating with us. Rather than rising up in injured pride, the Arab "street" would respect our resolve and move toward moderation, as would Arab leaders.

Perhaps so. But it does not take much imagination to conjure a darker picture, and the performance of our intelligence services in the region does not inspire confidence in the factual basis of the optimists' views. If a wave of public anger helped Islamic radicals unseat Pakistan's General Pervez Musharraf, for example, we would have exchanged a dangerous regime seeking nuclear weapons for an even more dangerous regime that possesses them.

All this, and I have not yet mentioned potential economic and diplomatic consequences. Even a relatively short war would likely produce an oil-price spike that could tip the fragile global economy into recession. Moreover, unlike the Gulf War, which the Japanese and Saudis largely financed, the United States would have to go it alone this time, with an estimated price tag of US\$ 60 billion for the war and \$15 billion to \$20 billion per year for the occupation.

Our closest allies have spoken out against an invasion of Iraq. Gerhard Schröder, leading a usually complaisant Germany but locked in a tough re-election fight, had gone so far as to label this possibility an "adventure," sparking a protest from our ambassador. Some Bush administration officials seem not to believe that our allies' views matter all that much. Others argue, more temperately, that the Europeans and other protesters will swallow their reservations after the fact, when they can see the military success of our action and its positive consequences. They may be right. But it is at least as likely that this disagreement will widen the already sizeable gap between European and American worldviews. Generations of young people could grow up resenting and resisting America, as they did after the Vietnam War. Whether or not these trends in the long run undermine our alliances, they could have a range of negative short-term consequences, including diminished intelligence sharing and cooperation.

BROADER IMPLICATIONS

Republicans have at least raised these prudential issues. For the most part, however, they have ignored broader questions of principle. But these questions cannot be evaded. An invasion of Iraq would be one of the most fateful deployments of American power since World War II. A global strategy based on the new Bush doctrine of preemption means the end of the system of international institutions, laws and norms that we have worked to build for more than half a century. To his credit, Kissinger recognizes this; he labels Bush's new approach "revolutionary" and declares, "Regime change as a goal for military intervention challenges the international system." The question is whether this revolution in international doctrine is justified and wise.

I think not. What is at stake is nothing less than a fundamental shift in America's place in the world. Rather than continuing to serve as first among equals in the postwar international system, the United States would act as a law unto itself, creating new rules of international engagement without the consent of other nations. In my judgment, this new stance would ill serve the long-term interests of the United States.

There is a reason why President Bush could build on the world's sympathy in framing the US response to al Qaeda after September 11, and why his father was able to sustain such a broad coalition to reverse Saddam Hussein's invasion of Kuwait. In those cases our policy fit squarely within established doctrines of self-defense By contrast, if we seek to overthrow Saddam Hussein, we will act outside the framework of global security that we have helped create.

In the first place, we are a signatory to (indeed, the principal drafter of) the United Nations Charter, which explicitly reserves to sovereign nations "the inherent right of individual or collective self-defense," but only in the event of armed attack. Unless the administration establishes Iraqi complicity in the terrorism of 9/11, it cannot invoke self-defense, as defined by the charter, as the justification for attacking Iraq. And if evidence of Iraqi involvement exists, the administration has a responsibility to present it to Congress, the American people and the world, much as John F. Kennedy and Adlai Stevenson did to justify the US naval blockade of Cuba during the 1962 missile crisis.

The broader structure of international law creates additional obstacles to an invasion of Iraq. To be sure, such law contains a doctrine of "anticipatory self-defense," and there is an ongoing argument concerning its scope. Daniel Webster, then secretary of state, offered the single most influential statement of the doctrine in 1837: There must be shown "a necessity of self-defense . . . instant, overwhelming, leaving no choice of means, and no moment for deliberation." Some contemporary scholars adopt a more permissive view. But even if that debate were resolved in the manner most favorable to the Bush administration, the concept of anticipatory self-defense would still be too narrow to support an attack on Iraq: The threat to the United States from Iraq is not sufficiently specific, clearly enough established or shown to be imminent.

The Bush doctrine of preemption goes well beyond the established bounds of anticipatory self-defense, as many supporters of the administration's Iraq policy privately concede. (They argue that the United States needs to make new law, using Iraq as a precedent.) If the administration wishes to argue that terrorism renders the imminence criterion obsolete, it must do what it has thus far failed to do—namely, to show that Iraq has both the capability of harming us and a serious intent to do so. The abstract logical possibility that Saddam Hussein could transfer weapons of mass destruction to stateless terrorists is not enough. If we cannot make our case, the world will see anticipatory self-defense as an international hunting license.

JUST WAR THEORY

We must also examine the proposed invasion of Iraq through the prism of just war theories developed by philosophers and theologians over a period of centuries. Just war theory begins with the proposition that universal moral reasoning can and should be applied to the activity of war, thereby helping us determine together whether a particular use of force is just or unjust. One of its most distinguished contemporary exponents, Michael Walzer, puts it this way: First strikes can occasionally be justified before the moment of imminent attack, if we have reached the point of "sufficient threat." This concept has three dimensions: "a manifest intent to injure, a degree of active preparation that makes that intent a positive danger, and a general situation in which waiting, or doing anything other than fighting, greatly magnifies the risk." The potential injury, moreover, must be of the gravest possible nature: the loss of territorial integrity or political independence.

Saddam Hussein may well endanger the survival of his neighbors, but he poses no such risk to the United States. And he knows full well that complicity in a 9/11-style terrorist attack on the United States would justify, and swiftly evoke, a regime-ending response. During the Gulf War, we invoked this threat to deter him from using weapons of mass destruction against our troops, and there is no reason to believe that this strategy would be less effective today. Dictators have much more to lose than do stateless terrorists; that is why deterrence directed against them has a good chance of working.

In short, the US cannot claim it undertakes a war of national defense. Iraq has not attacked the US and, in spite of determined efforts by some in the administration, it is not yet clearly implicated in attacks on us by others. The just war tradition suggests that four criteria exist that can justify preemption, and each of them is a continuum of possibilities rather than an on/off switch. These criteria are: 1) the severity of the threat; 2) the degree of probability of the threat; 3) the imminence of the threat; and 4) the cost of delay. But if one tests the proposed intervention in Iraq against these criteria, I suggest one finds the following: 1) the threat is high in the worst case—that is, the acquisition of transferable nuclear weapons; 2) the probability of the threat is contested—many experts have argued that a transfer of nuclear weapons by Saddam Hussein to terrorists is contrary not only to his past behavior but also to his clear and present interests; 3) no one has argued that the threat of attack is imminent; and 4) the cost of delay is low if it is measured in months as the US tries to exhaust other options.

According to this four-part analysis, then, the case has not been made that Iraq poses a sufficient threat to justify a preemptive strike. Further, in its segue from al Qaeda to Saddam Hussein, and from defense to preemption, the Bush administration has shifted its focus from stateless foes to state-based adversaries, and from terrorism in the precise sense to the possession of weapons of mass destruction. Each constitutes a threat. But they are not the same threat and do not warrant the same response. It serves no useful purpose to pretend that they are seamlessly connected, let alone one and the same.

The United Nations, international law, just war theory—it is not hard to imagine the impatience with which policy makers will greet arguments made on these bases. The first duty of every government, they will say, is to defend the lives and security of its citizens. The elimination of Saddam Hussein and, by extension, every regime that threatens to share weapons of mass destruction with anti-American terrorists, comports with this duty. To invoke international norms designed for a different world is to blind ourselves to the harsh necessities of international action in this new era of terrorism. Now that we have faced the facts about the axis of evil, it would be a dereliction of duty to shrink from their consequences for policy. Even if no other nation agrees, we have a duty to the American people to go it alone. The end justifies—indeed requires—the means.

These are powerful claims, not easily dismissed. But even if an invasion of Iraq succeeds in removing a threat here and now, it is not clear whether a policy of preemption would make us safer in the long run. Specifically, we must ask how the new norms of international action we employ would play out as nations around the world adopt them and shape them to their own purposes. (And they *will;* witness the instant appropriation of the United States' antiterrorism rhetoric by Russia and India, among others.) It is an illusion to believe that the United States can employ new norms of action while denying the rights of others to do so as well.

Also at stake are competing understandings of the international system and of our role within it. Some administration officials appear to believe that alliances and treaties are in the main counterproductive, constraining us from most effectively pursuing our national interest. Because the United States enjoys unprecedented military, economic and technological preeminence, we can do best by going it alone. The response to these unilateralists is that that there are many goals that we cannot hope to achieve without the cooperation of others. To pretend otherwise is to exchange short-term gains for long-term risks.

Even after we acknowledge the important distinctions between domestic and international politics, the fact remains: No push for international cooperation can succeed without international law and, therefore, without treaties that build the institutions for administering that law. This is one more reason, if one were needed, why the United States must resist the temptation to set itself apart from the system of international law. It will serve us poorly in the long run if we offer public justifications for an invasion of Iraq that we cannot square with established international legal norms.

BUT *IF* THERE BE WAR . . .

I have argued that war with Iraq *is* avoidable and *should be* avoided. But if the US does go to war, I contend that there are better and worse ways of prosecuting such a war. The US must make a visible and credible effort to explore and exhaust all other *reasonable* options—not logically possible options—but all reasonable ones. The US also must state a public rationale that focuses on enforcement within some viable international system. And most important of all, if regime change means the unconditional surrender of Iraq and abdication by Saddam Hussein of all reins of power, then the US must commit itself to doing for Iraq what it did for Germany after World War II. The US must commit itself to political, economic, and social reconstruction of Iraq such that a decent regime capable of standing on its own will

be the likely outcome of US efforts. If that means an occupation measured in decades rather than months, and it means the expenditures of tens of billions of dollars a year in order to sustain that—then we must commit ourselves to that here and now, because if what we really have in mind the destruction and abandonment of a nation, that, in my judgment, is absolutely the worse outcome imaginable.

We are the most powerful nation on earth, but we must remember we are not invulnerable. I conclude by stressing that to safeguard our own security, we need the assistance of the allies whose doubts we scorn, and the protection of the international restraints against which we chafe. We must therefore resist the easy seduction of unilateral action. In the long run, our interests will best be served by an international system that is as law-like and collaborative as possible, given the reality that we live in a world of sovereign states.

This article derives both from "Perils of Preemptive War," which appeared in *The American Prospect,* vol. 13, no. 17 (September 23, 2002) and also a presentation given at the symposium "Iraq and Just War: A Symposium," sponsored by The Pew Forum on Religion and Public Life, held September 30, 2002.

Sources: The text of President Bush's June 1, 2002 address at West Point is available at, among other sources, http://www.whitehouse.gov/news/releases/2002/06/20020601-3.html; Vice President Dick Cheney's August 26, 2002 remarks can be found, among other places, at: http://www.whitehouse.gov/news/releases/2002/08/20020826.html; Henry Kissinger's remarks concerning regime change can be found in the *Washington Post,* opinion and editorial section (August 12, 2002) and repeated in interviews in various media. The United Nations Charter, Ch. VII, art. 51; Daniel Webster's views of the necessity of self-defense were occasioned by the *Caroline* incident of 1837, in which the American ship was attacked by a Canadian naval force to end the ship's supplying of armed rebels plotting the liberation of French Canada. Michael Walzer, *Just and Unjust Wars* (Basic Books, 1977).

The War on Terrorism
and the End of Human Rights

(2002)

David Luban

David Luban is the Frederick Haas Professor of Law and Philosophy at Georgetown University's Law Center and Department of Philosophy. He works in legal ethics, international criminal law, human rights theory, and jurisprudence, among other topics. His books include Lawyers and Justice: An Ethical Study *(Princeton University Press, 1988),* Legal Modernism *(University of Michigan Press, 1994) and (with Deborah Rhode)* Legal Ethics *(3rd ed, Foundation Press, 2001).*

In the immediate aftermath of September 11, President Bush stated that the perpetrators of the deed would be brought to justice. Soon afterwards, the President announced that the United States would engage in a war on terrorism. The first of these statements adopts the familiar language of criminal law and criminal justice. It treats the September 11 attacks as horrific crimes—mass murders—and the government's mission as apprehending and punishing the surviving planners and conspirators for their roles in the crimes. The War on Terrorism is a different proposition, however, and a different model of governmental action—not law but war. Most obviously, it dramatically broadens the scope of action, because now terrorists who knew nothing about September 11 have been earmarked as enemies. But that is only the beginning.

THE HYBRID WAR-LAW APPROACH

The model of war offers much freer rein than that of law, and therein lies its appeal in the wake of 9/11. First, in war but not in law it is permissible to use lethal force on enemy troops regardless of their degree of personal involvement with the adversary. The conscripted cook is as legitimate a target as the enemy general. Second, in war but not in law "collateral damage," that is, foreseen but unintended killing of non-combatants, is permissible. (Police cannot blow up an apartment building full of people because a murderer is inside, but an air force can bomb the building if it contains a military target.) Third, the requirements of evidence and proof are drastically weaker in war than in criminal justice. Soldiers do not need proof beyond a reasonable doubt, or even proof by a preponderance of evidence, that someone is an enemy soldier before firing on him or capturing and imprisoning him. They don't need proof at all, merely plausible intelligence. Thus, the U.S. military remains regretful but unapologetic about its January 2002 attack on the Afghani town of Uruzgan, in which 21 innocent civilians were killed, based on faulty intelligence that they were al Qaeda fighters. Fourth, in war one can attack an enemy without concern over whether he has done anything. Legitimate targets are those who in the course of combat *might* harm us, not those who *have* harmed us. No doubt there are other significant differences as well. But the basic point should be clear: given Washington's mandate to eliminate the danger of future 9/11s, so far as humanly possible, the model of war offers important advantages over the model of law.

There are disadvantages as well. Most obviously, in war but not in law, fighting back is a *legitimate* response of the enemy. Second, when nations fight a war, other nations may opt for neutrality. Third, because fighting back is legitimate, in war the enemy soldier deserves special regard once he is rendered harmless through injury or surrender. It is impermissible to punish him for his role in fighting the war. Nor can he be harshly interrogated after he is captured. The Third Geneva Convention provides: "Prisoners of war who refuse to answer [questions] may not be threatened, insulted, or exposed to unpleasant or disadvantageous treatment of any kind." And, when the war concludes, the enemy soldier must be repatriated.

Here, however, Washington has different ideas, designed to eliminate these tactical disadvantages in the traditional war model. Washington regards international terrorism not only as a military adversary,

but also as a criminal activity and criminal conspiracy. In the law model, criminals don't get to shoot back, and their acts of violence subject them to legitimate punishment. That is what we see in Washington's prosecution of the War on Terrorism. Captured terrorists may be tried before military or civilian tribunals, and shooting back at Americans, including American troops, is a federal crime (for a statute under which John Walker Lindh was indicted criminalizes anyone regardless of nationality, who "outside the United States attempts to kill, or engages in a conspiracy to kill, a national of the United States" or "engages in physical violence with intent to cause serious bodily injury to a national of the United States; or with the result that serious bodily injury is caused to a national of the United States"). Furthermore, the U.S. may rightly demand that other countries not be neutral about murder and terrorism. Unlike the war model, a nation may insist that those who are not with us in fighting murder and terror are against us, because by not joining our operations they are providing a safe haven for terrorists or their bank accounts. By selectively combining elements of the war model and elements of the law model, Washington is able to maximize its own ability to mobilize lethal force against terrorists while eliminating most traditional rights of a military adversary, as well as the rights of innocent bystanders caught in the crossfire.

A LIMBO OF RIGHTLESSNESS

The legal status of al Qaeda suspects imprisoned at the Guantanamo Bay Naval Base in Cuba is emblematic of this hybrid war-law approach to the threat of terrorism. In line with the war model, they lack the usual rights of criminal suspects—the presumption of innocence, the right to a hearing to determine guilt, the opportunity to prove that the authorities have grabbed the wrong man. But, in line with the law model, they are considered *unlawful* combatants. Because they are not uniformed forces, they lack the rights of prisoners of war and are liable to criminal punishment. Initially, the American government declared that the Guantanamo Bay prisoners have no rights under the Geneva Conventions. In the face of international protests, Washington quickly backpedaled and announced that the Guantanamo Bay prisoners would indeed be treated as decently as POWs—but it also made clear that the prisoners have no right to such treatment. Neither criminal suspects nor POWs, neither fish nor fowl, they inhabit a limbo of rightlessness. Secretary of Defense Rumsfeld's assertion that the U.S. may continue to detain them even if they are acquitted by a military tribunal dramatizes the point.

To understand how extraordinary their status is, consider an analogy. Suppose that Washington declares a War on Organized Crime. Troops are dispatched to Sicily, and a number of Mafiosi are seized, brought to Guantanamo Bay, and imprisoned without a hearing for the indefinite future, maybe the rest of their lives. They are accused of no crimes, because their capture is based not on what they have done but on what they might do. After all, to become "made" they took oaths of obedience to the bad guys. Seizing them accords with the war model: they are enemy foot soldiers. But they are foot soldiers out of uniform; they lack a "fixed distinctive emblem," in the words of The Hague Convention. That makes them unlawful com-

batants, so they lack the rights of POWs. They may object that it is only a unilateral declaration by the American President that has turned them into combatants in the first place—he called it a war, they didn't—and that, since they do not regard themselves as literal foot soldiers it never occurred to them to wear a fixed distinctive emblem. They have a point. It seems too easy for the President to divest anyone in the world of rights and liberty simply by announcing that the U.S. is at war with them and then declaring them unlawful combatants if they resist. But, in the hybrid war-law model, they protest in vain.

Consider another example. In January 2002, U.S. forces in Bosnia seized five Algerians and a Yemeni suspected of al Qaeda connections and took them to Guantanamo Bay. The six had been jailed in Bosnia, but a Bosnian court released them for lack of evidence, and the Bosnian Human Rights Chamber issued an injunction that four of them be allowed to remain in the country pending further legal proceedings. The Human Rights Chamber, ironically, was created under U.S. auspices in the Dayton peace accords, and it was designed specifically to protect against treatment like this. Ruth Wedgwood, a well-known international law scholar at Yale and a member of the Council on Foreign Relations, defended the Bosnian seizure in war-model terms. "I think we would simply argue this was a matter of self-defense. One of the fundamental rules of military law is that you have a right ultimately to act in self-defense. And if these folks were actively plotting to blow up the U.S. embassy, they should be considered combatants and captured as combatants in a war." Notice that Professor Wedgwood argues in terms of what the men seized in Bosnia were *planning to do*, not what they *did;* notice as well that the decision of the Bosnian court that there was insufficient evidence does not matter. These are characteristics of the war model.

More recently, two American citizens alleged to be al Qaeda operatives (Jose Padilla, a.k.a. Abdullah al Muhajir, and Yasser Esam Hamdi) have been held in American military prisons, with no crimes charged, no opportunity to consult counsel, and no hearing. The President described Padilla as "a bad man" who aimed to build a nuclear "dirty" bomb and use it against America; and the Justice Department has classified both men as "enemy combatants" who may be held indefinitely. Yet, as military law expert Gary Solis points out, "Until now, as used by the attorney general, the term 'enemy combatant' appeared nowhere in U.S. criminal law, international law or in the law of war." The phrase comes from the 1942 Supreme Court case *Ex parte Quirin,* but all the Court says there is that "an enemy combatant who without uniform comes secretly through the lines for the purpose of waging war by destruction of life or property" would "not . . . be entitled to the status of prisoner of war, but . . . [they would] be offenders against the law of war subject to trial and punishment by military tribunals." For the Court, in other words, the status of a person as a nonuniformed enemy combatant makes him a criminal rather than a warrior, and determines *where* he is tried (in a military, rather than a civilian, tribunal) but not *whether* he is tried. Far from authorizing open-ended confinement, *Ex parte Quirin* presupposes that criminals are entitled to hearings: without a hearing how can suspects prove that the government made a mistake? *Quirin* embeds the concept of "enemy combatant" firmly in the law model. In the war model, by contrast,

POWs may be detained without a hearing until hostilities are over. But POWs were captured in uniform, and only their undoubted identity as enemy soldiers justifies such open-ended custody. Apparently, Hamdi and Padilla will get the worst of both models—open-ended custody with no trial, like POWs, but no certainty beyond the U.S. government's say-so that they really are "bad men." This is the hybrid war-law model. It combines the *Quirin* category of "enemy combatant without uniform," used in the law model to justify a military trial, with the war model's practice of indefinite confinement with no trial at all.

THE CASE FOR THE HYBRID APPROACH

Is there any justification for the hybrid war-law model, which so drastically diminishes the rights of the enemy? An argument can be offered along the following lines. In ordinary cases of war among states, enemy soldiers may well be morally and politically innocent. Many of them are conscripts, and those who aren't do not necessarily endorse the state policies they are fighting to defend. But enemy soldiers in the War on Terrorism are, by definition, those who have embarked on a path of terrorism. They are neither morally nor politically innocent. Their sworn aim—"Death to America!"—is to create more 9/11s. In this respect, they are much more akin to criminal conspirators than to conscript soldiers. Terrorists will fight as soldiers when they must, and metamorphose into mass murderers when they can.

Furthermore, suicide terrorists pose a special, unique danger. Ordinary criminals do not target innocent bystanders. They may be willing to kill them if necessary, but bystanders enjoy at least some measure of security because they are not primary targets. Not so with terrorists, who aim to kill as many innocent people as possible. Likewise, innocent bystanders are protected from ordinary criminals by whatever deterrent force the threat of punishment and the risk of getting killed in the act of committing a crime offer. For a suicide bomber, neither of these threats is a deterrent at all—after all, for the suicide bomber one of the hallmarks of a *successful* operation is that he winds up dead at day's end. Given the unique and heightened danger that suicide terrorists pose, a stronger response that grants potential terrorists fewer rights may be justified. Add to this the danger that terrorists may come to possess weapons of mass destruction, including nuclear devices in suitcases. Under circumstances of such dire menace, it is appropriate to treat terrorists as though they embody the most dangerous aspects of both warriors and criminals. That is the basis of the hybrid war-law model.

THE CASE AGAINST EXPEDIENCY

The argument against the hybrid war-law model is equally clear. The U.S. has simply chosen the bits of the law model and the bits of the war model that are most convenient for American interests, and ignored the rest. The model abolishes the rights of potential enemies (and their innocent shields) by fiat—not for reasons of moral or legal principle, but solely because the U.S. does not want them to have rights. The more rights they have, the more risk they pose. But Americans' urgent desire to minimize our risks doesn't make other people's rights disappear. Calling our policy a War on Terrorism obscures this point.

The theoretical basis of the objection is that the law model and the war model each comes as a package, with a kind of intellectual integrity. The law model grows out of relationships within states, while the war model arises from relationships between states. The law model imputes a ground-level community of values to those subject to the law—paradigmatically, citizens of a state, but also visitors and foreigners who choose to engage in conduct that affects a state. Only because law imputes shared basic values to the community can a state condemn the conduct of criminals and inflict punishment on them. Criminals deserve condemnation and punishment because their conduct violates norms that we are entitled to count on their sharing. But, for the same reason—the imputed community of values—those subject to the law ordinarily enjoy a presumption of innocence and an expectation of safety. The government cannot simply grab them and confine them without making sure they have broken the law, nor can it condemn them without due process for ensuring that it has the right person, nor can it knowingly place bystanders in mortal peril in the course of fighting crime. They are our fellows, and the community should protect them just as it protects us. The same imputed community of values that justifies condemnation and punishment creates rights to due care and due process.

War is different. War is the ultimate acknowledgment that human beings do not live in a single community with shared norms. If their norms conflict enough, communities pose a physical danger to each other, and nothing can safeguard a community against its enemies except force of arms. That makes enemy soldiers legitimate targets; but it makes our soldiers legitimate targets as well, and, once the enemy no longer poses a danger, he should be immune from punishment, because if he has fought cleanly he has violated no norms that we are entitled to presume he honors. Our norms are, after all, *our* norms, not his.

Because the law model and war model come as conceptual packages, it is unprincipled to wrench them apart and recombine them simply because it is in America's interest to do so. To declare that Americans can fight enemies with the latitude of warriors, but if the enemies fight back they are not warriors but criminals, amounts to a kind of heads-I-win-tails-you-lose international morality in which whatever it takes to reduce American risk, no matter what the cost to others, turns out to be justified. This, in brief, is the criticism of the hybrid war-law model.

To be sure, the law model could be made to incorporate the war model merely by rewriting a handful of statutes. Congress could enact laws permitting imprisonment or execution of persons who pose a significant threat of terrorism whether or not they have already done anything wrong. The standard of evidence could be set low and the requirement of a hearing eliminated. Finally, Congress could authorize the use of lethal force against terrorists regardless of the danger to innocent bystanders, and it could immunize officials from lawsuits or prosecution by victims of collateral damage. Such statutes would violate the Constitution, but the Constitution could be amended to incorporate anti-terrorist exceptions to the Fourth, Fifth, and Sixth Amendments. In the end, we would have a system of law that includes all the essential features of the war model.

It would, however, be a system that imprisons people for their intentions rather than their actions, and that offers the innocent few protections against mistaken detention or inadvertent death through collateral damage. Gone are the principles that people should never be punished for their thoughts, only for their deeds, and that innocent people must be protected rather than injured by their own government. In that sense, at any rate, repackaging war as law seems merely cosmetic, because it replaces the ideal of law as a protector of rights with the more problematic goal of protecting some innocent people by sacrificing others. The hypothetical legislation incorporates war into law only by making law as partisan and ruthless as war. It no longer resembles law as Americans generally understand it.

THE THREAT TO INTERNATIONAL HUMAN RIGHTS

In the War on Terrorism, what becomes of international human rights? It seems beyond dispute that the war model poses a threat to international human rights, because honoring human rights is neither practically possible nor theoretically required during war. Combatants are legitimate targets; non-combatants maimed by accident or mistake are regarded as collateral damage rather than victims of atrocities; cases of mistaken identity get killed or confined without a hearing because combat conditions preclude due process. To be sure, the laws of war specify minimum human rights, but these are far less robust than rights in peacetime—and the hybrid war-law model reduces this schedule of rights even further by classifying the enemy as unlawful combatants.

One striking example of the erosion of human rights is tolerance of torture. It should be recalled that a 1995 al Qaeda plot to bomb eleven U.S. airliners was thwarted by information tortured out of a Pakistani suspect by the Philippine police—an eerie real-life version of the familiar philosophical thought-experiment. The *Washington Post* reports that since September 11 the U.S. has engaged in the summary transfer of dozens of terrorism suspects to countries where they will be interrogated under torture. But it isn't just the United States that has proven willing to tolerate torture for security reasons. Last December, the Swedish government snatched a suspected Islamic extremist to whom it had previously granted political asylum, and the same day had him transferred to Egypt, where Amnesty International reports that he has been tortured to the point where he walks only with difficulty. Sweden is not, to say the least, a traditionally hard-line nation on human rights issues. None of this international transportation is lawful—indeed, it violates international treaty obligations under the Convention against Torture that in the U.S. have constitutional status as "supreme Law of the Land"—but that may not matter under the war model, in which even constitutional rights may be abrogated.

It is natural to suggest that this suspension of human rights is an exceptional emergency measure to deal with an unprecedented threat. This raises the question of how long human rights will remain suspended. When will the war be over?

Here, the chief problem is that the War on Terrorism is not like any other kind of war. The enemy, Terrorism, is not a territorial state or nation or government. There is no opposite number to negotiate with. There is no one on the other side to call a truce or declare a ceasefire, no one among the enemy authorized to surrender. In traditional wars among states, the war aim is, as Clausewitz argued, to impose one state's political will on another's. The *aim* of the war is not to kill the enemy—killing the enemy is the *means* used to achieve the real end, which is to force capitulation. In the War on Terrorism, no capitulation is possible. That means that the real aim of the war is, quite simply, to kill or capture all of the terrorists—to keep on killing and killing, capturing and capturing, until they are all gone.

Of course, no one expects that terrorism will ever disappear completely. Everyone understands that new anti-American extremists, new terrorists, will always arise and always be available for recruitment and deployment. Everyone understands that even if al Qaeda is destroyed or decapitated, other groups, with other leaders, will arise in its place. It follows, then, that the War on Terrorism will be a war that can only be abandoned, never concluded. The War has no natural resting point, no moment of victory or finality. It requires a mission of killing and capturing, in territories all over the globe, that will go on in perpetuity. It follows as well that the suspension of human rights implicit in the hybrid war-law model is not temporary but permanent.

Perhaps with this fear in mind, Congressional authorization of President Bush's military campaign limits its scope to those responsible for September 11 and their sponsors. But the War on Terrorism has taken on a life of its own that makes the Congressional authorization little more than a technicality. Because of the threat of nuclear terror, the American leadership actively debates a war on Iraq regardless of whether Iraq was implicated in September 11; and the President's yoking of Iraq, Iran, and North Korea into a single axis of evil because they back terror suggests that the War on Terrorism might eventually encompass all these nations. If the U.S. ever unearths tangible evidence that any of these countries is harboring or abetting terrorists with weapons of mass destruction, there can be little doubt that Congress will support military action. So too, Russia invokes the American War on Terrorism to justify its attacks on Chechen rebels, China uses it to deflect criticisms of its campaign against Uighur separatists, and Israeli Prime Minister Sharon explicitly links military actions against Palestinian insurgents to the American War on Terrorism. No doubt there is political opportunism at work in some or all of these efforts to piggy-back onto America's campaign, but the opportunity would not exist if "War on Terrorism" were merely the code-name of a discrete, neatly-boxed American operation. Instead, the War on Terrorism has become a model of politics, a world-view with its own distinctive premises and consequences. As I have argued, it includes a new model of state action, the hybrid war-law model, which depresses human rights from their peace-time standard to the war-time standard, and indeed even further. So long as it continues, the War on Terrorism means the end of human rights, at least for those near enough to be touched by the fire of battle.

Sources: On the January 2002 attack on the Afghani town of Uruzgan, see: John Ward Anderson, "Afghans Falsely Held by U.S. Tried to Explain; Fighters Recount Unanswered Pleas, Beatings—and an Apology on Their Release," *Washington Post* (March 26, 2002); see also Susan B. Glasser, "Afghans Live and Die With U.S. Mistakes; Villagers Tell of Over 100 Casualties," *Washington Post* (Feb. 20, 2002). On the Third Geneva Convention, see: Geneva Convention (III) Relative to the Treatment of Prisoners of War, 6 U.S.T. 3317, signed on August 12, 1949, at Geneva, Article 17. Although the U.S. has not ratified the Geneva Convention, it has become part of customary international law, and certainly belongs to the war model. Count One of the Lindh indictment charges him with violating 18 U.S.C. 2332(b), "Whoever outside the United States attempts to kill, or engages in a conspiracy to kill, a national of the United States" may be sentenced to 20 years (for attempts) or life imprisonment (for conspiracies). Subsection (c) likewise criminalizes "engag[ing] in physical violence with intent to cause serious bodily injury to a national of the United States; or with the result that serious bodily injury is caused to a national of the United States." Lawful combatants are defined in the Hague Convention (IV) Respecting the Laws and Customs of War on Land, Annex to the Convention, 1 Bevans 631, signed on October 18, 1907, at The Hague, Article 1. The definition requires that combatants "have a fixed distinctive emblem recognizable at a distance." Protocol I Additional to the Geneva Conventions of 1949, 1125 U.N.T.S. 3, adopted on June 8, 1977, at Geneva, Article 44 (3) makes an important change in the Hague Convention, expanding the definition of combatants to include non-uniformed irregulars. However, the United States has not agreed to Protocol I. The source of Ruth Wedgwood's remarks: Interview with Melissa Block, National Public Radio program, "All Things Considered" (January 18, 2002); Gary Solis, "Even a 'Bad Man' Has Rights," *Washington Post* (June 25, 2002); *Ex parte Quirin,* 317 U.S. 1, 31 (1942). On the torture of the Pakistani militant by Philippine police: Doug Struck et al., "Borderless Network Of Terror; Bin Laden Followers Reach Across Globe," *Washington Post* (September 23, 2001): " 'For weeks, agents hit him with a chair and a long piece of wood, forced water into his mouth, and crushed lighted cigarettes into his private parts,' wrote journalists Marites Vitug and Glenda Gloria in 'Under the Crescent Moon,' an acclaimed book on Abu Sayyaf. 'His ribs were almost totally broken and his captors were surprised he survived.' " On U.S. and Swedish transfers of Isamic militants to countries employing torture: Rajiv Chandrasakaran & Peter Finn, "U.S. Behind Secret Transfer of Terror Suspects," *Washington Post* (March 11, 2002); Peter Finn, "Europeans Tossing Terror Suspects Out the Door,"

Washington Post (January 29, 2002); Anthony Shadid, "Fighting Terror/Atmosphere in Europe, Military Campaign/Asylum Bids; in Shift, Sweden Extradites Militants to Egypt," *Boston Globe* (December 31, 2001). Article 3(1) of the Convention against Torture provides that "No State Party shall expel, return (*'refouler'*) or extradite a person to another State where there are substantial grounds for believing that he would be in danger of being subjected to torture." Article 2(2) cautions that "No exceptional circumstances whatsoever, whether a state of war or a threat of war, internal political instability or any other public emer-gency, may be invoked as a justification of torture." But no parallel caution is incorporated into Article 3(1)'s non-*refoulement* rule, and a lawyer might well argue that its absence implies that the rule may be abrogated during war or similar public emergency. *Convention against Torture and Other Cruel, Inhuman or Degrading Treatment or Punishment,* 1465 U.N.T.S. 85. Ratified by the United States, Oct. 2, 1994. Entered into force for the United States, Nov. 20, 1994. (Article VI of the U.S. Constitution provides that treaties are the "supreme Law of the Land.")

D. After War

When war is over, there is often a desire to hold those who commit immoral acts in war responsible for their conduct. One of the first questions that commonly arises is, can subordinates be held responsible for committing immoral acts even though they were obeying orders? The first selection of this section directly addresses this question. The next two selections also address this question, but they also provide insights into the difficulties of assigning moral responsibility in war more generally. The last selection addresses the issue of whether truth and reconciliation commissions provide justice.

In "Can I Be Blamed for Obeying Orders?" R. M. Hare seeks to explain what a moral decision is and, based on this, why subordinates are always (or almost always) at least partially morally responsible for their actions. For Hare, moral decision making concerns finding out what *ought* to be done, and discovering this cannot be inferred from the simple fact that someone told someone else to do something. Even if God were to command a person to do something, it could not be inferred from this fact alone that it *ought* to be done. A single factual premise does not provide the proper basis for a moral conclusion. A second moral premise is needed. Regarding God, the second premise might be something like "everything God commands ought to be done." This second premise would provide the moral reason why the thing commanded by God in the first premise ought to be done. This logical rule is often summarized as: One cannot derive an *ought* from an *is*.

With this logical rule in mind, it becomes clear that the simple fact that a superior commands something to be done does not morally justify a subordinate's performance of that action. More is needed. According to Hare, subordinates must make a moral inquiry into the truth of the other, required moral premise. Or, put another way, subordinates must ask why it is that they are morally obligated to follow their superior's command. For Hare, this necessary moral inquiry by subordinates has at least the following two ramifications. First, subordinates are required to judge, mostly on a case by case basis, whether the commands of their superior are morally justified. Second, subordinates are required to be involved in the decision-making process that leads to their performance of the act commanded; it makes the subordinate an accomplice. As accomplices, Hare concludes, subordinates are always (or almost always) at least partially morally responsible for performing acts commanded.

Like Hare, Larry May in "Superior Orders, Duress, and Moral Perception," thinks that soldiers can be held morally responsible though they were following orders. May states that even lower-ranking soldiers conspire with other soldiers in their unit to achieve certain objectives. As a co-conspirator, the lower-ranking soldier shares in the responsibility for performing the action commanded. Unlike Hare, however, May is concerned with why sometimes it might be wrong to hold a soldier or subordinate morally responsible, even though the soldier performs an action that is normally thought to be immoral.

According to the "Nuremberg defense," soldiers who invoke the "defense of superior orders" for war crimes in international criminal courts must be able to show that the action they took was moral and that it was the only morally reasonable action available given the circumstances. The Nuremberg defense is like the defense of duress. Generally, it is not thought that someone is legally or morally responsible if it is also thought that that person had "no other choice" given the circumstances. The Nuremberg trials put subordinates on notice that the fact that they were obeying orders would not excuse their immoral or illegal acts.

May points out that with regard to war adjudicating the defense of duress and the moral requirements incorporated in that defense is often more difficult than it might first appear. Even what appears to be the easy case, like holding Lieutenant Calley responsible for his actions taken at what is now known as the My Lai Massacre, can be difficult. May emphasizes that the circumstances of war are abnormal. As a result, the moral perceptions of soldiers in war do not correspond to the moral perceptions of a normal person who did not go through the same or similar experiences. According to May, "people's moral perceptions vary based on character and circumstance." Their moral perceptions differ with their experiences. May argues that any legal standard, e.g., the defense of superior orders, that incorporates a moral requirement for determining responsibility should take into account this difference in moral perception. For May, it is the moral perspective of the reasonable person on the battlefield, not the moral perception of the "normal person," that should be used in determining whether the act committed was moral or whether a moral choice was available.

Similar to May, David Cooper in "Collective Responsibility, "Moral Luck," and Reconciliation," emphasizes that any judgment concerning moral responsibility for actions taken in war must consider whether it was reasonable for that person, based on the context of war and their past experiences, to act as they did. Unlike May, however, Cooper argues that assigning moral responsibility is appropriate only when it can be concluded that the action was unreasonable for a person who was brought up under and exposed to the exact same conditions of the person in question. Cooper argues that many of the choices made in life can be attributed to circumstances "beyond our control." For Cooper, even identity "owes" to factors beyond one's control. In short, Cooper argues that many of our choices and actions are the result of luck, and luck cannot be used as the basis for assigning moral responsibility.

While Cooper thinks that many individuals are often in a sense free from moral blame because their actions are the result of luck, he also thinks that groups and some people can be held responsible for immoral acts committed in war. Cooper argues that the "architects of oppression" can still be singled out, and he states that the groups who fostered the oppression should be held responsible and judged in the "harshest terms." Regarding groups and those individuals who were not the "architects of oppression," Cooper argues that often an acknowledgement or apology rather than punishment is the preferred moral solution for the wrong committed. For Cooper, an acknowledgement or apology is appropriate because it allows groups and individuals to begin again as "fellow human beings" to engage in meaningful, moral relationships.

In "Moral Ambition Within and Beyond Political Constraints," Elizabeth Kiss asks whether truth and reconciliation commissions (TRC) that seek the kind of acknowledgments advocated by Cooper result in justice. Her answer is a cautious and thoughtful yes. Truth commissions promote restorative justice, not retributive justice. They are often contrasted with retributive justice, but they are not necessarily opposed to retributive justice. Kiss indicates that truth commissions, like the South African TRC, can work in conjunction with a threat of prosecution if the perpetrator fails to acknowledge and fully disclose the wrong committed.

Generally, Kiss examines the following four commitments of truth commissions: first, the healing power and utility of discovering the truth of past events; second, the need to hold perpetrators accountable for past acts; third, the need to create conditions in which human rights can again be respected; and finally, reconciliation. Kiss states that the first three commitments are compatible with the commitments of retributive justice. Because these three commitments are compatible, she claims that restorative justice differs from retributive justice only in degree, not in kind, with regard to these three commitments. It is only the last commitment, reconciliation, which differs in kind. Restorative justice privileges reconciliation over retribution. Because it does, Kiss states that it "seeks to transcend the traditional dichotomy between justice and mercy, incorporating dimensions of mercy into justice."

Can I Be Blamed for Obeying Orders?

(1972)

R. M. Hare

R. M. Hare was White's Professor of Moral Philosophy at Oxford University from 1966 to 1983 and graduate research professor at the University of Florida from 1983 to 1994. His books include The Language of Morals *(1952),* Freedom and Reason *(1963), and* Moral Thinking *(1981). He died in 2002 at the age of eighty-two.*

Many people, if asked for the distinctive feature of present-day British philosophy, would say that it lies in the peculiar attention which we tend to pay to the study of language. Perhaps most British philosophers would agree that the study of language, in some sense, is a very potent philosophical tool; and many would say that it is *the* philosophical method—that any problem which is properly philosophical reduces in the end to an elucidation of our use of words. Criticisms of this approach to philosophy are frequently made by those who have not practised the sort of method we use, and therefore do not understand either what the method is, or how fruitful it can be. It is alleged that we are turning philosophy away from matters of substance to trivial verbal matters (as if it were a trivial matter to understand the words we use); and it is also sometimes said that we are to be contrasted unfavourably in this respect with the great philosophers of the past.

The purpose of these talks is to indicate, by means of two examples taken from political philosophy, that both these criticisms arise from misunderstandings of the nature of philosophy in general and of our kind of philosophy in particular. The point could have been made by means of a general discussion about philosophical method; or it could have been made by taking examples out of the works of famous philosophers, and showing how much kinship there is between their methods of argumentation and ours. But I thought it better to take two practical problems of political morality—problems which exercise us currently, or ought to—and to show how a great deal of light can be shed on these by an understanding of the words used in discussing them: an understanding of the sort which it is the purpose of contemporary moral philosophy to achieve. None of the things I shall say will be original; indeed, it is part of the point of these talks that they are not original: I am merely translating into a new, and I think clearer, idiom things which have been said by great philosophers of the past, and thereby showing that the new idiom is a vehicle for philosophy as it has always been understood.

In the first of these talks I shall discuss a problem which arises frequently in wartime and in connection with war crimes trials. The thesis is sometimes maintained that a soldier's duty is always to obey orders; and this is often brought forward as a defense when someone is accused of having committed some atrocity. It is said that, since it is a soldier's duty to obey his orders, and he is liable to blame if he disobeys them, we cannot consistently also blame him if in a particular case he obeys them—even though the act which he has committed is of itself wrong. We may blame his superiors who gave the orders, but not the man who carried them out. Others, in opposition to this, maintain that the individual is always responsible for his own acts.

Can the study of moral language shed any light on this problem? I want to maintain that it can; and the way I shall do this is by exhibiting the formal features of the problem, as they arise out of the logical properties of the words used in discussing it. I wish to show that these formal features are common to a large range of questions which are not at first sight similar, and that the key to the whole matter is a purely linguistic and logical observation made a long time ago by Hume.

The formal features of this problem are brought out extremely clearly by Kant in a famous passage,[1] in which he is arguing that we have to make our own moral judgements, and cannot get them made for us, without any decision on our part, by God. Suppose that I am commanded by God to do something. The Bible is full of stories where this is said to have happened. Can I without further consideration conclude that I ought to do it? Kant argued (rightly) that I cannot—not without further consideration. For it does not follow automatically, as it were, from the fact that God wills me to do something, that I ought to do it. From the fact that God wills

me to do something, I can only conclude that I ought to do it if I am given the additional premise that God wills that and that only to be done, which ought to be done. This additional premise is one which indeed Christians all accept, because they believe that God is good; and part of what we mean by saying that God is good is that he wills that and that only to be done which ought to be done. But we have to assume this, if we are to pass from the fact that God wills us to do something to the conclusion that we ought to do it. So we can indeed, as it were, get out of making the particular moral decision as to whether we ought to do this particular thing, by putting it on the shoulders of God; but only at the cost of having to make for ourselves a more general moral decision, that we ought always to do what God commands (the very fundamental, crucial decision that is made when anyone decided to become, or to remain, an adherent of the Christian or some other religion). This more general moral judgement obviously cannot, without arguing in a circle, be shuffled off our shoulders in the same way.

Yet, if we do not assume that God is good, the only conception we have left of him is one of power without goodness— one, as Kant picturesquely puts it, compounded of lust for glory and domination, together with frightful ideas of power and vengefulness; and to make our duty the obedience to the will of such a being would be to adopt a highly immoral morality. We might rather be inclined to approve of disobeying an evil God, as Shelley portrays Prometheus doing, however appalling the consequences.

I want you to notice that this argument does not depend on its being God's will in particular upon which it is sought to base morality. The same argument would apply were we to substitute for 'God' the name of any other person whatever, divine or human. Kant is here making use of a principle in ethics which was, so far as I am aware, first stated by Hume. The actual passage is worth quoting, both because it is rightly held to be one of the two or three most important observations in moral philosophy, and because it illustrates very well my thesis that the subject matter of philosophy is the use of words. Hume says:

> In every system of authority, which I have hitherto met with, I have always remark'd, that the author proceeds for some time in the ordinary way of reasoning, and establishes the being of a God, or makes observations concerning human affairs; when of a sudden I am surpriz'd to find, that instead of the usual copulations of propositions, *is,* and *is not,* I meet with no proposition that is not connected with an *ought,* or an *ought not.* This change is imperceptible; -but is, however, of the last consequence. For as this *ought,* or *ought not,* expresses some new relation or affirmation, 'tis necessary that it shou'd be observ'd and explain'd; and at the same time that a reason should be given, for what seems altogether inconceivable, how this new relation can be a deduction from others, which are entirely different from it. But as authors do not commonly use this precaution, I shall presume to recommend it to the readers; and am persuaded that this small attention wou'd subvert all the vulgar systems of morality.[2]

It is easy to apply this canon of Hume's to our example. The proposition "*X*'s will is, that I do *A*" (where *X* is any person whatever and *A* is any act whatever) is a proposition of fact, an "is"-proposition. It does not matter who *X* is; in Kant's example it was God; but it might be some human ruler. From this "is"-proposition the "ought"-proposition "I ought to do *A*" cannot be derived. The first proposition states

a mere fact, a fact about what someone wills that I do. From this fact no moral proposition follows. Only if we are given the *moral* premise, "*X* wills that and that only to be done, which ought to be done" or "Everything which *X* wills to be done, ought to be done" can we, from this, in conjunction with the premise "*X*'s will is, that I do *A*," conclude that I ought to do *A*. This is all right, because we have added to our factual minor premise a moral major premise; and from the two together we can infer a moral conclusion; but not from the factual minor premise alone.

In the example with which I started, *X* was God. But I wish to discuss the first and most celebrated example of a philosopher who thought that moral decisions could be made on his subjects' behalf by a ruler, namely Plato. Plato thought that, just as there are experts in riding and in other skills, so there ought to be experts in morals. All we had to do, in order to solve all moral problems, was to get such an expert, make him our philosopher-king, and leave him to decide for us what was right and what was wrong. He would make the laws, and we, by obeying them, could be absolutely certain of living morally blameless lives. This program has an obvious and immediate appeal. For moral problems are difficult and tormenting; how fortunate it would be if we could leave them, like problems of engineering, to somebody who could solve them for us! To get rid of one's moral problems on to the shoulders of someone else—some political or military leader, some priest or commissar—is to be free of much worry; it is to exchange the tortured responsibility of the adult for the happy irresponsibility of the child; that is why so many have taken this course.

The flaw in this arrangement is that we could never know whether the philosopher-king really was a philosopher-king.

Plato himself admits that his ideal republic might degenerate. The maintenance of the republic depended on the correct calculation of the famous Platonic Number,[3] which was used for determining the correct mating-season to produce the philosopher-kings of the next generation. If the number were miscalculated, a person might be made ruler who did not really possess the required qualifications. Suppose that we are inhabitants of a Platonic republic, and are ordered by our so-called philosopher-king to do a certain act. And suppose that we are troubled about the morality of this act; suppose that it is the act of torturing some unfortunate person. It is perfectly true that if our ruler is a *true* philosopher-king, then, *ex hypothesi,* he knows infallibly what is right and what is wrong, and so we cannot do wrong to obey him. But the question is: Can we be sure that he is the genuine article? Can we be sure that they did not miscalculate the number a generation ago, so that what we have at this moment is not a philosopher-king, but the most wicked of tyrants masquerading as one?

We can tell whether a man is a good man, or, specifically, whether a king is a good king, only by considering his acts. So that it is no use saying of *all* our ruler's acts, "He is the philosopher-king, and the philosopher-king can do no wrong; therefore each and every act of his must be right." For this would be to argue in a circle. It is only if we are satisfied that his acts are right that we can be satisfied that he is a good king. Therefore if he commands us to perform what looks like an atrocity, the only thing we can do is look at the individual act and say, "What about this very thing that he is commanding me to do now? Could a good man command anyone to do this?" That is to say, we have

to make up our own minds about the morality of the king's acts and orders.

Governing is different from engineering in an important respect. The engineer as such is concerned with means only; but government involves the choice both of means and ends. If you know no engineering, you have to get the best engineer you can to build your bridge; but the engineer is not the man who decides that there shall be a bridge. Therefore, we can say to the engineer, "We want a bridge just here"; and leave him to build it. We judge him by his success in bringing about the end which we have set him. If his bridge falls into the river, we do not employ him again. Rulers also often have to find means to ends which are agreed upon. For example, it is recognized that it is a bad thing if large numbers of people starve through being unable to get employment; and we expect our rulers nowadays to see to it that this does not happen. The means to this end are very complicated, and only an economist can understand them; but we are content to leave our rulers to employ competent economists, understand their prescriptions as best they can, choose between them when, as often, they conflict, and generally do their best to realize the end of full employment without impairing any other of the ends which we also wish to realize. But in government someone has to decide on the ends of policy. In a democracy this is done by the voters. They do it in part explicitly and in advance, by choosing between parties with rival policies; but in the main they do it implicitly and by results, by turning out of office those parties who do not achieve the ends which the voters desire.

In Plato's republic it was different. The people were supposed to be entirely ignorant both about means and about ends; the rulers decided on both. And if the ruler decides both on the means and on the end, one cannot judge him as one judges the engineer. For one can say to the engineer, "You were told to produce a bridge that stood up to the weather, and your bridge has been blown into the river." But if we have not told our ruler to do anything—if we have just left it to him to decide on the ends of political action—then we cannot ever accuse him of not fulfilling the purposes which we intended him to fulfill. He can always say, "I did what I thought good, and I still think it good." This is the decisive point at which Plato's analogy between the ruler and the expert breaks down. The expert is an expert at getting something done, once it has been decided *what* is to be done. Plato's philosopher-king was supposed to do not merely this— he was supposed not merely to perform a task, but to decide what the task was to be. And this is a thing that cannot be left to experts; it is the responsibility of all of us.

If it is true that we cannot leave the moral problems about political ends to a Platonic philosopher-king, then it is still more obviously true that we cannot leave them to any ordinary human superior. As I said at the beginning, we often hear it said by someone who is accused of a war crime—for example of killing some innocent people in cold blood—"I did it on the orders of my superior officers; I am not morally guilty." If the superior officers could likewise be found and charged they would say the same thing, until we got back, perhaps, to some high-up ruler who initiated in some very general terms some policy whose detailed execution involved the slaughtering of the innocents. But how can the orders of somebody else absolve *me* from moral responsibility? It may indeed absolve me from legal responsibility: that

is a different matter, and depends on the law that is in force. But if we are speaking of a matter of morals, surely the man who is ordered to do such an act has to ask himself whether it is morally right for him to do it. It cannot follow, from the "is"-proposition that X orders me to kill these people, that I ought to kill them. The people who order these crimes, and I who execute them, are accomplices, and share the responsibility.

In many cases, admittedly, a person in such a position can plead that he is acting under duress; he, or his family, will be shot if he does not obey orders. We do tend to excuse a man in such a position, or at any rate to blame him less. Why we do so is also a matter upon which the study of moral language can shed a good deal of light; but I have no time to discuss it now. Let us exclude duress from the argument by assuming that the subordinate knows that his superiors will not find out whether he has obeyed orders or not: let us suppose that he is the head of a mental home who has been ordered to poison all incurables, and that he himself does the classification into curables and incurables.

Up to a certain point, indeed, a person in this position can plead ignorance of fact; his superiors, no doubt, have access to more information than he has, and can foresee consequences of the omission to murder these people which might not be known to the person who has to perform the act. Up to a point a subordinate can say, "I cannot see the whole picture; I must be content to leave the formulation of policy to my superiors, whose job it is to know what the consequences would be of various alternative policies, and to make a choice between evils." But the point must in the end come when a subordinate has to say, "Any policy which involves my doing this sort of thing (for example, slaughtering all these people in cold blood) must be a wicked policy, and anyone who has conceived it must be a wicked man; it cannot therefore be my duty to obey him." To decide just when this point has been reached is one of the most difficult problems in morals. But we must never banish from our minds the thought that it might be reached. We must never lose sight of the distinction between what we are told to do and what we ought to do. There is a point beyond which we cannot get rid of our own moral responsibilities by laying them on the shoulders of a superior, whether he be general, priest or politician, human or divine. Anyone who thinks otherwise has not understood what a moral decision is.

Notes

1. *Groundwork*, 2d ed., p. 92 (tr. Paton, *The Moral Law*, p. 104).
2. David Hume, *Treatise*, III I i.
3. Plato, *Republic*, 546c.

Superior Orders, Duress, and Moral Perception

(2004)

Larry May

Larry May is professor of philosophy at Washington University in St. Louis. He is the author of The Morality of Groups *(1987),* Sharing Responsibility *(1992),* The Socially Responsive Self *(1996), and* Masculinity and Morality *(1997). May is also the coeditor of* Collective Responsibility *(1991),* Rethinking Masculinity *(1992),* Mind and Morals *(1996),* Hannah Arendt: Twenty Years Later *(1996), and* Applied Ethics: A Multicultural Approach *(2002).*

In 1946 the Nuremberg trials were begun, attempting to bring to justice the perpetrators of the Holocaust, among others. Politically, what was groundbreaking was that the trials were based on international norms rather than the laws of any particular country, and that most of the defendants were former members of the German military forces, being tried on German soil largely by non-Germans. Philosophically, one of the most interesting things about these trials was that an attempt was made to refine the limits of the defense of "superior orders," the defense that exculpated individual soldiers, and some other minor players, from responsibility if they were merely following duly authorized orders. Legally, what has come to be called the "Nuremberg defense" is the result of the attempt to provide a set of limitations for the "superior orders" defense by reference to concepts of moral perception and moral choice.

The courts at Nuremberg subscribed to the relatively new idea that it was not sufficient for soldiers to show that they were following orders in order to be relieved from personal responsibility for what they did. In addition, these courts held that soldiers must show that they believed their actions to be: a) morally and legally permissible, and b) the only morally reasonable action available in the circumstances. In the first few sections of this chapter, I will be mainly interested in seeing whether the Nuremberg defense is a normatively plausible and serviceable basis for deciding when "following orders" should excuse one from responsibility. I will then consider the change in these conceptions, developed shortly after Nuremberg, that stressed that the test for superior orders is to be drawn in terms of the "moral sentiments of humankind," the chief way that the notions of natural law and human rights insert themselves into these deliberations about superior orders. . . .

Throughout, I will argue that the Nuremberg defense provides a normatively justifiable and workable defense, and indeed a more difficult one to rebut than is normally recognized, for many of the crimes that could be prosecuted in an international criminal court. To defend this claim, I will often traverse the difficult and philosophically rich terrain of the moral psychology of humans who are in hostile circumstances. . . .

I. THE NUREMBERG DEFENSE

The Charter of the International Military Tribunal, ratified in 1945, governed the war crimes tribunals that sat in Nuremberg Germany.[1] The Charter established

principles of individual responsibility for the consequences of the actions of military personnel during World War II.[2] Most controversially, it also specified conditions under which soldiers could be relieved of responsibility when in the act of carrying out duly authorized orders from their superiors. The idea underlying the traditional superior orders defense, which the Nuremberg defense replaced, was that soldiers do not really plan and intend to kill, but only intend to do what they are ordered to do. It is those who make the orders, not those who merely carry them out, who should be held responsible for what occurs in wartime. Such an idea is consistent with what I argued in the previous three chapters, namely, that minor players should rarely be prosecuted for group-based crimes and that instead prosecutions should focus on heads of state and other leaders.

At Nuremberg the superior orders defense was codified and also changed from its previous meaning. What is now called the "Nuremberg defense" is based on the following interpretation of the Charter made by the Nuremberg Tribunal:

> The true test, which is found in varying degrees in the criminal law of most nations, is not the existence of the order, but whether moral choice was in fact possible. . . A soldier could be relieved of personal responsibility for the soldier's acts only if the soldier could show that he or she did not have a moral choice to disobey his or her superior's orders.[3]

Thus the Nuremberg defense changed the traditional superior orders defense, which had relieved nearly all soldiers of responsibility for following orders, by stipulating that a soldier was only to be relieved of responsibility if the soldier had no moral choice but to obey the orders, a topic which is fraught with philosophical problems, as we will see.

As I indicated above, there are two aspects of moral choice that are of importance in the Nuremberg defense. The first is that the soldier reasonably believes that the superior's order was legally and morally valid. The second is that the soldier believes that following the superior's order was the only morally reasonable course of action open to the soldier. In this section of the chapter I will examine the first of these conditions. . . .

If a defendant lacks capacity to understand that his or her actions are wrong, at very least that person is said to have diminished responsibility for what the person does. In addition, if a person only contributes to a given result, then that person is often thought to be only partially responsible for what occurs. Both of these diminutions of responsibility are based on the idea that a person should be held responsible only for those consequences that the person knew to be wrong and personally caused. As we have seen, in criminal law generally only those people are held liable who had the capacity to understand, and intended, the wrongness of the their acts (*mens rea*) and whose acts causally contributed to a harm (*actus reus*).

I will begin by examining why soldiers, as opposed to everyday people, are held personally responsible for what they collectively bring about. One standard way to approach this issue is to think of soldiers as involved in a kind of conspiracy, where each displays complicity insofar as he or she contributes to a particular result under the direction of someone in authority who stands above him or her in a chain of command. While soldiers are often thought of as mere cogs in a larger "war machine," or as representatives for the entire nation that employs them, they are surely not really automatons either. The defense of "superior orders" is meant to allow some of these soldiers to diminish or eliminate their personal responsibility, but only under fairly restricted conditions. And the main reason for this restriction is that, after all, it is the soldiers who are actually doing the killing or destroying of property. While it is true that the soldiers are ordered to act, they are themselves also independent actors who should normally bear at least some of the responsibility for what they do, even while in the uniform of their respective states. The modern changes in the superior orders defense reflect the view that soldiers are normally to be considered autonomous agents, not mere cogs in a machine.

Many of the versions of the superior orders defense rely on something like a conspiracy model of understanding group behavior. The conspiracy model of responsibility is especially appropriate since soldiers truly do conspire to accomplish various objectives. An army unit is able to do things, that individual soldiers would not normally be able to do, because of the relationships that exist within the group, most importantly because some are leaders and others are followers - both groups often acting at risk to their own individual lives. Because of the structure of these military relationships, there are common goals and objectives that all of the members of the unit seek to accomplish and, most importantly, there is normally not disagreement about what those goals or objectives are. Of course, the chief reason for this nearly undisputed commonality of objective and goal is that there is a chain of command running from soldiers to their leaders who are the nearly sovereign determiners of what goals and objectives should be pursued...

The Nuremberg defense brings about a sea of change in understanding the idea of choice in soldier's actions. After Nuremberg it was thought that soldiers should be able to see that some of the orders they have been given are clearly immoral or illegal, and if the orders are seen as clearly immoral or illegal then the soldiers should not be excused for following these orders. The Nuremberg trials put soldiers on notice that they would not necessarily be relieved of responsibility for their acts merely because they were ordered to act. The idea behind the Nuremberg trials was that there are higher moral rules than those that are issued by commanding officers, and that should be obeyed, at least in some circumstances, even when the higher moral rules are countermanded by the orders of a commanding officer....

One of the chief difficulties here is that supporters of a clear moral norm that goes beyond a minimum rely on knowledge that any foot soldier should have known, even in the most distracting and demanding of circumstances. The fact of extremely distracting circumstances will make it very hard to specify what every soldier must be supposed to know, although there certainly are some easy cases.

In one notorious case from World War I, that had a profound impact on the Nuremberg trials, Lieutenant Patzig, a commander of a German U-Boat, "sunk a hospital ship and then destroyed two lifeboats with survivors." After the war, charges were brought against two of the U-boat's crew members when Lieutenant Patzig could not be found. "The court ruled that [the crew members] well knew that Patzig's order to attack the lifeboats was unlawful." Both were convicted of manslaughter, but both soon escaped "apparently with the connivance of the jailers."[4] The Court did not challenge the fact that the original order to sink the hospital ship may have been properly issued. Instead, the German court held that no reasonable person could think that it is morally or legally justifiable to sink lifeboats carrying medical personnel and patients....

In another case, greatly influenced by the Nuremberg proceedings, Lieutenant Calley of the United States army was tried for what came to be known as the My Lai massacre. On March 16th of 1968 hundreds of unarmed women, children, and elderly male Vietnamese were rounded up and killed by the soldiers of Charlie Company, 1st Battalion, 20th Infantry Division of the United States Army under Calley's direction. Calley declared that he himself was only following orders to kill everyone in the hamlet.[5] But Judge Kennedy, a United States military court judge, held that " 'a man of ordinary sense and understanding' would see that it was unlawful to kill civilians as at My Lai."[6] According to the court, even if Calley had been ordered to lead his men against the civilians of My Lai, he should have been able to see that such orders were illegal and immoral. As we will see in subsequent sections, it is not as clear that Calley should have seen these acts to be immoral as that the U-boat crew should have seen their acts to be immoral, and this is precisely because it was not clear that in the Calley case the security of the victims was the only security issue worthy of consideration.

It is interesting that in both of these cases, the imagery of "seeing" what is morally right is crucial. If it is self-evident to any normal person who perceives a certain situation that following an order is immoral, then a person cannot claim to be excused from responsibility in such cases merely because he or she was ordered to do a certain thing. But the question to ask is why an individual person's responsibility turns on what a normal person would see as morally right or wrong. In the context of wartime cases, should we hold people to standards for normal people given the abnormal conditions of the battlefield? The Nuremberg trials stand for the proposition that it is indeed just this standard of normalcy that should be applied in some cases to the abnormal circumstances of war. In the next section philosophical problems with this approach will be explored.

II. NORMAL PERCEPTION IN ABNORMAL TIMES

Moral perception generally refers to the ability to ascertain what is morally salient in a given set of circumstances.[7] Moral sensitivity is that part of moral perception that concerns the ability to ascertain an appropriate response to these circumstances given the moral character of these circumstances and the expected moral reactions of others.[8] "Normal" moral sensitivity, if there is such a thing, seems to involve some average or general way of ascertaining what is morally salient. But does it make sense to judge people in terms of what the normal or average person would see to be morally right or wrong? If this judgment is to make sense it should recognize that people's moral perceptions vary based on character and circumstance. . . .

In a previous book, I sketched an account of moral sensitivity as involving four overlapping components. Moral sensitivity involves: perceptiveness of the needs or feelings of others; caring about the effects of one's action; critical appreciation for what is morally relevant about the situation of those who are affected by one's behavior; and motivation to act so as to minimize the harms and offenses that might result from one's behavior.[9] While critical appreciation is the main moral motivator, it is at least a rudimentary moral perceptiveness that is absolutely necessary for sensitivity. One must be able to see what is, and is not, morally salient about a certain situation for one to be able to judge properly what is the right thing to do.

Part of moral sensitivity involves the sharing of perspectives where it is not sufficient for a person merely to perceive the world from his or her own 'normal' perspective. It can make sense, in certain cases, to think of the morally perceptive act as potentially average or general, but relying on this type of moral perception in all, or even most, cases would not be sensitive to the differences among people. I may justifiably believe that any normal person would not take offense at my remark, and yet, knowing that you are not normal, I will fail in moral sensitivity if I continue to think that you are like normal people and will not be offended by my remark. It would be insufficiently attentive of who you are merely to base my reactions on how a normal person would react.

Similarly, the Nuremberg defense asks us to postulate a normal moral perception in abnormal times where there may be, perhaps because of the times, abnormal people. There are several ways of understanding what is postulated by the Nuremberg defense. It may be that what we are asked to do is to imagine what a normal person, unexposed to the vagaries of war, would think about the moral and legal permissibility of killing civilians in certain situations. Or, perhaps more plausibly, it may be that what we are asked is how someone who had been exposed to just what the soldier in question had been exposed to would think about killing civilians in certain situations. Or finally, it may be that what we should be asking is whether someone just like this soldier, exposed to just what this soldier had been exposed to, would think about the killing of civilians in circumstances just like these. Of course, the last of these three alternatives would not get us very far since presumably someone just like the soldier in question *would* react just as the soldier in question *did* react. So, we are left with the first two possibilities, to which I will now turn in more detail.

In the Anglo-American legal tradition, it is common to ask jury members to place themselves in the shoes of the defendant and then ask themselves whether they think that the defendant's behavior was reasonable. The assumption is that any person on the street can tell whether some other person on the street is acting reasonably or not. This is because it is assumed that all humans have roughly the same capacities of moral perception and judgment. But what this seemingly fails to take into account is that even slight changes in the circumstances one faces, and even slight changes in the experiences through which one filters these circumstances, can make a profound difference in moral perception and judgment, perhaps making one person's moral situation opaque to that of another person.

In the discussion of wartime situations, differences in experience will make even a bigger difference in moral perceptions than would normally be true of two different people. Specifically, there is little in a person's normal experiences that can

compare to being in the military uniform of a country that is at war with the country on whose soil one is currently trespassing. It is no exaggeration to say that a person's whole outlook changes when on enemy soil.[10] The normal reaction to strangers, where it is assumed that the stranger is trustworthy until proven otherwise, is turned on its head so that the burden of proof is on the stranger to demonstrate trustworthiness, otherwise distrust will be the "norm." . . .

We need to ascertain whether someone on the battlefield would have the moral perception to see an order as immoral or illegal and be able to exercise the moral choice to resist the order. The drafters of the Nuremberg defense seem to have contemplated just this eventuality and chose generally not to prosecute ordinary soldiers, but instead to prosecute those officers in the Third Reich who were not blinded by the rhetoric of the Fuhrer or who did not feel coerced by the circumstances of their circumscribed roles.[11] The United Nations tried to codify this view when it established its own War Crimes Commission in 1948. For soldiers to be held responsible it would have to be clear that "they commit[ted] acts which both violate unchallenged rules of warfare and outrage the general sentiment of mankind."[12]

III. OUTRAGE AND THE SENTIMENTS OF HUMANKIND

The International Military Tribunal at Nuremberg was established to prosecute individuals for three kinds of action: a) crimes against peace, including starting an unjust war, b) war crimes, including murder or ill treatment of prisoners of war, and c) crimes against humanity, including an attack on a civilian population that involves the killing of innocent civilians and other human rights abuses.[13] This second category is the one that I have been focusing on and which I will now explore in greater detail in the rest of this section. For all three categories of action, the crimes are thought to be of sufficient importance and scope to warrant an international prosecution. These acts all have in common that something has been done that offends a basic human sense of justice, not merely a localized sense of what is fair or just.

The appeal to what would cause outrage in the general sentiments of humankind is a common way to think about the elements of normal moral perception of which each person is thought to be capable. Certain things are thought to be so heinous that any person would be outraged when perceiving them. The killing of civilians during wartime is one of the most commonly cited examples of just this kind of heinous act. But consider for a moment the conditions of warfare where one is acting in enemy territory. In some wartime situations, every person, soldier or civilian, is a potential threat. If the civilians seem to be unarmed, and the soldiers are armed, then the idea of the civilians as potential threats is only partially blunted since the soldiers often do not know which civilians are members of the enemy forces.

Is it clearly an outrage against the sentiments of humankind for soldiers at My Lai to kill civilian men, women, and children? Initially it seems that the answer would be clearly "yes," as in fact was held by the American military tribunal that convicted Lieutenant Calley. The shooting of seemingly unarmed civilians, especially children, at point blank range,

appeared to be morally outrageous. Virtually all societies have had strong moral prohibitions against the taking of innocent life. The standard morally acceptable bases for justified killing: self-defense or defense of others, cannot be seen to justify killing those who do not have the capacity to harm or kill a well armed, typically male, adult soldier. Soldiers have been trained to kill. When soldiers follow their training and kill it is not as much of an outrage as it would be for a non-soldier to engage in such killing. But when a soldier or non-soldier kills an innocent person, especially a child, this is considered to be enough of an outrage to our civilized instincts to think that it should be heavily sanctioned so as to prevent future acts of this sort at nearly any cost.

In the My Lai massacre, it is uncontested that Lieutenant Calley and his men killed over one hundred unarmed civilian men, women and children. But as one reads through the various court opinions in this case, there is quite a bit of disagreement of how best to characterize these killings. As I said, the military tribunal found Calley guilty of war crimes, and the Court of Military Review upheld the conviction. But the first civilian court to consider the case took a very different position. Here is how the US District Court characterized some of the facts:

> Petitioner was 25 years of age and . . . had been an enlisted man for approximately 14 months . . . The petitioner's first assignment in Vietnam was at Doc Pho. He had a short series of classes there and most of the instruction was given by ARVN instructors. This was his first indoctrination about the character of the potential enemy. He was told that women were as dangerous as men, and that children were even more dangerous because they were unsuspected. He was also informed that women were

frequently better shots than the men and that the children were used to plant mines and booby traps.[14]

During Calley's earlier limited missions

the unit was continually subject to fire from unknown and unseen individuals. A number of men in the company had been killed or wounded and prior to the operation at My Lai Four they had never seen the persons responsible for the death or injuries of their buddies. Consequently, they formed the opinion that civilians were in part responsible.[15]

When Calley was supposedly told to go to My Lai and kill everyone there, his background assumption seems to have been that all of the people in the village, including men, women and children, were enemies and potential threats. This US District Court grants Calley's petition for habeas corpus relief in part because of how they understand the facts.

The US Court of Appeals for the Fifth Circuit reverses the US District Court, also at least in part because of its very different construal of the factual record. Here is how the Circuit Court of Appeals views some of the relevant facts:

Lieutenant Calley was the 1st platoon leader in Company C . . . and had been stationed in Vietnam since December of 1967. Prior to March 16, 1968, his unit had received little combat experience. On March 15, members of the unit were briefed that they were to engage the enemy in an offensive action in the area of My Lai (4). The troops were informed that the area had long been controlled by the Viet Cong, and that they could expect heavy resistance . . .[16]

This report is fairly close to the lower Court opinion, but then an account is given of the massacre.

The attack began early in the morning of March 16. Calley's platoon was landed on the outskirts of My Lai after about five minutes of artillery and gunship fire. The assault met little resistance of hostile fire. After cautiously approaching My Lai (4), C Company discovered only unarmed, unresisting old men, women and children eating breakfast or beginning the day's chores although intelligence reports had indicated that the villagers would be gone to market. Encountering only civilians and no enemy soldiers, Calley's platoon, which was to lead the sweep through the hamlet, quickly became disorganized. Some soldiers undertook the destruction of livestock, foodstuffs and buildings as ordered. Others collected and evacuated the Vietnamese civilians and then proceeded systematically to slaughter the villagers.[17]

In reversing the US District Court, the Circuit Court of Appeals seems to have had little sympathy for seeing the My Lai incident as anything other than a "slaughter" of "unarmed, unresisting old men, women and children eating breakfast."

What complicated the picture in My Lai was that the border between civilian and combatant had become blurred, with even fairly small children used to transport weapons. So, while there may be strong sentiments against the killing of civilians, especially children, there was a possible defense in the case of My Lai that might have been an exception to the moral judgment of what was normally acceptable or appropriate behavior. For there was reason, according to the US District Court, to believe that some civilians, and even some children, could be trying to inflict injury or death on the American soldiers in this Vietnamese hamlet. At Calley's military trial, and also in the US Circuit Court of Appeals, such reasons were indeed considered and rejected, after much discussion and debate. But, the US District Court seems to believe that some of the civilians who were killed might have been thought to be threats to the soldiers in Lieutenant Calley's unit.

In retrospect, it seems to many that the District Court opinion was seriously flawed. For even if Calley had feared that the civilians in the My Lai hamlet might be enemy soldiers in disguise, they gave no indication that they were armed or that they were posing an immediate threat to Calley and his men.[18] But in partial defense of the District Court, I would point out that we do not always require that soldiers prove that enemy soldiers pose an immediate threat before it is considered justifiable to kill them. It may be too late by the time it is discovered that suspected enemy soldiers are concealing not only their identities but also their weapons. While I remain suspicious of such an argument, when applied to civilians it is not utterly implausible for the district court judges to have come to this conclusion. The point here is not to argue that Calley should have been relieved of responsibility, but only to indicate that even in this seemingly clear case, two courts came to very different opinions about how to regard this "massacre," based on how they reconstructed the threat faced by Calley and his men in Vietnam.

This discussion does not call into question the normal sentiment that innocent life should be preserved. Rather, what is uncertain is the very judgment that a certain adult, or even a child, is to be seen as an innocent person. And yet it is this judgment, really a matter of moral perception, which is crucial to the determination of whether it was indeed an outrage for Lieutenant Calley's unit to kill civilians in the hamlet of My Lai in Vietnam. Normally, things would be clearer. But we are here dealing with several levels of abnormality. First, of course, it is wartime and not the normality of peacetime. Second, even for a wartime situation, things were abnormal

given that the members of the enemy forces were often disguised as average-looking civilians. And there had been widespread reports of these "civilians" attacking U.S. army regulars. For these reasons, the perception that killing people who appear to be civilians is wrong was called into question. . . .

War crimes tribunals have had to decide what price is too high to pay in order to expect people reasonably to exercise due care not to injure one another. In the case of Lieutenant Calley, it may be true that he and his soldiers feared for their own lives if they did not do what they thought they had been legitimately ordered to do. . . . Calley never claimed that someone literally had a gun to his head forcing him to shoot the civilians. And even the worry that the seemingly innocent civilians might be enemies in disguise was not sufficient to establish that he had no other moral choice but to follow orders, for it is important to consider what sort of threat they posed. If the killing of civilians had been clearly and unambiguously wrong, then Calley would have needed a very strong showing that he had no moral choice but to do what was clearly and unambiguously wrong. The question to be asked, and one I am not in a position to answer, is whether a reasonable person in Calley's situation would believe that these civilians posed a threat to him, and his troops' safety? If so, then perhaps even here moral choice was restricted.

Notes

1. The Tribunal considered three types of crime: war crimes, crimes against humanity, and crimes against peace, even though it was only called a war crimes tribunal.
2. As it turned out, only the actions of soldiers of the German army were considered, even though

there were soldiers from many other armies who took part in World War II.

3. *The Judgment of the International Tribunal at Nuremberg,* Washington, DC: United States Government Printing Office, 1947, p. 53, reprinted in *War and Morality,* edited by Richard Wasserstrom, Belmont, CA: Wadsworth Publishing Co., 1970, p. 109.

4. Telford Taylor, *The Anatomy of the Nuremberg Trials,* Boston: Little Brown and Company, 1992, p. 17.

5. There is considerable disagreement about exactly what orders Calley was given.

6. Quoted in Richard Hammer, *The Court Martial of Lt. Calley,* NY: Coward, McCann, and Geoghegan, 1971, 337. See also David Cooper, "Responsibility and the System," in Peter French, ed., *Individual and Collective Responsibility: The Massacre at My Lai,* Cambridge, MA: Schenkman Publishing Co., 1962; Burleigh Wilkins, "Responsibility for the My Lai Massacre," in his book *Terrorism and Collective Responsibility,* NY: Routledge, 1992, p. 88; and Calley v. Callaway, 519 F.2d 184 (5th Cir. 1975) where a federal circuit court upheld Calley's conviction, reversing a lower federal court ruling.

7. See Lawrence Blum, *Moral Perception and Particularity,* Cambridge: Cambridge University Press, 1994.

8. See Larry May, *Sharing Responsibility,* Chicago: University of Chicago Press, 1992.

9. See my book, *Sharing Responsibility,* chapter 3.

10. See J. Glenn Gray's evocative descriptions of these experiences in *The Warriors: Reflection on Men in Battle,* NY: Harcourt Brace, 1959, especially chapter 5.

11. On this point see Guenter Lewy, "Superior Orders, Nuclear Warfare, and the Dictates of Conscience," *American Political Science Review,* vol. 55, 1961, reprinted in *War and Morality,* edited by Richard Wasserstrom, op. cit., pp. 119–120.

12. United Nations War Crimes Commission, *History of the United Nations War Crime Commission and the Development of the Laws of War,* London, 1948, Article 443, p. 282, quoted in Lewy, ibid, p. 116.

13. *The Judgment of the International Tribunal at Nuremberg,* op. cit., p. 102.

14. Calley v. Callaway, 382 F.Supp.650, 654.

15. Ibid.

16. Calley v. Callaway, 519 F.2d 184, 191.

17. Ibid., 191–192.

18. I am grateful to Bill Edmundson for this point.

Collective Responsibility, "Moral Luck," and Reconciliation

(2001)

David Cooper

David Cooper is professor of philosophy at the University of Durham. His several books include Existentialism: A Reconstruction *(1999),* World Philosophies: An Historical Introduction *(2nd ed., 2002),* The Measure of Things: Humanism, Humility and Mystery *(2002), and* Meaning *(2003). He has also written several articles on the topic of collective responsibility.*

I

Not a few philosophers experience an understandable reluctance toward "being clever" about—as Wittgenstein might have regarded it—"moral gassing" about subjects as sombre as genocide, "ethnic cleansing" and "administrative massacre." This can seem as distasteful as university courses with names like "Holocaust Studies," which subject Auschwitz or Cambodia's "killing fields" to the latest fashions in sociological theory. But perhaps that reluctance is too fastidious, an abdication of responsibility even. For if philosophy has anything, however modest, to contribute to reconciliations that render the occurrence of such evils less likely, it is surely obliged to do so.

It seems to me that it may contribute something, for the following reason. La Rochefoucauld defined "reconciliation with our enemies" as "nothing more than the desire to improve our position, war-weariness, or fear of some unlucky turn of events."[1] But this is a cynic's definition of what is only a charade of reconciliation. It is real reconciliation which is wanted, one which enables men to comport with one another, once more, as men, not as monsters. It is far from clear, however, what real reconciliation requires, what conditions must be met in order to judge. "Now there has been genuine reconciliation, not a bogus truce, a war-weary interlude." In what light must the parties regard one another and their past deeds for us to speak of true reconciliation between them? Such questions invite philosophical reflection.

I shall be suggesting answers to these questions by reflecting on the notions of collective responsibility and so-called "moral luck," on the relations between these notions, and on their bearing on the requirements for reconciliation.

II

The expression "collective responsibility" is variously used. Sometimes it seems to indicate little more than that responsibility or guilt is much more widely spread than is generally assumed—as when one is told that the West or Europe, and not just the warring parties, bear responsibility for the atrocities of the Bosnian war. A more precise sense is indicated in the following remark: "The thrust of the charge of collective guilt is that a person—regardless of that person's actions—is guilty merely by dint of his or her membership in a collectivity," such as a nation.[2] This is close to the sense in which, in British politics, one speaks of the collective responsibility of the Cabinet. Each member of the Cabinet is deemed responsible for a Cabinet decision, even if he or she opposed that decision.

There is a further sense, familiar in the philosophical literature, and the one with which I am primarily concerned. In this sense, unlike the previous one, collective responsibility is not understood as the responsibility of each and every member of some collective (a club, tribe, nation, or whatever). Rather it is a responsibility ascribed to the collective itself, as when, say, the tennis club *itself* is blamed for its closure or bankruptcy—irrespective of the blame, *if any,* attaching to individual members.

I think it is clear that we do operate with a concept of collective responsibility that is not reducible to, or definable in terms of, individual responsibilities.[3] Such a concept was employed at the Nuremburg trials, when the German High Command, and not just individual officers, were charged with planning and waging aggressive war. This concept lurks, too, in Karl Jaspers's famous discussion of German guilt during the Nazi era. Despite denouncing the "crudeness of collective thinking and collective condemnation," Jaspers allows for "a sort of collective moral guilt in a people's way of life," and "a collective morality contained in . . . ways of life and feeling, from which no individual can altogether escape." This collective guilt, he implies, is not the sum or product of each member's individual guilt. If each member, even one who was in opposition to the collective morality, nevertheless accepts "co-responsibility," this will be *because* of belonging to a collective which is *itself* guilty.[4] That is a point I shall return to at the end.

III

So much, for the moment, for the idea of collective guilt. I turn to the topic of "moral luck." This expression, though not the concept it expresses, was introduced by Thomas Nagel and Bernard Williams some twenty years ago. Nagel did so as follows:

> Where a significant aspect of what someone does depends on factors beyond his control, yet we continue to treat him in that respect as an object of moral judgement, it can be called moral luck.[5]

For example, of two drunken drivers one gets home safely, the other runs into a group of schoolchildren. Despite there being no difference between them in terms of degree of negligence, the latter will be condemned—and will probably condemn himself—much more harshly than the for-

mer. The latter's "bad luck," therefore, is moral unluck, for it has resulted in a harsher moral judgment.

Moral luck can, as in that example, be a matter of the unintended consequences of actions. But it can arise in other ways, including a way very relevant to our present concerns and one suggested by the following example of Nagel's:

> Ordinary citizens of Nazi Germany had an opportunity to behave heroically . . . and most of them are culpable for having failed this test. But it is a test to which the citizens of other countries were not subjected, with the result that even if they . . . would have behaved as badly . . . they simply did not and therefore are not similarly culpable.[6]

Ordinary Germans, that is, were genuinely culpable while their English contemporaries were not: but there is moral luck here, since those Germans would very likely not have behaved badly, while the Englishmen very likely would have, had their circumstances been reversed.

Why should "circumstantial" moral luck of this kind be germane to issues of wartime atrocities, collective responsibility, and prospects for authentic reconciliation? It certainly will be if, like many writers, one recognizes the pervasiveness of moral luck—the large degree, that is, to which moral judgment is affected by "factors beyond the control" of those being judged—*and* regards the phenomenon of moral luck as a profoundly irrational component in our moral thinking. How, such writers wonder, can it be sensible to regard some people as culpable, other people as not, when the difference in their behaviour is due to context and circumstance?

One way of pressing this argument would be as follows: if we concede that certain people would not have acted wrongly had it not been for their situation and background circumstances, we are implicitly conceding that we—their judges—would likely have acted badly too if we had been similarly placed. But now, to concede that "there, but for the grace of God and the chances of history, go we all,"[7] whilst continuing to condemn those whom grace and chance did not favor, sounds invidious and irrational.

Just such a line of argument has been followed in urging that the culpability of soldiers who have committed atrocities might at the very least be a "diminished" one. Richard Wasserstrom, for instance, argues that we need to bear in mind not only the dire penalties soldiers can face for disobedience, but a whole range of factors—training, "ethos," and so on—which make it understandable why "the ordinary soldier," who you or I might have been, "sometimes regards . . . behaviour as . . . appropriate, even though it is not." "Modern warfare," he maintains, "can be extraordinarily corruptive of the capacity to behave morally," and hence corruptive of the perfectly ordinary soldiers who, but for fortune, might have been us.[8]

A similar argument could be used to question the consistency of the moral position taken by Daniel Jonah Goldhagen in his remarkable book *Hitler's Willing Executioners,* and the similar position of some recent commentators on "ethnic cleansing" in Bosnia. Goldhagen's thesis is that the usual explanations of ordinary Germans' complicity in the Holocaust—economic hardship, fear of punishment, and the like—rest on the "grave error" of assuming that these Germans were "*un*willing executioners" and bystanders. In fact, he argues, "the central causal agent of the Holocaust" was massively shared anti-Semitic beliefs, an "eliminationist anti-Semi-

tism," which led millions of Germans to "conclude that the Jews *ought to die.*"[9] Germany, Goldhagen continues, had for centuries been in the grip of a "cognitive model" on which Jews were demonized. So powerful was this grip that "during the Nazi period, and even long before, most Germans could no more emerge with cognitive models foreign to their society . . . than they could speak fluent Romanian without ever having been exposed to it." During that period, children in particular "never had a chance" to reject that model, absorbing anti-Semitic beliefs as "matter-of-factly" as arithmetic lessons.[10]

The problem arises when, in the Foreword to the German Edition of his book, Goldhagen insists that these millions of "willing executioners" are to be "considered guilty" and "criminal." They were, he says, not "will-less cogs in a machine," but "the authors of their own actions."[11] This is problematical since it is not easy to square—according to the line of argument we are presently considering—with the clear cognitive model, of sincere and deep beliefs, which the young at least "never had a chance" to challenge rationally and resist.[12] What business do we have condemning these people if, as the analogy with one's native language suggests, we too would have naturally absorbed those beliefs had we been brought up in their society? As luck would have it, we were not: but luck, on the present argument, should not influence moral judgment.

Similarly problematical, on that argument, is the position taken by some writers towards "ethnic cleansing" in Bosnia, who also combine fierce moral condemnation of the participants with an explanation of their behavior which might suggest a more moderate verdict. In his powerful book *The Bridge Betrayed,* Michael A. Sells rejects what he regards as the flaccid judgment that, in war, "everyone is to blame, of course" and pins responsibility firmly, if not quite exclusively, on the Serbs. Rather in Goldhagen's manner, however, Sells tries to explain the Serbs' actions, not in terms of opportunism, spinelessness, or fear of punishment for nonparticipation, but of an "ideology of genocide"—this time, a "Christoslavism" informed by a demonization of the Turks, a doctrine of the "race betrayal" of those slaves who converted to Islam, and fear of a resurgent, aggressive Islam. Sells concedes that the motives of many Serbs were "deeply religious," and stresses that the component beliefs in Christoslavism constituted a "raging torrent" or "lethal brew" sufficiently powerful or intoxicating to inspire many ordinary people to act as they did.[13] The problem, once more, is that if the ideology was *that* powerful then nearly everyone subjected to it—ourselves included—would have gone along with its dictates.

IV

We have before us, then, the argument that, while the phenomenon of moral luck—of allowing factors outside people's control to influence moral judgments on them—may be a pervasive feature of our moral sensibility, it is also a deeply irrational one. It is irrational, not least, because it requires us to condemn people for behavior in which we too would likely have engaged had we been dealt a different hand in life. If this argument is to be employed in any particular case—like that of the Holocaust or "ethnic cleansing"—so as to preclude or mitigate moral blame, then,

of course, various empirical claims would need to be substantiated. It would be necessary, for example, to accept something like Goldhagen's explanation of the behavior of ordinary Germans if these are to be exonerated, in whole or in part, from moral guilt. The validity of such claims or explanations is not in my competence to assess. I take no sides, for instance, on President Chirac's impatient dismissal of the "Christoslavic" factor in the Bosnian war: "Don't speak to me about any religious war," he exclaimed, "these people are without any faith . . . they are terrorists."[14] I shall be concerned, rather, with a philosophical issue: *if* explanations like Goldhagen's are accepted—*if,* that is, we concede that we too would, under the circumstances, have behaved like those we are tempted to condemn—is that a good reason for resisting the temptation, for witholding or tempering blame?

Before I turn to that issue, however, I want to say a little about the possible connections between moral luck, collective responsibility, and reconciliation. The first thing to say is that if, as charged above, the phenomenon of moral luck is an irrational one, then the reality and importance of collective responsibility (in my primary sense) are confirmed. For what is confirmed is the possibility of holding a collective to blame for its actions without thereby blaming all—or conceivably *any*—of the individual members who participated in those actions. If, for example, it is correct to explain people's vicious behavior in terms of a collective "way of life," the grip of a culture's "cognitive model," or the power of a "raging torrent" of ideology, from which "no individual can altogether escape," then we shall harshly judge that way of life, model, or ideology. But the thought that we too would likely have behaved as many of those people did, had luck placed us in different circumstances, will prevent us from automatically extending our condemnation to them as individuals.

The second thing to say is that, with the notion of collective responsibility thereby vindicated, a certain obstacle to reconciliation might be removed. Many people, I suspect, find it impossible to exonerate, and so to imagine reconciliation with their oppressors because, they feel, there would then be nowhere to fix blame for the wrongs committed. And how can wrongs or evils have been done without people being to blame? The notion of collective responsibility suggests an answer: *a* people, a culture, a nation, or whatever can be held responsible and judged in the harshest terms without it being the case that the individual members of such a collective are blamed. (Not, at any rate, all or most of them. Doubtless there will be certain individuals, notably the architects of oppression, who can be singled out for specific responsibility.) And the possibility would thereby be opened up for exoneration, forgiveness, and reconciliation at the level of individual, personal intercourse between the erstwhile victims and oppressors.

That possibility will sound a welcome one to many ears. But whether it is a genuine one depends on finding acceptable the line of argument I was describing earlier—the argument to the effect that moral luck is an irrational phenomenon, that reflection on the truth of "There but for the grace of God . . ." can and, rationally, *ought* to preclude or mitigate moral condemnation of people whose actions were shaped by "factors beyond their control." So, as promised earlier, that line of argument needs to be assessed. Ought "grace of God"

considerations temper our moral judgments?

V

With one objection to that argument, I shall be brief. If Goldhagen's explanation of the behavior of ordinary Germans during the Nazi era is right, then there is a problem about asking myself whether I would have behaved in the same way under the circumstances. For the question is not whether I, with my current beliefs and moral commitments, might have so behaved through opportunism or out of fear of punishment for noncompliance. Rather, it is whether I, if brought up in a very different climate of beliefs and values, and subjected to a very different "cognitive model," would have acted as they did. And the problem is that this question seems to lack sense. For in what sense could it be *myself* whose behavior I am then trying to envisage? Is it not crucial to my self-understanding that I am a person with certain beliefs and commitments that lend shape to the life which is mine? The objection to the argument under consideration, then, is that the question it requires each of us to ask himself, "How would I have acted under those circumstances?," is not a question that gets off the ground when "those circumstances" are of the kind emphasized by Goldhagen. Hence, no implications can be drawn from reflection on that question for judgment on those who did act under those circumstances.

This objection is, as far as it goes, well-taken. But perhaps it doesn't go very far. Imagining oneself in the shoes, or circumstances, of other people is, after all, only a heuristic device for attending to the role which chance and contingency play in shaping contexts of action, and indeed the agents themselves. This is something we can still attend to even when those contexts are so different from our actual one that it cannot be we ourselves whom we imagine transplanted into those contexts. Indeed, reflecting that it couldn't be *us* in those contexts forces recognition of the role contingency plays, not only in explaining a person's behavior, but in shaping his or her identity. *Who* people are, not only what they do, owes to "factors beyond their control." And this recognition may seem to reinforce the argument for mitigating or even suspending judgments on people. Interestingly, in the *Bhagavadgita,* Krishna employs this reflection, among others, when persuading the warrior Arjuna to overcome his scruples about killing his own kith and kin in the impending battle.[15]

That very example, however, suggests another objection to the argument under consideration. Whatever the ultimate cogency of Krishna's reasons, it is surely appropriate that Arjuna himself should have scruples. It is appropriate, too, we feel, that he should have regrets, and feel some remorse, after the battle, and not simply shrug off his killing of uncles and cousins as an unfortunate episode for which fate or contingency is alone to blame. To recall an earlier example: however *we* might judge the two drunken drivers, we would be perturbed if the "unlucky" driver were to say "Yes, of course I shouldn't have driven after ten whiskies, but I can't blame myself any more than I would have blamed myself had I got home safely and not run over those schoolchildren."

The problem is this: according to the argument under consideration, detached reflection indicates that it is irrational to base moral judgments on "lucky" factors. But the above examples suggest that we

neither expect nor want people to adopt that detached stance toward *themselves*. In other words, it is remarkably hard—and far from obviously desirable—entirely to insulate moral judgment from considerations of luck or contingency. In cool moments, it may seem easy to say, of "an ordinary German" perhaps, "One cannot really blame someone for acting according to beliefs that he never had a chance to resist": but it would be hard to sympathize with the man himself were *he* calmly to say "Yes, I mustn't be too hard on myself for the atrocities I committed. After all, I was brought up in a rampantly anti-Semitic climate, the propaganda was extremely effective, etc. . . ."

VI

A dilemma seems to have been reached. On the one hand, the claim that recognition of the role of luck or contingency should preclude or temper moral condemnation sounds persuasive. On the other hand, it is important to us that the agents themselves should not, generally, seek to excuse themselves by appealing to such considerations. Put bluntly, it seems that we often want to refrain from blaming people whilst insisting that they blame themselves. And that sounds irrational: a reflection, arguably, of a more general tension between two opposed, yet ineradicable perspectives which, at different moments, we adopt towards human behavior—a detached, "objective" one, where actions are viewed as contingent events in the world, and a more engaged, "reactive" one, where the focus is squarely on the agents and the "quality" of their acts.[16]

The only escape from this dilemma is to argue for an asymmetry between self-ascription of responsibility and ascription of responsibility to others—an asymmetry which would make it intelligible for a person to refrain from holding a second person responsible while nevertheless insisting that the latter holds himself responsible. Some philosophers allow for this asymmetry. Thus, in the case of what he calls the "moral guilt" of Nazis, Jaspers holds that "moral sentence on *the other* is suspended," since such a sentence is a matter of "self-judgement . . . up to *the individual alone.*"[17] Nor is it an asymmetry unfamiliar in everyday moral discourse. At any rate, one often reads of people saying things like "No one else can judge you. That's for you alone to do." Still, it is hardly clear how sense can be made of this asymmetry. How, one wants to ask, can it be correct for you alone to judge your actions harshly? Surely the correctness of a verdict cannot depend on who pronounces it.

Here is a possible solution to the dilemma. Perhaps what is required of those who have wronged us is not a *judgment,* an assenting to some proposition, for then it is impossible to see how, if we accept their self-judgment, we can refuse to make the same judgment, assent to the same proposition. Perhaps what is required is an *act*—an apology, an expression of remorse, an owning to the harm they have done, an acknowledgment. (In such trivial cases, certainly, as someone's inadvertently treading on my toes, I expect him to say "I'm sorry," but I am not concerned whether he is passing some internal judgment on his clumsiness.) Why we find it so important that people perform such acts, even in cases where we are willing to withhold or temper condemnation, is a difficult question which I can only touch upon. I suspect that the following remark

by a witness to the Truth and Reconciliation Commission in South Africa contains the germ of an answer: "acknowledging responsibility" and "making apology" serve to "confirm one's membership" of the "moral order" and of the social fellowship.[18] (The clumsy man's "I'm sorry," one might say, shows that he regards, and relates to, me as a fellow person, and serves to restore a relation that his clumsiness threatened.) But whatever the explanation, it is undeniable that people do place great weight upon self-ascription of responsibility in the form of public acts of acknowledgement and apology. (Think of the 50-year-old but continuing demand by British prisoners of war for an apology from the Emperor of Japan.)

The above consideration offers a possible escape from our dilemma. In demanding that those who have harmed us accept a responsibility that we ourselves, after due reflection on the role of contingency and "factors beyond their control," are unwilling to ascribe to them, we are not (incoherently) insisting that they judge themselves differently from how we judge them. Rather, we are demanding that they *do* something—something to acknowledge the harm they have done. This acknowledgment is indeed something that they alone can do, and something which does not conflict with the exonerating judgment that we pass.

VII

Such reflections also offer, at long last, an indication of the requirements for genuine reconciliation between peoples, groups, or nations which have inflicted suffering on one another. There are, as I see it, two such requirements which have emerged from my discussion. The first is that the parties to be reconciled hold one another collectively responsible for the sufferings inflicted. That is, they will indeed condemn one another, but without condemning all, or even many, of the individuals who participated or colluded in the wrongs done. They will refrain from such individual condemnations because of their recognition of the role of contingency or luck in shaping people's behavior—of, for example, the terrible power that a distorted "cognitive model" or religious ideology can exert over ordinary people.

But there is a second requirement if members of the erstwhile warring parties are, once more, to comport with one another as fellow human beings. They must acknowledge and apologize for their participation or collusion in the sufferings inflicted, for their unprotesting membership of the guilty collective. For members of one group to take the same "objective" view of their actions as their former enemies are now willing to take, for *them* to "put it all down" to contingency, is a refusal on their part to perform those public acts of restoration which it is essential that people perform if they are to manifest a readiness to engage, once more, in a fellowship of human beings.

Notes

1. Duc de la Rochefoucauld, *Maxims* (Harmondsworth: Penguin, 1959), no. 82.

2. Daniel Jonah Goldhagen, *Hitler's Willing Executioners: Ordinary Germans and the Holocaust* (London: Abacus, 1996), p. 481.
3. See David E. Cooper, "Collective Responsibility," in L. May and S. Hoffman, eds., *Collective Responsibility: Five Decades of Debate in Theoretical and Applied Ethics* (Maryland: Rowman & Littlefield, 1991). This volume contains articles both defending and criticizing the notion of collective responsibility.
4. Karl Jaspers, *The Question of German Guilt,* excerpted in H. Morris, ed., *Guilt and Shame* (Belmont, CA: Wadsworth, 1971). pp. 49 ff.
5. Thomas Nagel, "Moral Luck," in his *Mortal Questions* (Cambridge: Cambridge University Press, 1979), p. 26.
6. Ibid., p. 34.
7. Geoffrey Scarre, "Understanding the Moral Phenomenology of the Third Reich," *Ethical Theory and Moral Practice,* forthcoming.
8. Richard Wasserstrom, "Conduct and Responsibility in War," in May and Hoffman, eds., *Collective Responsibility,* p. 185.
9. Goldhagen, *Hitler's Willing Executioners,* pp. 9 and 14.
10. Ibid., p. 609.
11. Ibid., p. 482.
12. See Geoffrey Scarre, *Ethical Theory and Moral Practice,* for a clear articulation of this problem with Goldhagen's book.
13. Michael A. Sells, *The Bridge Betrayed: Religion and Genocide in Bosnia* (Berkeley, CA: University of California Press, 1996), pp. 63, 69, and 87.
14. Quoted in David Rohde, *A Safe Area—Srebenica: Europe's Worst Massacre Since the Second World War* (London: Pocket Books, 1997), p. 363.
15. *The Bhagavadgita,* trans. W. J. Johnson (Oxford: Oxford University Press, 1994), esp. ch. 2.
16. On this tension, see P. F. Strawson, *Freedom and Resentment and Other Essays,* London: Methuen, 1974, and Thomas Nagel, "Moral Luck."
17. Jaspers, *The Question of German Guilt,* p. 41.
18. Hugo van der Merwe, quoted in Donald W. Shriver, "The International Criminal Court: Its Moral Urgency," Gopher://gopher.igc.apc.org:70/00/orgs/icc/ngodocs/monitor/seven/shriver.txt, 1997. p. 6.

Moral Ambition Within and Beyond Political Constraints: Reflections on Restorative Justice

(2000)

Elizabeth Kiss[1]

Elizabeth Kiss is Director of the Kenan Ethics Program and Associate Professor of the Practice of Political Science and Philosophy at Duke University. She specializes in moral and political philosophy. She has written and lectured on human rights, feminist theory, moral education, and issues of nationalism, group rights, and democracy in Central Europe.

"We've heard the truth. There is even talk about reconciliation. But where's the justice?" This, according to the *Final Report* issued in November 1998 by South Africa's Truth and Reconciliation Commission (TRC), was a "common refrain" among observers of the commission's work. . . .[2]

> If justice requires the prosecution and punishment of those who commit gross human rights violations—which the South African Parliament defined as "killing, abduction, torture, or severe ill-treatment"—then the amnesty offered by the TRC violates justice.[3] Can the TRC be defended against, or in spite of, this criticism?. . .

Truth commissions are a recent invention, designed to provide societies in transition with a way to deal with their legacies of mass violence, abuse, and injustice.[4] They are authoritative bodies given a mandate to develop an official account of past brutalities, in the hopes that doing so will help prevent a recurrence of such violations. In most cases, transitional regimes emerge under difficult and unstable conditions, con-

strained by limited resources and threatened by the continued presence of former elites who still possess considerable military, judicial, and economic power. This is certainly as true in South Africa as it was, for instance, in Chile, where former dictator Augusto Pinochet remained head of the armed forces, and in Argentina, where civilian president Raul Alfonsin needed to placate the same military establishment that had waged the dirty war. These conditions place severe constraints on what truth commissions can do. As a result, almost all commissions have exhibited some features—grants of amnesty to perpetrators, selective investigation of crimes, or a failure to "name names"—that revealed them to be, in Weschler's vivid phrase, "mired in the muck of forced compromise."[5]

But there is another side to the story. In their efforts to fulfill their mandates under these difficult circumstances, truth commissions have struggled with basic questions about what justice requires in relation to survivors, perpetrators, and entire nations scarred by a brutal past. Out of these struggles are emerging new vocabularies of truth and justice as well as a new institutional repertoire for pursuing them. Developed through a remarkable learning process involving participants from around the world, especially from Latin America, Eastern Europe, and Africa, this repertoire encompasses multiple tasks and aims.[6] Truth commissions generate authoritative historical accounts, issue recommendations for institutional change, and direct a national morality play that places victims of injustice on center stage. They combine investigative, judicial, political, educational, therapeutic, and even spiritual functions. This proliferation of functions and aims reflects what I call the *moral ambition* of truth commissions, their determination to honor multiple moral considerations and to pursue profound and nuanced moral ends. In the process, truth commissioners have affirmed the value of "narrative" as well as of "forensic" forms of truth, and have come to speak of justice as reconciliation, national healing, and moral reconstruction. More to the point, they have developed concrete practices aimed at furthering these goals, practices that stretch the conventional limits of judicial and political action. All of these features of truth commissions are clearly discernible in the South African TRC, the most morally ambitious commission to date. And they are dramatically encapsulated in the commission's efforts to promote what it calls "restorative justice."

Is such moral ambition legitimate or wise? In particular, is restorative justice truly a distinctive type or dimension of justice, one that is different from, and in some cases more important than, retributive justice? If so, can restorative justice be promoted through a truth commission? Or, as some critics charge, is restorative justice both conceptually muddled and politically illegitimate? I defend restorative justice as a coherent and legitimate, though risky, framework for seeking to rectify profound injustice. Although it cannot refute the legitimacy of retributive justice, restorative justice presents an ambitious and inspiring alternative. It is important, however, that its proponents be mindful of the risks involved in pursuing restorative justice, and of the limitations of truth commissions as instruments for accomplishing such a project.

THE ROLE OF TRUTH: ACKNOWLEDGMENT, THERAPY, AND JUSTICE

The "essence" of a commitment to restorative justice, according to the TRC's report, is an effort to restore and affirm the human and civil dignity of victims.[7] When truth commissions were first established two decades ago, this was not envisaged as an important, or even necessarily relevant, aspect of their purpose. Instead, it has emerged out of reflection on the actual experiences of truth commissions.

As their name implies, truth commissions are created, first and foremost, to establish the truth about past injustices. Sometimes this requires unearthing information that has been hidden from the public. The TRC for example, succeeded in exhuming the bodies of almost fifty activists who had been abducted, killed, and buried in unmarked graves.[8] But even when most of the facts about a crime or atrocity are well known, it is vital to a society's prospects for justice that they be publicly and officially acknowledged.[9]

Establishing the truth is instrumental to justice in at least two ways. Truth serves justice in a basic sense stressed by the Argentinian truth commission in its report *Nunca Mas:* without truth one cannot distinguish the innocent from the guilty.[10] Less directly, truth serves justice by overcoming fear and distrust and by breaking the cycles of violence and oppression that characterize profoundly unjust societies. As the TRC report put it,

> The Commission was founded in the belief that, in order to build the "historic bridge" of which the interim Constitution speaks [between "a deeply divided past of untold suffering and injustice" and "a future founded on the recognition of human rights"], one must establish "as complete a picture as possible" of the injustices committed in the past. This must be coupled with a public, official acknowledgement of the "untold suffering" which resulted from those injustices.[11]

Some have cast doubt on the value of revealing such truths, worrying that there is already too much fixation on past wounds and that, as Elon put it, "A little forgetfulness might be in order."[12] The past, they warn, can become an indulgence and an obsession, playing into our capacity for what Breytenbach has called "scab-picking curiosity."[13] There may well be some wisdom in these warnings. But a policy of enforced amnesia is simply not a viable alternative for fledgling democracies emerging from a period of gross human rights violations. Moreover, many people have concluded that, just as wounds fester when they are not exposed to the open air, so unacknowledged injustice can poison societies and produce the cycles of distrust, hatred, and violence we have witnessed in many parts of the world, including the Balkans, Rwanda, and the Middle East.

Even more dangerous, perhaps, than ignored injustices are distortions and disinformation. The TRC made a special point of emphasizing how its work has decisively discredited some widely circulated accusations and counteraccusations.[14] In addition, "partisan" or "selective" accounts of past conflicts can "easily provide the basis for mobilisation towards further conflicts."[15] For instance, selective narratives of suffering can lead previously victimized groups to victimize others in turn. Krog has speculated that the atrocities suffered by Afrikaners at the hands of the British in the Anglo-Boer War (1899–1902) helped to shape the brutalities of apartheid.[16] A similar argument might be made about Israeli behavior toward Palestinians. What is needed to counteract these tendencies is "an inclusive remembering of painful truths about the past."[17] Thus, while Archbishop Desmond Tutu's assertion that there is "no healing without truth" is more of a working hypothesis than a demonstrated fact, it is reasonable, on the available evidence, to believe that truth-gathering can help to prevent a recurrence of the injustices of the past.[18]

Truth commissions originally gathered victim testimony in order to construct an official account of past abuses. However, a growing number of commission participants have begun to find value in the process of listening to such testimony. Some highlight the therapeutic value of giving testimony; for others, it represents a form of doing justice to victims. Both views signal important shifts in the theory and practice of truth commissions.

Many survivors of human rights violations—whether in Chile, Sri Lanka, or South Africa—attest to the healing power of telling their story to an official commission after a lifetime of being ignored, disrespected, and abused by state officials.[19] For instance, when asked by a commissioner how he felt after testifying before the TRC, one South African man, blinded as the result of an assault by a police officer, replied, "I feel what has been making me sick all the time is the fact that I couldn't tell my story. But now . . . it feels like I got my sight back by coming here."[20] Telling the truth about their wounds can heal the wounded—and perhaps listening to such stories can help heal societies.[21]

Of course, the therapeutic aspects of the work of truth commissions can be viewed as incidental to their core mission of establishing the truth. Indeed, some critics have referred dismissively to the TRC's Human Rights Violations Committee as a "kleenex commission."[22] Others, more thoughtfully, warn that an overemphasis on the therapeutic does a disservice to survivors who regard themselves not as patients in need of healing but as citizens entitled to justice.[23] While such warnings are important, healing deserves attention as an important part of what truth commissions can accomplish.

But the taking of survivor testimony has another dimension beyond, and independent of, its potential as a source of healing: it is an important means of doing justice to victims. In an article entitled "Truth as Justice," Popkin and Roht-Arriaza contend that providing a platform for victims is one of the core tasks of truth commissions, not merely as a way of obtaining information but also from the standpoint of justice.[24] Truth and justice are intrinsically, and not just instrumentally, connected. Those whose lives were shattered are entitled to have their suffering acknowledged and their dignity affirmed, to know that their "pain is real and worthy of attention."[25] We have an obliga-

tion to tell them, in the words of TRC commissioner Pumla Gobodo-Madikizela, "You are right, you were damaged, and *it was wrong*."[26] More important, we have an obligation to listen, to "give them an opportunity to relate their own accounts of the violations of which they are the victim."[27] Justice requires that we treat people as ends in themselves. We affirm the dignity and agency of those who have been brutalized by attending to their voices and making their stories a part of the historical record. . . .

Moreover, in its effort to develop as complete a picture as possible of past injustices, the TRC was not only concerned with victims' perspectives; its mandate also extended to an effort to understand "the motives and perspectives of the persons responsible" for gross human rights violations.[28] This meant that the commission gave amnesty applicants opportunities to explain themselves, and regarded the testimony of perpetrators as an important feature of what it called "social, or dialogue truth."[29] In his foreword to the commission's report, Tutu provided a striking illustration of this spirit of understanding when he noted that, although he firmly believed that "apartheid was an intrinsically evil system," he tried to understand the "insights and perspectives" of its supporters and believed that some of them "were not driven by malicious motives," but "genuinely believed" that apartheid offered "the best solution to the complexities of a multiracial land with citizens at very different levels of economic, social, and educational development."[30]

While perpetrators deserved a fair hearing, the commission sought, not to excuse them, but to assign "political accountability and moral responsibility" to those who had committed some of apartheid's most egregious crimes.[31] Whether truth commissions that lack the power of prosecution can achieve such accountability is one of the most difficult questions confronting defenders of restorative justice.

JUSTICE AND ACCOUNTABILITY: THE PROBLEM OF AMNESTY

If truth commissions have a moral Achilles' heel, it is the issue of amnesty. Doing justice to the past and to its victims entails holding those who committed abuses accountable. Accountability, in turn, evokes the idea of retributive justice, of legal prosecution and punishment. In principle, truth commissions are compatible with, and indeed can be precursors to, judicial prosecutions. This was in fact the assumption underlying the work of the Argentinian Truth Commission in the early 1980s: that its findings would subsequently be used by the Argentinian judiciary to prosecute members of the military junta who had committed gross human rights violations. Five hundred officers were indeed tried on the basis of the truth commission's report. In the end, however, the effort to punish perpetrators of the dirty war foundered on legal and political obstacles. Faced with judicial chaos and the threat of a coup, the government halted the prosecutions and issued a blanket amnesty for soldiers and police. Since then, truth commissions have come to be viewed more as alternatives to trials than as precursors to them. . . .

Even as they have continued to be shaped by these constraints and compromises, however, truth commissions have sought to reach beyond them in order to achieve some degree of accountability. For instance, commissions have sought to identify those responsible for human rights violations even in circumstances in which they could not publish this information, much less use it as the basis for legal prosecutions. Thus, for instance, the Chilean Truth Commission submitted a list of alleged perpetrators to the country's president. In addition, most truth commissions prepare a report offering specific recommendations for legislative, political, institutional, educational, or other changes that are needed to ensure that abuses do not recur. While attenuated, this, too, provides a measure of accountability, for it establishes as a matter of public record the institutional mechanisms responsible for past abuses. By identifying structural causes of human rights violations, commission reports reveal systematic patterns of accountability that may be a valuable resource for future political mobilization.

The South African TRC presents the most striking example of an innovative attempt to establish mechanisms of accountability in the face of severe political constraints. With a commitment to amnesty guaranteed by the interim constitution, the new government needed to determine the exact form amnesty would take. After extensive parliamentary and public debate, a policy was drafted that made amnesty individual rather than collective, and conditional on full, public, disclosure by perpetrators. This novel approach to amnesty was morally innovative in three ways. First, it upheld the principle usually repudiated by amnesties, the principle of individual moral accountability. As the TRC's final report rightly stresses, the amnesty provisions did not give perpetrators impunity but provided "a considerable degree of accountability."[32] Perpetrators had to disclose publicly what they had done. The TRC firmly upheld this principle over the objections of some in the ANC who argued that antiapartheid activists were involved in a just war and therefore should not be held accountable for gross human rights violations.[33]

The second moral innovation accomplished by South Africa's amnesty provisions was that applicants for amnesty were tried in the court of public opinion. Previous truth commissions had met in private. In South Africa, public hearings and extensive coverage by the media ensured that perpetrators could not hide behind the wall of silence and anonymity that has protected the torturers and murderers of so many regimes. Victims had a right to confront their abusers during amnesty hearings, holding them accountable in an especially powerful way. These confrontations sometimes achieved what the TRC characterizes as one of the key elements of restorative justice, the idea that crimes and offenses are injuries done to another person, violations against individual human beings rather than against "faceless" institutions.[34] So, for instance, Ashley Forbes was able to confront his torturer, policeman Jeffrey Benzien, and compel him to "demonstrate" his torture techniques at the amnesty hearing. Forbes then asked Benzien, "What kind of a man does this to another human being?"[35]

South Africa's third moral innovation was that its amnesty law created incentives for truth-telling, so that applications for amnesty became vehicles for uncovering truths about past abuses. Those who failed to apply for amnesty remained vulnerable to criminal or civil charges. Persons named as perpetrators in testimony given to the Committee on Human Rights were contacted and invited to apply for amnesty. Perpetrators could be denied amnesty if they failed to make full disclosure of their participation in gross human rights violations, or if they failed to persuade the commission that they had acted out of political motives.[36] Given the requirements of "full disclosure," the incentive to close ranks was eroded and a substantial number of perpetrators sought to explain or excuse themselves by naming those who had ordered them to act. For instance, five officers who had killed unarmed demonstrators implicated General Johan van der Merwe as the one who had given them orders to fire. The general applied for amnesty in turn, and implicated two of his superiors. In this way accountability could be established along a chain of command, a feat that has proved almost impossible to accomplish through trials.[37] This model of individual amnesty represents an important innovation and a positive precedent for future truth commissions.

These accomplishments of the South African amnesty provisions do not alter the fact that some people who had committed brutal crimes were granted amnesty and allowed to continue with their lives. In this sense, as the TRC report rightly acknowledges, retributive justice was not done. For some human rights advocates this amounts to the failure to uphold an absolute moral and legal imperative to prosecute those who have committed gross human rights violations.[38] Many critics also noted that, while the commission's Amnesty Committee was empowered to grant or deny amnesty, victims who testified before the commission would wait for years to receive reparations. The TRC came in for particular criticism for its failure to obtain more substantial interim reparations for victims.[39] Moreover, since amnesty was not contingent on expressions of remorse or contrition, on the grounds that these could be feigned so easily, some applicants pointedly refused to apologize and adopted a self-righteous and supercilious tone. Others, seemingly untouched by the process, mechanically confessed only the bare minimum to satisfy the requirements of disclosure and sought to excuse their own conduct by portraying themselves as obedient functionaries or victims of "ideological brainwashing." Small wonder that some victims and their families were frustrated or enraged by the TRC process.[40]

On the other hand, the case of General Magnus Malan, former army chief and defense minister, is instructive. While the TRC was doing its work, Malan was prosecuted for authorizing hit squads and assassinations. After eighteen months and twelve million rand in taxpayer-supported court costs, he was acquitted. Later, however, Malan appeared before the commission and told his own story, denying some allegations but admitting to much more than his trial had disclosed.[41]

While the TRC's encounters with the highest-ranking leaders of apartheid, former prime ministers/presidents Pieter W. Botha and Frederik W. de Klerk, were frustratingly inconclusive, it is clear that the truth commission process led to the identification of many more perpetrators than would have been revealed through prosecutions. Two large, high-profile post-apartheid trials yielded only one conviction. By contrast, the TRC received amnesty applications from more than 7,000 people, an astonishing number given initial estimates that about 200 would apply.[42] . . .

As part of its effort to "establish as complete a picture as possible of the causes, nature and extent of the gross vio-

lations of human rights" and of the "antecedents, circumstances, factors and context of such violations," the TRC organized hearings on the roles of the media, the medical profession, business, political parties, the churches, and the legal system under apartheid.[43] These hearings attempted to establish the extent to which these institutions collaborated with both the extralegal and legal violence of apartheid. While the hearings were decidedly a mixed success—with the legal hearings, in particular, thwarted by the refusal of judges to appear before the commission—they nevertheless prompted a national debate about broader questions of what the TRC called "direct and indirect, individual and shared responsibility" for human rights violations.[44]

The TRC also encouraged ordinary South Africans to consider their accountability in upholding apartheid. For instance, it created a Register of Reconciliation, inviting people who were neither victims of gross human rights violations nor applicants for amnesty to send personal reflections.[45] People were encouraged to recognize "the little perpetrator in each one of us" and to acknowledge their "direct or indirect responsibility" for the "mundane but nonetheless traumatizing dimensions of apartheid life that had affected every single black South African."[46]

In the end, the TRC's ability to overcome the culture of impunity that has plagued so many countries in transition depends on the overall pattern of its own grants and denials of amnesty as well as on how the debate over whether to prosecute alleged perpetrators who were denied amnesty or who declined to apply for it is ultimately resolved. The TRC took a clear stand in this debate in 1999, when it presented to the National Director of Public Proseclutions a list of over one hundred names of persons it recommended for prosecution.[47] However, questions over the wisdom of post-TRC prosecutions continue to divide human rights advocates both inside and outside South Africa.[48]

Justice, whether retributive or restorative, demands full and fair accountability. In practice, such accountability is difficult to achieve in transitional situations like postapartheid South Africa. Nevertheless, despite the severe constraints of a politically imposed amnesty process, the TRC achieved a robust degree of accountability and reinforced the links between justice, accountability, and truth.

RECONCILIATION, REPARATION, AND RESTORATIVE JUSTICE

Restorative justice includes a three-fold commitment (1) to affirm and restore the dignity of those whose human rights have been violated; (2) to hold perpetrators accountable, emphasizing the harm that they have done to individual human beings; and (3) to create social conditions in which human rights will be respected. As yet, all of these features are perfectly compatible with retributive justice. To be sure, trials rarely do justice to victims' voices in the way truth commissions have the capacity to do, and traditional conceptions of retributive justice place relatively little emphasis on restoring victims' dignity. Nevertheless, legal punishment of rights violators remains a powerful way of affirming the dignity of victims. Thus far, the difference between retributive and restorative justice appears to be one in emphasis and degree rather than in kind. It becomes

much sharper when we consider a fourth aspect of restorative justice, its commitment to reconciliation. For while retributive justice demands that the guilty be punished, restorative justice, in Tutu's words, "is concerned not so much with punishment as with correcting imbalances, restoring broken relationships—with healing, harmony and reconciliation."[49] Thus, a key defining element of restorative justice is its privileging of reconciliation over retribution. . . .

The transformative aspirations of truth commissions have been articulated more fully by Zalaquett, a lawyer and Chilean truth commissioner. Zalaquett argues that the ultimate goal of truth commissions, and indeed of any attempt to deal systematically with past human rights abuses, is "to put back in place a moral order that has broken down or has been severely undermined, or to build up a just political order if none existed in historical memory."[50] The task of creating a just society is one of moral reconstruction. It entails efforts to repair the broken quality of human relationships throughout a society, including those between the former oppressor and the oppressed, and sets as its overriding goal the creation of conditions in which all citizens are accorded dignity and respect.

Moral reconstruction cannot be accomplished through judicial means alone; it is at once political, legal, cultural, moral, psychological, and spiritual. Many of those who participated in deliberations about a possible South African truth commission shared this expansive vision of the work a truth commission needed to do to contribute to such moral reconstruction. For instance, Justice Goldstone commented that he hoped the commission would merge two "streams," the "vital legal underpinning . . . without which such a commission could not succeed" and the "philosophical, religious and moral aspects without which the commission would be an empty legal vessel which would do a great deal of harm and achieve nothing."[51] And Justice Sachs noted with approval that the commission was being envisioned as an enterprise "that is primarily moral, cultural, psychological and human rather than one which is solely legal or instrumental."[52] He argued that the commission represented "what we have spent our whole lives fighting for. . . . It is the creation of a nation."[53]

Restorative justice does not *preclude* punishing the guilty. Indeed, punishment can be justified as a way of restoring moral order. Arendt characterized punishment and forgiveness as alternatives but not opposites, because both were "ways of attempting to put an end" to a cycle of vengeance, of action and reaction that "without interference could go on endlessly."[54] Nevertheless, proponents of restorative justice tend to privilege forgiveness or reconciliation over punishment, to emphasize the humanity of both victim and offender, and to seek personal and institutional transformation ahead of retribution.[55] As Zalaquett put it,

> There is a long-standing tradition, both religious and humanistic, that establishes a moral superiority of forgiveness and reconciliation over punishment. This is not a pious renunciation of justice. Rather, it means that if the reestablishment of a moral order may be similarly achieved through either path, the road of forgiveness and reconciliation should be preferred.[56]

The reason for this preference is that forgiveness is "more conducive to re-establishing the broken moral order because it presupposes the perpetrator's voluntary submission to the values that were violated. Such a solution is a better solution than to have to subdue the . . . perpetrator by punishing him."[57] Zalaquett makes clear that forgiveness and reconciliation require that past injustices be uncovered and acknowledged, that perpetrators be held accountable, and that reparations be provided to those who were harmed. Thus justice as truth and accountability are essential elements of his vision of restorative justice. But he prefers the path of forgiveness and reconciliation because he believes it opens up moral possibilities for reconstructing a just society that are harder to achieve via the path of punishment.

During the South African transition, the priority of reconciliation over retribution was powerfully expressed through the exemplary magnanimity of President Nelson Mandela and through the ANC's willingness, unprecedented on the part of a victorious liberation movement, to acknowledge officially that there were victims and perpetrators on all sides. Indeed, the ANC appointed three commissions prior to the establishment of the TRC specifically to investigate allegations of human rights violations in ANC camps and detention centers. To be sure, subsequent relations between the ANC and the TRC were frequently stormy, and the ANC even mounted a court challenge to the *Final Report*. But it was a credit to both parties that these tensions never derailed the TRC process.

The postamble to the interim constitution set the tone for the TRC's work when it proclaimed "a need for understanding but not for vengeance, a need for reparation but not for retaliation, a need for *ubuntu* but not for victimization," invoking the African concept of *ubuntu,* or humaneness. As the commission's name indicated, its "overarching task" was not only to seek the truth but also to promote "national unity and reconciliation."[58] In his foreword to the TRC report, Tutu pointed to the necessity of reconciliation by invoking an image of South Africa "soaked in the blood of her children of all races and of all political persuasions."[59] The pervasive violence of apartheid and of the brutal struggles that it spawned had left South Africans bitterly divided by hatred and fear. The country's prospects for a more just and peaceful future depended on a willingness to reconcile and move forward. Reconciliation was not, however, a policy of "forgive and forget." As the TRC motto ("Truth . . . the Road to Reconciliation") emphasized, its vision of reconciliation was premised on reconstructing as complete a picture as possible of the injustices of the past. Nor did reconciliation involve impunity or moral amnesty, for the commission sought to establish accountability for the crimes of the apartheid period. What was required was a renunciation of vengeance and violence in favor of a willingness to work together as South Africans.

As the commission's work proceeded, reconciliation and restorative justice became more and more explicitly its animating moral vision.[60] Its rhetoric and practice persistently championed reconciliation at the personal, interpersonal, community, and national levels in ways that were breathtakingly ambitious in a society emerging from years of brutal repression and communal violence. While the amnesty process did not require perpetrators to apologize for their actions, commission hearings created an opportunity for repentance and forgiveness. The most extraordinary, and publicly celebrated, moments of those hearings occurred when individual

victims and perpetrators reached out to one another and achieved some measure of reconciliation. Commissioners applauded those who repented and forgave, exhorted white South Africans to acknowledge their complicity in apartheid, and called on all South Africans to "forego bitterness, renounce resentment," "move past old hurt," and approach one another in a spirit of "generosity" and "magnanimity."[61] The TRC thus became an advocate and facilitator of reconciliation, challenging conventional models of judicial proceedings and commissions of inquiry.

Some people, both within and outside of the commission, were uneasy about this ambitious vision of reconciliation and argued that a more limited notion of peaceful coexistence was all that could and should be promoted. The commission's report acknowledged this concern and noted that it was also shared by some of those who gave testimony at the victims hearings.[62] Yet even those who most vigorously advocate criminal prosecutions in the aftermath of the TRC acknowledge that the participation of perpetrators within the TRC process had transformative significance for South Africa. In calling for the prosecution of rights violators who "snubbed" the TRC, human rights groups emphasized that perpetrators who came before the TRC and accepted "public shaming or accountability" thereby contributed to the creation of "a culture of human rights and respect for . . . institutions of justice."[63]

By privileging reconciliation over punishment, restorative justice seeks to transcend the traditional dichotomy between justice and mercy, incorporating dimensions of mercy into justice.[64] Yet the reconciliation sought through restorative justice does not come cheaply, either for perpetrators or for victims. Because neither remorse nor forgiveness can be demanded, or even expected, in South Africa's deeply divided and grossly unequal society, restorative justice requires a difficult balancing act between an insistence on accountability and a readiness to reconcile.[65] It also demands a recognition that reconciliation will be a lengthy and difficult project.

Three points emphasized in the *Final Report* serve as a useful corrective to any temptation to overstate the commission's success in achieving reconciliation. First, the report repeatedly stresses that reconciliation is a long-term goal and vision, and that the TRC can be no more than one part of a much larger process.[66] Second, the commission acknowledged that its task of promoting truth and reconciliation proved to be "riddled with tension." Disclosure of painful truths sometimes evoked anger and alienation rather than reconciliation, and the commission's efforts exacerbated some community conflicts even as they moderated others.[67] Finally, the report emphasizes that genuine reconciliation cannot occur without material reparations and redistribution of resources. The reparations proposed by the TRC, which include monetary payments to individuals as well as collective and symbolic reparations such as clinics to provide medical and counseling services, monuments, and the renaming of parks and schools to honor the victims of repression, are inadequate in themselves.[68] Only a commitment to mitigate the pervasive inequities of apartheid and to provide social justice for black South Africans can sustain progress on the "road to reconciliation." A spirit of reconciliation, while necessary, is insufficient; "wide-ranging structural and institutional transformation" has to occur.[69] Ultimately, therefore, the TRC sought to honor its ambitious vision of reconciliation by emphasizing its own limitations and pointing beyond itself to the many tasks still left to be done in the name of restorative justice.

Notes

1. I would like to thank the organizers and participants of two meetings on truth commissions, one at Harvard Law School in May 1996 organized by the World Peace Foundation, the Harvard Human Rights Program, and the Harvard Program in Ethics and the Professions, and one in Somerset West, South Africa, in May 1998 organized by the World Peace Foundation and attended by commissioners and staff of the Truth and Reconciliation Commission. It was a privilege to be present at both of these gatherings. I especially wish to thank Amy Gutmann, Martha Minow, Robert Rotberg, Graeme Simpson, Dennis Thompson, and Wilhelm Verwoerd for their responses to my paper. I also presented the paper to the University of Toronto Department of Political Science in December 1999, and I am grateful to all present for their stimulating questions and comments, most especially to David Dyzenhaus, Ran Hirschl, Cheryl Misak, Edward Morgan, Jennifer Nedelsky, Ayelet Shachar, and Melissa Williams. My thanks also to Lincoln Hancock for exceptional research assistance; to students in my class, Human Rights in Theory and Practice, for lively discussions about truth commissions; to my colleague Sheridan Johns for an excellent presentation to my class on the subject—and, as always, to Jeff Holzgrefe for his invaluable editorial and moral support.
2. TRC, *Final Report* (Cape Town, 1998), I, chap. 5, par. 3.
3. Promotion of the National Unity and Reconciliation Act of 1995, section 1(1)(xix). This act established the TRC.
4. For a useful comparative study, see Priscilla B. Hayner, "Fifteen Truth Commission—1974 to 1994: A Comparative Study," in Neil J. Kritz (ed.), *Transitional Justice* (Washington, D.C., 1995), I, 225–261.
5. Lawrence Weschler, "Afterword," *A Miracle, A Universe: Settling Accounts with Torturers* (New York, 1990).
6. For a vivid description of this process see the forewords and introductions to Alex Boraine, Janet Levy, and Ronel Scheffer (eds.), *Dealing with the Past: Truth and Reconciliation in South Africa* (Cape Town, 1994); and Alex Boraine and Janet Levy (eds.), *The Healing of a Nation?* (Cape Town, 1995).

7. *Final Report,* I, chap. 5, par. 89.
8. Ibid., chap. 1, par. 29.
9. This crucial difference between knowledge and acknowledgment, which is stressed in most of the literature on truth commissions, has been attributed to Thomas Nagel. See Weschler, *A Miracle, A Universe,* 4.
10. Ernesto Sabato, "Prologue," to *Nunca Mas* (New York, 1986), 5.
11. *Final Report,* I, chap. 5, par. 2.
12. Amos Elon, "The Politics of Memory," *New York Review of Books,* 7 October 1995, 5.
13. Breyten Breytenbach, "Appendix," in Boraine, Levy, and Scheffer, *Dealing with the Past,* 162.
14. *Final Report,* I, ch. 5, par. 34.
15. Ibid., 51.
16. Antjie Krog, "The South African Road," in Boraine and Levy, *Healing of a Nation?* 112–119.
17. *Final Report,* I, chap. 5, par. 51.
18. Ibid., chap. 1, par. 16.
19. See Henry J. Steiner (ed.), *Truth Commissions: A Comparative Assessment* (Cambridge, Mass., 1997), especially comments by José Zalaquett and Manouri Muttetuwegama.
20. Testimony of Lucas Baba Sikwepere, quoted in Martha Minow, *Between Vengeance and Forgiveness* (Boston, 1998), 67.
21. For an insightful discussion of the capacity of truth commissions to heal individuals and collectivities, see ibid., 61–79.
22. This criticism is cited by TRC member Pumla Gobodo-Madikizela, in "On Reconciliation: Reflecting on the Truth Commission," December 1996, on the official website of the Truth and Reconciliation Commission at http://www.truth .org.za.
23. For arguments for and against the therapeutic value of truth commissions, see Steiner, *Truth Commissions.*
24. Margaret Popkin and Naomi Roht-Arriaza, "Truth as Justice: Investigatory Commissions in Latin America," in Kritz, *Transitional Justice,* I, 262.
25. *Final Report,* I, chap. 5, par. 22, 45.
26. Comments of Gobodo-Madikizela, quoted in Minow, *Between Vengeance and Forgiveness,* 60; emphasis added.
27. *Final Report,* I, chap. 5, par. 89.
28. Ibid., par. 97.
29. Ibid., par. 39–42.
30. Ibid., chap. 1, par. 56.
31. Ibid., chap. 5, par. 96.
32. Ibid., par. 57–61.
33. Ibid., chap. 1, par. 41, and chap. 4, par. 64–81.
34. Ibid., chap. 5, par. 89, 82.
35. Lindy Wilson, "Can Truth Bring Reconciliation?" a public lecture at the Center for Documentary Studies, Duke University, 21 April 1998.
36. For an example of a finding denying amnesty on grounds of failure to make full disclosure, see "Amnesty Decision: Gerhardus Johannes Nieuwoudt (AM3920/96)"; http://www.truth.org.za/ amnesty/45.html.
37. Minow, *Between Vengeance and Forgiveness,* 59.
38. Aryeh Neier is among the most vocal advocates of an imperative to prosecute violators of human rights. For a good summary of his arguments and his ongoing debate with José Zalaquett, see Boraine, Levy, and Scheffer, *Dealing with the Past,* 2–15. See also Diane Orentlicher, "The Duty to Prosecute Human Rights Violations of a Prior Regime," *Yale Law Journal* C (1991): 2537–2615.
39. Antjie Krog, *Country of My Skull* (Johannesburg, 1998), 278.
40. David Dyzenhaus, *Judging the Judges, Judging Ourselves* (Oxford, 1998), 10.
41. *Final Report,* I, chap. 5, par. 73; Minow, *Between Vengeance and Forgiveness,* 89–90.
42. Krog, *Country of My Skull,* 121.
43. Dyzenhaus, *Judging the Judges,* 25–26.
44. Dyzenhaus, *Judging the Judges,* is an excellent analysis of the hearing on the legal profession. See also *Final Report,* I, chap. 5, par. 110.
45. Minow, *Between Vengeance and Forgiveness,* 75.
46. *Final Report,* I, chap. 5, par. 107–108.
47. "TRC Urges that Scores Be Charged," *The Star,* 25 May 1999 (available at http://archive.iol.co .za/Archives/1999/9905/25/freedom3day4.htm).
48. See, for instance, the *Call for Prosecutions* issued by a coalition on nongovernmental organizations in November 1998, as well as the heated public debate between Barney Pityana, chair of the South African Human Rights Commission, and human rights organizations and other commentators in July 1999. The text of the *Call for Prosecutions* and further information about these debates may be found at the website of the Centre for the Study of Violence and Reconciliation, http://www.wits.ac.za/csvr/press.htm. See also Piers Pigon, "No Reconciliation Possible without Investigation," *Daily Mail and Guardian,* 4 August 1999 (available at http://www.mg .co.za/mg/news/99aug1/4augboipatong.html.), and "South Africa: No Impunity for Perpetrators of Human Rights Abuses," Amnesty International Press Release, 30 July 1999 (http://www .amnesty.org.uk/news/press/releases/30_july_ 1999-2.shtml).
49. *Final Report,* chap. 1, par. 36.
50. José Zalaquett in Boraine and Levy, *The Healing of a Nation?* 45.
51. Comments by Richard Goldstone, in ibid., 120.
52. Comments by Albie Sachs, in ibid., 103.
53. Comments by Albie Sachs, in Boraine, Levy, and Scheffer, *Dealing with the Past,* 146.

54. Hannah Arendt, *The Human Condition* (Chicago, 1958), 241.

55. Minow, *Between Vengeance and Forgiveness,* 92; Dyzenhaus, *Judging the Judges,* 6.

56. Zalaquett, in Boraine and Levy, *The Healing of Nation?* 46.

57. Ibid., 46–47.

58. *Final Report,* I, chap. 5, par. 10.

59. Ibid., chap. 1, par. 1.

60. See, for instance, the press club speech by Archbishop Tutu on 21 October 1997 and Howard Zehr, "South Africa's Truth and Reconciliation Commission Is an Unprecedented Experiment of Breathtaking Stakes," *Mennonite Central Committee News Service,* 7 March 1997; both on http://www. truth.org.za.

61. *Final Report,* I, chap. 5, par. 50–52, and chap. 1, par. 67, 71.

62. Ibid., chap. 5, par. 20.

63. "NGO Response to Dr. Barney Pityana's Call to Stop Apartheid Prosecutions," 30 July 1999 (http://www.wits.ac.za/csvr/press.htm).

64. My thanks to Robert Keohane for a discussion that helped me formulate this point. The dichotomy between justice and mercy is one of the archetypal "right versus right" dilemmas discussed in Rushworth Kidder, *How Good People Make Tough Choices* (New York, 1995), 109–126. See also 13–29.

65. Jonathan Allen offers an acute analysis of this balancing act as a principled compromise between justice and reconciliation in "Balancing Justice and Social Unity: Political Theory and the Idea of a Truth and Reconciliation Commission," *University of Toronto, Law Journal* XLIX (1999): 320, 325, 338.

66. *Final Report,* par. 1, 6, 27, and chap. 4, par. 42–59.

67. Ibid., par. 3, 14, 18.

68. Minow, *Between Vengeance and Forgiveness,* 92–93. Reparations continue to be an unfinished item on the South African government's agenda. See "One Year Since the TRC Report: Where Are the Reparations? (http://www.wits.ac.za/csvr/press.htm).

69. *Final Report,* I, chap. 5, par. 26, 52.

Credits

Seneca, ON MERCY, (De Clementia), (c. 56), Book I. Chs. 3–8, translated by John M. Cooper and J.F. Procope, in SENECA: MORAL AND POLITICAL ESSAYS, Cambridge: Cambridge University Press, 1995, pp. 131–137. Copyright © 1995 by Cambridge University Press. Reprinted with the permission of Cambridge University Press.   8

Tertullian, "The Soldier's Chaplet," (c. 210), Chs. 11 and 12, in DISCIPLINARY, MORAL and ASCETICAL WORKS, translated by Rudolph Arbersmann, Sister Emily Joseph Daly, and Edwin Quain, NY: Fathers of the Church, Inc., 1959, pp. 255–260   12

Excerpts from CONCERNING THE CITY OF GOD AGAINST THE PAGANS by St. Augustine, translated by Henry Bettenson (Pelican Books, 1972.) Translation © Henry Bettenson, 1972. Reproduced by permission of Penguin Books Ltd.   15

Reprinted from JIHAD IN CLASSICAL AND MODERN TIMES by Rudolph Peters, Marcus Wiener Publishers, Princeton, NJ. Reprinted by permission of the publisher.   21

Alberico Gentili, THE LAW OF WAR, (De Jure Belli), (1598), Bk. I, chs. 5, 6, 13, 14 (first 10 paras.), translated by John C. Rolfe, Oxford: Clarendon Press, 1933, pp. 27–33, 58–63. This article was originally published by Carnegie Endowment for International Peace, www.CarnegieEndowment.org   49

Francisco Suarez, "On War," (Disputation XIII of DE TRIPLICI VIRTUTE THEOLOGICA: CHARITATE, Disputation XIII, (c. 1610), sec. 1, 2 (subsection 1), 4 (first 5 subsections), sec 7 (subsection 15), translated by Gladys L. Williams, Ammi Brown, and John Waldron, Oxford: Clarendon Press, 1944, pp. 800–806, 815–818, 845–846. This article was originally published by Carnegie Endowment for International Peace, www.CarnegieEndowment .org   58

Hugo Grotius, ON THE LAW OF WAR AND PEACE (*De Jure Belli ac Pacis*), (1625), Bk. I, Ch. 2, sec. 1 and 2; Bk. II., Ch. 1, sec. 1–7, Ch. 23, sec. 13; Book III, Ch. 10, sec. 1–4, Ch. 11, sec. 1–3, translated by Francis W. Kelsey, Oxford: Clarendon Press, 1925, pp. 51–55, 169–175, 565–566, 716–719, 722–725. This article was originally published by Carnegie Endowment for International Peace, www.CarnegieEndowment.org   66

Thomas Hobbes, LEVIATHAN, (1651), edited by Edwin Curley, Indianapolis: Hackett, 1994, pp. 74–82, 89–92, 99–100. Copyright © 1994 by Hackett Publishing Company, Inc. Reprinted by permission of Hackett Publishing Company, Inc. All rights reserved.   80

Samuel Pufendorf, ON THE LAW OF NATURE AND NATIONS, (De Jure Naturae et Gentium), (1672), Bk. VIII, Ch. 6, para. 1–8., translated by C.H. and W.A. Oldfather, Oxford: Clarendon Press, 1934, pp. 1292–1299. This article was originally published by Carnegie Endowment for International Peace, www.CarnegieEndowment.org   89

Immanuel Kant, "Perceptual Peace," (Zum ewigen Frieden), (1795), Section 1, 2 (first para.) in KANT'S POLITICAL WRITINGS, translated by H.B. Nisbett, Cambridge: Cambridge University Press, 1970, pp. 93–98. Copyright © 1970 by Cambridge University Press. Reprinted with the permission of Cambridge University Press.   110

Carl von Clausewitz, ON THE ART OF WAR, (Vom Kriege), (1832), Chapter 1, sections 1–9, 21–24, translated by J.J. Graham, London: Penguin Books, 1968, pp. 101–108, 116–119.   115

Excerpts from Narveson, J., "Pacificism: A Philosophical Analysis," ETHICS 75:4 (1965), pp. 623–670. Copyright © 1965 by The University of Chicago. Reprinted by permission of The University of Chicago Press.   141

Michael Walzer, "Terrorism: A Critique of Excuses," from PROBLEMS OF INTERNATIONAL JUSTICE, ed. by Steven Luper-Foy, Boulder, CO: Westview Press, 1988, pp. 237–247. Reprinted by permission of Michael Walzer.   296

Robert K. Fullinwider, "Understanding Terrorism" from PROBLEMS OF INTERNATIONAL JUSTICE, ed. by Steven Luper-Foy, Boulder, CO: Westview Press, 1988, pp. 248–259. Reprinted by permission of the author.   305

Andrew Valls, "Can Terrorism Be Justified?" from ETHICS IN INTERNATIONAL AFFAIRS, edited by Andrew Valls, Lanham, MD: Rowman and Littlefield, 2000, pp. 65–79. Reprinted by permission.   315

Joseph Boyle, "Just War Doctrine and the Military Response to Terrorism," THE JOURNAL OF POLITICAL PHILOSOPHY, volume 11, number 2, (2003), pp. 153–170. Reprinted by permission of Blackwell Publishing.   326

David Luban, "The Romance of the Nation-State," PHILOSOPHY AND PUBLIC AFFAIRS, volume 9, number 4 (Summer 1980), pp. 392–397. Reprinted by permission Blackwell Publishing.   343